30127085125826

The

HOLY
BIBLE

NEW INTERNATIONAL VERSION:
INCLUSIVE LANGUAGE EDITION

THE NEW TESTAMENT,
PSALMS AND PROVERBS

The

HOLY
BIBLE

NEW INTERNATIONAL VERSION:
INCLUSIVE LANGUAGE EDITION

THE NEW TESTAMENT,
PSALMS AND PROVERBS

HODDER AND STOUGHTON
LONDON   SYDNEY   AUCKLAND

You will be pleased to know that a portion of the purchase price of your new NIV Bible has been allocated to the International Bible Society to help spread the Gospel of Jesus Christ around the world.

This publication is not included under licences issued by the Copyright Licensing Agency. Photoset by Rowland Phototypesetting Ltd, Bury St Edmunds, Suffolk. Printed in Great Britain for Hodder and Stoughton Ltd, a member of the Hodder Headline Plc Group, 338 Euston Road, London NW1 3BH by Clays Ltd, St Ives plc.

PREFACE

THE NEW INTERNATIONAL VERSION is a completely new translation of the Holy Bible made by over a hundred scholars working directly from the best available Hebrew, Aramaic and Greek texts. It had its beginning in 1965 when, after several years of exploratory study by committees from the Christian Reformed Church and the National Association of Evangelicals, a group of scholars met at Palos Heights, Illinois, and concurred in the need for a new translation of the Bible in contemporary English. This group, though not made up of official church representatives, was transdenominational. Its conclusion was endorsed by a large number of leaders from many denominations who met in Chicago in 1966.

Responsibility for the new version was delegated by the Palos Heights group to a self-governing body of fifteen, the Committee on Bible Translation, composed for the most part of biblical scholars from colleges, universities and seminaries. In 1967 the New York Bible Society (now the International Bible Society) generously undertook the financial sponsorship of the project – a sponsorship that made it possible to enlist the help of many distinguished scholars. The fact that participants from the United States, Great Britain, Canada, Australia and New Zealand worked together gave the project its international scope. That they were from many denominations – including Anglican, Assemblies of God, Baptist, Brethren, Christian Reformed, Church of Christ, Evangelical Free, Lutheran, Mennonite, Methodist, Nazarene, Presbyterian, Wesleyan and other churches – helped to safeguard the translation from sectarian bias.

How it was made helps to give the New International Version its distinctiveness. The translation of each book was assigned to a team of scholars. Next, one of the Intermediate Editorial Committees revised the initial translation, with constant reference to the Hebrew, Aramaic or Greek. Their work then went to one of the General Editorial Committees, which checked it in detail and made another thorough revision. This revision in turn was carefully reviewed by the Committee on Bible Translation, which made further changes and then released the final version for publication. In this way the entire Bible underwent three revisions, during each of which the translation was examined for its faithfulness to the original languages and for its English style.

All this involved many thousands of hours of research and discussion regarding the meaning of the texts and the precise way of putting them into English. It may well be that no other translation has been made by a more thorough process of review and revision from committee to committee than this one.

From the beginning of the project, the Committee on Bible Translation held to certain goals for the New International Version: that it would be an accurate translation and one that would have clarity and literary quality and so prove suitable for public and private reading, teaching, preaching, memorising and liturgical use. The Committee also sought to preserve some measure of continuity with the long tradition of translating the Scriptures into English.

In working towards these goals, the translators were united in their commitment to the authority and infallibility of the Bible as God's Word in written form. They believe that it contains the divine answer to the deepest needs of humanity, that it sheds unique light on our path in a dark world, and that it sets forth the way to our eternal well-being.

The first concern of the translators has been the accuracy of the translation and its fidelity to the thought of the biblical writers. They have weighed the significance of the lexical and grammatical details of the Hebrew, Aramaic and Greek texts. At the same time, they have striven for more than a word-for-word translation. Because thought patterns and syntax differ from language to language, faithful communication of the meaning of the writers of the Bible demands frequent modifications in sentence structure and constant regard for the contextual meanings of words.

A sensitive feeling for style does not always accompany scholarship. Accordingly the Committee on Bible Translation submitted the developing version to a number of stylistic consultants. Two of them read every book of both Old and New Testaments twice – once before and once after the last major revision – and made invaluable suggestions. Samples of the translation were tested for clarity and ease of reading by various kinds of people – young and old, highly educated and less well educated, ministers and laymen.

Concern for clear and natural English – that the New International Version should be idiomatic but not indiosyncratic, contemporary but not dated – motivated the translators and consultants. At the same time, they tried to reflect the differing styles of the biblical writers. In view of the international use of English, the translators sought to avoid obvious Americanisms on the one hand and obvious Anglicisms on the other. A British edition reflects the comparatively few differences of significant idiom and of spelling.

As for the traditional pronouns 'thou,' 'thee' and 'thine' in reference to the Deity, the translators judged that to use these archaisms (along with the old verb forms such as 'doest,' 'wouldest' and 'hadst') would violate accuracy in translation. Neither Hebrew, Aramaic nor Greek uses special pronouns for the persons of the Godhead. A present-day translation is not enhanced by forms that in the time of the King James Version were used in everyday speech, whether referring to God or human beings.

For the Old Testament the standard Hebrew text, the Masoretic Text as published in the latest editions of *Biblia Hebraica*, was used throughout. The Dead Sea Scrolls contain material bearing on an earlier stage of the Hebrew text. They were consulted, as were the Samaritan Pentateuch and the ancient scribal traditions relating to textual changes. Sometimes a variant Hebrew reading in the margin of the Masoretic Text was followed instead of the text itself. Such instances, being variants within the Masoretic tradition, are not specified by footnotes. In rare cases, words in consonantal text were divided differently from the way they appear in the Masoretic Text. Footnotes indicate this. The translators also consulted the more important early versions – the Septuagint; Aquila, Symmachus and Theodotion; the Vulgate; the Syriac Peshitta; the Targums; and for the Psalms the *Juxta Hebraica* of Jerome. Readings from these versions were occasionally followed where the Masoretic Text seemed doubtful and where accepted principles of textual criticism showed that one or more of these textual witnesses appeared to provide the correct reading. Such instances are footnoted. Sometimes vowel letters and vowel signs did not, in the judgment of the translators, represent the correct vowels for the original consonantal text. Accordingly some words were read with a different set of vowels. These instances are usually not indicated by footnotes.

The Greek text used in translating the New Testament was an eclectic one. No other piece of ancient literature has such an abundance of manuscript witnesses as does the New Testament. Where existing manuscripts differ, the translators made their choice of readings according to accepted principles of New Testament textual criticism. Footnotes call attention to places where there was uncertainty about what the original text was. The best current printed texts of the Greek New Testament were used.

There is a sense in which the work of translation is never wholly finished. This applies to all great literature and uniquely so to the Bible. In 1973 the New Testament in the New International Version was published. Since then, suggestions for corrections and revisions have been received from various sources. The Committee on Bible Translation carefully considered the suggestions and adopted a number of them. These were incorporated in the first printing of the entire Bible in 1978. Additional revisions were made by the Committee on Bible Translation in 1983 and appear in printings after that date.

As in other ancient documents, the precise meaning of the biblical texts is sometimes uncertain. This is more often the case with the Hebrew and Aramaic texts than with the Greek text. Although archaeological and linguistic discoveries in this century aid in understanding difficult passages, some uncertainties remain. The more significant of these have been called to the reader's attention in the footnotes.

In regard to the divine name *YHWH*, commonly referred to as the *Tetragrammaton*, the translators adopted the device used in most English versions of rendering that name as 'Lord,' in capital letters to distinguish it from *Adonai*, another Hebrew word rendered 'Lord,' for which small letters are used. Wherever the two names stand together in the Old Testament as a compound name of God, they are rendered 'Sovereign Lord.'

Because for most readers today the phrases 'the Lord of hosts' and 'God of hosts' have little meaning, this version renders them 'the Lord Almighty' and 'God Almighty.' These renderings convey the sense of the Hebrew, namely, 'he who is soveriegn over all the "hosts" (powers) in heaven and on earth, especially over the "hosts" (armies) of Israel.' For readers unacquainted with Hebrew this does not make clear the distinction between *Sabaoth* ('hosts' or 'Almighty') and *Shaddai* (which can also be translated 'Almighty'), but the latter occurs infrequently and is always footnoted. When *Adonai* and *YHWH Sabaoth* occur together, they are rendered 'the Lord, the Lord Almighty.'

As for other proper nouns, the familiar spellings of the King James Version are generally retained. Names traditionally spelled with 'ch,' except where it is final, are usually spelled in this translation with 'k' or 'c,' since the biblical languages do not have the sound that 'ch' frequently indicates in English – for example, in *chant*. For well-known names such as Zechariah, however, the traditional spelling has been retained. Variation in the spelling of names in the original languages has usually not been indicated. Where a person or place has two or more different names in the Hebrew, Aramaic or Greek texts, the more familiar one has generally been used, with footnotes where needed.

To achieve clarity the translators sometimes supplied words not in the original texts but required by the context. If there was uncertainty about such material, it is enclosed in brackets. Also for the sake of clarity or style, nouns, including some proper nouns, are sometimes substituted for pronouns, and vice versa. And though the Hebrew writers often shifted back and forth between first, second and third personal pronouns without change of antecedent, this translation often makes them uniform, in accordance with English style and without the use of footnotes.

Poetical passages are printed as poetry, that is, with indentation of lines and with separate stanzas. These are generally designed to reflect the structure of Hebrew poetry. This poetry is normally characterised by parallelism in balanced lines. Most of the poetry in the Bible is in the Old Testament, and scholars differ regarding the scansion of Hebrew lines. The translators determined the stanza divisions for the most part by analysis of the subject matter. The stanzas therefore serve as poetic paragraphs.

As an aid to the reader, italicised sectional headings are inserted in most of the books. They are not to be regarded as part of the NIV text, are not for oral reading, and are not intended to dictate the interpretation of the sections they head.

The footnotes in this version are of several kinds, most of which need no explanation. Those giving alternative translations begin with 'Or' and generally introduce the alternative with the last word preceding it in the text, except when it is a single-word alternative; in poetry quoted in a footnote a slant mark indicates a line division. Footnotes introduced by 'Or' do not have uniform significance. In some cases two possible translations were considered to have about equal validity. In other cases, though the translators were convinced that the translation in the text was correct, they judged that another interpretation was possible and of sufficient importance to be represented in a footnote.

In the New Testament, footnotes that refer to uncertainty regarding the original text are introduced by 'Some manuscripts' or similar expressions. In the Old Testament, evidence for the reading chosen is given first and evidence for the alternative is added after a semicolon (for example: Septuagint; Hebrew *father*). In such notes the term 'Hebrew' refers to the Masoretic Text.

It should be noted that minerals, flora and fauna, architectural details, articles of clothing and jewellery, musical instruments and other articles cannot always be identified with precision. Also measures of capacity in the biblical period are particularly uncertain (see the table of weights and measures following the text).

Like all translations of the Bible, made as they are by imperfect human beings, this one undoubtedly falls short of its goals. Yet we are grateful to God for the extent to which he has enabled us to realise these goals and for the strength he has given us and our colleagues to complete our task. We offer this version of the Bible to him in whose name and for whose glory it has been made. We pray that it will lead many into a better understanding of the Holy Scriptures and a fuller knowledge of Jesus Christ the incarnate Word, of whom the Scriptures so faithfully testify.

The Committee on Bible Translation

June 1978
(Revised August 1983)

Names of the translators and editors may be secured
from the International Bible Society,
translation sponsors of the New International Version,
1820 Jet Stream Drive, Colorado Springs,
Co 80921–3696, USA.

PREFACE TO INCLUSIVE
LANGUAGE NIV

Soon after its first appearance in 1978, the New International Version established its place among the leading translations of the Bible. It received wide acceptance in the English-speaking world as a Bible suitable for both church and private use.

No living language ever stands still, however, and the English language in particular is continuously subject to influences and developments worldwide. Even though only a comparatively short time has elapsed since the New International Version was first produced, it is already clear that it needs to be brought up to date in certain areas. The Committee on Bible Translation have therefore given themselves to the task of continuing to keep this translation available in contemporary English while remaining faithful to its established text.

A major challenge facing the Committee is how to respond to the significant changes that are taking place within the English language in regard to gender issues. The word 'man', for example, is now widely understood to refer only to males, even though that is often not the intention of the corresponding Greek or Hebrew words. Instances of potential confusion abound, as in instructions about preparing for the Lord's Supper ('A man ought to examine himself', 1 Corinthians 11:28), or in pronouncements of beatitude such as in Psalm 1:1 ('Blessed is the man . . .'). In these and many other passages, it has become increasingly necessary to have a translation that makes it clear that women and men are both included.

Recognising this need, the Committee on Bible Translation made a decision in 1992 that the New International Version should be made available in an inclusive language edition. Many of the issues are of a sensitive nature. So to guide its inclusive language revision, the Committee adopted a set of principles.

The first principle was to retain the gender used in the original languages when referring to God, angels and demons. At the same time, it was recognised that it was often appropriate to mute the patriarchalism of the culture of the biblical writers through gender-inclusive language when this could be done without compromising the message of the Spirit. This involved distinguishing between those passages in which an activity was normally carried out by either males or females, and other cases where the gender of the people concerned was less precisely identified. While in cases of the former the text could be left unaltered, in cases of the latter words like 'workmen' could be changed to 'worker' or 'craftsman' to 'skilled worker'.

A further problem presented itself in handling pronouns. In order to avoid gender-specific language in statements of a general kind, it was agreed that the plural might be substituted for the singular and the second person for the third person. On the other hand, inclusive singular subjects such as 'everyone' or 'whoever' would only occasionally be followed by plural pronouns such as 'they' or 'their'.

Female words such as 'maid' or 'girl', which in recent years have developed a more pejorative connotation, would usually be replaced. Awkward generic terms like 'human' used as a noun or 'humankind' would be used as sparingly as possible. Some expressions, however, would be left unchanged, as in specific references to either males or females or in wisdom literature where young men on the threshold of adult life were being addressed. The feminine gender of cities and states or nations would also be retained.

It was further determined that the revisions must be sensitive to the varying demands of context. Gender-specific features in literary genres such as parables or exemplary stories were not to be altered without good reason, nor were specific features of metaphorical language.

A common feature in the language of both Old and New Testaments is the use of 'brothers' to refer to members of social units broader than the nuclear family. In cases where reference is to communities that are inclusive of women, 'brothers' should be replaced with some more gender-inclusive expression. Where the noun is vocative (and in a few other passages), the rendering should be expanded to 'brothers and sisters', without the addition of a footnote.

The Committee on Bible Translation have sought to keep faith with the original principles of the New International Version, and at the same time ensure that the recognised text of the New International Version reflects the contemporary use of English around the world. We believe that the changes introduced will remove the obstacles to understanding experienced by some readers, and so enable a new generation to read the Word of God in language they can understand. We pray that God will bless this modern revision as richly as he has done the earlier editions of the New International Version.

The Committee on Bible Translation
1995

CONTENTS

THE BOOKS OF THE NEW TESTAMENT, PSALMS AND PROVERBS

	Page		*Page*
Matthew	3	2 Timothy	233
Mark	40	Titus	236
Luke	63	Philemon	238
John	101	Hebrews	239
Acts	130	James	251
Romans	166	1 Peter	255
1 Corinthians	182	2 Peter	260
2 Corinthians	196	1 John	263
Galatians	206	2 John	267
Ephesians	211	3 John	268
Philippians	216	Jude	269
Colossians	220	Revelation	271
1 Thessalonians	224	Psalms	293
2 Thessalonians	227	Proverbs	385
1 Timothy	229		

THE
NEW TESTAMENT

Matthew

The Genealogy of Jesus

1 A record of the genealogy of Jesus Christ the son of David, the son of Abraham:

2 Abraham was the father of Isaac,
Isaac the father of Jacob,
Jacob the father of Judah and his brothers,
3 Judah the father of Perez and Zerah, whose mother was Tamar,
Perez the father of Hezron,
Hezron the father of Ram,
4 Ram the father of Amminadab,
Amminadab the father of Nahshon,
Nahshon the father of Salmon,
5 Salmon the father of Boaz, whose mother was Rahab,
Boaz the father of Obed, whose mother was Ruth,
Obed the father of Jesse,
6 and Jesse the father of King David.

David was the father of Solomon, whose mother had been Uriah's wife,
7 Solomon the father of Rehoboam,
Rehoboam the father of Abijah,
Abijah the father of Asa,
8 Asa the father of Jehoshaphat,
Jehoshaphat the father of Jehoram,
Jehoram the father of Uzziah,
9 Uzziah the father of Jotham,
Jotham the father of Ahaz,
Ahaz the father of Hezekiah,
10 Hezekiah the father of Manasseh,
Manasseh the father of Amon,
Amon the father of Josiah,
11 and Josiah the father of Jeconiah[a] and his brothers at the time of the exile to Babylon.

12 After the exile to Babylon:
Jeconiah was the father of Shealtiel,
Shealtiel the father of Zerubbabel,
13 Zerubbabel the father of Abiud,
Abiud the father of Eliakim,
Eliakim the father of Azor,
14 Azor the father of Zadok,
Zadok the father of Akim,
Akim the father of Eliud,
15 Eliud the father of Eleazar,
Eleazar the father of Matthan,
Matthan the father of Jacob,
16 and Jacob the father of Joseph, the husband of Mary, of whom was born Jesus, who is called Christ.

17 Thus there were fourteen generations in all from Abraham to David, fourteen from David to the exile to Babylon, and fourteen from the exile to the Christ.[b]

The Birth of Jesus Christ

18 This is how the birth of Jesus Christ came about: His mother Mary was pledged to be married to Joseph, but before they came together, she was found to be with child through the Holy Spirit. 19 Because Joseph her husband was a righteous man and did not want to expose

[a]11 That is, Jehoiachin; also in verse 12
[b]17 Or *Messiah*. "The Christ" (Greek) and "the Messiah" (Hebrew) both mean "the Anointed One".

her to public disgrace, he had in mind to divorce her quietly.

[20] But after he had considered this, an angel of the Lord appeared to him in a dream and said, "Joseph son of David, do not be afraid to take Mary home as your wife, because what is conceived in her is from the Holy Spirit. [21] She will give birth to a son, and you are to give him the name Jesus,[c] because he will save his people from their sins."

[22] All this took place to fulfil what the Lord had said through the prophet: [23] "The virgin will be with child and will give birth to a son, and they will call him Immanuel"[d]—which means, "God with us."

[24] When Joseph woke up, he did what the angel of the Lord had commanded him and took Mary home as his wife. [25] But he had no union with her until she gave birth to a son. And he gave him the name Jesus.

The Visit of the Magi

2 After Jesus was born in Bethlehem in Judea, during the time of King Herod, Magi[a] from the east came to Jerusalem [2] and asked, "Where is the one who has been born king of the Jews? We saw his star in the east[b] and have come to worship him."

[3] When King Herod heard this he was disturbed, and all Jerusalem with him. [4] When he had called together all the people's chief priests and teachers of the law, he asked them where the Christ[c] was to be born. [5] "In Bethlehem in Judea," they replied, "for this is what the prophet has written:

[6] " 'But you, Bethlehem, in the land of Judah,
  are by no means least among the rulers of Judah;
for out of you will come a ruler
  who will be the shepherd of my people Israel.'[d] "

[7] Then Herod called the Magi secretly and found out from them the exact time the star had appeared. [8] He sent them to Bethlehem and said, "Go and make a careful search for the child. As soon as you find him, report to me, so that I too may go and worship him."

[9] After they had heard the king, they went on their way, and the star they had seen in the east[e] went ahead of them until it stopped over the place where the child was. [10] When they saw the star, they were overjoyed. [11] On coming to the house, they saw the child with his mother Mary, and they bowed down and worshipped him. Then they opened their treasures and presented him with gifts of gold and of incense and of myrrh. [12] And having been warned in a dream not to go back to Herod, they returned to their country by another route.

The Escape to Egypt

[13] When they had gone, an angel of the Lord appeared to Joseph in a dream. "Get up," he said, "take the child and his mother and escape to Egypt. Stay there until I tell you, for Herod is going to search for the child to kill him."

[14] So he got up, took the child and his mother during the night and left for Egypt, [15] where he stayed until the death of Herod. And so was fulfilled what the Lord had said through the prophet: "Out of Egypt I called my son."[f]

[16] When Herod realised that he had been outwitted by the Magi, he was furious, and he gave orders to kill all the boys in Bethlehem and its vicinity who were two years old and under, in accordance with the time he had learned from the Magi. [17] Then what was said through the prophet Jeremiah was fulfilled:

[18] "A voice is heard in Ramah,
  weeping and great mourning,
Rachel weeping for her children
  and refusing to be comforted,
because they are no more."[g]

---

[c]21 *Jesus* is the Greek form of *Joshua*, which means *the LORD saves.*   [d]23 Isaiah 7:14
[a]1 Traditionally *Wise Men*   [b]2 Or *star when it rose*   [c]4 Or *Messiah*   [d]6 Micah 5:2
[e]9 Or *seen when it rose*   [f]15 Hosea 11:1   [g]18 Jer. 31:15

The Return to Nazareth

¹⁹ After Herod died, an angel of the Lord appeared in a dream to Joseph in Egypt ²⁰ and said, "Get up, take the child and his mother and go to the land of Israel, for those who were trying to take the child's life are dead."

²¹ So he got up, took the child and his mother and went to the land of Israel. ²² But when he heard that Archelaus was reigning in Judea in place of his father Herod, he was afraid to go there. Having been warned in a dream, he withdrew to the district of Galilee, ²³ and he went and lived in a town called Nazareth. So was fulfilled what was said through the prophets: "He will be called a Nazarene."

John the Baptist Prepares the Way

3 In those days John the Baptist came, preaching in the Desert of Judea ² and saying, "Repent, for the kingdom of heaven is near." ³ This is he who was spoken of through the prophet Isaiah:

"A voice of one calling in the desert,
'Prepare the way for the Lord,
    make straight paths for him.' "ᵃ

⁴ John's clothes were made of camel's hair, and he had a leather belt round his waist. His food was locusts and wild honey. ⁵ People went out to him from Jerusalem and all Judea and the whole region of the Jordan. ⁶ Confessing their sins, they were baptised by him in the Jordan River.

⁷ But when he saw many of the Pharisees and Sadducees coming to where he was baptising, he said to them: "You brood of vipers! Who warned you to flee from the coming wrath? ⁸ Produce fruit in keeping with repentance. ⁹ And do not think you can say to yourselves, 'We have Abraham as our father.' I tell you that out of these stones God can raise up children for Abraham. ¹⁰ The axe is already at the root of the trees, and every tree that does not produce good fruit will be cut down and thrown into the fire.

¹¹ "I baptise you with ᵇ water for repentance. But after me will come one who is more powerful than I, whose sandals I am not fit to carry. He will baptise you with the Holy Spirit and with fire. ¹² His winnowing fork is in his hand, and he will clear his threshing-floor, gathering his wheat into the barn and burning up the chaff with unquenchable fire."

The Baptism of Jesus

¹³ Then Jesus came from Galilee to the Jordan to be baptised by John. ¹⁴ But John tried to deter him, saying, "I need to be baptised by you, and do you come to me?" ¹⁵ Jesus replied, "Let it be so now; it is proper for us to do this to fulfil all righteousness." Then John consented.

¹⁶ As soon as Jesus was baptised, he went up out of the water. At that moment heaven was opened, and he saw the Spirit of God descending like a dove and lighting on him. ¹⁷ And a voice from heaven said, "This is my Son, whom I love; with him I am well pleased."

The Temptation of Jesus

4 Then Jesus was led by the Spirit into the desert to be tempted by the devil. ² After fasting for forty days and forty nights, he was hungry. ³ The tempter came to him and said, "If you are the Son of God, tell these stones to become bread."

⁴ Jesus answered, "It is written: 'People do not live on bread alone, but on every word that comes from the mouth of God.'ᵃ"

⁵ Then the devil took him to the holy city and had him stand on the highest point of the temple. ⁶ "If you are the Son of God," he said, "throw yourself down. For it is written:

" 'He will command his angels
    concerning you,
  and they will lift you up in their
    hands,
so that you will not strike your foot
    against a stone.'ᵇ "

ᵃ3 Isaiah 40:3   ᵇ11 Or *in*   ᵃ4 Deut. 8:3   ᵇ6 Psalm 91:11,12

7 Jesus answered him, "It is also written: 'Do not put the Lord your God to the test.'^{c}"

8 Again, the devil took him to a very high mountain and showed him all the kingdoms of the world and their splendour. 9 "All this I will give you," he said, "if you will bow down and worship me."

10 Jesus said to him, "Away from me, Satan! For it is written: 'Worship the Lord your God, and serve him only.'^{d}"

11 Then the devil left him, and angels came and attended him.

Jesus Begins to Preach

12 When Jesus heard that John had been put in prison, he returned to Galilee. 13 Leaving Nazareth, he went and lived in Capernaum, which was by the lake in the area of Zebulun and Naphtali—14 to fulfil what was said through the prophet Isaiah:

15 "Land of Zebulun and land of Naphtali,
　the way to the sea, along the Jordan,
　Galilee of the Gentiles—
16 the people living in darkness
　have seen a great light;
　on those living in the land of the shadow of death
　a light has dawned."^{e}

17 From that time on Jesus began to preach, "Repent, for the kingdom of heaven is near."

The Calling of the First Disciples

18 As Jesus was walking beside the Sea of Galilee, he saw two brothers, Simon called Peter and his brother Andrew. They were casting a net into the lake, for they were fishermen. 19 "Come, follow me," Jesus said, "and I will make you fishers of men and women." 20 At once they left their nets and followed him.

21 Going on from there, he saw two other brothers, James son of Zebedee and his brother John. They were in a boat with their father Zebedee, preparing their nets. Jesus called them, 22 and immediately they left the boat and their father and followed him.

Jesus Heals the Sick

23 Jesus went throughout Galilee, teaching in their synagogues, preaching the good news of the kingdom, and healing every disease and sickness among the people. 24 News about him spread all over Syria, and people brought to him all who were ill with various diseases, those suffering severe pain, the demon-possessed, those having seizures, and the paralysed, and he healed them. 25 Large crowds from Galilee, the Decapolis,^{f} Jerusalem, Judea and the region across the Jordan followed him.

The Beatitudes

5 Now when he saw the crowds, he went up on a mountainside and sat down. His disciples came to him, 2 and he began to teach them, saying:

3 "Blessed are the poor in spirit,
　for theirs is the kingdom of heaven.
4 Blessed are those who mourn,
　for they will be comforted.
5 Blessed are the meek,
　for they will inherit the earth.
6 Blessed are those who hunger and thirst for righteousness,
　for they will be filled.
7 Blessed are the merciful,
　for they will be shown mercy.
8 Blessed are the pure in heart,
　for they will see God.
9 Blessed are the peacemakers,
　for they will be called children of God.
10 Blessed are those who are persecuted because of righteousness,
　for theirs is the kingdom of heaven.

11 "Blessed are you when people insult you, persecute you and falsely say all

---

^{c}7 Deut. 6:16　　^{d}10 Deut. 6:13　　^{e}16 Isaiah 9:1,2　　^{f}25 That is, the Ten Cities kinds of evil against you because of me. [12] Rejoice and be glad, because great is your reward in heaven, for in the same way they persecuted the prophets who were before you.

Salt and Light

[13] "You are the salt of the earth. But if the salt loses its saltiness, how can it be made salty again? It is no longer good for anything, except to be thrown out and trampled under foot.

[14] "You are the light of the world. A city on a hill cannot be hidden. [15] Neither do people light a lamp and put it under a bowl. Instead they put it on its stand, and it gives light to everyone in the house. [16] In the same way, let your light shine before others, that they may see your good deeds and praise your Father in heaven.

The Fulfilment of the Law

[17] "Do not think that I have come to abolish the Law or the Prophets; I have not come to abolish them but to fulfil them. [18] I tell you the truth, until heaven and earth disappear, not the smallest letter, not the least stroke of a pen, will by any means disappear from the Law until everything is accomplished. [19] Anyone who breaks one of the least of these commandments and teaches others to do the same will be called least in the kingdom of heaven, but whoever practises and teaches these commands will be called great in the kingdom of heaven. [20] For I tell you that unless your righteousness surpasses that of the Pharisees and the teachers of the law, you will certainly not enter the kingdom of heaven.

Murder

[21] "You have heard that it was said to the people long ago, 'Do not murder,[a] and anyone who murders will be subject to judgment.' [22] But I tell you that anyone who is angry with a brother or sister[b] will be subject to judgment. Again, anyone who says to a brother or sister, 'Raca,'[c] is answerable to the Sanhedrin. But anyone who says, 'You fool!' will be in danger of the fire of hell.

[23] "Therefore, if you are offering your gift at the altar and there remember that your brother or sister has something against you, [24] leave your gift there in front of the altar. First go and be reconciled to them; then come and offer your gift.

[25] "Settle matters quickly with your adversary who is taking you to court. Do it while you are still together on the way, or your adversary may hand you over to the judge, and the judge may hand you over to the officer, and you may be thrown into prison. [26] I tell you the truth, you will not get out until you have paid the last penny.[d]

Adultery

[27] "You have heard that it was said, 'Do not commit adultery.'[e] [28] But I tell you that anyone who looks at a woman lustfully has already committed adultery with her in his heart. [29] If your right eye causes you to sin, gouge it out and throw it away. It is better for you to lose one part of your body than for your whole body to be thrown into hell. [30] And if your right hand causes you to sin, cut it off and throw it away. It is better for you to lose one part of your body than for your whole body to go into hell.

Divorce

[31] "It has been said, 'Anyone who divorces his wife must give her a certificate of divorce.'[f] [32] But I tell you that anyone who divorces his wife, except for marital unfaithfulness, causes her to become an adulteress, and anyone who marries the divorced woman commits adultery.

Oaths

[33] "Again, you have heard that it was said to the people long ago, 'Do not break

[a]21 Exodus 20:13　　[b]22 Some manuscripts *brother or sister without cause*　　[c]22 An Aramaic term of contempt
[d]26 Greek *kodrantes*　　[e]27 Exodus 20:14　　[f]31 Deut. 24:1

your oath, but keep the oaths you have made to the Lord.' ³⁴ But I tell you, Do not swear at all: either by heaven, for it is God's throne; ³⁵ or by the earth, for it is his footstool; or by Jerusalem, for it is the city of the Great King. ³⁶ And do not swear by your head, for you cannot make even one hair white or black. ³⁷ Simply let your 'Yes' be 'Yes', and your 'No', 'No'; anything beyond this comes from the evil one.

An Eye for an Eye

³⁸ "You have heard that it was said, 'Eye for eye, and tooth for tooth.'ᵍ ³⁹ But I tell you, Do not resist an evil person. If someone strikes you on the right cheek, turn the other cheek also. ⁴⁰ And if someone wants to sue you and take your tunic, hand over your cloak as well. ⁴¹ If someone forces you to go one mile, go two miles. ⁴² Give to the one who asks you, and do not turn away from the one who wants to borrow from you.

Love for Enemies

⁴³ "You have heard that it was said, 'Love your neighbourʰ and hate your enemy.' ⁴⁴ But I tell you: Love your enemiesⁱ and pray for those who persecute you, ⁴⁵ that you may be children of your Father in heaven. He causes his sun to rise on the evil and the good, and sends rain on the righteous and the unrighteous. ⁴⁶ If you love those who love you, what reward will you get? Are not even the tax collectors doing that? ⁴⁷ And if you greet only your own people, what are you doing more than others? Do not even pagans do that? ⁴⁸ Be perfect, therefore, as your heavenly Father is perfect.

Giving to the Needy

6 "Be careful not to do your 'acts of righteousness' before others, to be seen by them. If you do, you will have no reward from your Father in heaven.

² "So when you give to the needy, do not announce it with trumpets, as the hypocrites do in the synagogues and on the streets, to be honoured by others. I tell you the truth, they have received their reward in full. ³ But when you give to the needy, do not let your left hand know what your right hand is doing, ⁴ so that your giving may be in secret. Then your Father, who sees what is done in secret, will reward you.

Prayer

⁵ "And when you pray, do not be like the hypocrites, for they love to pray standing in the synagogues and on the street corners to be seen by others. I tell you the truth, they have received their reward in full. ⁶ But when you pray, go into your room, close the door and pray to your Father, who is unseen. Then your Father, who sees what is done in secret, will reward you. ⁷ And when you pray, do not keep on babbling like pagans, for they think they will be heard because of their many words. ⁸ Do not be like them, for your Father knows what you need before you ask him.

⁹ "This, then, is how you should pray:

" 'Our Father in heaven,
  hallowed be your name,
¹⁰ your kingdom come,
  your will be done
    on earth as it is in heaven.
¹¹ Give us today our daily bread.
¹² Forgive us our debts,
    as we also have forgiven our
      debtors.
¹³ And lead us not into temptation,
  but deliver us from the evil one.'ᵃ

¹⁴ For if you forgive others when they sin against you, your heavenly Father will also forgive you. ¹⁵ But if you do not forgive others their sins, your Father will not forgive your sins.

ᵍ38 Exodus 21:24; Lev. 24:20 and Deut. 19:21   ʰ43 Lev. 19:18
ⁱ44 Some late manuscripts enemies, bless those who curse you, do good to those who hate you
ᵃ13 Or from evil; some late manuscripts one, / for yours is the kingdom and the power and the glory for ever. Amen.

Fasting

16 "When you fast, do not look sombre as the hypocrites do, for they disfigure their faces to show others they are fasting. I tell you the truth, they have received their reward in full. 17 But when you fast, put oil on your head and wash your face, 18 so that it will not be obvious to others that you are fasting, but only to your Father, who is unseen; and your Father, who sees what is done in secret, will reward you.

Treasures in Heaven

19 "Do not store up for yourselves treasures on earth, where moth and rust destroy, and where thieves break in and steal. 20 But store up for yourselves treasures in heaven, where moth and rust do not destroy, and where thieves do not break in and steal. 21 For where your treasure is, there your heart will be also.

22 "The eye is the lamp of the body. If your eyes are good, your whole body will be full of light. 23 But if your eyes are bad, your whole body will be full of darkness. If then the light within you is darkness, how great is that darkness!

24 "No-one can be a slave to two masters. Either you will hate the one and love the other, or you will be devoted to the one and despise the other. You cannot be a slave to both God and Money.

Do not Worry

25 "Therefore I tell you, do not worry about your life, what you will eat or drink; or about your body, what you will wear. Is not life more important than food, and the body more important than clothes? 26 Look at the birds of the air; they do not sow or reap or store away in barns, and yet your heavenly Father feeds them. Are you not much more valuable than they? 27 Who of you by worrying can add a single hour to your life?[b] 28 "And why do you worry about clothes? See how the lilies of the field grow. They do not labour or spin. 29 Yet I tell you that not even Solomon in all his splendour was dressed like one of these. 30 If that is how God clothes the grass of the field, which is here today and tomorrow is thrown into the fire, will he not much more clothe you, O you of little faith? 31 So do not worry, saying, 'What shall we eat?' or 'What shall we drink?' or 'What shall we wear?' 32 For the pagans run after all these things, and your heavenly Father knows that you need them. 33 But seek first his kingdom and his righteousness, and all these things will be given to you as well. 34 Therefore do not worry about tomorrow, for tomorrow will worry about itself. Each day has enough trouble of its own.

Judging Others

7 "Do not judge, or you too will be judged. 2 For in the same way as you judge others, you will be judged, and with the measure you use, it will be measured to you.

3 "Why do you look at the speck of sawdust in someone else's eye and pay no attention to the plank in your own eye? 4 How can you say, 'Let me take the speck out of your eye,' when all the time there is a plank in your own eye? 5 You hypocrite, first take the plank out of your own eye, and then you will see clearly to remove the speck from the other person's eye.

6 "Do not give dogs what is sacred; do not throw your pearls to pigs. If you do, they may trample them under their feet, and then turn and tear you to pieces.

Ask, Seek, Knock

7 "Ask and it will be given to you; seek and you will find; knock and the door will be opened to you. 8 For everyone who asks receives; everyone who seeks finds; and to everyone who knocks, the door will be opened.

9 "Which of you, if your children ask for bread, will give them a stone? 10 Or if they ask for a fish, will give them a snake? 11 If you, then, though you are evil, know how

b27 Or single cubit to your height

to give good gifts to your children, how much more will your Father in heaven give good gifts to those who ask him! ¹²So in everything, do to others what you would have them do to you, for this sums up the Law and the Prophets.

The Narrow and Wide Gates

¹³"Enter through the narrow gate. For wide is the gate and broad is the road that leads to destruction, and many enter through it. ¹⁴But small is the gate and narrow the road that leads to life, and only a few find it.

A Tree and Its Fruit

¹⁵"Watch out for false prophets. They come to you in sheep's clothing, but inwardly they are ferocious wolves. ¹⁶By their fruit you will recognise them. Do people pick grapes from thornbushes, or figs from thistles? ¹⁷Likewise every good tree bears good fruit, but a bad tree bears bad fruit. ¹⁸A good tree cannot bear bad fruit, and a bad tree cannot bear good fruit. ¹⁹Every tree that does not bear good fruit is cut down and thrown into the fire. ²⁰Thus, by their fruit you will recognise them.

²¹"Not everyone who says to me, 'Lord, Lord,' will enter the kingdom of heaven, but only those who do the will of my Father who is in heaven. ²²Many will say to me on that day, 'Lord, Lord, did we not prophesy in your name, and in your name drive out demons and perform many miracles?' ²³Then I will tell them plainly, 'I never knew you. Away from me, you evildoers!'

The Wise and Foolish Builders

²⁴"Therefore everyone who hears these words of mine and puts them into practice is like a wise man who built his house on the rock. ²⁵The rain came down, the streams rose, and the winds blew and beat against that house; yet it did not fall, because it had its foundation on the rock.

²⁶But everyone who hears these words of mine and does not put them into practice is like a foolish man who built his house on sand. ²⁷The rain came down, the streams rose, and the winds blew and beat against that house, and it fell with a great crash."

²⁸When Jesus had finished saying these things, the crowds were amazed at his teaching, ²⁹because he taught as one who had authority, and not as their teachers of the law.

The Man with Leprosy

8 When he came down from the mountainside, large crowds followed him. ²A man with leprosy[a] came and knelt before him and said, "Lord, if you are willing, you can make me clean."

³Jesus reached out his hand and touched the man. "I am willing," he said. "Be clean!" Immediately he was cured[b] of his leprosy. ⁴Then Jesus said to him, "See that you don't tell anyone. But go, show yourself to the priest and offer the gift Moses commanded, as a testimony to them."

The Faith of the Centurion

⁵When Jesus had entered Capernaum, a centurion came to him, asking for help. ⁶"Lord," he said, "my servant lies at home paralysed and in terrible suffering."

⁷Jesus said to him, "I will go and heal him."

⁸The centurion replied, "Lord, I do not deserve to have you come under my roof. But just say the word, and my servant will be healed. ⁹For I myself am a man under authority, with soldiers under me. I tell this one, 'Go,' and he goes; and that one, 'Come,' and he comes. I say to my servant, 'Do this,' and he does it."

¹⁰When Jesus heard this, he was astonished and said to those following him, "I tell you the truth, I have not found anyone in Israel with such great faith. ¹¹I say to you that many will come from the east and the west, and will take their places at the

---

[a]2 The Greek word was used for various diseases affecting the skin—not necessarily leprosy.
[b]3 Greek made clean

feast with Abraham, Isaac and Jacob in the kingdom of heaven. [12] But the subjects of the kingdom will be thrown outside, into the darkness, where there will be weeping and gnashing of teeth."

[13] Then Jesus said to the centurion, "Go! It will be done just as you believed it would." And his servant was healed at that very hour.

Jesus Heals Many

[14] When Jesus came into Peter's house, he saw Peter's mother-in-law lying in bed with a fever. [15] He touched her hand and the fever left her, and she got up and began to wait on him.

[16] When evening came, many who were demon-possessed were brought to him, and he drove out the spirits with a word and healed all the sick. [17] This was to fulfil what was spoken through the prophet Isaiah:

"He took up our infirmities
and carried our diseases."[c]

The Cost of Following Jesus

[18] When Jesus saw the crowd around him, he gave orders to cross to the other side of the lake. [19] Then a teacher of the law came to him and said, "Teacher, I will follow you wherever you go."

[20] Jesus replied, "Foxes have holes and birds of the air have nests, but the Son of Man has nowhere to lay his head."

[21] Another disciple said to him, "Lord, first let me go and bury my father."

[22] But Jesus told him, "Follow me, and let the dead bury their own dead."

Jesus Calms the Storm

[23] Then he got into the boat and his disciples followed him. [24] Without warning, a furious storm came up on the lake, so that the waves swept over the boat. But Jesus was sleeping. [25] The disciples went and woke him, saying, "Lord, save us! We're going to drown!"

[26] He replied, "You of little faith, why are you so afraid?" Then he got up and rebuked the winds and the waves, and it was completely calm.

[27] The disciples were amazed and asked, "What kind of man is this? Even the winds and the waves obey him!"

The Healing of Two Demon-possessed Men

[28] When he arrived at the other side in the region of the Gadarenes,[d] two demon-possessed men coming from the tombs met him. They were so violent that no-one could pass that way. [29] "What do you want with us, Son of God?" they shouted. "Have you come here to torture us before the appointed time?"

[30] Some distance from them a large herd of pigs was feeding. [31] The demons begged Jesus, "If you drive us out, send us into the herd of pigs."

[32] He said to them, "Go!" So they came out and went into the pigs, and the whole herd rushed down the steep bank into the lake and died in the water. [33] Those tending the pigs ran off, went into the town and reported all this, including what had happened to the demon-possessed men. [34] Then the whole town went out to meet Jesus. And when they saw him, they pleaded with him to leave their region.

Jesus Heals a Paralytic

9 Jesus stepped into a boat, crossed over and came to his own town. [2] Some people brought to him a paralytic, lying on a mat. When Jesus saw their faith, he said to the paralytic, "Take heart, son; your sins are forgiven."

[3] At this, some of the teachers of the law said to themselves, "This fellow is blaspheming!"

[4] Knowing their thoughts, Jesus said, "Why do you entertain evil thoughts in your hearts? [5] Which is easier: to say, 'Your sins are forgiven,' or to say, 'Get up and walk'? [6] But so that you may know that the Son of Man has authority on earth to forgive sins. . . ." Then he said to the

[c]17 Isaiah 53:4   [d]28 Some manuscripts *Gergesenes*; others *Gerasenes*

paralytic, "Get up, take your mat and go home." [7] And the man got up and went home. [8] When the crowd saw this, they were filled with awe; and they praised God, who had given such authority to human beings.

The Calling of Matthew

[9] As Jesus went on from there, he saw a man named Matthew sitting at the tax collector's booth. "Follow me," he told him, and Matthew got up and followed him.
[10] While Jesus was having dinner at Matthew's house, many tax collectors and "sinners" came and ate with him and his disciples. [11] When the Pharisees saw this, they asked his disciples, "Why does your teacher eat with tax collectors and 'sinners'?"
[12] On hearing this, Jesus said, "It is not the healthy who need a doctor, but the sick. [13] But go and learn what this means: 'I desire mercy, not sacrifice.'[a] For I have not come to call the righteous, but sinners."

Jesus Questioned About Fasting

[14] Then John's disciples came and asked him, "How is it that we and the Pharisees fast, but your disciples do not fast?"
[15] Jesus answered, "How can the guests of the bridegroom mourn while he is with them? The time will come when the bridegroom will be taken from them; then they will fast.
[16] "No-one sews a patch of unshrunk cloth on an old garment, for the patch will pull away from the garment, making the tear worse. [17] Neither do people pour new wine into old wineskins. If they do, the skins will burst, the wine will run out and the wineskins will be ruined. No, they pour new wine into new wineskins, and both are preserved."

A Dead Girl and a Sick Woman

[18] While he was saying this, a ruler came and knelt before him and said, "My daughter has just died. But come and put your hand on her, and she will live."
[19] Jesus got up and went with him, and so did his disciples.
[20] Just then a woman who had been subject to bleeding for twelve years came up behind him and touched the edge of his cloak. [21] She said to herself, "If I only touch his cloak, I will be healed."
[22] Jesus turned and saw her. "Take heart, daughter," he said, "your faith has healed you." And the woman was healed from that moment.
[23] When Jesus entered the ruler's house and saw the flute players and the noisy crowd, [24] he said, "Go away. The girl is not dead but asleep." But they laughed at him. [25] After the crowd had been put outside, he went in and took the girl by the hand, and she got up. [26] News of this spread through all that region.

Jesus Heals the Blind and Mute

[27] As Jesus went on from there, two blind men followed him, calling out, "Have mercy on us, Son of David!"
[28] When he had gone indoors, the blind men came to him, and he asked them, "Do you believe that I am able to do this?"
"Yes, Lord," they replied.
[29] Then he touched their eyes and said, "According to your faith will it be done to you"; [30] and their sight was restored. Jesus warned them sternly, "See that no-one knows about this." [31] But they went out and spread the news about him all over that region.
[32] While they were going out, a man who was demon-possessed and could not talk was brought to Jesus. [33] And when the demon was driven out, the man who had been mute spoke. The crowd was amazed and said, "Nothing like this has ever been seen in Israel."
[34] But the Pharisees said, "It is by the prince of demons that he drives out demons."

The Workers Are Few

[35] Jesus went through all the towns and villages, teaching in their synagogues,

[a]13 Hosea 6:6

preaching the good news of the kingdom and healing every disease and sickness. ³⁶When he saw the crowds, he had compassion on them, because they were harassed and helpless, like sheep without a shepherd. ³⁷Then he said to his disciples, "The harvest is plentiful but the workers are few. ³⁸Ask the Lord of the harvest, therefore, to send out workers into his harvest field."

Jesus Sends Out the Twelve

10 He called his twelve disciples to him and gave them authority to drive out evil*ᵃ* spirits and to heal every disease and sickness.

²These are the names of the twelve apostles: first, Simon (who is called Peter) and his brother Andrew; James son of Zebedee, and his brother John; ³Philip and Bartholomew; Thomas and Matthew the tax collector; James son of Alphaeus, and Thaddaeus; ⁴Simon the Zealot and Judas Iscariot, who betrayed him.

⁵These twelve Jesus sent out with the following instructions: "Do not go among the Gentiles or enter any town of the Samaritans. ⁶Go rather to the lost sheep of Israel. ⁷As you go, preach this message: 'The kingdom of heaven is near.' ⁸Heal the sick, raise the dead, cleanse those who have leprosy,*ᵇ* drive out demons. Freely you have received, freely give. ⁹Do not take along any gold or silver or copper in your belts; ¹⁰take no bag for the journey, or extra tunic, or sandals or a staff; for workers are worth their keep.

¹¹"Whatever town or village you enter, search for some worthy person there and stay at that house until you leave. ¹²As you enter the home, give it your greeting. ¹³If the home is deserving, let your peace rest on it; if it is not, let your peace return to you. ¹⁴If anyone will not welcome you or listen to your words, shake the dust off your feet when you leave that home or town. ¹⁵I tell you the truth, it will be more bearable for Sodom and Gomorrah on the day of judgment than for that town. ¹⁶I am

sending you out like sheep among wolves. Therefore be as shrewd as snakes and as innocent as doves.

¹⁷"Be on your guard against other people; they will hand you over to the local councils and flog you in their synagogues. ¹⁸On my account you will be brought before governors and kings as witnesses to them and to the Gentiles. ¹⁹But when they arrest you, do not worry about what to say or how to say it. At that time you will be given what to say, ²⁰for it will not be you speaking, but the Spirit of your Father speaking through you.

²¹"Brother will betray brother to death, and a father his child; children will rebel against their parents and have them put to death. ²²Everyone will hate you because of me, but those who stand firm to the end will be saved. ²³When you are persecuted in one place, flee to another. I tell you the truth, you will not finish going through the cities of Israel before the Son of Man comes.

²⁴"Students are not above their teachers, nor servants above their masters. ²⁵It is enough for students to be like their teachers, and the servants like their masters. If the head of the house has been called Beelzebub,*ᶜ* how much more the members of the household!

²⁶"So do not be afraid of them. There is nothing concealed that will not be disclosed, or hidden that will not be made known. ²⁷What I tell you in the dark, speak in the daylight; what is whispered in your ear, proclaim from the roofs. ²⁸Do not be afraid of those who kill the body but cannot kill the soul. Rather, be afraid of the One who can destroy both soul and body in hell. ²⁹Are not two sparrows sold for a penny?*ᵈ* Yet not one of them will fall to the ground apart from the will of your Father. ³⁰And even the very hairs of your head are all numbered. ³¹So don't be afraid; you are worth more than many sparrows.

³²"Those who acknowledge me before others, I will also acknowledge before my Father in heaven. ³³But those who disown

---

*ᵃ*1 Greek *unclean*
*ᵇ*8 The Greek word was used for various diseases affecting the skin—not necessarily leprosy.
*ᶜ*25 Greek *Beezeboul* or *Beelzeboul*   *ᵈ*29 Greek *an assarion*

me before others, I will disown before my Father in heaven.

34 "Do not suppose that I have come to bring peace to the earth. I did not come to bring peace, but a sword. 35 For I have come to turn

" 'a man against his father,
     a daughter against her mother,
a daughter-in-law against her
     mother-in-law—
36   Your enemies will be the members
     of your own household.'*e*

37 "Anyone who loves father or mother more than me is not worthy of me; anyone who loves son or daughter more than me is not worthy of me; 38 Those who do not take up their cross and follow me are not worthy of me. 39 Those who find their lives will lose them, and those who lose their lives for my sake will find them.

40 "Anyone who receives you receives me, and anyone who receives me receives the one who sent me. 41 Anyone who receives a prophet as a prophet will receive a prophet's reward, and anyone who receives a righteous person as a righteous person will receive a righteous person's reward. 42 And if anyone gives even a cup of cold water to one of these little ones who is my disciple, I tell you the truth, that person will certainly be rewarded."

Jesus and John the Baptist

11 After Jesus had finished instructing his twelve disciples, he went on from there to teach and preach in the towns of Galilee.*a*

2 When John heard in prison what Christ was doing, he sent his disciples 3 to ask him, "Are you the one who was to come, or should we expect someone else?"

4 Jesus replied, "Go back and report to John what you hear and see: 5 The blind receive sight, the lame walk, those who have leprosy*b* are cured, the deaf hear, the dead are raised, and the good news is preached to the poor. 6 Blessed is anyone

who does not fall away on account of me."

7 As John's disciples were leaving, Jesus began to speak to the crowd about John: "What did you go out into the desert to see? A reed swayed by the wind? 8 If not, what did you go out to see? A man dressed in fine clothes? No, those who wear fine clothes are in kings' palaces. 9 Then what did you go out to see? A prophet? Yes, I tell you, and more than a prophet. 10 This is the one about whom it is written:

" 'I will send my messenger ahead of
     you,
   who will prepare your way before
     you.'*c*

11 I tell you the truth: Among those born of women there has not risen anyone greater than John the Baptist; yet whoever is least in the kingdom of heaven is greater than he. 12 From the days of John the Baptist until now, the kingdom of heaven has been forcefully advancing, and forceful people lay hold of it. 13 For all the Prophets and the Law prophesied until John. 14 And if you are willing to accept it, he is the Elijah who was to come. 15 Those who have ears, let them hear.

16 "To what can I compare this generation? They are like children sitting in the market-places and calling out to others:

17 " 'We played the flute for you,
     and you did not dance;
   we sang a dirge,
     and you did not mourn.'

18 For John came neither eating nor drinking, and they say, 'He has a demon.' 19 The Son of Man came eating and drinking, and they say, 'Here is a glutton and a drunkard, a friend of tax collectors and "sinners".' But wisdom is proved right by her actions."

Woe on Unrepentant Cities

20 Then Jesus began to denounce the cities in which most of his miracles had been performed, because they did not

*e*36 Micah 7:6   *a*1 Greek *in their towns*
*b*5 The Greek word was used for various diseases affecting the skin—not necessarily leprosy.   *c*10 Mal. 3:1

repent. ²¹ "Woe to you, Korazin! Woe to you, Bethsaida! If the miracles that were performed in you had been performed in Tyre and Sidon, they would have repented long ago in sackcloth and ashes. ²² But I tell you, it will be more bearable for Tyre and Sidon on the day of judgment than for you. ²³ And you, Capernaum, will you be lifted up to the skies? No, you will go down to the depths.*d* If the miracles that were performed in you had been performed in Sodom, it would have remained to this day. ²⁴ But I tell you that it will be more bearable for Sodom on the day of judgment than for you."

Rest for the Weary

²⁵ At that time Jesus said, "I praise you, Father, Lord of heaven and earth, because you have hidden these things from the wise and learned, and revealed them to little children. ²⁶ Yes, Father, for this was your good pleasure.

²⁷ "All things have been committed to me by my Father. No-one knows the Son except the Father, and no-one knows the Father except the Son and those to whom the Son chooses to reveal him.

²⁸ "Come to me, all you who are weary and burdened, and I will give you rest. ²⁹ Take my yoke upon you and learn from me, for I am gentle and humble in heart, and you will find rest for your souls. ³⁰ For my yoke is easy and my burden is light."

Lord of the Sabbath

12 At that time Jesus went through the cornfields on the Sabbath. His disciples were hungry and began to pick some ears of corn and eat them. ² When the Pharisees saw this, they said to him, "Look! Your disciples are doing what is unlawful on the Sabbath."

³ He answered, "Haven't you read what David did when he and his companions were hungry? ⁴ He entered the house of God, and he and his companions ate the consecrated bread—which was not lawful for them to do, but only for the priests. ⁵ Or haven't you read in the Law that on the Sabbath the priests in the temple desecrate the day and yet are innocent? ⁶ I tell you that one*a* greater than the temple is here. ⁷ If you had known what these words mean, 'I desire mercy, not sacrifice,'*b* you would not have condemned the innocent. ⁸ For the Son of Man is Lord of the Sabbath."

⁹ Going on from that place, he went into their synagogue, ¹⁰ and a man with a shrivelled hand was there. Looking for a reason to accuse Jesus, they asked him, "Is it lawful to heal on the Sabbath?"

¹¹ He said to them, "If any of you has a sheep and it falls into a pit on the Sabbath, will you not take hold of it and lift it out? ¹² How much more valuable is a human being than a sheep! Therefore it is lawful to do good on the Sabbath."

¹³ Then he said to the man, "Stretch out your hand." So he stretched it out and it was completely restored, just as sound as the other. ¹⁴ But the Pharisees went out and plotted how they might kill Jesus.

God's Chosen Servant

¹⁵ Aware of this, Jesus withdrew from that place. Many followed him, and he healed all their sick, ¹⁶ warning them not to tell who he was. ¹⁷ This was to fulfil what was spoken through the prophet Isaiah:

¹⁸ "Here is my servant whom I have chosen,
    the one I love, in whom I delight;
I will put my Spirit on him,
    and he will proclaim justice to the nations.
¹⁹ He will not quarrel or cry out;
    no-one will hear his voice in the streets.
²⁰ A bruised reed he will not break,
    and a smouldering wick he will not snuff out,
till he leads justice to victory.
²¹   In his name the nations will put their hope."*c*

---

*d*23 Greek *Hades*   *a*6 Or *something*; also in verses 41 and 42   *b*7 Hosea 6:6   *c*21 Isaiah 42:1–4

Jesus and Beelzebub

22 Then they brought him a demon-possessed man who was blind and mute, and Jesus healed him, so that he could both talk and see. 23 All the people were astonished and said, "Could this be the Son of David?"

24 But when the Pharisees heard this, they said, "It is only by Beelzebub,*d* the prince of demons, that this fellow drives out demons."

25 Jesus knew their thoughts and said to them, "Every kingdom divided against itself will be ruined, and every city or household divided against itself will not stand. 26 If Satan drives out Satan, he is divided against himself. How then can his kingdom stand? 27 And if I drive out demons by Beelzebub, by whom do your people drive them out? So then, they will be your judges. 28 But if I drive out demons by the Spirit of God, then the kingdom of God has come upon you.

29 "Or again, how can anyone enter a strong man's house and carry off his possessions without first tying up the strong man? Then his house can be plundered.

30 "Whoever is not with me is against me, and whoever does not gather with me scatters. 31 And so I tell you, people will be forgiven every sin and blasphemy. But the blasphemy against the Spirit will not be forgiven. 32 Anyone who speaks a word against the Son of Man will be forgiven, but anyone who speaks against the Holy Spirit will not be forgiven, either in this age or in the age to come.

33 "Make a tree good and its fruit will be good, or make a tree bad and its fruit will be bad, for a tree is recognised by its fruit. 34 You brood of vipers, how can you who are evil say anything good? For out of the overflow of the heart the mouth speaks. 35 Good people bring good things out of the good stored up in them, and evil people bring evil things out of the evil stored up in them. 36 But I tell you that people will have to give account on the day of judgment for every careless word they have spoken. 37 For by your words

you will be acquitted, and by your words you will be condemned."

The Sign of Jonah

38 Then some of the Pharisees and teachers of the law said to him, "Teacher, we want to see a miraculous sign from you."

39 He answered, "A wicked and adulterous generation asks for a miraculous sign! But none will be given it except the sign of the prophet Jonah. 40 For as Jonah was three days and three nights in the belly of a huge fish, so the Son of Man will be three days and three nights in the heart of the earth. 41 The people of Nineveh will stand up at the judgment with this generation and condemn it; for they repented at the preaching of Jonah, and now one*e* greater than Jonah is here. 42 The Queen of the South will rise at the judgment with this generation and condemn it; for she came from the ends of the earth to listen to Solomon's wisdom, and now one greater than Solomon is here.

43 "When an evil*f* spirit comes out of anyone, it goes through arid places seeking rest and does not find it. 44 Then it says, 'I will return to the house I left.' When it arrives, it finds the house unoccupied, swept clean and put in order. 45 Then it goes and takes with it seven other spirits more wicked than itself, and they go in and live there. And the final condition of that person is worse than the first. That is how it will be with this wicked generation."

Jesus' Mother and Brothers

46 While Jesus was still talking to the crowd, his mother and brothers stood outside, wanting to speak to him. 47 Someone told him, "Your mother and brothers are standing outside, wanting to speak to you."*g*

48 He replied to him, "Who is my mother, and who are my brothers?" 49 Pointing to his disciples, he said, "Here are my mother and my brothers. 50 For

---

*d*24 Greek *Beezeboul* or *Beelzeboul*; also in verse 27   *e*41 Or *something*; also in verse 42   *f*43 Greek *unclean*   *g*47 Some manuscripts do not have verse 47.

whoever does the will of my Father in heaven is my brother and sister and mother."

The Parable of the Sower

13 That same day Jesus went out of the house and sat by the lake. ² Such large crowds gathered round him that he got into a boat and sat in it, while all the people stood on the shore. ³ Then he told them many things in parables, saying: "A farmer went out to sow his seed. ⁴ As he was scattering the seed, some fell along the path, and the birds came and ate it up. ⁵ Some fell on rocky places, where it did not have much soil. It sprang up quickly, because the soil was shallow. ⁶ But when the sun came up, the plants were scorched, and they withered because they had no root. ⁷ Other seed fell among thorns, which grew up and choked the plants. ⁸ Still other seed fell on good soil, where it produced a crop—a hundred, sixty or thirty times what was sown. ⁹ Those who have ears, let them hear."

¹⁰ The disciples came to him and asked, "Why do you speak to the people in parables?"

¹¹ He replied, "The knowledge of the secrets of the kingdom of heaven has been given to you, but not to them. ¹² Those who have will be given more, and they will have an abundance. Those who do not have, even what they have will be taken from them. ¹³ This is why I speak to them in parables:

"Though seeing, they do not see;
    though hearing, they do not hear or understand.

¹⁴ In them is fulfilled the prophecy of Isaiah:

" 'You will be ever hearing but never understanding;
    you will be ever seeing but never perceiving.
¹⁵ For this people's heart has become calloused;

they hardly hear with their ears,
    and they have closed their eyes.
Otherwise they might see with their eyes,
hear with their ears,
    understand with their hearts
and turn, and I would heal them.'ᵃ

¹⁶ "But blessed are your eyes because they see, and your ears because they hear. ¹⁷ For I tell you the truth, many prophets and righteous people longed to see what you see but did not see it, and to hear what you hear but did not hear it.

¹⁸ "Listen then to what the parable of the sower means: ¹⁹ When people hear the message about the kingdom and do not understand it, the evil one comes and snatches away what was sown in their hearts. This is the seed sown along the path. ²⁰ Those who received the seed that fell on rocky places are people who hear the word and at once receive it with joy. ²¹ But since they have no root, they last only a short time. When trouble or persecution comes because of the word, they quickly fall away. ²² Those who received the seed that fell among the thorns are people who hear the word, but the worries of this life and the deceitfulness of wealth choke it, making it unfruitful. ²³ But those who received the seed that fell on good soil are people who hear the word and understand it. They produce a crop, yielding a hundred, sixty or thirty times what was sown."

The Parable of the Weeds

²⁴ Jesus told them another parable: "The kingdom of heaven is like a man who sowed good seed in his field. ²⁵ But while everyone was sleeping, his enemy came and sowed weeds among the wheat, and went away. ²⁶ When the wheat sprouted and formed ears, then the weeds also appeared.

²⁷ "The owner's servants came to him and said, 'Sir, didn't you sow good seed in your field? Where then did the weeds come from?'

ᵃ15 Isaiah 6:9,10

28 " 'An enemy did this,' he replied.

"The servants asked him, 'Do you want us to go and pull them up?'

29 " 'No,' he answered, 'because while you are pulling the weeds, you may root up the wheat with them. 30 Let both grow together until the harvest. At that time I will tell the harvesters: First collect the weeds and tie them in bundles to be burned; then gather the wheat and bring it into my barn.' "

The Parables of the Mustard Seed and the Yeast

31 He told them another parable: "The kingdom of heaven is like a mustard seed, which a man took and planted in his field. 32 Though it is the smallest of all your seeds, yet when it grows, it is the largest of garden plants and becomes a tree, so that the birds of the air come and perch in its branches."

33 He told them still another parable: "The kingdom of heaven is like yeast that a woman took and mixed into a large amount[b] of flour until it worked all through the dough."

34 Jesus spoke all these things to the crowd in parables; he did not say anything to them without using a parable. 35 So was fulfilled what was spoken through the prophet:

"I will open my mouth in parables,
  I will utter things hidden since the creation of the world."[c]

The Parable of the Weeds Explained

36 Then he left the crowd and went into the house. His disciples came to him and said, "Explain to us the parable of the weeds in the field."

37 He answered, "The one who sowed the good seed is the Son of Man. 38 The field is the world, and the good seed stands for the people of the kingdom. The weeds are the people of the evil one, 39 and the enemy who sows them is the devil. The harvest is the end of the age, and the harvesters are angels.

40 "As the weeds are pulled up and burned in the fire, so it will be at the end of the age. 41 The Son of Man will send out his angels, and they will weed out of his kingdom everything that causes sin and all who do evil. 42 They will throw them into the fiery furnace, where there will be weeping and gnashing of teeth. 43 Then the righteous will shine like the sun in the kingdom of their Father. Those who have ears, let them hear.

The Parables of the Hidden Treasure and the Pearl

44 "The kingdom of heaven is like treasure hidden in a field. When a man found it, he hid it again, and then in his joy went and sold all he had and bought that field.

45 "Again, the kingdom of heaven is like a merchant looking for fine pearls. 46 When he found one of great value, he went away and sold everything he had and bought it.

The Parable of the Net

47 "Once again, the kingdom of heaven is like a net that was let down into the lake and caught all kinds of fish. 48 When it was full, the fishermen pulled it up on the shore. Then they sat down and collected the good fish in baskets, but threw the bad away. 49 This is how it will be at the end of the age. The angels will come and separate the wicked from the righteous 50 and throw them into the fiery furnace, where there will be weeping and gnashing of teeth.

51 "Have you understood all these things?" Jesus asked.

"Yes," they replied.

52 He said to them, "Therefore every teacher of the law who has been instructed about the kingdom of heaven is like the owner of a house who brings out of the storeroom new treasures as well as old."

A Prophet Without Honour

53 When Jesus had finished these parables, he moved on from there. 54 Coming

[b]33 Greek *three satas* (probably about 3/5 bushel or 22 litres)   [c]35 Psalm 78:2

to his home town, he began teaching the people in their synagogue, and they were amazed. "Where did this man get this wisdom and these miraculous powers?" they asked. ⁵⁵"Isn't this the carpenter's son? Isn't his mother's name Mary, and aren't his brothers James, Joseph, Simon and Judas? ⁵⁶Aren't all his sisters with us? Where then did this man get all these things?" ⁵⁷And they took offence at him.

But Jesus said to them, "Only in their hometowns and in their own homes are prophets without honour."

⁵⁸And he did not do many miracles there because of their lack of faith.

John the Baptist Beheaded

14 At that time Herod the tetrarch heard the reports about Jesus, ²and he said to his attendants, "This is John the Baptist; he has risen from the dead! That is why miraculous powers are at work in him."

³Now Herod had arrested John and bound him and put him in prison because of Herodias, his brother Philip's wife, ⁴for John had been saying to him: "It is not lawful for you to have her." ⁵Herod wanted to kill John, but he was afraid of the people, because they considered him a prophet.

⁶On Herod's birthday the daughter of Herodias danced for them and pleased Herod so much ⁷that he promised with an oath to give her whatever she asked. ⁸Prompted by her mother, she said, "Give me here on a platter the head of John the Baptist." ⁹The king was distressed, but because of his oaths and his dinner guests, he ordered that her request be granted ¹⁰and had John beheaded in the prison. ¹¹His head was brought in on a platter and given to the girl, who carried it to her mother. ¹²John's disciples came and took his body and buried it. Then they went and told Jesus.

Jesus Feeds the Five Thousand

¹³When Jesus heard what had happened, he withdrew by boat privately to a solitary place. Hearing of this, the crowds followed him on foot from the towns. ¹⁴When Jesus landed and saw a large crowd, he had compassion on them and healed their sick.

¹⁵As evening approached, the disciples came to him and said, "This is a remote place, and it's already getting late. Send the crowds away, so that they can go to the villages and buy themselves some food."

¹⁶Jesus replied, "They do not need to go away. You give them something to eat."

¹⁷"We have here only five loaves of bread and two fish," they answered.

¹⁸"Bring them here to me," he said. ¹⁹And he directed the people to sit down on the grass. Taking the five loaves and the two fish and looking up to heaven, he gave thanks and broke the loaves. Then he gave them to the disciples, and the disciples gave them to the people. ²⁰They all ate and were satisfied, and the disciples picked up twelve basketfuls of broken pieces that were left over. ²¹The number of those who ate was about five thousand men, besides women and children.

Jesus Walks on the Water

²²Immediately Jesus made the disciples get into the boat and go on ahead of him to the other side, while he dismissed the crowd. ²³After he had dismissed them, he went up on a mountainside by himself to pray. When evening came, he was there alone, ²⁴but the boat was already a considerable distance*a* from land, buffeted by the waves because the wind was against it.

²⁵During the fourth watch of the night Jesus went out to them, walking on the lake. ²⁶When the disciples saw him walking on the lake, they were terrified. "It's a ghost," they said, and cried out in fear.

²⁷But Jesus immediately said to them: "Take courage! It is I. Don't be afraid."

²⁸"Lord, if it's you," Peter replied, "tell me to come to you on the water."

²⁹"Come," he said.

Then Peter got down out of the boat, walked on the water and came towards

*a*24 Greek *many stadia*

Jesus. 30 But when he saw the wind, he was afraid and, beginning to sink, cried out, "Lord, save me!"

31 Immediately Jesus reached out his hand and caught him. "You of little faith," he said, "why did you doubt?"

32 And when they climbed into the boat, the wind died down. 33 Then those who were in the boat worshipped him, saying, "Truly you are the Son of God."

34 When they had crossed over, they landed at Gennesaret. 35 And when the people of that place recognised Jesus, they sent word to all the surrounding country. People brought all their sick to him 36 and begged him to let the sick just touch the edge of his cloak, and all who touched him were healed.

Clean and Unclean

15 Then some Pharisees and teachers of the law came to Jesus from Jerusalem and asked, 2 "Why do your disciples break the tradition of the elders? They don't wash their hands before they eat!"

3 Jesus replied, "And why do you break the command of God for the sake of your tradition? 4 For God said, 'Honour your father and mother'*a* and 'Anyone who curses father or mother must be put to death.'*b* 5 But you say that if any say to their father or mother, 'Whatever help you might otherwise have received from me is a gift devoted to God,' 6 they are not to 'honour their father or mother' with it. Thus you nullify the word of God for the sake of your tradition. 7 You hypocrites! Isaiah was right when he prophesied about you:

8 " 'These people honour me with their lips,
but their hearts are far from me.
9 They worship me in vain;
their teachings are merely human rules.'*c* "

10 Jesus called the crowd to him and said, "Listen and understand. 11 What goes into your mouth does not make you 'unclean', but what comes out of your mouth, that is what makes you 'unclean'."

12 Then the disciples came to him and asked, "Do you know that the Pharisees were offended when they heard this?"

13 He replied, "Every plant that my heavenly Father has not planted will be pulled up by the roots. 14 Leave them; they are blind guides.*d* If the blind lead the blind, both will fall into a pit."

15 Peter said, "Explain the parable to us."

16 "Are you still so dull?" Jesus asked them. 17 "Don't you see that whatever enters the mouth goes into the stomach and then out of the body? 18 But the things that come out of the mouth come from the heart, and these make you 'unclean'. 19 For out of the heart come evil thoughts, murder, adultery, sexual immorality, theft, false testimony, slander. 20 These are what make you 'unclean'; but eating with unwashed hands does not make you 'unclean'."

The Faith of the Canaanite Woman

21 Leaving that place, Jesus withdrew to the region of Tyre and Sidon. 22 A Canaanite woman from that vicinity came to him, crying out, "Lord, Son of David, have mercy on me! My daughter is suffering terribly from demon-possession."

23 Jesus did not answer a word. So his disciples came to him and urged him, "Send her away, for she keeps crying out after us."

24 He answered, "I was sent only to the lost sheep of Israel."

25 The woman came and knelt before him. "Lord, help me!" she said.

26 He replied, "It is not right to take the children's bread and toss it to their dogs."

27 "Yes, Lord," she said, "but even the dogs eat the crumbs that fall from their masters' table."

28 Then Jesus answered, "Woman, you have great faith! Your request is granted." And her daughter was healed from that very hour.

*a*4 Exodus 20:12; Deut. 5:16   *b*4 Exodus 21:17; Lev. 20:9   *c*9 Isaiah 29:13
*d*14 Some manuscripts *guides of the blind*

Jesus Feeds the Four Thousand

²⁹Jesus left there and went along the Sea of Galilee. Then he went up on a mountainside and sat down. ³⁰Great crowds came to him, bringing the lame, the blind, the crippled, the mute and many others, and laid them at his feet; and he healed them. ³¹The people were amazed when they saw the mute speaking, the crippled made well, the lame walking and the blind seeing. And they praised the God of Israel.

³²Jesus called his disciples to him and said, "I have compassion for these people; they have already been with me three days and have nothing to eat. I do not want to send them away hungry, or they may collapse on the way."

³³His disciples answered, "Where could we get enough bread in this remote place to feed such a crowd?"

³⁴"How many loaves do you have?" Jesus asked.

"Seven," they replied, "and a few small fish."

³⁵He told the crowd to sit down on the ground. ³⁶Then he took the seven loaves and the fish, and when he had given thanks, he broke them and gave them to the disciples, and they in turn to the people. ³⁷They all ate and were satisfied. Afterwards the disciples picked up seven basketfuls of broken pieces that were left over. ³⁸The number of those who ate was four thousand men, besides women and children. ³⁹After Jesus had sent the crowd away, he got into the boat and went to the vicinity of Magadan.

The Demand for a Sign

16 The Pharisees and Sadducees came to Jesus and tested him by asking him to show them a sign from heaven.

²He replied,ᵃ "When evening comes, you say, 'It will be fair weather, for the sky is red,' ³and in the morning, 'Today it will be stormy, for the sky is red and overcast.' You know how to interpret the appearance of the sky, but you cannot interpret the signs of the times. ⁴A wicked and adulterous generation looks for a miraculous sign, but none will be given it except the sign of Jonah." Jesus then left them and went away.

The Yeast of the Pharisees and Sadducees

⁵When they went across the lake, the disciples forgot to take bread. ⁶"Be careful," Jesus said to them. "Be on your guard against the yeast of the Pharisees and Sadducees."

⁷They discussed this among themselves and said, "It is because we didn't bring any bread."

⁸Aware of their discussion, Jesus asked, "You of little faith, why are you talking among yourselves about having no bread? ⁹Do you still not understand? Don't you remember the five loaves for the five thousand, and how many basketfuls you gathered? ¹⁰Or the seven loaves for the four thousand, and how many basketfuls you gathered? ¹¹How is it you don't understand that I was not talking to you about bread? But be on your guard against the yeast of the Pharisees and Sadducees." ¹²Then they understood that he was not telling them to guard against the yeast used in bread, but against the teaching of the Pharisees and Sadducees.

Peter's Confession of Christ

¹³When Jesus came to the region of Caesarea Philippi, he asked his disciples, "Who do people say the Son of Man is?"

¹⁴They replied, "Some say John the Baptist; others say Elijah; and still others, Jeremiah or one of the prophets."

¹⁵"But what about you?" he asked. "Who do you say I am?"

¹⁶Simon Peter answered, "You are the Christ,ᵇ the Son of the living God."

¹⁷Jesus replied, "Blessed are you, Simon son of Jonah, for this was not revealed to you by flesh and blood, but by my Father in heaven. ¹⁸And I tell you that you are Peter,ᶜ and on this rock I will build

---

ᵃ2 Some early manuscripts do not have the rest of verse 2 and all of verse 3.   ᵇ16 Or *Messiah*; also in verse 20
ᶜ18 *Peter* means *rock*.

my church, and the gates of Hades*d* will not overcome it. *e* 19 I will give you the keys of the kingdom of heaven; whatever you bind on earth will be*f* bound in heaven, and whatever you loose on earth will be*g* loosed in heaven." 20 Then he warned his disciples not to tell anyone that he was the Christ.

Jesus Predicts His Death

21 From that time on Jesus began to explain to his disciples that he must go to Jerusalem and suffer many things at the hands of the elders, chief priests and teachers of the law, and that he must be killed and on the third day be raised to life.

22 Peter took him aside and began to rebuke him. "Never, Lord!" he said. "This shall never happen to you!"

23 Jesus turned and said to Peter, "Get behind me, Satan! You are a stumbling-block to me; you do not have in mind the concerns of God, but human concerns."

24 Then Jesus said to his disciples, "Those who would come after me must deny themselves and take up their cross and follow me. 25 For those who want to save their lives*h* will lose them, but those who lose their lives for me will find them. 26 What good will it be for you to gain the whole world, yet forfeit your soul? Or what can you give in exchange for your soul? 27 For the Son of Man is going to come in his Father's glory with his angels, and then he will reward everyone according to what they have done. 28 I tell you the truth, some who are standing here will not taste death before they see the Son of Man coming in his kingdom."

The Transfiguration

17 After six days Jesus took with him Peter, James and John the brother of James, and led them up a high mountain by themselves. 2 There he was transfigured before them. His face shone like the sun, and his clothes became as white as the light. 3 Just then there appeared before

them Moses and Elijah, talking with Jesus.

4 Peter said to Jesus, "Lord, it is good for us to be here. If you wish, I will put up three shelters—one for you, one for Moses and one for Elijah."

5 While he was still speaking, a bright cloud enveloped them, and a voice from the cloud said, "This is my Son, whom I love; with him I am well pleased. Listen to him!"

6 When the disciples heard this, they fell face down to the ground, terrified. 7 But Jesus came and touched them. "Get up," he said. "Don't be afraid." 8 When they looked up, they saw no-one except Jesus.

9 As they were coming down the mountain, Jesus instructed them, "Don't tell anyone what you have seen, until the Son of Man has been raised from the dead."

10 The disciples asked him, "Why then do the teachers of the law say that Elijah must come first?"

11 Jesus replied, "To be sure, Elijah comes and will restore all things. 12 But I tell you, Elijah has already come, and they did not recognise him, but have done to him everything they wished. In the same way the Son of Man is going to suffer at their hands." 13 Then the disciples understood that he was talking to them about John the Baptist.

The Healing of a Boy With a Demon

14 When they came to the crowd, a man approached Jesus and knelt before him. 15 "Lord, have mercy on my son," he said. "He has seizures and is suffering greatly. He often falls into the fire or into the water. 16 I brought him to your disciples, but they could not heal him."

17 "O unbelieving and perverse generation," Jesus replied, "how long shall I stay with you? How long shall I put up with you? Bring the boy here to me." 18 Jesus rebuked the demon, and it came out of the boy, and he was healed from that moment.

19 Then the disciples came to Jesus in

*d*18 Or *hell*   *e*18 Or *not prove stronger than it*   *f,g*19 Or *have been*
*h*25 The Greek word means either *life* or *soul*; also in verse 26.

private and asked, "Why couldn't we drive it out?"

20 He replied, "Because you have so little faith. I tell you the truth, if you have faith as small as a mustard seed, you can say to this mountain, 'Move from here to there' and it will move. Nothing will be impossible for you."[a]

22 When they came together in Galilee, he said to them, "The Son of Man is going to be betrayed into human hands. 23 People will kill him, and on the third day he will be raised to life." And the disciples were filled with grief.

The Temple Tax

24 After Jesus and his disciples arrived in Capernaum, the collectors of the two-drachma tax came to Peter and asked, "Doesn't your teacher pay the temple tax?"[b]

25 "Yes, he does," he replied.

When Peter came into the house, Jesus was the first to speak. "What do you think, Simon?" he asked. "From whom do the kings of the earth collect duty and taxes—from their own children or from others?"

26 "From others," Peter answered.

"Then the children are exempt," Jesus said to him. 27 "But so that we may not offend them, go to the lake and throw out your line. Take the first fish you catch; open its mouth and you will find a four-drachma coin. Take it and give it to them for my tax and yours."

The Greatest in the Kingdom of Heaven

18 At that time the disciples came to Jesus and asked, "Who is the greatest in the kingdom of heaven?"

2 He called a little child whom he placed among them. 3 And he said: "I tell you the truth, unless you change and become like little children, you will never enter the kingdom of heaven. 4 Therefore, those who humble themselves like this child are the greatest in the kingdom of heaven.

5 "And whoever welcomes a little child like this in my name welcomes me. 6 But if any of you causes one of these little ones who believe in me to sin, it would be better for you to have a large millstone hung around your neck and to be drowned in the depths of the sea.

7 "Woe to the world because of the things that cause people to sin! Such things must come, but woe to the person through whom they come! 8 If your hand or your foot causes you to sin, cut it off and throw it away. It is better for you to enter life maimed or crippled than to have two hands or two feet and be thrown into eternal fire. 9 And if your eye causes you to sin, gouge it out and throw it away. It is better for you to enter life with one eye than to have two eyes and be thrown into the fire of hell.

The Parable of the Lost Sheep

10 "See that you do not look down on one of these little ones. For I tell you that their angels in heaven always see the face of my Father in heaven.[a]

12 "What do you think? If a man owns a hundred sheep, and one of them wanders away, will he not leave the ninety-nine on the hills and go to look for the one that wandered off? 13 And if he finds it, I tell you the truth, he is happier about that one sheep than about the ninety-nine that did not wander off. 14 In the same way your Father in heaven is not willing that any of these little ones should be lost.

Dealing with Sin in the Church

15 "If your brother or sister sins against you,[b] go and show them their fault, just between the two of you. If they listen to you, you have won them over. 16 But if they will not listen, take one or two others along, so that 'every matter may be established by the testimony of two or three witnesses.'[c] 17 If they refuse to listen to them, tell it to the church; and if they

[a]20 Some manuscripts you. 21But this kind does not go out except by prayer and fasting.
[b]24 Greek the two drachmas   [a]10 Some manuscripts heaven. 11The Son of Man came to save what was lost.
[b]15 Some manuscripts do not have against you.   [c]16 Deut. 19:15

refuse to listen even to the church, treat them as you would a pagan or a tax collector.

18 "I tell you the truth, whatever you bind on earth will be[d] bound in heaven, and whatever you loose on earth will be[d] loosed in heaven.

19 "Again, I tell you that if two of you on earth agree about anything you ask for, it will be done for you by my Father in heaven. 20 For where two or three come together in my name, there am I with them."

The Parable of the Unmerciful Servant

21 Then Peter came to Jesus and asked, "Lord, how many times shall I forgive someone who sins against me? Up to seven times?"

22 Jesus answered, "I tell you, not seven times, but seventy-seven times.[e]

23 "Therefore, the kingdom of heaven is like a king who wanted to settle accounts with his servants. 24 As he began the settlement, a man who owed him ten thousand talents[f] was brought to him. 25 Since he was not able to pay, the master ordered that he and his wife and his children and all that he had be sold to repay the debt.

26 "The servant fell on his knees before him. 'Be patient with me,' he begged, 'and I will pay back everything.' 27 The servant's master took pity on him, cancelled the debt and let him go.

28 "But when that servant went out, he found one of his fellow-servants who owed him a hundred denarii.[g] He grabbed him and began to choke him. 'Pay back what you owe me!' he demanded.

29 "His fellow-servant fell to his knees and begged him, 'Be patient with me, and I will pay you back.'

30 "But he refused. Instead, he went off and had the man thrown into prison until he could pay the debt. 31 When the other servants saw what had happened, they were greatly distressed and went and told their master everything that had happened.

32 "Then the master called the servant in. 'You wicked servant,' he said, 'I cancelled all that debt of yours because you begged me to. 33 Shouldn't you have had mercy on your fellow-servant just as I had on you?' 34 In anger his master turned him over to the jailers to be tortured, until he should pay back all he owed.

35 "This is how my heavenly Father will treat each of you unless you forgive one another from your heart."

Divorce

19 When Jesus had finished saying these things, he left Galilee and went into the region of Judea to the other side of the Jordan. 2 Large crowds followed him, and he healed them there.

3 Some Pharisees came to him to test him. They asked, "Is it lawful for a man to divorce his wife for any and every reason?"

4 "Haven't you read," he replied, "that at the beginning the Creator 'made them male and female',[a] 5 and said, 'For this reason a man will leave his father and mother and be united to his wife, and the two will become one flesh'[b]? 6 So they are no longer two, but one. Therefore what God has joined together, let no-one separate."

7 "Why then," they asked, "did Moses command that a man give his wife a certificate of divorce and send her away?"

8 Jesus replied, "Moses permitted you to divorce your wives because your hearts were hard. But it was not this way from the beginning. 9 I tell you that anyone who divorces his wife, except for marital unfaithfulness, and marries another woman commits adultery."

10 The disciples said to him, "If this is the situation between a husband and wife, it is better not to marry."

11 Jesus replied, "Not everyone can accept this word, but only those to whom it has been given. 12 For some are eunuchs because they were born that way; others have been made eunuchs; and others have renounced marriage[c] because of the

---

[d]18 Or *have been*   [e]22 Or *seventy times seven*   [f]24 That is, millions of pounds
[g]28 That is, a few pounds   [a]4 Gen. 1:27   [b]5 Gen. 2:24   [c]12 Or *have made themselves eunuchs*

kingdom of heaven. The one who can accept this should accept it."

The Little Children and Jesus

13 Then little children were brought to Jesus for him to place his hands on them and pray for them. But the disciples rebuked those who brought them.

14 Jesus said, "Let the little children come to me, and do not hinder them, for the kingdom of heaven belongs to such as these." 15 When he had placed his hands on them, he went on from there.

The Rich Young Man

16 Now someone came up to Jesus and asked, "Teacher, what good thing must I do to get eternal life?"

17 "Why do you ask me about what is good?" Jesus replied. "There is only One who is good. If you want to enter life, obey the commandments."

18 "Which ones?" he enquired.

Jesus replied, " 'Do not murder, do not commit adultery, do not steal, do not give false testimony, 19 honour your father and mother,'*d* and 'love your neighbour as yourself.'*e* "

20 "All these I have kept," the young man said. "What do I still lack?"

21 Jesus answered, "If you want to be perfect, go, sell your possessions and give to the poor, and you will have treasure in heaven. Then come, follow me."

22 When the young man heard this, he went away sad, because he had great wealth.

23 Then Jesus said to his disciples, "I tell you the truth, it is hard for the rich to enter the kingdom of heaven. 24 Again I tell you, it is easier for a camel to go through the eye of a needle than for the rich to enter the kingdom of God."

25 When the disciples heard this, they were greatly astonished and asked, "Who then can be saved?"

26 Jesus looked at them and said, "Humanly, this is impossible, but with God all things are possible."

27 Peter answered him, "We have left everything to follow you! What then will there be for us?"

28 Jesus said to them, "I tell you the truth, at the renewal of all things, when the Son of Man sits on his glorious throne, you who have followed me will also sit on twelve thrones, judging the twelve tribes of Israel. 29 And everyone who has left houses or brothers or sisters or father or mother*f* or children or fields for my sake will receive a hundred times as much and will inherit eternal life. 30 But many who are first will be last, and many who are last will be first.

The Parable of the Workers in the Vineyard

20 "For the kingdom of heaven is like a landowner who went out early in the morning to hire workers for his vineyard. 2 He agreed to pay them a denarius for the day and sent them into his vineyard.

3 "About the third hour he went out and saw others standing in the market-place doing nothing. 4 He told them, 'You also go and work in my vineyard, and I will pay you whatever is right.' 5 So they went.

"He went out again about the sixth hour and the ninth hour and did the same thing. 6 About the eleventh hour he went out and found still others standing around. He asked them, 'Why have you been standing here all day long doing nothing?'

7 " 'Because no-one has hired us,' they answered.

"He said to them, 'You also go and work in my vineyard.'

8 "When evening came, the owner of the vineyard said to his manager, 'Call the workers and pay them their wages, beginning with the last ones hired and going on to the first.'

9 "The workers who were hired about the eleventh hour came and each received a denarius. 10 So when those came who were hired first, they expected to receive more. But each one of them also received

a denarius. [11] When they received it, they began to grumble against the landowner. [12] 'These people who were hired last worked only one hour,' they said, 'and you have made them equal to us who have borne the burden of the work and the heat of the day.'

[13] 'But he answered one of them, 'Friend, I am not being unfair to you. Didn't you agree to work for a denarius? [14] Take your pay and go. I want to give the one who was hired last the same as I gave you. [15] Don't I have the right to do what I want with my own money? Or are you envious because I am generous?'

[16] 'So the last will be first, and the first will be last.'

Jesus Again Predicts His Death

[17] Now as Jesus was going up to Jerusalem, he took the twelve disciples aside and said to them, [18] 'We are going up to Jerusalem, and the Son of Man will be betrayed to the chief priests and the teachers of the law. They will condemn him to death [19] and will turn him over to the Gentiles to be mocked and flogged and crucified. On the third day he will be raised to life!'

A Mother's Request

[20] Then the mother of Zebedee's sons came to Jesus with her sons and, kneeling down, asked a favour of him.

[21] 'What is it you want?' he asked.

She said, 'Grant that one of these two sons of mine may sit at your right and the other at your left in your kingdom.'

[22] 'You don't know what you are asking,' Jesus said to them. 'Can you drink the cup I am going to drink?'

'We can,' they answered.

[23] Jesus said to them, 'You will indeed drink from my cup, but to sit at my right or left is not for me to grant. These places belong to those for whom they have been prepared by my Father.'

[24] When the ten heard about this, they were indignant with the two brothers. [25] Jesus called them together and said,

'You know that the rulers of the Gentiles lord it over them, and their high officials exercise authority over them. [26] Not so with you. Instead, whoever wants to become great among you must be your servant, [27] and whoever wants to be first must be your slave—[28] just as the Son of Man did not come to be served, but to serve, and to give his life as a ransom for many.'

Two Blind Men Receive Sight

[29] As Jesus and his disciples were leaving Jericho, a large crowd followed him. [30] Two blind men were sitting by the roadside, and when they heard that Jesus was going by, they shouted, 'Lord, Son of David, have mercy on us!'

[31] The crowd rebuked them and told them to be quiet, but they shouted all the louder, 'Lord, Son of David, have mercy on us!'

[32] Jesus stopped and called them. 'What do you want me to do for you?' he asked.

[33] 'Lord,' they answered, 'we want our sight.'

[34] Jesus had compassion on them and touched their eyes. Immediately they received their sight and followed him.

The Triumphal Entry

21 As they approached Jerusalem and came to Bethphage on the Mount of Olives, Jesus sent two disciples, [2] saying to them, 'Go to the village ahead of you, and at once you will find a donkey tied there, with her colt by her. Untie them and bring them to me. [3] If anyone says anything to you, say that the Lord needs them, and he will send them right away.'

[4] This took place to fulfil what was spoken through the prophet:

[5] 'Say to the Daughter of Zion,
  'See, your king comes to you,
gentle and riding on a donkey,
  on a colt, the foal of a donkey.' '[a]

[6] The disciples went and did as Jesus had instructed them. [7] They brought the

[a] 5 Zech. 9:9

donkey and the colt, placed their cloaks on them, and Jesus sat on them. 8 A very large crowd spread their cloaks on the road, while others cut branches from the trees and spread them on the road. 9 The crowds that went ahead of him and those that followed shouted,

"Hosanna*b* to the Son of David!"

"Blessed is he who comes in the name of the Lord!"*c*

"Hosanna*b* in the highest!"

10 When Jesus entered Jerusalem, the whole city was stirred and asked, "Who is this?"
11 The crowds answered, "This is Jesus, the prophet from Nazareth in Galilee."

Jesus at the Temple

12 Jesus entered the temple area and drove out all who were buying and selling there. He overturned the tables of the money-changers and the benches of those selling doves. 13 "It is written," he said to them, " 'My house will be called a house of prayer,'*d* but you are making it a 'den of robbers'.*e* "
14 The blind and the lame came to him at the temple, and he healed them. 15 But when the chief priests and the teachers of the law saw the wonderful things he did and the children shouting in the temple area, "Hosanna to the Son of David," they were indignant.
16 "Do you hear what these children are saying?" they asked him.
"Yes," replied Jesus, "have you never read,

" 'From the lips of children and
     infants
    you have ordained praise'*f* ?"

17 And he left them and went out of the city to Bethany, where he spent the night.

The Fig-Tree Withers

18 Early in the morning, as he was on his way back to the city, he was hungry. 19 Seeing a fig-tree by the road, he went up to it but found nothing on it except leaves. Then he said to it, "May you never bear fruit again!" Immediately the tree withered.
20 When the disciples saw this, they were amazed. "How did the fig-tree wither so quickly?" they asked.
21 Jesus replied, "I tell you the truth, if you have faith and do not doubt, not only can you do what was done to the fig-tree, but also you can say to this mountain, 'Go, throw yourself into the sea,' and it will be done. 22 If you believe, you will receive whatever you ask for in prayer."

The Authority of Jesus Questioned

23 Jesus entered the temple courts, and, while he was teaching, the chief priests and the elders of the people came to him. "By what authority are you doing these things?" they asked. "And who gave you this authority?"
24 Jesus replied, "I will also ask you one question. If you answer me, I will tell you by what authority I am doing these things. 25 John's baptism—where did it come from? Was it from heaven, or of human origin?"
They discussed it among themselves and said, "If we say, 'From heaven', he will ask, 'Then why didn't you believe him?' 26 But if we say, 'Of human origin'—we are afraid of the people, for they all hold that John was a prophet."
27 So they answered Jesus, "We don't know."
Then he said, "Neither will I tell you by what authority I am doing these things.

The Parable of the Two Sons

28 "What do you think? There was a man who had two sons. He went to the first and said, 'Son, go and work today in the vineyard.'

b9 A Hebrew expression meaning "Save!" which became an exclamation of praise; also in verse 15
c9 Psalm 118:26   d13 Isaiah 56:7   e13 Jer. 7:11   f16 Psalm 8:2

²⁹ " 'I will not,' he answered, but later he changed his mind and went.

³⁰ "Then the father went to the other son and said the same thing. He answered, 'I will, sir,' but he did not go.

³¹ "Which of the two did what his father wanted?"

"The first," they answered.

Jesus said to them, "I tell you the truth, the tax collectors and the prostitutes are entering the kingdom of God ahead of you. ³² For John came to you to show you the way of righteousness, and you did not believe him, but the tax collectors and the prostitutes did. And even after you saw this, you did not repent and believe him.

The Parable of the Tenants

³³ "Listen to another parable: There was a landowner who planted a vineyard. He put a wall around it, dug a winepress in it and built a watchtower. Then he rented the vineyard to some farmers and went away on a journey. ³⁴ When the harvest time approached, he sent his servants to the tenants to collect his fruit.

³⁵ "The tenants seized his servants; they beat one, killed another, and stoned a third. ³⁶ Then he sent other servants to them, more than the first time, and the tenants treated them in the same way. ³⁷ Last of all, he sent his son to them. 'They will respect my son,' he said.

³⁸ "But when the tenants saw the son, they said to each other, 'This is the heir. Come, let's kill him and take his inheritance.' ³⁹ So they took him and threw him out of the vineyard and killed him.

⁴⁰ "Therefore, when the owner of the vineyard comes, what will he do to those tenants?"

⁴¹ "He will bring those wretches to a wretched end," they replied, "and he will rent the vineyard to other tenants, who will give him his share of the crop at harvest time."

⁴² Jesus said to them, "Have you never read in the Scriptures:

" 'The stone the builders rejected
   has become the capstone;ᵍ

the Lord has done this,
   and it is marvellous in our
    eyes'ʰ?

⁴³ "Therefore I tell you that the kingdom of God will be taken away from you and given to a people who will produce its fruit. ⁴⁴ Anyone who falls on this stone will be broken to pieces, but anyone on whom it falls will be crushed."ⁱ

⁴⁵ When the chief priests and the Pharisees heard Jesus' parables, they knew he was talking about them. ⁴⁶ They looked for a way to arrest him, but they were afraid of the crowd because the people held that he was a prophet.

The Parable of the Wedding Banquet

22 Jesus spoke to them again in parables, saying: ² "The kingdom of heaven is like a king who prepared a wedding banquet for his son. ³ He sent his servants to those who had been invited to the banquet to tell them to come, but they refused to come.

⁴ "Then he sent some more servants and said, 'Tell those who have been invited that I have prepared my dinner: My oxen and fattened cattle have been slaughtered, and everything is ready. Come to the wedding banquet.'

⁵ "But they paid no attention and went off—one to his field, another to his business. ⁶ The rest seized his servants, ill-treated them and killed them. ⁷ The king was enraged. He sent his army and destroyed those murderers and burned their city.

⁸ "Then he said to his servants, 'The wedding banquet is ready, but those I invited did not deserve to come. ⁹ Go to the street corners and invite to the banquet anyone you find.' ¹⁰ So the servants went out into the streets and gathered all the people they could find, both good and bad, and the wedding hall was filled with guests.

¹¹ "But when the king came in to see the guests, he noticed someone there who was not wearing wedding clothes. ¹² 'Friend,' he asked, 'how did you get in here without

---

ᵍ42 Or *cornerstone*   ʰ42 Psalm 118:22,23   ⁱ44 Some manuscripts do not have verse 44.

wedding clothes?' The man was speechless.

¹³ "Then the king told the attendants, 'Tie him hand and foot, and throw him outside, into the darkness, where there will be weeping and gnashing of teeth.'

¹⁴ "For many are invited, but few are chosen."

Paying Taxes to Caesar

¹⁵ Then the Pharisees went out and laid plans to trap him in his words. ¹⁶ They sent their disciples to him along with the Herodians. "Teacher," they said, "we know you are a man of integrity and that you teach the way of God in accordance with the truth. You aren't swayed by others, because you pay no attention to who they are. ¹⁷ Tell us then, what is your opinion? Is it right to pay taxes to Caesar or not?"

¹⁸ But Jesus, knowing their evil intent, said, "You hypocrites, why are you trying to trap me? ¹⁹ Show me the coin used for paying the tax." They brought him a denarius, ²⁰ and he asked them, "Whose portrait is this? And whose inscription?"

²¹ "Caesar's," they replied.

Then he said to them, "Give to Caesar what is Caesar's, and to God what is God's."

²² When they heard this, they were amazed. So they left him and went away.

Marriage at the Resurrection

²³ That same day the Sadducees, who say there is no resurrection, came to him with a question. ²⁴ "Teacher," they said, "Moses told us that if a man dies without having children, his brother must marry the widow and have children for him. ²⁵ Now there were seven brothers among us. The first one married and died, and since he had no children, he left his wife to his brother. ²⁶ The same thing happened to the second and third brother, right on down to the seventh. ²⁷ Finally, the woman died. ²⁸ Now then, at the resurrection, whose wife will she be of the seven, since all of them were married to her?"

²⁹ Jesus replied, "You are in error because you do not know the Scriptures or the power of God. ³⁰ At the resurrection people will neither marry nor be given in marriage; they will be like the angels in heaven. ³¹ But about the resurrection of the dead—have you not read what God said to you, ³² 'I am the God of Abraham, the God of Isaac, and the God of Jacob'ᵃ? He is not the God of the dead but of the living."

³³ When the crowds heard this, they were astonished at his teaching.

The Greatest Commandment

³⁴ Hearing that Jesus had silenced the Sadducees, the Pharisees got together. ³⁵ One of them, an expert in the law, tested him with this question: ³⁶ "Teacher, which is the greatest commandment in the Law?"

³⁷ Jesus replied: " 'Love the Lord your God with all your heart and with all your soul and with all your mind.'ᵇ ³⁸ This is the first and greatest commandment. ³⁹ And the second is like it: 'Love your neighbour as yourself.'ᶜ ⁴⁰ All the Law and the Prophets hang on these two commandments."

Whose Son Is the Christ?

⁴¹ While the Pharisees were gathered together, Jesus asked them, ⁴² "What do you think about the Christ?ᵈ Whose son is he?"

"The son of David," they replied.

⁴³ He said to them, "How is it then that David, speaking by the Spirit, calls him 'Lord'? For he says,

⁴⁴ " 'The Lord said to my Lord:
    "Sit at my right hand
until I put your enemies
    under your feet." 'ᵉ

⁴⁵ If then David calls him 'Lord', how can he be his son?" ⁴⁶ No-one could say a word in reply, and from that day on no-one dared to ask him any more questions.

ᵃ32 Exodus 3:6   ᵇ37 Deut. 6:5   ᶜ39 Lev. 19:18   ᵈ42 Or *Messiah*   ᵉ44 Psalm 110:1

Seven Woes

23 Then Jesus said to the crowds and to his disciples: 2 "The teachers of the law and the Pharisees sit in Moses' seat. 3 So you must obey them and do everything they tell you. But do not do what they do, for they do not practise what they preach. 4 They tie up heavy loads and put them on other people's shoulders, but they themselves are not willing to lift a finger to move them.

5 "Everything they do is done for others to see: They make their phylacteries*a* wide and the tassels on their garments long; 6 they love the place of honour at banquets and the most important seats in the synagogues; 7 they love to be greeted in the market-places and to have people call them 'Rabbi'.

8 "But you are not to be called 'Rabbi', for you have only one Master and you are all brothers and sisters. 9 And do not call anyone on earth 'father', for you have one Father, and he is in heaven. 10 Nor are you to be called 'teacher', for you have one Teacher, the Christ.*b* 11 The greatest among you will be your servant. 12 For those who exalt themselves will be humbled, and those who humble themselves will be exalted.

13 "Woe to you, teachers of the law and Pharisees, you hypocrites! You shut the kingdom of heaven in people's faces. You yourselves do not enter, nor will you let those enter who are trying to.*c*

15 "Woe to you, teachers of the law and Pharisees, you hypocrites! You travel over land and sea to win a single convert, and then you make that convert twice as much a child of hell as you are.

16 "Woe to you, blind guides! You say, 'If anyone swears by the temple, it means nothing; but whoever swears by the gold of the temple is bound by the oath.' 17 You blind fools! Which is greater: the gold, or the temple that makes the gold sacred? 18 You also say, 'If anyone swears by the altar, it means nothing; but if anyone swears by the gift on it, he is bound by his oath.' 19 You blind men! Which is greater: the gift, or the altar that makes the gift sacred? 20 Therefore, anyone who swears by the altar swears by it and by everything on it. 21 And anyone who swears by the temple swears by it and by the one who dwells in it. 22 And anyone who swears by heaven swears by God's throne and by the one who sits on it.

23 "Woe to you, teachers of the law and Pharisees, you hypocrites! You give a tenth of your spices—mint, dill and cummin. But you have neglected the more important matters of the law—justice, mercy and faithfulness. You should have practised the latter, without neglecting the former. 24 You blind guides! You strain out a gnat but swallow a camel.

25 "Woe to you, teachers of the law and Pharisees, you hypocrites! You clean the outside of the cup and dish, but inside they are full of greed and self-indulgence. 26 Blind Pharisee! First clean the inside of the cup and dish, and then the outside also will be clean.

27 "Woe to you, teachers of the law and Pharisees, you hypocrites! You are like whitewashed tombs, which look beautiful on the outside but on the inside are full of the bones of the dead and everything unclean. 28 In the same way, on the outside you appear to people as righteous but on the inside you are full of hypocrisy and wickedness.

29 "Woe to you, teachers of the law and Pharisees, you hypocrites! You build tombs for the prophets and decorate the graves of the righteous. 30 And you say, 'If we had lived in the days of our ancestors, we would not have taken part with them in shedding the blood of the prophets.' 31 So you testify against yourselves that you are the descendants of those who murdered the prophets. 32 Fill up, then, the measure of the sin of your ancestors!

33 "You snakes! You brood of vipers! How will you escape being condemned to hell? 34 Therefore I am sending you prophets and sages and teachers. Some of them you will kill and crucify; others you

---

*a*5 That is, boxes containing Scripture verses, worn on forehead and arm   *b*10 Or *Messiah*
*c*13 Some manuscripts *to.* 14 *Woe to you, teachers of the law and Pharisees, you hypocrites! You devour widows' houses and for a show make lengthy prayers. Therefore you will be punished more severely.*

will flog in your synagogues and pursue from town to town. 35 And so upon you will come all the righteous blood that has been shed on earth, from the blood of righteous Abel to the blood of Zechariah son of Barakiah, whom you murdered between the temple and the altar. 36 I tell you the truth, all this will come upon this generation.

37 "O Jerusalem, Jerusalem, you who kill the prophets and stone those sent to you, how often I have longed to gather your children together, as a hen gathers her chicks under her wings, but you were not willing. 38 Look, your house is left to you desolate. 39 For I tell you, you will not see me again until you say, 'Blessed is he who comes in the name of the Lord.'*d* "

Signs of the End of the Age

24 Jesus left the temple and was walking away when his disciples came up to him to call his attention to its buildings. 2 "Do you see all these things?" he asked. "I tell you the truth, not one stone here will be left on another; every one will be thrown down."

3 As Jesus was sitting on the Mount of Olives, the disciples came to him privately. "Tell us," they said, "when will this happen, and what will be the sign of your coming and of the end of the age?"

4 Jesus answered: "Watch out that no-one deceives you. 5 For many will come in my name, claiming, 'I am the Christ,'*a* and will deceive many. 6 You will hear of wars and rumours of wars, but see to it that you are not alarmed. Such things must happen, but the end is still to come. 7 Nation will rise against nation, and kingdom against kingdom. There will be famines and earthquakes in various places. 8 All these are the beginning of birth-pains.

9 "Then you will be handed over to be persecuted and put to death, and you will be hated by all nations because of me. 10 At that time many will turn away from the faith and will betray and hate each other, 11 and many false prophets will appear and deceive many people. 12 Because

of the increase of wickedness, the love of most will grow cold, 13 but whoever stands firm to the end will be saved. 14 And this gospel of the kingdom will be preached in the whole world as a testimony to all nations, and then the end will come.

15 "So when you see standing in the holy place 'the abomination that causes desolation',*b* spoken of through the prophet Daniel—let the reader understand— 16 then let those who are in Judea flee to the mountains. 17 Let no-one on the housetop go down to take anything out of the house. 18 Let no-one in the field go back to get a cloak. 19 How dreadful it will be in those days for pregnant women and nursing mothers! 20 Pray that your flight will not take place in winter or on the Sabbath. 21 For then there will be great distress, unequalled from the beginning of the world until now—and never to be equalled again. 22 If those days had not been cut short, no-one would survive, but for the sake of the elect those days will be shortened. 23 At that time if anyone says to you, 'Look, here is the Christ!' or, 'There he is!' do not believe it. 24 For false Christs and false prophets will appear and perform great signs and miracles to deceive even the elect—if that were possible. 25 See, I have told you ahead of time.

26 "So if anyone tells you, 'There he is, out in the desert,' do not go out; or, 'Here he is, in the inner rooms,' do not believe it. 27 For as lightning that comes from the east is visible even in the west, so will be the coming of the Son of Man. 28 Wherever there is a carcass, there the vultures will gather.

29 "Immediately after the distress of those days

" 'the sun will be darkened,
    and the moon will not give its light;
  the stars will fall from the sky,
    and the heavenly bodies will be
      shaken.'*c*

30 "At that time the sign of the Son of Man will appear in the sky, and all the nations of the earth will mourn. They will see the Son of Man coming on the clouds

of the sky, with power and great glory.
[31] And he will send his angels with a loud
trumpet call, and they will gather his elect
from the four winds, from one end of the
heavens to the other.

[32] "Now learn this lesson from the fig-
tree: As soon as its twigs get tender and its
leaves come out, you know that summer is
near. [33] Even so, when you see all these
things, you know that it[d] is near, right at
the door. [34] I tell you the truth, this generation[e] will certainly not pass away until
all these things have happened. [35] Heaven
and earth will pass away, but my words
will never pass away.

The Day and Hour Unknown

[36] "No-one knows about that day or
hour, not even the angels in heaven, nor
the Son,[f] but only the Father. [37] As it was
in the days of Noah, so it will be at the
coming of the Son of Man. [38] For in the
days before the flood, people were eating
and drinking, marrying and giving in marriage, up to the day Noah entered the ark;
[39] and they knew nothing about what
would happen until the flood came and
took them all away. That is how it will be
at the coming of the Son of Man. [40] Two
men will be in the field; one will be taken
and the other left. [41] Two women will be
grinding with a hand mill; one will be
taken and the other left.

[42] "Therefore keep watch, because you
do not know on what day your Lord will
come. [43] But understand this: If the owner
of the house had known at what time of
night the thief was coming, he would have
kept watch and would not have let his
house be broken into. [44] So you also must
be ready, because the Son of Man will
come at an hour when you do not expect
him.

[45] "Who then is the faithful and wise
servant, whom the master has put in
charge of the servants in his household to
give them their food at the proper time?
[46] It will be good for that servant whose
master finds him doing so when he returns. [47] I tell you the truth, he will put

him in charge of all his possessions. [48] But
suppose that servant is wicked and says to
himself, 'My master is staying away a long
time,' [49] and he then begins to beat his
fellow-servants and to eat and drink with
drunkards. [50] The master of that servant
will come on a day when he does not expect him and at an hour he is not aware
of. [51] He will cut him to pieces and assign
him a place with the hypocrites, where
there will be weeping and gnashing of
teeth.

The Parable of the Ten Virgins

25 "At that time the kingdom of
heaven will be like ten virgins who
took their lamps and went out to meet the
bridegroom. [2] Five of them were foolish
and five were wise. [3] The foolish ones took
their lamps but did not take any oil with
them. [4] The wise, however, took oil in jars
along with their lamps. [5] The bridegroom
was a long time in coming, and they all
became drowsy and fell asleep.

[6] "At midnight the cry rang out: 'Here's
the bridegroom! Come out to meet him!'

[7] "Then all the virgins woke up and
trimmed their lamps. [8] The foolish ones
said to the wise, 'Give us some of your oil;
our lamps are going out.'

[9] " 'No,' they replied, 'there may not be
enough for both us and you. Instead, go
to those who sell oil and buy some for
yourselves.'

[10] "But while they were on their way to
buy the oil, the bridegroom arrived. The
virgins who were ready went in with him
to the wedding banquet. And the door
was shut.

[11] "Later the others also came. 'Sir! Sir!'
they said. 'Open the door for us!'

[12] "But he replied, 'I tell you the truth,
I don't know you.'

[13] "Therefore keep watch, because you
do not know the day or the hour.

The Parable of the Talents

[14] "Again, it will be like a man going
on a journey, who called his servants and

---

[d]33 Or he   [e]34 Or race   [f]36 Some manuscripts do not have *nor the Son*.

entrusted his property to them. [15] To one he gave five talents[a] of money, to another two talents, and to another one talent, each according to his ability. Then he went on his journey. [16] The man who had received the five talents went at once and put his money to work and gained five more. [17] So also, the one with the two talents gained two more. [18] But the man who had received the one talent went off, dug a hole in the ground and hid his master's money.

[19] "After a long time the master of those servants returned and settled accounts with them. [20] The man who had received the five talents brought the other five. 'Master,' he said, 'you entrusted me with five talents. See, I have gained five more.'

[21] "His master replied, 'Well done, good and faithful servant! You have been faithful with a few things; I will put you in charge of many things. Come and share your master's happiness!'

[22] "The man with the two talents also came. 'Master,' he said, 'you entrusted me with two talents; see, I have gained two more.'

[23] "His master replied, 'Well done, good and faithful servant! You have been faithful with a few things; I will put you in charge of many things. Come and share your master's happiness!'

[24] "Then the man who had received the one talent came. 'Master,' he said, 'I knew that you are a hard man, harvesting where you have not sown and gathering where you have not scattered seed. [25] So I was afraid and went out and hid your talent in the ground. See, here is what belongs to you.'

[26] "His master replied, 'You wicked, lazy servant! So you knew that I harvest where I have not sown and gather where I have not scattered seed? [27] Well then, you should have put my money on deposit with the bankers, so that when I returned I would have received it back with interest.

[28] " 'Take the talent from him and give it to the one who has the ten talents. [29] For those who have will be given more, and they will have an abundance. Those who

do not have, even what they have will be taken from them. [30] And throw that worthless servant outside, into the darkness, where there will be weeping and gnashing of teeth.'

The Sheep and the Goats

[31] "When the Son of Man comes in his glory, and all the angels with him, he will sit on his throne in heavenly glory. [32] All the nations will be gathered before him, and he will separate the people one from another as a shepherd separates the sheep from the goats. [33] He will put the sheep on his right and the goats on his left.

[34] "Then the King will say to those on his right, 'Come, you who are blessed by my Father; take your inheritance, the kingdom prepared for you since the creation of the world. [35] For I was hungry and you gave me something to eat, I was thirsty and you gave me something to drink, I was a stranger and you invited me in, [36] I needed clothes and you clothed me, I was sick and you looked after me, I was in prison and you came to visit me.'

[37] "Then the righteous will answer him, 'Lord, when did we see you hungry and feed you, or thirsty and give you something to drink? [38] When did we see you a stranger and invite you in, or needing clothes and clothe you? [39] When did we see you sick or in prison and go to visit you?'

[40] "The King will reply, 'I tell you the truth, whatever you did for one of the least of these brothers and sisters of mine, you did for me.'

[41] "Then he will say to those on his left, 'Depart from me, you who are cursed, into the eternal fire prepared for the devil and his angels. [42] For I was hungry and you gave me nothing to eat, I was thirsty and you gave me nothing to drink, [43] I was a stranger and you did not invite me in, I needed clothes and you did not clothe me, I was sick and in prison and you did not look after me.'

[44] "They also will answer, 'Lord, when did we see you hungry or thirsty or a

---

[a]15 A talent was worth several hundred pounds.

stranger or needing clothes or sick or in prison, and did not help you?'

45 "He will reply, 'I tell you the truth, whatever you did not do for one of the least of these, you did not do for me.'

46 "Then they will go away to eternal punishment, but the righteous to eternal life."

The Plot Against Jesus

26 When Jesus had finished saying all these things, he said to his disciples, 2 "As you know, the Passover is two days away—and the Son of Man will be handed over to be crucified."

3 Then the chief priests and the elders of the people assembled in the palace of the high priest, whose name was Caiaphas, 4 and they plotted to arrest Jesus in some sly way and kill him. 5 "But not during the Feast," they said, "or there may be a riot among the people."

Jesus Anointed at Bethany

6 While Jesus was in Bethany in the home of Simon the Leper, 7 a woman came to him with an alabaster jar of very expensive perfume, which she poured on his head as he was reclining at the table.

8 When the disciples saw this, they were indignant. "Why this waste?" they asked. 9 "This perfume could have been sold at a high price and the money given to the poor."

10 Aware of this, Jesus said to them, "Why are you bothering this woman? She has done a beautiful thing to me. 11 The poor you will always have with you, but you will not always have me. 12 When she poured this perfume on my body, she did it to prepare me for burial. 13 I tell you the truth, wherever this gospel is preached throughout the world, what she has done will also be told, in memory of her."

Judas Agrees to Betray Jesus

14 Then one of the Twelve—the one called Judas Iscariot—went to the chief priests 15 and asked, "What are you willing to give me if I hand him over to you?" So they counted out for him thirty silver coins. 16 From then on Judas watched for an opportunity to hand him over.

The Lord's Supper

17 On the first day of the Feast of Unleavened Bread, the disciples came to Jesus and asked, "Where do you want us to make preparations for you to eat the Passover?"

18 He replied, "Go into the city to a certain man and tell him, 'The Teacher says: My appointed time is near. I am going to celebrate the Passover with my disciples at your house.'" 19 So the disciples did as Jesus had directed them and prepared the Passover.

20 When evening came, Jesus was reclining at the table with the Twelve. 21 And while they were eating, he said, "I tell you the truth, one of you will betray me."

22 They were very sad and began to say to him one after the other, "Surely not I, Lord?"

23 Jesus replied, "The one who has dipped his hand into the bowl with me will betray me. 24 The Son of Man will go just as it is written about him. But woe to that man who betrays the Son of Man! It would be better for him if he had not been born."

25 Then Judas, the one who would betray him, said, "Surely not I, Rabbi?"

Jesus answered, "Yes, it is you."[a]

26 While they were eating, Jesus took bread, gave thanks and broke it, and gave it to his disciples, saying, "Take and eat; this is my body."

27 Then he took the cup, gave thanks and offered it to them, saying, "Drink from it, all of you. 28 This is my blood of the[b] covenant, which is poured out for many for the forgiveness of sins. 29 I tell you, I will not drink of this fruit of the vine from now on until that day when I drink it anew with you in my Father's kingdom."

30 When they had sung a hymn, they went out to the Mount of Olives.

---

[a]25 Or "You yourself have said it"   [b]28 Some manuscripts the new

Jesus Predicts Peter's Denial

[31] Then Jesus told them, "This very night you will all fall away on account of me, for it is written:

> " 'I will strike the shepherd,
>   and the sheep of the flock will be
>   scattered.'[c]

[32] But after I have risen, I will go ahead of you into Galilee."

[33] Peter replied, "Even if all fall away on account of you, I never will."

[34] "I tell you the truth," Jesus answered, "this very night, before the cock crows, you will disown me three times."

[35] But Peter declared, "Even if I have to die with you, I will never disown you." And all the other disciples said the same.

Gethsemane

[36] Then Jesus went with his disciples to a place called Gethsemane, and he said to them, "Sit here while I go over there and pray." [37] He took Peter and the two sons of Zebedee along with him, and he began to be sorrowful and troubled. [38] Then he said to them, "My soul is overwhelmed with sorrow to the point of death. Stay here and keep watch with me."

[39] Going a little farther, he fell with his face to the ground and prayed, "My Father, if it is possible, may this cup be taken from me. Yet not as I will, but as you will."

[40] Then he returned to his disciples and found them sleeping. "Couldn't you keep watch with me for one hour?" he asked Peter. [41] "Watch and pray so that you will not fall into temptation. The spirit is willing, but the body is weak."

[42] He went away a second time and prayed, "My Father, if it is not possible for this cup to be taken away unless I drink it, may your will be done."

[43] When he came back, he again found them sleeping, because their eyes were heavy. [44] So he left them and went away once more and prayed the third time, saying the same thing.

[45] Then he returned to the disciples and said to them, "Are you still sleeping and resting? Look, the hour is near, and the Son of Man is betrayed into the hands of sinners. [46] Rise, let us go! Here comes my betrayer!"

Jesus Arrested

[47] While he was still speaking, Judas, one of the Twelve, arrived. With him was a large crowd armed with swords and clubs, sent from the chief priests and the elders of the people. [48] Now the betrayer had arranged a signal with them: "The one I kiss is the man; arrest him." [49] Going at once to Jesus, Judas said, "Greetings, Rabbi!" and kissed him.

[50] Jesus replied, "Friend, do what you came for."[d]

Then the men stepped forward, seized Jesus and arrested him. [51] With that, one of Jesus' companions reached for his sword, drew it out and struck the servant of the high priest, cutting off his ear.

[52] "Put your sword back in its place," Jesus said to him, "for all who draw the sword will die by the sword. [53] Do you think I cannot call on my Father, and he will at once put at my disposal more than twelve legions of angels? [54] But how then would the Scriptures be fulfilled that say it must happen in this way?"

[55] At that time Jesus said to the crowd, "Am I leading a rebellion, that you have come out with swords and clubs to capture me? Every day I sat in the temple courts teaching, and you did not arrest me. [56] But this has all taken place that the writings of the prophets might be fulfilled." Then all the disciples deserted him and fled.

Before the Sanhedrin

[57] Those who had arrested Jesus took him to Caiaphas, the high priest, where the teachers of the law and the elders had assembled. [58] But Peter followed him at a distance, right up to the courtyard of the

---

[c]31 Zech. 13:7   [d]50 Or *"Friend, why have you come?"*

high priest. He entered and sat down with the guards to see the outcome.

⁵⁹ The chief priests and the whole Sanhedrin were looking for false evidence against Jesus so that they could put him to death. ⁶⁰ But they did not find any, though many false witnesses came forward.

Finally two came forward ⁶¹ and declared, "This fellow said, 'I am able to destroy the temple of God and rebuild it in three days.'"

⁶² Then the high priest stood up and said to Jesus, "Are you not going to answer? What is this testimony that these men are bringing against you?" ⁶³ But Jesus remained silent.

The high priest said to him, "I charge you under oath by the living God: Tell us if you are the Christ,ᵉ the Son of God."

⁶⁴ "Yes, it is as you say," Jesus replied. "But I say to all of you: In the future you will see the Son of Man sitting at the right hand of the Mighty One and coming on the clouds of heaven."

⁶⁵ Then the high priest tore his clothes and said, "He has spoken blasphemy! Why do we need any more witnesses? Look, now you have heard the blasphemy. ⁶⁶ What do you think?"

"He is worthy of death," they answered.

⁶⁷ Then they spat in his face and struck him with their fists. Others slapped him ⁶⁸ and said, "Prophesy to us, Christ. Who hit you?"

Peter Disowns Jesus

⁶⁹ Now Peter was sitting out in the courtyard, and a woman servant came to him. "You also were with Jesus of Galilee," she said.

⁷⁰ But he denied it before them all. "I don't know what you're talking about," he said.

⁷¹ Then he went out to the gateway, where another woman servant saw him and said to the people there, "This fellow was with Jesus of Nazareth."

⁷² He denied it again, with an oath: "I don't know the man!"

⁷³ After a little while, those standing there went up to Peter and said, "Surely you are one of them, for your accent gives you away."

⁷⁴ Then he began to call down curses on himself and he swore to them, "I don't know the man!"

Immediately a cock crowed. ⁷⁵ Then Peter remembered the word Jesus had spoken: "Before the cock crows, you will disown me three times." And he went outside and wept bitterly.

Judas Hangs Himself

27 Early in the morning, all the chief priests and the elders of the people came to the decision to put Jesus to death. ² They bound him, led him away and handed him over to Pilate, the governor.

³ When Judas, who had betrayed him, saw that Jesus was condemned, he was seized with remorse and returned the thirty silver coins to the chief priests and the elders. ⁴ "I have sinned," he said, "for I have betrayed innocent blood."

"What is that to us?" they replied. "That's your responsibility."

⁵ So Judas threw the money into the temple and left. Then he went away and hanged himself.

⁶ The chief priests picked up the coins and said, "It is against the law to put this into the treasury, since it is blood money." ⁷ So they decided to use the money to buy the potter's field as a burial place for foreigners. ⁸ That is why it has been called the Field of Blood to this day. ⁹ Then what was spoken by Jeremiah the prophet was fulfilled: "They took the thirty silver coins, the price set on him by the people of Israel, ¹⁰ and they used them to buy the potter's field, as the Lord commanded me."ᵃ

Jesus Before Pilate

¹¹ Meanwhile Jesus stood before the governor, and the governor asked him, "Are you the king of the Jews?"

"Yes, it is as you say," Jesus replied.

ᵉ63 Or *Messiah*; also in verse 68   ᵃ10 See Zech. 11:12,13; Jer. 19:1–13; 32:6–9.

[12] When he was accused by the chief priests and the elders, he gave no answer. [13] Then Pilate asked him, "Don't you hear the testimony they are bringing against you?" [14] But Jesus made no reply, not even to a single charge—to the great amazement of the governor.

[15] Now it was the governor's custom at the Feast to release a prisoner chosen by the crowd. [16] At that time they had a notorious prisoner, called Barabbas. [17] So when the crowd had gathered, Pilate asked them, "Which one do you want me to release to you: Barabbas, or Jesus who is called Christ?" [18] For he knew it was out of envy that they had handed Jesus over to him.

[19] While Pilate was sitting on the judge's seat, his wife sent him this message: "Don't have anything to do with that innocent man, for I have suffered a great deal today in a dream because of him."

[20] But the chief priests and the elders persuaded the crowd to ask for Barabbas and to have Jesus executed.

[21] "Which of the two do you want me to release to you?" asked the governor.

"Barabbas," they answered.

[22] "What shall I do, then, with Jesus who is called Christ?" Pilate asked.

They all answered, "Crucify him!"

[23] "Why? What crime has he committed?" asked Pilate.

But they shouted all the louder, "Crucify him!"

[24] When Pilate saw that he was getting nowhere, but that instead an uproar was starting, he took water and washed his hands in front of the crowd. "I am innocent of this man's blood," he said. "It is your responsibility!"

[25] All the people answered, "Let his blood be on us and on our children!"

[26] Then he released Barabbas to them. But he had Jesus flogged, and handed him over to be crucified.

The Soldiers Mock Jesus

[27] Then the governor's soldiers took Jesus into the Praetorium and gathered the whole company of soldiers round him. [28] They stripped him and put a scarlet robe on him, [29] and then twisted together a crown of thorns and set it on his head. They put a staff in his right hand and knelt in front of him and mocked him. "Hail, king of the Jews!" they said. [30] They spat on him, and took the staff and struck him on the head again and again. [31] After they had mocked him, they took off the robe and put his own clothes on him. Then they led him away to crucify him.

The Crucifixion

[32] As they were going out, they met a man from Cyrene, named Simon, and they forced him to carry the cross. [33] They came to a place called Golgotha (which means The Place of the Skull). [34] There they offered Jesus wine to drink, mixed with gall; but after tasting it, he refused to drink it. [35] When they had crucified him, they divided up his clothes by casting lots.*b* [36] And sitting down, they kept watch over him there. [37] Above his head they placed the written charge against him: THIS IS JESUS, THE KING OF THE JEWS. [38] Two robbers were crucified with him, one on his right and one on his left. [39] Those who passed by hurled insults at him, shaking their heads [40] and saying, "You who are going to destroy the temple and build it in three days, save yourself! Come down from the cross, if you are the Son of God!"

[41] In the same way the chief priests, the teachers of the law and the elders mocked him. [42] "He saved others," they said, "but he can't save himself! He's the King of Israel! Let him come down now from the cross, and we will believe in him. [43] He trusts in God. Let God rescue him now if he wants him, for he said, 'I am the Son of God.' " [44] In the same way the robbers who were crucified with him also heaped insults on him.

The Death of Jesus

[45] From the sixth hour until the ninth hour darkness came over all the land.

---

b 35 A few late manuscripts *lots that the word spoken by the prophet might be fulfilled: "They divided my garments among themselves and cast lots for my clothing."* (Psalm 22:18)

[46] About the ninth hour Jesus cried out in a loud voice, "*Eloi, Eloi,[c] lama sabachthani?*"—which means, "My God, my God, why have you forsaken me?"[d]

[47] When some of those standing there heard this, they said, "He's calling Elijah." [48] Immediately one of them ran and got a sponge. He filled it with wine vinegar, put it on a stick, and offered it to Jesus to drink. [49] The rest said, "Now leave him alone. Let's see if Elijah comes to save him."

[50] And when Jesus had cried out again in a loud voice, he gave up his spirit.

[51] At that moment the curtain of the temple was torn in two from top to bottom. The earth shook and the rocks split. [52] The tombs broke open and the bodies of many holy people who had died were raised to life. [53] They came out of the tombs, and after Jesus' resurrection they went into the holy city and appeared to many people.

[54] When the centurion and those with him who were guarding Jesus saw the earthquake and all that had happened, they were terrified, and exclaimed, "Surely he was the Son[e] of God!"

[55] Many women were there, watching from a distance. They had followed Jesus from Galilee to care for his needs. [56] Among them were Mary Magdalene, Mary the mother of James and Joses, and the mother of Zebedee's sons.

The Burial of Jesus

[57] As evening approached, there came a rich man from Arimathea, named Joseph, who had himself become a disciple of Jesus. [58] Going to Pilate, he asked for Jesus' body, and Pilate ordered that it be given to him. [59] Joseph took the body, wrapped it in a clean linen cloth, [60] and placed it in his own new tomb that he had cut out of the rock. He rolled a big stone in front of the entrance to the tomb and went away. [61] Mary Magdalene and the other Mary were sitting there opposite the tomb.

The Guard at the Tomb

[62] The next day, the one after Preparation Day, the chief priests and the Pharisees went to Pilate. [63] "Sir," they said, "we remember that while he was still alive that deceiver said, 'After three days I will rise again.' [64] So give the order for the tomb to be made secure until the third day. Otherwise, his disciples may come and steal the body and tell the people that he has been raised from the dead. This last deception will be worse than the first."

[65] "Take a guard," Pilate answered. "Go, make the tomb as secure as you know how." [66] So they went and made the tomb secure by putting a seal on the stone and posting the guard.

The Resurrection

28 After the Sabbath, at dawn on the first day of the week, Mary Magdalene and the other Mary went to look at the tomb.

[2] There was a violent earthquake, for an angel of the Lord came down from heaven and, going to the tomb, rolled back the stone and sat on it. [3] His appearance was like lightning, and his clothes were white as snow. [4] The guards were so afraid of him that they shook and became like dead men.

[5] The angel said to the women, "Do not be afraid, for I know that you are looking for Jesus, who was crucified. [6] He is not here; he has risen, just as he said. Come and see the place where he lay. [7] Then go quickly and tell his disciples: 'He has risen from the dead and is going ahead of you into Galilee. There you will see him.' Now I have told you."

[8] So the women hurried away from the tomb, afraid yet filled with joy, and ran to tell his disciples. [9] Suddenly Jesus met them. "Greetings," he said. They came to him, clasped his feet and worshipped him. [10] Then Jesus said to them, "Do not be afraid. Go and tell my brothers to go to Galilee; there they will see me."

---

*c*46 Some manuscripts *Eli, Eli*   *d*46 Psalm 22:1   *e*54 Or *a son*

The Guards' Report

[11] While the women were on their way, some of the guards went into the city and reported to the chief priests everything that had happened. [12] When the chief priests had met with the elders and devised a plan, they gave the soldiers a large sum of money, [13] telling them, "You are to say, 'His disciples came during the night and stole him away while we were asleep.' [14] If this report gets to the governor, we will satisfy him and keep you out of trouble." [15] So the soldiers took the money and did as they were instructed. And this story has been widely circulated among the Jews to this very day.

The Great Commission

[16] Then the eleven disciples went to Galilee, to the mountain where Jesus had told them to go. [17] When they saw him, they worshipped him; but some doubted. [18] Then Jesus came to them and said, "All authority in heaven and on earth has been given to me. [19] Therefore go and make disciples of all nations, baptising them in[a] the name of the Father and of the Son and of the Holy Spirit, [20] and teaching them to obey everything I have commanded you. And surely I am with you always, to the very end of the age."

Mark

John the Baptist Prepares the Way

1 The beginning of the gospel about Jesus Christ, the Son of God.[a]

[2] It is written in Isaiah the prophet:

"I will send my messenger ahead of
    you,
    who will prepare your way"[b] —
[3] "a voice of one calling in the desert,
    'Prepare the way for the Lord,
    make straight paths for him.'"[c]

[4] And so John came, baptising in the desert region and preaching a baptism of repentance for the forgiveness of sins. [5] The whole Judean countryside and all the people of Jerusalem went out to him. Confessing their sins, they were baptised by him in the Jordan River. [6] John wore clothing made of camel's hair, with a leather belt round his waist, and he ate locusts and wild honey. [7] And this was his message: "After me will come one more powerful than I, the thongs of whose sandals I am not worthy to stoop down and untie. [8] I baptise you with[d] water, but he will baptise you with the Holy Spirit."

The Baptism and Temptation of Jesus

[9] At that time Jesus came from Nazareth in Galilee and was baptised by John in the Jordan. [10] As Jesus was coming up out of the water, he saw heaven being torn open and the Spirit descending on him like a dove. [11] And a voice came from heaven: "You are my Son, whom I love; with you I am well pleased."

[12] At once the Spirit sent him out into the desert, [13] and he was in the desert for forty days, being tempted by Satan. He was with the wild animals, and angels attended him.

The Calling of the First Disciples

[14] After John was put in prison, Jesus went into Galilee, proclaiming the good news of God. [15] "The time has come," he said. "The kingdom of God is near. Repent and believe the good news!"

[16] As Jesus walked beside the Sea of Galilee, he saw Simon and his brother Andrew casting a net into the lake, for they were fishermen. [17] "Come, follow me," Jesus said, "and I will make you fishers of men and women." [18] At once they left their nets and followed him.

[19] When he had gone a little farther, he saw James son of Zebedee and his brother John in a boat, preparing their nets. [20] Without delay he called them, and they left their father Zebedee in the boat with the hired men and followed him.

Jesus Drives Out an Evil Spirit

[21] They went to Capernaum, and when the Sabbath came, Jesus went into the synagogue and began to teach. [22] The people were amazed at his teaching, because he taught them as one who had

---

[a]1 Some manuscripts do not have *the Son of God.*   [b]2 Mal. 3:1   [c]3 Isaiah 40:3   [d]8 Or *in*

authority, not as the teachers of the law.

²³ Just then a man in their synagogue who was possessed by an evil*ᵉ* spirit cried out, ²⁴ "What do you want with us, Jesus of Nazareth? Have you come to destroy us? I know who you are—the Holy One of God!"

²⁵ "Be quiet!" said Jesus sternly. "Come out of him!" ²⁶ The evil spirit shook the man violently and came out of him with a shriek.

²⁷ The people were all so amazed that they asked each other, "What is this? A new teaching—and with authority! He even gives orders to evil spirits and they obey him." ²⁸ News about him spread quickly over the whole region of Galilee.

Jesus Heals Many

²⁹ As soon as they left the synagogue, they went with James and John to the home of Simon and Andrew. ³⁰ Simon's mother-in-law was in bed with a fever, and they told Jesus about her. ³¹ So he went to her, took her hand and helped her up. The fever left her and she began to wait on them.

³² That evening after sunset the people brought to Jesus all the sick and demon-possessed. ³³ The whole town gathered at the door, ³⁴ and Jesus healed many who had various diseases. He also drove out many demons, but he would not let the demons speak because they knew who he was.

Jesus Prays in a Solitary Place

³⁵ Very early in the morning, while it was still dark, Jesus got up, left the house and went off to a solitary place, where he prayed. ³⁶ Simon and his companions went to look for him, ³⁷ and when they found him, they exclaimed: "Everyone is looking for you!"

³⁸ Jesus replied, "Let us go somewhere else—to the nearby villages—so that I can preach there also. That is why I have come." ³⁹ So he travelled throughout Galilee, preaching in their synagogues and driving out demons.

A Man With Leprosy

⁴⁰ A man with leprosy*ᶠ* came to him and begged him on his knees, "If you are willing, you can make me clean."

⁴¹ Filled with compassion, Jesus reached out his hand and touched the man. "I am willing," he said. "Be clean!" ⁴² Immediately the leprosy left him and he was cured.

⁴³ Jesus sent him away at once with a strong warning: ⁴⁴ "See that you don't tell this to anyone. But go, show yourself to the priest and offer the sacrifices that Moses commanded for your cleansing, as a testimony to them." ⁴⁵ Instead he went out and began to talk freely, spreading the news. As a result, Jesus could no longer enter a town openly but stayed outside in lonely places. Yet the people still came to him from everywhere.

Jesus Heals a Paralytic

2 A few days later, when Jesus again entered Capernaum, the people heard that he had come home. ² So many gathered that there was no room left, not even outside the door, and he preached the word to them. ³ Some people came, bringing to him a paralytic, carried by four of them. ⁴ Since they could not get him to Jesus because of the crowd, they made an opening in the roof above Jesus and, after digging through it, lowered the mat the paralysed man was lying on. ⁵ When Jesus saw their faith, he said to the paralytic, "Son, your sins are forgiven."

⁶ Now some teachers of the law were sitting there, thinking to themselves, ⁷ "Why does this fellow talk like that? He's blaspheming! Who can forgive sins but God alone?"

⁸ Immediately Jesus knew in his spirit that this was what they were thinking in their hearts, and he said to them, "Why are you thinking these things? ⁹ Which is easier: to say to the paralytic, 'Your sins are forgiven,' or to say, 'Get up, take your mat and walk'? ¹⁰ But that you may know that the Son of Man has authority on earth

*ᵉ*23 Greek *unclean*; also in verses 26 and 27
*ᶠ*40 The Greek word was used for various diseases affecting the skin—not necessarily leprosy.

to forgive sins . . . ." He said to the paralytic, [11]"I tell you, get up, take your mat and go home." [12]He got up, took his mat and walked out in full view of them all. This amazed everyone and they praised God, saying, "We have never seen anything like this!"

The Calling of Levi

[13]Once again Jesus went out beside the lake. A large crowd came to him, and he began to teach them. [14]As he walked along, he saw Levi son of Alphaeus sitting at the tax collector's booth. "Follow me," Jesus told him, and Levi got up and followed him.

[15]While Jesus was having dinner at Levi's house, many tax collectors and "sinners" were eating with him and his disciples, for there were many who followed him. [16]When the teachers of the law who were Pharisees saw him eating with the "sinners" and tax collectors, they asked his disciples: "Why does he eat with tax collectors and 'sinners'?"

[17]On hearing this, Jesus said to them, "It is not the healthy who need a doctor, but the sick. I have not come to call the righteous, but sinners."

Jesus Questioned About Fasting

[18]Now John's disciples and the Pharisees were fasting. Some people came and asked Jesus, "How is it that John's disciples and the disciples of the Pharisees are fasting, but yours are not?"

[19]Jesus answered, "How can the guests of the bridegroom fast while he is with them? They cannot, so long as they have him with them. [20]But the time will come when the bridegroom will be taken from them, and on that day they will fast.

[21]"People do not sew a patch of unshrunk cloth on an old garment. If they do, the new piece will pull away from the old, making the tear worse. [22]And people do not pour new wine into old wineskins. If they do, the wine will burst the skins, and both the wine and the wineskins will be ruined. No, they pour new wine into new wineskins."

Lord of the Sabbath

[23]One Sabbath Jesus was going through the cornfields, and as his disciples walked along, they began to pick some ears of corn. [24]The Pharisees said to him, "Look, why are they doing what is unlawful on the Sabbath?"

[25]He answered, "Have you never read what David did when he and his companions were hungry and in need? [26]In the days of Abiathar the high priest, he entered the house of God and ate the consecrated bread, which is lawful only for priests to eat. And he also gave some to his companions."

[27]Then he said to them, "The Sabbath was made for people, not people for the Sabbath. [28]So the Son of Man is Lord even of the Sabbath."

3 Another time he went into the synagogue, and a man with a shrivelled hand was there. [2]Some of them were looking for a reason to accuse Jesus, so they watched him closely to see if he would heal him on the Sabbath. [3]Jesus said to the man with the shrivelled hand, "Stand up in front of everyone."

[4]Then Jesus asked them, "Which is lawful on the Sabbath: to do good or to do evil, to save life or to kill?" But they remained silent.

[5]He looked round at them in anger and, deeply distressed at their stubborn hearts, said to the man, "Stretch out your hand." He stretched it out, and his hand was completely restored. [6]Then the Pharisees went out and began to plot with the Herodians how they might kill Jesus.

Crowds Follow Jesus

[7]Jesus withdrew with his disciples to the lake, and a large crowd from Galilee followed. [8]When they heard all he was doing, many people came to him from Judea, Jerusalem, Idumea, and the regions across the Jordan and around Tyre and Sidon. [9]Because of the crowd he told his disciples to have a small boat ready for him, to keep the people from crowding him. [10]For he had healed many, so that those with diseases were pushing forward

to touch him. [11] Whenever the evil[a] spirits saw him, they fell down before him and cried out, "You are the Son of God." [12] But he gave them strict orders not to tell who he was.

The Appointing of the Twelve Apostles

[13] Jesus went up on a mountainside and called to him those he wanted, and they came to him. [14] He appointed twelve—designating them apostles[b]—that they might be with him and that he might send them out to preach [15] and to have authority to drive out demons. [16] These are the twelve he appointed: Simon (to whom he gave the name Peter); [17] James son of Zebedee and his brother John (to them he gave the name Boanerges, which means Sons of Thunder); [18] Andrew, Philip, Bartholomew, Matthew, Thomas, James son of Alphaeus, Thaddaeus, Simon the Zealot [19] and Judas Iscariot, who betrayed him.

Jesus and Beelzebub

[20] Then Jesus entered a house, and again a crowd gathered, so that he and his disciples were not even able to eat. [21] When his family heard about this, they went to take charge of him, for they said, "He is out of his mind."

[22] And the teachers of the law who came down from Jerusalem said, "He is possessed by Beelzebub![c] By the prince of demons he is driving out demons."

[23] So Jesus called them and spoke to them in parables: "How can Satan drive out Satan? [24] If a kingdom is divided against itself, that kingdom cannot stand. [25] If a house is divided against itself, that house cannot stand. [26] And if Satan opposes himself and is divided, he cannot stand; his end has come. [27] In fact, no-one can enter a strong man's house and carry off his possessions without first tying up the strong man. Then his house can be plundered. [28] I tell you the truth, people will be forgiven all their sins and all the blasphemies they utter. [29] But whoever

blasphemes against the Holy Spirit will never be forgiven, but is guilty of an eternal sin."

[30] He said this because they were saying, "He has an evil spirit."

Jesus' Mother and Brothers

[31] Then Jesus' mother and brothers arrived. Standing outside, they sent someone in to call him. [32] A crowd was sitting around him, and they told him, "Your mother and brothers are outside looking for you."

[33] "Who are my mother and my brothers?" he asked.

[34] Then he looked at those seated in a circle around him and said, "Here are my mother and my brothers! [35] Whoever does God's will is my brother and sister and mother."

The Parable of the Sower

4 Again Jesus began to teach by the lake. The crowd that gathered round him was so large that he got into a boat and sat in it out on the lake, while all the people were along the shore at the water's edge. [2] He taught them many things by parables, and in his teaching said: [3] "Listen! A farmer went out to sow his seed. [4] As he was scattering the seed, some fell along the path, and the birds came and ate it up. [5] Some fell on rocky places, where it did not have much soil. It sprang up quickly, because the soil was shallow. [6] But when the sun came up, the plants were scorched, and they withered because they had no root. [7] Other seed fell among thorns, which grew up and choked the plants, so that they did not bear grain. [8] Still other seed fell on good soil. It came up, grew and produced a crop, multiplying thirty, sixty, or even a hundred times."

[9] Then Jesus said, "Those who have ears to hear, let them hear."

[10] When he was alone, the Twelve and the others around him asked him about the parables. [11] He told them, "The secret of the kingdom of God has been given to

---

[a]11 Greek *unclean*; also in verse 30   [b]14 Some manuscripts do not have *designating them apostles*.
[c]22 Greek *Beezeboul* or *Beelzeboul*

you. But to those on the outside everything is said in parables [12] so that,

> " 'they may be ever seeing but never
> perceiving,
> and ever hearing but never
> understanding;
> otherwise they might turn and be
> forgiven!'[a]"

[13] Then Jesus said to them, "Don't you understand this parable? How then will you understand any parable? [14] The farmer sows the word. [15] Some people are like seed along the path, where the word is sown. As soon as they hear it, Satan comes and takes away the word that was sown in them. [16] Others, like seed sown on rocky places, hear the word and at once receive it with joy. [17] But since they have no root, they last only a short time. When trouble or persecution comes because of the word, they quickly fall away. [18] Still others, like seed sown among thorns, hear the word; [19] but the worries of this life, the deceitfulness of wealth and the desires for other things come in and choke the word, making it unfruitful. [20] Others, like seed sown on good soil, hear the word, accept it, and produce a crop—thirty, sixty or even a hundred times what was sown."

A Lamp on a Stand

[21] He said to them, "Do you bring in a lamp to put it under a bowl or a bed? Instead, don't you put it on its stand? [22] For whatever is hidden is meant to be disclosed, and whatever is concealed is meant to be brought out into the open. [23] If any have ears to hear, let them hear."

[24] "Consider carefully what you hear," he continued. "With the measure you use, it will be measured to you—and even more. [25] Those who have will be given more; those who do not have, even what they have will be taken from them."

The Parable of the Growing Seed

[26] He also said, "This is what the kingdom of God is like. A man scatters

seed on the ground. [27] Night and day, whether he sleeps or gets up, the seed sprouts and grows, though he does not know how. [28] All by itself the soil produces corn—first the stalk, then the ear, then the full grain in the ear. [29] As soon as the grain is ripe, he puts the sickle to it, because the harvest has come."

The Parable of the Mustard Seed

[30] Again he said, "What shall we say the kingdom of God is like, or what parable shall we use to describe it? [31] It is like a mustard seed, which is the smallest seed you plant in the ground. [32] Yet when planted, it grows and becomes the largest of all garden plants, with such big branches that the birds of the air can perch in its shade."

[33] With many similar parables Jesus spoke the word to them, as much as they could understand. [34] He did not say anything to them without using a parable. But when he was alone with his own disciples, he explained everything.

Jesus Calms the Storm

[35] That day when evening came, he said to his disciples, "Let us go over to the other side." [36] Leaving the crowd behind, they took him along, just as he was, in the boat. There were also other boats with him. [37] A furious squall came up, and the waves broke over the boat, so that it was nearly swamped. [38] Jesus was in the stern, sleeping on a cushion. The disciples woke him and said to him, "Teacher, don't you care if we drown?"

[39] He got up, rebuked the wind and said to the waves, "Quiet! Be still!" Then the wind died down and it was completely calm.

[40] He said to his disciples, "Why are you so afraid? Do you still have no faith?"

[41] They were terrified and asked each other, "Who is this? Even the wind and the waves obey him!"

[a] 12 Isaiah 6:9,10

The Healing of a Demon-possessed Man

5 They went across the lake to the region of the Gerasenes.[a] 2 When Jesus got out of the boat, a man with an evil[b] spirit came from the tombs to meet him. 3 This man lived in the tombs, and no-one could bind him any more, not even with a chain. 4 For he had often been chained hand and foot, but he tore the chains apart and broke the irons on his feet. No-one was strong enough to subdue him. 5 Night and day among the tombs and in the hills he would cry out and cut himself with stones.

6 When he saw Jesus from a distance, he ran and fell on his knees in front of him. 7 He shouted at the top of his voice, "What do you want with me, Jesus, Son of the Most High God? Swear to God that you won't torture me!" 8 For Jesus had said to him, "Come out of this man, you evil spirit!"

9 Then Jesus asked him, "What is your name?"

"My name is Legion," he replied, "for we are many." 10 And he begged Jesus again and again not to send them out of the area.

11 A large herd of pigs was feeding on the nearby hillside. 12 The demons begged Jesus, "Send us among the pigs; allow us to go into them." 13 He gave them permission, and the evil spirits came out and went into the pigs. The herd, about two thousand in number, rushed down the steep bank into the lake and were drowned.

14 Those tending the pigs ran off and reported this in the town and countryside, and the people went out to see what had happened. 15 When they came to Jesus, they saw the man who had been possessed by the legion of demons, sitting there, dressed and in his right mind; and they were afraid. 16 Those who had seen it told the people what had happened to the demon-possessed man—and told about the pigs as well. 17 Then the people began to plead with Jesus to leave their region.

18 As Jesus was getting into the boat, the man who had been demon-possessed begged to go with him. 19 Jesus did not let him, but said, "Go home to your family and tell them how much the Lord has done for you, and how he has had mercy on you." 20 So the man went away and began to tell in the Decapolis[c] how much Jesus had done for him. And all the people were amazed.

A Dead Girl and a Sick Woman

21 When Jesus had again crossed over by boat to the other side of the lake, a large crowd gathered round him while he was by the lake. 22 Then one of the synagogue rulers, named Jairus, came there. Seeing Jesus, he fell at his feet 23 and pleaded earnestly with him, "My little daughter is dying. Please come and put your hands on her so that she will be healed and live." 24 So Jesus went with him.

A large crowd followed and pressed around him. 25 And a woman was there who had been subject to bleeding for twelve years. 26 She had suffered a great deal under the care of many doctors and had spent all she had, yet instead of getting better she grew worse. 27 When she heard about Jesus, she came up behind him in the crowd and touched his cloak, 28 because she thought, "If I just touch his clothes, I will be healed." 29 Immediately her bleeding stopped and she felt in her body that she was freed from her suffering.

30 At once Jesus realised that power had gone out from him. He turned around in the crowd and asked, "Who touched my clothes?"

31 "You see the people crowding against you," his disciples answered, "and yet you can ask, 'Who touched me?' "

32 But Jesus kept looking around to see who had done it. 33 Then the woman, knowing what had happened to her, came and fell at his feet and, trembling with fear, told him the whole truth. 34 He said to her, "Daughter, your faith has healed you. Go in peace and be freed from your suffering."

---

[a]1 Some manuscripts *Gadarenes*; other manuscripts *Gergesenes*   [b]2 Greek *unclean*; also in verses 8 and 13
[c]20 That is, the Ten Cities

35 While Jesus was still speaking, some people came from the house of Jairus, the synagogue ruler. "Your daughter is dead," they said. "Why bother the teacher any more?"

36 Ignoring what they said, Jesus told the synagogue ruler, "Don't be afraid; just believe."

37 He did not let anyone follow him except Peter, James and John the brother of James. 38 When they came to the home of the synagogue ruler, Jesus saw a commotion, with people crying and wailing loudly. 39 He went in and said to them, "Why all this commotion and wailing? The child is not dead but asleep." 40 But they laughed at him.

After he put them all out, he took the child's father and mother and the disciples who were with him, and went in where the child was. 41 He took her by the hand and said to her, *"Talitha koum!"* (which means, "Little girl, I say to you, get up!"). 42 Immediately the girl stood up and walked around (she was twelve years old). At this they were completely astonished. 43 He gave strict orders not to let anyone know about this, and told them to give her something to eat.

A Prophet Without Honour

6 Jesus left there and went to his home town, accompanied by his disciples. 2 When the Sabbath came, he began to teach in the synagogue, and many who heard him were amazed.

"Where did this man get these things?" they asked. "What's this wisdom that has been given him, that he even does miracles! 3 Isn't this the carpenter? Isn't this Mary's son and the brother of James, Joseph,[a] Judas and Simon? Aren't his sisters here with us?" And they took offence at him.

4 Jesus said to them, "Only in their home towns, among their relatives and in their own homes are prophets without honour." 5 He could not do any miracles there, except lay his hands on a few sick people and heal them. 6 And he was amazed at their lack of faith.

Jesus Sends Out the Twelve

Then Jesus went round teaching from village to village. 7 Calling the Twelve to him, he sent them out two by two and gave them authority over evil[b] spirits.

8 These were his instructions: "Take nothing for the journey except a staff— no bread, no bag, no money in your belts. 9 Wear sandals but not an extra tunic. 10 Whenever you enter a house, stay there until you leave that town. 11 And if any place will not welcome you or listen to you, shake the dust off your feet when you leave, as a testimony against them."

12 They went out and preached that people should repent. 13 They drove out many demons and anointed many sick people with oil and healed them.

John the Baptist Beheaded

14 King Herod heard about this, for Jesus' name had become well known. Some were saying,[c] "John the Baptist has been raised from the dead, and that is why miraculous powers are at work in him."

15 Others said, "He is Elijah."

And still others claimed, "He is a prophet, like one of the prophets of long ago."

16 But when Herod heard this, he said, "John, whom I beheaded, has been raised from the dead!"

17 For Herod himself had given orders to have John arrested, and he had him bound and put in prison. He did this because of Herodias, his brother Philip's wife, whom he had married. 18 For John had been saying to Herod, "It is not lawful for you to have your brother's wife." 19 So Herodias nursed a grudge against John and wanted to kill him. But she was not able to, 20 because Herod feared John and protected him, knowing him to be a righteous and holy man. When Herod heard John, he was greatly puzzled;[d] yet he liked to listen to him.

---

[a]3 Greek *Joses*, a variant of *Joseph*   [b]7 Greek *unclean*
[d]20 Some early manuscripts *he did many things*   [c]14 Some early manuscripts *He was saying*

21 Finally the opportune time came. On his birthday Herod gave a banquet for his high officials and military commanders and the leading men of Galilee. 22 When the daughter of Herodias came in and danced, she pleased Herod and his dinner guests.

The king said to the girl, "Ask me for anything you want, and I'll give it to you." 23 And he promised her with an oath, "Whatever you ask I will give you, up to half my kingdom."

24 She went out and said to her mother, "What shall I ask for?"

"The head of John the Baptist," she answered.

25 At once the girl hurried in to the king with the request: "I want you to give me right now the head of John the Baptist on a platter."

26 The king was greatly distressed, but because of his oaths and his dinner guests, he did not want to refuse her. 27 So he immediately sent an executioner with orders to bring John's head. The man went, beheaded John in the prison, 28 and brought back his head on a platter. He presented it to the girl, and she gave it to her mother. 29 On hearing of this, John's disciples came and took his body and laid it in a tomb.

Jesus Feeds the Five Thousand

30 The apostles gathered round Jesus and reported to him all they had done and taught. 31 Then, because so many people were coming and going that they did not even have a chance to eat, he said to them, "Come with me by yourselves to a quiet place and get some rest."

32 So they went away by themselves in a boat to a solitary place. 33 But many who saw them leaving recognised them and ran on foot from all the towns and got there ahead of them. 34 When Jesus landed and saw a large crowd, he had compassion on them, because they were like sheep without a shepherd. So he began teaching them many things.

35 By this time it was late in the day, so his disciples came to him. "This is a remote place," they said, "and it's already very late. 36 Send the people away so that they can go to the surrounding countryside and villages and buy themselves something to eat."

37 But he answered, "You give them something to eat."

They said to him, "That would take eight months' wages.[e] Are we to go and spend that much on bread and give it to them to eat?"

38 "How many loaves do you have?" he asked. "Go and see."

When they found out, they said, "Five—and two fish."

39 Then Jesus directed them to have all the people sit down in groups on the green grass. 40 So they sat down in groups of hundreds and fifties. 41 Taking the five loaves and the two fish and looking up to heaven, he gave thanks and broke the loaves. Then he gave them to his disciples to set before the people. He also divided the two fish among them all. 42 They all ate and were satisfied, 43 and the disciples picked up twelve basketfuls of broken pieces of bread and fish. 44 The number of the men who had eaten was five thousand.

Jesus Walks on the Water

45 Immediately Jesus made his disciples get into the boat and go on ahead of him to Bethsaida, while he dismissed the crowd. 46 After leaving them, he went up on a mountainside to pray.

47 When evening came, the boat was in the middle of the lake, and he was alone on land. 48 He saw the disciples straining at the oars, because the wind was against them. About the fourth watch of the night he went out to them, walking on the lake. He was about to pass by them, 49 but when they saw him walking on the lake, they thought he was a ghost. They cried out, 50 because they all saw him and were terrified.

Immediately he spoke to them and said, "Take courage! It is I. Don't be afraid." 51 Then he climbed into the boat with them, and the wind died down. They were

e 37 Greek *take two hundred denarii*

completely amazed, [52]for they had not understood about the loaves; their hearts were hardened.

[53]When they had crossed over, they landed at Gennesaret and anchored there. [54]As soon as they got out of the boat, people recognised Jesus. [55]They ran throughout that whole region and carried the sick on mats to wherever they heard he was. [56]And wherever he went—into villages, towns or countryside—they placed the sick in the market-places. They begged him to let them touch even the edge of his cloak, and all who touched him were healed.

Clean and Unclean

7 The Pharisees and some of the teachers of the law who had come from Jerusalem gathered round Jesus and [2]saw some of his disciples eating food with hands that were "unclean", that is, unwashed. [3](The Pharisees and all the Jews do not eat unless they give their hands a ceremonial washing, holding to the tradition of the elders. [4]When they come from the market-place they do not eat unless they wash. And they observe many other traditions, such as the washing of cups, pitchers and kettles.[a])

[5]So the Pharisees and teachers of the law asked Jesus, "Why don't your disciples live according to the tradition of the elders instead of eating their food with 'unclean' hands?"

[6]He replied, "Isaiah was right when he prophesied about you hypocrites; as it is written:

" 'These people honour me with their
        lips,
    but their hearts are far from me.
[7]They worship me in vain;
    their teachings are merely human
        rules.'[b]

[8]You have let go of the commands of God and are holding on to human traditions."

[9]And he said to them: "You have a fine way of setting aside the commands of God in order to observe[c] your own traditions! [10]For Moses said, 'Honour your father and your mother,'[d] and, 'Anyone who curses father or mother must be put to death.'[e] [11]But you say that if anyone says to father or mother: 'Whatever help you might otherwise have received from me is Corban' (that is, a gift devoted to God), [12]then you no longer let them do anything for their father or mother. [13]Thus you nullify the word of God by your tradition that you have handed down. And you do many things like that."

[14]Again Jesus called the crowd to him and said, "Listen to me, everyone, and understand this. [15]Nothing outside you can make you 'unclean' by going into you. Rather, it is what comes out of you that makes you 'unclean'."[f]

[17]After he had left the crowd and entered the house, his disciples asked him about this parable. [18]"Are you so dull?" he asked. "Don't you see that nothing that enters you from the outside can make you 'unclean'? [19]For it doesn't go into your heart but into your stomach, and then out of your body." (In saying this, Jesus declared all foods "clean".)

[20]He went on: "What comes out of you is what makes you 'unclean'. [21]For from within, out of your hearts, come evil thoughts, sexual immorality, theft, murder, adultery, [22]greed, malice, deceit, lewdness, envy, slander, arrogance and folly. [23]All these evils come from inside and make you 'unclean'."

The Faith of a Syro-Phoenician Woman

[24]Jesus left that place and went to the vicinity of Tyre.[g] He entered a house and did not want anyone to know it; yet he could not keep his presence secret. [25]In fact, as soon as she heard about him, a woman whose little daughter was possessed by an evil[h] spirit came and fell at

---

[a]4 Some early manuscripts *pitchers, kettles and dining couches*   [b]6,7 Isaiah 29:13   [c]9 Some manuscripts *set up*
[d]10 Exodus 20:12; Deut. 5:16   [e]10 Exodus 21:17; Lev. 20:9
[f]15 Some early manuscripts *'unclean'.* [16]*If any have ears to hear, let them hear."*
[g]24 Many early manuscripts *Tyre and Sidon*   [h]25 Greek *unclean*

his feet. 26 The woman was a Greek, born in Syrian Phoenicia. She begged Jesus to drive the demon out of her daughter.

27 "First let the children eat all they want," he told her, "for it is not right to take the children's bread and toss it to their dogs."

28 "Yes, Lord," she replied, "but even the dogs under the table eat the children's crumbs."

29 Then he told her, "For such a reply, you may go; the demon has left your daughter."

30 She went home and found her child lying on the bed, and the demon gone.

The Healing of a Deaf and Mute Man

31 Then Jesus left the vicinity of Tyre and went through Sidon, down to the Sea of Galilee and into the region of the Decapolis.*i* 32 There some people brought to him a man who was deaf and could hardly talk, and they begged him to place his hand on him.

33 After he took him aside, away from the crowd, Jesus put his fingers into the man's ears. Then he spat and touched the man's tongue. 34 He looked up to heaven and with a deep sigh said to him, "*Ephphatha!*" (which means, "Be opened!").

35 At this, the man's ears were opened, his tongue was loosened and he began to speak plainly.

36 Jesus commanded them not to tell anyone. But the more he did so, the more they kept talking about it. 37 People were overwhelmed with amazement. "He has done everything well," they said. "He even makes the deaf hear and the mute speak."

Jesus Feeds the Four Thousand

8 During those days another large crowd gathered. Since they had nothing to eat, Jesus called his disciples to him and said, 2 "I have compassion for these people; they have already been with me three days and have nothing to eat. 3 If I send them home hungry, they will collapse on the way, because some of them have come a long distance."

4 His disciples answered, "But where in this remote place can anyone get enough bread to feed them?"

5 "How many loaves do you have?" Jesus asked.

"Seven," they replied.

6 He told the crowd to sit down on the ground. When he had taken the seven loaves and given thanks, he broke them and gave them to his disciples to set before the people, and they did so. 7 They had a few small fish as well; he gave thanks for them also and told the disciples to distribute them. 8 The people ate and were satisfied. Afterwards the disciples picked up seven basketfuls of broken pieces that were left over. 9 About four thousand were present. And having sent them away, 10 he got into the boat with his disciples and went to the region of Dalmanutha.

11 The Pharisees came and began to question Jesus. To test him, they asked him for a sign from heaven. 12 He sighed deeply and said, "Why does this generation ask for a miraculous sign? I tell you the truth, no sign will be given to it." 13 Then he left them, got back into the boat and crossed to the other side.

The Yeast of the Pharisees and Herod

14 The disciples had forgotten to bring bread, except for one loaf they had with them in the boat. 15 "Be careful," Jesus warned them. "Watch out for the yeast of the Pharisees and that of Herod."

16 They discussed this with one another and said, "It is because we have no bread."

17 Aware of their discussion, Jesus asked them: "Why are you talking about having no bread? Do you still not see or understand? Are your hearts hardened? 18 Do you have eyes but fail to see, and ears but fail to hear? And don't you remember? 19 When I broke the five loaves for the five thousand, how many basketfuls of pieces did you pick up?"

*i*31 That is, the Ten Cities

"Twelve," they replied.

20 "And when I broke the seven loaves for the four thousand, how many basketfuls of pieces did you pick up?"

They answered, "Seven."

21 He said to them, "Do you still not understand?"

The Healing of a Blind Man at Bethsaida

22 They came to Bethsaida, and some people brought a blind man and begged Jesus to touch him. 23 He took the blind man by the hand and led him outside the village. When he had spat on the man's eyes and put his hands on him, Jesus asked, "Do you see anything?"

24 He looked up and said, "I see people; they look like trees walking around."

25 Once more Jesus put his hands on the man's eyes. Then his eyes were opened, his sight was restored, and he saw everything clearly. 26 Jesus sent him home, saying, "Don't go into the village."[a]

Peter's Confession of Christ

27 Jesus and his disciples went on to the villages around Caesarea Philippi. On the way he asked them, "Who do people say I am?"

28 They replied, "Some say John the Baptist; others say Elijah; and still others, one of the prophets."

29 "But what about you?" he asked. "Who do you say I am?"

Peter answered, "You are the Christ."[b]

30 Jesus warned them not to tell anyone about him.

Jesus Predicts His Death

31 He then began to teach them that the Son of Man must suffer many things and be rejected by the elders, chief priests and teachers of the law, and that he must be killed and after three days rise again. 32 He spoke plainly about this, and Peter took him aside and began to rebuke him.

33 But when Jesus turned and looked at his disciples, he rebuked Peter. "Get behind me, Satan!" he said. "You do not have in mind the concerns of God, but human concerns."

34 Then he called the crowd to him along with his disciples and said: "Those who would come after me must deny themselves and take up their cross and follow me. 35 For those who want to save their lives[c] will lose them, but those who lose their lives for me and for the gospel will save them. 36 What good is it for you to gain the whole world, yet forfeit your soul? 37 Or what can you give in exchange for your soul? 38 All who are ashamed of me and my words in this adulterous and sinful generation the Son of Man will be ashamed of when he comes in his Father's glory with the holy angels."

9 And he said to them, "I tell you the truth, some who are standing here will not taste death before they see the kingdom of God come with power."

The Transfiguration

2 After six days Jesus took Peter, James and John with him and led them up a high mountain, where they were all alone. There he was transfigured before them. 3 His clothes became dazzling white, whiter than anyone in the world could bleach them. 4 And there appeared before them Elijah and Moses, who were talking with Jesus.

5 Peter said to Jesus, "Rabbi, it is good for us to be here. Let us put up three shelters—one for you, one for Moses and one for Elijah." 6 (He did not know what to say, they were so frightened.)

7 Then a cloud appeared and enveloped them, and a voice came from the cloud: "This is my Son, whom I love. Listen to him!"

8 Suddenly, when they looked round, they no longer saw anyone with them except Jesus.

9 As they were coming down the mountain, Jesus gave them orders not to tell anyone what they had seen until the Son

---

[a]26 Some manuscripts *Don't go and tell anyone in the village*

[b]29 Or *Messiah*. "The Christ" (Greek) and "the Messiah" (Hebrew) both mean "the Anointed One".

[c]35 The Greek word means either *life* or *soul*; also in verse 36.

of Man had risen from the dead. ¹⁰They kept the matter to themselves, discussing what "rising from the dead" meant.

¹¹And they asked him, "Why do the teachers of the law say that Elijah must come first?"

¹²Jesus replied, "To be sure, Elijah does come first, and restores all things. Why then is it written that the Son of Man must suffer much and be rejected? ¹³But I tell you, Elijah has come, and they have done to him everything they wished, just as it is written about him."

The Healing of a Boy With an Evil Spirit

¹⁴When they came to the other disciples, they saw a large crowd around them and the teachers of the law arguing with them. ¹⁵As soon as all the people saw Jesus, they were overwhelmed with wonder and ran to greet him.

¹⁶"What are you arguing with them about?" he asked.

¹⁷A man in the crowd answered, "Teacher, I brought you my son, who is possessed by a spirit that has robbed him of speech. ¹⁸Whenever it seizes him, it throws him to the ground. He foams at the mouth, gnashes his teeth and becomes rigid. I asked your disciples to drive out the spirit, but they could not."

¹⁹"O unbelieving generation," Jesus replied, "how long shall I stay with you? How long shall I put up with you? Bring the boy to me."

²⁰So they brought him. When the spirit saw Jesus, it immediately threw the boy into a convulsion. He fell to the ground and rolled around, foaming at the mouth.

²¹Jesus asked the boy's father, "How long has he been like this?"

"From childhood," he answered. ²²"It has often thrown him into fire or water to kill him. But if you can do anything, take pity on us and help us."

²³"'If you can'?" said Jesus. "Everything is possible for one who believes."

²⁴Immediately the boy's father exclaimed, "I do believe; help me overcome my unbelief!"

²⁵When Jesus saw that a crowd was running to the scene, he rebuked the evil*ᵃ* spirit. "You deaf and mute spirit," he said, "I command you, come out of him and never enter him again."

²⁶The spirit shrieked, convulsed him violently and came out. The boy looked so much like a corpse that many said, "He's dead." ²⁷But Jesus took him by the hand and lifted him to his feet, and he stood up.

²⁸After Jesus had gone indoors, his disciples asked him privately, "Why couldn't we drive it out?"

²⁹He replied, "This kind can come out only by prayer."*ᵇ*

³⁰They left that place and passed through Galilee. Jesus did not want anyone to know where they were, ³¹because he was teaching his disciples. He said to them, "The Son of Man is going to be betrayed into human hands. People will kill him, and after three days he will rise." ³²But they did not understand what he meant and were afraid to ask him about it.

Who Is the Greatest?

³³They came to Capernaum. When he was in the house, he asked them, "What were you arguing about on the road?" ³⁴But they kept quiet because on the way they had argued about who was the greatest.

³⁵Sitting down, Jesus called the Twelve and said, "Anyone who wants to be first must be the very last, and the servant of all."

³⁶He took a little child whom he placed among them. Taking the child in his arms, he said to them, ³⁷"Whoever welcomes one of these little children in my name welcomes me; and whoever welcomes me does not welcome me but the one who sent me."

Whoever Is Not Against Us Is for Us

³⁸"Teacher," said John, "we saw someone driving out demons in your name and we told him to stop, because he was not one of us."

*ᵃ*25 Greek *unclean*   *ᵇ*29 Some manuscripts *prayer and fasting*

39 "Do not stop him," Jesus said. "No-one who does a miracle in my name can in the next moment say anything bad about me, 40 for whoever is not against us is for us. 41 I tell you the truth, anyone who gives you a cup of water in my name because you belong to Christ will certainly be rewarded.

Causing to Sin

42 "And if any of you causes one of these little ones who believe in me to sin, it would be better for you to be thrown into the sea with a large millstone tied around your neck. 43 If your hand causes you to sin, cut it off. It is better for you to enter life maimed than with two hands to go into hell, where the fire never goes out.*c* 45 And if your foot causes you to sin, cut it off. It is better for you to enter life crippled than to have two feet and be thrown into hell.*d* 47 And if your eye causes you to sin, pluck it out. It is better for you to enter the kingdom of God with one eye than to have two eyes and be thrown into hell, 48 where

" 'their worm does not die,
and the fire is not quenched.'*e*

49 Everyone will be salted with fire. 50 "Salt is good, but if it loses its saltiness, how can you make it salty again? Have salt in yourselves, and be at peace with each other."

Divorce

10 Jesus then left that place and went into the region of Judea and across the Jordan. Again crowds of people came to him, and as was his custom, he taught them.

2 Some Pharisees came and tested him by asking, "Is it lawful for a man to divorce his wife?"

3 "What did Moses command you?" he replied.

4 They said, "Moses permitted a man to write a certificate of divorce and send her away."

5 "It was because your hearts were hard that Moses wrote you this law," Jesus replied. 6 "But at the beginning of creation God 'made them male and female'.*a* 7 'For this reason a man will leave his father and mother and be united to his wife,*b* 8 and the two will become one flesh.'*c* So they are no longer two, but one. 9 Therefore what God has joined together, let no-one separate."

10 When they were in the house again, the disciples asked Jesus about this. 11 He answered, "Anyone who divorces his wife and marries another woman commits adultery against her. 12 And if she divorces her husband and marries another man, she commits adultery."

The Little Children and Jesus

13 People were bringing little children to Jesus to have him touch them, but the disciples rebuked them. 14 When Jesus saw this, he was indignant. He said to them, "Let the little children come to me, and do not hinder them, for the kingdom of God belongs to such as these. 15 I tell you the truth, anyone who will not receive the kingdom of God like a little child will never enter it." 16 And he took the children in his arms, put his hands on them and blessed them.

The Rich Young Man

17 As Jesus started on his way, someone ran up to him and fell on his knees before him. "Good teacher," he asked, "what must I do to inherit eternal life?"

18 "Why do you call me good?" Jesus answered. "No-one is good—except God alone. 19 You know the commandments: 'Do not murder, do not commit adultery, do not steal, do not give false testimony, do not defraud, honour your father and mother.'*d* "

*c*43 Some manuscripts *out,* 44*where* / "'*their worm does not die,* / *and the fire is not quenched.*'
*d*45 Some manuscripts *hell,* 46*where* / "'*their worm does not die,* / *and the fire is not quenched.*'
*e*48 Isaiah 66:24   *a*6 Gen. 1:27   *b*7 Some early manuscripts do not have *and be united to his wife.*
*c*8 Gen. 2:24   *d*19 Exodus 20:12–16; Deut. 5:16–20

20 "Teacher," he declared, "all these I have kept since I was a boy."

21 Jesus looked at him and loved him. "One thing you lack," he said. "Go, sell everything you have and give to the poor, and you will have treasure in heaven. Then come, follow me."

22 At this the man's face fell. He went away sad, because he had great wealth.

23 Jesus looked around and said to his disciples, "How hard it is for the rich to enter the kingdom of God!"

24 The disciples were amazed at his words. But Jesus said again, "Children, how hard it is[e] to enter the kingdom of God! 25 It is easier for a camel to go through the eye of a needle than for the rich to enter the kingdom of God."

26 The disciples were even more amazed, and said to each other, "Who then can be saved?"

27 Jesus looked at them and said, "Humanly, this is impossible, but not with God; all things are possible with God."

28 Peter said to him, "We have left everything to follow you!"

29 "I tell you the truth," Jesus replied, "no-one who has left home or brothers or sisters or mother or father or children or fields for me and the gospel 30 will fail to receive a hundred times as much in this present age (homes, brothers, sisters, mothers, children and fields—and with them, persecutions) and in the age to come, eternal life. 31 But many who are first will be last, and the last first."

Jesus Again Predicts His Death

32 They were on their way up to Jerusalem, with Jesus leading the way, and the disciples were astonished, while those who followed were afraid. Again he took the Twelve aside and told them what was going to happen to him. 33 "We are going up to Jerusalem," he said, "and the Son of Man will be betrayed to the chief priests and teachers of the law. They will condemn him to death and will hand him over to the Gentiles, 34 who will mock him and spit on him, flog him and kill him. Three days later he will rise."

The Request of James and John

35 Then James and John, the sons of Zebedee, came to him. "Teacher," they said, "we want you to do for us whatever we ask."

36 "What do you want me to do for you?" he asked.

37 They replied, "Let one of us sit at your right and the other at your left in your glory."

38 "You don't know what you are asking," Jesus said. "Can you drink the cup I drink or be baptised with the baptism I am baptised with?"

39 "We can," they answered.

Jesus said to them, "You will drink the cup I drink and be baptised with the baptism I am baptised with, 40 but to sit at my right or left is not for me to grant. These places belong to those for whom they have been prepared."

41 When the ten heard about this, they became indignant with James and John. 42 Jesus called them together and said, "You know that those who are regarded as rulers of the Gentiles lord it over them, and their high officials exercise authority over them. 43 Not so with you. Instead, whoever wants to become great among you must be your servant, 44 and whoever wants to be first must be slave of all. 45 For even the Son of Man did not come to be served, but to serve, and to give his life as a ransom for many."

Blind Bartimaeus Receives His Sight

46 Then they came to Jericho. As Jesus and his disciples, together with a large crowd, were leaving the city, a blind man, Bartimaeus (that is, the Son of Timaeus), was sitting by the roadside begging. 47 When he heard that it was Jesus of Nazareth, he began to shout, "Jesus, Son of David, have mercy on me!"

48 Many rebuked him and told him to be quiet, but he shouted all the more, "Son of David, have mercy on me!"

49 Jesus stopped and said, "Call him."

So they called to the blind man, "Cheer up! On your feet! He's calling you."

[e]24 Some manuscripts *is for those who trust in riches*

50 Throwing his cloak aside, he jumped to his feet and came to Jesus.

51 "What do you want me to do for you?" Jesus asked him.

The blind man said, "Rabbi, I want to see."

52 "Go," said Jesus, "your faith has healed you." Immediately he received his sight and followed Jesus along the road.

The Triumphal Entry

11 As they approached Jerusalem and came to Bethphage and Bethany at the Mount of Olives, Jesus sent two of his disciples, 2 saying to them, "Go to the village ahead of you, and just as you enter it, you will find a colt tied there, which no-one has ever ridden. Untie it and bring it here. 3 If anyone asks you, 'Why are you doing this?' say, 'The Lord needs it and will send it back here shortly.' "

4 They went and found a colt outside in the street, tied at a doorway. As they untied it, 5 some people standing there asked, "What are you doing, untying that colt?" 6 They answered as Jesus had told them to, and the people let them go. 7 When they brought the colt to Jesus and threw their cloaks over it, he sat on it. 8 Many people spread their cloaks on the road, while others spread branches they had cut in the fields. 9 Those who went ahead and those who followed shouted,

"Hosanna!"*a*

"Blessed is he who comes in the name of the Lord!"*b*

10 "Blessed is the coming kingdom of our father David!"

"Hosanna in the highest!"

11 Jesus entered Jerusalem and went to the temple. He looked around at everything, but since it was already late, he went out to Bethany with the Twelve.

Jesus Clears the Temple

12 The next day as they were leaving Bethany, Jesus was hungry. 13 Seeing in the distance a fig-tree in leaf, he went to find out if it had any fruit. When he reached it, he found nothing but leaves, because it was not the season for figs. 14 Then he said to the tree, "May no-one ever eat fruit from you again." And his disciples heard him say it.

15 On reaching Jerusalem, Jesus entered the temple area and began driving out those who were buying and selling there. He overturned the tables of the money-changers and the benches of those selling doves, 16 and would not allow anyone to carry merchandise through the temple courts. 17 And as he taught them, he said, "Is it not written:

" 'My house will be called
    a house of prayer for all nations'*c* ?

But you have made it 'a den of robbers'.*d*"

18 The chief priests and the teachers of the law heard this and began looking for a way to kill him, for they feared him, because the whole crowd was amazed at his teaching.

19 When evening came, they*e* went out of the city.

The Withered Fig-Tree

20 In the morning, as they went along, they saw the fig-tree withered from the roots. 21 Peter remembered and said to Jesus, "Rabbi, look! The fig-tree you cursed has withered!"

22 "Have*f* faith in God," Jesus answered. 23 "I tell you the truth, if you say to this mountain, 'Go, throw yourself into the sea,' and do not doubt in your heart but believe that what you say will happen, it will be done for you. 24 Therefore I tell you, whatever you ask for in prayer, believe that you have received it, and it will be yours. 25 And when you stand praying,

---

*a*9 A Hebrew expression meaning "Save!" which became an exclamation of praise; also in verse 10.
*b*9 Psalm 118:25,26   *c*17 Isaiah 56:7   *d*17 Jer. 7:11   *e*19 Some early manuscripts *he*
*f*22 Some early manuscripts *If you have*

if you hold anything against anyone, forgive them, so that your Father in heaven may forgive you your sins."[8]

The Authority of Jesus Questioned

[27]They arrived again in Jerusalem, and while Jesus was walking in the temple courts, the chief priests, the teachers of the law and the elders came to him. [28]"By what authority are you doing these things?" they asked. "And who gave you authority to do this?"

[29]Jesus replied, "I will ask you one question. Answer me, and I will tell you by what authority I am doing these things. [30]John's baptism—was it from heaven, or of human origin? Tell me!"

[31]They discussed it among themselves and said, "If we say, 'From heaven', he will ask, 'Then why didn't you believe him?' [32]But if we say, 'Of human origin'. . . .'" (They feared the people, for everyone held that John really was a prophet.)

[33]So they answered Jesus, "We don't know."

Jesus said, "Neither will I tell you by what authority I am doing these things."

The Parable of the Tenants

12 He then began to speak to them in parables: "A man planted a vineyard. He put a wall around it, dug a pit for the winepress and built a watchtower. Then he rented the vineyard to some farmers and went away on a journey. [2]At harvest time he sent a servant to the tenants to collect from them some of the fruit of the vineyard. [3]But they seized him, beat him and sent him away empty-handed. [4]Then he sent another servant to them; they struck this man on the head and treated him shamefully. [5]He sent still another, and that one they killed. He sent many others; some of them they beat, others they killed.

[6]"He had one left to send, a son, whom he loved. He sent him last of all, saying, 'They will respect my son.'

[7]"But the tenants said to one another, 'This is the heir. Come, let's kill him, and the inheritance will be ours.' [8]So they took him and killed him, and threw him out of the vineyard.

[9]"What then will the owner of the vineyard do? He will come and kill those tenants and give the vineyard to others. [10]Haven't you read this scripture:

" 'The stone the builders rejected
    has become the capstone;[a]
[11]the Lord has done this,
    and it is marvellous in our
    eyes'[b]?"

[12]Then they looked for a way to arrest him because they knew he had spoken the parable against them. But they were afraid of the crowd; so they left him and went away.

Paying Taxes to Caesar

[13]Later they sent some of the Pharisees and Herodians to Jesus to catch him in his words. [14]They came to him and said, "Teacher, we know you are a man of integrity. You aren't swayed by others, because you pay no attention to who they are; but you teach the way of God in accordance with the truth. Is it right to pay taxes to Caesar or not? [15]Should we pay or shouldn't we?"

But Jesus knew their hypocrisy. "Why are you trying to trap me?" he asked. "Bring me a denarius and let me look at it." [16]They brought the coin, and he asked them, "Whose portrait is this? And whose inscription?"

"Caesar's," they replied.

[17]Then Jesus said to them, "Give to Caesar what is Caesar's and to God what is God's."

And they were amazed at him.

Marriage at the Resurrection

[18]Then the Sadducees, who say there is no resurrection, came to him with a question. [19]"Teacher," they said, "Moses

---

[8]25 Some manuscripts *sins. [26]But if you do not forgive, neither will your Father who is in heaven forgive your sins.*
[a]10 Or *cornerstone*   [b]11 Psalm 118:22,23

wrote for us that if a man's brother dies and leaves a wife but no children, the man must marry the widow and have children for his brother. 20 Now there were seven brothers. The first one married and died without leaving any children. 21 The second one married the widow, but he also died, leaving no child. It was the same with the third. 22 In fact, none of the seven left any children. Last of all, the woman died too. 23 At the resurrection[c] whose wife will she be, since the seven were married to her?"

24 Jesus replied, "Are you not in error because you do not know the Scriptures or the power of God? 25 When the dead rise, they will neither marry nor be given in marriage; they will be like the angels in heaven. 26 Now about the dead rising—have you not read in the book of Moses, in the account of the bush, how God said to him, 'I am the God of Abraham, the God of Isaac, and the God of Jacob'[d]? 27 He is not the God of the dead, but of the living. You are badly mistaken!"

The Greatest Commandment

28 One of the teachers of the law came and heard them debating. Noticing that Jesus had given them a good answer, he asked him, "Of all the commandments, which is the most important?"

29 "The most important one," answered Jesus, "is this: 'Hear, O Israel, the Lord our God, the Lord is one.[e] 30 Love the Lord your God with all your heart and with all your soul and with all your mind and with all your strength.'[f] 31 The second is this: 'Love your neighbour as yourself.'[g] There is no commandment greater than these."

32 "Well said, teacher," the man replied. "You are right in saying that God is one and there is no other but him. 33 To love him with all your heart, with all your understanding and with all your strength, and to love your neighbour as yourself is more important than all burnt offerings and sacrifices."

34 When Jesus saw that he had answered wisely, he said to him, "You are not far from the kingdom of God." And from then on no-one dared ask him any more questions.

Whose Son Is the Christ?

35 While Jesus was teaching in the temple courts, he asked, "How is it that the teachers of the law say that the Christ[h] is the son of David? 36 David himself, speaking by the Holy Spirit, declared:

" 'The Lord said to my Lord:
"Sit at my right hand
until I put your enemies
under your feet." '[i]

37 David himself calls him 'Lord'. How then can he be his son?"

The large crowd listened to him with delight.

38 As he taught, Jesus said, "Watch out for the teachers of the law. They like to walk around in flowing robes and be greeted in the market-places, 39 and have the most important seats in the synagogues and the places of honour at banquets. 40 They devour widows' houses and for a show make lengthy prayers. Such people will be punished most severely."

The Widow's Offering

41 Jesus sat down opposite the place where the offerings were put and watched the crowd putting their money into the temple treasury. Many rich people threw in large amounts. 42 But a poor widow came and put in two very small copper coins,[j] worth only a fraction of a penny.[k]

43 Calling his disciples to him, Jesus said, "I tell you the truth, this poor widow has put more into the treasury than all the others. 44 They all gave out of their wealth; but she, out of her poverty, put in everything—all she had to live on."

---

[c]23 Some manuscripts *resurrection, when men rise from the dead,*   [d]26 Exodus 3:6
[e]29 Or *the Lord our God is one Lord*   [f]30 Deut. 6:4,5   [g]31 Lev. 19:18   [h]35 Or *Messiah*
[i]36 Psalm 110:1   [j]42 Greek *two lepta*   [k]42 Greek *kodrantes*

Signs of the End of the Age

13 As he was leaving the temple, one of his disciples said to him, "Look, Teacher! What massive stones! What magnificent buildings!"

2 "Do you see all these great buildings?" replied Jesus. "Not one stone here will be left on another; every one will be thrown down."

3 As Jesus was sitting on the Mount of Olives opposite the temple, Peter, James, John and Andrew asked him privately, 4 "Tell us, when will these things happen? And what will be the sign that they are all about to be fulfilled?"

5 Jesus said to them: "Watch out that no-one deceives you. 6 Many will come in my name, claiming, 'I am he,' and will deceive many. 7 When you hear of wars and rumours of wars, do not be alarmed. Such things must happen, but the end is still to come. 8 Nation will rise against nation, and kingdom against kingdom. There will be earthquakes in various places, and famines. These are the beginning of birth-pains.

9 "You must be on your guard. You will be handed over to the local councils and flogged in the synagogues. On account of me you will stand before governors and kings as witnesses to them. 10 And the gospel must first be preached to all nations. 11 Whenever you are arrested and brought to trial, do not worry beforehand about what to say. Just say whatever is given you at the time, for it is not you speaking, but the Holy Spirit.

12 "Brother will betray brother to death, and a father his child. Children will rebel against their parents and have them put to death. 13 Everyone will hate you because of me, but those who stand firm to the end will be saved.

14 "When you see 'the abomination that causes desolation'*a* standing where it*b* does not belong—let the reader understand—then let those who are in Judea flee to the mountains. 15 Let no-one on the housetop go down or enter the house to take anything out. 16 Let no-one in

the field go back to get a cloak. 17 How dreadful it will be in those days for pregnant women and nursing mothers! 18 Pray that this will not take place in winter, 19 because those will be days of distress unequalled from the beginning, when God created the world, until now—and never to be equalled again. 20 If the Lord had not cut short those days, no-one would survive. But for the sake of the elect, whom he has chosen, he has shortened them. 21 At that time if anyone says to you, 'Look, here is the Christ!'*c* or, 'Look, there he is!' do not believe it. 22 For false Christs and false prophets will appear and perform signs and miracles to deceive the elect—if that were possible. 23 So be on your guard; I have told you everything ahead of time.

24 "But in those days, following that distress,

" 'the sun will be darkened,
    and the moon will not give its light;
25 the stars will fall from the sky,
    and the heavenly bodies will be
      shaken.'*d*

26 "At that time people will see the Son of Man coming in clouds with great power and glory. 27 And he will send his angels and gather his elect from the four winds, from the ends of the earth to the ends of the heavens.

28 "Now learn this lesson from the figtree: As soon as its twigs get tender and its leaves come out, you know that summer is near. 29 Even so, when you see these things happening, you know that it is near, right at the door. 30 I tell you the truth, this generation*e* will certainly not pass away until all these things have happened. 31 Heaven and earth will pass away, but my words will never pass away.

The Day and Hour Unknown

32 "No-one knows about that day or hour, not even the angels in heaven, nor the Son, but only the Father. 33 Be on guard! Be alert!*f* You do not know when

*a*14 Daniel 9:27; 11:31; 12:11   *b*14 Or *he*; also in verse 29   *c*21 Or *Messiah*   *d*25 Isaiah 13:10; 34:4
*e*30 Or *race*   *f*33 Some manuscripts *alert and pray*

that time will come. ³⁴It's like a man going away: He leaves his house and puts his servants in charge, each with an assigned task, and tells the one at the door to keep watch.

³⁵"Therefore keep watch because you do not know when the owner of the house will come back—whether in the evening, or at midnight, or when the cock crows, or at dawn. ³⁶If he comes suddenly, do not let him find you sleeping. ³⁷What I say to you, I say to everyone: 'Watch!' "

Jesus Anointed at Bethany

14 Now the Passover and the Feast of Unleavened Bread were only two days away, and the chief priests and the teachers of the law were looking for some sly way to arrest Jesus and kill him. ²"But not during the Feast," they said, "or the people may riot."

³While he was in Bethany, reclining at the table in the home of Simon the Leper, a woman came with an alabaster jar of very expensive perfume, made of pure nard. She broke the jar and poured the perfume on his head.

⁴Some of those present were saying indignantly to one another, "Why this waste of perfume? ⁵It could have been sold for more than a year's wages[a] and the money given to the poor." And they rebuked her harshly.

⁶"Leave her alone," said Jesus. "Why are you bothering her? She has done a beautiful thing to me. ⁷The poor you will always have with you, and you can help them any time you want. But you will not always have me. ⁸She did what she could. She poured perfume on my body beforehand to prepare for my burial. ⁹I tell you the truth, wherever the gospel is preached throughout the world, what she has done will also be told, in memory of her."

¹⁰Then Judas Iscariot, one of the Twelve, went to the chief priests to betray Jesus to them. ¹¹They were delighted to hear this and promised to give him money. So he watched for an opportunity to hand him over.

The Lord's Supper

¹²On the first day of the Feast of Unleavened Bread, when it was customary to sacrifice the Passover lamb, Jesus' disciples asked him, "Where do you want us to go and make preparations for you to eat the Passover?"

¹³So he sent two of his disciples, telling them, "Go into the city, and a man carrying a jar of water will meet you. Follow him. ¹⁴Say to the owner of the house he enters, 'The Teacher asks: Where is my guest room, where I may eat the Passover with my disciples?' ¹⁵He will show you a large upper room, furnished and ready. Make preparations for us there."

¹⁶The disciples left, went into the city and found things just as Jesus had told them. So they prepared the Passover.

¹⁷When evening came, Jesus arrived with the Twelve. ¹⁸While they were reclining at the table eating, he said, "I tell you the truth, one of you will betray me—one who is eating with me."

¹⁹They were saddened, and one by one they said to him, "Surely not I?"

²⁰"It is one of the Twelve," he replied, "one who dips bread into the bowl with me. ²¹The Son of Man will go just as it is written about him. But woe to that man who betrays the Son of Man! It would be better for him if he had not been born."

²²While they were eating, Jesus took bread, gave thanks and broke it, and gave it to his disciples, saying, "Take it; this is my body."

²³Then he took the cup, gave thanks and offered it to them, and they all drank from it.

²⁴"This is my blood of the[b] covenant, which is poured out for many," he said to them. ²⁵"I tell you the truth, I will not drink again of the fruit of the vine until that day when I drink it anew in the kingdom of God."

²⁶When they had sung a hymn, they went out to the Mount of Olives.

---

[a]5 Greek *than three hundred denarii*   [b]24 Some manuscripts *the new*

Jesus Predicts Peter's Denial

27 "You will all fall away," Jesus told them, "for it is written:

" 'I will strike the shepherd,
    and the sheep will be scattered.'[c]

28 But after I have risen, I will go ahead of you into Galilee."

29 Peter declared, "Even if all fall away, I will not."

30 "I tell you the truth," Jesus answered, "today—yes, tonight—before the cock crows twice[d] you yourself will disown me three times."

31 But Peter insisted emphatically, "Even if I have to die with you, I will never disown you." And all the others said the same.

Gethsemane

32 They went to a place called Gethsemane, and Jesus said to his disciples, "Sit here while I pray." 33 He took Peter, James and John along with him, and he began to be deeply distressed and troubled. 34 "My soul is overwhelmed with sorrow to the point of death," he said to them. "Stay here and keep watch."

35 Going a little farther, he fell to the ground and prayed that if possible the hour might pass from him. 36 "Abba,[e] Father," he said, "everything is possible for you. Take this cup from me. Yet not what I will, but what you will."

37 Then he returned to his disciples and found them sleeping. "Simon," he said to Peter, "are you asleep? Could you not keep watch for one hour? 38 Watch and pray so that you will not fall into temptation. The spirit is willing, but the body is weak."

39 Once more he went away and prayed the same thing. 40 When he came back, he again found them sleeping, because their eyes were heavy. They did not know what to say to him.

41 Returning the third time, he said to them, "Are you still sleeping and resting? Enough! The hour has come. Look, the Son of Man is betrayed into the hands of sinners. 42 Rise! Let us go! Here comes my betrayer!"

Jesus Arrested

43 Just as he was speaking, Judas, one of the Twelve, appeared. With him was a crowd armed with swords and clubs, sent from the chief priests, the teachers of the law, and the elders. 44 Now the betrayer had arranged a signal with them: "The one I kiss is the man; arrest him and lead him away under guard." 45 Going at once to Jesus, Judas said, "Rabbi!" and kissed him. 46 The men seized Jesus and arrested him. 47 Then one of those standing near drew his sword and struck the servant of the high priest, cutting off his ear.

48 "Am I leading a rebellion," said Jesus, "that you have come out with swords and clubs to capture me? 49 Every day I was with you, teaching in the temple courts, and you did not arrest me. But the Scriptures must be fulfilled." 50 Then everyone deserted him and fled.

51 A young man, wearing nothing but a linen garment, was following Jesus. When they seized him, 52 he fled naked, leaving his garment behind.

Before the Sanhedrin

53 They took Jesus to the high priest, and all the chief priests, elders and teachers of the law came together. 54 Peter followed him at a distance, right into the courtyard of the high priest. There he sat with the guards and warmed himself at the fire.

55 The chief priests and the whole Sanhedrin were looking for evidence against Jesus so that they could put him to death, but they did not find any. 56 Many testified falsely against him, but their statements did not agree.

57 Then some stood up and gave this false testimony against him: 58 "We heard him say, 'I will destroy this temple made with human hands and in three days will build another, not made with hands.' "

---

[c]27 Zech. 13:7   [d]30 Some early manuscripts do not have *twice*.   [e]36 Aramaic for *Father*

⁵⁹ Yet even then their testimony did not agree.

⁶⁰ Then the high priest stood up before them and asked Jesus, "Are you not going to answer? What is this testimony that these men are bringing against you?" ⁶¹ But Jesus remained silent and gave no answer.

Again the high priest asked him, "Are you the Christ,ᶠ the Son of the Blessed One?"

⁶² "I am," said Jesus. "And you will see the Son of Man sitting at the right hand of the Mighty One and coming on the clouds of heaven."

⁶³ The high priest tore his clothes. "Why do we need any more witnesses?" he asked. ⁶⁴ "You have heard the blasphemy. What do you think?"

They all condemned him as worthy of death. ⁶⁵ Then some began to spit at him; they blindfolded him, struck him with their fists, and said, "Prophesy!" And the guards took him and beat him.

Peter Disowns Jesus

⁶⁶ While Peter was below in the courtyard, one of the woman servants of the high priest came by. ⁶⁷ When she saw Peter warming himself, she looked closely at him.

"You also were with that Nazarene, Jesus," she said.

⁶⁸ But he denied it. "I don't know or understand what you're talking about," he said, and went out into the entrance.ᵍ

⁶⁹ When the woman servant saw him there, she said again to those standing around, "This fellow is one of them." ⁷⁰ Again he denied it.

After a little while, those standing near said to Peter, "Surely you are one of them, for you are a Galilean."

⁷¹ He began to call down curses on himself, and he swore to them, "I don't know this man you're talking about."

⁷² Immediately the cock crowed the second time.ʰ Then Peter remembered the word Jesus had spoken to him: "Before the cock crows twiceⁱ you will disown

me three times." And he broke down and wept.

Jesus Before Pilate

15 Very early in the morning, the chief priests, with the elders, the teachers of the law and the whole Sanhedrin, reached a decision. They bound Jesus, led him away and turned him over to Pilate.

² "Are you the king of the Jews?" asked Pilate.

"Yes, it is as you say," Jesus replied.

³ The chief priests accused him of many things. ⁴ So again Pilate asked him, "Aren't you going to answer? See how many things they are accusing you of."

⁵ But Jesus still made no reply, and Pilate was amazed.

⁶ Now it was the custom at the Feast to release a prisoner whom the people requested. ⁷ A man called Barabbas was in prison with the insurrectionists who had committed murder in the uprising. ⁸ The crowd came up and asked Pilate to do for them what he usually did.

⁹ "Do you want me to release to you the king of the Jews?" asked Pilate, ¹⁰ knowing it was out of envy that the chief priests had handed Jesus over to him. ¹¹ But the chief priests stirred up the crowd to have Pilate release Barabbas instead.

¹² "What shall I do, then, with the one you call the king of the Jews?" Pilate asked them.

¹³ "Crucify him!" they shouted.

¹⁴ "Why? What crime has he committed?" asked Pilate.

But they shouted all the louder, "Crucify him!"

¹⁵ Wanting to satisfy the crowd, Pilate released Barabbas to them. He had Jesus flogged, and handed him over to be crucified.

The Soldiers Mock Jesus

¹⁶ The soldiers led Jesus away into the palace (that is, the Praetorium) and called together the whole company of soldiers.

ᶠ61 Or *Messiah*   ᵍ68 Some early manuscripts *entrance and the cock crowed*
ʰ72 Some early manuscripts do not have *the second time.*   ⁱ72 Some early manuscripts do not have *twice.*

[17] They put a purple robe on him, then twisted together a crown of thorns and set it on him. [18] And they began to call out to him, "Hail, king of the Jews!" [19] Again and again they struck him on the head with a staff and spat on him. Falling on their knees, they paid homage to him. [20] And when they had mocked him, they took off the purple robe and put his own clothes on him. Then they led him out to crucify him.

The Crucifixion

[21] A certain man from Cyrene, Simon, the father of Alexander and Rufus, was passing by on his way in from the country, and they forced him to carry the cross. [22] They brought Jesus to the place called Golgotha (which means The Place of the Skull). [23] Then they offered him wine mixed with myrrh, but he did not take it. [24] And they crucified him. Dividing up his clothes, they cast lots to see what each would get.

[25] It was the third hour when they crucified him. [26] The written notice of the charge against him read: THE KING OF THE JEWS. [27] They crucified two robbers with him, one on his right and one on his left.[a]

[29] Those who passed by hurled insults at him, shaking their heads and saying, "So! You who are going to destroy the temple and build it in three days, [30] come down from the cross and save yourself!"

[31] In the same way the chief priests and the teachers of the law mocked him among themselves. "He saved others," they said, "but he can't save himself! [32] Let this Christ,[b] this King of Israel, come down now from the cross, that we may see and believe." Those crucified with him also heaped insults on him.

The Death of Jesus

[33] At the sixth hour darkness came over the whole land until the ninth hour. [34] And at the ninth hour Jesus cried out in a loud voice, "*Eloi, Eloi, lama sabachthani?*" — which means, "My God, my God, why have you forsaken me?"[c]

[35] When some of those standing near heard this, they said, "Listen, he's calling Elijah."

[36] Someone ran, filled a sponge with wine vinegar, put it on a stick, and offered it to Jesus to drink. "Now leave him alone. Let's see if Elijah comes to take him down," he said.

[37] With a loud cry, Jesus breathed his last.

[38] The curtain of the temple was torn in two from top to bottom. [39] And when the centurion, who stood there in front of Jesus, heard his cry and[d] saw how he died, he said, "Surely this man was the Son[e] of God!"

[40] Some women were watching from a distance. Among them were Mary Magdalene, Mary the mother of James the younger and of Joses, and Salome. [41] In Galilee these women had followed him and cared for his needs. Many other women who had come up with him to Jerusalem were also there.

The Burial of Jesus

[42] It was Preparation Day (that is, the day before the Sabbath). So as evening approached, [43] Joseph of Arimathea, a prominent member of the Council, who was himself waiting for the kingdom of God, went boldly to Pilate and asked for Jesus' body. [44] Pilate was surprised to hear that he was already dead. Summoning the centurion, he asked him if Jesus had already died. [45] When he learned from the centurion that it was so, he gave the body to Joseph. [46] So Joseph bought some linen cloth, took down the body, wrapped it in the linen, and placed it in a tomb cut out of rock. Then he rolled a stone against the entrance of the tomb. [47] Mary Magdalene and Mary the mother of Joses saw where he was laid.

---

[a]27 Some manuscripts *left,* [28]*and the scripture was fulfilled which says, "He was counted with the lawless ones"* (Isaiah 53:12)   [b]32 Or *Messiah*   [c]34 Psalm 22:1   [d]39 Some manuscripts do not have *heard his cry and.* [e]39 Or *a son*

The Resurrection

16 When the Sabbath was over, Mary Magdalene, Mary the mother of James, and Salome bought spices so that they might go to anoint Jesus' body. [2] Very early on the first day of the week, just after sunrise, they were on their way to the tomb [3] and they asked each other, "Who will roll the stone away from the entrance of the tomb?"

[4] But when they looked up, they saw that the stone, which was very large, had been rolled away. [5] As they entered the tomb, they saw a young man dressed in a white robe sitting on the right side, and they were alarmed.

[6] "Don't be alarmed," he said. "You are looking for Jesus the Nazarene, who was crucified. He has risen! He is not here. See the place where they laid him. [7] But go, tell his disciples and Peter, 'He is going ahead of you into Galilee. There you will see him, just as he told you.'"

[8] Trembling and bewildered, the women went out and fled from the tomb. They said nothing to anyone, because they were afraid.

[The earliest manuscripts and some other ancient witnesses do not have Mark 16:9 – 20.]

[9] When Jesus rose early on the first day of the week, he appeared first to Mary Magdalene, out of whom he had driven seven demons. [10] She went and told those who had been with him and who were mourning and weeping. [11] When they heard that Jesus was alive and that she had seen him, they did not believe it.

[12] Afterwards Jesus appeared in a different form to two of them while they were walking in the country. [13] These returned and reported it to the rest; but they did not believe them either.

[14] Later Jesus appeared to the Eleven as they were eating; he rebuked them for their lack of faith and their stubborn refusal to believe those who had seen him after he had risen.

[15] He said to them, "Go into all the world and preach the good news to all creation. [16] Whoever believes and is baptised will be saved, but whoever does not believe will be condemned. [17] And these signs will accompany those who believe: In my name they will drive out demons; they will speak in new tongues; [18] they will pick up snakes with their hands; and when they drink deadly poison, it will not hurt them at all; they will place their hands on sick people, and they will get well."

[19] After the Lord Jesus had spoken to them, he was taken up into heaven and he sat at the right hand of God. [20] Then the disciples went out and preached everywhere, and the Lord worked with them and confirmed his word by the signs that accompanied it.

Luke

Introduction

1 Many have undertaken to draw up an account of the things that have been fulfilled*a* among us, ²just as they were handed down to us by those who from the first were eye-witnesses and servants of the word. ³Therefore, since I myself have carefully investigated everything from the beginning, it seemed good also to me to write an orderly account for you, most excellent Theophilus, ⁴so that you may know the certainty of the things you have been taught.

The Birth of John the Baptist Foretold

⁵In the time of Herod king of Judea there was a priest named Zechariah, who belonged to the priestly division of Abijah; his wife Elizabeth was also a descendant of Aaron. ⁶Both of them were upright in the sight of God, observing all the Lord's commandments and regulations blamelessly. ⁷But they had no children, because Elizabeth was barren; and they were both well on in years.

⁸Once when Zechariah's division was on duty and he was serving as priest before God, ⁹he was chosen by lot, according to the custom of the priesthood, to go into the temple of the Lord and burn incense. ¹⁰And when the time for the burning of incense came, all the assembled worshippers were praying outside.

¹¹Then an angel of the Lord appeared to him, standing at the right side of the altar of incense. ¹²When Zechariah saw him, he was startled and was gripped with fear. ¹³But the angel said to him: "Do not be afraid, Zechariah; your prayer has been heard. Your wife Elizabeth will bear you a son, and you are to give him the name John. ¹⁴He will be a joy and delight to you, and many will rejoice because of his birth, ¹⁵for he will be great in the sight of the Lord. He is never to take wine or other fermented drink, and he will be filled with the Holy Spirit even from birth.*b* ¹⁶Many of the people of Israel will he bring back to the Lord their God. ¹⁷And he will go on before the Lord, in the spirit and power of Elijah, to turn the hearts of the parents to their children and the disobedient to the wisdom of the righteous—to make ready a people prepared for the Lord."

¹⁸Zechariah asked the angel, "How can I be sure of this? I am an old man and my wife is well on in years."

¹⁹The angel answered, "I am Gabriel. I stand in the presence of God, and I have been sent to speak to you and to tell you this good news. ²⁰And now you will be silent and not able to speak until the day this happens, because you did not believe my words, which will come true at their proper time."

²¹Meanwhile, the people were waiting for Zechariah and wondering why he stayed so long in the temple. ²²When he came out, he could not speak to them. They realised he had seen a vision in the temple, for he kept making signs to them but remained unable to speak.

---

*a*1 Or *been surely believed*   *b*15 Or *from his mother's womb*

23 When his time of service was completed, he returned home. 24 After this his wife Elizabeth became pregnant and for five months remained in seclusion. 25 "The Lord has done this for me," she said. "In these days he has shown his favour and taken away my disgrace among the people."

The Birth of Jesus Foretold

26 In the sixth month, God sent the angel Gabriel to Nazareth, a town in Galilee, 27 to a virgin pledged to be married to a man named Joseph, a descendant of David. The virgin's name was Mary. 28 The angel went to her and said, "Greetings, you who are highly favoured! The Lord is with you."

29 Mary was greatly troubled at his words and wondered what kind of greeting this might be. 30 But the angel said to her, "Do not be afraid, Mary, you have found favour with God. 31 You will be with child and give birth to a son, and you are to give him the name Jesus. 32 He will be great and will be called the Son of the Most High. The Lord God will give him the throne of his father David, 33 and he will reign over the house of Jacob for ever; his kingdom will never end."

34 "How will this be," Mary asked the angel, "since I am a virgin?"

35 The angel answered, "The Holy Spirit will come upon you, and the power of the Most High will overshadow you. So the holy one to be born will be called[c] the Son of God. 36 Even Elizabeth your relative is going to have a child in her old age, and she who was said to be barren is in her sixth month. 37 For nothing is impossible with God."

38 "I am the Lord's servant," Mary answered. "May it be to me as you have said." Then the angel left her.

Mary Visits Elizabeth

39 At that time Mary got ready and hurried to a town in the hill country of Judea, 40 where she entered Zechariah's home and greeted Elizabeth. 41 When Elizabeth heard Mary's greeting, the baby leaped in her womb, and Elizabeth was filled with the Holy Spirit. 42 In a loud voice she exclaimed: "Blessed are you among women, and blessed is the child you will bear! 43 But why am I so favoured, that the mother of my Lord should come to me? 44 As soon as the sound of your greeting reached my ears, the baby in my womb leaped for joy. 45 Blessed is she who has believed that what the Lord has said to her will be accomplished!"

Mary's Song

46 And Mary said:

"My soul glorifies the Lord
47   and my spirit rejoices in God my Saviour,
48 for he has been mindful
     of the humble state of his servant.
From now on all generations will call me blessed,
49   for the Mighty One has done great things for me—
     holy is his name.
50 His mercy extends to those who fear him,
     from generation to generation.
51 He has performed mighty deeds with his arm;
     he has scattered those who are proud in their inmost thoughts.
52 He has brought down rulers from their thrones
     but has lifted up the humble.
53 He has filled the hungry with good things
     but has sent the rich away empty.
54 He has helped his servant Israel,
     remembering to be merciful
55 to Abraham and his descendants for ever,
     even as he said to our ancestors."

56 Mary stayed with Elizabeth for about three months and then returned home.

---

c 35 Or So the child to be born will be called holy,

The Birth of John the Baptist

57 When it was time for Elizabeth to have her baby, she gave birth to a son. 58 Her neighbours and relatives heard that the Lord had shown her great mercy, and they shared her joy. 59 On the eighth day they came to circumcise the child, and they were going to name him after his father Zechariah, 60 but his mother spoke up and said, "No! He is to be called John."

61 They said to her, "There is no-one among your relatives who has that name." 62 Then they made signs to his father, to find out what he would like to name the child. 63 He asked for a writing tablet, and to everyone's astonishment he wrote, "His name is John." 64 Immediately his mouth was opened and his tongue was loosed, and he began to speak, praising God. 65 The neighbours were all filled with awe, and throughout the hill country of Judea people were talking about all these things. 66 Everyone who heard this wondered about it, asking, "What then is this child going to be?" For the Lord's hand was with him.

Zechariah's Song

67 His father Zechariah was filled with the Holy Spirit and prophesied:

68 "Praise be to the Lord, the God of Israel,
   because he has come and has
     redeemed his people.
69 He has raised up a horn[d] of salvation
     for us
   in the house of his servant David
70 (as he said through his holy prophets
     of long ago),
71 salvation from our enemies
   and from the hand of all who
     hate us—
72 to show mercy to our ancestors
   and to remember his holy
     covenant,
73 the oath he swore to our father
     Abraham:
74 to rescue us from the hand of our
     enemies,

and to enable us to serve him
   without fear
75 in holiness and righteousness
     before him all our days.

76 And you, my child, will be called a
     prophet of the Most High;
   for you will go on before the Lord
     to prepare the way for him,
77 to give his people the knowledge of
     salvation
   through the forgiveness of their
     sins,
78 because of the tender mercy of our
     God,
   by which the rising sun will come to
     us from heaven
79 to shine on those living in darkness
   and in the shadow of death,
   to guide our feet into the path of
     peace."

80 And the child grew and became strong in spirit; and he lived in the desert until he appeared publicly to Israel.

The Birth of Jesus

2 In those days Caesar Augustus issued a decree that a census should be taken of the entire Roman world. (2 This was the first census that took place while Quirinius was governor of Syria.) 3 And all went to their own towns to register.

4 So Joseph also went up from the town of Nazareth in Galilee to Judea, to Bethlehem the town of David, because he belonged to the house and line of David. 5 He went there to register with Mary, who was pledged to be married to him and was expecting a child. 6 While they were there, the time came for the baby to be born, 7 and she gave birth to her firstborn, a son. She wrapped him in cloths and placed him in a manger, because there was no room for them in the inn.

The Shepherds and the Angels

8 And there were shepherds living out in the fields near by, keeping watch over their flocks at night. 9 An angel of the Lord

d69 *Horn* here symbolises strength.

appeared to them, and the glory of the Lord shone around them, and they were terrified. ¹⁰But the angel said to them, "Do not be afraid. I bring you good news of great joy that will be for all the people. ¹¹Today in the town of David a Saviour has been born to you; he is Christ*a* the Lord. ¹²This will be a sign to you: You will find a baby wrapped in cloths and lying in a manger."

¹³Suddenly a great company of the heavenly host appeared with the angel, praising God and saying,

¹⁴"Glory to God in the highest,
    and on earth peace to those on
        whom his favour rests."

¹⁵When the angels had left them and gone into heaven, the shepherds said to one another, "Let's go to Bethlehem and see this thing that has happened, which the Lord has told us about."

¹⁶So they hurried off and found Mary and Joseph, and the baby, who was lying in the manger. ¹⁷When they had seen him, they spread the word concerning what had been told them about this child, ¹⁸and all who heard it were amazed at what the shepherds said to them. ¹⁹But Mary treasured up all these things and pondered them in her heart. ²⁰The shepherds returned, glorifying and praising God for all the things they had heard and seen, which were just as they had been told.

Jesus Presented in the Temple

²¹On the eighth day, when it was time to circumcise him, he was named Jesus, the name the angel had given him before he had been conceived.

²²When the time of their purification according to the Law of Moses had been completed, Joseph and Mary took him to Jerusalem to present him to the Lord ²³(as it is written in the Law of the Lord, "Every firstborn male is to be consecrated to the Lord"*b*), ²⁴and to offer a sacrifice in keeping with what is said in the Law of

the Lord: "a pair of doves or two young pigeons".*c*

²⁵Now there was a man in Jerusalem called Simeon, who was righteous and devout. He was waiting for the consolation of Israel, and the Holy Spirit was upon him. ²⁶It had been revealed to him by the Holy Spirit that he would not die before he had seen the Lord's Christ. ²⁷Moved by the Spirit, he went into the temple courts. When the parents brought in the child Jesus to do for him what the custom of the Law required, ²⁸Simeon took him in his arms and praised God, saying:

²⁹"Sovereign Lord, as you have
        promised,
    you now dismiss*d* your servant in
        peace.
³⁰For my eyes have seen your salvation,
³¹   which you have prepared in the
        sight of all people,
³²a light for revelation to the Gentiles
    and for glory to your people
        Israel."

³³The child's father and mother marvelled at what was said about him. ³⁴Then Simeon blessed them and said to Mary, his mother: "This child is destined to cause the falling and rising of many in Israel, and to be a sign that will be spoken against, ³⁵so that the thoughts of many hearts will be revealed. And a sword will pierce your own soul too."

³⁶There was also a prophetess, Anna, the daughter of Phanuel, of the tribe of Asher. She was very old; she had lived with her husband seven years after her marriage, ³⁷and then was a widow until she was eighty-four.*e* She never left the temple but worshipped night and day, fasting and praying. ³⁸Coming up to them at that very moment, she gave thanks to God and spoke about the child to all who were looking forward to the redemption of Jerusalem.

³⁹When Joseph and Mary had done everything required by the Law of the Lord, they returned to Galilee to their

---

*a*11 Or *Messiah*. "The Christ" (Greek) and "the Messiah" (Hebrew) both mean "the Anointed One"; also in verse 26.
*b*23 Exodus 13:2,12   *c*24 Lev. 12:8   *d*29 Or *promised, / now dismiss*
*e*37 Or *widow for eighty-four years*

own town of Nazareth. ⁴⁰And the child grew and became strong; he was filled with wisdom, and the grace of God was upon him.

The Boy Jesus at the Temple

⁴¹Every year his parents went to Jerusalem for the Feast of the Passover. ⁴²When he was twelve years old, they went up to the Feast, according to the custom. ⁴³After the Feast was over, while his parents were returning home, the boy Jesus stayed behind in Jerusalem, but they were unaware of it. ⁴⁴Thinking he was in their company, they travelled on for a day. Then they began looking for him among their relatives and friends. ⁴⁵When they did not find him, they went back to Jerusalem to look for him. ⁴⁶After three days they found him in the temple courts, sitting among the teachers, listening to them and asking them questions. ⁴⁷Everyone who heard him was amazed at his understanding and his answers. ⁴⁸When his parents saw him, they were astonished. His mother said to him, "Son, why have you treated us like this? Your father and I have been anxiously searching for you."

⁴⁹"Why were you searching for me?" he asked. "Didn't you know I had to be in my Father's house?" ⁵⁰But they did not understand what he was saying to them.

⁵¹Then he went down to Nazareth with them and was obedient to them. But his mother treasured all these things in her heart. ⁵²And Jesus grew in wisdom and stature, and in favour with God and people.

John the Baptist Prepares the Way

3 In the fifteenth year of the reign of Tiberius Caesar—when Pontius Pilate was governor of Judea, Herod tetrarch of Galilee, his brother Philip tetrarch of Iturea and Traconitis, and Lysanias tetrarch of Abilene—²during the high priesthood of Annas and Caiaphas, the word of God came to John son of Zechariah in the desert. ³He went into all the country around the Jordan, preaching a baptism of repentance for the forgiveness of sins. ⁴As is written in the book of the words of Isaiah the prophet:

> "A voice of one calling in the desert,
> 'Prepare the way for the Lord,
>   make straight paths for him.
> ⁵Every valley shall be filled in,
>   every mountain and hill made low.
> The crooked roads shall become
>   straight,
>   the rough ways smooth.
> ⁶And the whole human race will see
>   God's salvation.' "ᵃ

⁷John said to the crowds coming out to be baptised by him, "You brood of vipers! Who warned you to flee from the coming wrath? ⁸Produce fruit in keeping with repentance. And do not begin to say to yourselves, 'We have Abraham as our father.' For I tell you that out of these stones God can raise up children for Abraham. ⁹The axe is already at the root of the trees, and every tree that does not produce good fruit will be cut down and thrown into the fire."

¹⁰"What should we do then?" the crowd asked.

¹¹John answered, "The person with two tunics should share with the one who has none, and the one who has food should do the same."

¹²Tax collectors also came to be baptised. "Teacher," they asked, "what should we do?"

¹³"Don't collect any more than you are required to," he told them.

¹⁴Then some soldiers asked him, "And what should we do?"

He replied, "Don't extort money and don't accuse people falsely—be content with your pay."

¹⁵The people were waiting expectantly and were all wondering in their hearts if John might possibly be the Christ.ᵇ ¹⁶John answered them all, "I baptise you withᶜ water. But one more powerful than I will come, the thongs of whose sandals I am not worthy to untie. He will baptise you with the Holy Spirit and with fire. ¹⁷His winnowing fork is in his hand to clear his threshing-floor and to gather the wheat

---

ᵃ6 Isaiah 40:3–5   ᵇ15 Or *Messiah*   ᶜ16 Or *in*

into his barn, but he will burn up the chaff with unquenchable fire." [18] And with many other words John exhorted the people and preached the good news to them.

[19] But when John rebuked Herod the tetrarch because of Herodias, his brother's wife, and all the other evil things he had done, [20] Herod added this to them all: He locked John up in prison.

The Baptism and Genealogy of Jesus

[21] When all the people were being baptised, Jesus was baptised too. And as he was praying, heaven was opened [22] and the Holy Spirit descended on him in bodily form like a dove. And a voice came from heaven: "You are my Son, whom I love; with you I am well pleased."

[23] Now Jesus himself was about thirty years old when he began his ministry. He was the son, so it was thought, of Joseph,

the son of Heli, [24] the son of Matthat,
the son of Levi, the son of Melki,
the son of Jannai, the son of Joseph,
[25] the son of Mattathias, the son of Amos,
the son of Nahum, the son of Esli,
the son of Naggai, [26] the son of Maath,
the son of Mattathias, the son of
Semein,
the son of Josech, the son of Joda,
[27] the son of Joanan, the son of Rhesa,
the son of Zerubbabel, the son of
Shealtiel,
the son of Neri, [28] the son of Melki,
the son of Addi, the son of Cosam,
the son of Elmadam, the son of Er,
[29] the son of Joshua, the son of Eliezer,
the son of Jorim, the son of Matthat,
the son of Levi, [30] the son of Simeon,
the son of Judah, the son of Joseph,
the son of Jonam, the son of Eliakim,
[31] the son of Melea, the son of Menna,
the son of Mattatha, the son of
Nathan,
the son of David, [32] the son of Jesse,
the son of Obed, the son of Boaz,
the son of Salmon,[d] the son of
Nahshon,

[33] the son of Amminadab, the son of
Ram,[e]
the son of Hezron, the son of Perez,
the son of Judah, [34] the son of Jacob,
the son of Isaac, the son of Abraham,
the son of Terah, the son of Nahor,
[35] the son of Serug, the son of Reu,
the son of Peleg, the son of Eber,
the son of Shelah, [36] the son of Cainan,
the son of Arphaxad, the son of Shem,
the son of Noah, the son of Lamech,
[37] the son of Methuselah, the son of
Enoch,
the son of Jared, the son of Mahalalel,
the son of Kenan, [38] the son of Enosh,
the son of Seth, the son of Adam,
the son of God.

The Temptation of Jesus

4 Jesus, full of the Holy Spirit, returned from the Jordan and was led by the Spirit in the desert, [2] where for forty days he was tempted by the devil. He ate nothing during those days, and at the end of them he was hungry.

[3] The devil said to him, "If you are the Son of God, tell this stone to become bread."

[4] Jesus answered, "It is written: 'People do not live on bread alone.'[a]"

[5] The devil led him up to a high place and showed him in an instant all the kingdoms of the world. [6] And he said to him, "I will give you all their authority and splendour, for it has been given to me, and I can give it to anyone I want to. [7] So if you worship me, it will all be yours."

[8] Jesus answered, "It is written: 'Worship the Lord your God and serve him only.'[b]"

[9] The devil led him to Jerusalem and had him stand on the highest point of the temple. "If you are the Son of God," he said, "throw yourself down from here. [10] For it is written:

" 'He will command his angels
    concerning you
to guard you carefully;

---

[d]32 Some early manuscripts *Sala*
[e]33 Some manuscripts *Amminadab, the son of Admin, the son of Arni* ; other manuscripts vary widely.
[a]4 Deut. 8:3   [b]8 Deut. 6:13

[11] they will lift you up in their hands,
    so that you will not strike your foot
        against a stone.'[c] "

[12] Jesus answered, "It says: 'Do not put the Lord your God to the test.'[d] "

[13] When the devil had finished all this tempting, he left him until an opportune time.

Jesus Rejected at Nazareth

[14] Jesus returned to Galilee in the power of the Spirit, and news about him spread through the whole countryside. [15] He taught in their synagogues, and everyone praised him.

[16] He went to Nazareth, where he had been brought up, and on the Sabbath day he went into the synagogue, as was his custom. And he stood up to read. [17] The scroll of the prophet Isaiah was handed to him. Unrolling it, he found the place where it is written:

[18] "The Spirit of the Lord is on me,
    because he has anointed me
      to preach good news to the poor.
He has sent me to proclaim freedom
      for the prisoners
    and recovery of sight for the blind,
to release the oppressed,
[19]   to proclaim the year of the Lord's
    favour."[e]

[20] Then he rolled up the scroll, gave it back to the attendant and sat down. The eyes of everyone in the synagogue were fastened on him, [21] and he began by saying to them, "Today this scripture is fulfilled in your hearing."

[22] All spoke well of him and were amazed at the gracious words that came from his lips. "Isn't this Joseph's son?" they asked.

[23] Jesus said to them, "Surely you will quote this proverb to me: 'Physician, heal yourself! Do here in your home town what we have heard that you did in Capernaum.' "

[24] "I tell you the truth," he continued,

"prophets are not accepted in their home towns. [25] I assure you that there were many widows in Israel in Elijah's time, when the sky was shut for three and a half years and there was a severe famine throughout the land. [26] Yet Elijah was not sent to any of them, but to a widow in Zarephath in the region of Sidon. [27] And there were many in Israel with leprosy[f] in the time of Elisha the prophet, yet not one of them was cleansed—only Naaman the Syrian."

[28] All the people in the synagogue were furious when they heard this. [29] They got up, drove him out of the town, and took him to the brow of the hill on which the town was built, in order to throw him down the cliff. [30] But he walked right through the crowd and went on his way.

Jesus Drives Out an Evil Spirit

[31] Then he went down to Capernaum, a town in Galilee, and on the Sabbath began to teach the people. [32] They were amazed at his teaching, because his message had authority.

[33] In the synagogue there was a man possessed by a demon, an evil[g] spirit. He cried out at the top of his voice, [34] "Ha! What do you want with us, Jesus of Nazareth? Have you come to destroy us? I know who you are—the Holy One of God!"

[35] "Be quiet!" Jesus said sternly. "Come out of him!" Then the demon threw the man down before them all and came out without injuring him.

[36] All the people were amazed and said to each other, "What is this teaching? With authority and power he gives orders to evil spirits and they come out!" [37] And the news about him spread throughout the surrounding area.

Jesus Heals Many

[38] Jesus left the synagogue and went to the home of Simon. Now Simon's mother-in-law was suffering from a high fever, and they asked Jesus to help her. [39] So he bent

---

[c]11 Psalm 91:11,12   [d]12 Deut. 6:16   [e]19 Isaiah 61:1,2
[f]27 The Greek word was used for various diseases affecting the skin—not necessarily leprosy.
[g]33 Greek *unclean*; also in verse 36

over her and rebuked the fever, and it left her. She got up at once and began to wait on them.

⁴⁰When the sun was setting, the people brought to Jesus all who had various kinds of sickness, and laying his hands on each one, he healed them. ⁴¹Moreover, demons came out of many people, shouting, "You are the Son of God!" But he rebuked them and would not allow them to speak, because they knew he was the Christ.ʰ

⁴²At daybreak Jesus went out to a solitary place. The people were looking for him and when they came to where he was, they tried to keep him from leaving them. ⁴³But he said, "I must preach the good news of the kingdom of God to the other towns also, because that is why I was sent." ⁴⁴And he kept on preaching in the synagogues of Judea.ⁱ

The Calling of the First Disciples

5 One day as Jesus was standing by the Lake of Gennesaret,ᵃ with the people crowding round him and listening to the word of God, ²he saw at the water's edge two boats, left there by the fishermen, who were washing their nets. ³He got into one of the boats, the one belonging to Simon, and asked him to put out a little from shore. Then he sat down and taught the people from the boat.

⁴When he had finished speaking, he said to Simon, "Put out into deep water, and let downᵇ the nets for a catch."

⁵Simon answered, "Master, we've worked hard all night and haven't caught anything. But because you say so, I will let down the nets."

⁶When they had done so, they caught such a large number of fish that their nets began to break. ⁷So they signalled to their partners in the other boat to come and help them, and they came and filled both boats so full that they began to sink.

⁸When Simon Peter saw this, he fell at Jesus' knees and said, "Go away from me, Lord; I am a sinful man!" ⁹For he and

all his companions were astonished at the catch of fish they had taken, ¹⁰and so were James and John, the sons of Zebedee, Simon's partners.

Then Jesus said to Simon, "Don't be afraid; from now on you will catch men and women." ¹¹So they pulled their boats up on shore, left everything and followed him.

The Man With Leprosy

¹²While Jesus was in one of the towns, a man came along who was covered with leprosy.ᶜ When he saw Jesus, he fell with his face to the ground and begged him, "Lord, if you are willing, you can make me clean."

¹³Jesus reached out his hand and touched the man. "I am willing," he said. "Be clean!" And immediately the leprosy left him.

¹⁴Then Jesus ordered him, "Don't tell anyone, but go, show yourself to the priest and offer the sacrifices that Moses commanded for your cleansing, as a testimony to them."

¹⁵Yet the news about him spread all the more, so that crowds of people came to hear him and to be healed of their sicknesses. ¹⁶But Jesus often withdrew to lonely places and prayed.

Jesus Heals a Paralytic

¹⁷One day as he was teaching, Pharisees and teachers of the law, who had come from every village of Galilee and from Judea and Jerusalem, were sitting there. And the power of the Lord was present for him to heal the sick. ¹⁸Some people came carrying a paralytic on a mat and tried to take him into the house to lay him before Jesus. ¹⁹When they could not find a way to do this because of the crowd, they went up on the roof and lowered him on his mat through the tiles into the middle of the crowd, right in front of Jesus.

²⁰When Jesus saw their faith, he said, "Friend, your sins are forgiven."

²¹The Pharisees and the teachers of the

ʰ41 Or *Messiah*   ⁱ44 Or *the land of the Jews*; some manuscripts *Galilee*
ᵃ1 That is, Sea of Galilee   ᵇ4 The Greek verb is plural.
ᶜ12 The Greek word was used for various diseases affecting the skin—not necessarily leprosy.

law began thinking to themselves, "Who is this fellow who speaks blasphemy? Who can forgive sins but God alone?"

²² Jesus knew what they were thinking and asked, "Why are you thinking these things in your hearts? ²³ Which is easier: to say, 'Your sins are forgiven,' or to say, 'Get up and walk'? ²⁴ But that you may know that the Son of Man has authority on earth to forgive sins. . . ." He said to the paralysed man, "I tell you, get up, take your mat and go home." ²⁵ Immediately he stood up in front of them, took what he had been lying on and went home praising God. ²⁶ Everyone was amazed and gave praise to God. They were filled with awe and said, "We have seen remarkable things today."

The Calling of Levi

²⁷ After this, Jesus went out and saw a tax collector by the name of Levi sitting at his tax booth. "Follow me," Jesus said to him, ²⁸ and Levi got up, left everything and followed him.

²⁹ Then Levi held a great banquet for Jesus at his house, and a large crowd of tax collectors and others were eating with them. ³⁰ But the Pharisees and the teachers of the law who belonged to their sect complained to his disciples, "Why do you eat and drink with tax collectors and 'sinners'?"

³¹ Jesus answered them, "It is not the healthy who need a doctor, but the sick. ³² I have not come to call the righteous, but sinners to repentance."

Jesus Questioned About Fasting

³³ They said to him, "John's disciples often fast and pray, and so do the disciples of the Pharisees, but yours go on eating and drinking."

³⁴ Jesus answered, "Can you make the guests of the bridegroom fast while he is with them? ³⁵ But the time will come when the bridegroom will be taken from them; in those days they will fast."

³⁶ He told them this parable: "No-one tears a patch from a new garment and sews it on an old one. Whoever does will have torn the new garment, and the patch from the new will not match the old. ³⁷ And no-one pours new wine into old wineskins. If anyone does, the new wine will burst the skins, the wine will run out and the wineskins will be ruined. ³⁸ No, new wine must be poured into new wineskins. ³⁹ And none of you, after drinking old wine, wants the new, for you say, 'The old is better.' "

Lord of the Sabbath

6 One Sabbath Jesus was going through the cornfields, and his disciples began to pick some ears of corn, rub them in their hands and eat the grain. ² Some of the Pharisees asked, "Why are you doing what is unlawful on the Sabbath?"

³ Jesus answered them, "Have you never read what David did when he and his companions were hungry? ⁴ He entered the house of God, and taking the consecrated bread, he ate what is lawful only for priests to eat. And he also gave some to his companions." ⁵ Then Jesus said to them, "The Son of Man is Lord of the Sabbath."

⁶ On another Sabbath he went into the synagogue and was teaching, and a man was there whose right hand was shrivelled. ⁷ The Pharisees and the teachers of the law were looking for a reason to accuse Jesus, so they watched him closely to see if he would heal on the Sabbath. ⁸ But Jesus knew what they were thinking and said to the man with the shrivelled hand, "Get up and stand in front of everyone." So he got up and stood there.

⁹ Then Jesus said to them, "I ask you, which is lawful on the Sabbath: to do good or to do evil, to save life or to destroy it?" ¹⁰ He looked round at them all, and then said to the man, "Stretch out your hand." He did so, and his hand was completely restored. ¹¹ But they were furious and began to discuss with one another what they might do to Jesus.

The Twelve Apostles

¹² One of those days Jesus went out to a mountainside to pray, and spent the night praying to God. ¹³ When morning came,

he called his disciples to him and chose twelve of them, whom he also designated apostles: ¹⁴Simon (whom he named Peter), his brother Andrew, James, John, Philip, Bartholomew, ¹⁵Matthew, Thomas, James son of Alphaeus, Simon who was called the Zealot, ¹⁶Judas son of James, and Judas Iscariot, who became a traitor.

Blessings and Woes

¹⁷He went down with them and stood on a level place. A large crowd of his disciples was there and a great number of people from all over Judea, from Jerusalem, and from the coast of Tyre and Sidon, ¹⁸who had come to hear him and to be healed of their diseases. Those troubled by evil[a] spirits were cured, ¹⁹and the people all tried to touch him, because power was coming from him and healing them all.

²⁰Looking at his disciples, he said:

"Blessed are you who are poor,
for yours is the kingdom of God.
²¹Blessed are you who hunger now,
for you will be satisfied.
Blessed are you who weep now,
for you will laugh.
²²Blessed are you when people hate you,
when they exclude you and insult
you
and reject your name as evil,
because of the Son of Man.

²³"Rejoice in that day and leap for joy, because great is your reward in heaven. For that is how their ancestors treated the prophets.

²⁴"But woe to you who are rich,
for you have already received your
comfort.
²⁵Woe to you who are well fed now,
for you will go hungry.
Woe to you who laugh now,
for you will mourn and weep.
²⁶Woe to you when everyone speaks
well of you,
for that is how their ancestors
treated the false prophets.

Love for Enemies

²⁷"But I tell you who hear me: Love your enemies, do good to those who hate you, ²⁸bless those who curse you, pray for those who ill-treat you. ²⁹If someone strikes you on one cheek, turn the other also. If someone takes your cloak, do not withhold your tunic. ³⁰Give to everyone who asks you, and if anyone takes what belongs to you, do not demand it back. ³¹Do to others as you would have them do to you.

³²"If you love those who love you, what credit is that to you? Even 'sinners' love those who love them. ³³And if you do good to those who are good to you, what credit is that to you? Even 'sinners' do that. ³⁴And if you lend to those from whom you expect repayment, what credit is that to you? Even 'sinners' lend to 'sinners', expecting to be repaid in full. ³⁵But love your enemies, do good to them, and lend to them without expecting to get anything back. Then your reward will be great, and you will be sons of the Most High, because he is kind to the ungrateful and wicked. ³⁶Be merciful, just as your Father is merciful.

Judging Others

³⁷"Do not judge, and you will not be judged. Do not condemn, and you will not be condemned. Forgive, and you will be forgiven. ³⁸Give, and it will be given to you. A good measure, pressed down, shaken together and running over, will be poured into your lap. For with the measure you use, it will be measured to you."

³⁹He also told them this parable: "Can a blind man lead a blind man? Will they not both fall into a pit? ⁴⁰A student is not above his teacher, but everyone who is fully trained will be like his teacher.

⁴¹"Why do you look at the speck of sawdust in someone else's eye and pay no attention to the plank in your own eye? ⁴²How can you say, 'Friend, let me take the speck out of your eye,' when you yourself fail to see the plank in your own eye?

---

[a]18 Greek *unclean*

You hypocrite, first take the plank out of your eye, and then you will see clearly to remove the speck from the other person's eye.

A Tree and Its Fruit

43 "No good tree bears bad fruit, nor does a bad tree bear good fruit. 44 Each tree is recognised by its own fruit. People do not pick figs from thorn-bushes, or grapes from briers. 45 Good people bring good things out of the good stored up in their hearts, and evil people bring evil things out of the evil stored up in their hearts. For out of the overflow of one's heart the mouth speaks.

The Wise and Foolish Builders

46 "Why do you call me, 'Lord, Lord,' and do not do what I say? 47 I will show you what people are like who come to me and hear my words and put them into practice. 48 They are like a man building a house, who dug down deep and laid the foundation on rock. When the flood came, the torrent struck that house but could not shake it, because it was well built. 49 But those who hear my words and do not put them into practice are like a man who built a house on the ground without a foundation. The moment the torrent struck that house, it collapsed and its destruction was complete."

The Faith of the Centurion

7 When Jesus had finished saying all this in the hearing of the people, he entered Capernaum. 2 There a centurion's servant, whom his master valued highly, was sick and about to die. 3 The centurion heard of Jesus and sent some elders of the Jews to him, asking him to come and heal his servant. 4 When they came to Jesus, they pleaded earnestly with him, "This man deserves to have you do this, 5 because he loves our nation and has built our synagogue." 6 So Jesus went with them.

He was not far from the house when the centurion sent friends to say to him:

"Lord, don't trouble yourself, for I do not deserve to have you come under my roof. 7 That is why I did not even consider myself worthy to come to you. But say the word, and my servant will be healed. 8 For I myself am a man under authority, with soldiers under me. I tell this one, 'Go', and he goes; and that one, 'Come', and he comes. I say to my servant, 'Do this', and he does it."

9 When Jesus heard this, he was amazed at him, and turning to the crowd following him, he said, "I tell you, I have not found such great faith even in Israel." 10 Then the men who had been sent returned to the house and found the servant well.

Jesus Raises a Widow's Son

11 Soon afterwards, Jesus went to a town called Nain, and his disciples and a large crowd went along with him. 12 As he approached the town gate, a dead person was being carried out—the only son of his mother, and she was a widow. And a large crowd from the town was with her. 13 When the Lord saw her, his heart went out to her and he said, "Don't cry."

14 Then he went up and touched the coffin, and those carrying it stood still. He said, "Young man, I say to you, get up!" 15 The dead man sat up and began to talk, and Jesus gave him back to his mother.

16 They were all filled with awe and praised God. "A great prophet has appeared among us," they said. "God has come to help his people." 17 This news about Jesus spread throughout Judea[a] and the surrounding country.

Jesus and John the Baptist

18 John's disciples told him about all these things. Calling two of them, 19 he sent them to the Lord to ask, "Are you the one who was to come, or should we expect someone else?"

20 When the men came to Jesus, they said, "John the Baptist sent us to you to ask, 'Are you the one who was to come, or should we expect someone else?'"

[a] 17 Or *the land of the Jews*

21 At that very time Jesus cured many who had diseases, sicknesses and evil spirits, and gave sight to many who were blind. 22 So he replied to the messengers, "Go back and report to John what you have seen and heard: The blind receive sight, the lame walk, those who have leprosy[b] are cured, the deaf hear, the dead are raised, and the good news is preached to the poor. 23 Blessed is anyone who does not fall away on account of me."

24 After John's messengers left, Jesus began to speak to the crowd about John: "What did you go out into the desert to see? A reed swayed by the wind? 25 If not, what did you go out to see? A man dressed in fine clothes? No, those who wear expensive clothes and indulge in luxury are in palaces. 26 But what did you go out to see? A prophet? Yes, I tell you, and more than a prophet. 27 This is the one about whom it is written:

" 'I will send my messenger ahead of
      you,
   who will prepare your way before
      you.'[c]

28 I tell you, among those born of women there is no-one greater than John; yet the one who is least in the kingdom of God is greater than he."

(29 All the people, even the tax collectors, when they heard Jesus' words, acknowledged that God's way was right, because they had been baptised by John. 30 But the Pharisees and experts in the law rejected God's purpose for themselves, because they had not been baptised by John.)

31 "To what, then, can I compare the people of this generation? What are they like? 32 They are like children sitting in the market-place and calling out to each other:

" 'We played the flute for you,
      and you did not dance;
   we sang a dirge,
      and you did not cry.'

33 For John the Baptist came neither eating bread nor drinking wine, and you say, 'He has a demon.' 34 The Son of Man came eating and drinking, and you say, 'Here is a glutton and a drunkard, a friend of tax collectors and "sinners".' 35 But wisdom is proved right by all her children."

Jesus Anointed by a Sinful Woman

36 Now one of the Pharisees invited Jesus to have dinner with him, so he went to the Pharisee's house and reclined at the table. 37 When a woman who had lived a sinful life in that town learned that Jesus was eating at the Pharisee's house, she brought an alabaster jar of perfume, 38 and as she stood behind him at his feet weeping, she began to wet his feet with her tears. Then she wiped them with her hair, kissed them and poured perfume on them.

39 When the Pharisee who had invited him saw this, he said to himself, "If this man were a prophet, he would know who is touching him and what kind of woman she is—that she is a sinner."

40 Jesus answered him, "Simon, I have something to tell you."

"Tell me, teacher," he said.

41 "Two people owed money to a certain money-lender. One owed him five hundred denarii,[d] and the other fifty. 42 Neither of them had the money to pay him back, so he cancelled the debts of both. Now which of them will love him more?"

43 Simon replied, "I suppose the one who had the bigger debt cancelled."

"You have judged correctly," Jesus said.

44 Then he turned towards the woman and said to Simon, "Do you see this woman? I came into your house. You did not give me any water for my feet, but she wet my feet with her tears and wiped them with her hair. 45 You did not give me a kiss, but this woman, from the time I entered, has not stopped kissing my feet. 46 You did not put oil on my head, but she

---

[b]22 The Greek word was used for various diseases affecting the skin—not necessarily leprosy.
[c]27 Mal. 3:1   [d]41 A denarius was a coin worth about a day's wages.

has poured perfume on my feet. [47]Therefore, I tell you, her many sins have been forgiven—for she loved much. But the one who has been forgiven little loves little."

[48]Then Jesus said to her, "Your sins are forgiven."

[49]The other guests began to say among themselves, "Who is this who even forgives sins?"

[50]Jesus said to the woman, "Your faith has saved you; go in peace."

The Parable of the Sower

8 After this, Jesus travelled about from one town and village to another, proclaiming the good news of the kingdom of God. The Twelve were with him, [2]and also some women who had been cured of evil spirits and diseases: Mary (called Magdalene) from whom seven demons had come out; [3]Joanna the wife of Chuza, the manager of Herod's household; Susanna; and many others. These women were helping to support them out of their own means.

[4]While a large crowd was gathering and people were coming to Jesus from town after town, he told this parable: [5]"A farmer went out to sow his seed. As he was scattering the seed, some fell along the path; it was trampled on, and the birds of the air ate it up. [6]Some fell on rock, and when it came up, the plants withered because they had no moisture. [7]Other seed fell among thorns, which grew up with it and choked the plants. [8]Still other seed fell on good soil. It came up and yielded a crop, a hundred times more than was sown."

When he said this, he called out, "Those who have ears to hear, let them hear."

[9]His disciples asked him what this parable meant. [10]He said, "The knowledge of the secrets of the kingdom of God has been given to you, but to others I speak in parables, so that,

" 'though seeing, they may not see;
    though hearing, they may not
        understand.'[a]

[11]"This is the meaning of the parable: The seed is the word of God. [12]Those along the path are the ones who hear, and then the devil comes and takes away the word from their hearts, so that they may not believe and be saved. [13]Those on the rock are the ones who receive the word with joy when they hear it, but they have no root. They believe for a while, but in the time of testing they fall away. [14]The seed that fell among thorns stands for those who hear, but as they go on their way they are choked by life's worries, riches and pleasures, and they do not mature. [15]But the seed on good soil stands for those with a noble and good heart, who hear the word, retain it, and by persevering produce a crop.

A Lamp on a Stand

[16]"People do not light a lamp and hide it in a jar or put it under a bed. Instead, they put it on a stand, so that those who come in can see the light. [17]For there is nothing hidden that will not be disclosed, and nothing concealed that will not be known or brought out into the open. [18]Therefore consider carefully how you listen. Those who have will be given more; Those who do not have, even what they think they have will be taken from them."

Jesus' Mother and Brothers

[19]Now Jesus' mother and brothers came to see him, but they were not able to get near him because of the crowd. [20]Someone told him, "Your mother and brothers are standing outside, wanting to see you."

[21]He replied, "My mother and brothers are those who hear God's word and put it into practice."

Jesus Calms the Storm

[22]One day Jesus said to his disciples, "Let's go over to the other side of the lake." So they got into a boat and set out. [23]As they sailed, he fell asleep. A squall

[a]10 Isaiah 6:9

came down on the lake, so that the boat was being swamped, and they were in great danger.

24 The disciples went and woke him, saying, "Master, Master, we're going to drown!"

He got up and rebuked the wind and the raging waters; the storm subsided, and all was calm. 25 "Where is your faith?" he asked his disciples.

In fear and amazement they asked one another, "Who is this? He commands even the winds and the water, and they obey him."

The Healing of a Demon-possessed Man

26 They sailed to the region of the Gerasenes,*b* which is across the lake from Galilee. 27 When Jesus stepped ashore, he was met by a demon-possessed man from the town. For a long time this man had not worn clothes or lived in a house, but had lived in the tombs. 28 When he saw Jesus, he cried out and fell at his feet, shouting at the top of his voice, "What do you want with me, Jesus, Son of the Most High God? I beg you, don't torture me!" 29 For Jesus had commanded the evil*c* spirit to come out of the man. Many times it had seized him, and though he was chained hand and foot and kept under guard, he had broken his chains and had been driven by the demon into solitary places.

30 Jesus asked him, "What is your name?"

"Legion," he replied, because many demons had gone into him. 31 And they begged him repeatedly not to order them to go into the Abyss.

32 A large herd of pigs was feeding there on the hillside. The demons begged Jesus to let them go into them, and he gave them permission. 33 When the demons came out of the man, they went into the pigs, and the herd rushed down the steep bank into the lake and was drowned.

34 When those tending the pigs saw what had happened, they ran off and reported this in the town and countryside, 35 and the people went out to see what had happened. When they came to Jesus, they found the man from whom the demons had gone out, sitting at Jesus' feet, dressed and in his right mind; and they were afraid. 36 Those who had seen it told the people how the demon-possessed man had been cured. 37 Then all the people of the region of the Gerasenes asked Jesus to leave them, because they were overcome with fear. So he got into the boat and left.

38 The man from whom the demons had gone out begged to go with him, but Jesus sent him away, saying, 39 "Return home and tell how much God has done for you."
So the man went away and told all over the town how much Jesus had done for him.

A Dead Girl and a Sick Woman

40 Now when Jesus returned, a crowd welcomed him, for they were all expecting him. 41 Then a man named Jairus, a ruler of the synagogue, came and fell at Jesus' feet, pleading with him to come to his house 42 because his only daughter, a girl of about twelve, was dying.

As Jesus was on his way, the crowds almost crushed him. 43 And a woman was there who had been subject to bleeding for twelve years,*d* but no-one could heal her. 44 She came up behind him and touched the edge of his cloak, and immediately her bleeding stopped.

45 "Who touched me?" Jesus asked.

When they all denied it, Peter said, "Master, the people are crowding and pressing against you."

46 But Jesus said, "Someone touched me; I know that power has gone out from me."

47 Then the woman, seeing that she could not go unnoticed, came trembling and fell at his feet. In the presence of all the people, she told why she had touched him and how she had been instantly healed. 48 Then he said to her, "Daughter, your faith has healed you. Go in peace."

49 While Jesus was still speaking, someone came from the house of Jairus, the synagogue ruler. "Your daughter is dead," he said. "Don't bother the teacher any more."

*b*26 Some manuscripts *Gadarenes*; other manuscripts *Gergesenes*; also in verse 37
*c*29 Greek *unclean*   *d*43 Many manuscripts *years, and she had spent all she had on doctors*

⁵⁰Hearing this, Jesus said to Jairus, "Don't be afraid; just believe, and she will be healed."

⁵¹When he arrived at the house of Jairus, he did not let anyone go in with him except Peter, John and James, and the child's father and mother. ⁵²Meanwhile, all the people were wailing and mourning for her. "Stop wailing," Jesus said. "She is not dead but asleep." ⁵³They laughed at him, knowing that she was dead. ⁵⁴But he took her by the hand and said, "My child, get up!" ⁵⁵Her spirit returned, and at once she stood up. Then Jesus told them to give her something to eat. ⁵⁶Her parents were astonished, but he ordered them not to tell anyone what had happened.

Jesus Sends Out the Twelve

9 When Jesus had called the Twelve together, he gave them power and authority to drive out all demons and to cure diseases, ²and he sent them out to preach the kingdom of God and to heal the sick. ³He told them: "Take nothing for the journey—no staff, no bag, no bread, no money, no extra tunic. ⁴Whatever house you enter, stay there until you leave that town. ⁵If people do not welcome you, shake the dust off your feet when you leave their town, as a testimony against them." ⁶So they set out and went from village to village, preaching the gospel and healing people everywhere.

⁷Now Herod the tetrarch heard about all that was going on. And he was perplexed, because some were saying that John had been raised from the dead, ⁸others that Elijah had appeared, and still others that one of the prophets of long ago had come back to life. ⁹But Herod said, "I beheaded John. Who, then, is this I hear such things about?" And he tried to see him.

Jesus Feeds the Five Thousand

¹⁰When the apostles returned, they reported to Jesus what they had done. Then he took them with him and they withdrew by themselves to a town called Bethsaida, ¹¹but the crowds learned about it and followed him. He welcomed them and spoke to them about the kingdom of God, and healed those who needed healing.

¹²Late in the afternoon the Twelve came to him and said, "Send the crowd away so they can go to the surrounding villages and countryside and find food and lodging, because we are in a remote place here."

¹³He replied, "You give them something to eat."

They answered, "We have only five loaves of bread and two fish—unless we go and buy food for all this crowd." ¹⁴(About five thousand men were there.)

But he said to his disciples, "Make them sit down in groups of about fifty each." ¹⁵The disciples did so, and everybody sat down. ¹⁶Taking the five loaves and the two fish and looking up to heaven, he gave thanks and broke them. Then he gave them to the disciples to set before the people. ¹⁷They all ate and were satisfied, and the disciples picked up twelve basketfuls of broken pieces that were left over.

Peter's Confession of Christ

¹⁸Once when Jesus was praying in private and his disciples were with him, he asked them, "Who do the crowds say I am?"

¹⁹They replied, "Some say John the Baptist; others say Elijah; and still others, that one of the prophets of long ago has come back to life."

²⁰"But what about you?" he asked. "Who do you say I am?"

Peter answered, "The Christ[a] of God."

²¹Jesus strictly warned them not to tell this to anyone. ²²And he said, "The Son of Man must suffer many things and be rejected by the elders, chief priests and teachers of the law, and he must be killed and on the third day be raised to life."

²³Then he said to them all: "Those who would come after me must deny themselves and take up their cross daily and

[a]20 Or *Messiah*

follow me. 24 For those who want to save their lives will lose them, but those who lose their lives for me will save them. 25 What good is it for you to gain the whole world, and yet lose or forfeit your very self? 26 All who are ashamed of me and my words, the Son of Man will be ashamed of them when he comes in his glory and in the glory of the Father and of the holy angels. 27 I tell you the truth, some who are standing here will not taste death before they see the kingdom of God."

The Transfiguration

28 About eight days after Jesus said this, he took Peter, John and James with him and went up onto a mountain to pray. 29 As he was praying, the appearance of his face changed, and his clothes became as bright as a flash of lightning. 30 Two men, Moses and Elijah, 31 appeared in glorious splendour, talking with Jesus. They spoke about his departure, which he was about to bring to fulfilment at Jerusalem. 32 Peter and his companions were very sleepy, but when they became fully awake, they saw his glory and the two men standing with him. 33 As the men were leaving Jesus, Peter said to him, "Master, it is good for us to be here. Let us put up three shelters—one for you, one for Moses and one for Elijah." (He did not know what he was saying.) 34 While he was speaking, a cloud appeared and enveloped them, and they were afraid as they entered the cloud. 35 A voice came from the cloud, saying, "This is my Son, whom I have chosen; listen to him." 36 When the voice had spoken, they found that Jesus was alone. The disciples kept this to themselves, and told no-one at that time what they had seen.

The Healing of a Boy With an Evil Spirit

37 The next day, when they came down from the mountain, a large crowd met him. 38 A man in the crowd called out, "Teacher, I beg you to look at my son, for he is my only child. 39 A spirit seizes him and he suddenly screams; it throws him into convulsions so that he foams at the mouth. It scarcely ever leaves him and is destroying him. 40 I begged your disciples to drive it out, but they could not."

41 "O unbelieving and perverse generation," Jesus replied, "how long shall I stay with you and put up with you? Bring your son here."

42 Even while the boy was coming, the demon threw him to the ground in a convulsion. But Jesus rebuked the evil*b* spirit, healed the boy and gave him back to his father. 43 And they were all amazed at the greatness of God.

While everyone was marvelling at all that Jesus did, he said to his disciples, 44 "Listen carefully to what I am about to tell you: The Son of Man is going to be betrayed into human hands." 45 But they did not understand what this meant. It was hidden from them, so that they did not grasp it, and they were afraid to ask him about it.

Who Will Be the Greatest?

46 An argument started among the disciples as to which of them would be the greatest. 47 Jesus, knowing their thoughts, took a little child and made him stand beside him. 48 Then he said to them, "Whoever welcomes this little child in my name welcomes me; and whoever welcomes me welcomes the one who sent me. For whoever is least among you all is the greatest."

49 "Master," said John, "we saw someone driving out demons in your name and we tried to stop him, because he is not one of us."

50 "Do not stop him," Jesus said, "for whoever is not against you is for you."

Samaritan Opposition

51 As the time approached for him to be taken up to heaven, Jesus resolutely set out for Jerusalem. 52 And he sent messengers on ahead, who went into a Samaritan village to get things ready for him; 53 but

*b*42 Greek *unclean*

the people there did not welcome him, because he was heading for Jerusalem. [54] When the disciples James and John saw this, they asked, "Lord, do you want us to call fire down from heaven to destroy them?"[c] [55] But Jesus turned and rebuked them, [56] and[d] they went to another village.

The Cost of Following Jesus

[57] As they were walking along the road, someone said to him, "I will follow you wherever you go."

[58] Jesus replied, "Foxes have holes and birds of the air have nests, but the Son of Man has nowhere to lay his head."

[59] He said to another man, "Follow me."

But he replied, "Lord, first let me go and bury my father."

[60] Jesus said to him, "Let the dead bury their own dead, but you go and proclaim the kingdom of God."

[61] Still another said, "I will follow you, Lord; but first let me go back and say good-bye to my family."

[62] Jesus replied, "No-one who takes hold of the plough and looks back is fit for service in the kingdom of God."

Jesus Sends Out the Seventy-two

10 After this the Lord appointed seventy-two[a] others and sent them two by two ahead of him to every town and place where he was about to go. [2] He told them, "The harvest is plentiful, but the workers are few. Ask the Lord of the harvest, therefore, to send out workers into his harvest field. [3] Go! I am sending you out like lambs among wolves. [4] Do not take a purse or bag or sandals; and do not greet anyone on the road.

[5] "When you enter a house, first say, 'Peace to this house.' [6] If anyone there loves peace, your peace will rest on that person; if not, it will return to you. [7] Stay in that house, eating and drinking whatever they give you, for workers deserve their wages. Do not move around from house to house.

[8] "When you enter a town and are welcomed, eat what is set before you. [9] Heal the sick who are there and tell them, 'The kingdom of God is near you.' [10] But when you enter a town and are not welcomed, go into its streets and say, [11] 'Even the dust of your town that sticks to our feet we wipe off against you. Yet be sure of this: The kingdom of God is near.' [12] I tell you, it will be more bearable on that day for Sodom than for that town.

[13] "Woe to you, Korazin! Woe to you, Bethsaida! For if the miracles that were performed in you had been performed in Tyre and Sidon, they would have repented long ago, sitting in sackcloth and ashes. [14] But it will be more bearable for Tyre and Sidon at the judgment than for you. [15] And you, Capernaum, will you be lifted up to the skies? No, you will go down to the depths.[b]

[16] "Whoever listens to you listens to me; whoever rejects you rejects me; but whoever rejects me rejects him who sent me."

[17] The seventy-two returned with joy and said, "Lord, even the demons submit to us in your name."

[18] He replied, "I saw Satan fall like lightning from heaven. [19] I have given you authority to trample on snakes and scorpions and to overcome all the power of the enemy; nothing will harm you. [20] However, do not rejoice that the spirits submit to you, but rejoice that your names are written in heaven."

[21] At that time Jesus, full of joy through the Holy Spirit, said, "I praise you, Father, Lord of heaven and earth, because you have hidden these things from the wise and learned, and revealed them to little children. Yes, Father, for this was your good pleasure.

[22] "All things have been committed to me by my Father. No-one knows who the Son is except the Father, and no-one knows who the Father is except the Son and those to whom the Son chooses to reveal him."

[23] Then he turned to his disciples and said privately, "Blessed are the eyes that

---

[c]54 Some manuscripts *them, even as Elijah did*
[d]55,56 Some manuscripts *them. And he said, "You do not know what kind of spirit you are of, for the Son of Man did not come to destroy people's lives, but to save them." 56And*   [a]1 Some manuscripts *seventy*; also in verse 17
[b]15 Greek *Hades*

see what you see. 24 For I tell you that many prophets and kings wanted to see what you see but did not see it, and to hear what you hear but did not hear it."

The Parable of the Good Samaritan

25 On one occasion an expert in the law stood up to test Jesus. "Teacher," he asked, "what must I do to inherit eternal life?"

26 "What is written in the Law?" he replied. "How do you read it?"

27 He answered: " 'Love the Lord your God with all your heart and with all your soul and with all your strength and with all your mind';*c* and, 'Love your neighbour as yourself.'*d* "

28 "You have answered correctly," Jesus replied. "Do this and you will live."

29 But he wanted to justify himself, so he asked Jesus, "And who is my neighbour?"

30 In reply Jesus said: "A man was going down from Jerusalem to Jericho, when he fell into the hands of robbers. They stripped him of his clothes, beat him and went away, leaving him half-dead. 31 A priest happened to be going down the same road, and when he saw the man, he passed by on the other side. 32 So too, a Levite, when he came to the place and saw him, passed by on the other side. 33 But a Samaritan, as he travelled, came where the man was; and when he saw him, he took pity on him. 34 He went to him and bandaged his wounds, pouring on oil and wine. Then he put the man on his own donkey, brought him to an inn and took care of him. 35 The next day he took out two silver coins*e* and gave them to the innkeeper. 'Look after him,' he said, 'and when I return, I will reimburse you for any extra expense you may have.'

36 "Which of these three do you think was a neighbour to the man who fell into the hands of robbers?"

37 The expert in the law replied, "The one who had mercy on him."

Jesus told him, "Go and do likewise."

At the Home of Martha and Mary

38 As Jesus and his disciples were on their way, he came to a village where a woman named Martha opened her home to him. 39 She had a sister called Mary, who sat at the Lord's feet listening to what he said. 40 But Martha was distracted by all the preparations that had to be made. She came to him and asked, "Lord, don't you care that my sister has left me to do the work by myself? Tell her to help me!"

41 "Martha, Martha," the Lord answered, "you are worried and upset about many things, 42 but only one thing is needed.*f* Mary has chosen what is better, and it will not be taken away from her."

Jesus' Teaching on Prayer

11 One day Jesus was praying in a certain place. When he finished, one of his disciples said to him, "Lord, teach us to pray, just as John taught his disciples."

2 He said to them, "When you pray, say:

" 'Father,*a*
hallowed be your name,
your kingdom come.*b*
3 Give us each day our daily bread.
4 Forgive us our sins,
    for we also forgive everyone who
        sins against us.*c*
And lead us not into temptation.' "*d*

5 Then he said to them, "Suppose one of you has a friend, and he goes to him at midnight and says, 'Friend, lend me three loaves of bread, 6 because a friend of mine on a journey has come to me, and I have nothing to set before him.'

7 "Then the one inside answers, 'Don't bother me. The door is already locked, and my children are with me in bed. I can't get up and give you anything.' 8 I tell you, though he will not get up and give him the bread because he is his friend, yet because of the man's boldness*e* he will get up and give him as much as he needs.

*c*27 Deut. 6:5   *d*27 Lev. 19:18   *e*35 Greek *two denarii*
*f*42 Some manuscripts *but few things are needed—or only one*   *a*2 Some manuscripts *Our Father in heaven*
*b*2 Some manuscripts *come. May your will be done on earth as it is in heaven.*   *c*4 Greek *everyone who is indebted to us*
*d*4 Some manuscripts *temptation but deliver us from the evil one*   *e*8 Or *persistence*

9 "So I say to you: Ask and it will be given to you; seek and you will find; knock and the door will be opened to you. 10 For everyone who asks receives; everyone who seeks finds; and to everyone who knocks, the door will be opened. 11 "Which of you fathers, if your children ask for*f* a fish, will give them a snake instead? 12 Or if they ask for an egg, will give them a scorpion? 13 If you then, though you are evil, know how to give good gifts to your children, how much more will your Father in heaven give the Holy Spirit to those who ask him!"

Jesus and Beelzebub

14 Jesus was driving out a demon that was mute. When the demon left, the man who had been mute spoke, and the crowd was amazed. 15 But some of them said, "By Beelzebub,*g* the prince of demons, he is driving out demons." 16 Others tested him by asking for a sign from heaven.

17 Jesus knew their thoughts and said to them: "Any kingdom divided against itself will be ruined, and a house divided against itself will fall. 18 If Satan is divided against himself, how can his kingdom stand? I say this because you claim that I drive out demons by Beelzebub. 19 Now if I drive out demons by Beelzebub, by whom do your followers drive them out? So then, they will be your judges. 20 But if I drive out demons by the finger of God, then the kingdom of God has come to you.

21 "When a strong man, fully armed, guards his own house, his possessions are safe. 22 But when someone stronger attacks and overpowers him, he takes away the armour in which the man trusted and divides up the spoils.

23 "Whoever is not with me is against me, and whoever does not gather with me, scatters.

24 "When an evil*h* spirit comes out of anyone, it goes through arid places seeking rest and does not find it. Then it says, 'I will return to the house I left.' 25 When it arrives, it finds the house swept clean and put in order. 26 Then it goes and takes seven other spirits more wicked than itself, and they go in and live there. And the final condition of that person is worse than the first."

27 As Jesus was saying these things, a woman in the crowd called out, "Blessed is the mother who gave you birth and nursed you."

28 He replied, "Blessed rather are those who hear the word of God and obey it."

The Sign of Jonah

29 As the crowds increased, Jesus said, "This is a wicked generation. It asks for a miraculous sign, but none will be given it except the sign of Jonah. 30 For as Jonah was a sign to the Ninevites, so also will the Son of Man be to this generation. 31 The Queen of the South will rise at the judgment with the people of this generation and condemn them; for she came from the ends of the earth to listen to Solomon's wisdom, and now one*i* greater than Solomon is here. 32 The people of Nineveh will stand up at the judgment with this generation and condemn it; for they repented at the preaching of Jonah, and now one greater than Jonah is here.

The Lamp of the Body

33 "None of you lights a lamp and puts it in a place where it will be hidden, or under a bowl. Instead you put it on its stand, so that those who come in may see the light. 34 Your eye is the lamp of your body. When your eyes are good, your whole body also is full of light. But when they are bad, your body also is full of darkness. 35 See to it, then, that the light within you is not darkness. 36 Therefore, if your whole body is full of light, and no part of it dark, it will be completely lighted, as when the light of a lamp shines on you."

Six Woes

37 When Jesus had finished speaking, a Pharisee invited him to eat with him; so

---

f 11 Some manuscripts *for bread, will give them a stone; or if they ask for*
g 15 Greek *Beezeboul* or *Beelzeboul* ; also in verses 18 and 19　　　*h* 24 Greek *unclean*
i 31 Or *something*; also in verse 32

he went in and reclined at the table. [38] But the Pharisee, noticing that Jesus did not first wash before the meal, was surprised.

[39] Then the Lord said to him, "Now then, you Pharisees clean the outside of the cup and dish, but inside you are full of greed and wickedness. [40] You foolish people! Did not the one who made the outside make the inside also? [41] But give what is inside ˪the dish⸆ⱼ to the poor, and everything will be clean for you.

[42] "Woe to you Pharisees, because you give God a tenth of your mint, rue and all other kinds of garden herbs, but you neglect justice and the love of God. You should have practised the latter without leaving the former undone.

[43] "Woe to you Pharisees, because you love the most important seats in the synagogues and greetings in the market-places.

[44] "Woe to you, because you are like unmarked graves, which people walk over without knowing it."

[45] One of the experts in the law answered him, "Teacher, when you say these things, you insult us also."

[46] Jesus replied, "And you experts in the law, woe to you, because you load people down with burdens they can hardly carry, and you yourselves will not lift one finger to help them.

[47] "Woe to you, because you build tombs for the prophets, and it was your ancestors who killed them. [48] So you testify that you approve of what your ancestors did; they killed the prophets, and you build their tombs. [49] Because of this, God in his wisdom said, 'I will send them prophets and apostles, some of whom they will kill and others they will persecute.' [50] Therefore this generation will be held responsible for the blood of all the prophets that has been shed since the beginning of the world, [51] from the blood of Abel to the blood of Zechariah, who was killed between the altar and the sanctuary. Yes, I tell you, this generation will be held responsible for it all.

[52] "Woe to you experts in the law, because you have taken away the key to knowledge. You yourselves have not entered, and you have hindered those who were entering."

[53] When Jesus left there, the Pharisees and the teachers of the law began to oppose him fiercely and to besiege him with questions, [54] waiting to catch him in something he might say.

Warnings and Encouragements

12 Meanwhile, when a crowd of many thousands had gathered, so that they were trampling on one another, Jesus began to speak first to his disciples, saying: "Be on your guard against the yeast of the Pharisees, which is hypocrisy. [2] There is nothing concealed that will not be disclosed, or hidden that will not be made known. [3] What you have said in the dark will be heard in the daylight, and what you have whispered in the ear in the inner rooms will be proclaimed from the roofs.

[4] "I tell you, my friends, do not be afraid of those who kill the body and after that can do no more. [5] But I will show you whom you should fear: Fear him who, after the killing of the body, has power to throw you into hell. Yes, I tell you, fear him. [6] Are not five sparrows sold for two pennies?[a] Yet not one of them is forgotten by God. [7] Indeed, the very hairs of your head are all numbered. Don't be afraid; you are worth more than many sparrows.

[8] "I tell you, those who acknowledge me before others the Son of Man will also acknowledge before the angels of God. [9] But those who disown me before others will be disowned before the angels of God. [10] And everyone who speaks a word against the Son of Man will be forgiven, but anyone who blasphemes against the Holy Spirit will not be forgiven.

[11] "When you are brought before synagogues, rulers and authorities, do not worry about how you will defend yourselves or what you will say, [12] for the Holy Spirit will teach you at that time what you should say."

---

*j*41 Or *what you have*   *a*6 Greek *two assaria*

The Parable of the Rich Fool

13 Someone in the crowd said to him, "Teacher, tell my brother to divide the inheritance with me."

14 Jesus replied, "Friend, who appointed me a judge or an arbiter between you?" 15 Then he said to them, "Watch out! Be on your guard against all kinds of greed; life does not consist in the abundance of possessions."

16 And he told them this parable: "The ground of a certain rich man produced a good crop. 17 He thought to himself, 'What shall I do? I have no place to store my crops.'

18 "Then he said, 'This is what I'll do. I will tear down my barns and build bigger ones, and there I will store all my grain and my goods. 19 And I'll say to myself, "You have plenty of good things laid up for many years. Take life easy; eat, drink and be merry." '

20 "But God said to him, 'You fool! This very night your life will be demanded from you. Then who will get what you have prepared for yourself?'

21 "This is how it will be with those who store up things for themselves but are not rich towards God."

Do Not Worry

22 Then Jesus said to his disciples: "Therefore I tell you, do not worry about your life, what you will eat; or about your body, what you will wear. 23 Life is more than food, and the body more than clothes. 24 Consider the ravens: They do not sow or reap, they have no storeroom or barn; yet God feeds them. And how much more valuable you are than birds! 25 Who of you by worrying can add a single hour to your life?*b* 26 Since you cannot do this very little thing, why do you worry about the rest?

27 "Consider how the lilies grow. They do not labour or spin. Yet I tell you, not even Solomon in all his splendour was dressed like one of these. 28 If that is how God clothes the grass of the field, which is here today, and tomorrow is thrown into the fire, how much more will he clothe you, O you of little faith! 29 And do not set your heart on what you will eat or drink; do not worry about it. 30 For the pagan world runs after all such things, and your Father knows that you need them. 31 But seek his kingdom, and these things will be given to you as well.

32 "Do not be afraid, little flock, for your Father has been pleased to give you the kingdom. 33 Sell your possessions and give to the poor. Provide purses for yourselves that will not wear out, a treasure in heaven that will not be exhausted, where no thief comes near and no moth destroys. 34 For where your treasure is, there your heart will be also.

Watchfulness

35 "Be dressed ready for service and keep your lamps burning, 36 like those waiting for their master to return from a wedding banquet, so that when he comes and knocks they can immediately open the door for him. 37 It will be good for those servants whose master finds them watching when he comes. I tell you the truth, he will dress himself to serve, will have them recline at the table and will come and wait on them. 38 It will be good for those servants whose master finds them ready, even if he comes in the second or third watch of the night. 39 But understand this: If the owner of the house had known at what hour the thief was coming, he would not have let his house be broken into. 40 You also must be ready, because the Son of Man will come at an hour when you do not expect him."

41 Peter asked, "Lord, are you telling this parable to us, or to everyone?"

42 The Lord answered, "Who then is the faithful and wise manager, whom the master puts in charge of his servants to give them their food allowance at the proper time? 43 It will be good for that servant whom the master finds doing so when he returns. 44 I tell you the truth, he will put him in charge of all his possessions.

*b*25 Or *single cubit to your height*

45 But suppose the servant says to himself, 'My master is taking a long time in coming,' and he then begins to beat the other servants, both men and women, and to eat and drink and get drunk. 46 The master of that servant will come on a day when he does not expect him and at an hour he is not aware of. He will cut him to pieces and assign him a place with the unbelievers.

47 "The servant who knows the master's will and does not get ready or does not do what the master wants will be beaten with many blows. 48 But the one who does not know and does things deserving punishment will be beaten with few blows. From everyone who has been given much, much will be demanded; and from the one who has been entrusted with much, much more will be asked.

Not Peace but Division

49 "I have come to bring fire on the earth, and how I wish it were already kindled! 50 But I have a baptism to undergo, and how distressed I am until it is completed! 51 Do you think I came to bring peace on earth? No, I tell you, but division. 52 From now on there will be five in one family divided against each other, three against two and two against three. 53 They will be divided, father against son and son against father, mother against daughter and daughter against mother, mother-in-law against daughter-in-law and daughter-in-law against mother-in-law."

Interpreting the Times

54 He said to the crowd: "When you see a cloud rising in the west, immediately you say, 'It's going to rain,' and it does. 55 And when the south wind blows, you say, 'It's going to be hot,' and it is. 56 Hypocrites! You know how to interpret the appearance of the earth and the sky. How is it that you don't know how to interpret this present time?

57 "Why don't you judge for yourselves

what is right? 58 As you are going with your adversary to the magistrate, try hard to be reconciled on the way, or your adversary may drag you off to the judge, and the judge turn you over to the officer, and the officer throw you into prison. 59 I tell you, you will not get out until you have paid the last penny."c

Repent or Perish

13 Now there were some present at that time who told Jesus about the Galileans whose blood Pilate had mixed with their sacrifices. 2 Jesus answered, "Do you think that these Galileans were worse sinners than all the other Galileans because they suffered this way? 3 I tell you, no! But unless you repent, you too will all perish. 4 Or those eighteen who died when the tower in Siloam fell on them—do you think they were more guilty than all the others living in Jerusalem? 5 I tell you, no! But unless you repent, you too will all perish."

6 Then he told this parable: "A man had a fig-tree, planted in his vineyard, and he went to look for fruit on it, but did not find any. 7 So he said to the man who took care of the vineyard, 'For three years now I've been coming to look for fruit on this fig-tree and haven't found any. Cut it down! Why should it use up the soil?'

8 " 'Sir,' the man replied, 'leave it alone for one more year, and I'll dig round it and fertilise it. 9 If it bears fruit next year, fine! If not, then cut it down.' "

A Crippled Woman Healed on the Sabbath

10 On a Sabbath Jesus was teaching in one of the synagogues, 11 and a woman was there who had been crippled by a spirit for eighteen years. She was bent over and could not straighten up at all. 12 When Jesus saw her, he called her forward and said to her, "Woman, you are set free from your infirmity." 13 Then he put his hands on her, and immediately she straightened up and praised God.

14 Indignant because Jesus had healed

c59 Greek lepton

on the Sabbath, the synagogue ruler said to the people, "There are six days for work. So come and be healed on those days, not on the Sabbath."

15 The Lord answered him, "You hypocrites! Doesn't each of you on the Sabbath untie his ox or donkey from the stall and lead it out to give it water? 16 Then should not this woman, a daughter of Abraham, whom Satan has kept bound for eighteen long years, be set free on the Sabbath day from what bound her?"

17 When he said this, all his opponents were humiliated, but the people were delighted with all the wonderful things he was doing.

The Parables of the Mustard Seed and the Yeast

18 Then Jesus asked, "What is the kingdom of God like? What shall I compare it to? 19 It is like a mustard seed, which a man took and planted in his garden. It grew and became a tree, and the birds of the air perched in its branches."

20 Again he asked, "What shall I compare the kingdom of God to? 21 It is like yeast that a woman took and mixed into a large amount*a* of flour until it worked all through the dough."

The Narrow Door

22 Then Jesus went through the towns and villages, teaching as he made his way to Jerusalem. 23 Someone asked him, "Lord, are only a few people going to be saved?"

He said to them, 24 "Make every effort to enter through the narrow door, because many, I tell you, will try to enter and will not be able to. 25 Once the owner of the house gets up and closes the door, you will stand outside knocking and pleading, 'Sir, open the door for us.'

"But he will answer, 'I don't know you or where you come from.'

26 "Then you will say, 'We ate and drank with you, and you taught in our streets.'

27 "But he will reply, 'I don't know you or where you come from. Away from me, all you evildoers!'

28 "There will be weeping there, and gnashing of teeth, when you see Abraham, Isaac and Jacob and all the prophets in the kingdom of God, but you yourselves thrown out. 29 People will come from east and west and north and south, and will take their places at the feast in the kingdom of God. 30 Indeed there are those who are last who will be first, and first who will be last."

Jesus' Sorrow for Jerusalem

31 At that time some Pharisees came to Jesus and said to him, "Leave this place and go somewhere else. Herod wants to kill you."

32 He replied, "Go tell that fox, 'I will drive out demons and heal people today and tomorrow, and on the third day I will reach my goal.' 33 In any case, I must keep going today and tomorrow and the next day—for surely no prophet can die outside Jerusalem!

34 "O Jerusalem, Jerusalem, you who kill the prophets and stone those sent to you, how often I have longed to gather your children together, as a hen gathers her chicks under her wings, but you were not willing! 35 Look, your house is left to you desolate. I tell you, you will not see me again until you say, 'Blessed is he who comes in the name of the Lord.'*b* "

Jesus at a Pharisee's House

14 One Sabbath, when Jesus went to eat in the house of a prominent Pharisee, he was being carefully watched. 2 There in front of him was a man suffering from dropsy. 3 Jesus asked the Pharisees and experts in the law, "Is it lawful to heal on the Sabbath or not?" 4 But they remained silent. So taking hold of the man, he healed him and sent him away.

5 Then he asked them, "If one of you has a child*a* or an ox that falls into a well on the Sabbath day, will you not immediately pull it out?" 6 And they had nothing to say.

7 When he noticed how the guests

---

*a*21 Greek *three satas* (probably about 3/5 bushel or 22 litres)   *b*35 Psalm 118:26   *a*5 Some manuscripts *donkey* picked the places of honour at the table, he told them this parable: 8 "When someone invites you to a wedding feast, do not take the place of honour, for a person more distinguished than you may have been invited. 9 If so, the host who invited both of you will come and say to you, 'Give this person your seat.' Then, humiliated, you will have to take the least important place. 10 But when you are invited, take the lowest place, so that when your host comes, he will say to you, 'Friend, move up to a better place.' Then you will be honoured in the presence of all the other guests. 11 For all those who exalt themselves will be humbled, and those who humble themselves will be exalted."

12 Then Jesus said to his host, "When you give a luncheon or dinner, do not invite your friends, brothers, sisters, relatives, or your rich neighbours; if you do, they may invite you back and so you will be repaid. 13 But when you give a banquet, invite the poor, the crippled, the lame, the blind, 14 and you will be blessed. Although they cannot repay you, you will be repaid at the resurrection of the righteous."

The Parable of the Great Banquet

15 When one of those at the table with him heard this, he said to Jesus, "Blessed is the one who will eat at the feast in the kingdom of God."

16 Jesus replied: "A certain man was preparing a great banquet and invited many guests. 17 At the time of the banquet he sent his servant to tell those who had been invited, 'Come, for everything is now ready.'

18 "But they all alike began to make excuses. The first said, 'I have just bought a field, and I must go and see it. Please excuse me.'

19 "Another said, 'I have just bought five yoke of oxen, and I'm on my way to try them out. Please excuse me.'

20 "Still another said, 'I have just got married, so I can't come.'

21 "The servant came back and reported this to his master. Then the owner of the house became angry and ordered his servant, 'Go out quickly into the streets and alleys of the town and bring in the poor, the crippled, the blind and the lame.'

22 "'Sir,' the servant said, 'what you ordered has been done, but there is still room.'

23 "Then the master told his servant, 'Go out to the roads and country lanes and make them come in, so that my house will be full. 24 I tell you, not one of those who were invited will get a taste of my banquet.'"

The Cost of Being a Disciple

25 Large crowds were travelling with Jesus, and turning to them he said: 26 "If anyone comes to me and does not hate father and mother, wife and children, brothers and sisters—yes, even life itself—such a person cannot be my disciple. 27 And those who do not carry their cross and follow me cannot be my disciples.

28 "Suppose one of you wants to build a tower. Will you not first sit down and estimate the cost to see if you have enough money to complete it? 29 For if you lay the foundation and are not able to finish it, everyone who sees it will ridicule you, 30 saying, 'This person began to build and was not able to finish.'

31 "Or suppose a king is about to go to war against another king. Will he not first sit down and consider whether he is able with ten thousand men to oppose the one coming against him with twenty thousand? 32 If he is not able, he will send a delegation while the other is still a long way off and will ask for terms of peace. 33 In the same way, those of you who do not give up everything you have cannot be my disciples.

34 "Salt is good, but if it loses its saltiness, how can it be made salty again? 35 It is fit neither for the soil nor for the manure heap; it is thrown out.

"Those who have ears to hear, let them hear."

The Parable of the Lost Sheep

15 Now the tax collectors and "sinners" were all gathering round to hear him. 2 But the Pharisees and the

teachers of the law muttered, "This man welcomes sinners, and eats with them."

[3] Then Jesus told them this parable: [4] "Suppose one of you has a hundred sheep and loses one of them. Does he not leave the ninety-nine in the open country and go after the lost sheep until he finds it? [5] And when he finds it, he joyfully puts it on his shoulders [6] and goes home. Then he calls his friends and neighbours together and says, 'Rejoice with me; I have found my lost sheep.' [7] I tell you that in the same way there will be more rejoicing in heaven over one sinner who repents than over ninety-nine righteous persons who do not need to repent.

The Parable of the Lost Coin

[8] "Or suppose a woman has ten silver coins[a] and loses one. Does she not light a lamp, sweep the house and search carefully until she finds it? [9] And when she finds it, she calls her friends and neighbours together and says, 'Rejoice with me; I have found my lost coin.' [10] In the same way, I tell you, there is rejoicing in the presence of the angels of God over one sinner who repents."

The Parable of the Lost Son

[11] Jesus continued: "There was a man who had two sons. [12] The younger one said to his father, 'Father, give me my share of the estate.' So he divided his property between them.

[13] "Not long after that, the younger son got together all he had, set off for a distant country and there squandered his wealth in wild living. [14] After he had spent everything, there was a severe famine in that whole country, and he began to be in need. [15] So he went and hired himself out to a citizen of that country, who sent him to his fields to feed pigs. [16] He longed to fill his stomach with the pods that the pigs were eating, but no-one gave him anything.

[17] "When he came to his senses, he said,

'How many of my father's hired servants have food to spare, and here I am starving to death! [18] I will set out and go back to my father and say to him: Father, I have sinned against heaven and against you. [19] I am no longer worthy to be called your son; make me like one of your hired servants.' [20] So he got up and went to his father.

"But while he was still a long way off, his father saw him and was filled with compassion for him; he ran to his son, threw his arms around him and kissed him.

[21] "The son said to him, 'Father, I have sinned against heaven and against you. I am no longer worthy to be called your son.'[b]

[22] "But the father said to his servants, 'Quick! Bring the best robe and put it on him. Put a ring on his finger and sandals on his feet. [23] Bring the fattened calf and kill it. Let's have a feast and celebrate. [24] For this son of mine was dead and is alive again; he was lost and is found.' So they began to celebrate.

[25] "Meanwhile, the older son was in the field. When he came near the house, he heard music and dancing. [26] So he called one of the servants and asked him what was going on. [27] 'Your brother has come,' he replied, 'and your father has killed the fattened calf because he has him back safe and sound.'

[28] "The older brother became angry and refused to go in. So his father went out and pleaded with him. [29] But he answered his father, 'Look! All these years I've been slaving for you and never disobeyed your orders. Yet you never gave me even a young goat so I could celebrate with my friends. [30] But when this son of yours who has squandered your property with prostitutes comes home, you kill the fattened calf for him!'

[31] " 'My son,' the father said, 'you are always with me, and everything I have is yours. [32] But we had to celebrate and be glad, because this brother of yours was dead and is alive again; he was lost and is found.' "

---

[a]8 Greek ten drachmas, each worth about a day's wages
[b]21 Some early manuscripts son. Make me like one of your hired men.

The Parable of the Shrewd Manager

16 Jesus told his disciples: "There was a rich man whose manager was accused of wasting his possessions. ²So he called him in and asked him, 'What is this I hear about you? Give an account of your management, because you cannot be manager any longer.'

³"The manager said to himself, 'What shall I do now? My master is taking away my job. I'm not strong enough to dig, and I'm ashamed to beg—⁴I know what I'll do so that, when I lose my job here, people will welcome me into their houses.'

⁵"So he called in each one of his master's debtors. He asked the first, 'How much do you owe my master?'

⁶" 'Eight hundred gallons*ᵃ* of olive oil,' he replied.

"The manager told him, 'Take your bill, sit down quickly, and make it four hundred.'

⁷"Then he asked the second, 'And how much do you owe?'

" 'A thousand bushels*ᵇ* of wheat,' he replied.

"He told him, 'Take your bill and make it eight hundred.'

⁸"The master commended the dishonest manager because he had acted shrewdly. For the people of this world are more shrewd in dealing with their own kind than are the people of the light. ⁹I tell you, use worldly wealth to gain friends for yourselves, so that when it is gone, you will be welcomed into eternal dwellings.

¹⁰"Whoever can be trusted with very little can also be trusted with much, and whoever is dishonest with very little will also be dishonest with much. ¹¹So if you have not been trustworthy in handling worldly wealth, who will trust you with true riches? ¹²And if you have not been trustworthy with someone else's property, who will give you property of your own?

¹³"No one can be a slave to two masters. Either you will hate the one and love the other, or you will be devoted to the one and despise the other. You cannot be a slave to both God and Money."

¹⁴The Pharisees, who loved money, heard all this and were sneering at Jesus. ¹⁵He said to them, "You are the ones who justify yourselves in the eyes of others, but God knows your hearts. What is highly valued by people is detestable in God's sight.

Additional Teachings

¹⁶"The Law and the Prophets were proclaimed until John. Since that time, the good news of the kingdom of God is being preached, and people are forcing their way into it. ¹⁷It is easier for heaven and earth to disappear than for the least stroke of a pen to drop out of the Law.

¹⁸"Anyone who divorces his wife and marries another woman commits adultery, and the man who marries a divorced woman commits adultery.

The Rich Man and Lazarus

¹⁹"There was a rich man who was dressed in purple and fine linen and lived in luxury every day. ²⁰At his gate was laid a beggar named Lazarus, covered with sores ²¹and longing to eat what fell from the rich man's table. Even the dogs came and licked his sores.

²²"The time came when the beggar died and the angels carried him to Abraham's side. The rich man also died and was buried. ²³In hell,*ᶜ* where he was in torment, he looked up and saw Abraham far away, with Lazarus by his side. ²⁴So he called to him, 'Father Abraham, have pity on me and send Lazarus to dip the tip of his finger in water and cool my tongue, because I am in agony in this fire.'

²⁵"But Abraham replied, 'Son, remember that in your lifetime you received your good things, while Lazarus received bad things, but now he is comforted here and you are in agony. ²⁶And besides all this, between us and you a great chasm has been fixed, so that those who want to go from here to you cannot, nor can anyone cross over from there to us.'

---

*ᵃ*6 Greek *one hundred batous* (probably about 3 kilolitres)
*ᵇ*7 Greek *one hundred korous* (probably about 35 kilolitres)
*ᶜ*23 Greek *Hades*

[27] "He answered, 'Then I beg you, father, send Lazarus to my father's house, [28] for I have five brothers. Let him warn them, so that they will not also come to this place of torment.'

[29] "Abraham replied, 'They have Moses and the Prophets; let them listen to them.'

[30] 'No, father Abraham,' he said, 'but if someone from the dead goes to them, they will repent.'

[31] "He said to him, 'If they do not listen to Moses and the Prophets, they will not be convinced even if someone rises from the dead.' "

Sin, Faith, Duty

17 Jesus said to his disciples: "Things that cause people to sin are bound to come, but woe to that person through whom they come. [2] It would be better for you to be thrown into the sea with a millstone tied round your neck than for you to cause one of these little ones to sin. [3] So watch yourselves.

"Rebuke a brother or sister who sins, and if they repent, forgive them. [4] If anyone sins against you seven times in a day, and seven times comes back to you and says, 'I repent,' you must forgive them."

[5] The apostles said to the Lord, "Increase our faith!"

[6] He replied, "If you have faith as small as a mustard seed, you can say to this mulberry tree, 'Be uprooted and planted in the sea,' and it will obey you.

[7] "Suppose one of you had a servant ploughing or looking after the sheep. Would he say to the servant when he comes in from the field, 'Come along now and sit down to eat'? [8] Would he not rather say, 'Prepare my supper, get yourself ready and wait on me while I eat and drink; after that you may eat and drink'? [9] Would he thank the servant because he did what he was told to do? [10] So you also, when you have done everything you were told to do, should say, 'We are unworthy servants; we have only done our duty.' "

Ten Healed of Leprosy

[11] Now on his way to Jerusalem, Jesus travelled along the border between Samaria and Galilee. [12] As he was going into a village, ten men who had leprosy[a] met him. They stood at a distance [13] and called out in a loud voice, "Jesus, Master, have pity on us!"

[14] When he saw them, he said, "Go, show yourselves to the priests." And as they went, they were cleansed.

[15] One of them, when he saw he was healed, came back, praising God in a loud voice. [16] He threw himself at Jesus' feet and thanked him—and he was a Samaritan.

[17] Jesus asked, "Were not all ten cleansed? Where are the other nine? [18] Was no-one found to return and give praise to God except this foreigner?" [19] Then he said to him, "Rise and go; your faith has made you well."

The Coming of the Kingdom of God

[20] Once, having been asked by the Pharisees when the kingdom of God would come, Jesus replied, "The kingdom of God does not come with your careful observation, [21] nor will people say, 'Here it is,' or 'There it is,' because the kingdom of God is within[b] you."

[22] Then he said to his disciples, "The time is coming when you will long to see one of the days of the Son of Man, but you will not see it. [23] People will tell you, 'There he is!' or 'Here he is!' Do not go running off after them. [24] For the Son of Man in his day[c] will be like the lightning, which flashes and lights up the sky from one end to the other. [25] But first he must suffer many things and be rejected by this generation.

[26] "Just as it was in the days of Noah, so also will it be in the days of the Son of Man. [27] People were eating, drinking, marrying and being given in marriage up to the day Noah entered the ark. Then the flood came and destroyed them all.

---

[a]12 The Greek word was used for various diseases affecting the skin—not necessarily leprosy.
[b]21 Or *among*   [c]24 Some manuscripts do not have *in his day.*

28 "It was the same in the days of Lot. People were eating and drinking, buying and selling, planting and building. 29 But the day Lot left Sodom, fire and sulphur rained down from heaven and destroyed them all.

30 "It will be just like this on the day the Son of Man is revealed. 31 On that day no-one who is on the top of the house, with possessions inside, should go down to get them. Likewise, no-one in the field should go back for anything. 32 Remember Lot's wife! 33 Those who try to keep their lives will lose them, and those who lose their lives will preserve them. 34 I tell you, on that night two people will be in one bed; one will be taken and the other left. 35 Two women will be grinding grain together; one will be taken and the other left."d

37 "Where, Lord?" they asked.

He replied, "Where there is a dead body, there the vultures will gather."

The Parable of the Persistent Widow

18 Then Jesus told his disciples a parable to show them that they should always pray and not give up. 2 He said: "In a certain town there was a judge who neither feared God nor cared about people. 3 And there was a widow in that town who kept coming to him with the plea, 'Grant me justice against my adversary.'

4 "For some time he refused. But finally he said to himself, 'Even though I don't fear God or care about people, 5 yet because this widow keeps bothering me, I will see that she gets justice, so that she won't eventually wear me out with her coming!' "

6 And the Lord said, "Listen to what the unjust judge says. 7 And will not God bring about justice for his chosen ones, who cry out to him day and night? Will he keep putting them off? 8 I tell you, he will see that they get justice, and quickly. However, when the Son of Man comes, will he find faith on the earth?"

The Parable of the Pharisee and the Tax Collector

9 To some who were confident of their own righteousness and looked down on everybody else, Jesus told this parable: 10 "Two men went up to the temple to pray, one a Pharisee and the other a tax collector. 11 The Pharisee stood up and prayed about a himself: 'God, I thank you that I am not like other people—robbers, evildoers, adulterers—or even like this tax collector. 12 I fast twice a week and give a tenth of all I get.'

13 "But the tax collector stood at a distance. He would not even look up to heaven, but beat his breast and said, 'God, have mercy on me, a sinner.'

14 "I tell you that this man, rather than the other, went home justified before God. For all those who exalt themselves will be humbled, and those who humble themselves will be exalted."

The Little Children and Jesus

15 People were also bringing babies to Jesus to have him touch them. When the disciples saw this, they rebuked them. 16 But Jesus called the children to him and said, "Let the little children come to me, and do not hinder them, for the kingdom of God belongs to such as these. 17 I tell you the truth, anyone who will not receive the kingdom of God like a little child will never enter it."

The Rich Ruler

18 A certain ruler asked him, "Good teacher, what must I do to inherit eternal life?"

19 "Why do you call me good?" Jesus answered. "No-one is good—except God alone. 20 You know the commandments: 'Do not commit adultery, do not murder, do not steal, do not give false testimony, honour your father and mother.'b "

21 "All these I have kept since I was a boy," he said.

22 When Jesus heard this, he said to

d35 Some manuscripts left. 36 Two men will be in the field; one will be taken and the other left.
a11 Or to   b20 Exodus 20:12–16; Deut. 5:16–20

him, "You still lack one thing. Sell everything you have and give to the poor, and you will have treasure in heaven. Then come, follow me."

23 When he heard this, he became very sad, because he was very wealthy. 24 Jesus looked at him and said, "How hard it is for the rich to enter the kingdom of God! 25 Indeed, it is easier for a camel to go through the eye of a needle than for the rich to enter the kingdom of God."

26 Those who heard this asked, "Who then can be saved?"

27 Jesus replied, "What is humanly impossible is possible with God."

28 Peter said to him, "We have left all we had to follow you!"

29 "I tell you the truth," Jesus said to them, "no-one who has left home or wife or brothers or sisters or parents or children for the sake of the kingdom of God 30 will fail to receive many times as much in this age and, in the age to come, eternal life."

Jesus Again Predicts His Death

31 Jesus took the Twelve aside and told them, "We are going up to Jerusalem, and everything that is written by the prophets about the Son of Man will be fulfilled. 32 He will be turned over to the Gentiles. They will mock him, insult him, spit on him, flog him and kill him. 33 On the third day he will rise again."

34 The disciples did not understand any of this. Its meaning was hidden from them, and they did not know what he was talking about.

A Blind Beggar Receives His Sight

35 As Jesus approached Jericho, a blind man was sitting by the roadside begging. 36 When he heard the crowd going by, he asked what was happening. 37 They told him, "Jesus of Nazareth is passing by."

38 He called out, "Jesus, Son of David, have mercy on me!"

39 Those who led the way rebuked him and told him to be quiet, but he shouted all the more, "Son of David, have mercy on me!"

40 Jesus stopped and ordered the man to be brought to him. When he came near, Jesus asked him, 41 "What do you want me to do for you?"

"Lord, I want to see," he replied.

42 Jesus said to him, "Receive your sight; your faith has healed you." 43 Immediately he received his sight and followed Jesus, praising God. When all the people saw it, they also praised God.

Zacchaeus the Tax Collector

19 Jesus entered Jericho and was passing through. 2 A man was there by the name of Zacchaeus; he was a chief tax collector and was wealthy. 3 He wanted to see who Jesus was, but being a short man he could not, because of the crowd. 4 So he ran ahead and climbed a sycamore-fig tree to see him, since Jesus was coming that way.

5 When Jesus reached the spot, he looked up and said to him, "Zacchaeus, come down immediately. I must stay at your house today." 6 So he came down at once and welcomed him gladly.

7 All the people saw this and began to mutter, "He has gone to be the guest of a 'sinner'."

8 But Zacchaeus stood up and said to the Lord, "Look, Lord! Here and now I give half of my possessions to the poor, and if I have cheated anybody out of anything, I will pay back four times the amount."

9 Jesus said to him, "Today salvation has come to this house, because this man, too, is a son of Abraham. 10 For the Son of Man came to seek and to save what was lost."

The Parable of the Ten Minas

11 While they were listening to this, he went on to tell them a parable, because he was near Jerusalem and the people thought that the kingdom of God was going to appear at once. 12 He said: "A man of noble birth went to a distant country to have himself appointed king and then to return. 13 So he called ten of his servants and gave them ten minas.[a]

---

[a]13 A mina was about three months' wages.

'Put this money to work,' he said, 'until I come back.'

14 "But his subjects hated him and sent a delegation after him to say, 'We don't want this man to be our king.'

15 "He was made king, however, and returned home. Then he sent for the servants to whom he had given the money, in order to find out what they had gained with it.

16 "The first one came and said, 'Sir, your mina has earned ten more.'

17 "'Well done, my good servant!' his master replied. 'Because you have been trustworthy in a very small matter, take charge of ten cities.'

18 "The second came and said, 'Sir, your mina has earned five more.'

19 "His master answered, 'You take charge of five cities.'

20 "Then another servant came and said, 'Sir, here is your mina; I have kept it laid away in a piece of cloth. 21 I was afraid of you, because you are a hard man. You take out what you did not put in and reap what you did not sow.'

22 "His master replied, 'I will judge you by your own words, you wicked servant! You knew, did you, that I am a hard man, taking out what I did not put in, and reaping what I did not sow? 23 Why then didn't you put my money on deposit, so that when I came back, I could have collected it with interest?'

24 "Then he said to those standing by, 'Take his mina away from him and give it to the one who has ten minas.'

25 "'Sir,' they said, 'he already has ten!'

26 "He replied, 'I tell you that to everyone who has, more will be given, but as for those who have nothing, even what they have will be taken away. 27 But those enemies of mine who did not want me to be a king over them—bring them here and kill them in front of me.' "

The Triumphal Entry

28 After Jesus had said this, he went on ahead, going up to Jerusalem. 29 As he approached Bethphage and Bethany at the hill called the Mount of Olives, he sent two of his disciples, saying to them, 30 "Go to the village ahead of you, and as you enter it, you will find a colt tied there, which no-one has ever ridden. Untie it and bring it here. 31 If anyone asks you, 'Why are you untying it?' say, 'The Lord needs it.' "

32 Those who were sent ahead went and found it just as he had told them. 33 As they were untying the colt, its owners asked them, "Why are you untying the colt?"

34 They replied, "The Lord needs it."

35 They brought it to Jesus, threw their cloaks on the colt and put Jesus on it. 36 As he went along, people spread their cloaks on the road.

37 When he came near the place where the road goes down the Mount of Olives, the whole crowd of disciples began joyfully to praise God in loud voices for all the miracles they had seen:

38 "Blessed is the king who comes in the
    name of the Lord!"*b*

"Peace in heaven and glory in the
    highest!"

39 Some of the Pharisees in the crowd said to Jesus, "Teacher, rebuke your disciples!"

40 "I tell you," he replied, "if they keep quiet, the stones will cry out."

41 As he approached Jerusalem and saw the city, he wept over it 42 and said, "If you, even you, had only known on this day what would bring you peace—but now it is hidden from your eyes. 43 The days will come upon you when your enemies will build an embankment against you and encircle you and hem you in on every side. 44 They will dash you to the ground, you and the children within your walls. They will not leave one stone on another, because you did not recognise the time of God's coming to you."

Jesus at the temple

45 Then he entered the temple area and began driving out those who were selling.

*b*38 Psalm 118:26

46 "It is written," he said to them, " 'My house will be a house of prayer';*c* but you have made it 'a den of robbers'.*d* "

47 Every day he was teaching at the temple. But the chief priests, the teachers of the law and the leaders among the people were trying to kill him. 48 Yet they could not find any way to do it, because all the people hung on his words.

The Authority of Jesus Questioned

20 One day as he was teaching the people in the temple courts and preaching the gospel, the chief priests and the teachers of the law, together with the elders, came up to him. 2 "Tell us by what authority you are doing these things," they said. "Who gave you this authority?"

3 He replied, "I will also ask you a question. Tell me, 4 John's baptism—was it from heaven, or of human origin?"

5 They discussed it among themselves and said, "If we say, 'From heaven', he will ask, 'Why didn't you believe him?' 6 But if we say, 'Of human origin', all the people will stone us, because they are persuaded that John was a prophet."

7 So they answered, "We don't know where it was from."

8 Jesus said, "Neither will I tell you by what authority I am doing these things."

The Parable of the Tenants

9 He went on to tell the people this parable: "A man planted a vineyard, rented it to some farmers and went away for a long time. 10 At harvest time he sent a servant to the tenants so they would give him some of the fruit of the vineyard. But the tenants beat him and sent him away empty-handed. 11 He sent another servant, but that one also they beat and treated shamefully and sent away empty-handed. 12 He sent still a third, and they wounded him and threw him out.

13 "Then the owner of the vineyard said; 'What shall I do? I will send my son, whom I love; perhaps they will respect him.'

14 "But when the tenants saw him, they talked the matter over. 'This is the heir,' they said. 'Let's kill him, and the inheritance will be ours.' 15 So they threw him out of the vineyard and killed him.

"What then will the owner of the vineyard do to them? 16 He will come and kill those tenants and give the vineyard to others."

When the people heard this, they said, "May this never be!"

17 Jesus looked directly at them and asked, "Then what is the meaning of that which is written:

" 'The stone the builders rejected
has become the capstone'*a, b*?

18 Everyone who falls on that stone will be broken to pieces, but anyone on whom it falls will be crushed."

19 The teachers of the law and the chief priests looked for a way to arrest him immediately, because they knew he had spoken this parable against them. But they were afraid of the people.

Paying Taxes to Caesar

20 Keeping a close watch on him, they sent spies, who pretended to be honest. They hoped to catch Jesus in something he said so that they might hand him over to the power and authority of the governor. 21 So the spies questioned him: "Teacher, we know that you speak and teach what is right, and that you do not show partiality but teach the way of God in accordance with the truth. 22 Is it right for us to pay taxes to Caesar or not?"

23 He saw through their duplicity and said to them, 24 "Show me a denarius. Whose portrait and inscription are on it?"

25 "Caesar's," they replied.

He said to them, "Then give to Caesar what is Caesar's, and to God what is God's."

26 They were unable to trap him in what he had said there in public. And astonished by his answer, they became silent.

---

*c*46 Isaiah 56:7   *d*46 Jer. 7:11   *a*17 Or *cornerstone*   *b*17 Psalm 118:22

The Resurrection and Marriage

27 Some of the Sadducees, who say there is no resurrection, came to Jesus with a question. 28 "Teacher," they said, "Moses wrote for us that if a man's brother dies and leaves a wife but no children, the man must marry the widow and have children for his brother. 29 Now there were seven brothers. The first one married a woman and died childless. 30 The second 31 and then the third married her, and in the same way the seven died, leaving no children. 32 Finally, the woman died too. 33 Now then, at the resurrection whose wife will she be, since the seven were married to her?"

34 Jesus replied, "The people of this age marry and are given in marriage. 35 But those who are considered worthy of taking part in that age and in the resurrection from the dead will neither marry nor be given in marriage, 36 and they can no longer die; for they are like the angels. They are God's children, since they are children of the resurrection. 37 But in the account of the bush, even Moses showed that the dead rise, for he calls the Lord 'the God of Abraham, and the God of Isaac, and the God of Jacob'.*c* 38 He is not the God of the dead, but of the living, for to him all are alive."

39 Some of the teachers of the law responded, "Well said, teacher!" 40 And no-one dared to ask him any more questions.

Whose Son Is the Christ?

41 Then Jesus said to them, "How is it that they say the Christ*d* is the Son of David? 42 David himself declares in the Book of Psalms:

" 'The Lord said to my Lord:
    "Sit at my right hand
43 until I make your enemies
    a footstool for your feet." '*e*

44 David calls him 'Lord'. How then can he be his son?"

45 While all the people were listening, Jesus said to his disciples, 46 "Beware of the teachers of the law. They like to walk around in flowing robes and love to be greeted in the market-places and have the most important seats in the synagogues and the places of honour at banquets. 47 They devour widows' houses and for a show make lengthy prayers. Such men will be punished most severely."

The Widow's Offering

21 As he looked up, Jesus saw the rich putting their gifts into the temple treasury. 2 He also saw a poor widow put in two very small copper coins.*a* 3 "I tell you the truth," he said, "this poor widow has put in more than all the others. 4 All these people gave their gifts out of their wealth; but she out of her poverty put in all she had to live on."

Signs of the End of the Age

5 Some of his disciples were remarking about how the temple was adorned with beautiful stones and with gifts dedicated to God. But Jesus said, 6 "As for what you see here, the time will come when not one stone will be left on another; every one of them will be thrown down."

7 "Teacher," they asked, "when will these things happen? And what will be the sign that they are about to take place?"

8 He replied: "Watch out that you are not deceived. For many will come in my name, claiming, 'I am he,' and 'The time is near.' Do not follow them. 9 When you hear of wars and revolutions, do not be frightened. These things must happen first, but the end will not come right away."

10 Then he said to them: "Nation will rise against nation, and kingdom against kingdom. 11 There will be great earthquakes, famines and pestilences in various places, and fearful events and great signs from heaven.

12 "But before all this, they will lay hands on you and persecute you. They will deliver you to synagogues and prisons, and you will be brought before kings and

---

*c*37 Exodus 3:6   *d*41 Or *Messiah*   *e*43 Psalm 110:1   *a*2 Greek *two lepta* governors, and all on account of my name. [13] This will result in your being witnesses to them. [14] But make up your mind not to worry beforehand how you will defend yourselves. [15] For I will give you words and wisdom that none of your adversaries will be able to resist or contradict. [16] You will be betrayed even by parents, brothers, sisters, relatives and friends, and they will put some of you to death. [17] Everyone will hate you because of me. [18] But not a hair of your head will perish. [19] By standing firm you will gain life.

[20] "When you see Jerusalem being surrounded by armies, you will know that its desolation is near. [21] Then let those who are in Judea flee to the mountains, let those in the city get out, and let those in the country not enter the city. [22] For this is the time of punishment in fulfilment of all that has been written. [23] How dreadful it will be in those days for pregnant women and nursing mothers! There will be great distress in the land and wrath against this people. [24] They will fall by the sword and will be taken as prisoners to all the nations. Jerusalem will be trampled on by the Gentiles until the times of the Gentiles are fulfilled.

[25] "There will be signs in the sun, moon and stars. On the earth, nations will be in anguish and perplexity at the roaring and tossing of the sea. [26] People will faint from terror, apprehensive of what is coming on the world, for the heavenly bodies will be shaken. [27] At that time they will see the Son of Man coming in a cloud with power and great glory. [28] When these things begin to take place, stand up and lift up your heads, because your redemption is drawing near."

[29] He told them this parable: "Look at the fig-tree and all the trees. [30] When they sprout leaves, you can see for yourselves and know that summer is near. [31] Even so, when you see these things happening, you know that the kingdom of God is near.

[32] "I tell you the truth, this generation[b] will certainly not pass away until all these things have happened. [33] Heaven and earth will pass away, but my words will never pass away.

[34] "Be careful, or your hearts will be weighed down with dissipation, drunkenness and the anxieties of life, and that day will close on you unexpectedly like a trap. [35] For it will come upon all those who live on the face of the whole earth. [36] Be always on the watch, and pray that you may be able to escape all that is about to happen, and that you may be able to stand before the Son of Man."

[37] Each day Jesus was teaching at the temple, and each evening he went out to spend the night on the hill called the Mount of Olives, [38] and all the people came early in the morning to hear him at the temple.

Judas Agrees to Betray Jesus

22 Now the Feast of Unleavened Bread, called the Passover, was approaching, [2] and the chief priests and the teachers of the law were looking for some way to get rid of Jesus, for they were afraid of the people. [3] Then Satan entered Judas, called Iscariot, one of the Twelve. [4] And Judas went to the chief priests and the officers of the temple guard and discussed with them how he might betray Jesus. [5] They were delighted and agreed to give him money. [6] He consented, and watched for an opportunity to hand Jesus over to them when no crowd was present.

The Last Supper

[7] Then came the day of Unleavened Bread on which the Passover lamb had to be sacrificed. [8] Jesus sent Peter and John, saying, "Go and make preparations for us to eat the Passover."

[9] "Where do you want us to prepare for it?" they asked.

[10] He replied, "As you enter the city, a man carrying a jar of water will meet you. Follow him to the house that he enters, [11] and say to the owner of the house, 'The Teacher asks: Where is the guest room, where I may eat the Passover with my disciples?' [12] He will show you a large upper room, all furnished. Make preparations there."

[b]32 Or *race*

13 They left and found things just as Jesus had told them. So they prepared the Passover.

14 When the hour came, Jesus and his apostles reclined at the table. 15 And he said to them, "I have eagerly desired to eat this Passover with you before I suffer. 16 For I tell you, I will not eat it again until it finds fulfilment in the kingdom of God."

17 After taking the cup, he gave thanks and said, "Take this and divide it among you. 18 For I tell you I will not drink again of the fruit of the vine until the kingdom of God comes."

19 And he took bread, gave thanks and broke it, and gave it to them, saying, "This is my body given for you; do this in remembrance of me."

20 In the same way, after the supper he took the cup, saying, "This cup is the new covenant in my blood, which is poured out for you. 21 But the hand of him who is going to betray me is with mine on the table. 22 The Son of Man will go as it has been decreed, but woe to that man who betrays him." 23 They began to question among themselves which of them it might be who would do this.

24 Also a dispute arose among them as to which of them was considered to be greatest. 25 Jesus said to them, "The kings of the Gentiles lord it over them; and those who exercise authority over them call themselves Benefactors. 26 But you are not to be like that. Instead, the greatest among you should be like the youngest, and the one who rules like the one who serves. 27 For who is greater, the one who is at the table or the one who serves? Is it not the one who is at the table? But I am among you as one who serves. 28 You are those who have stood by me in my trials. 29 And I confer on you a kingdom, just as my Father conferred one on me, 30 so that you may eat and drink at my table in my kingdom and sit on thrones, judging the twelve tribes of Israel.

31 "Simon, Simon, Satan has asked to sift you*a* as wheat. 32 But I have prayed for you, Simon, that your faith may not fail. And when you have turned back, strengthen your brothers."

33 But he replied, "Lord, I am ready to go with you to prison and to death."

34 Jesus answered, "I tell you, Peter, before the cock crows today, you will deny three times that you know me."

35 Then Jesus asked them, "When I sent you without purse, bag or sandals, did you lack anything?"

"Nothing," they answered.

36 He said to them, "But now if you have a purse, take it, and also a bag; and if you don't have a sword, sell your cloak and buy one. 37 It is written: 'And he was numbered with the transgressors';*b* and I tell you that this must be fulfilled in me. Yes, what is written about me is reaching its fulfilment."

38 The disciples said, "See, Lord, here are two swords."

"That is enough," he replied.

Jesus Prays on the Mount of Olives

39 Jesus went out as usual to the Mount of Olives, and his disciples followed him. 40 On reaching the place, he said to them, "Pray that you will not fall into temptation." 41 He withdrew about a stone's throw beyond them, knelt down and prayed, 42 "Father, if you are willing, take this cup from me; yet not my will, but yours be done." 43 An angel from heaven appeared to him and strengthened him. 44 And being in anguish, he prayed more earnestly, and his sweat was like drops of blood falling to the ground.*c*

45 When he rose from prayer and went back to the disciples, he found them asleep, exhausted from sorrow. 46 "Why are you sleeping?" he asked them. "Get up and pray so that you will not fall into temptation."

Jesus Arrested

47 While he was still speaking a crowd came up, and the man who was called Judas, one of the Twelve, was leading them. He approached Jesus to kiss him,

---

*a*31 The Greek is plural.   *b*37 Isaiah 53:12   *c*44 Some early manuscripts do not have verses 43 and 44.

⁴⁸but Jesus asked him, "Judas, are you betraying the Son of Man with a kiss?"

⁴⁹When Jesus' followers saw what was going to happen, they said, "Lord, should we strike with our swords?" ⁵⁰And one of them struck the servant of the high priest, cutting off his right ear.

⁵¹But Jesus answered, "No more of this!" And he touched the man's ear and healed him.

⁵²Then Jesus said to the chief priests, the officers of the temple guard, and the elders, who had come for him, "Am I leading a rebellion, that you have come with swords and clubs? ⁵³Every day I was with you in the temple courts, and you did not lay a hand on me. But this is your hour—when darkness reigns."

Peter Disowns Jesus

⁵⁴Then seizing him, they led him away and took him into the house of the high priest. Peter followed at a distance. ⁵⁵But when they had kindled a fire in the middle of the courtyard and had sat down together, Peter sat down with them. ⁵⁶A woman servant saw him seated there in the firelight. She looked closely at him and said, "This man was with him."

⁵⁷But he denied it. "Woman, I don't know him," he said.

⁵⁸A little later someone else saw him and said, "You also are one of them."

"Man, I am not!" Peter replied.

⁵⁹About an hour later another asserted, "Certainly this fellow was with him, for he is a Galilean."

⁶⁰Peter replied, "Man, I don't know what you're talking about!" Just as he was speaking, the cock crowed. ⁶¹The Lord turned and looked straight at Peter. Then Peter remembered the word the Lord had spoken to him: "Before the cock crows today, you will disown me three times." ⁶²And he went outside and wept bitterly.

The Guards Mock Jesus

⁶³The men who were guarding Jesus began mocking and beating him. ⁶⁴They blindfolded him and demanded, "Prophesy! Who hit you?" ⁶⁵And they said many other insulting things to him.

Jesus Before Pilate and Herod

⁶⁶At daybreak the council of the elders of the people, both the chief priests and teachers of the law, met together, and Jesus was led before them. ⁶⁷"If you are the Christ,"*d* they said, "tell us."

Jesus answered, "If I tell you, you will not believe me, ⁶⁸and if I asked you, you would not answer. ⁶⁹But from now on, the Son of Man will be seated at the right hand of the mighty God."

⁷⁰They all asked, "Are you then the Son of God?"

He replied, "You are right in saying I am."

⁷¹Then they said, "Why do we need any more testimony? We have heard it from his own lips."

23 Then the whole assembly rose and led him off to Pilate. ²And they began to accuse him, saying, "We have found this man subverting our nation. He opposes payment of taxes to Caesar and claims to be Christ,*a* a king."

³So Pilate asked Jesus, "Are you the king of the Jews?"

"Yes, it is as you say," Jesus replied.

⁴Then Pilate announced to the chief priests and the crowd, "I find no basis for a charge against this man."

⁵But they insisted, "He stirs up the people all over Judea*b* by his teaching. He started in Galilee and has come all the way here."

⁶On hearing this, Pilate asked if the man was a Galilean. ⁷When he learned that Jesus was under Herod's jurisdiction, he sent him to Herod, who was also in Jerusalem at that time.

⁸When Herod saw Jesus, he was greatly pleased, because for a long time he had been wanting to see him. From what he had heard about him, he hoped to see him perform some miracle. ⁹He plied him with many questions, but Jesus gave him no answer. ¹⁰The chief priests and the teachers

---

*d*67 Or *Messiah*   *a*2 Or *Messiah*; also in verses 35 and 39   *b*5 Or *over the land of the Jews* of the law were standing there, vehemently accusing him. [11] Then Herod and his soldiers ridiculed and mocked him. Dressing him in an elegant robe, they sent him back to Pilate. [12] That day Herod and Pilate became friends—before this they had been enemies.

[13] Pilate called together the chief priests, the rulers and the people, [14] and said to them, "You brought me this man as one who was inciting the people to rebellion. I have examined him in your presence and have found no basis for your charges against him. [15] Neither has Herod, for he sent him back to us; as you can see, he has done nothing to deserve death. [16] Therefore, I will punish him and then release him."[c]

[18] With one voice they cried out, "Away with this man! Release Barabbas to us!" ([19] Barabbas had been thrown into prison for an insurrection in the city, and for murder.)

[20] Wanting to release Jesus, Pilate appealed to them again. [21] But they kept shouting, "Crucify him! Crucify him!"

[22] For the third time he spoke to them: "Why? What crime has this man committed? I have found in him no grounds for the death penalty. Therefore I will have him punished and then release him."

[23] But with loud shouts they insistently demanded that he be crucified, and their shouts prevailed. [24] So Pilate decided to grant their demand. [25] He released the man who had been thrown into prison for insurrection and murder, the one they asked for, and surrendered Jesus to their will.

The Crucifixion

[26] As they led him away, they seized Simon from Cyrene, who was on his way in from the country, and put the cross on him and made him carry it behind Jesus. [27] A large number of people followed him, including women who mourned and wailed for him. [28] Jesus turned and said to them, "Daughters of Jerusalem, do not weep for me; weep for yourselves and for your children. [29] For the time will come when you will say, 'Blessed are the barren women, the wombs that never bore and the breasts that never nursed!' [30] Then

> " 'they will say to the mountains,
>   "Fall on us!"
> and to the hills "Cover us!" ' [d]

[31] For if people do these things when the tree is green, what will happen when it is dry?"

[32] Two other men, both criminals, were also led out with him to be executed. [33] When they came to the place called the Skull, there they crucified him, along with the criminals—one on his right, the other on his left. [34] Jesus said, "Father, forgive them, for they do not know what they are doing."[e] And they divided up his clothes by casting lots.

[35] The people stood watching, and the rulers even sneered at him. They said, "He saved others; let him save himself if he is the Christ of God, the Chosen One."

[36] The soldiers also came up and mocked him. They offered him wine vinegar [37] and said, "If you are the king of the Jews, save yourself."

[38] There was a written notice above him, which read: THIS IS THE KING OF THE JEWS.

[39] One of the criminals who hung there hurled insults at him: "Aren't you the Christ? Save yourself and us!"

[40] But the other criminal rebuked him. "Don't you fear God," he said, "since you are under the same sentence? [41] We are punished justly, for we are getting what our deeds deserve. But this man has done nothing wrong."

[42] Then he said, "Jesus, remember me when you come into your kingdom.[f] "

[43] Jesus answered him, "I tell you the truth, today you will be with me in paradise."

Jesus' Death

[44] It was now about the sixth hour, and darkness came over the whole land until

---

[c]16 Some manuscripts *him.*" [17]*Now he was obliged to release one man to them at the Feast.*   [d]30 Hosea 10:8
[e]34 Some early manuscripts do not have this sentence.   [f]42 Some manuscripts *come with your kingly power*

the ninth hour, [45] for the sun stopped shining. And the curtain of the temple was torn in two. [46] Jesus called out with a loud voice, "Father, into your hands I commit my spirit." When he had said this, he breathed his last.

[47] The centurion, seeing what had happened, praised God and said, "Surely this was a righteous man." [48] When all the people who had gathered to witness this sight saw what took place, they beat their breasts and went away. [49] But all those who knew him, including the women who had followed him from Galilee, stood at a distance, watching these things.

Jesus' Burial

[50] Now there was a man named Joseph, a member of the Council, a good and upright man, [51] who had not consented to their decision and action. He came from the Judean town of Arimathea and he was waiting for the kingdom of God. [52] Going to Pilate, he asked for Jesus' body. [53] Then he took it down, wrapped it in linen cloth and placed it in a tomb cut in the rock, one in which no-one had yet been laid. [54] It was Preparation Day, and the Sabbath was about to begin.

[55] The women who had come with Jesus from Galilee followed Joseph and saw the tomb and how his body was laid in it. [56] Then they went home and prepared spices and perfumes. But they rested on the Sabbath in obedience to the commandment.

The Resurrection

24 On the first day of the week, very early in the morning, the women took the spices they had prepared and went to the tomb. [2] They found the stone rolled away from the tomb, [3] but when they entered, they did not find the body of the Lord Jesus. [4] While they were wondering about this, suddenly two men in clothes that gleamed like lightning stood beside them. [5] In their fright the women bowed down with their faces to the ground, but the men said to them, "Why do you look for the living among the dead? [6] He is not here; he has risen! Remember how he told you, while he was still with you in Galilee: [7] 'The Son of Man must be delivered into the hands of sinful men, be crucified and on the third day be raised again.' " [8] Then they remembered his words.

[9] When they came back from the tomb, they told all these things to the Eleven and to all the others. [10] It was Mary Magdalene, Joanna, Mary the mother of James, and the others with them who told this to the apostles. [11] But they did not believe the women, because their words seemed to them like nonsense. [12] Peter, however, got up and ran to the tomb. Bending over, he saw the strips of linen lying by themselves, and he went away, wondering to himself what had happened.

On the Road to Emmaus

[13] Now that same day two of them were going to a village called Emmaus, about seven miles[a] from Jerusalem. [14] They were talking with each other about everything that had happened. [15] As they talked and discussed these things with each other, Jesus himself came up and walked along with them; [16] but they were kept from recognising him. [17] He asked them, "What are you discussing together as you walk along?"

They stood still, their faces downcast. [18] One of them, named Cleopas, asked him, "Are you only a visitor to Jerusalem and do not know the things that have happened there in these days?"

[19] "What things?" he asked.

"About Jesus of Nazareth," they replied. "He was a prophet, powerful in word and deed before God and all the people. [20] The chief priests and our rulers handed him over to be sentenced to death, and they crucified him; [21] but we had hoped that he was the one who was going to redeem Israel. And what is more, it is the third day since all this took place. [22] In addition, some of our women amazed us.

---

[a] 13 Greek *sixty stadia* (about 11 kilometres)

They went to the tomb early this morning [23] but didn't find his body. They came and told us that they had seen a vision of angels, who said he was alive. [24] Then some of our companions went to the tomb and found it just as the women had said, but him they did not see."

[25] He said to them, "How foolish you are, and how slow of heart to believe all that the prophets have spoken! [26] Did not the Christ[b] have to suffer these things and then enter his glory?" [27] And beginning with Moses and all the Prophets, he explained to them what was said in all the Scriptures concerning himself.

[28] As they approached the village to which they were going, Jesus acted as if he were going further. [29] But they urged him strongly, "Stay with us, for it is nearly evening; the day is almost over." So he went in to stay with them.

[30] When he was at the table with them, he took bread, gave thanks, broke it and began to give it to them. [31] Then their eyes were opened and they recognised him, and he disappeared from their sight. [32] They asked each other, "Were not our hearts burning within us while he talked with us on the road and opened the Scriptures to us?"

[33] They got up and returned at once to Jerusalem. There they found the Eleven and those with them, assembled together [34] and saying, "It is true! The Lord has risen and has appeared to Simon." [35] Then the two told what had happened on the way, and how Jesus was recognised by them when he broke the bread.

Jesus Appears to the Disciples

[36] While they were still talking about this, Jesus himself stood among them and said to them, "Peace be with you."

[37] They were startled and frightened, thinking they saw a ghost. [38] He said to them, "Why are you troubled, and why do doubts rise in your minds? [39] Look at my hands and my feet. It is I myself! Touch me and see; a ghost does not have flesh and bones, as you see I have."

[40] When he had said this, he showed them his hands and feet. [41] And while they still did not believe it because of joy and amazement, he asked them, "Do you have anything here to eat?" [42] They gave him a piece of broiled fish, [43] and he took it and ate it in their presence.

[44] He said to them, "This is what I told you while I was still with you: Everything must be fulfilled that is written about me in the Law of Moses, the Prophets and the Psalms."

[45] Then he opened their minds so they could understand the Scriptures. [46] He told them, "This is what is written: The Christ will suffer and rise from the dead on the third day, [47] and repentance and forgiveness of sins will be preached in his name to all nations, beginning at Jerusalem. [48] You are witnesses of these things. [49] I am going to send you what my Father has promised; but stay in the city until you have been clothed with power from on high."

The Ascension

[50] When he had led them out to the vicinity of Bethany, he lifted up his hands and blessed them. [51] While he was blessing them, he left them and was taken up into heaven. [52] Then they worshipped him and returned to Jerusalem with great joy. [53] And they stayed continually at the temple, praising God.

b26 Or Messiah; also in verse 46

John

The Word Became Flesh

1 In the beginning was the Word, and the Word was with God, and the Word was God. ²He was with God in the beginning.

³Through him all things were made; without him nothing was made that has been made. ⁴In him was life, and that life was the light of all people. ⁵The light shines in the darkness, but the darkness has not understood*ᵃ* it.

⁶There came a man who was sent from God; his name was John. ⁷He came as a witness to testify concerning that light, so that through him all might believe. ⁸He himself was not the light; he came only as a witness to the light. ⁹The true light that gives light to everyone was coming into the world.*ᵇ*

¹⁰He was in the world, and though the world was made through him, the world did not recognise him. ¹¹He came to that which was his own, but his own did not receive him. ¹²Yet to all who received him, to those who believed in his name, he gave the right to become children of God—¹³children born not of natural descent,*ᶜ* nor of human decision or a husband's will, but born of God.

¹⁴The Word became flesh and made his dwelling among us. We have seen his glory, the glory of the One and Only,*ᵈ* who came from the Father, full of grace and truth.

¹⁵John testifies concerning him. He cries out, saying, "This was he of whom I said, 'He who comes after me has surpassed me because he was before me.'" ¹⁶From the fulness of his grace we have all received one blessing after another. ¹⁷For the law was given through Moses; grace and truth came through Jesus Christ. ¹⁸No-one has ever seen God, but God the One and Only,*ᵉ,ᶠ* who is at the Father's side, has made him known.

John the Baptist Denies Being the Christ

¹⁹Now this was John's testimony when the Jews of Jerusalem sent priests and Levites to ask him who he was. ²⁰He did not fail to confess, but confessed freely, "I am not the Christ."*ᵍ*

²¹They asked him, "Then who are you? Are you Elijah?"

He said, "I am not."

"Are you the Prophet?"

He answered, "No."

²²Finally they said, "Who are you? Give us an answer to take back to those who sent us. What do you say about yourself?"

²³John replied in the words of Isaiah the prophet, "I am the voice of one calling in the desert, 'Make straight the way for the Lord.'*ʰ*"

²⁴Now some Pharisees who had been sent ²⁵questioned him, "Why then do you baptise if you are not the Christ, nor Elijah, nor the Prophet?"

---

*ᵃ*5 Or *darkness, and the darkness has not overcome*
*ᵇ*9 Or *This was the true light that gives light to everyone who comes into the world*   *ᶜ*13 Greek *of bloods*
*ᵈ*14 Or *the Only Begotten*   *ᵉ*14 Or *the Only Begotten*   *ᶠ*18 Some manuscripts *but the only* (or *only begotten*) *Son*
*ᵍ*20 Or *Messiah.* "The Christ" (Greek) and "the Messiah" (Hebrew) both mean "the Anointed One"; also in verse 25.
*ʰ*23 Isaiah 40:3

26 "I baptise with*i* water," John replied, "but among you stands one you do not know. 27 He is the one who comes after me, the thongs of whose sandals I am not worthy to untie."

28 This all happened at Bethany on the other side of the Jordan, where John was baptising.

Jesus the Lamb of God

29 The next day John saw Jesus coming towards him and said, "Look, the Lamb of God, who takes away the sin of the world! 30 This is the one I meant when I said, 'A man who comes after me has surpassed me because he was before me.' 31 I myself did not know him, but the reason I came baptising with water was that he might be revealed to Israel."

32 Then John gave this testimony: "I saw the Spirit come down from heaven as a dove and remain on him. 33 I would not have known him, except that the one who sent me to baptise with water told me, 'The man on whom you see the Spirit come down and remain is the one who will baptise with the Holy Spirit.' 34 I have seen and I testify that this is the Son of God."

Jesus' First Disciples

35 The next day John was there again with two of his disciples. 36 When he saw Jesus passing by, he said, "Look, the Lamb of God!"

37 When the two disciples heard him say this, they followed Jesus. 38 Turning round, Jesus saw them following and asked, "What do you want?"

They said, "Rabbi" (which means Teacher), "where are you staying?"

39 "Come," he replied, "and you will see."

So they went and saw where he was staying, and spent that day with him. It was about the tenth hour.

40 Andrew, Simon Peter's brother, was one of the two who heard what John had said and who had followed Jesus. 41 The first thing Andrew did was to find his brother Simon and tell him, "We have found the Messiah" (that is, the Christ). 42 And he brought him to Jesus.

Jesus looked at him and said, "You are Simon son of John. You will be called Cephas" (which, when translated, is Peter*j*).

Jesus Calls Philip and Nathanael

43 The next day Jesus decided to leave for Galilee. Finding Philip, he said to him, "Follow me."

44 Philip, like Andrew and Peter, was from the town of Bethsaida. 45 Philip found Nathanael and told him, "We have found the one Moses wrote about in the Law, and about whom the prophets also wrote—Jesus of Nazareth, the son of Joseph."

46 "Nazareth! Can anything good come from there?" Nathanael asked.

"Come and see," said Philip.

47 When Jesus saw Nathanael approaching, he said of him, "Here is a true Israelite, in whom there is nothing false."

48 "How do you know me?" Nathanael asked.

Jesus answered, "I saw you while you were still under the fig-tree before Philip called you."

49 Then Nathanael declared, "Rabbi, you are the Son of God; you are the King of Israel."

50 Jesus said, "You believe*k* because I told you I saw you under the fig-tree. You shall see greater things than that." 51 He then added, "I tell you*l* the truth, you*l* shall see heaven open, and the angels of God ascending and descending on the Son of Man."

Jesus Changes Water to Wine

2 On the third day a wedding took place at Cana in Galilee. Jesus' mother was there, 2 and Jesus and his disciples had also been invited to the wedding. 3 When the wine was gone, Jesus'

---

*i*26 Or *in*; also in verses 31 and 33   *j*42 Both *Cephas* (Aramaic) and *Peter* (Greek) mean *rock*.
*k*50 Or *Do you believe . . . ?*   *l*51 The Greek is plural.

mother said to him, "They have no more wine."

4 "Dear woman, why do you involve me?" Jesus replied. "My time has not yet come."

5 His mother said to the servants, "Do whatever he tells you."

6 Nearby stood six stone water jars, the kind used by the Jews for ceremonial washing, each holding from twenty to thirty gallons.[a]

7 Jesus said to the servants, "Fill the jars with water"; so they filled them to the brim.

8 Then he told them, "Now draw some out and take it to the master of the banquet."

They did so, 9 and the master of the banquet tasted the water that had been turned into wine. He did not realise where it had come from, though the servants who had drawn the water knew. Then he called the bridegroom aside 10 and said, "Everyone brings out the choice wine first and then the cheaper wine after the guests have had too much to drink; but you have saved the best till now."

11 This, the first of his miraculous signs, Jesus performed at Cana in Galilee. He thus revealed his glory, and his disciples put their faith in him.

Jesus Clears the Temple

12 After this he went down to Capernaum with his mother and brothers and his disciples. There they stayed for a few days.

13 When it was almost time for the Jewish Passover, Jesus went up to Jerusalem. 14 In the temple courts he found people selling cattle, sheep and doves, and others sitting at tables exchanging money. 15 So he made a whip out of cords, and drove all from the temple area, both sheep and cattle; he scattered the coins of the money-changers and overturned their tables. 16 To those who sold doves he said, "Get these out of here! How dare you turn my Father's house into a market!"

17 His disciples remembered that it is written: "Zeal for your house will consume me."[b]

18 Then the Jews demanded of him, "What miraculous sign can you show us to prove your authority to do all this?"

19 Jesus answered them, "Destroy this temple, and I will raise it again in three days."

20 The Jews replied, "It has taken forty-six years to build this temple, and you are going to raise it in three days?" 21 But the temple he had spoken of was his body. 22 After he was raised from the dead, his disciples recalled what he had said. Then they believed the Scripture and the words that Jesus had spoken.

23 Now while he was in Jerusalem at the Passover Feast, many people saw the miraculous signs he was doing and believed in his name.[c] 24 But Jesus would not entrust himself to them, for he knew all people. 25 He did not need human testimony about them, for he knew what was in people.

Jesus Teaches Nicodemus

3 Now there was a Pharisee named Nicodemus, a member of the Jewish ruling council. 2 He came to Jesus at night and said, "Rabbi, we know you are a teacher who has come from God. For you could not perform the miraculous signs you are doing if God were not with you."

3 In reply Jesus declared, "I tell you the truth, no-one can see the kingdom of God without being born again."[a]

4 "How can anyone be born in old age?" Nicodemus asked. "Surely they cannot enter a second time into their mother's womb to be born!"

5 Jesus answered, "I tell you the truth, no-one can enter the kingdom of God without being born of water and the Spirit. 6 Flesh gives birth to flesh, but the Spirit[b] gives birth to spirit. 7 You should not be surprised at my saying, 'You[c] must be born again.' 8 The wind blows wherever

---

*a*6 Greek *two to three metretes* (probably about 75 to 115 litres)   *b*17 Psalm 69:9   *c*23 Or *and believed in him*
*a*3 Or *born from above*; also in verse 7   *b*6 Or *but spirit*   *c*7 The Greek is plural.

it pleases. You hear its sound, but you cannot tell where it comes from or where it is going. So it is with everyone born of the Spirit."

9 "How can this be?" Nicodemus asked.

10 "You are Israel's teacher," said Jesus, "and do you not understand these things? 11 I tell you the truth, we speak of what we know, and we testify to what we have seen, but still you people do not accept our testimony. 12 I have spoken to you of earthly things and you do not believe; how then will you believe if I speak of heavenly things? 13 No-one has ever gone into heaven except the one who came from heaven—the Son of Man.*d* 14 Just as Moses lifted up the snake in the desert, so the Son of Man must be lifted up, 15 that everyone who believes in him may have eternal life.*e*

16 "For God so loved the world that he gave his one and only Son,*f* that whoever believes in him shall not perish but have eternal life. 17 For God did not send his Son into the world to condemn the world, but to save the world through him. 18 Those who believe in him are not condemned, but those who do not believe stand condemned already because they have not believed in the name of God's one and only Son.*g* 19 This is the verdict: Light has come into the world, but people loved darkness instead of light because their deeds were evil. 20 All those who do evil hate the light, and will not come into the light for fear that their deeds will be exposed. 21 But those who live by the truth come into the light, so that it may be seen plainly that what they have done has been done through God."*h*

John the Baptist's Testimony About Jesus

22 After this, Jesus and his disciples went out into the Judean countryside, where he spent some time with them, and baptised. 23 Now John also was baptising at Aenon near Salim, because there was plenty of water, and people were constantly coming to be baptised. 24 (This was before John was put in prison.) 25 An argument developed between some of John's disciples and a certain Jew*i* over the matter of ceremonial washing. 26 They came to John and said to him, "Rabbi, that man who was with you on the other side of the Jordan—the one you testified about—well, he is baptising, and everyone is going to him."

27 To this John replied, "A person can receive only what is given from heaven. 28 You yourselves can testify that I said, 'I am not the Christ*j* but am sent ahead of him.' 29 The bride belongs to the bridegroom. The friend who attends the bridegroom waits and listens for him, and is full of joy when he hears the bridegroom's voice. That joy is mine, and it is now complete. 30 He must become greater; I must become less.

31 "The one who comes from above is above all; the one who is from the earth belongs to the earth, and speaks as one from the earth. The one who comes from heaven is above all. 32 He testifies to what he has seen and heard, but no-one accepts his testimony. 33 The person who has accepted it has certified that God is truthful. 34 For the one whom God has sent speaks the words of God, for God*k* gives the Spirit without limit. 35 The Father loves the Son and has placed everything in his hands. 36 Those who believe in the Son have eternal life, but those who reject the Son will not see life, for God's wrath remains on them."*l*

Jesus Talks With a Samaritan Woman

4 The Pharisees heard that Jesus was gaining and baptising more disciples than John, 2 although in fact it was not Jesus who baptised, but his disciples. 3 When the Lord learned of this, he left Judea and went back once more to Galilee.

4 Now he had to go through Samaria.

---

*d*13 Some manuscripts *Man, who is in heaven*   *e*15 Or *believes may have eternal life in him*
*f*16 Or *his only begotten Son*   *g*18 Or *God's only begotten Son*
*h*21 Some interpreters end the quotation after verse 15.   *i*25 Some manuscripts *and certain Jews*
*j*28 Or *Messiah*   *k*34 Greek *he*   *l*36 Some interpreters end the quotation after verse 30.

⁵ So he came to a town in Samaria called Sychar, near the plot of ground Jacob had given to his son Joseph. ⁶ Jacob's well was there, and Jesus, tired as he was from the journey, sat down by the well. It was about the sixth hour.

⁷ When a Samaritan woman came to draw water, Jesus said to her, "Will you give me a drink?" ⁸ (His disciples had gone into the town to buy food.)

⁹ The Samaritan woman said to him, "You are a Jew and I am a Samaritan woman. How can you ask me for a drink?" (For Jews do not associate with Samaritans.ᵃ)

¹⁰ Jesus answered her, "If you knew the gift of God and who it is that asks you for a drink, you would have asked him and he would have given you living water."

¹¹ "Sir," the woman said, "you have nothing to draw with and the well is deep. Where can you get this living water? ¹² Are you greater than our father Jacob, who gave us the well and drank from it himself, as did also his sons and his flocks and herds?"

¹³ Jesus answered, "All who drink this water will be thirsty again, ¹⁴ but those who drink the water I give them will never thirst. Indeed, the water I give them will become in them a spring of water welling up to eternal life."

¹⁵ The woman said to him, "Sir, give me this water so that I won't get thirsty and have to keep coming here to draw water."

¹⁶ He told her, "Go, call your husband and come back."

¹⁷ "I have no husband," she replied.

Jesus said to her, "You are right when you say you have no husband. ¹⁸ The fact is, you have had five husbands, and the man you now have is not your husband. What you have just said is quite true."

¹⁹ "Sir," the woman said, "I can see that you are a prophet. ²⁰ Our ancestors worshipped on this mountain, but you Jews claim that the place where we must worship is in Jerusalem."

²¹ Jesus declared, "Believe me, woman, a time is coming when you will worship the Father neither on this mountain nor in Jerusalem. ²² You Samaritans worship what you do not know; we worship what we do know, for salvation is from the Jews. ²³ Yet a time is coming and has now come when the true worshippers will worship the Father in spirit and truth, for they are the kind of worshippers the Father seeks. ²⁴ God is spirit, and his worshippers must worship in spirit and in truth."

²⁵ The woman said, "I know that Messiah" (called Christ) "is coming. When he comes, he will explain everything to us."

²⁶ Then Jesus declared, "I who speak to you am he."

The Disciples Rejoin Jesus

²⁷ Just then his disciples returned and were surprised to find him talking with a woman. But no-one asked, "What do you want?" or "Why are you talking with her?"

²⁸ Then, leaving her water jar, the woman went back to the town and said to the people, ²⁹ "Come, see a man who told me everything I ever did. Could this be the Christ?"ᵇ ³⁰ They came out of the town and made their way towards him.

³¹ Meanwhile his disciples urged him, "Rabbi, eat something."

³² But he said to them, "I have food to eat that you know nothing about."

³³ Then his disciples said to each other, "Could someone have brought him food?"

³⁴ "My food," said Jesus, "is to do the will of him who sent me and to finish his work. ³⁵ Do you not say, 'Four months more and then the harvest'? I tell you, open your eyes and look at the fields! They are ripe for harvest. ³⁶ Even now those who reap draw their wages, even now they harvest the crop for eternal life, so that the sower and the reaper may be glad together. ³⁷ Thus the saying 'One sows and another reaps' is true. ³⁸ I sent you to reap what you have not worked for. Others have done the hard work, and you have reaped the benefits of their labour."

ᵃ9 Or *do not use dishes Samaritans have used*   ᵇ29 Or *Messiah*

Many Samaritans Believe

³⁹ Many of the Samaritans from that town believed in him because of the woman's testimony, "He told me everything I ever did." ⁴⁰ So when the Samaritans came to him, they urged him to stay with them, and he stayed two days. ⁴¹ And because of his words many more became believers.

⁴² They said to the woman, "We no longer believe just because of what you said; now we have heard for ourselves, and we know that this man really is the Saviour of the world."

Jesus Heals the Official's Son

⁴³ After the two days he left for Galilee. ⁴⁴ (Now Jesus himself had pointed out that prophets have no honour in their own country.) ⁴⁵ When he arrived in Galilee, the Galileans welcomed him. They had seen all that he had done in Jerusalem at the Passover Feast, for they also had been there.

⁴⁶ Once more he visited Cana in Galilee, where he had turned the water into wine. And there was a certain royal official whose son lay sick at Capernaum. ⁴⁷ When this man heard that Jesus had arrived in Galilee from Judea, he went to him and begged him to come and heal his son, who was close to death.

⁴⁸ "Unless you people see miraculous signs and wonders," Jesus told him, "you will never believe."

⁴⁹ The royal official said, "Sir, come down before my child dies."

⁵⁰ Jesus replied, "You may go. Your son will live."

The man took Jesus at his word and departed. ⁵¹ While he was still on the way, his servants met him with the news that his boy was living. ⁵² When he enquired as to the time when his son got better, they said to him, "The fever left him yesterday at the seventh hour."

⁵³ Then the father realised that this was the exact time at which Jesus had said to him, "Your son will live." So he and all his household believed.

⁵⁴ This was the second miraculous sign that Jesus performed, having come from Judea to Galilee.

The Healing at the Pool

5 Some time later, Jesus went up to Jerusalem for a feast of the Jews. ² Now there is in Jerusalem near the Sheep Gate a pool, which in Aramaic is called Bethesda*a* and which is surrounded by five covered colonnades. ³ Here a great number of disabled people used to lie— the blind, the lame, the paralysed.*b* ⁵ One who was there had been an invalid for thirty-eight years. ⁶ When Jesus saw him lying there and learned that he had been in this condition for a long time, he asked him, "Do you want to get well?"

⁷ "Sir," the invalid replied, "I have no-one to help me into the pool when the water is stirred. While I am trying to get in, someone else goes down ahead of me."

⁸ Then Jesus said to him, "Get up! Pick up your mat and walk." ⁹ At once the man was cured; he picked up his mat and walked.

The day on which this took place was a Sabbath, ¹⁰ and so the Jews said to the man who had been healed, "It is the Sabbath; the law forbids you to carry your mat."

¹¹ But he replied, "The man who made me well said to me, 'Pick up your mat and walk.' "

¹² So they asked him, "Who is this fellow who told you to pick it up and walk?"

¹³ The man who was healed had no idea who it was, for Jesus had slipped away into the crowd that was there.

¹⁴ Later Jesus found him at the temple and said to him, "See, you are well again. Stop sinning or something worse may happen to you." ¹⁵ The man went away and told the Jews that it was Jesus who had made him well.

---

*a*2 Some manuscripts *Bethzatha*; other manuscripts *Bethsaida*
*b*3 Some less important manuscripts *paralysed—and they waited for the moving of the waters. ⁴From time to time an angel of the Lord would come down and stir up the waters. The first one into the pool after each such disturbance would be cured of whatever disease they had.*

Life Through the Son

¹⁶ So, because Jesus was doing these things on the Sabbath, the Jews persecuted him. ¹⁷ Jesus said to them, "My Father is always at his work to this very day, and I, too, am working." ¹⁸ For this reason the Jews tried all the harder to kill him; not only was he breaking the Sabbath, but he was even calling God his own Father, making himself equal with God.

¹⁹ Jesus gave them this answer: "I tell you the truth, the Son can do nothing by himself; he can do only what he sees his Father doing, because whatever the Father does the Son also does. ²⁰ For the Father loves the Son and shows him all he does. Yes, to your amazement he will show him even greater things than these. ²¹ For just as the Father raises the dead and gives them life, even so the Son gives life to whom he is pleased to give it. ²² Moreover, the Father judges no-one, but has entrusted all judgment to the Son, ²³ that all may honour the Son just as they honour the Father. Whoever does not honour the Son does not honour the Father, who sent him.

²⁴ "I tell you the truth, those who hear my word and believe him who sent me have eternal life and will not be condemned; they have crossed over from death to life. ²⁵ I tell you the truth, a time is coming and has now come when the dead will hear the voice of the Son of God and those who hear will live. ²⁶ For as the Father has life in himself, so he has granted the Son to have life in himself. ²⁷ And he has given him authority to judge because he is the Son of Man.

²⁸ "Do not be amazed at this, for a time is coming when all who are in their graves will hear his voice ²⁹ and come out—those who have done good will rise to live, and those who have done evil will rise to be condemned. ³⁰ By myself I can do nothing; I judge only as I hear, and my judgment is just, for I seek not to please myself but him who sent me.

Testimonies About Jesus

³¹ "If I testify about myself, my testimony is not valid. ³² There is another who testifies in my favour, and I know that his testimony about me is valid.

³³ "You have sent to John and he has testified to the truth. ³⁴ Not that I accept human testimony; but I mention it that you may be saved. ³⁵ John was a lamp that burned and gave light, and you chose for a time to enjoy his light.

³⁶ "I have testimony weightier than that of John. For the very work that the Father has given me to finish, and which I am doing, testifies that the Father has sent me. ³⁷ And the Father who sent me has himself testified concerning me. You have never heard his voice nor seen his form, ³⁸ nor does his word dwell in you, for you do not believe the one he sent. ³⁹ You diligently study^c the Scriptures because you think that by them you possess eternal life. These are the Scriptures that testify about me, ⁴⁰ yet you refuse to come to me to have life.

⁴¹ "I do not accept human praise, ⁴² but I know you. I know that you do not have the love of God in your hearts. ⁴³ I have come in my Father's name, and you do not accept me; but if others come in their own names, you will accept them. ⁴⁴ How can you believe if you accept praise from one another, yet make no effort to obtain the praise that comes from the only God?^d

⁴⁵ "But do not think I will accuse you before the Father. Your accuser is Moses, on whom your hopes are set. ⁴⁶ If you believed Moses, you would believe me, for he wrote about me. ⁴⁷ But since you do not believe what he wrote, how are you going to believe what I say?"

Jesus Feeds the Five Thousand

6 Some time after this, Jesus crossed to the far shore of the Sea of Galilee (that is, the Sea of Tiberias), ² and a great crowd of people followed him because they saw the miraculous signs he had performed on the sick. ³ Then Jesus went up on a

---

^c39 Or *Study diligently* (the imperative)   ^d44 Some early manuscripts *the Only One*

mountainside and sat down with his disciples. [4] The Jewish Passover Feast was near.

[5] When Jesus looked up and saw a great crowd coming towards him, he said to Philip, "Where shall we buy bread for these people to eat?" [6] He asked this only to test him, for he already had in mind what he was going to do.

[7] Philip answered him, "Eight months' wages[a] would not buy enough bread for each one to have a bite!"

[8] Another of his disciples, Andrew, Simon Peter's brother, spoke up, [9] "Here is a boy with five small barley loaves and two small fish, but how far will they go among so many?"

[10] Jesus said, "Make the people sit down." There was plenty of grass in that place, and they sat down, about five thousand of them. [11] Jesus then took the loaves, gave thanks, and distributed to those who were seated as much as they wanted. He did the same with the fish.

[12] When they had all had enough to eat, he said to his disciples, "Gather the pieces that are left over. Let nothing be wasted." [13] So they gathered them and filled twelve baskets with the pieces of the five barley loaves left over by those who had eaten.

[14] After the people saw the miraculous sign that Jesus did, they began to say, "Surely this is the Prophet who is to come into the world." [15] Jesus, knowing that they intended to come and make him king by force, withdrew again to a mountain by himself.

Jesus Walks on the Water

[16] When evening came, his disciples went down to the lake, [17] where they got into a boat and set off across the lake for Capernaum. By now it was dark, and Jesus had not yet joined them. [18] A strong wind was blowing and the waters grew rough. [19] When they had rowed three or three and a half miles,[b] they saw Jesus approaching the boat, walking on the water; and they were terrified. [20] But he said to them, "It is I; don't be afraid."

[21] Then they were willing to take him into the boat, and immediately the boat reached the shore where they were heading.

[22] The next day the crowd that had stayed on the opposite shore of the lake realised that only one boat had been there, and that Jesus had not entered it with his disciples, but that they had gone away alone. [23] Then some boats from Tiberias landed near the place where the people had eaten the bread after the Lord had given thanks. [24] Once the crowd realised that neither Jesus nor his disciples were there, they got into the boats and went to Capernaum in search of Jesus.

Jesus the Bread of Life

[25] When they found him on the other side of the lake, they asked him, "Rabbi, when did you get here?"

[26] Jesus answered, "I tell you the truth, you are looking for me, not because you saw miraculous signs but because you ate the loaves and had your fill. [27] Do not work for food that spoils, but for food that endures to eternal life, which the Son of Man will give you. On him God the Father has placed his seal of approval."

[28] Then they asked him, "What must we do to do the works God requires?"

[29] Jesus answered, "The work of God is this: to believe in the one he has sent."

[30] So they asked him, "What miraculous sign then will you give that we may see it and believe you? What will you do? [31] Our ancestors ate the manna in the desert; as it is written: 'He gave them bread from heaven to eat.'[c]"

[32] Jesus said to them, "I tell you the truth, it is not Moses who has given you the bread from heaven, but it is my Father who gives you the true bread from heaven. [33] For the bread of God is he who comes down from heaven and gives life to the world."

[34] "Sir," they said, "from now on give us this bread."

[35] Then Jesus declared, "I am the bread of life. Whoever comes to me will never

---

[a]7 Greek *two hundred denarii*   [b]19 Greek *rowed twenty-five or thirty stadia* (about 5 or 6 kilometres)
[c]31 Exodus 16:4; Neh. 9:15; Psalm 78:24,25

go hungry, and whoever believes in me will never be thirsty. ³⁶But as I told you, you have seen me and still you do not believe. ³⁷All that the Father gives me will come to me, and whoever comes to me I will never drive away. ³⁸For I have come down from heaven not to do my will but to do the will of him who sent me. ³⁹And this is the will of him who sent me, that I shall lose none of all that he has given me, but raise them up at the last day. ⁴⁰For my Father's will is that all those who look to the Son and believe in him shall have eternal life, and I will raise them up at the last day."

⁴¹At this the Jews began to grumble about him because he said, "I am the bread that came down from heaven." ⁴²They said, "Is this not Jesus, the son of Joseph, whose father and mother we know? How can he now say, 'I came down from heaven'?"

⁴³"Stop grumbling among yourselves," Jesus answered. ⁴⁴"No-one can come to me unless the Father who sent me draws them, and I will raise them up at the last day. ⁴⁵It is written in the Prophets: 'They will all be taught by God.'ᵈ Everyone who listens to the Father and learns from him comes to me. ⁴⁶No-one has seen the Father except the one who is from God; only he has seen the Father. ⁴⁷I tell you the truth, whoever believes has everlasting life. ⁴⁸I am the bread of life. ⁴⁹Your ancestors ate the manna in the desert, yet they died. ⁵⁰But here is the bread that comes down from heaven, which people may eat and not die. ⁵¹I am the living bread that came down from heaven. Whoever eats of this bread will live for ever. This bread is my flesh, which I will give for the life of the world."

⁵²Then the Jews began to argue sharply among themselves, "How can this man give us his flesh to eat?"

⁵³Jesus said to them, "I tell you the truth, unless you eat the flesh of the Son of Man and drink his blood, you have no life in you. ⁵⁴Those who eat my flesh and drink my blood have eternal life, and I will raise them up at the last day. ⁵⁵For my

flesh is real food and my blood is real drink. ⁵⁶Those who eat my flesh and drink my blood remain in me, and I in them. ⁵⁷Just as the living Father sent me and I live because of the Father, so the one who feeds on me will live because of me. ⁵⁸This is the bread that came down from heaven. Your ancestors ate manna and died, but whoever feeds on this bread will live for ever." ⁵⁹He said this while teaching in the synagogue in Capernaum.

Many Disciples Desert Jesus

⁶⁰On hearing it, many of his disciples said, "This is a hard teaching. Who can accept it?"

⁶¹Aware that his disciples were grumbling about this, Jesus said to them, "Does this offend you? ⁶²What if you see the Son of Man ascend to where he was before! ⁶³The Spirit gives life; the flesh counts for nothing. The words I have spoken to you are spiritᵉ and they are life. ⁶⁴Yet there are some of you who do not believe." For Jesus had known from the beginning which of them did not believe and who would betray him. ⁶⁵He went on to say, "This is why I told you that no-one can come to me unless the Father has enabled them."

⁶⁶From this time many of his disciples turned back and no longer followed him.

⁶⁷"You do not want to leave too, do you?" Jesus asked the Twelve.

⁶⁸Simon Peter answered him, "Lord, to whom shall we go? You have the words of eternal life. ⁶⁹We believe and know that you are the Holy One of God."

⁷⁰Then Jesus replied, "Have I not chosen you, the Twelve? Yet one of you is a devil!" ⁷¹(He meant Judas, the son of Simon Iscariot, who, though one of the Twelve, was later to betray him.)

Jesus Goes to the Feast of Tabernacles

7 After this, Jesus went around in Galilee, purposely staying away from Judea because the Jews there were waiting to take his life. ²But when the

ᵈ45 Isaiah 54:13 ᵉ63 Or *Spirit*

Jewish Feast of Tabernacles was near, [3] Jesus' brothers said to him, "You ought to leave here and go to Judea, so that your disciples may see the miracles you do. [4] No-one who wants to become a public figure acts in secret. Since you are doing these things, show yourself to the world." [5] For even his own brothers did not believe in him.

[6] Therefore Jesus told them, "The right time for me has not yet come; for you any time is right. [7] The world cannot hate you, but it hates me because I testify that what it does is evil. [8] You go to the Feast. I am not yet[a] going up to this Feast, because for me the right time has not yet come." [9] Having said this, he stayed in Galilee.

[10] However, after his brothers had left for the Feast, he went also, not publicly, but in secret. [11] Now at the Feast the Jews were watching for Jesus and asking, "Where is he?"

[12] Among the crowds there was widespread whispering about him. Some said, "He is a good man."

Others replied, "No, he deceives the people." [13] But no-one would say anything publicly about him for fear of the Jews.

Jesus Teaches at the Feast

[14] Not until halfway through the Feast did Jesus go up to the temple courts and begin to teach. [15] The Jews were amazed and asked, "How did this man get such learning without having studied?"

[16] Jesus answered, "My teaching is not my own. It comes from him who sent me. [17] Anyone who chooses to do the will of God will find out whether my teaching comes from God or whether I speak on my own. [18] Those who speak on their own do so to gain honour for themselves, but he who works for the honour of the one who sent him is a man of truth; there is nothing false about him. [19] Has not Moses given you the law? Yet not one of you keeps the law. Why are you trying to kill me?"

[20] "You are demon-possessed," the crowd answered. "Who is trying to kill you?"

[21] Jesus said to them, "I did one miracle, and you are all astonished. [22] Yet, because Moses gave you circumcision (though actually it did not come from Moses, but from the patriarchs), you circumcise a child on the Sabbath. [23] Now if a child can be circumcised on the Sabbath so that the law of Moses may not be broken, why are you angry with me for healing the whole person on the Sabbath? [24] Stop judging by mere appearances, and make a right judgment."

Is Jesus the Christ?

[25] At that point some of the people of Jerusalem began to ask, "Isn't this the man they are trying to kill? [26] Here he is, speaking publicly, and they are not saying a word to him. Have the authorities really concluded that he is the Christ?[b] [27] But we know where this man is from; when the Christ comes, no-one will know where he is from."

[28] Then Jesus, still teaching in the temple courts, cried out, "Yes, you know me, and you know where I am from. I am not here on my own, but he who sent me is true. You do not know him, [29] but I know him because I am from him and he sent me."

[30] At this they tried to seize him, but no-one laid a hand on him, because his time had not yet come. [31] Still, many in the crowd put their faith in him. They said, "When the Christ comes, will he do more miraculous signs than this man?"

[32] The Pharisees heard the crowd whispering such things about him. Then the chief priests and the Pharisees sent temple guards to arrest him.

[33] Jesus said, "I am with you for only a short time, and then I go to the one who sent me. [34] You will look for me, but you will not find me; and where I am, you cannot come."

[35] The Jews said to one another, "Where does this man intend to go that we cannot find him? Will he go where our people live scattered among the Greeks, and teach the Greeks? [36] What did he mean when he said, 'You will look for me,

---

[a]8 Some early manuscripts do not have yet.   [b]26 Or Messiah; also in verses 27, 31, 41 and 42

but you will not find me,' and 'Where I am, you cannot come'?"

[37] On the last and greatest day of the Feast, Jesus stood and said in a loud voice, "Let anyone who is thirsty come to me and drink. [38] Whoever believes in me, as the Scripture has said, will[c] have streams of living water flowing from within." [39] By this he meant the Spirit, whom those who believed in him were later to receive. Up to that time the Spirit had not been given, since Jesus had not yet been glorified.

[40] On hearing his words, some of the people said, "Surely this man is the Prophet."

[41] Others said, "He is the Christ."

Still others asked, "How can the Christ come from Galilee? [42] Does not the Scripture say that the Christ will come from David's family[d] and from Bethlehem, the town where David lived?" [43] Thus the people were divided because of Jesus. [44] Some wanted to seize him, but no-one laid a hand on him.

Unbelief of the Jewish Leaders

[45] Finally the temple guards went back to the chief priests and Pharisees, who asked them, "Why didn't you bring him in?"

[46] "No-one ever spoke the way this man does," the guards declared.

[47] "You mean he has deceived you also?" the Pharisees retorted. [48] "Has any of the rulers or of the Pharisees believed in him? [49] No! But this mob that knows nothing of the law—there is a curse on them."

[50] Nicodemus, who had gone to Jesus earlier and who was one of their own number, asked, [51] "Does our law condemn people without first hearing them to find out what they are doing?"

[52] They replied, "Are you from Galilee, too? Look into it, and you will find that a prophet[e] does not come out of Galilee."

[The earliest manuscripts and other ancient witnesses do not have John 7:53 –8:11.]

[53] Then they all went home.

8 But Jesus went to the Mount of Olives. [2] At dawn he appeared again in the temple courts, where all the people gathered round him, and he sat down to teach them. [3] The teachers of the law and the Pharisees brought in a woman caught in adultery. They made her stand before the group [4] and said to Jesus, "Teacher, this woman was caught in the act of adultery. [5] In the Law Moses commanded us to stone such women. Now what do you say?" [6] They were using this question as a trap, in order to have a basis for accusing him.

But Jesus bent down and started to write on the ground with his finger. [7] When they kept on questioning him, he straightened up and said to them, "Let anyone of you who is without sin be the first to throw a stone at her." [8] Again he stooped down and wrote on the ground.

[9] At this, those who heard began to go away one at a time, the older ones first, until only Jesus was left, with the woman still standing there. [10] Jesus straightened up and asked her, "Woman, where are they? Has no-one condemned you?"

[11] "No-one, sir," she said.

"Then neither do I condemn you," Jesus declared. "Go now and leave your life of sin."

The Validity of Jesus' Testimony

[12] When Jesus spoke again to the people, he said, "I am the light of the world. Whoever follows me will never walk in darkness, but will have the light of life."

[13] The Pharisees challenged him, "Here you are, appearing as your own witness; your testimony is not valid."

[14] Jesus answered, "Even if I testify on my own behalf, my testimony is valid, for I know where I came from and where I am going. But you have no idea where I come from or where I am going. [15] You judge by human standards; I pass judgment on no-one. [16] But if I do judge, my

---

*c*37, 38 Or *Let anyone who is thirsty come to me. / And let anyone drink* *38who believes in me. / As the Scripture has said, they will*   *d*42 Greek *seed*   *e*52 Two early manuscripts *the Prophet* decisions are right, because I am not alone. I stand with the Father, who sent me. [17] In your own Law it is written that the testimony of two witnesses is valid. [18] I am one who testifies for myself; my other witness is the Father, who sent me."

[19] Then they asked him, "Where is your father?"

"You do not know me or my Father," Jesus replied. "If you knew me, you would know my Father also." [20] He spoke these words while teaching in the temple area near the place where the offerings were put. Yet no-one seized him, because his time had not yet come.

[21] Once more Jesus said to them, "I am going away, and you will look for me, and you will die in your sin. Where I go, you cannot come."

[22] This made the Jews ask, "Will he kill himself? Is that why he says, 'Where I go, you cannot come'?"

[23] But he continued, "You are from below; I am from above. You are of this world; I am not of this world. [24] I told you that you would die in your sins; if you do not believe that I am ˌthe one I claim to be˩,[a] you will indeed die in your sins."

[25] "Who are you?" they asked.

"Just what I have been claiming all along," Jesus replied. [26] "I have much to say in judgment of you. But he who sent me is reliable, and what I have heard from him I tell the world."

[27] They did not understand that he was telling them about his Father. [28] So Jesus said, "When you have lifted up the Son of Man, then you will know that I am ˌthe one I claim to be˩ and that I do nothing on my own but speak just what the Father has taught me. [29] The one who sent me is with me; he has not left me alone, for I always do what pleases him." [30] Even as he spoke, many put their faith in him.

The Children of Abraham

[31] To the Jews who had believed him, Jesus said, "If you hold to my teaching,

you are really my disciples. [32] Then you will know the truth, and the truth will set you free."

[33] They answered him, "We are Abraham's descendants[b] and have never been slaves of anyone. How can you say that we shall be set free?"

[34] Jesus replied, "I tell you the truth, everyone who sins is a slave to sin. [35] Now a slave has no permanent place in the family, but a son belongs to it for ever. [36] So if the Son sets you free, you will be free indeed. [37] I know you are Abraham's descendants. Yet you are ready to kill me, because you have no room for my word. [38] I am telling you what I have seen in the Father's presence, and you do what you have heard from your father."[c]

[39] "Abraham is our father," they answered.

"If you were Abraham's children," said Jesus, "then you would[d] do the things Abraham did. [40] As it is, you are determined to kill me, a man who has told you the truth that I heard from God. Abraham did not do such things. [41] You are doing the things your own father does."

"We are not illegitimate children," they protested. "The only Father we have is God himself."

The Children of the Devil

[42] Jesus said to them, "If God were your Father, you would love me, for I came from God and now am here. I have not come on my own; but he sent me. [43] Why is my language not clear to you? Because you are unable to hear what I say. [44] You belong to your father, the devil, and you want to carry out your father's desire. He was a murderer from the beginning, not holding to the truth, for there is no truth in him. When he lies, he speaks his native language, for he is a liar and the father of lies. [45] Yet because I tell the truth, you do not believe me! [46] Can any of you prove me guilty of sin? If I am telling the truth, why don't you believe me? [47] Whoever belongs to God hears what God says. The

[a]24 Or *I am he*; also in verse 28   [b]33 Greek *seed*; also in verse 37
[c]38 Or *presence. Therefore do what you have heard from the Father.*
[d]39 Some early manuscripts *"If you are Abraham's children," said Jesus, "then*

reason you do not hear is that you do not belong to God."

The Claims of Jesus About Himself

48 The Jews answered him, "Aren't we right in saying that you are a Samaritan and demon-possessed?"

49 "I am not possessed by a demon," said Jesus, "but I honour my Father and you dishonour me. 50 I am not seeking glory for myself; but there is one who seeks it, and he is the judge. 51 I tell you the truth, whoever keeps my word will never see death."

52 At this the Jews exclaimed, "Now we know that you are demon-possessed! Abraham died and so did the prophets, yet you say that whoever keeps your word will never taste death. 53 Are you greater than our father Abraham? He died, and so did the prophets. Who do you think you are?"

54 Jesus replied, "If I glorify myself, my glory means nothing. My Father, whom you claim as your God, is the one who glorifies me. 55 Though you do not know him, I know him. If I said I did not, I would be a liar like you, but I do know him and keep his word. 56 Your father Abraham rejoiced at the thought of seeing my day; he saw it and was glad."

57 "You are not yet fifty years old," the Jews said to him, "and you have seen Abraham!"

58 "I tell you the truth," Jesus answered, "before Abraham was born, I am!" 59 At this, they picked up stones to stone him, but Jesus hid himself, slipping away from the temple grounds.

Jesus Heals a Man Born Blind

9 As he went along, he saw a man blind from birth. 2 His disciples asked him, "Rabbi, who sinned, this man or his parents, that he was born blind?"

3 "Neither this man nor his parents sinned," said Jesus, "but this happened so that the work of God might be displayed in his life. 4 As long as it is day, we must do the work of him who sent me. Night is coming, when no-one can work. 5 While I am in the world, I am the light of the world."

6 Having said this, he spat on the ground, made some mud with the saliva, and put it on the man's eyes. 7 "Go," he told him, "wash in the Pool of Siloam" (this word means Sent). So the man went and washed, and came home seeing.

8 His neighbours and those who had formerly seen him begging asked, "Isn't this the same man who used to sit and beg?" 9 Some claimed that he was.

Others said, "No, he only looks like him."

But he himself insisted, "I am the man."

10 "How then were your eyes opened?" they demanded.

11 He replied, "The man they call Jesus made some mud and put it on my eyes. He told me to go to Siloam and wash. So I went and washed, and then I could see."

12 "Where is this man?" they asked him. "I don't know," he said.

The Pharisees Investigate the Healing

13 They brought to the Pharisees the man who had been blind. 14 Now the day on which Jesus had made the mud and opened the man's eyes was a Sabbath. 15 Therefore the Pharisees also asked him how he had received his sight. "He put mud on my eyes," the man replied, "and I washed, and now I see."

16 Some of the Pharisees said, "This man is not from God, for he does not keep the Sabbath."

But others asked, "How can a sinner do such miraculous signs?" So they were divided.

17 Finally they turned again to the blind man, "What have you to say about him? It was your eyes he opened."

The man replied, "He is a prophet."

18 The Jews still did not believe that he had been blind and had received his sight until they sent for the man's parents. 19 "Is this your son?" they asked. "Is this the one you say was born blind? How is it that now he can see?"

20 "We know he is our son," the parents answered, "and we know he was born

blind. 21 But how he can see now, or who opened his eyes, we don't know. Ask him. He is of age; he will speak for himself." 22 His parents said this because they were afraid of the Jews, for already the Jews had decided that anyone who acknowledged that Jesus was the Christ[a] would be put out of the synagogue. 23 That was why his parents said, "He is of age; ask him."

24 A second time they summoned the man who had been blind. "Give glory to God,"[b] they said. "We know this man is a sinner."

25 He replied, "Whether he is a sinner or not, I don't know. One thing I do know. I was blind but now I see!"

26 Then they asked him, "What did he do to you? How did he open your eyes?"

27 He answered, "I have told you already and you did not listen. Why do you want to hear it again? Do you want to become his disciples, too?"

28 Then they hurled insults at him and said, "You are this fellow's disciple! We are disciples of Moses! 29 We know that God spoke to Moses, but as for this fellow, we don't even know where he comes from."

30 The man answered, "Now that is remarkable! You don't know where he comes from, yet he opened my eyes. 31 We know that God does not listen to sinners. He listens to the godly person who does his will. 32 Nobody has ever heard of opening the eyes of someone born blind. 33 If this man were not from God, he could do nothing."

34 To this they replied, "You were steeped in sin at birth; how dare you lecture us!" And they threw him out.

Spiritual Blindness

35 Jesus heard that they had thrown him out, and when he found him, he said, "Do you believe in the Son of Man?"

36 "Who is he, sir?" the man asked. "Tell me so that I may believe in him."

37 Jesus said, "You have now seen him; in fact, he is the one speaking with you."

38 Then the man said, "Lord, I believe," and he worshipped him.

39 Jesus said, "For judgment I have come into this world, so that the blind will see and those who see will become blind."

40 Some Pharisees who were with him heard him say this and asked, "What? Are we blind too?"

41 Jesus said, "If you were blind, you would not be guilty of sin; but now that you claim you can see, your guilt remains.

The Shepherd and His Flock

10 "I tell you the truth, anyone who does not enter the sheep pen by the gate, but climbs in by some other way, is a thief and a robber. 2 The one who enters by the gate is the shepherd of his sheep. 3 The gatekeeper opens the gate for him, and the sheep listen to his voice. He calls his own sheep by name and leads them out. 4 When he has brought out all his own, he goes on ahead of them, and his sheep follow him because they know his voice. 5 But they will never follow a stranger; in fact, they will run away from him because they do not recognise a stranger's voice." 6 Jesus used this figure of speech, but they did not understand what he was telling them.

7 Therefore Jesus said again, "I tell you the truth, I am the gate for the sheep. 8 All who ever came before me were thieves and robbers, but the sheep did not listen to them. 9 I am the gate; all who enter through me will be saved.[a] They will come in and go out, and find pasture. 10 The thief comes only to steal and kill and destroy; I have come that they may have life, and have it to the full.

11 "I am the good shepherd. The good shepherd lays down his life for the sheep. 12 The hired hand is not the shepherd who owns the sheep. So when he sees the wolf coming, he abandons the sheep and runs away. Then the wolf attacks the flock and scatters it. 13 The man runs away because he is a hired hand and cares nothing for the sheep.

14 "I am the good shepherd; I know my sheep and my sheep know me—15 just as the Father knows me and I know the Father—and I lay down my life for the

---

[a]22 Or Messiah   [b]24 A solemn charge to tell the truth (see Joshua 7:19)   [a]9 Or kept safe

sheep. [16] I have other sheep that are not of this sheep pen. I must bring them also. They too will listen to my voice, and there shall be one flock and one shepherd. [17] The reason my Father loves me is that I lay down my life—only to take it up again. [18] No-one takes it from me, but I lay it down of my own accord. I have authority to lay it down and authority to take it up again. This command I received from my Father."

[19] At these words the Jews were again divided. [20] Many of them said, "He is demon-possessed and raving mad. Why listen to him?"

[21] But others said, "These are not the sayings of someone possessed by a demon. Can a demon open the eyes of the blind?"

The Unbelief of the Jews

[22] Then came the Feast of Dedication[b] at Jerusalem. It was winter, [23] and Jesus was in the temple area walking in Solomon's Colonnade. [24] The Jews gathered round him, saying, "How long will you keep us in suspense? If you are the Christ,[c] tell us plainly."

[25] Jesus answered, "I did tell you, but you do not believe. The miracles I do in my Father's name speak for me, [26] but you do not believe because you are not my sheep. [27] My sheep listen to my voice; I know them, and they follow me. [28] I give them eternal life, and they shall never perish; no-one can snatch them out of my hand. [29] My Father, who has given them to me, is greater than all;[d] no-one can snatch them out of my Father's hand. [30] I and the Father are one."

[31] Again the Jews picked up stones to stone him, [32] but Jesus said to them, "I have shown you many great miracles from the Father. For which of these do you stone me?"

[33] "We are not stoning you for any of these," replied the Jews, "but for blasphemy, because you, a mere human being, claim to be God."

[34] Jesus answered them, "Is it not written in your Law, 'I have said you are gods'[e]? [35] If he called them 'gods', to whom the word of God came—and the Scripture cannot be broken—[36] what about the one whom the Father set apart as his very own and sent into the world? Why then do you accuse me of blasphemy because I said, 'I am God's Son'? [37] Do not believe me unless I do what my Father does. [38] But if I do it, even though you do not believe me, believe the miracles, that you may know and understand that the Father is in me, and I in the Father." [39] Again they tried to seize him, but he escaped their grasp.

[40] Then Jesus went back across the Jordan to the place where John had been baptising in the early days. Here he stayed [41] and many people came to him. They said, "Though John never performed a miraculous sign, all that John said about this man was true." [42] And in that place many believed in Jesus.

The Death of Lazarus

11 Now a man named Lazarus was sick. He was from Bethany, the village of Mary and her sister Martha. [2] This Mary, whose brother Lazarus now lay sick, was the same one who poured perfume on the Lord and wiped his feet with her hair. [3] So the sisters sent word to Jesus, "Lord, the one you love is sick."

[4] When he heard this, Jesus said, "This sickness will not end in death. No, it is for God's glory so that God's Son may be glorified through it." [5] Jesus loved Martha and her sister and Lazarus. [6] Yet when he heard that Lazarus was sick, he stayed where he was two more days.

[7] Then he said to his disciples, "Let us go back to Judea."

[8] "But Rabbi," they said, "a short while ago the Jews tried to stone you, and yet you are going back there?"

[9] Jesus answered, "Are there not twelve hours of daylight? Those who walk by day will not stumble, for they see by this world's light. [10] It is when they walk by

---

[b]22 That is, Hanukkah [c]24 Or *Messiah*
[d]29 Many early manuscripts *What my Father has given me is greater than all* [e]34 Psalm 82:6

night that they stumble, for they have no light."

11 After he had said this, he went on to tell them, "Our friend Lazarus has fallen asleep; but I am going there to wake him up."

12 His disciples replied, "Lord, if he sleeps, he will get better." 13 Jesus had been speaking of his death, but his disciples thought he meant natural sleep.

14 So then he told them plainly, "Lazarus is dead, 15 and for your sake I am glad I was not there, so that you may believe. But let us go to him."

16 Then Thomas (called Didymus) said to the rest of the disciples, "Let us also go, that we may die with him."

Jesus Comforts the Sisters

17 On his arrival, Jesus found that Lazarus had already been in the tomb for four days. 18 Bethany was less than two miles[a] from Jerusalem, 19 and many Jews had come to Martha and Mary to comfort them in the loss of their brother. 20 When Martha heard that Jesus was coming, she went out to meet him, but Mary stayed at home.

21 "Lord," Martha said to Jesus, "if you had been here, my brother would not have died. 22 But I know that even now God will give you whatever you ask."

23 Jesus said to her, "Your brother will rise again."

24 Martha answered, "I know he will rise again in the resurrection at the last day."

25 Jesus said to her, "I am the resurrection and the life. Those who believe in me will live, even though they die; 26 and whoever lives and believes in me will never die. Do you believe this?"

27 "Yes, Lord," she told him, "I believe that you are the Christ,[b] the Son of God, who was to come into the world."

28 And after she had said this, she went back and called her sister Mary aside. "The Teacher is here," she said, "and is asking for you." 29 When Mary heard this, she got up quickly and went to him. 30 Now

Jesus had not yet entered the village, but was still at the place where Martha had met him. 31 When the Jews who had been with Mary in the house, comforting her, noticed how quickly she got up and went out, they followed her, supposing she was going to the tomb to mourn there.

32 When Mary reached the place where Jesus was and saw him, she fell at his feet and said, "Lord, if you had been here, my brother would not have died."

33 When Jesus saw her weeping, and the Jews who had come along with her also weeping, he was deeply moved in spirit and troubled. 34 "Where have you laid him?" he asked.

"Come and see, Lord," they replied.

35 Jesus wept.

36 Then the Jews said, "See how he loved him!"

37 But some of them said, "Could not he who opened the eyes of the blind man have kept this man from dying?"

Jesus Raises Lazarus From the Dead

38 Jesus, once more deeply moved, came to the tomb. It was a cave with a stone laid across the entrance. 39 "Take away the stone," he said.

"But, Lord," said Martha, the sister of the dead man, "by this time there is a bad odour, for he has been there four days."

40 Then Jesus said, "Did I not tell you that if you believed, you would see the glory of God?"

41 So they took away the stone. Then Jesus looked up and said, "Father, I thank you that you have heard me. 42 I knew that you always hear me, but I said this for the benefit of the people standing here, that they may believe that you sent me."

43 When he had said this, Jesus called in a loud voice, "Lazarus, come out!" 44 The dead man came out, his hands and feet wrapped with strips of linen, and a cloth around his face.

Jesus said to them, "Take off the grave clothes and let him go."

---

[a]18 Greek *fifteen stadia* (about 3 kilometres)   [b]27 Or *Messiah*

The Plot to Kill Jesus

45 Therefore many of the Jews who had come to visit Mary, and had seen what Jesus did, put their faith in him. 46 But some of them went to the Pharisees and told them what Jesus had done. 47 Then the chief priests and the Pharisees called a meeting of the Sanhedrin.

"What are we accomplishing?" they asked. "Here is this man performing many miraculous signs. 48 If we let him go on like this, everyone will believe in him, and then the Romans will come and take away both our place[c] and our nation."

49 Then one of them, named Caiaphas, who was high priest that year, spoke up, "You know nothing at all! 50 You do not realise that it is better for you that one person die for the people than that the whole nation perish."

51 He did not say this on his own, but as high priest that year he prophesied that Jesus would die for the Jewish nation, 52 and not only for that nation but also for the scattered children of God, to bring them together and make them one. 53 So from that day on they plotted to take his life.

54 Therefore Jesus no longer moved about publicly among the Jews. Instead he withdrew to a region near the desert, to a village called Ephraim, where he stayed with his disciples.

55 When it was almost time for the Jewish Passover, many went up from the country to Jerusalem for their ceremonial cleansing before the Passover. 56 They kept looking for Jesus, and as they stood in the temple area they asked one another, "What do you think? Isn't he coming to the Feast at all?" 57 But the chief priests and Pharisees had given orders that if anyone found out where Jesus was, he should report it so that they might arrest him.

Jesus Anointed at Bethany

12 Six days before the Passover, Jesus arrived at Bethany, where Lazarus lived, whom Jesus had raised from the dead. 2 Here a dinner was given in Jesus' honour. Martha served, while Lazarus was among those reclining at the table with him. 3 Then Mary took about a pint[a] of pure nard, an expensive perfume; she poured it on Jesus' feet and wiped his feet with her hair. And the house was filled with the fragrance of the perfume.

4 But one of his disciples, Judas Iscariot, who was later to betray him, objected, 5 "Why wasn't this perfume sold and the money given to the poor? It was worth a year's wages."[b] 6 He did not say this because he cared about the poor but because he was a thief; as keeper of the money bag, he used to help himself to what was put into it.

7 "Leave her alone," Jesus replied. "It was intended that she should save this perfume for the day of my burial. 8 You will always have the poor among you, but you will not always have me."

9 Meanwhile a large crowd of Jews found out that Jesus was there and came, not only because of him but also to see Lazarus, whom he had raised from the dead. 10 So the chief priests made plans to kill Lazarus as well, 11 for on account of him many of the Jews were going over to Jesus and putting their faith in him.

The Triumphal Entry

12 The next day the great crowd that had come for the Feast heard that Jesus was on his way to Jerusalem. 13 They took palm branches and went out to meet him, shouting,

"Hosanna!"[c]

"Blessed is he who comes in the name of the Lord!"[d]

"Blessed is the King of Israel!"

14 Jesus found a young donkey and sat upon it, as it is written,

c48 Or temple   a3 Greek a litra (probably about 0.5 litre)   b5 Greek three hundred denarii
c13 A Hebrew expression meaning "Save!" which became an exclamation of praise   d13 Psalm 118:25,26

15 "Do not be afraid, O Daughter of
Zion;
  see, your king is coming,
  seated on a donkey's colt."*e*

16 At first his disciples did not understand all this. Only after Jesus was glorified did they realise that these things had
been written about him and that they had
done these things to him.

17 Now the crowd that was with him
when he called Lazarus from the tomb and
raised him from the dead continued to
spread the word. 18 Many people, because
they had heard that he had given this miraculous sign, went out to meet him. 19 So
the Pharisees said to one another, "See,
this is getting us nowhere. Look how the
whole world has gone after him!"

Jesus Predicts His Death

20 Now there were some Greeks among
those who went up to worship at the Feast.
21 They came to Philip, who was from
Bethsaida in Galilee, with a request.
"Sir," they said, "we would like to see
Jesus." 22 Philip went to tell Andrew; Andrew and Philip in turn told Jesus.

23 Jesus replied, "The hour has come for
the Son of Man to be glorified. 24 I tell you
the truth, unless a grain of wheat falls to
the ground and dies, it remains only a
single seed. But if it dies, it produces many
seeds. 25 Those who love their lives will
lose them, while those who hate their lives
in this world will keep them for eternal
life. 26 Whoever serves me must follow
me; and where I am, my servant also will
be. My Father will honour the one who
serves me.

27 "Now my heart is troubled, and what
shall I say? 'Father, save me from this
hour'? No, it was for this very reason I
came to this hour. 28 Father, glorify your
name!"

Then a voice came from heaven, "I
have glorified it, and will glorify it again."
29 The crowd that was there and heard it
said it had thundered; others said an angel
had spoken to him.

30 Jesus said, "This voice was for your
benefit, not mine. 31 Now is the time for
judgment on this world; now the prince of
this world will be driven out. 32 But I,
when I am lifted up from the earth, will
draw all people to myself." 33 He said this
to show the kind of death he was going to
die.

34 The crowd spoke up, "We have heard
from the Law that the Christ*f* will remain
for ever, so how can you say, 'The Son of
Man must be lifted up'? Who is this 'Son
of Man'?"

35 Then Jesus told them, "You are going
to have the light just a little while longer.
Walk while you have the light, before
darkness overtakes you. Those who walk
in the dark do not know where they are
going. 36 Put your trust in the light while
you have it, so that you may become children of light." When he had finished
speaking, Jesus left and hid himself from
them.

The Jews Continue in Their Unbelief

37 Even after Jesus had done all these
miraculous signs in their presence, they
still would not believe in him. 38 This was
to fulfil the word of Isaiah the prophet:

"Lord, who has believed our message
  and to whom has the arm of the
    Lord been revealed?"*g*

39 For this reason they could not believe, because, as Isaiah says elsewhere:

40 "He has blinded their eyes
  and deadened their hearts,
so they can neither see with their eyes,
  nor understand with their hearts,
  nor turn—and I would heal
    them."*h*

41 Isaiah said this because he saw Jesus'
glory and spoke about him.

42 Yet at the same time many even
among the leaders believed in him. But
because of the Pharisees they would not
confess their faith for fear they would be

*e*15 Zech. 9:9   *f*34 Or *Messiah*   *g*38 Isaiah 53:1   *h*40 Isaiah 6:10

put out of the synagogue; [43] for they loved human praise more than praise from God.

[44] Then Jesus cried out, "Those who believe in me do not believe in me only, but in the one who sent me. [45] When they look at me, they see the one who sent me. [46] I have come into the world as a light, so that no-one who believes in me should stay in darkness.

[47] "As for those who hear my words but do not keep them, I do not judge them. For I did not come to judge the world, but to save it. [48] There is a judge for those who reject me and do not accept my words; that very word which I spoke will condemn them at the last day. [49] For I did not speak of my own accord, but the Father who sent me commanded me what to say and how to say it. [50] I know that his command leads to eternal life. So whatever I say is just what the Father has told me to say."

Jesus Washes His Disciples' Feet

13 It was just before the Passover Feast. Jesus knew that the time had come for him to leave this world and go to the Father. Having loved his own who were in the world, he now showed them the full extent of his love.[a]

[2] The evening meal was being served, and the devil had already prompted Judas Iscariot, son of Simon, to betray Jesus. [3] Jesus knew that the Father had put all things under his power, and that he had come from God and was returning to God; [4] so he got up from the meal, took off his outer clothing, and wrapped a towel round his waist. [5] After that, he poured water into a basin and began to wash his disciples' feet, drying them with the towel that was wrapped round him.

[6] He came to Simon Peter, who said to him, "Lord, are you going to wash my feet?"

[7] Jesus replied, "You do not realise now what I am doing, but later you will understand."

[8] "No," said Peter, "you shall never wash my feet."

Jesus answered, "Unless I wash you, you have no part with me."

[9] "Then, Lord," Simon Peter replied, "not just my feet but my hands and my head as well!"

[10] Jesus answered, "Those who have had a bath need only to wash their feet; their whole body is clean. And you are clean, though not every one of you." [11] For he knew who was going to betray him, and that was why he said not every one was clean.

[12] When he had finished washing their feet, he put on his clothes and returned to his place. "Do you understand what I have done for you?" he asked them. [13] "You call me 'Teacher' and 'Lord', and rightly so, for that is what I am. [14] Now that I, your Lord and Teacher, have washed your feet, you also should wash one another's feet. [15] I have set you an example that you should do as I have done for you. [16] I tell you the truth, servants are not greater than their masters, nor are messengers greater than those who sent them. [17] Now that you know these things, you will be blessed if you do them.

Jesus Predicts His Betrayal

[18] "I am not referring to all of you; I know those I have chosen. But this is to fulfil the scripture: 'He who shares my bread has lifted up his heel against me.'[b]

[19] "I am telling you now before it happens, so that when it does happen you will believe that I am He. [20] I tell you the truth, whoever accepts anyone I send accepts me; and whoever accepts me accepts the one who sent me."

[21] After he had said this, Jesus was troubled in spirit and testified, "I tell you the truth, one of you is going to betray me."

[22] His disciples stared at one another, at a loss to know which of them he meant. [23] One of them, the disciple whom Jesus loved, was reclining next to him. [24] Simon Peter motioned to this disciple and said, "Ask him which one he means."

---

[a]1 Or *he loved them to the last*   [b]18 Psalm 41:9

25 Leaning back against Jesus, he asked him, "Lord, who is it?"

26 Jesus answered, "It is the one to whom I will give this piece of bread when I have dipped it in the dish." Then, dipping the piece of bread, he gave it to Judas Iscariot, son of Simon. 27 As soon as Judas took the bread, Satan entered into him.

"What you are about to do, do quickly," Jesus told him, 28 but no-one at the meal understood why Jesus said this to him. 29 Since Judas had charge of the money, some thought Jesus was telling him to buy what was needed for the Feast, or to give something to the poor. 30 As soon as Judas had taken the bread, he went out. And it was night.

Jesus Predicts Peter's Denial

31 When he was gone, Jesus said, "Now is the Son of Man glorified and God is glorified in him. 32 If God is glorified in him,^{c} God will glorify the Son in himself, and will glorify him at once.

33 "My children, I will be with you only a little longer. You will look for me, and just as I told the Jews, so I tell you now: Where I am going, you cannot come.

34 "A new command I give you: Love one another. As I have loved you, so you must love one another. 35 By this everyone will know that you are my disciples, if you love one another."

36 Simon Peter asked him, "Lord, where are you going?"

Jesus replied, "Where I am going, you cannot follow now, but you will follow later."

37 Peter asked, "Lord, why can't I follow you now? I will lay down my life for you."

38 Then Jesus answered, "Will you really lay down your life for me? I tell you the truth, before the cock crows, you will disown me three times!

Jesus Comforts His Disciples

14 "Do not let your hearts be troubled. Trust in God;^{a} trust also in me. 2 In my Father's house are many rooms; if it were not so, I would have told you. I am going there to prepare a place for you. 3 And if I go and prepare a place for you, I will come back and take you to be with me that you also may be where I am. 4 You know the way to the place where I am going."

Jesus the Way to the Father

5 Thomas said to him, "Lord, we don't know where you are going, so how can we know the way?"

6 Jesus answered, "I am the way and the truth and the life. No-one comes to the Father except through me. 7 If you really knew me, you would know^b my Father as well. From now on, you do know him and have seen him."

8 Philip said, "Lord, show us the Father and that will be enough for us."

9 Jesus answered: "Don't you know me, Philip, even after I have been among you such a long time? Anyone who has seen me has seen the Father. How can you say, 'Show us the Father'? 10 Don't you believe that I am in the Father, and that the Father is in me? The words I say to you are not just my own. Rather, it is the Father, living in me, who is doing his work. 11 Believe me when I say that I am in the Father and the Father is in me; or at least believe on the evidence of the miracles themselves. 12 I tell you the truth, all who have faith in me will do what I have been doing, and they will do even greater things than these, because I am going to the Father. 13 And I will do whatever you ask in my name, so that the Son may bring glory to the Father. 14 You may ask me for anything in my name, and I will do it.

Jesus Promises the Holy Spirit

15 "If you love me, you will obey what I command. 16 And I will ask the Father, and he will give you another Counsellor to be with you for ever—17 the Spirit of truth. The world cannot accept him, because it neither sees him nor knows him. But you know him, for he lives with you

---

^{c}32 Many early manuscripts do not have *If God is glorified in him.* ^{a}1 Or *You trust in God*
^{b}7 Some early manuscripts *If you really have known me, you will know* ^{c}17 Some early manuscripts *and is*

and will be*c* in you. [18] I will not leave you as orphans; I will come to you. [19] Before long, the world will not see me any more, but you will see me. Because I live, you also will live. [20] On that day you will realise that I am in my Father, and you are in me, and I am in you. [21] Those who have my commands and obey them are the ones who love me. Those who love me will be loved by my Father, and I too will love them and show myself to them.''

[22] Then Judas (not Judas Iscariot) said, ''But, Lord, why do you intend to show yourself to us and not to the world?''

[23] Jesus replied, ''Those who love me will obey my teaching. My Father will love them, and we will come to them and make our home with them. [24] Anyone who does not love me will not obey my teaching. These words you hear are not my own; they belong to the Father who sent me.

[25] ''All this I have spoken while still with you. [26] But the Counsellor, the Holy Spirit, whom the Father will send in my name, will teach you all things and will remind you of everything I have said to you. [27] Peace I leave with you; my peace I give you. I do not give to you as the world gives. Do not let your hearts be troubled and do not be afraid.

[28] ''You heard me say, 'I am going away and I am coming back to you.' If you loved me, you would be glad that I am going to the Father, for the Father is greater than I. [29] I have told you now before it happens, so that when it does happen you will believe. [30] I will not speak with you much longer, for the prince of this world is coming. He has no hold on me, [31] but the world must learn that I love the Father and that I do exactly what my Father has commanded me.

''Come now; let us leave.''

The Vine and the Branches

15 ''I am the true vine, and my Father is the gardener. [2] He cuts off every branch in me that bears no fruit, while every branch that does bear fruit he prunes*a* so that it will be even more fruitful. [3] You are already clean because of the word I have spoken to you. [4] Remain in me, and I will remain in you. No branch can bear fruit by itself; it must remain in the vine. Neither can you bear fruit unless you remain in me.

[5] ''I am the vine; you are the branches. If you remain in me and I you, you will bear much fruit; apart from me you can do nothing. [6] If you do not remain in me, you are like a branch that is thrown away and withers; such branches are picked up, thrown into the fire and burned. [7] If you remain in me and my words remain in you, ask whatever you wish, and it will be given you. [8] This is to my Father's glory, that you bear much fruit, showing yourselves to be my disciples.

[9] ''As the Father has loved me, so have I loved you. Now remain in my love. [10] If you obey my commands, you will remain in my love, just as I have obeyed my Father's commands and remain in his love. [11] I have told you this so that my joy may be in you and that your joy may be complete. [12] My command is this: Love each other as I have loved you. [13] Greater love has no-one than this, to lay down one's life for one's friends. [14] You are my friends if you do what I command. [15] I no longer call you servants, because servants do not know their master's business. Instead, I have called you friends, for everything that I learned from my Father I have made known to you. [16] You did not choose me, but I chose you and appointed you to go and bear fruit—fruit that will last. Then the Father will give you whatever you ask in my name. [17] This is my command: Love each other.

The World Hates the Disciples

[18] ''If the world hates you, keep in mind that it hated me first. [19] If you belonged to the world, it would love you as its own. As it is, you do not belong to the world, but I have chosen you out of the world. That is why the world hates you. [20] Remember the words I spoke to you: 'Servants are not greater than their masters.'*b*

---

*a*2 The Greek for *prunes* also means *cleans.*   *b*20 John 13:16

If they persecuted me, they will persecute you also. If they obeyed my teaching, they will obey yours also. 21 They will treat you this way because of my name, for they do not know the One who sent me. 22 If I had not come and spoken to them, they would not be guilty of sin. Now, however, they have no excuse for their sin. 23 Those who hate me hate my Father as well. 24 If I had not done among them what no-one else did, they would not be guilty of sin. But now they have seen these miracles, and yet they have hated both me and my Father. 25 But this is to fulfil what is written in their Law: 'They hated me without reason.'c

26 "When the Counsellor comes, whom I will send to you from the Father, the Spirit of truth who goes out from the Father, he will testify about me. 27 And you also must testify, for you have been with me from the beginning.

16 "All this I have told you so that you will not go astray. 2 They will put you out of the synagogue; in fact, a time is coming when those who kill you will think they are offering a service to God. 3 They will do such things because they have not known the Father or me. 4 I have told you this, so that when the time comes you will remember that I warned you. I did not tell you this at first because I was with you.

The Work of the Holy Spirit

5 "Now I am going to him who sent me, yet none of you asks me, 'Where are you going?' 6 Because I have said these things, you are filled with grief. 7 But I tell you the truth: It is for your good that I am going away. Unless I go away, the Counsellor will not come to you; but if I go, I will send him to you. 8 When he comes, he will convict the world of guilta in regard to sin and righteousness and judgment: 9 in regard to sin, because people do not believe in me; 10 in regard to righteousness, because I am going to the Father, where you can see me no longer; 11 and in regard to judgment, because the prince of this world now stands condemned.

12 "I have much more to say to you, more than you can now bear. 13 But when he, the Spirit of truth, comes, he will guide you into all truth. He will not speak on his own; he will speak only what he hears, and he will tell you what is yet to come. 14 He will bring glory to me by taking from what is mine and making it known to you. 15 All that belongs to the Father is mine. That is why I said the Spirit will take from what is mine and make it known to you.

16 "In a little while you will see me no more, and then after a little while you will see me."

The Disciples' Grief Will Turn to Joy

17 Some of his disciples said to one another, "What does he mean by saying, 'In a little while you will see me no more, and then after a little while you will see me,' and 'Because I am going to the Father'?" 18 They kept asking, "What does he mean by 'a little while'? We don't understand what he is saying."

19 Jesus saw that they wanted to ask him about this, so he said to them, "Are you asking one another what I meant when I said, 'In a little while you will see me no more, and then after a little while you will see me'? 20 I tell you the truth, you will weep and mourn while the world rejoices. You will grieve, but your grief will turn to joy. 21 A woman giving birth to a child has pain because her time has come; but when her baby is born she forgets the anguish because of her joy that a child is born into the world. 22 So with you: Now is your time of grief, but I will see you again and you will rejoice, and no-one will take away your joy. 23 In that day you will no longer ask me anything. I tell you the truth, my Father will give you whatever you ask in my name. 24 Until now you have not asked for anything in my name. Ask and you will receive, and your joy will be complete.

25 "Though I have been speaking figuratively, a time is coming when I will no longer use this kind of language but will tell you plainly about my Father. 26 In that

c25 Psalms 35:19; 69:4   a8 Or *will expose the guilt of the world* day you will ask in my name. I am not saying that I will ask the Father on your behalf. 27 No, the Father himself loves you because you have loved me and have believed that I came from God. 28 I came from the Father and entered the world; now I am leaving the world and going back to the Father."

29 Then Jesus' disciples said, "Now you are speaking clearly and without figures of speech. 30 Now we can see that you know all things and that you do not even need to have anyone ask you questions. This makes us believe that you came from God."

31 "You believe at last!"*b* Jesus answered. 32 "But a time is coming, and has come, when you will be scattered, each to your own home. You will leave me all alone. Yet I am not alone, for my Father is with me.

33 "I have told you these things, so that in me you may have peace. In this world you will have trouble. But take heart! I have overcome the world."

Jesus Prays for Himself

17 After Jesus said this, he looked towards heaven and prayed:

"Father, the time has come. Glorify your Son, that your Son may glorify you. 2 For you granted him authority over all people that he might give eternal life to all those you have given him. 3 Now this is eternal life: that they may know you, the only true God, and Jesus Christ, whom you have sent. 4 I have brought you glory on earth by completing the work you gave me to do. 5 And now, Father, glorify me in your presence with the glory I had with you before the world began.

Jesus Prays for His Disciples

6 "I have revealed you*a* to those whom you gave me out of the world. They were yours; you gave them to me and they have obeyed your word. 7 Now they know that

everything you have given me comes from you. 8 For I gave them the words you gave me and they accepted them. They knew with certainty that I came from you, and they believed that you sent me. 9 I pray for them. I am not praying for the world, but for those you have given me, for they are yours. 10 All I have is yours, and all you have is mine. And glory has come to me through them. 11 I will remain in the world no longer, but they are still in the world, and I am coming to you. Holy Father, protect them by the power of your name—the name you gave me—so that they may be one as we are one. 12 While I was with them, I protected them and kept them safe by that name you gave me. None has been lost except the one doomed to destruction so that Scripture would be fulfilled.

13 "I am coming to you now, but I say these things while I am still in the world, so that they may have the full measure of my joy within them. 14 I have given them your word and the world has hated them, for they are not of the world any more than I am of the world. 15 My prayer is not that you take them out of the world but that you protect them from the evil one. 16 They are not of the world, even as I am not of it. 17 Sanctify*b* them by the truth; your word is truth. 18 As you sent me into the world, I have sent them into the world. 19 For them I sanctify myself, that they too may be truly sanctified.

Jesus Prays for All Believers

20 "My prayer is not for them alone. I pray also for those who will believe in me through their message, 21 that all of them may be one, Father, just as you are in me and I am in you. May they also be in us so that the world may believe that you have sent me. 22 I have given them the glory that you gave me, that they may be one as we are one: 23 I in them and you in me. May they be brought to complete unity to let the world know that you sent me and have loved them even as you have loved me.

24 "Father, I want those you have given

*b*31 Or *"Do you now believe?"*　　*a*6 Greek *your name*; also in verse 26
*b*17 Greek *hagiazo* (*set apart for sacred use* or *make holy*); also in verse 19

me to be with me where I am, and to see my glory, the glory you have given me because you loved me before the creation of the world.

25 "Righteous Father, though the world does not know you, I know you, and they know that you have sent me. 26 I have made you known to them, and will continue to make you known in order that the love you have for me may be in them and that I myself may be in them."

Jesus Arrested

18 When he had finished praying, Jesus left with his disciples and crossed the Kidron Valley. On the other side there was an olive grove, and he and his disciples went into it.

2 Now Judas, who betrayed him, knew the place, because Jesus had often met there with his disciples. 3 So Judas came to the grove, guiding a detachment of soldiers and some officials from the chief priests and Pharisees. They were carrying torches, lanterns and weapons.

4 Jesus, knowing all that was going to happen to him, went out and asked them, "Who is it you want?"

5 "Jesus of Nazareth," they replied.

"I am he," Jesus said. (And Judas the traitor was standing there with them.) 6 When Jesus said, "I am he," they drew back and fell to the ground.

7 Again he asked them, "Who is it you want?"

And they said, "Jesus of Nazareth."

8 "I told you that I am he," Jesus answered. "If you are looking for me, then let these men go." 9 This happened so that the words he had spoken would be fulfilled: "I have not lost one of those you gave me."*a*

10 Then Simon Peter, who had a sword, drew it and struck the high priest's servant, cutting off his right ear. (The servant's name was Malchus.)

11 Jesus commanded Peter, "Put your sword away! Shall I not drink the cup the Father has given me?"

Jesus Taken to Annas

12 Then the detachment of soldiers with its commander and the Jewish officials arrested Jesus. They bound him 13 and brought him first to Annas, who was the father-in-law of Caiaphas, the high priest that year. 14 Caiaphas was the one who had advised the Jews that it would be good if one person died for the people.

Peter's First Denial

15 Simon Peter and another disciple were following Jesus. Because this disciple was known to the high priest, he went with Jesus into the high priest's courtyard, 16 but Peter had to wait outside at the door. The other disciple, who was known to the high priest, came back, spoke to the woman on duty there and brought Peter in.

17 "You are not one of his disciples, are you?" the woman at the door asked Peter.

He replied, "I am not."

18 It was cold, and the servants and officials stood round a fire they had made to keep warm. Peter also was standing with them, warming himself.

The High Priest Questions Jesus

19 Meanwhile, the high priest questioned Jesus about his disciples and his teaching.

20 "I have spoken openly to the world," Jesus replied. "I always taught in synagogues or at the temple, where all the Jews come together. I said nothing in secret. 21 Why question me? Ask those who heard me. Surely they know what I said."

22 When Jesus said this, one of the officials near by struck him in the face. "Is this the way you answer the high priest?" he demanded.

23 "If I said something wrong," Jesus replied, "testify as to what is wrong. But if I spoke the truth, why did you strike me?" 24 Then Annas sent him, still bound, to Caiaphas the high priest.*b*

*a*9 John 6:39 *b*24 Or (Now Annas had sent him, still bound, to Caiaphas the high priest.)

Peter's Second and Third Denials

25 As Simon Peter stood warming himself, he was asked, "You are not one of his disciples, are you?"

He denied it, saying, "I am not."

26 One of the high priest's servants, a relative of the man whose ear Peter had cut off, challenged him, "Didn't I see you with him in the olive grove?" 27 Again Peter denied it, and at that moment a cock began to crow.

Jesus Before Pilate

28 Then the Jews led Jesus from Caiaphas to the palace of the Roman governor. By now it was early morning, and to avoid ceremonial uncleanness the Jews did not enter the palace; they wanted to be able to eat the Passover. 29 So Pilate came out to them and asked, "What charges are you bringing against this man?"

30 "If he were not a criminal," they replied, "we would not have handed him over to you."

31 Pilate said, "Take him yourselves and judge him by your own law."

"But we have no right to execute anyone," the Jews objected. 32 This happened so that the words Jesus had spoken indicating the kind of death he was going to die would be fulfilled.

33 Pilate then went back inside the palace, summoned Jesus and asked him, "Are you the king of the Jews?"

34 "Is that your own idea," Jesus asked, "or did others talk to you about me?"

35 "Am I a Jew?" Pilate replied. "It was your people and your chief priests who handed you over to me. What is it you have done?"

36 Jesus said, "My kingdom is not of this world. If it were, my servants would fight to prevent my arrest by the Jews. But now my kingdom is from another place."

37 "You are a king, then!" said Pilate.

Jesus answered, "You are right in saying I am a king. In fact, for this reason I was born, and for this I came into the world, to testify to the truth. Everyone on the side of truth listens to me."

38 "What is truth?" Pilate asked. With this he went out again to the Jews and said, "I find no basis for a charge against him. 39 But it is your custom for me to release to you one prisoner at the time of the Passover. Do you want me to release 'the king of the Jews'?"

40 They shouted back, "No, not him! Give us Barabbas!" Now Barabbas had taken part in a rebellion.

Jesus Sentenced to be Crucified

19 Then Pilate took Jesus and had him flogged. 2 The soldiers twisted together a crown of thorns and put it on his head. They clothed him in a purple robe 3 and went up to him again and again, saying, "Hail, king of the Jews!" And they struck him in the face.

4 Once more Pilate came out and said to the Jews, "Look, I am bringing him out to you to let you know that I find no basis for a charge against him." 5 When Jesus came out wearing the crown of thorns and the purple robe, Pilate said to them, "Here is the man!"

6 As soon as the chief priests and their officials saw him, they shouted, "Crucify! Crucify!"

But Pilate answered, "You take him and crucify him. As for me, I find no basis for a charge against him."

7 The Jews insisted, "We have a law, and according to that law he must die, because he claimed to be the Son of God."

8 When Pilate heard this, he was even more afraid, 9 and he went back inside the palace. "Where do you come from?" he asked Jesus, but Jesus gave him no answer. 10 "Do you refuse to speak to me?" Pilate said. "Don't you realise I have power either to free you or to crucify you?"

11 Jesus answered, "You would have no power over me if it were not given to you from above. Therefore the one who handed me over to you is guilty of a greater sin."

12 From then on, Pilate tried to set Jesus free, but the Jews kept shouting, "If you let this man go, you are no friend of

Caesar. Anyone who claims to be a king opposes Caesar."

13 When Pilate heard this, he brought Jesus out and sat down on the judge's seat at a place known as the Stone Pavement (which in Aramaic is Gabbatha). 14 It was the day of Preparation of Passover Week, about the sixth hour.

"Here is your king," Pilate said to the Jews.

15 But they shouted, "Take him away! Take him away! Crucify him!"

"Shall I crucify your king?" Pilate asked.

"We have no king but Caesar," the chief priests answered.

16 Finally Pilate handed him over to them to be crucified.

The Crucifixion

So the soldiers took charge of Jesus. 17 Carrying his own cross, he went out to the place of the Skull (which in Aramaic is called Golgotha). 18 Here they crucified him, and with him two others—one on each side and Jesus in the middle.

19 Pilate had a notice prepared and fastened to the cross. It read: JESUS OF NAZARETH, THE KING OF THE JEWS. 20 Many of the Jews read this sign, for the place where Jesus was crucified was near the city, and the sign was written in Aramaic, Latin and Greek. 21 The chief priests of the Jews protested to Pilate, "Do not write 'The King of the Jews', but that this man claimed to be king of the Jews."

22 Pilate answered, "What I have written, I have written."

23 When the soldiers crucified Jesus, they took his clothes, dividing them into four shares, one for each of them, with the undergarment remaining. This garment was seamless, woven in one piece from top to bottom.

24 "Let's not tear it," they said to one another. "Let's decide by lot who will get it."

This happened that the scripture might be fulfilled which said,

"They divided my garments among them
and cast lots for my clothing."[a]

So this is what the soldiers did.

25 Near the cross of Jesus stood his mother, his mother's sister, Mary the wife of Clopas, and Mary Magdalene. 26 When Jesus saw his mother there, and the disciple whom he loved standing near by, he said to his mother, "Dear woman, here is your son," 27 and to the disciple, "Here is your mother." From that time on, this disciple took her into his home.

The Death of Jesus

28 Later, knowing that all was now completed, and so that the Scripture would be fulfilled, Jesus said, "I am thirsty." 29 A jar of wine vinegar was there, so they soaked a sponge in it, put the sponge on a stalk of the hyssop plant, and lifted it to Jesus' lips. 30 When he had received the drink, Jesus said, "It is finished." With that, he bowed his head and gave up his spirit.

31 Now it was the day of Preparation, and the next day was to be a special Sabbath. Because the Jews did not want the bodies left on the crosses during the Sabbath, they asked Pilate to have the legs broken and the bodies taken down. 32 The soldiers therefore came and broke the legs of the first man who had been crucified with Jesus, and then those of the other. 33 But when they came to Jesus and found that he was already dead, they did not break his legs. 34 Instead, one of the soldiers pierced Jesus' side with a spear, bringing a sudden flow of blood and water. 35 The man who saw it has given testimony, and his testimony is true. He knows that he tells the truth, and he testifies so that you also may believe. 36 These things happened so that the scripture would be fulfilled: "Not one of his bones will be broken,"[b] 37 and, as another scripture says, "They will look on the one they have pierced."[c]

---

[a]24 Psalm 22:18   [b]36 Exodus 12:46; Num. 9:12; Psalm 34:20   [c]37 Zech. 12:10

The Burial of Jesus

38 Later, Joseph of Arimathea asked Pilate for the body of Jesus. Now Joseph was a disciple of Jesus, but secretly because he feared the Jews. With Pilate's permission, he came and took the body away. 39 He was accompanied by Nicodemus, the man who earlier had visited Jesus at night. Nicodemus brought a mixture of myrrh and aloes, about seventy-five pounds.*d* 40 Taking Jesus' body, the two of them wrapped it, with the spices, in strips of linen. This was in accordance with Jewish burial customs. 41 At the place where Jesus was crucified, there was a garden, and in the garden a new tomb, in which no-one had ever been laid. 42 Because it was the Jewish day of Preparation and since the tomb was near by, they laid Jesus there.

The Empty Tomb

20 Early on the first day of the week, while it was still dark, Mary Magdalene went to the tomb and saw that the stone had been removed from the entrance. 2 So she came running to Simon Peter and the other disciple, the one Jesus loved, and said, "They have taken the Lord out of the tomb, and we don't know where they have put him!"

3 So Peter and the other disciple started for the tomb. 4 Both were running, but the other disciple outran Peter and reached the tomb first. 5 He bent over and looked in at the strips of linen lying there but did not go in. 6 Then Simon Peter, who was behind him, arrived and went into the tomb. He saw the strips of linen lying there, 7 as well as the burial cloth that had been around Jesus' head. The cloth was folded up by itself, separate from the linen. 8 Finally the other disciple, who had reached the tomb first, also went inside. He saw and believed. 9 (They still did not understand from Scripture that Jesus had to rise from the dead.)

Jesus Appears to Mary Magdalene

10 Then the disciples went back to their homes, 11 but Mary stood outside the tomb crying. As she wept, she bent over to look into the tomb 12 and saw two angels in white, seated where Jesus' body had been, one at the head and the other at the foot.

13 They asked her, "Woman, why are you crying?"

"They have taken my Lord away," she said, "and I don't know where they have put him." 14 At this, she turned round and saw Jesus standing there, but she did not realise that it was Jesus.

15 "Woman," he said, "why are you crying? Who is it you are looking for?"

Thinking he was the gardener, she said, "Sir, if you have carried him away, tell me where you have put him, and I will get him."

16 Jesus said to her, "Mary."

She turned towards him and cried out in Aramaic, "Rabboni!" (which means Teacher).

17 Jesus said, "Do not hold on to me, for I have not yet returned to the Father. Go instead to my brothers and tell them, 'I am returning to my Father and your Father, to my God and your God.' "

18 Mary Magdalene went to the disciples with the news: "I have seen the Lord!" And she told them that he had said these things to her.

Jesus Appears to His Disciples

19 On the evening of that first day of the week, when the disciples were together, with the doors locked for fear of the Jews, Jesus came and stood among them and said, "Peace be with you!" 20 After he said this, he showed them his hands and side. The disciples were overjoyed when they saw the Lord.

21 Again Jesus said, "Peace be with you! As the Father has sent me, I am sending you." 22 And with that he breathed on them and said, "Receive the Holy Spirit. 23 If you forgive the sins of anyone, their

*d*39 Greek *a hundred litrai* (about 34 kilograms)

sins are forgiven; if you do not forgive them, they are not forgiven."

Jesus Appears to Thomas

24 Now Thomas (called Didymus), one of the Twelve, was not with the disciples when Jesus came. 25 So the other disciples told him, "We have seen the Lord!"

But he said to them, "Unless I see the nail marks in his hands and put my finger where the nails were, and put my hand into his side, I will not believe it."

26 A week later his disciples were in the house again, and Thomas was with them. Though the doors were locked, Jesus came and stood among them and said, "Peace be with you!" 27 Then he said to Thomas, "Put your finger here; see my hands. Reach out your hand and put it into my side. Stop doubting and believe."

28 Thomas said to him, "My Lord and my God!"

29 Then Jesus told him, "Because you have seen me, you have believed; blessed are those who have not seen and yet have believed."

30 Jesus did many other miraculous signs in the presence of his disciples, which are not recorded in this book. 31 But these are written that you may[a] believe that Jesus is the Christ, the Son of God, and that by believing you may have life in his name.

Jesus and the Miraculous Catch of Fish

21 Afterwards Jesus appeared again to his disciples, by the Sea of Tiberias.[a] It happened this way: 2 Simon Peter, Thomas (called Didymus), Nathanael from Cana in Galilee, the sons of Zebedee, and two other disciples were together. 3 "I'm going out to fish," Simon Peter told them, and they said, "We'll go with you." So they went out and got into the boat, but that night they caught nothing.

4 Early in the morning, Jesus stood on the shore, but the disciples did not realise that it was Jesus.

5 He called out to them, "Friends, haven't you any fish?"

"No," they answered.

6 He said, "Throw your net on the right side of the boat and you will find some." When they did, they were unable to haul the net in because of the large number of fish.

7 Then the disciple whom Jesus loved said to Peter, "It is the Lord!" As soon as Simon Peter heard him say, "It is the Lord," he wrapped his outer garment around him (for he had taken it off) and jumped into the water. 8 The other disciples followed in the boat, towing the net full of fish, for they were not far from shore, about a hundred yards.[b] 9 When they landed, they saw a fire of burning coals there with fish on it, and some bread.

10 Jesus said to them, "Bring some of the fish you have just caught."

11 Simon Peter climbed aboard and dragged the net ashore. It was full of large fish, 153, but even with so many the net was not torn. 12 Jesus said to them, "Come and have breakfast." None of the disciples dared ask him, "Who are you?" They knew it was the Lord. 13 Jesus came, took the bread and gave it to them, and did the same with the fish. 14 This was now the third time Jesus appeared to his disciples after he was raised from the dead.

Jesus Reinstates Peter

15 When they had finished eating, Jesus said to Simon Peter, "Simon son of John, do you truly love me more than these?"

"Yes, Lord," he said, "you know that I love you."

Jesus said, "Feed my lambs."

16 Again Jesus said, "Simon son of John, do you truly love me?"

He answered, "Yes, Lord, you know that I love you."

Jesus said, "Take care of my sheep."

17 The third time he said to him, "Simon son of John, do you love me?"

---

[a]31 Some manuscripts *may continue to*   [a]1 That is, Sea of Galilee
[b]8 Greek *about two hundred cubits* (about 90 metres)

Peter was hurt because Jesus asked him the third time, "Do you love me?" He said, "Lord, you know all things; you know that I love you."

Jesus said, "Feed my sheep. 18 I tell you the truth, when you were younger you dressed yourself and went where you wanted; but when you are old you will stretch out your hands, and someone else will dress you and lead you where you do not want to go." 19 Jesus said this to indicate the kind of death by which Peter would glorify God. Then he said to him, "Follow me!"

20 Peter turned and saw that the disciple whom Jesus loved was following them. (This was the one who had leaned back against Jesus at the supper and had said, "Lord, who is going to betray you?")

21 When Peter saw him, he asked, "Lord, what about him?"

22 Jesus answered, "If I want him to remain alive until I return, what is that to you? You must follow me." 23 Because of this, the rumour spread among the believers that this disciple would not die. But Jesus did not say that he would not die; he only said, "If I want him to remain alive until I return, what is that to you?"

24 This is the disciple who testifies to these things and who wrote them down. We know that his testimony is true.

25 Jesus did many other things as well. If every one of them were written down, I suppose that even the whole world would not have room for the books that would be written.

Acts

Jesus Taken Up Into Heaven

1 In my former book, Theophilus, I wrote about all that Jesus began to do and to teach ² until the day he was taken up to heaven, after giving instructions through the Holy Spirit to the apostles he had chosen. ³ After his suffering, he showed himself to them and gave many convincing proofs that he was alive. He appeared to them over a period of forty days and spoke about the kingdom of God. ⁴ On one occasion, while he was eating with them, he gave them this command: "Do not leave Jerusalem, but wait for the gift my Father promised, which you have heard me speak about. ⁵ For John baptised with*ᵃ* water, but in a few days you will be baptised with the Holy Spirit."

⁶ So when they met together, they asked him, "Lord, are you at this time going to restore the kingdom to Israel?"

⁷ He said to them: "It is not for you to know the times or dates the Father has set by his own authority. ⁸ But you will receive power when the Holy Spirit comes on you; and you will be my witnesses in Jerusalem, and in all Judea and Samaria, and to the ends of the earth."

⁹ After he said this, he was taken up before their very eyes, and a cloud hid him from their sight.

¹⁰ They were looking intently up into the sky as he was going, when suddenly two men dressed in white stood beside them. ¹¹ "You Galileans," they said, "why do you stand here looking into the sky? This same Jesus, who has been taken from you into heaven, will come back in the same way you have seen him go into heaven."

Matthias Chosen to Replace Judas

¹² Then they returned to Jerusalem from the hill called the Mount of Olives, a Sabbath day's walk*ᵇ* from the city. ¹³ When they arrived, they went upstairs to the room where they were staying. Those present were Peter, John, James and Andrew; Philip and Thomas, Bartholomew and Matthew; James son of Alphaeus and Simon the Zealot, and Judas son of James. ¹⁴ They all joined together constantly in prayer, along with the women and Mary the mother of Jesus, and with his brothers.

¹⁵ In those days Peter stood up among the believers*ᶜ* (a group numbering about a hundred and twenty) ¹⁶ and said, "Brothers and sisters, the Scripture had to be fulfilled which the Holy Spirit spoke long ago through the mouth of David concerning Judas, who served as guide for those who arrested Jesus—¹⁷ he was one of our number and shared in this ministry."

¹⁸ (With the reward he got for his wickedness, Judas bought a field; there he fell headlong, his body burst open and all his intestines spilled out. ¹⁹ Everyone in Jerusalem heard about this, so they called that field in their language Akeldama, that is, Field of Blood.)

²⁰ "For," said Peter, "it is written in the Book of Psalms,

*ᵃ*5 Or *in*   *ᵇ*12 That is, about ¾ of a mile (about 1,100 metres)   *ᶜ*15 Greek *brothers*

" 'May his place be deserted;
  let there be no-one to dwell in it,'[d]

and,

" 'May another take his place of
  leadership.'[e]

[21] Therefore it is necessary to choose one of those who have been with us the whole time the Lord Jesus went in and out among us, [22] beginning from John's baptism to the time when Jesus was taken up from us. For one of these must become a witness with us of his resurrection."

[23] So they proposed two names: Joseph called Barsabbas (also known as Justus) and Matthias. [24] Then they prayed, "Lord, you know everyone's heart. Show us which of these two you have chosen [25] to take over this apostolic ministry, which Judas left to go where he belongs." [26] Then they cast lots, and the lot fell to Matthias; so he was added to the eleven apostles.

The Holy Spirit Comes at Pentecost

2 When the day of Pentecost came, they were all together in one place. [2] Suddenly a sound like the blowing of a violent wind came from heaven and filled the whole house where they were sitting. [3] They saw what seemed to be tongues of fire that separated and came to rest on each of them. [4] All of them were filled with the Holy Spirit and began to speak in other tongues[a] as the Spirit enabled them.

[5] Now there were staying in Jerusalem God-fearing Jews from every nation under heaven. [6] When they heard this sound, a crowd came together in bewilderment, because each one heard them speaking in his or her own language. [7] Utterly amazed, they asked: "Are not all these who are speaking Galileans? [8] Then how is it that each of us hears them in our own native language? [9] Parthians, Medes and Elamites; residents of Mesopotamia, Judea and Cappadocia, Pontus and Asia, [10] Phrygia and Pamphylia, Egypt and the parts of Libya near Cyrene;

visitors from Rome [11] (both Jews and converts to Judaism); Cretans and Arabs—we hear them declaring the wonders of God in our own tongues!" [12] Amazed and perplexed, they asked one another, "What does this mean?" [13] Some, however, made fun of them and said, "They have had too much wine."[b]

Peter Addresses the Crowd

[14] Then Peter stood up with the Eleven, raised his voice and addressed the crowd: "Fellow Jews and all of you who live in Jerusalem, let me explain this to you; listen carefully to what I say. [15] These people are not drunk, as you suppose. It's only nine in the morning! [16] No, this is what was spoken by the prophet Joel:

[17] " 'In the last days, God says,
      I will pour out my Spirit on all
        people.
    Your sons and daughters will
        prophesy,
      your young men will see visions,
      your old men will dream dreams.
[18] Even on my servants, both men and
        women,
      I will pour out my Spirit in those
        days,
      and they will prophesy.
[19] I will show wonders in the heaven
        above
      and signs on the earth below,
      blood and fire and billows of
        smoke.
[20] The sun will be turned to darkness
      and the moon to blood
      before the coming of the great and
        glorious day of the Lord.
[21] And everyone who calls
      on the name of the Lord will be
        saved.'[c]

[22] "People of Israel, listen to this: Jesus of Nazareth was a man accredited by God to you by miracles, wonders and signs, which God did among you through him, as you yourselves know. [23] This man was handed over to you by God's set purpose and foreknowledge; and you, with the

---

[d]20 Psalm 69:25   [e]20 Psalm 109:8   [a]4 Or *languages*; also in verse 11   [b]13 Or *sweet wine*
[c]21 Joel 2:28–32

help of wicked people,*d* put him to death by nailing him to the cross. 24 But God raised him from the dead, freeing him from the agony of death, because it was impossible for death to keep its hold on him. 25 David said about him:

" 'I saw the Lord always before me.
        Because he is at my right hand,
        I will not be shaken.
26 Therefore my heart is glad and my
        tongue rejoices;
    my body also will live in hope,
27 because you will not abandon me to
        the grave,
    nor will you let your Holy One see
        decay.
28 You have made known to me the
        paths of life;
    you will fill me with joy in your
        presence.'*e*

29 "Brothers and sisters, I can tell you confidently that the patriarch David died and was buried, and his tomb is here to this day. 30 But he was a prophet and knew that God had promised him on oath that he would place one of his descendants on his throne. 31 Seeing what was ahead, he spoke of the resurrection of the Christ,*f* that he was not abandoned to the grave, nor did his body see decay. 32 God has raised this Jesus to life, and we are all witnesses of the fact. 33 Exalted to the right hand of God, he has received from the Father the promised Holy Spirit and has poured out what you now see and hear. 34 For David did not ascend to heaven, and yet he said,

" 'The Lord said to my Lord:
    "Sit at my right hand
35 until I make your enemies
    a footstool for your feet." '*g*

36 "Therefore let all Israel be assured of this: God has made this Jesus, whom you crucified, both Lord and Christ."

37 When the people heard this, they were cut to the heart and said to Peter and the other apostles, "Brothers, what shall we do?"

38 Peter replied, "Repent and be baptised, every one of you, in the name of Jesus Christ for the forgiveness of your sins. And you will receive the gift of the Holy Spirit. 39 The promise is for you and your children and for all who are far off— for all whom the Lord our God will call."

40 With many other words he warned them; and he pleaded with them, "Save yourselves from this corrupt generation." 41 Those who accepted his message were baptised, and about three thousand were added to their number that day.

The Fellowship of the Believers

42 They devoted themselves to the apostles' teaching and to the fellowship, to the breaking of bread and to prayer. 43 Everyone was filled with awe, and many wonders and miraculous signs were done by the apostles. 44 All the believers were together and had everything in common. 45 Selling their possessions and goods, they gave to anyone who had need. 46 Every day they continued to meet together in the temple courts. They broke bread in their homes and ate together with glad and sincere hearts, 47 praising God and enjoying the favour of all the people. And the Lord added to their number daily those who were being saved.

Peter Heals the Crippled Beggar

3 One day Peter and John were going up to the temple at the time of prayer—at three in the afternoon. 2 Now a man crippled from birth was being carried to the temple gate called Beautiful, where he was put every day to beg from those going into the temple courts. 3 When he saw Peter and John about to enter, he asked them for money. 4 Peter looked straight at him, as did John. Then Peter said, "Look at us!" 5 So the man gave them his attention, expecting to get something from them.

---

*d*23 Or *of those not having the law* (that is, Gentiles)   *e*28 Psalm 16:8 –11
*f*31 Or *Messiah.* "The Christ" (Greek) and "the Messiah" (Hebrew) both mean "the Anointed One"; also in verse 36.
*g*35 Psalm 110:1

6 Then Peter said, "Silver or gold I do not have, but what I have I give you. In the name of Jesus Christ of Nazareth, walk." 7 Taking him by the right hand, he helped him up, and instantly the man's feet and ankles became strong. 8 He jumped to his feet and began to walk. Then he went with them into the temple courts, walking and jumping, and praising God. 9 When all the people saw him walking and praising God, 10 they recognised him as the same man who used to sit begging at the temple gate called Beautiful, and they were filled with wonder and amazement at what had happened to him.

Peter Speaks to the Onlookers

11 While the beggar held on to Peter and John, all the people were astonished and came running to them in the place called Solomon's Colonnade. 12 When Peter saw this, he said to them: "People of Israel, why does this surprise you? Why do you stare at us as if by our own power or godliness we had made this man walk? 13 The God of Abraham, Isaac and Jacob, the God of our fathers, has glorified his servant Jesus. You handed him over to be killed, and you disowned him before Pilate, though he had decided to let him go. 14 You disowned the Holy and Righteous One and asked that a murderer be released to you. 15 You killed the author of life, but God raised him from the dead. We are witnesses of this. 16 By faith in the name of Jesus, this man whom you see and know was made strong. It is Jesus' name and the faith that comes through him that has given this complete healing to him, as you can all see.

17 "Now, brothers and sisters, I know that you acted in ignorance, as did your leaders. 18 But this is how God fulfilled what he had foretold through all the prophets, saying that his Christ[a] would suffer. 19 Repent, then, and turn to God, so that your sins may be wiped out, that times of refreshing may come from the Lord, 20 and that he may send the Christ, who has been appointed for you—even

Jesus. 21 He must remain in heaven until the time comes for God to restore everything, as he promised long ago through his holy prophets. 22 For Moses said, 'The Lord your God will raise up for you a prophet like me from among your own people; you must listen to everything he tells you. 23 Anyone who does not listen to him will be completely cut off from among the people.'[b]

24 "Indeed, all the prophets from Samuel on, as many as have spoken, have foretold these days. 25 And you are heirs of the prophets and of the covenant God made with your fathers. He said to Abraham, 'Through your offspring all peoples on earth will be blessed.'[c] 26 When God raised up his servant, he sent him first to you to bless you by turning each of you from your wicked ways."

Peter and John Before the Sanhedrin

4 The priests and the captain of the temple guard and the Sadducees came up to Peter and John while they were speaking to the people. 2 They were greatly disturbed because the apostles were teaching the people and proclaiming in Jesus the resurrection of the dead. 3 They seized Peter and John, and because it was evening, they put them in jail until the next day. 4 But many who heard the message believed, and their number[a] grew to about five thousand.

5 The next day the rulers, elders and teachers of the law met in Jerusalem. 6 Annas the high priest was there, and so were Caiaphas, John, Alexander and others of the high priest's family. 7 They had Peter and John brought before them and began to question them: "By what power or what name did you do this?"

8 Then Peter, filled with the Holy Spirit, said to them: "Rulers and elders of the people! 9 If we are being called to account today for an act of kindness shown to a cripple and are asked how he was healed, 10 then know this, you and all the people of Israel: It is by the name of Jesus Christ of Nazareth, whom you crucified but

---

[a] 18 Or *Messiah*; also in verse 20   [b] 23 Deut. 18:15,18,19   [c] 25 Gen. 22:18; 26:4
[a] 4 Or *and the number of men*

whom God raised from the dead, that this man stands before you healed. ¹¹He is

" 'the stone you builders rejected,
  which has become the capstone.*b, c*

¹²Salvation is found in no-one else, for there is no other name under heaven given to people by which we must be saved."

¹³When they saw the courage of Peter and John and realised that they were unschooled, ordinary men, they were astonished and they took note that these men had been with Jesus. ¹⁴But since they could see the man who had been healed standing there with them, there was nothing they could say. ¹⁵So they ordered them to withdraw from the Sanhedrin and then conferred together. ¹⁶"What are we going to do with these men?" they asked. "Everybody living in Jerusalem knows they have done an outstanding miracle, and we cannot deny it. ¹⁷But to stop this thing from spreading any further among the people, we must warn them to speak no longer to anyone in this name."

¹⁸Then they called them in again and commanded them not to speak or teach at all in the name of Jesus. ¹⁹But Peter and John replied, "Judge for yourselves whether it is right in God's sight to obey you rather than God. ²⁰For we cannot help speaking about what we have seen and heard."

²¹After further threats they let them go. They could not decide how to punish them, because all the people were praising God for what had happened. ²²For the man who was miraculously healed was over forty years old.

The Believers' Prayer

²³On their release, Peter and John went back to their own people and reported all that the chief priests and elders had said to them. ²⁴When they heard this, they raised their voices together in prayer to God. "Sovereign Lord," they said, "you made the heaven and the earth and the sea, and everything in them. ²⁵You spoke by the

Holy Spirit through the mouth of your servant, our father David:

" 'Why do the nations rage
  and the peoples plot in vain?
²⁶The kings of the earth take their stand
  and the rulers gather together
against the Lord
  and against his Anointed One.*d, e*

²⁷Indeed Herod and Pontius Pilate met together with the Gentiles and the people*f* of Israel in this city to conspire against your holy servant Jesus, whom you anointed. ²⁸They did what your power and will had decided beforehand should happen. ²⁹Now, Lord, consider their threats and enable your servants to speak your word with great boldness. ³⁰Stretch out your hand to heal and perform miraculous signs and wonders through the name of your holy servant Jesus."

³¹After they prayed, the place where they were meeting was shaken. And they were all filled with the Holy Spirit and spoke the word of God boldly.

The Believers Share Their Possessions

³²All the believers were one in heart and mind. No-one claimed that any of their possessions was their own, but they shared everything they had. ³³With great power the apostles continued to testify to the resurrection of the Lord Jesus, and much grace was upon them all. ³⁴There were no needy persons among them. For from time to time those who owned lands or houses sold them, brought the money from the sales ³⁵and put it at the apostles' feet, and it was distributed to anyone who had need.

³⁶Joseph, a Levite from Cyprus, whom the apostles called Barnabas (which means Son of Encouragement), ³⁷sold a field he owned and brought the money and put it at the apostles' feet.

Ananias and Sapphira

5 Now a man named Ananias, together with his wife Sapphira, also sold a piece of property. ²With his wife's full

---

*b*11 Or *cornerstone* *c*11 Psalm 118:22 *d*26 That is, Christ or Messiah *e*26 Psalm 2:1,2
*f*27 The Greek is plural.

knowledge he kept back part of the money for himself, but brought the rest and put it at the apostles' feet.

3 Then Peter said, "Ananias, how is it that Satan has so filled your heart that you have lied to the Holy Spirit and have kept for yourself some of the money you received for the land? 4 Didn't it belong to you before it was sold? And after it was sold, wasn't the money at your disposal? What made you think of doing such a thing? You have not lied to us men but to God."

5 When Ananias heard this, he fell down and died. And great fear seized all who heard what had happened. 6 Then the young men came forward, wrapped up his body, and carried him out and buried him.

7 About three hours later his wife came in, not knowing what had happened. 8 Peter asked her, "Tell me, is this the price you and Ananias got for the land?"

"Yes," she said, "that is the price."

9 Peter said to her, "How could you agree to test the Spirit of the Lord? Look! The feet of those who buried your husband are at the door, and they will carry you out also."

10 At that moment she fell down at his feet and died. Then the young men came in and, finding her dead, carried her out and buried her beside her husband. 11 Great fear seized the whole church and all who heard about these events.

The Apostles Heal Many

12 The apostles performed many miraculous signs and wonders among the people. And all the believers used to meet together in Solomon's Colonnade. 13 No-one else dared join them, even though they were highly regarded by the people. 14 Nevertheless, more and more men and women believed in the Lord and were added to their number. 15 As a result, people brought the sick into the streets and laid them on beds and mats so that at least Peter's shadow might fall on some of them as he passed by. 16 Crowds gathered also from the towns around Jerusalem, bringing their sick and those tormented by evil^a spirits, and all of them were healed.

The Apostles Persecuted

17 Then the high priest and all his associates, who were members of the party of the Sadducees, were filled with jealousy. 18 They arrested the apostles and put them in the public jail. 19 But during the night an angel of the Lord opened the doors of the jail and brought them out. 20 "Go, stand in the temple courts," he said, "and tell the people the full message of this new life."

21 At daybreak they entered the temple courts, as they had been told, and began to teach the people.

When the high priest and his associates arrived, they called together the Sanhedrin—the full assembly of the elders of Israel—and sent to the jail for the apostles. 22 But on arriving at the jail, the officers did not find them there. So they went back and reported, 23 "We found the jail securely locked, with the guards standing at the doors; but when we opened them, we found no-one inside." 24 On hearing this report, the captain of the temple guard and the chief priests were puzzled, wondering what would come of this.

25 Then someone came and said, "Look! The men you put in jail are standing in the temple courts teaching the people." 26 At that, the captain went with his officers and brought the apostles. They did not use force, because they feared that the people would stone them.

27 Having brought the apostles, they made them appear before the Sanhedrin to be questioned by the high priest. 28 "We gave you strict orders not to teach in this name," he said. "Yet you have filled Jerusalem with your teaching and are determined to make us guilty of this man's blood."

29 Peter and the other apostles replied: "We must obey God rather than human beings! 30 The God of our ancestors raised Jesus from the dead—whom you had killed by hanging him on a tree. 31 God

^{a}16 Greek unclean

exalted him to his own right hand as Prince and Saviour that he might give repentance and forgiveness of sins to Israel. [32] We are witnesses of these things, and so is the Holy Spirit, whom God has given to those who obey him."

[33] When they heard this, they were furious and wanted to put them to death. [34] But a Pharisee named Gamaliel, a teacher of the law, who was honoured by all the people, stood up in the Sanhedrin and ordered that the men be put outside for a little while. [35] Then he addressed them: "Men of Israel, consider carefully what you intend to do to these men. [36] Some time ago Theudas appeared, claiming to be somebody, and about four hundred men rallied to him. He was killed, all his followers were dispersed, and it all came to nothing. [37] After him, Judas the Galilean appeared in the days of the census and led a band of people in revolt. He too was killed, and all his followers were scattered. [38] Therefore, in the present case I advise you: Leave these men alone! Let them go! For if their purpose or activity is of human origin, it will fail. [39] But if it is from God, you will not be able to stop these men; you will only find yourselves fighting against God."

[40] His speech persuaded them. They called the apostles in and had them flogged. Then they ordered them not to speak in the name of Jesus, and let them go.

[41] The apostles left the Sanhedrin, rejoicing because they had been counted worthy of suffering disgrace for the Name. [42] Day after day, in the temple courts and from house to house, they never stopped teaching and proclaiming the good news that Jesus is the Christ.[b]

The Choosing of the Seven

6 In those days when the number of disciples was increasing, the Grecian Jews among them complained against the Hebraic Jews because their widows were being overlooked in the daily distribution of food. [2] So the Twelve gathered all the disciples together and said, "It would not be right for us to neglect the ministry of the word of God in order to wait on tables. [3] Brothers and sisters, choose seven men from among you who are known to be full of the Spirit and wisdom. We will turn this responsibility over to them [4] and will give our attention to prayer and the ministry of the word."

[5] This proposal pleased the whole group. They chose Stephen, a man full of faith and of the Holy Spirit; also Philip, Procorus, Nicanor, Timon, Parmenas, and Nicolas from Antioch, a convert to Judaism. [6] They presented them to the apostles, who prayed and laid their hands on them.

[7] So the word of God spread. The number of disciples in Jerusalem increased rapidly, and a large number of priests became obedient to the faith.

Stephen Seized

[8] Now Stephen, a man full of God's grace and power, did great wonders and miraculous signs among the people. [9] Opposition arose, however, from members of the Synagogue of the Freedmen (as it was called)—Jews of Cyrene and Alexandria as well as the provinces of Cilicia and Asia, who began to argue with Stephen, [10] but they could not stand up against his wisdom or the Spirit by whom he spoke.

[11] Then they secretly persuaded some men to say, "We have heard Stephen speak words of blasphemy against Moses and against God."

[12] So they stirred up the people and the elders and the teachers of the law. They seized Stephen and brought him before the Sanhedrin. [13] They produced false witnesses, who testified, "This fellow never stops speaking against this holy place and against the law. [14] For we have heard him say that this Jesus of Nazareth will destroy this place and change the customs Moses handed down to us."

[15] All who were sitting in the Sanhedrin looked intently at Stephen, and they saw that his face was like the face of an angel.

[b]42 Or Messiah

Stephen's Speech to the Sanhedrin

7 Then the high priest asked him, "Are these charges true?"

2 To this he replied: "Brothers and fathers, listen to me! The God of glory appeared to our father Abraham while he was still in Mesopotamia, before he lived in Haran. 3 'Leave your country and your people,' God said, 'and go to the land I will show you.'*a*

4 "So he left the land of the Chaldeans and settled in Haran. After the death of his father, God sent him to this land where you are now living. 5 He gave him no inheritance here, not even a foot of ground. But God promised him that he and his descendants after him would possess the land, even though at that time Abraham had no child. 6 God spoke to him in this way: 'Your descendants will be strangers in a country not their own, and they will be enslaved and ill-treated for four hundred years. 7 But I will punish the nation they serve as slaves,' God said, 'and afterwards they will come out of that country and worship me in this place.'*b* 8 Then he gave Abraham the covenant of circumcision. And Abraham became the father of Isaac and circumcised him eight days after his birth. Later Isaac became the father of Jacob, and Jacob became the father of the twelve patriarchs.

9 "Because the patriarchs were jealous of Joseph, they sold him as a slave into Egypt. But God was with him 10 and rescued him from all his troubles. He gave Joseph wisdom and enabled him to gain the goodwill of Pharaoh king of Egypt; so he made him ruler over Egypt and all his palace.

11 "Then a famine struck all Egypt and Canaan, bringing great suffering, and our people could not find food. 12 When Jacob heard that there was grain in Egypt, he sent our ancestors on their first visit. 13 On their second visit, Joseph told his brothers who he was, and Pharaoh learned about Joseph's family. 14 After this, Joseph sent for his father Jacob and his whole family, seventy-five in all. 15 Then Jacob went down to Egypt, where he and our ancestors died. 16 Their bodies were brought back to Shechem and placed in the tomb that Abraham had bought from the sons of Hamor at Shechem for a certain sum of money.

17 "As the time drew near for God to fulfil his promise to Abraham, the number of our people in Egypt greatly increased. 18 Then another king, who knew nothing about Joseph, became ruler of Egypt. 19 He dealt treacherously with our people and oppressed our ancestors by forcing them to throw out their newborn babies so that they would die.

20 "At that time Moses was born, and he was no ordinary child.*c* For three months he was cared for in his parents' house. 21 When he was placed outside, Pharaoh's daughter took him and brought him up as her own son. 22 Moses was educated in all the wisdom of the Egyptians and was powerful in speech and action.

23 "When Moses was forty years old, he decided to visit his own people, the Israelites. 24 He saw one of them being ill-treated by an Egyptian, so he went to his defence and avenged him by killing the Egyptian. 25 Moses thought that his own people would realise that God was using him to rescue them, but they did not. 26 The next day Moses came upon two Israelites who were fighting. He tried to reconcile them by saying, 'Men, you are brothers; why do you want to hurt each other?'

27 "But the man who was ill-treating the other pushed Moses aside and said, 'Who made you ruler and judge over us? 28 Do you want to kill me as you killed the Egyptian yesterday?'*d* 29 When Moses heard this, he fled to Midian, where he settled as a foreigner and had two sons.

30 "After forty years had passed, an angel appeared to Moses in the flames of a burning bush in the desert near Mount Sinai. 31 When he saw this, he was amazed at the sight. As he went over to look more closely, he heard the Lord's voice: 32 'I am the God of your fathers, the God of Abraham, Isaac and Jacob.'*e* Moses trembled with fear and did not dare to look.

*a*3 Gen. 12:1   *b*7 Gen. 15:13,14   *c*20 Or *was fair in the sight of God*   *d*28 Exodus 2:14   *e*32 Exodus 3:6

33 "Then the Lord said to him, 'Take off your sandals; the place where you are standing is holy ground. 34 I have indeed seen the oppression of my people in Egypt. I have heard their groaning and have come down to set them free. Now come, I will send you back to Egypt.'*f*

35 "This is the same Moses whom they had rejected with the words, 'Who made you ruler and judge?' He was sent to be their ruler and deliverer by God himself, through the angel who appeared to him in the bush. 36 He led them out of Egypt and did wonders and miraculous signs in Egypt, at the Red Sea*g* and for forty years in the desert.

37 "This is that Moses who told the Israelites, 'God will send you a prophet like me from your own people.'*h* 38 He was in the assembly in the desert, with the angel who spoke to him on Mount Sinai, and with our ancestors; and he received living words to pass on to us.

39 "But our ancestors refused to obey him. Instead, they rejected him and in their hearts turned back to Egypt. 40 They told Aaron, 'Make us gods who will go before us. As for this fellow Moses who led us out of Egypt—we don't know what has happened to him!'*i* 41 That was the time they made an idol in the form of a calf. They brought sacrifices to it and held a celebration in honour of what their hands had made. 42 But God turned away and gave them over to the worship of the heavenly bodies. This agrees with what is written in the book of the prophets:

" 'Did you bring me sacrifices and
    offerings
  for forty years in the desert,
    O house of Israel?
43 You have lifted up the shrine of
    Molech
  and the star of your god Rephan,
    the idols you made to worship.
  Therefore I will send you into exile'*j*
    beyond Babylon.

44 "Our ancestors had the tabernacle of the Testimony with them in the desert. It had been made as God directed Moses, according to the pattern he had seen. 45 Having received the tabernacle, our ancestors under Joshua brought it with them when they took the land from the nations God drove out before them. It remained in the land until the time of David, 46 who enjoyed God's favour and asked that he might provide a dwelling-place for the God of Jacob.*k* 47 But it was Solomon who built the house for him.

48 "However, the Most High does not live in houses made by human hands. As the prophet says:

49 " 'Heaven is my throne,
    and the earth is my footstool.
  What kind of house will you build for
    me?
                    says the Lord.
  Or where will my resting place be?
50 Has not my hand made all these
    things?'*l*

51 "You stiff-necked people, with uncircumcised hearts and ears! You are just like your ancestors: You always resist the Holy Spirit! 52 Was there ever a prophet your ancestors did not persecute? They even killed those who predicted the coming of the Righteous One. And now you have betrayed and murdered him— 53 you who have received the law that was put into effect through angels but have not obeyed it."

The Stoning of Stephen

54 When they heard this, they were furious and gnashed their teeth at him. 55 But Stephen, full of the Holy Spirit, looked up to heaven and saw the glory of God, and Jesus standing at the right hand of God. 56 "Look," he said, "I see heaven open and the Son of Man standing at the right hand of God."

57 At this they covered their ears and, yelling at the top of their voices, they all rushed at him, 58 dragged him out of the city and began to stone him. Meanwhile,

*f*34 Exodus 3:5,7,8,10   *g*36 That is, Sea of Reeds   *h*37 Deut. 18:15   *i*40 Exodus 32:1
*j*43 Amos 5:25–27   *k*46 Some early manuscripts *the house of Jacob*   *l*50 Isaiah 66:1,2

the witnesses laid their clothes at the feet of a young man named Saul.

59 While they were stoning him, Stephen prayed, "Lord Jesus, receive my spirit." 60 Then he fell on his knees and cried out, "Lord, do not hold this sin against them." When he had said this, he fell asleep.

8 And Saul was there, giving approval to his death.

The Church Persecuted and Scattered

On that day a great persecution broke out against the church at Jerusalem, and all except the apostles were scattered throughout Judea and Samaria. 2 Godly men buried Stephen and mourned deeply for him. 3 But Saul began to destroy the church. Going from house to house, he dragged off both men and women and put them in prison.

Philip in Samaria

4 Those who had been scattered preached the word wherever they went. 5 Philip went down to a city in Samaria and proclaimed the Christ*a* there. 6 When the crowds heard Philip and saw the miraculous signs he did, they all paid close attention to what he said. 7 With shrieks, evil*b* spirits came out of many, and many paralytics and cripples were healed. 8 So there was great joy in that city.

Simon the Sorcerer

9 Now for some time a man named Simon had practised sorcery in the city and amazed all the people of Samaria. He boasted that he was someone great, 10 and all the people, both high and low, gave him their attention and exclaimed, "This man is the divine power known as the Great Power." 11 They followed him because he had amazed them for a long time with his magic. 12 But when they believed Philip as he preached the good news of the kingdom of God and the name of Jesus Christ, they were baptised, both men and

women. 13 Simon himself believed and was baptised. And he followed Philip everywhere, astonished by the great signs and miracles he saw.

14 When the apostles in Jerusalem heard that Samaria had accepted the word of God, they sent Peter and John to them. 15 When they arrived, they prayed for them that they might receive the Holy Spirit, 16 because the Holy Spirit had not yet come upon any of them; they had simply been baptised into*c* the name of the Lord Jesus. 17 Then Peter and John placed their hands on them, and they received the Holy Spirit.

18 When Simon saw that the Spirit was given at the laying on of the apostles' hands, he offered them money 19 and said, "Give me also this ability so that everyone on whom I lay my hands may receive the Holy Spirit."

20 Peter answered: "May your money perish with you, because you thought you could buy the gift of God with money! 21 You have no part or share in this ministry, because your heart is not right before God. 22 Repent of this wickedness and pray to the Lord. Perhaps he will forgive you for having such a thought in your heart. 23 For I see that you are full of bitterness and captive to sin."

24 Then Simon answered, "Pray to the Lord for me so that nothing you have said may happen to me."

25 When they had testified and proclaimed the word of the Lord, Peter and John returned to Jerusalem, preaching the gospel in many Samaritan villages.

Philip and the Ethiopian

26 Now an angel of the Lord said to Philip, "Go south to the road—the desert road—that goes down from Jerusalem to Gaza." 27 So he started out, and on his way he met an Ethiopian*d* eunuch, an important official in charge of all the treasury of Candace, queen of the Ethiopians. This man had gone to Jerusalem to worship, 28 and on his way home was sitting in his chariot reading the book of Isaiah the

---

*a*5 Or *Messiah*   *b*7 Greek *unclean*   *c*16 Or *in*   *d*27 That is, from the upper Nile region prophet. ²⁹The Spirit told Philip, "Go to that chariot and stay near it."

³⁰Then Philip ran up to the chariot and heard the man reading Isaiah the prophet. "Do you understand what you are reading?" Philip asked.

³¹"How can I," he said, "unless someone explains it to me?" So he invited Philip to come up and sit with him.

³²The eunuch was reading this passage of Scripture:

"He was led like a sheep to the
        slaughter,
    and as a lamb before the shearer is
        silent,
    so he did not open his mouth.
³³In his humiliation he was deprived of
        justice.
    Who can speak of his descendants?
    For his life was taken from the
        earth."^e

³⁴The eunuch asked Philip, "Tell me, please, who is the prophet talking about, himself or someone else?" ³⁵Then Philip began with that very passage of Scripture and told him the good news about Jesus.

³⁶As they travelled along the road, they came to some water and the eunuch said, "Look, here is water. Why shouldn't I be baptised?"^f ³⁸And he gave orders to stop the chariot. Then both Philip and the eunuch went down into the water and Philip baptised him. ³⁹When they came up out of the water, the Spirit of the Lord suddenly took Philip away, and the eunuch did not see him again, but went on his way rejoicing. ⁴⁰Philip, however, appeared at Azotus and travelled about, preaching the gospel in all the towns until he reached Caesarea.

Saul's Conversion

9 Meanwhile, Saul was still breathing out murderous threats against the Lord's disciples. He went to the high priest ²and asked him for letters to the synagogues in Damascus, so that if he found any there who belonged to the Way, whether men or women, he might take them as prisoners to Jerusalem. ³As he neared Damascus on his journey, suddenly a light from heaven flashed around him. ⁴He fell to the ground and heard a voice say to him, "Saul, Saul, why do you persecute me?"

⁵"Who are you, Lord?" Saul asked.

"I am Jesus, whom you are persecuting," he replied. ⁶"Now get up and go into the city, and you will be told what you must do."

⁷Those who were travelling with Saul stood there speechless; they heard the sound but did not see anyone. ⁸Saul got up from the ground, but when he opened his eyes he could see nothing. So they led him by the hand into Damascus. ⁹For three days he was blind, and did not eat or drink anything.

¹⁰In Damascus there was a disciple named Ananias. The Lord called to him in a vision, "Ananias!"

"Yes, Lord," he answered.

¹¹The Lord told him, "Go to the house of Judas on Straight Street and ask for a man from Tarsus named Saul, for he is praying. ¹²In a vision he has seen a man named Ananias come and place his hands on him to restore his sight."

¹³"Lord," Ananias answered, "I have heard many reports about this man and all the harm he has done to your saints in Jerusalem. ¹⁴And he has come here with authority from the chief priests to arrest all who call on your name."

¹⁵But the Lord said to Ananias, "Go! This man is my chosen instrument to carry my name before the Gentiles and their kings and before the people of Israel. ¹⁶I will show him how much he must suffer for my name."

¹⁷Then Ananias went to the house and entered it. Placing his hands on Saul, he said, "Brother Saul, the Lord—Jesus, who appeared to you on the road as you were coming here—has sent me so that you may see again and be filled with the Holy Spirit." ¹⁸Immediately, something like scales fell from Saul's eyes, and he

^e33 Isaiah 53:7,8
^f36 Some late manuscripts *baptised?"* ³⁷*Philip said, "If you believe with all your heart, you may." The eunuch answered, "I believe that Jesus Christ is the Son of God."*

could see again. He got up and was baptised, [19] and after taking some food, he regained his strength.

Saul in Damascus and Jerusalem

Saul spent several days with the disciples in Damascus. [20] At once he began to preach in the synagogues that Jesus is the Son of God. [21] All those who heard him were astonished and asked, "Isn't he the man who caused havoc in Jerusalem among those who call on this name? And hasn't he come here to take them as prisoners to the chief priests?" [22] Yet Saul grew more and more powerful and baffled the Jews living in Damascus by proving that Jesus is the Christ.[a]

[23] After many days had gone by, the Jews conspired to kill him, [24] but Saul learned of their plan. Day and night they kept close watch on the city gates in order to kill him. [25] But his followers took him by night and lowered him in a basket through an opening in the wall.

[26] When he came to Jerusalem, he tried to join the disciples, but they were all afraid of him, not believing that he really was a disciple. [27] But Barnabas took him and brought him to the apostles. He told them how Saul on his journey had seen the Lord and that the Lord had spoken to him, and how in Damascus he had preached fearlessly in the name of Jesus. [28] So Saul stayed with them and moved about freely in Jerusalem, speaking boldly in the name of the Lord. [29] He talked and debated with the Grecian Jews, but they tried to kill him. [30] When the believers learned of this, they took him down to Caesarea and sent him off to Tarsus.

[31] Then the church throughout Judea, Galilee and Samaria enjoyed a time of peace. It was strengthened; and encouraged by the Holy Spirit, it grew in numbers, living in the fear of the Lord.

Aeneas and Dorcas

[32] As Peter travelled about the country, he went to visit the saints in Lydda. [33] There he found a man named Aeneas, a paralytic who had been bedridden for eight years. [34] "Aeneas," Peter said to him, "Jesus Christ heals you. Get up and tidy up your mat." Immediately Aeneas got up. [35] All those who lived in Lydda and Sharon saw him and turned to the Lord.

[36] In Joppa there was a disciple named Tabitha (which, when translated, is Dorcas[b]), who was always doing good and helping the poor. [37] About that time she became sick and died, and her body was washed and placed in an upstairs room. [38] Lydda was near Joppa; so when the disciples heard that Peter was in Lydda, they sent two men to him and urged him, "Please come at once!"

[39] Peter went with them, and when he arrived he was taken upstairs to the room. All the widows stood around him, crying and showing him the robes and other clothing that Dorcas had made while she was still with them.

[40] Peter sent them all out of the room; then he got down on his knees and prayed. Turning towards the dead woman, he said, "Tabitha, get up." She opened her eyes, and seeing Peter she sat up. [41] He took her by the hand and helped her to her feet. Then he called the believers and the widows and presented her to them alive. [42] This became known all over Joppa, and many people believed in the Lord. [43] Peter stayed in Joppa for some time with a tanner named Simon.

Cornelius Calls for Peter

10 At Caesarea there was a man named Cornelius, a centurion in what was known as the Italian Regiment. [2] He and all his family were devout and God-fearing; he gave generously to those in need and prayed to God regularly. [3] One day at about three in the afternoon he had a vision. He distinctly saw an angel of God, who came to him and said, "Cornelius!"

[4] Cornelius stared at him in fear. "What is it, Lord?" he asked.

The angel answered, "Your prayers and gifts to the poor have come up as a memorial offering before God. [5] Now

---

[a]22 Or *Messiah*   [b]36 Both *Tabitha* (Aramaic) and *Dorcas* (Greek) mean *gazelle*.

send men to Joppa to bring back a man named Simon who is called Peter. ⁶He is staying with Simon the tanner, whose house is by the sea."

⁷When the angel who spoke to him had gone, Cornelius called two of his servants and a devout soldier who was one of his attendants. ⁸He told them everything that had happened and sent them to Joppa.

Peter's Vision

⁹About noon the following day as they were on their journey and approaching the city, Peter went up on the roof to pray. ¹⁰He became hungry and wanted something to eat, and while the meal was being prepared, he fell into a trance. ¹¹He saw heaven opened and something like a large sheet being let down to earth by its four corners. ¹²It contained all kinds of four-footed animals, as well as reptiles of the earth and birds of the air. ¹³Then a voice told him, "Get up, Peter. Kill and eat."

¹⁴"Surely not, Lord!" Peter replied. "I have never eaten anything impure or unclean."

¹⁵The voice spoke to him a second time, "Do not call anything impure that God has made clean."

¹⁶This happened three times, and immediately the sheet was taken back to heaven.

¹⁷While Peter was wondering about the meaning of the vision, the men sent by Cornelius found out where Simon's house was and stopped at the gate. ¹⁸They called out, asking if Simon who was known as Peter was staying there.

¹⁹While Peter was still thinking about the vision, the Spirit said to him, "Simon, three*a* men are looking for you. ²⁰So get up and go downstairs. Do not hesitate to go with them, for I have sent them."

²¹Peter went down and said to the men, "I'm the one you're looking for. Why have you come?"

²²The men replied, "We have come from Cornelius the centurion. He is a righteous and God-fearing man, who is respected by all the Jewish people. A

holy angel told him to have you come to his house so that he could hear what you have to say." ²³Then Peter invited the men into the house to be his guests.

Peter at Cornelius' House

The next day Peter started out with them, and some of the believers from Joppa went along. ²⁴The following day he arrived in Caesarea. Cornelius was expecting them and had called together his relatives and close friends. ²⁵As Peter entered the house, Cornelius met him and fell at his feet in reverence. ²⁶But Peter made him get up. "Stand up," he said, "I am only human myself."

²⁷Talking with him, Peter went inside and found a large gathering of people. ²⁸He said to them: "You are well aware that it is against our law for a Jew to associate with Gentiles or visit them. But God has shown me that I should not call anyone impure or unclean. ²⁹So when I was sent for, I came without raising any objection. May I ask why you sent for me?"

³⁰Cornelius answered: "Four days ago I was in my house praying at this hour, at three in the afternoon. Suddenly a man in shining clothes stood before me ³¹and said, 'Cornelius, God has heard your prayer and remembered your gifts to the poor. ³²Send to Joppa for Simon who is called Peter. He is a guest in the home of Simon the tanner, who lives by the sea.' ³³So I sent for you immediately, and it was good of you to come. Now we are all here in the presence of God to listen to everything the Lord has commanded you to tell us."

³⁴Then Peter began to speak: "I now realise how true it is that God does not show favouritism ³⁵but accepts those from every nation who fear him and do what is right. ³⁶You know the message God sent to the people of Israel, telling the good news of peace through Jesus Christ, who is Lord of all. ³⁷You know what has happened throughout Judea, beginning in Galilee after the baptism that John

*a*19 One early manuscript *two*; other manuscripts do not have the number.

preached—[38] how God anointed Jesus of Nazareth with the Holy Spirit and power, and how he went around doing good and healing all who were under the power of the devil, because God was with him.

[39] "We are witnesses of everything he did in the country of the Jews and in Jerusalem. They killed him by hanging him on a tree, [40] but God raised him from the dead on the third day and caused him to be seen. [41] He was not seen by all the people, but by witnesses whom God had already chosen—by us who ate and drank with him after he rose from the dead. [42] He commanded us to preach to the people and to testify that he is the one whom God appointed as judge of the living and the dead. [43] All the prophets testify about him that everyone who believes in him receives forgiveness of sins through his name."

[44] While Peter was still speaking these words, the Holy Spirit came on all who heard the message. [45] The circumcised believers who had come with Peter were astonished that the gift of the Holy Spirit had been poured out even on the Gentiles. [46] For they heard them speaking in tongues[b] and praising God.

Then Peter said, [47] "Can anyone keep these people from being baptised with water? They have received the Holy Spirit just as we have." [48] So he ordered that they be baptised in the name of Jesus Christ. Then they asked Peter to stay with them for a few days.

Peter Explains His Actions

11 The apostles and the believers throughout Judea heard that the Gentiles also had received the word of God. [2] So when Peter went up to Jerusalem, the circumcised believers criticised him [3] and said, "You went into the house of uncircumcised men and ate with them."

[4] Peter began and explained everything to them precisely as it had happened: [5] "I was in the city of Joppa praying, and in a trance I saw a vision. I saw something like a large sheet being let down from heaven by its four corners, and it came down to where I was. [6] I looked into it and saw four-footed animals of the earth, wild beasts, reptiles, and birds of the air. [7] Then I heard a voice telling me, 'Get up, Peter. Kill and eat.'

[8] "I replied, 'Surely not, Lord! Nothing impure or unclean has ever entered my mouth.'

[9] "The voice spoke from heaven a second time, 'Do not call anything impure that God has made clean.' [10] This happened three times, and then it was pulled up to heaven again.

[11] "Right then three men who had been sent to me from Caesarea stopped at the house where I was staying. [12] The Spirit told me to have no hesitation about going with them. These six brothers also went with me, and we entered the man's house. [13] He told us how he had seen an angel appear in his house and say, 'Send to Joppa for Simon who is called Peter. [14] He will bring you a message through which you and all your household will be saved.'

[15] "As I began to speak, the Holy Spirit came on them as he had come on us at the beginning. [16] Then I remembered what the Lord had said: 'John baptised with[a] water, but you will be baptised with the Holy Spirit.' [17] So if God gave them the same gift as he gave us, who believed in the Lord Jesus Christ, who was I to think that I could oppose God?"

[18] When they heard this, they had no further objections and praised God, saying, "So then, God has granted even the Gentiles repentance unto life."

The Church in Antioch

[19] Now those who had been scattered by the persecution in connection with Stephen travelled as far as Phoenicia, Cyprus and Antioch, telling the message only to Jews. [20] Some of them, however, men from Cyprus and Cyrene, went to Antioch and began to speak to Greeks also, telling them the good news about the Lord Jesus. [21] The Lord's hand was with them, and a great number of people believed and turned to the Lord.

[b]46 Or *other languages*   [a]16 Or *in*

22 News of this reached the ears of the church at Jerusalem, and they sent Barnabas to Antioch. 23 When he arrived and saw the evidence of the grace of God, he was glad and encouraged them all to remain true to the Lord with all their hearts. 24 He was a good man, full of the Holy Spirit and faith, and a great number of people were brought to the Lord. 25 Then Barnabas went to Tarsus to look for Saul, 26 and when he found him, he brought him to Antioch. So for a whole year Barnabas and Saul met with the church and taught great numbers of people. The disciples were called Christians first at Antioch.

27 During this time some prophets came down from Jerusalem to Antioch. 28 One of them, named Agabus, stood up and through the Spirit predicted that a severe famine would spread over the entire Roman world. (This happened during the reign of Claudius.) 29 The disciples, each according to his ability, decided to provide help for the believers living in Judea. 30 This they did, sending their gift to the elders by Barnabas and Saul.

Peter's Miraculous Escape From Prison

12 It was about this time that King Herod arrested some who belonged to the church, intending to persecute them. 2 He had James, the brother of John, put to death with the sword. 3 When he saw that this pleased the Jews, he proceeded to seize Peter also. This happened during the Feast of Unleavened Bread. 4 After arresting him, he put him in prison, handing him over to be guarded by four squads of four soldiers each. Herod intended to bring him out for public trial after the Passover.

5 So Peter was kept in prison, but the church was earnestly praying to God for him.

6 The night before Herod was to bring him to trial, Peter was sleeping between two soldiers, bound with two chains, and sentries stood guard at the entrance. 7 Suddenly an angel of the Lord appeared and a light shone in the cell. He struck Peter on the side and woke him up. "Quick, get

up!" he said, and the chains fell off Peter's wrists.

8 Then the angel said to him, "Put on your clothes and sandals." And Peter did so. "Wrap your cloak around you and follow me," the angel told him. 9 Peter followed him out of the prison, but he had no idea that what the angel was doing was really happening; he thought he was seeing a vision. 10 They passed the first and second guards and came to the iron gate leading to the city. It opened for them by itself, and they went through it. When they had walked the length of one street, suddenly the angel left him.

11 Then Peter came to himself and said, "Now I know without a doubt that the Lord sent his angel and rescued me from Herod's clutches and from everything the Jewish people were anticipating."

12 When this had dawned on him, he went to the house of Mary the mother of John, also called Mark, where many people had gathered and were praying. 13 Peter knocked at the outer entrance, and a servant named Rhoda came to answer the door. 14 When she recognised Peter's voice, she was so overjoyed she ran back without opening it and exclaimed, "Peter is at the door!"

15 "You're out of your mind," they told her. When she kept insisting that it was so, they said, "It must be his angel."

16 But Peter kept on knocking, and when they opened the door and saw him, they were astonished. 17 Peter motioned with his hand for them to be quiet and described how the Lord had brought him out of prison. "Tell James and the believers about this," he said, and then he left for another place.

18 In the morning, there was no small commotion among the soldiers as to what had become of Peter. 19 After Herod had a thorough search made for him and did not find him, he cross-examined the guards and ordered that they be executed.

Herod's Death

Then Herod went from Judea to Caesarea and stayed there a while. 20 He had been quarrelling with the people of

Tyre and Sidon; they now joined together and sought an audience with him. Having secured the support of Blastus, a trusted personal servant of the king, they asked for peace, because they depended on the king's country for their food supply.

21 On the appointed day Herod, wearing his royal robes, sat on his throne and delivered a public address to the people. 22 They shouted, "This is the voice of a god, not of a mere mortal." 23 Immediately, because Herod did not give praise to God, an angel of the Lord struck him down, and he was eaten by worms and died.

24 But the word of God continued to increase and spread.

25 When Barnabas and Saul had finished their mission, they returned from[a] Jerusalem, taking with them John, also called Mark.

Barnabas and Saul Sent Off

13 In the church at Antioch there were prophets and teachers: Barnabas, Simeon called Niger, Lucius of Cyrene, Manaen (who had been brought up with Herod the tetrarch) and Saul. 2 While they were worshipping the Lord and fasting, the Holy Spirit said, "Set apart for me Barnabas and Saul for the work to which I have called them." 3 So after they had fasted and prayed, they placed their hands on them and sent them off.

On Cyprus

4 The two of them, sent on their way by the Holy Spirit, went down to Seleucia and sailed from there to Cyprus. 5 When they arrived at Salamis, they proclaimed the word of God in the Jewish synagogues. John was with them as their helper.

6 They travelled through the whole island until they came to Paphos. There they met a Jewish sorcerer and false prophet named Bar-Jesus, 7 who was an attendant of the proconsul, Sergius Paulus. The proconsul, an intelligent man, sent for Barnabas and Saul because he wanted to hear the word of God. 8 But Elymas the sorcerer (for that is what his name means) opposed them and tried to turn the proconsul from the faith. 9 Then Saul, who was also called Paul, filled with the Holy Spirit, looked straight at Elymas and said, 10 "You are a child of the devil and an enemy of everything that is right! You are full of all kinds of deceit and trickery. Will you never stop perverting the right ways of the Lord? 11 Now the hand of the Lord is against you. You are going to be blind, and for a time you will be unable to see the light of the sun."

Immediately mist and darkness came over him, and he groped about, seeking someone to lead him by the hand. 12 When the proconsul saw what had happened, he believed, for he was amazed at the teaching about the Lord.

In Pisidian Antioch

13 From Paphos, Paul and his companions sailed to Perga in Pamphylia, where John left them to return to Jerusalem. 14 From Perga they went on to Pisidian Antioch. On the Sabbath they entered the synagogue and sat down. 15 After the reading from the Law and the Prophets, the synagogue rulers sent word to them, saying, "Brothers, if you have a message of encouragement for the people, please speak."

16 Standing up, Paul motioned with his hand and said: "People of Israel and you Gentiles who worship God, listen to me! 17 The God of the people of Israel chose our ancestors; he made the people prosper during their stay in Egypt, with mighty power he led them out of that country, 18 he endured their conduct[a] for about forty years in the desert, 19 he overthrew seven nations in Canaan and gave their land to his people as their inheritance. 20 All this took about 450 years.

"After this, God gave them judges until the time of Samuel the prophet. 21 Then the people asked for a king, and he gave them Saul son of Kish, of the tribe of Benjamin, who ruled for forty years. 22 After

---

[a]25 Some manuscripts *to*   [a]18 Some manuscripts *and cared for them*

removing Saul, he made David their king. He testified concerning him: 'I have found David son of Jesse a man after my own heart; he will do everything I want him to do.'

²³"From this man's descendants God has brought to Israel the Saviour Jesus, as he promised. ²⁴Before the coming of Jesus, John preached repentance and baptism to all the people of Israel. ²⁵As John was completing his work, he said: 'Who do you think I am? I am not that one. No, but he is coming after me, whose sandals I am not worthy to untie.'

²⁶"Brothers and sisters from the children of Abraham and you God-fearing Gentiles, it is to us that this message of salvation has been sent. ²⁷The people of Jerusalem and their rulers did not recognise Jesus, yet in condemning him they fulfilled the words of the prophets that are read every Sabbath. ²⁸Though they found no proper ground for a death sentence, they asked Pilate to have him executed. ²⁹When they had carried out all that was written about him, they took him down from the tree and laid him in a tomb. ³⁰But God raised him from the dead, ³¹and for many days he was seen by those who had travelled with him from Galilee to Jerusalem. They are now his witnesses to our people.

³²"We tell you the good news: What God promised our ancestors³³he has fulfilled for us, their children, by raising up Jesus. As it is written in the second Psalm:

" 'You are my Son;
    today I have become your
      Father.'*b, c*

³⁴The fact that God raised him from the dead, never to decay, is stated in these words:

" 'I will give you the holy and sure
    blessings promised to David.'*d*

³⁵So it is stated elsewhere:

" 'You will not let your Holy One see
    decay.'*e*

³⁶"For when David had served God's purpose in his own generation, he fell asleep; he was buried with his ancestors and his body decayed. ³⁷But the one whom God raised from the dead did not see decay.

³⁸"Therefore, my brothers and sisters, I want you to know that through Jesus the forgiveness of sins is proclaimed to you. ³⁹Through him everyone who believes is justified from everything you could not be justified from by the law of Moses. ⁴⁰Take care that what the prophets have said does not happen to you:

⁴¹" 'Look, you scoffers,
      wonder and perish,
    for I am going to do something in your
      days
      that you would never believe,
      even if someone told you.'*f*"

⁴²As Paul and Barnabas were leaving the synagogue, the people invited them to speak further about these things on the next Sabbath. ⁴³When the congregation was dismissed, many of the Jews and devout converts to Judaism followed Paul and Barnabas, who talked with them and urged them to continue in the grace of God.

⁴⁴On the next Sabbath almost the whole city gathered to hear the word of the Lord. ⁴⁵When the Jews saw the crowds, they were filled with jealousy and talked abusively against what Paul was saying.

⁴⁶Then Paul and Barnabas answered them boldly: "We had to speak the word of God to you first. Since you reject it and do not consider yourselves worthy of eternal life, we now turn to the Gentiles. ⁴⁷For this is what the Lord has commanded us:

" 'I have made you*g* a light for the
      Gentiles,
    that you*g* may bring salvation to the
      ends of the earth.'*h*"

⁴⁸When the Gentiles heard this, they were glad and honoured the word of the

---

*b*33 Or *have begotten you*   *c*33 Psalm 2:7   *d*34 Isaiah 55:3   *e*35 Psalm 16:10   *f*41 Hab. 1:5
*g*47 The Greek is singular.   *h*47 Isaiah 49:6

Lord; and all who were appointed for eternal life believed.

[49] The word of the Lord spread through the whole region. [50] But the Jews incited the God-fearing women of high standing and the leading men of the city. They stirred up persecution against Paul and Barnabas, and expelled them from their region. [51] So they shook the dust from their feet in protest against them and went to Iconium. [52] And the disciples were filled with joy and with the Holy Spirit.

In Iconium

14 At Iconium Paul and Barnabas went as usual into the Jewish synagogue. There they spoke so effectively that a great number of Jews and Gentiles believed. [2] But the Jews who refused to believe stirred up the Gentiles and poisoned their minds against the brothers. [3] So Paul and Barnabas spent considerable time there, speaking boldly for the Lord, who confirmed the message of his grace by enabling them to do miraculous signs and wonders. [4] The people of the city were divided; some sided with the Jews, others with the apostles. [5] There was a plot afoot among the Gentiles and Jews, together with their leaders, to ill-treat them and stone them. [6] But they found out about it and fled to the Lycaonian cities of Lystra and Derbe and to the surrounding country, [7] where they continued to preach the good news.

In Lystra and Derbe

[8] In Lystra there sat a man crippled in his feet, who was lame from birth and had never walked. [9] He listened to Paul as he was speaking. Paul looked directly at him, saw that he had faith to be healed [10] and called out, "Stand up on your feet!" At that, the man jumped up and began to walk.

[11] When the crowd saw what Paul had done, they shouted in the Lycaonian language, "The gods have come down to us in human form!" [12] Barnabas they called Zeus, and Paul they called Hermes because he was the chief speaker. [13] The priest of Zeus, whose temple was just outside the city, brought bulls and wreaths to the city gates because he and the crowd wanted to offer sacrifices to them.

[14] But when the apostles Barnabas and Paul heard of this, they tore their clothes and rushed out into the crowd, shouting: [15] "Friends, why are you doing this? We too are only human like you. We are bringing you good news, telling you to turn from these worthless things to the living God, who made heaven and earth and sea and everything in them. [16] In the past, he let all nations go their own way. [17] Yet he has not left himself without testimony: He has shown kindness by giving you rain from heaven and crops in their seasons; he provides you with plenty of food and fills your hearts with joy." [18] Even with these words, they had difficulty keeping the crowd from sacrificing to them.

[19] Then some Jews came from Antioch and Iconium and won the crowd over. They stoned Paul and dragged him outside the city, thinking he was dead. [20] But after the disciples had gathered round him, he got up and went back into the city. The next day he and Barnabas left for Derbe.

The Return to Antioch in Syria

[21] They preached the good news in that city and won a large number of disciples. Then they returned to Lystra, Iconium and Antioch, [22] strengthening the disciples and encouraging them to remain true to the faith. "We must go through many hardships to enter the kingdom of God," they said. [23] Paul and Barnabas appointed elders[a] for them in each church and, with prayer and fasting, committed them to the Lord, in whom they had put their trust. [24] After going through Pisidia, they came into Pamphylia, [25] and when they had preached the word in Perga, they went down to Attalia.

[26] From Attalia they sailed back to

---

[a]23 Or *Barnabas ordained elders*; or *Barnabas had elders elected*

Antioch, where they had been committed to the grace of God for the work they had now completed. ²⁷On arriving there, they gathered the church together and reported all that God had done through them and how he had opened the door of faith to the Gentiles. ²⁸And they stayed there a long time with the disciples.

The Council at Jerusalem

15 Certain individuals came down from Judea to Antioch and were teaching the believers: "Unless you are circumcised, according to the custom taught by Moses, you cannot be saved." ²This brought Paul and Barnabas into sharp dispute and debate with them. So Paul and Barnabas were appointed, along with some other believers, to go up to Jerusalem to see the apostles and elders about this question. ³The church sent them on their way, and as they travelled through Phoenicia and Samaria, they told how the Gentiles had been converted. This news made all the believers very glad. ⁴When they came to Jerusalem, they were welcomed by the church and the apostles and elders, to whom they reported everything God had done through them.

⁵Then some of the believers who belonged to the party of the Pharisees stood up and said, "The Gentiles must be circumcised and required to obey the law of Moses."

⁶The apostles and elders met to consider this question. ⁷After much discussion, Peter got up and addressed them: "Brothers, you know that some time ago God made a choice among you that the Gentiles might hear from my lips the message of the gospel and believe. ⁸God, who knows the heart, showed that he accepted them by giving the Holy Spirit to them, just as he did to us. ⁹He made no distinction between us and them, for he purified their hearts by faith. ¹⁰Now then, why do you try to test God by putting on the necks of the disciples a yoke that neither we nor our ancestors have been able to bear? ¹¹No! We believe it is

through the grace of our Lord Jesus that we are saved, just as they are."

¹²The whole assembly became silent as they listened to Barnabas and Paul telling about the miraculous signs and wonders God had done among the Gentiles through them. ¹³When they finished, James spoke up: "Brothers, listen to me. ¹⁴Simon[a] has described to us how God at first showed his concern by taking from the Gentiles a people for himself. ¹⁵The words of the prophets are in agreement with this, as it is written:

¹⁶" 'After this I will return
      and rebuild David's fallen tent.
  Its ruins I will rebuild,
      and I will restore it,
¹⁷that the remnant of humanity may
      seek the Lord,
  and all the Gentiles who bear my
      name,
  says the Lord, who does these things'[b]
  ¹⁸that have been known for ages.[c]

¹⁹"It is my judgment, therefore, that we should not make it difficult for the Gentiles who are turning to God. ²⁰Instead we should write to them, telling them to abstain from food polluted by idols, from sexual immorality, from the meat of strangled animals and from blood. ²¹For Moses has been preached in every city from the earliest times and is read in the synagogues on every Sabbath."

The Council's Letter to Gentile Believers

²²Then the apostles and elders, with the whole church, decided to choose some of their own men and send them to Antioch with Paul and Barnabas. They chose Judas (called Barsabbas) and Silas, who were leaders among the believers. ²³With them they sent the following letter:

The apostles and elders, your brothers,

To the Gentile believers in Antioch, Syria and Cilicia:

---

[a]14 Greek *Simeon*, a variant of *Simon*; that is, Peter   [b]17 Amos 9:11,12
[c]17,18 Some manuscripts *things'* — / ¹⁸*known to the Lord for ages is his work*

Greetings.

[24] We have heard that some went out from us without our authorisation and disturbed you, troubling your minds by what they said. [25] So we all agreed to choose some men and send them to you with our dear friends Barnabas and Paul—[26] men who have risked their lives for the name of our Lord Jesus Christ. [27] Therefore we are sending Judas and Silas to confirm by word of mouth what we are writing. [28] It seemed good to the Holy Spirit and to us not to burden you with anything beyond the following requirements: [29] You are to abstain from food sacrificed to idols, from blood, from the meat of strangled animals and from sexual immorality. You will do well to avoid these things.

Farewell.

[30] So they were sent off and went down to Antioch, where they gathered the church together and delivered the letter. [31] The people read it and were glad for its encouraging message. [32] Judas and Silas, who themselves were prophets, said much to encourage and strengthen the believers. [33] After spending some time there, they were sent off by the believers with the blessing of peace to return to those who had sent them.[d] [35] But Paul and Barnabas remained in Antioch, where they and many others taught and preached the word of the Lord.

Disagreement Between Paul and Barnabas

[36] Some time later Paul said to Barnabas, "Let us go back and visit the believers in all the towns where we preached the word of the Lord and see how they are doing." [37] Barnabas wanted to take John, also called Mark, with them, [38] but Paul did not think it wise to take him, because he had deserted them in Pamphylia and

had not continued with them in the work. [39] They had such a sharp disagreement that they parted company. Barnabas took Mark and sailed for Cyprus, [40] but Paul chose Silas and left, commended by the believers to the grace of the Lord. [41] He went through Syria and Cilicia, strengthening the churches.

Timothy Joins Paul and Silas

16 He came to Derbe and then to Lystra, where a disciple named Timothy lived, whose mother was a Jewess and a believer, but whose father was a Greek. [2] The believers at Lystra and Iconium spoke well of him. [3] Paul wanted to take him along on the journey, so he circumcised him because of the Jews who lived in that area, for they all knew that his father was a Greek. [4] As they travelled from town to town, they delivered the decisions reached by the apostles and elders in Jerusalem for the people to obey. [5] So the churches were strengthened in the faith and grew daily in numbers.

Paul's Vision of the Man of Macedonia

[6] Paul and his companions travelled throughout the region of Phrygia and Galatia, having been kept by the Holy Spirit from preaching the word in the province of Asia. [7] When they came to the border of Mysia, they tried to enter Bithynia, but the Spirit of Jesus would not allow them to. [8] So they passed by Mysia and went down to Troas. [9] During the night Paul had a vision of a man of Macedonia standing and begging him, "Come over to Macedonia and help us." [10] After Paul had seen the vision, we got ready at once to leave for Macedonia, concluding that God had called us to preach the gospel to them.

Lydia's Conversion in Philippi

[11] From Troas we put out to sea and sailed straight for Samothrace, and the

---

*d*33 Some manuscripts *them,* *34but Silas decided to remain there* next day on to Neapolis. [12] From there we travelled to Philippi, a Roman colony and the leading city of that district of Macedonia. And we stayed there several days.

[13] On the Sabbath we went outside the city gate to the river, where we expected to find a place of prayer. We sat down and began to speak to the women who had gathered there. [14] One of those listening was a woman named Lydia, a dealer in purple cloth from the city of Thyatira, who was a worshipper of God. The Lord opened her heart to respond to Paul's message. [15] When she and the members of her household were baptised, she invited us to her home. "If you consider me a believer in the Lord," she said, "come and stay at my house." And she persuaded us.

Paul and Silas in Prison

[16] Once when we were going to the place of prayer, we were met by a female slave who had a spirit by which she predicted the future. She earned a great deal of money for her owners by fortune-telling. [17] She followed Paul and the rest of us, shouting, "These men are servants of the Most High God, who are telling you the way to be saved." [18] She kept this up for many days. Finally Paul became so troubled that he turned round and said to the spirit, "In the name of Jesus Christ I command you to come out of her!" At that moment the spirit left her.

[19] When her owners realised that their hope of making money was gone, they seized Paul and Silas and dragged them into the market-place to face the authorities. [20] They brought them before the magistrates and said, "These men are Jews, and are throwing our city into an uproar [21] by advocating customs unlawful for us Romans to accept or practise."

[22] The crowd joined in the attack against Paul and Silas, and the magistrates ordered them to be stripped and beaten. [23] After they had been severely flogged, they were thrown into prison, and the jailer was commanded to guard them carefully. [24] Upon receiving such orders, he put them in the inner cell and fastened their feet in the stocks.

[25] About midnight Paul and Silas were praying and singing hymns to God, and the other prisoners were listening to them. [26] Suddenly there was such a violent earthquake that the foundations of the prison were shaken. At once all the prison doors flew open, and everybody's chains came loose. [27] The jailer woke up, and when he saw the prison doors open, he drew his sword and was about to kill himself because he thought the prisoners had escaped. [28] But Paul shouted, "Don't harm yourself! We are all here!"

[29] The jailer called for lights, rushed in and fell trembling before Paul and Silas. [30] He then brought them out and asked, "Sirs, what must I do to be saved?"

[31] They replied, "Believe in the Lord Jesus, and you will be saved—you and your household." [32] Then they spoke the word of the Lord to him and to all the others in his house. [33] At that hour of the night the jailer took them and washed their wounds; then immediately he and all his family were baptised. [34] The jailer brought them into his house and set a meal before them; he was filled with joy because he had come to believe in God—he and his whole family.

[35] When it was daylight, the magistrates sent their officers to the jailer with the order: "Release those men." [36] The jailer told Paul, "The magistrates have ordered that you and Silas be released. Now you can leave. Go in peace."

[37] But Paul said to the officers: "They beat us publicly without a trial, even though we are Roman citizens, and threw us into prison. And now do they want to get rid of us quietly? No! Let them come themselves and escort us out."

[38] The officers reported this to the magistrates, and when they heard that Paul and Silas were Roman citizens, they were alarmed. [39] They came to appease them and escorted them from the prison, requesting them to leave the city. [40] After Paul and Silas came out of the prison, they went to Lydia's house, where they met with the believers and encouraged them. Then they left.

In Thessalonica

17 When they had passed through Amphipolis and Apollonia, they came to Thessalonica, where there was a Jewish synagogue. 2 As his custom was, Paul went into the synagogue, and on three Sabbath days he reasoned with them from the Scriptures, 3 explaining and proving that the Christ*a* had to suffer and rise from the dead. "This Jesus I am proclaiming to you is the Christ,"*a* he said. 4 Some of the Jews were persuaded and joined Paul and Silas, as did a large number of God-fearing Greeks and not a few prominent women.

5 But the Jews were jealous; so they rounded up some bad characters from the market-place, formed a mob and started a riot in the city. They rushed to Jason's house in search of Paul and Silas in order to bring them out to the crowd.*b* 6 But when they did not find them, they dragged Jason and some other believers before the city officials, shouting: "These people who have caused trouble all over the world have now come here, 7 and Jason has welcomed them into his house. They are all defying Caesar's decrees, saying that there is another king, one called Jesus." 8 When they heard this, the crowd and the city officials were thrown into turmoil. 9 Then they put Jason and the others on bail and let them go.

In Berea

10 As soon as it was night, the believers sent Paul and Silas away to Berea. On arriving there, they went to the Jewish synagogue. 11 Now the Bereans were of more noble character than the Thessalonians, for they received the message with great eagerness and examined the Scriptures every day to see if what Paul said was true. 12 Many of the Jews believed, as did also a number of prominent Greek women and many Greek men. 13 When the Jews in Thessalonica learned that Paul was preaching the word of God at Berea, they went there too,

agitating the crowds and stirring them up. 14 The believers immediately sent Paul to the coast, but Silas and Timothy stayed at Berea. 15 Those who escorted Paul brought him to Athens and then left with instructions for Silas and Timothy to join him as soon as possible.

In Athens

16 While Paul was waiting for them in Athens, he was greatly distressed to see that the city was full of idols. 17 So he reasoned in the synagogue with the Jews and the God-fearing Greeks, as well as in the market-place day by day with those who happened to be there. 18 A group of Epicurean and Stoic philosophers began to dispute with him. Some of them asked, "What is this babbler trying to say?" Others remarked, "He seems to be advocating foreign gods." They said this because Paul was preaching the good news about Jesus and the resurrection. 19 Then they took him and brought him to a meeting of the Areopagus, where they said to him, "May we know what this new teaching is that you are presenting? 20 You are bringing some strange ideas to our ears, and we want to know what they mean." 21 (All the Athenians and the foreigners who lived there spent their time doing nothing but talking about and listening to the latest ideas.)

22 Paul then stood up in the meeting of the Areopagus and said: "People of Athens! I see that in every way you are very religious. 23 For as I walked around and looked carefully at your objects of worship, I even found an altar with this inscription: TO AN UNKNOWN GOD. Now what you worship as something unknown I am going to proclaim to you.

24 "The God who made the world and everything in it is the Lord of heaven and earth and does not live in temples built by hands. 25 And he is not served by human hands, as if he needed anything, because he himself gives all life and breath and everything else. 26 From one man he made all the nations, that they should inhabit

---

*a*3 Or *Messiah*   *b*5 Or *the assembly of the people*

the whole earth; and he determined the times set for them and the exact places where they should live. ²⁷God did this so that they would seek him and perhaps reach out for him and find him, though he is not far from each one of us. ²⁸'For in him we live and move and have our being.' As some of your own poets have said, 'We are his offspring.'

²⁹"Therefore since we are God's offspring, we should not think that the divine being is like gold or silver or stone—an image made by human design and skill. ³⁰In the past God overlooked such ignorance, but now he commands all people everywhere to repent. ³¹For he has set a day when he will judge the world with justice by the man he has appointed. He has given proof of this to everyone by raising him from the dead."

³²When they heard about the resurrection of the dead, some of them sneered, but others said, "We want to hear you again on this subject." ³³At that, Paul left the Council. ³⁴Some of the people became followers of Paul and believed. Among them was Dionysius, a member of the Areopagus, also a woman named Damaris, and a number of others.

In Corinth

18 After this, Paul left Athens and went to Corinth. ²There he met a Jew named Aquila, a native of Pontus, who had recently come from Italy with his wife Priscilla, because Claudius had ordered all the Jews to leave Rome. Paul went to see them, ³and because he was a tentmaker as they were, he stayed and worked with them. ⁴Every Sabbath he reasoned in the synagogue, trying to persuade Jews and Greeks.

⁵When Silas and Timothy came from Macedonia, Paul devoted himself exclusively to preaching, testifying to the Jews that Jesus was the Christ.[a] ⁶But when the Jews opposed Paul and became abusive, he shook out his clothes in protest and said to them, "Your blood be on your own heads! I am clear of my responsibility. From now on I will go to the Gentiles."

⁷Then Paul left the synagogue and went next door to the house of Titius Justus, a worshipper of God. ⁸Crispus, the synagogue ruler, and his entire household believed in the Lord; and many of the Corinthians who heard him believed and were baptised.

⁹One night the Lord spoke to Paul in a vision: "Do not be afraid; keep on speaking, do not be silent. ¹⁰For I am with you, and no-one is going to attack and harm you, because I have many people in this city." ¹¹So Paul stayed for a year and a half, teaching them the word of God.

¹²While Gallio was proconsul of Achaia, the Jews made a united attack on Paul and brought him into court. ¹³"This man," they charged, "is persuading the people to worship God in ways contrary to the law."

¹⁴Just as Paul was about to speak, Gallio said to the Jews, "If you Jews were making a complaint about some misdemeanour or serious crime, it would be reasonable for me to listen to you. ¹⁵But since it involves questions about words and names and your own law—settle the matter yourselves. I will not be a judge of such things." ¹⁶So he had them ejected from the court. ¹⁷Then they all turned on Sosthenes the synagogue ruler and beat him in front of the court. But Gallio showed no concern whatever.

Priscilla, Aquila and Apollos

¹⁸Paul stayed on in Corinth for some time. Then he left the believers and sailed for Syria, accompanied by Priscilla and Aquila. Before he sailed, he had his hair cut off at Cenchrea because of a vow he had taken. ¹⁹They arrived at Ephesus, where Paul left Priscilla and Aquila. He himself went into the synagogue and reasoned with the Jews. ²⁰When they asked him to spend more time with them, he declined. ²¹But as he left, he promised, "I will come back if it is God's will." Then he set sail from Ephesus. ²²When he landed at Caesarea, he went up and greeted the church and then went down to Antioch.

---

[a]5 Or *Messiah*; also in verse 28

23 After spending some time in Antioch, Paul set out from there and travelled from place to place throughout the region of Galatia and Phrygia, strengthening all the disciples.

24 Meanwhile a Jew named Apollos, a native of Alexandria, came to Ephesus. He was a learned man, with a thorough knowledge of the Scriptures. 25 He had been instructed in the way of the Lord, and he spoke with great fervour[b] and taught about Jesus accurately, though he knew only the baptism of John. 26 He began to speak boldly in the synagogue. When Priscilla and Aquila heard him, they invited him to their home and explained to him the way of God more adequately.

27 When Apollos wanted to go to Achaia, the believers encouraged him and wrote to the disciples there to welcome him. On arriving, he was a great help to those who by grace had believed. 28 For he vigorously refuted the Jews in public debate, proving from the Scriptures that Jesus was the Christ.

Paul in Ephesus

19 While Apollos was at Corinth, Paul took the road through the interior and arrived at Ephesus. There he found some disciples 2 and asked them, "Did you receive the Holy Spirit when[a] you believed?"

They answered, "No, we have not even heard that there is a Holy Spirit."

3 So Paul asked, "Then what baptism did you receive?"

"John's baptism," they replied.

4 Paul said, "John's baptism was a baptism of repentance. He told the people to believe in the one coming after him, that is, in Jesus." 5 On hearing this, they were baptised into[b] the name of the Lord Jesus. 6 When Paul placed his hands on them, the Holy Spirit came on them, and they spoke in tongues[c] and prophesied. 7 There were about twelve men in all.

8 Paul entered the synagogue and spoke boldly there for three months, arguing persuasively about the kingdom of God. 9 But some of them became obstinate; they refused to believe and publicly maligned the Way. So Paul left them. He took the disciples with him and had discussions daily in the lecture hall of Tyrannus. 10 This went on for two years, so that all the Jews and Greeks who lived in the province of Asia heard the word of the Lord.

11 God did extraordinary miracles through Paul, 12 so that even handkerchiefs and aprons that had touched him were taken to the sick, and their illnesses were cured and the evil spirits left them.

13 Some Jews who went around driving out evil spirits tried to invoke the name of the Lord Jesus over those who were demon-possessed. They would say, "In the name of Jesus, whom Paul preaches, I command you to come out." 14 Seven sons of Sceva, a Jewish chief priest, were doing this. 15 ⌞One day⌟ the evil spirit answered them, "Jesus I know, and I know about Paul, but who are you?" 16 Then the man who had the evil spirit jumped on them and overpowered them all. He gave them such a beating that they ran out of the house naked and bleeding.

17 When this became known to the Jews and Greeks living in Ephesus, they were all seized with fear, and the name of the Lord Jesus was held in high honour. 18 Many of those who believed now came and openly confessed their evil deeds. 19 A number who had practised sorcery brought their scrolls together and burned them publicly. When they calculated the value of the scrolls, the total came to fifty thousand drachmas.[d] 20 In this way the word of the Lord spread widely and grew in power.

21 After all this had happened, Paul decided to go to Jerusalem, passing through Macedonia and Achaia. "After I have been there," he said, "I must visit Rome also." 22 He sent two of his helpers, Timothy and Erastus, to Macedonia, while he stayed in the province of Asia a little longer.

---

b25 Or *with fervour in the Spirit*   a2 Or *after*   b5 Or *in*   c6 Or *other languages*
d19 A drachma was a silver coin worth about a day's wages.

The Riot in Ephesus

23 About that time there arose a great disturbance about the Way. 24 A silversmith named Demetrius, who made silver shrines of Artemis, brought in no little business for the skilled workers. 25 He called them together, along with the workers in related trades, and said: "Men, you know we receive a good income from this business. 26 And you see and hear how this fellow Paul has convinced and led astray large numbers of people here in Ephesus and in practically the whole province of Asia. He says that gods made by human hands are no gods at all. 27 There is danger not only that our trade will lose its good name, but also that the temple of the great goddess Artemis will be discredited, and the goddess herself, who is worshipped throughout the province of Asia and the world, will be robbed of her divine majesty."

28 When they heard this, they were furious and began shouting: "Great is Artemis of the Ephesians!" 29 Soon the whole city was in an uproar. The people seized Gaius and Aristarchus, Paul's travelling companions from Macedonia, and they all rushed into the theatre. 30 Paul wanted to appear before the crowd, but the disciples would not let him. 31 Even some of the officials of the province, friends of Paul, sent him a message begging him not to venture into the theatre.

32 The assembly was in confusion: Some were shouting one thing, some another. Most of the people did not even know why they were there. 33 The Jews pushed Alexander to the front, and some of the crowd shouted instructions to him. He motioned for silence in order to make a defence before the people. 34 But when they realised he was a Jew, they all shouted in unison for about two hours: "Great is Artemis of the Ephesians!"

35 The city clerk quietened the crowd and said: "People of Ephesus, doesn't all the world know that the city of Ephesus is the guardian of the temple of the great Artemis and of her image, which fell from heaven? 36 Therefore, since these facts are undeniable, you ought to be quiet and not do anything rash. 37 You have brought these men here, though they have neither robbed temples nor blasphemed our goddess. 38 If, then, Demetrius and his associates have a grievance against anybody, the courts are open and there are proconsuls. They can press charges. 39 If there is anything further you want to bring up, it must be settled in a legal assembly. 40 As it is, we are in danger of being charged with rioting because of today's events. In that case we would not be able to account for this commotion, since there is no reason for it." 41 After he had said this, he dismissed the assembly.

Through Macedonia and Greece

20 When the uproar had ended, Paul sent for the disciples and, after encouraging them, said good-bye and set out for Macedonia. 2 He travelled through that area, speaking many words of encouragement to the people, and finally arrived in Greece, 3 where he stayed three months. Because the Jews made a plot against him just as he was about to sail for Syria, he decided to go back through Macedonia. 4 He was accompanied by Sopater son of Pyrrhus from Berea, Aristarchus and Secundus from Thessalonica, Gaius from Derbe, Timothy also, and Tychicus and Trophimus from the province of Asia. 5 These men went on ahead and waited for us at Troas. 6 But we sailed from Philippi after the Feast of Unleavened Bread, and five days later joined the others at Troas, where we stayed seven days.

Eutychus Raised From the Dead at Troas

7 On the first day of the week we came together to break bread. Paul spoke to the people and, because he intended to leave the next day, kept on talking until midnight. 8 There were many lamps in the upstairs room where we were meeting. 9 Seated in a window was a young man named Eutychus, who was sinking into a deep sleep as Paul talked on and on. When he was sound asleep, he fell to the ground from the third storey and was

picked up dead. ¹⁰Paul went down, threw himself on the young man and put his arms around him. "Don't be alarmed," he said. "He's alive!" ¹¹Then he went upstairs again and broke bread and ate. After talking until daylight, he left. ¹²The people took the young man home alive and were greatly comforted.

Paul's Farewell to the Ephesian Elders

¹³We went on ahead to the ship and sailed for Assos, where we were going to take Paul aboard. He had made this arrangement because he was going there on foot. ¹⁴When he met us at Assos, we took him aboard and went on to Mitylene. ¹⁵The next day we set sail from there and arrived off Kios. The day after that we crossed over to Samos, and on the following day arrived at Miletus. ¹⁶Paul had decided to sail past Ephesus to avoid spending time in the province of Asia, for he was in a hurry to reach Jerusalem, if possible, by the day of Pentecost.

¹⁷From Miletus, Paul sent to Ephesus for the elders of the church. ¹⁸When they arrived, he said to them: "You know how I lived the whole time I was with you, from the first day I came into the province of Asia. ¹⁹I served the Lord with great humility and with tears, although I was severely tested by the plots of the Jews. ²⁰You know that I have not hesitated to preach anything that would be helpful to you but have taught you publicly and from house to house. ²¹I have declared to both Jews and Greeks that they must turn to God in repentance and have faith in our Lord Jesus.

²²"And now, compelled by the Spirit, I am going to Jerusalem, not knowing what will happen to me there. ²³I only know that in every city the Holy Spirit warns me that prison and hardships are facing me. ²⁴However, I consider my life worth nothing to me, if only I may finish the race and complete the task the Lord Jesus has given me—the task of testifying to the gospel of God's grace.

²⁵"Now I know that none of you among whom I have gone about preaching the kingdom will ever see me again. ²⁶Therefore, I declare to you today that I am innocent of the blood of everyone. ²⁷For I have not hesitated to proclaim to you the whole will of God. ²⁸Keep watch over yourselves and all the flock of which the Holy Spirit has made you overseers.ᵃ Be shepherds of the church of God,ᵇ which he bought with his own blood. ²⁹I know that after I leave, savage wolves will come in among you and will not spare the flock. ³⁰Even from your own number some will arise and distort the truth in order to draw away disciples after them. ³¹So be on your guard! Remember that for three years I never stopped warning each of you night and day with tears.

³²"Now I commit you to God and to the word of his grace, which can build you up and give you an inheritance among all those who are sanctified. ³³I have not coveted anyone's silver or gold or clothing. ³⁴You yourselves know that these hands of mine have supplied my own needs and the needs of my companions. ³⁵In everything I did, I showed you that by this kind of hard work we must help the weak, remembering the words the Lord Jesus himself said: 'It is more blessed to give than to receive.' "

³⁶When he had said this, he knelt down with all of them and prayed. ³⁷They all wept as they embraced him and kissed him. ³⁸What grieved them most was his statement that they would never see his face again. Then they accompanied him to the ship.

On to Jerusalem

21 After we had torn ourselves away from them, we put out to sea and sailed straight to Cos. The next day we went to Rhodes and from there to Patara. ²We found a ship crossing over to Phoenicia, went on board and set sail. ³After sighting Cyprus and passing to the south of it, we sailed on to Syria. We landed at Tyre, where our ship was to unload its cargo. ⁴Finding the disciples there, we stayed with them seven days. Through the Spirit they urged Paul not to go on to Jerusalem. [5] But when our time was up, we left and continued on our way. All of them, including wives and children accompanied us out of the city, and there on the beach we knelt to pray. [6] After saying good-bye to each other, we went aboard the ship, and they returned home.

[7] We continued our voyage from Tyre and landed at Ptolemais, where we greeted the believers and stayed with them for a day. [8] Leaving the next day, we reached Caesarea and stayed at the house of Philip the evangelist, one of the Seven. [9] He had four unmarried daughters who prophesied.

[10] After we had been there a number of days, a prophet named Agabus came down from Judea. [11] Coming over to us, he took Paul's belt, tied his own hands and feet with it and said, "The Holy Spirit says, 'In this way the Jews of Jerusalem will bind the owner of this belt and will hand him over to the Gentiles.' "

[12] When we heard this, we and the people there pleaded with Paul not to go up to Jerusalem. [13] Then Paul answered, "Why are you weeping and breaking my heart? I am ready not only to be bound, but also to die in Jerusalem for the name of the Lord Jesus." [14] When he would not be dissuaded, we gave up and said, "The Lord's will be done."

[15] After this, we got ready and went up to Jerusalem. [16] Some of the disciples from Caesarea accompanied us and brought us to the home of Mnason, where we were to stay. He was a man from Cyprus and one of the early disciples.

Paul's Arrival at Jerusalem

[17] When we arrived at Jerusalem, the believers received us warmly. [18] The next day Paul and the rest of us went to see James, and all the elders were present. [19] Paul greeted them and reported in detail what God had done among the Gentiles through his ministry.

[20] When they heard this, they praised God. Then they said to Paul: "You see, brother, how many thousands of Jews have believed, and all of them are zealous for the law. [21] They have been informed that you teach all the Jews who live among the Gentiles to turn away from Moses, telling them not to circumcise their children or live according to our customs. [22] What shall we do? They will certainly hear that you have come, [23] so do what we tell you. There are four men with us who have made a vow. [24] Take these men, join in their purification rites and pay their expenses, so that they can have their heads shaved. Then everybody will know there is no truth in these reports about you, but that you yourself are living in obedience to the law. [25] As for the Gentile believers, we have written to them our decision that they should abstain from food sacrificed to idols, from blood, from the meat of strangled animals and from sexual immorality."

[26] The next day Paul took the men and purified himself along with them. Then he went to the temple to give notice of the date when the days of purification would end and the offering would be made for each of them.

Paul Arrested

[27] When the seven days were nearly over, some Jews from the province of Asia saw Paul at the temple. They stirred up the whole crowd and seized him, [28] shouting, "People of Israel, help us! This is the man who teaches everyone everywhere against our people and our law and this place. And besides, he has brought Greeks into the temple area and defiled this holy place." [29] (They had previously seen Trophimus the Ephesian in the city with Paul and assumed that Paul had brought him into the temple area.)

[30] The whole city was aroused, and the people came running from all directions. Seizing Paul, they dragged him from the temple, and immediately the gates were shut. [31] While they were trying to kill him, news reached the commander of the Roman troops that the whole city of Jerusalem was in an uproar. [32] He at once took some officers and soldiers and ran down to the crowd. When the rioters saw

the commander and his soldiers, they stopped beating Paul.

33 The commander came up and arrested him and ordered him to be bound with two chains. Then he asked who he was and what he had done. 34 Some in the crowd shouted one thing and some another, and since the commander could not get at the truth because of the uproar, he ordered that Paul be taken into the barracks. 35 When Paul reached the steps, the violence of the mob was so great he had to be carried by the soldiers. 36 The crowd that followed kept shouting, "Away with him!"

Paul Speaks to the Crowd

37 As the soldiers were about to take Paul into the barracks, he asked the commander, "May I say something to you?"

"Do you speak Greek?" he replied. 38 "Aren't you the Egyptian who started a revolt and led four thousand terrorists out into the desert some time ago?"

39 Paul answered, "I am a Jew, from Tarsus in Cilicia, a citizen of no ordinary city. Please let me speak to the people."

40 Having received the commander's permission, Paul stood on the steps and motioned to the crowd. When they were all silent, he said to them in Aramaic[a]:

22 1 "Brothers and fathers, listen now to my defence."

2 When they heard him speak to them in Aramaic, they became very quiet.

Then Paul said: 3 "I am a Jew, born in Tarsus of Cilicia, but brought up in this city. Under Gamaliel I was thoroughly trained in the law of our ancestors and was just as zealous for God as any of you are today. 4 I persecuted the followers of this Way to their death, arresting both men and women and throwing them into prison, 5 as also the high priest and all the Council can testify. I even obtained letters from them to their associates in Damascus, and went there to bring these people as prisoners to Jerusalem to be punished.

6 "About noon as I came near Damascus, suddenly a bright light from heaven flashed around me. 7 I fell to the ground and heard a voice say to me, 'Saul! Saul! Why do you persecute me?'

8 " 'Who are you, Lord?' I asked.

" 'I am Jesus of Nazareth, whom you are persecuting,' he replied. 9 My companions saw the light, but they did not understand the voice of him who was speaking to me.

10 " 'What shall I do, Lord?' I asked.

" 'Get up,' the Lord said, 'and go into Damascus. There you will be told all that you have been assigned to do.' 11 My companions led me by the hand into Damascus, because the brilliance of the light had blinded me.

12 "A man named Ananias came to see me. He was a devout observer of the law and highly respected by all the Jews living there. 13 He stood beside me and said, 'Brother Saul, receive your sight!' And at that very moment I was able to see him.

14 "Then he said: 'The God of our ancestors has chosen you to know his will and to see the Righteous One and to hear words from his mouth. 15 You will be his witness to all people of what you have seen and heard. 16 And now what are you waiting for? Get up, be baptised and wash your sins away, calling on his name.'

17 "When I returned to Jerusalem and was praying at the temple, I fell into a trance 18 and saw the Lord speaking. 'Quick!' he said to me. 'Leave Jerusalem immediately, because they will not accept your testimony about me.'

19 " 'Lord,' I replied, 'these people know that I went from one synagogue to another to imprison and beat those who believe in you. 20 And when the blood of your martyr[a] Stephen was shed, I stood there giving my approval and guarding the clothes of those who were killing him.'

21 "Then the Lord said to me, 'Go; I will send you far away to the Gentiles.' "

Paul the Roman Citizen

22 The crowd listened to Paul until he said this. Then they raised their voices and

---

[a]40 Or possibly *Hebrew*; also in 22:2 [a]20 Or *witness*

shouted, "Rid the earth of him! He's not fit to live!"

23 As they were shouting and throwing off their cloaks and flinging dust into the air, 24 the commander ordered Paul to be taken into the barracks. He directed that he be flogged and questioned in order to find out why the people were shouting at him like this. 25 As they stretched him out to flog him, Paul said to the centurion standing there, "Is it legal for you to flog a Roman citizen who hasn't even been found guilty?"

26 When the centurion heard this, he went to the commander and reported it. "What are you going to do?" he asked. "This man is a Roman citizen."

27 The commander went to Paul and asked, "Tell me, are you a Roman citizen?"

"Yes, I am," he answered.

28 Then the commander said, "I had to pay a big price for my citizenship."

"But I was born a citizen," Paul replied.

29 Those who were about to question him withdrew immediately. The commander himself was alarmed when he realised that he had put Paul, a Roman citizen, in chains.

Before the Sanhedrin

30 The next day, since the commander wanted to find out exactly why Paul was being accused by the Jews, he released him and ordered the chief priests and all the Sanhedrin to assemble. Then he brought Paul and had him stand before them.

23 Paul looked straight at the Sanhedrin and said, "My brothers, I have fulfilled my duty to God in all good conscience to this day." 2 At this the high priest Ananias ordered those standing near Paul to strike him on the mouth. 3 Then Paul said to him, "God will strike you, you whitewashed wall! You sit there to judge me according to the law, yet you yourself violate the law by commanding that I be struck!"

4 Those who were standing near Paul said, "You dare to insult God's high priest?"

5 Paul replied, "Brothers, I did not realise that he was the high priest; for it is written: 'Do not speak evil about the ruler of your people.'a"

6 Then Paul, knowing that some of them were Sadducees and the others Pharisees, called out in the Sanhedrin, "My brothers, I am a Pharisee, the son of a Pharisee. I stand on trial because of my hope in the resurrection of the dead." 7 When he said this, a dispute broke out between the Pharisees and the Sadducees, and the assembly was divided. 8 (The Sadducees say that there is no resurrection, and that there are neither angels nor spirits, but the Pharisees acknowledge them all.)

9 There was a great uproar, and some of the teachers of the law who were Pharisees stood up and argued vigorously. "We find nothing wrong with this man," they said. "What if a spirit or an angel has spoken to him?" 10 The dispute became so violent that the commander was afraid Paul would be torn to pieces by them. He ordered the troops to go down and take him away from them by force and bring him into the barracks.

11 The following night the Lord stood near Paul and said, "Take courage! As you have testified about me in Jerusalem, so you must also testify in Rome."

The Plot to Kill Paul

12 The next morning the Jews formed a conspiracy and bound themselves with an oath not to eat or drink until they had killed Paul. 13 More than forty men were involved in this plot. 14 They went to the chief priests and elders and said, "We have taken a solemn oath not to eat anything until we have killed Paul. 15 Now then, you and the Sanhedrin petition the commander to bring him before you on the pretext of wanting more accurate information about his case. We are ready to kill him before he gets here."

---

a5 Exodus 22:28

16 But when the son of Paul's sister heard of this plot, he went into the barracks and told Paul.

17 Then Paul called one of the centurions and said, "Take this young man to the commander; he has something to tell him." 18 So he took him to the commander.

The centurion said, "Paul, the prisoner, sent for me and asked me to bring this young man to you because he has something to tell you."

19 The commander took the young man by the hand, drew him aside and asked, "What is it you want to tell me?"

20 He said: "The Jews have agreed to ask you to bring Paul before the Sanhedrin tomorrow on the pretext of wanting more accurate information about him. 21 Don't give in to them, because more than forty of them are waiting in ambush for him. They have taken an oath not to eat or drink until they have killed him. They are ready now, waiting for your consent to their request."

22 The commander dismissed the young man and cautioned him, "Don't tell anyone that you have reported this to me."

Paul Transferred to Caesarea

23 Then he called two of his centurions and ordered them, "Get ready a detachment of two hundred soldiers, seventy horsemen and two hundred spearmen[b] to go to Caesarea at nine tonight. 24 Provide mounts for Paul so that he may be taken safely to Governor Felix."

25 He wrote a letter as follows:

26 Claudius Lysias,

To His Excellency, Governor Felix:

Greetings.

27 This man was seized by the Jews and they were about to kill him, but I came with my troops and rescued him, for I had learned that he is a Roman citizen. 28 I wanted to know why they were accusing him, so I brought him to their Sanhedrin. 29 I found that the accusation had to do with questions about their law, but there was no charge against him that deserved death or imprisonment. 30 When I was informed of a plot to be carried out against the man, I sent him to you at once. I also ordered his accusers to present to you their case against him.

31 So the soldiers, carrying out their orders, took Paul with them during the night and brought him as far as Antipatris. 32 The next day they let the cavalry go on with him, while they returned to the barracks. 33 When the cavalry arrived in Caesarea, they delivered the letter to the governor and handed Paul over to him. 34 The governor read the letter and asked what province he was from. Learning that he was from Cilicia, 35 he said, "I will hear your case when your accusers get here." Then he ordered that Paul be kept under guard in Herod's palace.

The Trial Before Felix

24 Five days later the high priest Ananias went down to Caesarea with some of the elders and a lawyer named Tertullus, and they brought their charges against Paul before the governor. 2 When Paul was called in, Tertullus presented his case before Felix: "We have enjoyed a long period of peace under you, and your foresight has brought about reforms in this nation. 3 Everywhere and in every way, most excellent Felix, we acknowledge this with profound gratitude. 4 But in order not to weary you further, I would request that you be kind enough to hear us briefly.

5 "We have found this man to be a troublemaker, stirring up riots among the Jews all over the world. He is a ringleader of the Nazarene sect 6 and even tried to desecrate the temple; so we seized him. 8 By[a] examining him yourself you will be able to learn the truth about all these

---

b23 The meaning of the Greek for this word is uncertain.
a6 –8 Some manuscripts *him and wanted to judge him according to our law.* 7*But the commander, Lysias, came and with the use of much force snatched him from our hands* 8*and ordered his accusers to come before you. By*

charges we are bringing against him."

⁹ The Jews joined in the accusation, asserting that these things were true.

¹⁰ When the governor motioned for him to speak, Paul replied: "I know that for a number of years you have been a judge over this nation; so I gladly make my defence. ¹¹ You can easily verify that no more than twelve days ago I went up to Jerusalem to worship. ¹² My accusers did not find me arguing with anyone at the temple, or stirring up a crowd in the synagogues or anywhere else in the city. ¹³ And they cannot prove to you the charges they are now making against me. ¹⁴ However, I admit that I worship the God of our ancestors as a follower of the Way, which they call a sect. I believe everything that agrees with the Law and that is written in the Prophets, ¹⁵ and I have the same hope in God as these people themselves have, that there will be a resurrection of both the righteous and the wicked. ¹⁶ So I strive always to keep my conscience clear before God and all people.

¹⁷ "After an absence of several years, I came to Jerusalem to bring my people gifts for the poor and to present offerings. ¹⁸ I was ceremonially clean when they found me in the temple courts doing this. There was no crowd with me, nor was I involved in any disturbance. ¹⁹ But there are some Jews from the province of Asia, who ought to be here before you and bring charges if they have anything against me. ²⁰ Or these who are here should state what crime they found in me when I stood before the Sanhedrin—²¹ unless it was this one thing I shouted as I stood in their presence: 'It is concerning the resurrection of the dead that I am on trial before you today.'"

²² Then Felix, who was well acquainted with the Way, adjourned the proceedings. "When Lysias the commander comes," he said, "I will decide your case." ²³ He ordered the centurion to keep Paul under guard but to give him some freedom and permit his friends to take care of his needs.

²⁴ Several days later Felix came with his wife Drusilla, who was a Jewess. He sent for Paul and listened to him as he spoke about faith in Christ Jesus. ²⁵ As Paul discoursed on righteousness, self-control and the judgment to come, Felix was afraid and said, "That's enough for now! You may leave. When I find it convenient, I will send for you." ²⁶ At the same time he was hoping that Paul would offer him a bribe, so he sent for him frequently and talked with him.

²⁷ When two years had passed, Felix was succeeded by Porcius Festus, but because Felix wanted to grant a favour to the Jews, he left Paul in prison.

The Trial Before Festus

25 Three days after arriving in the province, Festus went up from Caesarea to Jerusalem, ² where the chief priests and Jewish leaders appeared before him and presented the charges against Paul. ³ They urgently requested Festus, as a favour to them, to have Paul transferred to Jerusalem, for they were preparing an ambush to kill him along the way. ⁴ Festus answered, "Paul is being held at Caesarea, and I myself am going there soon. ⁵ Let some of your leaders come with me and press charges against the man there, if he has done anything wrong."

⁶ After spending eight or ten days with them, he went down to Caesarea, and the next day he convened the court and ordered that Paul be brought before him. ⁷ When Paul appeared, the Jews who had come down from Jerusalem stood around him, bringing many serious charges against him, which they could not prove.

⁸ Then Paul made his defence: "I have done nothing wrong against the law of the Jews or against the temple or against Caesar."

⁹ Festus, wishing to do the Jews a favour, said to Paul, "Are you willing to go up to Jerusalem and stand trial before me there on these charges?"

¹⁰ Paul answered: "I am now standing before Caesar's court, where I ought to be tried. I have not done any wrong to the Jews, as you yourself know very well. ¹¹ If, however, I am guilty of doing anything deserving death, I do not refuse to die. But if the charges brought against me by

these Jews are not true, no-one has the right to hand me over to them. I appeal to Caesar!"

¹²After Festus had conferred with his council, he declared: "You have appealed to Caesar. To Caesar you will go!"

Festus Consults King Agrippa

¹³A few days later King Agrippa and Bernice arrived at Caesarea to pay their respects to Festus. ¹⁴Since they were spending many days there, Festus discussed Paul's case with the king. He said: "There is a man here whom Felix left as a prisoner. ¹⁵When I went to Jerusalem, the chief priests and elders of the Jews brought charges against him and asked that he be condemned.

¹⁶"I told them that it is not the Roman custom to hand over anyone before the accused has faced the accusers and has had an opportunity to make a defence against their charges. ¹⁷When they came here with me, I did not delay the case, but convened the court the next day and ordered the man to be brought in. ¹⁸When his accusers got up to speak, they did not charge him with any of the crimes I had expected. ¹⁹Instead, they had some points of dispute with him about their own religion and about a dead man named Jesus whom Paul claimed was alive. ²⁰I was at a loss how to investigate such matters; so I asked if he would be willing to go to Jerusalem and stand trial there on these charges. ²¹When Paul made his appeal to be held over for the Emperor's decision, I ordered him to be held until I could send him to Caesar."

²²Then Agrippa said to Festus, "I would like to hear this man myself."

He replied, "Tomorrow you will hear him."

Paul Before Agrippa

²³The next day Agrippa and Bernice came with great pomp and entered the audience room with the high ranking officers and the leading men of the city. At the command of Festus, Paul was brought in. ²⁴Festus said: "King Agrippa, and all who are present with us, you see this man! The whole Jewish community has petitioned me about him in Jerusalem and here in Caesarea, shouting that he ought not to live any longer. ²⁵I found he had done nothing deserving of death, but because he made his appeal to the Emperor I decided to send him to Rome. ²⁶But I have nothing definite to write to His Majesty about him. Therefore I have brought him before all of you, and especially before you, King Agrippa, so that as a result of this investigation I may have something to write. ²⁷For I think it is unreasonable to send on a prisoner without specifying the charges against him."

26 Then Agrippa said to Paul, "You have permission to speak for yourself."

So Paul motioned with his hand and began his defence: ²"King Agrippa, I consider myself fortunate to stand before you today as I make my defence against all the accusations of the Jews, ³and especially so because you are well acquainted with all the Jewish customs and controversies. Therefore, I beg you to listen to me patiently.

⁴"The Jews all know the way I have lived ever since I was a child, from the beginning of my life in my own country, and also in Jerusalem. ⁵They have known me for a long time and can testify, if they are willing, that according to the strictest sect of our religion, I lived as a Pharisee. ⁶And now it is because of my hope in what God has promised our ancestors that I am on trial today. ⁷This is the promise our twelve tribes are hoping to see fulfilled as they earnestly serve God day and night. O King, it is because of this hope that the Jews are accusing me. ⁸Why should any of you consider it incredible that God raises the dead?

⁹"I too was convinced that I ought to do all that was possible to oppose the name of Jesus of Nazareth. ¹⁰And that is just what I did in Jerusalem. On the authority of the chief priests I put many of the saints in prison, and when they were put to death, I cast my vote against them. ¹¹Many a time I went from one synagogue to another to have them punished, and I tried

to force them to blaspheme. In my obsession against them, I even went to foreign cities to persecute them.

12 "On one of these journeys I was going to Damascus with the authority and commission of the chief priests. 13 About noon, O King, as I was on the road, I saw a light from heaven, brighter than the sun, blazing around me and my companions. 14 We all fell to the ground, and I heard a voice saying to me in Aramaic,[a] 'Saul, Saul, why do you persecute me? It is hard for you to kick against the goads.'

15 "Then I asked, 'Who are you, Lord?'

" 'I am Jesus, whom you are persecuting,' the Lord replied. 16 'Now get up and stand on your feet. I have appeared to you to appoint you as a servant and as a witness of what you have seen of me and what I will show you. 17 I will rescue you from your own people and from the Gentiles. I am sending you to them 18 to open their eyes and turn them from darkness to light, and from the power of Satan to God, so that they may receive forgiveness of sins and a place among those who are sanctified by faith in me.'

19 "So then, King Agrippa, I was not disobedient to the vision from heaven. 20 First to those in Damascus, then to those in Jerusalem and in all Judea, and to the Gentiles also, I preached that they should repent and turn to God and prove their repentance by their deeds. 21 That is why the Jews seized me in the temple courts and tried to kill me. 22 But I have had God's help to this very day, and so I stand here and testify to small and great alike. I am saying nothing beyond what the prophets and Moses said would happen—23 that the Christ[b] would suffer and, as the first to rise from the dead, would proclaim light to his own people and to the Gentiles."

24 At this point Festus interrupted Paul's defence. "You are out of your mind, Paul!" he shouted. "Your great learning is driving you insane."

25 "I am not insane, most excellent Festus," Paul replied. "What I am saying is true and reasonable. 26 The king is familiar with these things, and I can speak

freely to him. I am convinced that none of this has escaped his notice, because it was not done in a corner. 27 King Agrippa, do you believe the prophets? I know you do."

28 Then Agrippa said to Paul, "Do you think that in such a short time you can persuade me to be a Christian?"

29 Paul replied, "Short time or long—I pray God that not only you but all who are listening to me today may become what I am, except for these chains."

30 The king rose, and with him the governor and Bernice and those sitting with them. 31 They left the room, and while talking with one another, they said, "This man is not doing anything that deserves death or imprisonment."

32 Agrippa said to Festus, "This man could have been set free if he had not appealed to Caesar."

Paul Sails for Rome

27 When it was decided that we would sail for Italy, Paul and some other prisoners were handed over to a centurion named Julius, who belonged to the Imperial Regiment. 2 We boarded a ship from Adramyttium about to sail for ports along the coast of the province of Asia, and we put out to sea. Aristarchus, a Macedonian from Thessalonica, was with us.

3 The next day we landed at Sidon; and Julius, in kindness to Paul, allowed him to go to his friends so they might provide for his needs. 4 From there we put out to sea again and passed to the lee of Cyprus because the winds were against us. 5 When we had sailed across the open sea off the coast of Cilicia and Pamphylia, we landed at Myra in Lycia. 6 There the centurion found an Alexandrian ship sailing for Italy and put us on board. 7 We made slow headway for many days and had difficulty arriving off Cnidus. When the wind did not allow us to hold our course, we sailed to the lee of Crete, opposite Salmone. 8 We moved along the coast with difficulty and came to a place called Fair Havens, near the town of Lasea.

9 Much time had been lost, and sailing

[a]14 Or Hebrew   [b]23 Or Messiah

had already become dangerous because by now it was after the Fast.[a] So Paul warned them, 10 "Men, I can see that our voyage is going to be disastrous and bring great loss to ship and cargo, and to our own lives also." 11 But the centurion, instead of listening to what Paul said, followed the advice of the pilot and of the owner of the ship. 12 Since the harbour was unsuitable to winter in, the majority decided that we should sail on, hoping to reach Phoenix and winter there. This was a harbour in Crete, facing both south-west and north-west.

The Storm

13 When a gentle south wind began to blow, they thought they had obtained what they wanted; so they weighed anchor and sailed along the shore of Crete. 14 Before very long, a wind of hurricane force, called the "north-easter", swept down from the island. 15 The ship was caught by the storm and could not head into the wind; so we gave way to it and were driven along. 16 As we passed to the lee of a small island called Cauda, we were hardly able to make the lifeboat secure. 17 When the men had hoisted it aboard, they passed ropes under the ship itself to hold it together. Fearing that they would run aground on the sand-bars of Syrtis, they lowered the sea anchor and let the ship be driven along. 18 We took such a violent battering from the storm that the next day they began to throw the cargo overboard. 19 On the third day, they threw the ship's tackle overboard with their own hands. 20 When neither sun nor stars appeared for many days and the storm continued raging, we finally gave up all hope of being saved.

21 After they had gone a long time without food, Paul stood up before them and said: "Men, you should have taken my advice not to sail from Crete; then you would have spared yourselves this damage and loss. 22 But now I urge you to keep up your courage, because not one of you will

be lost; only the ship will be destroyed. 23 Last night an angel of the God whose I am and whom I serve stood beside me 24 and said, 'Do not be afraid, Paul. You must stand trial before Caesar; and God has graciously given you the lives of all who sail with you.' 25 So keep up your courage, men, for I have faith in God that it will happen just as he told me. 26 Nevertheless, we must run aground on some island."

The Shipwreck

27 On the fourteenth night we were still being driven across the Adriatic[b] Sea, when about midnight the sailors sensed they were approaching land. 28 They took soundings and found that the water was one hundred and twenty feet[c] deep. A short time later they took soundings again and found it was ninety feet[d] deep. 29 Fearing that we would be dashed against the rocks, they dropped four anchors from the stern and prayed for daylight. 30 In an attempt to escape from the ship, the sailors let the lifeboat down into the sea, pretending they were going to lower some anchors from the bow. 31 Then Paul said to the centurion and the soldiers, "Unless these men stay with the ship, you cannot be saved." 32 So the soldiers cut the ropes that held the lifeboat and let it fall away.

33 Just before dawn Paul urged them all to eat. "For the last fourteen days," he said, "you have been in constant suspense and have gone without food—you haven't eaten anything. 34 Now I urge you to take some food. You need it to survive. Not one of you will lose a single hair from his head." 35 After he said this, he took some bread and gave thanks to God in front of them all. Then he broke it and began to eat. 36 They were all encouraged and ate some food themselves. 37 Altogether there were 276 of us on board. 38 When they had eaten as much as they wanted, they lightened the ship by throwing the grain into the sea.

---

[a]9 That is, the Day of Atonement (Yom Kippur)
[b]27 In ancient times the name referred to an area extending well south of Italy.
[c]28 Greek *twenty orguias* (about 37 metres)   [d]28 Greek *fifteen orguias* (about 27 metres)

[39] When daylight came, they did not recognise the land, but they saw a bay with a sandy beach, where they decided to run the ship aground if they could. [40] Cutting loose the anchors, they left them in the sea and at the same time untied the ropes that held the rudders. Then they hoisted the foresail to the wind and made for the beach. [41] But the ship struck a sand-bar and ran aground. The bow stuck fast and would not move, and the stern was broken to pieces by the pounding of the surf.

[42] The soldiers planned to kill the prisoners to prevent any of them from swimming away and escaping. [43] But the centurion wanted to spare Paul's life and kept them from carrying out their plan. He ordered those who could swim to jump overboard first and get to land. [44] The rest were to get there on planks or on pieces of the ship. In this way everyone reached land in safety.

Ashore on Malta

28 Once safely on shore, we found out that the island was called Malta. [2] The islanders showed us unusual kindness. They built a fire and welcomed us all because it was raining and cold. [3] Paul gathered a pile of brushwood and, as he put it on the fire, a viper, driven out by the heat, fastened itself on his hand. [4] When the islanders saw the snake hanging from his hand, they said to each other, "This man must be a murderer; for though he escaped from the sea, Justice has not allowed him to live." [5] But Paul shook the snake off into the fire and suffered no ill effects. [6] The people expected him to swell up or suddenly fall dead, but after waiting a long time and seeing nothing unusual happen to him, they changed their minds and said he was a god.

[7] There was an estate near by that belonged to Publius, the chief official of the island. He welcomed us to his home and for three days entertained us hospitably. [8] His father was sick in bed, suffering from fever and dysentery. Paul went in to see him and, after prayer, placed his hands on him and healed him. [9] When this had happened, the rest of the sick on the island came and were cured. [10] They honoured us in many ways and when we were ready to sail, they furnished us with the supplies we needed.

Arrival at Rome

[11] After three months we put out to sea in a ship that had wintered in the island. It was an Alexandrian ship with the figurehead of the twin gods Castor and Pollux. [12] We put in at Syracuse and stayed there three days. [13] From there we set sail and arrived at Rhegium. The next day the south wind came up, and on the following day we reached Puteoli. [14] There we found some believers who invited us to spend a week with them. And so we came to Rome. [15] The believers there had heard that we were coming, and they travelled as far as the Forum of Appius and the Three Taverns to meet us. At the sight of these people Paul thanked God and was encouraged. [16] When we got to Rome, Paul was allowed to live by himself, with a soldier to guard him.

Paul Preaches at Rome Under Guard

[17] Three days later he called together the leaders of the Jews. When they had assembled, Paul said to them: "My brothers, although I have done nothing against our people or against the customs of our ancestors, I was arrested in Jerusalem and handed over to the Romans. [18] They examined me and wanted to release me, because I was not guilty of any crime deserving death. [19] But when the Jews objected, I was compelled to appeal to Caesar—not that I had any charge to bring against my own people. [20] For this reason I have asked to see you and talk with you. It is because of the hope of Israel that I am bound with this chain."

[21] They replied, "We have not received any letters from Judea concerning you, and none of our people who have come from there has reported or said anything bad about you. [22] But we want to hear

what your views are, for we know that people everywhere are talking against this sect."

²³ They arranged to meet Paul on a certain day, and came in even larger numbers to the place where he was staying. From morning till evening he explained and declared to them the kingdom of God and tried to convince them about Jesus from the Law of Moses and from the Prophets. ²⁴ Some were convinced by what he said, but others would not believe. ²⁵ They disagreed among themselves and began to leave after Paul had made this final statement: "The Holy Spirit spoke the truth to your ancestors when he said through Isaiah the prophet:

²⁶ " 'Go to this people and say,
  "You will be ever hearing but never
    understanding;

  you will be ever seeing but never
    perceiving."
²⁷ For this people's heart has become
    calloused;
  they hardly hear with their ears,
  and they have closed their eyes.
Otherwise they might see with their
    eyes,
  hear with their ears,
  understand with their hearts
and turn, and I would heal them.'ᵃ

²⁸ "Therefore I want you to know that God's salvation has been sent to the Gentiles, and they will listen!"ᵇ

³⁰ For two whole years Paul stayed there in his own rented house and welcomed all who came to see him. ³¹ Boldly and without hindrance he preached the kingdom of God and taught about the Lord Jesus Christ.

ᵃ27 Isaiah 6:9,10
ᵇ28 Some manuscripts *listen!" ²⁹After he said this, the Jews left, arguing vigorously among themselves.*

Romans

1 Paul, a servant of Christ Jesus, called to be an apostle and set apart for the gospel of God—²the gospel he promised beforehand through his prophets in the Holy Scriptures ³regarding his Son, who as to his human nature was a descendant of David, ⁴and who through the Spirit*a* of holiness was declared with power to be the Son of God,*b* by his resurrection from the dead: Jesus Christ our Lord. ⁵Through him and for his name's sake, we received grace and apostleship to call people from among all the Gentiles to the obedience that comes from faith. ⁶And you also are among those who are called to belong to Jesus Christ.

⁷To all in Rome who are loved by God and called to be saints:

Grace and peace to you from God our Father and from the Lord Jesus Christ.

Paul's Longing to Visit Rome

⁸First, I thank my God through Jesus Christ for all of you, because your faith is being reported all over the world. ⁹God, whom I serve with my whole heart in preaching the gospel of his Son, is my witness how constantly I remember you ¹⁰in my prayers at all times; and I pray that now at last by God's will the way may be opened for me to come to you.

¹¹I long to see you so that I may impart to you some spiritual gift to make you strong—¹²that is, that you and I may be mutually encouraged by each other's faith. ¹³I do not want you to be unaware, brothers and sisters, that I planned many times to come to you (but have been prevented from doing so until now) in order that I might have a harvest among you, just as I have had among the other Gentiles.

¹⁴I am bound both to Greeks and non-Greeks, both to the wise and the foolish. ¹⁵That is why I am so eager to preach the gospel also to you who are at Rome.

¹⁶I am not ashamed of the gospel, because it is the power of God for the salvation of everyone who believes: first for the Jew, then for the Gentile. ¹⁷For in the gospel a righteousness from God is revealed, a righteousness that is by faith from first to last,*c* just as it is written: "The righteous will live by faith."*d*

God's Wrath Against Human Beings

¹⁸The wrath of God is being revealed from heaven against all the godlessness and wickedness of those who suppress the truth by their wickedness, ¹⁹since what may be known about God is plain to them, because God has made it plain to them. ²⁰For since the creation of the world God's invisible qualities—his eternal power and divine nature—have been clearly seen, being understood from what has been made, so that they are without excuse.

²¹For although they knew God, they neither glorified him as God nor gave thanks to him, but their thinking became

---

*a*4 Or *who as to his spirit*   *b*4 Or *was appointed to be the Son of God with power*
*c*17 Or *is from faith to faith*   *d*17 Hab. 2:4

futile and their foolish hearts were darkened. [22] Although they claimed to be wise, they became fools [23] and exchanged the glory of the immortal God for images made to look like mortal human beings and birds and animals and reptiles.

[24] Therefore God gave them over in the sinful desires of their hearts to sexual impurity for the degrading of their bodies with one another. [25] They exchanged the truth of God for a lie, and worshipped and served created things rather than the Creator—who is for ever praised. Amen.

[26] Because of this, God gave them over to shameful lusts. Even their women exchanged natural relations for unnatural ones. [27] In the same way the men also abandoned natural relations with women and were inflamed with lust for one another. Men committed indecent acts with other men, and received in themselves the due penalty for their perversion.

[28] Furthermore, since they did not think it worth while to retain the knowledge of God, he gave them over to a depraved mind, to do what ought not to be done. [29] They have become filled with every kind of wickedness, evil, greed and depravity. They are full of envy, murder, strife, deceit and malice. They are gossips, [30] slanderers, God-haters, insolent, arrogant and boastful; they invent ways of doing evil; they disobey their parents; [31] they are senseless, faithless, heartless, ruthless. [32] Although they know God's righteous decree that those who do such things deserve death, they not only continue to do these very things but also approve of those who practise them.

God's Righteous Judgment

2 You, therefore, have no excuse, you who pass judgment on someone else, for at whatever point you judge the other, you are condemning yourself, because you who pass judgment do the same things. [2] Now we know that God's judgment against those who do such things is based on truth. [3] So when you, a mere human being, pass judgment on them and yet do the same things, do you think you will escape God's judgment? [4] Or do you show contempt for the riches of his kindness, tolerance and patience, not realising that God's kindness leads you towards repentance?

[5] But because of your stubbornness and your unrepentant heart, you are storing up wrath against yourself for the day of God's wrath, when his righteous judgment will be revealed. [6] God "will give to everyone according to what they have done".[a] [7] To those who by persistence in doing good seek glory, honour and immortality, he will give eternal life. [8] But for those who are self-seeking and who reject the truth and follow evil, there will be wrath and anger. [9] There will be trouble and distress for every human being who does evil: first for the Jew, then for the Gentile; [10] but glory, honour and peace for everyone who does good: first for the Jew, then for the Gentile. [11] For God does not show favouritism.

[12] All who sin apart from the law will also perish apart from the law, and all who sin under the law will be judged by the law. [13] For it is not those who hear the law who are righteous in God's sight, but it is those who obey the law who will be declared righteous. [14] (Indeed, when Gentiles, who do not have the law, do by nature things required by the law, they are a law for themselves, even though they do not have the law, [15] since they show that the requirements of the law are written on their hearts, their consciences also bearing witness, and their thoughts now accusing, now even defending them.) [16] This will take place on the day when God will judge everyone's secrets through Jesus Christ, as my gospel declares.

The Jews and the Law

[17] Now you, if you call yourself a Jew; if you rely on the law and brag about your relationship to God; [18] if you know his will and approve of what is superior because you are instructed by the law; [19] if you are

[a]6 Psalm 62:12; Prov. 24:12

convinced that you are a guide for the blind, a light for those who are in the dark, [20] an instructor of the foolish, a teacher of infants, because you have in the law the embodiment of knowledge and truth— [21] you, then, who teach others, do you not teach yourself? You who preach against stealing, do you steal? [22] You who say that people should not commit adultery, do you commit adultery? You who abhor idols, do you rob temples? [23] You who brag about the law, do you dishonour God by breaking the law? [24] As it is written: "God's name is blasphemed among the Gentiles because of you."[b]

[25] Circumcision has value if you observe the law, but if you break the law, you have become as though you had not been circumcised. [26] If those who are not circumcised keep the law's requirements, will they not be regarded as though they were circumcised? [27] The one who is not circumcised physically and yet obeys the law will condemn you who, even though you have the[c] written code and circumcision, are a law-breaker.

[28] A person is not a Jew who is only one outwardly, nor is circumcision merely outward and physical. [29] No, a person is a Jew who is one inwardly; and circumcision is circumcision of the heart, by the Spirit, not by the written code. Such a person's praise is not from others, but from God.

God's Faithfulness

3 What advantage, then, is there in being a Jew, or what value is there in circumcision? [2] Much in every way! First of all, they have been entrusted with the very words of God.

[3] What if some did not have faith? Will their lack of faith nullify God's faithfulness? [4] Not at all! Let God be true, and every person a liar. As it is written:

"So that you may be proved right
    when you speak
and prevail when you judge."[a]

[5] But if our unrighteousness brings out God's righteousness more clearly, what shall we say? That God is unjust in bringing his wrath on us? (I am using a human argument.) [6] Certainly not! If that were so, how could God judge the world? [7] Someone might argue, "If my falsehood enhances God's truthfulness and so increases his glory, why am I still condemned as a sinner?" [8] Why not say—as we are being slanderously reported as saying and as some claim that we say— "Let us do evil that good may result"? Their condemnation is deserved.

No-one Is Righteous

[9] What shall we conclude then? Are we any better?[b] Not at all! We have already made the charge that Jews and Gentiles alike are all under sin. [10] As it is written:

"There is no-one righteous, not even
    one;
[11]   there is no-one who understands,
    no-one who seeks God.
[12] All have turned away,
    they have together become
        worthless;
there is no-one who does good,
    not even one."[c]
[13] "Their throats are open graves;
    their tongues practise deceit."[d]
"The poison of vipers is on their lips."[e]
[14]   "Their mouths are full of cursing
        and bitterness."[f]
[15] "Their feet are swift to shed blood;
[16]   ruin and misery mark their ways,
[17] and the way of peace they do not
        know."[g]
[18]   "There is no fear of God before
        their eyes."[h]

[19] Now we know that whatever the law says, it says to those who are under the law, so that every mouth may be silenced and the whole world held accountable to God. [20] Therefore no-one will be declared righteous in his sight by observing the law; rather, through the law we become conscious of sin.

---

[b]24 Isaiah 52:5; Ezek. 36:22   [c]27 Or who, by means of a
[c]12 Psalms 14:1–3; 53:1–3; Eccles. 7:20   [d]13 Psalm 5:9
[g]17 Isaiah 59:7,8   [h]18 Psalm 36:1

[a]4 Psalm 51:4   [b]9 Or worse
[e]13 Psalm 140:3   [f]14 Psalm 10:7

Righteousness Through Faith

21 But now a righteousness from God, apart from law, has been made known, to which the Law and the Prophets testify. 22 This righteousness from God comes through faith in Jesus Christ to all who believe. There is no difference, 23 for all have sinned and fall short of the glory of God, 24 and are justified freely by his grace through the redemption that came by Christ Jesus. 25 God presented him as a sacrifice of atonement,*i* through faith in his blood. He did this to demonstrate his justice, because in his forbearance he had left the sins committed beforehand unpunished 26 —he did it to demonstrate his justice at the present time, so as to be just and the one who justifies those who have faith in Jesus.

27 Where, then, is boasting? It is excluded. On what principle? On that of observing the law? No, but on that of faith. 28 For we maintain that a person is justified by faith apart from observing the law. 29 Is God the God of Jews only? Is he not the God of Gentiles too? Yes, of Gentiles too, 30 since there is only one God, who will justify the circumcised by faith and the uncircumcised through that same faith. 31 Do we, then, nullify the law by this faith? Not at all! Rather, we uphold the law.

Abraham Justified by Faith

4 What then shall we say that Abraham, our father, discovered in this matter? 2 If, in fact, Abraham was justified by works, he had something to boast about— but not before God. 3 What does the Scripture say? "Abraham believed God, and it was credited to him as righteousness."*a*

4 Now to one who works, wages are not credited as a gift, but as an obligation. 5 However, to the one who does not work but trusts God who justifies the wicked, that person's faith is credited as righteousness. 6 David says the same thing when he speaks of the blessedness of those to whom God credits righteousness apart from works:

7 "Blessed are those
    whose transgressions are forgiven,
    whose sins are covered.
8 Blessed are those
    whose sin the Lord will never count
    against them."*b*

9 Is this blessedness only for the circumcised, or also for the uncircumcised? We have been saying that Abraham's faith was credited to him as righteousness. 10 Under what circumstances was it credited? Was it after he was circumcised, or before? It was not after, but before! 11 And he received the sign of circumcision, a seal of the righteousness that he had by faith while he was still uncircumcised. So then, he is the father of all who believe but have not been circumcised, in order that righteousness might be credited to them. 12 And he is also the father of the circumcised who not only are circumcised but who also walk in the footsteps of the faith that our father Abraham had before he was circumcised.

13 It was not through law that Abraham and his offspring received the promise that he would be heir of the world, but through the righteousness that comes by faith. 14 For if those who live by law are heirs, faith has no value and the promise is worthless, 15 because law brings wrath. And where there is no law there is no transgression.

16 Therefore, the promise comes by faith, so that it may be by grace and may be guaranteed to all Abraham's offspring—not only to those who are of the law but also to those who are of the faith of Abraham. He is the father of us all. 17 As it is written: "I have made you a father of many nations."*c* He is our father in the sight of God, in whom he believed—the God who gives life to the dead and calls things that are not as though they were.

18 Against all hope, Abraham in hope believed and so became the father of many nations, just as it had been said to him, "So shall your offspring be."*d* 19 Without weakening in his faith, he faced

---

*i*25 Or *as the one who would turn aside his wrath, taking away sin*   *a*3 Gen. 15:6; also in verse 22
*b*8 Psalm 32:1,2   *c*17 Gen. 17:5   *d*18 Gen. 15:5

the fact that his body was as good as dead—since he was about a hundred years old—and that Sarah's womb was also dead. 20 Yet he did not waver through unbelief regarding the promise of God, but was strengthened in his faith and gave glory to God, 21 being fully persuaded that God had power to do what he had promised. 22 This is why "it was credited to him as righteousness." 23 The words "it was credited to him" were written not for him alone, 24 but also for us, to whom God will credit righteousness—for us who believe in him who raised Jesus our Lord from the dead. 25 He was delivered over to death for our sins and was raised to life for our justification.

Peace and Joy

5 Therefore, since we have been justified through faith, we[a] have peace with God through our Lord Jesus Christ, 2 through whom we have gained access by faith into this grace in which we now stand. And we[a] rejoice in the hope of the glory of God. 3 Not only so, but we[a] also rejoice in our sufferings, because we know that suffering produces perseverance; 4 perseverance, character; and character, hope. 5 And hope does not disappoint us, because God has poured out his love into our hearts by the Holy Spirit, whom he has given us.

6 You see, at just the right time, when we were still powerless, Christ died for the ungodly. 7 Very rarely will anyone die for a righteous person, though for a good person someone might possibly dare to die. 8 But God demonstrates his own love for us in this: While we were still sinners, Christ died for us.

9 Since we have now been justified by his blood, how much more shall we be saved from God's wrath through him! 10 For if, when we were God's enemies, we were reconciled to him through the death of his Son, how much more, having been reconciled, shall we be saved through his life! 11 Not only is this so, but we also rejoice in God through our Lord Jesus Christ, through whom we have now received reconciliation.

Death Through Adam, Life Through Christ

12 Therefore, just as sin entered the world through one man, and death through sin, and in this way death came to all people, because all sinned— 13 for before the law was given, sin was in the world. But sin is not taken into account when there is no law. 14 Nevertheless, death reigned from the time of Adam to the time of Moses, even over those who did not sin by breaking a command, as did Adam, who was a pattern of the one to come.

15 But the gift is not like the trespass. For if the many died by the trespass of the one man, how much more did God's grace and the gift that came by the grace of the one man, Jesus Christ, overflow to the many! 16 Again, the gift of God is not like the result of the one man's sin: The judgment followed one sin and brought condemnation, but the gift followed many trespasses and brought justification. 17 For if, by the trespass of the one man, death reigned through that one man, how much more will those who receive God's abundant provision of grace and of the gift of righteousness reign in life through the one man, Jesus Christ.

18 Consequently, just as the result of one trespass was condemnation for all people, so also the result of one act of righteousness was justification that brings life for all people. 19 For just as through the disobedience of the one man the many were made sinners, so also through the obedience of the one man the many will be made righteous.

20 The law was added so that the trespass might increase. But where sin increased, grace increased all the more, 21 so that, just as sin reigned in death, so also grace might reign through righteousness to bring eternal life through Jesus Christ our Lord.

Dead to Sin, Alive in Christ

6 What shall we say, then? Shall we go on sinning, so that grace may increase? 2 By no means! We died to sin; how can we live in it any longer? 3 Or don't

---

[a]1,2,3 Or let us

you know that all of us who were baptised into Christ Jesus were baptised into his death? [4] We were therefore buried with him through baptism into death in order that, just as Christ was raised from the dead through the glory of the Father, we too may live a new life.

[5] If we have been united with him like this in his death, we will certainly also be united with him in his resurrection. [6] For we know that our old self was crucified with him so that the body of sin might be done away with,[a] that we should no longer be slaves to sin—[7] because anyone who has died has been freed from sin.

[8] Now if we died with Christ, we believe that we will also live with him. [9] For we know that since Christ was raised from the dead, he cannot die again; death no longer has mastery over him. [10] The death he died, he died to sin once for all; but the life he lives, he lives to God.

[11] In the same way, count yourselves dead to sin but alive to God in Christ Jesus. [12] Therefore do not let sin reign in your mortal body so that you obey its evil desires. [13] Do not offer the parts of your body to sin, as instruments of wickedness, but rather offer yourselves to God, as those who have been brought from death to life; and offer the parts of your body to him as instruments of righteousness. [14] For sin shall not be your master, because you are not under law, but under grace.

Slaves to Righteousness

[15] What then? Shall we sin because we are not under law but under grace? By no means! [16] Don't you know that when you offer yourselves to someone as obedient slaves, you are slaves to the one whom you obey—whether you are slaves to sin, which leads to death, or to obedience, which leads to righteousness? [17] But thanks be to God that, though you used to be slaves to sin, you wholeheartedly obeyed the form of teaching to which you were entrusted. [18] You have been set free from sin and have become slaves to righteousness.

[19] I put this in human terms because you are weak in your natural selves. Just as you used to offer the parts of your body in slavery to impurity and to ever-increasing wickedness, so now offer them in slavery to righteousness leading to holiness. [20] When you were slaves to sin, you were free from the control of righteousness. [21] What benefit did you reap at that time from the things you are now ashamed of? Those things result in death! [22] But now that you have been set free from sin and have become slaves to God, the benefit you reap leads to holiness, and the result is eternal life. [23] For the wages of sin is death, but the gift of God is eternal life in[b] Christ Jesus our Lord.

An Illustration From Marriage

7 Do you not know, brothers and sisters—for I am speaking to those who know the law—that the law has authority over someone only as long as that person lives? [2] For example, by law a married woman is bound to her husband as long as he is alive, but if her husband dies, she is released from the law of marriage. [3] So then, if she marries another man while her husband is still alive, she is called an adulteress. But if her husband dies, she is released from that law and is not an adulteress, even though she marries another man.

[4] So, my brothers and sisters, you also died to the law through the body of Christ, that you might belong to another, to him who was raised from the dead, in order that we might bear fruit to God. [5] For when we were controlled by the sinful nature,[a] the sinful passions aroused by the law were at work in our bodies, so that we bore fruit for death. [6] But now, by dying to what once bound us, we have been released from the law so that we serve in the new way of the Spirit, and not in the old way of the written code.

Struggling With Sin

[7] What shall we say, then? Is the law sin? Certainly not! Indeed I would not

---

[a]6 Or *be rendered powerless*   [b]23 Or *through*   [a]5 Or *the flesh*; also in verse 25

have known what sin was except through the law. For I would not have known what coveting really was if the law had not said, "Do not covet."[b] [8]But sin, seizing the opportunity afforded by the commandment, produced in me every kind of covetous desire. For apart from law, sin is dead. [9]Once I was alive apart from law; but when the commandment came, sin sprang to life and I died. [10]I found that the very commandment that was intended to bring life actually brought death. [11]For sin, seizing the opportunity afforded by the commandment, deceived me, and through the commandment put me to death. [12]So then, the law is holy, and the commandment is holy, righteous and good.

[13]Did that which is good, then, become death to me? By no means! But in order that sin might be recognised as sin, it produced death in me through what was good, so that through the commandment sin might become utterly sinful.

[14]We know that the law is spiritual; but I am unspiritual, sold as a slave to sin. [15]I do not understand what I do. For what I want to do I do not do, but what I hate I do. [16]And if I do what I do not want to do, I agree that the law is good. [17]As it is, it is no longer I myself who do it, but it is sin living in me. [18]I know that nothing good lives in me, that is, in my sinful nature.[c] For I have the desire to do what is good, but I cannot carry it out. [19]For what I do is not the good I want to do; no, the evil I do not want to do—this I keep on doing. [20]Now if I do what I do not want to do, it is no longer I who do it, but it is sin living in me that does it.

[21]So I find this law at work: When I want to do good, evil is right there with me. [22]For in my inner being I delight in God's law; [23]but I see another law at work in the members of my body, waging war against the law of my mind and making me a prisoner of the law of sin at work within my members. [24]What a wretched man I am! Who will rescue me from this body of death? [25]Thanks be to God—through Jesus Christ our Lord!

So then, I myself in my mind am a slave to God's law, but in the sinful nature a slave to the law of sin.

Life Through the Spirit

8 Therefore, there is now no condemnation for those who are in Christ Jesus,[a] [2]because through Christ Jesus the law of the Spirit of life set me free from the law of sin and death. [3]For what the law was powerless to do in that it was weakened by the sinful nature,[b] God did by sending his own Son in the likeness of sinful humanity to be a sin offering.[c] And so he condemned sin in our sinful nature,[d] [4]in order that the righteous requirements of the law might be fully met in us, who do not live according to the sinful nature but according to the Spirit.

[5]Those who live according to the sinful nature have their minds set on what that nature desires; but those who live in accordance with the Spirit have their minds set on what the Spirit desires. [6]The mind controlled by the sinful nature[e] is death, but the mind controlled by the Spirit is life and peace; [7]the sinful mind[f] is hostile to God. It does not submit to God's law, nor can it do so. [8]Those controlled by the sinful nature cannot please God.

[9]You, however, are controlled not by the sinful nature but by the Spirit, if the Spirit of God lives in you. And if anyone does not have the Spirit of Christ, that person does not belong to Christ. [10]But if Christ is in you, your body is dead because of sin, yet your spirit is alive because of righteousness. [11]And if the Spirit of him who raised Jesus from the dead is living in you, he who raised Christ from the dead will also give life to your mortal bodies through his Spirit, who lives in you.

[12]Therefore, brothers and sisters, we have an obligation—but it is not to the sinful nature, to live according to it. [13]For if you live according to the sinful nature, you will die; but if by the Spirit you put to death the misdeeds of the body, you will

---

[b]7 Exodus 20:17; Deut. 5:21   [c]18 Or *my flesh*
[a]1 Some later manuscripts *Jesus, who do not live according to the sinful nature but according to the Spirit,*
[b]3 Or *the flesh;* also in verses 4, 5, 8, 9, 12 and 13   [c]3 Or *man, for sin*   [d]3 Or *in the flesh*
[e]6 Or *mind set on the flesh*   [f]7 Or *the mind set on the flesh*

live, [14]because those who are led by the Spirit of God are children of God. [15]For you did not receive a spirit that makes you a slave again to fear, but you received the Spirit of adoption.[g] And by him we cry, "Abba,[h] Father." [16]The Spirit himself testifies with our spirit that we are God's children. [17]Now if we are children, then we are heirs—heirs of God and co-heirs with Christ, if indeed we share in his sufferings in order that we may also share in his glory.

Future Glory

[18]I consider that our present sufferings are not worth comparing with the glory that will be revealed in us. [19]The creation waits in eager expectation for the children of God to be revealed. [20]For the creation was subjected to frustration, not by its own choice, but by the will of the one who subjected it, in hope [21]that[i] the creation itself will be liberated from its bondage to decay and brought into the glorious freedom of the children of God.

[22]We know that the whole creation has been groaning as in the pains of childbirth right up to the present time. [23]Not only so, but we ourselves, who have the firstfruits of the Spirit, groan inwardly as we wait eagerly for our adoption, the redemption of our bodies. [24]For in this hope we were saved. But hope that is seen is no hope at all. Who hopes for what one already has? [25]But if we hope for what we do not yet have, we wait for it patiently.

[26]In the same way, the Spirit helps us in our weakness. We do not know what we ought to pray for, but the Spirit himself intercedes for us with groans that words cannot express. [27]And he who searches our hearts knows the mind of the Spirit, because the Spirit intercedes for the saints in accordance with God's will.

More Than Conquerors

[28]And we know that in all things God works for the good of those who love

him,[j] who[k] have been called according to his purpose. [29]For those God foreknew he also predestined to be conformed to the likeness of his Son, that he might be the firstborn among many brothers and sisters. [30]And those he predestined, he also called; those he called, he also justified; those he justified, he also glorified.

[31]What, then, shall we say in response to this? If God is for us, who can be against us? [32]He who did not spare his own Son, but gave him up for us all—how will he not also, along with him, graciously give us all things? [33]Who will bring any charge against those whom God has chosen? It is God who justifies. [34]Who then can condemn? Christ Jesus, who died—more than that, who was raised to life—is at the right hand of God and is also interceding for us. [35]Who shall separate us from the love of Christ? Shall trouble or hardship or persecution or famine or nakedness or danger or sword? [36]As it is written:

"For your sake we face death all day
        long;
    we are considered as sheep to be
        slaughtered."[l]

[37]No, in all these things we are more than conquerors through him who loved us. [38]For I am convinced that neither death nor life, neither angels nor demons,[m] neither the present nor the future, nor any powers, [39]neither height nor depth, nor anything else in all creation, will be able to separate us from the love of God that is in Christ Jesus our Lord.

God's Sovereign Choice

9 I speak the truth in Christ—I am not lying, my conscience confirms it in the Holy Spirit—[2]I have great sorrow and unceasing anguish in my heart. [3]For I could wish that I myself were cursed and cut off from Christ for the sake of my people, those of my own race, [4]the people of Israel. Theirs is the adoption; theirs the divine glory, the covenants, the receiving

---

g15 Or *adoption*   h15 Aramaic for *Father*
i20,21 Or *subjected it in hope.* 21*For*
j28 Some manuscripts *And we know that all things work together for good to those who love God*
k28 Or *works together with those who love him to bring about what is good—with those who*
l36 Psalm 44:22   m38 Or *no heavenly rulers*

of the law, the temple worship and the promises. ⁵ Theirs are the patriarchs, and from them is traced the human ancestry of Christ, who is God over all, for ever praised!ᵃ Amen.

⁶ It is not as though God's word had failed. For not all who are descended from Israel are Israel. ⁷ Nor because they are his descendants are they all Abraham's children. On the contrary, "It is through Isaac that your offspring will be reckoned."ᵇ ⁸ In other words, it is not the natural children who are God's children, but it is the children of the promise who are regarded as Abraham's offspring. ⁹ For this was how the promise was stated: "At the appointed time I will return, and Sarah will have a son."ᶜ

¹⁰ Not only that, but Rebekah's children had one and the same father, our father Isaac. ¹¹ Yet, before the twins were born or had done anything good or bad—in order that God's purpose in election might stand: ¹² not by works but by him who calls—she was told, "The older will serve the younger."ᵈ ¹³ Just as it is written: "Jacob I loved, but Esau I hated."ᵉ

¹⁴ What then shall we say? Is God unjust? Not at all! ¹⁵ For he says to Moses,

"I will have mercy on whom I have
mercy,
and I will have compassion on
whom I have compassion."ᶠ

¹⁶ It does not, therefore, depend on human desire or effort, but on God's mercy. ¹⁷ For the Scripture says to Pharaoh: "I raised you up for this very purpose, that I might display my power in you and that my name might be proclaimed in all the earth."ᵍ ¹⁸ Therefore God has mercy on whom he wants to have mercy, and he hardens whom he wants to harden.

¹⁹ One of you will say to me: "Then why does God still blame us? For who resists his will?" ²⁰ But you, a mere mortal, who are you to talk back to God? "Shall what is formed say to him who

formed it, 'Why did you make me like this?' "ʰ ²¹ Does not the potter have the right to make out of the same lump of clay some pottery for noble purposes and some for common use?

²² What if God, choosing to show his wrath and make his power known, bore with great patience the objects of his wrath—prepared for destruction? ²³ What if he did this to make the riches of his glory known to the objects of his mercy, whom he prepared in advance for glory—²⁴ even us, whom he also called, not only from the Jews but also from the Gentiles? ²⁵ As he says in Hosea:

"I will call them 'my people' who are
not my people;
and I will call her 'my loved one'
who is not my loved one,"ⁱ

²⁶ and,

"It will happen that in the very place
where it was said to them,
'You are not my people,'
they will be called 'children of the
living God'."ʲ

²⁷ Isaiah cries out concerning Israel:

"Though the number of the Israelites
be like the sand by the sea,
only the remnant will be saved.
²⁸ For the Lord will carry out
his sentence on earth with speed
and finality."ᵏ

²⁹ It is just as Isaiah said previously:

"Unless the Lord Almighty
had left us descendants,
we would have become like Sodom,
we would have been like
Gomorrah."ˡ

Israel's Unbelief

³⁰ What then shall we say? That the Gentiles, who did not pursue righteousness,

ᵃ5 Or *Christ, who is over all. God be for ever praised!* Or *Christ. God who is over all be for ever praised!*
ᵇ7 Gen. 21:12   ᶜ9 Gen. 18:10,14   ᵈ12 Gen. 25:23   ᵉ13 Mal. 1:2,3   ᶠ15 Exodus 33:19
ᵍ17 Exodus 9:16   ʰ20 Isaiah 29:16; 45:9   ⁱ25 Hosea 2:23   ʲ26 Hosea 1:10   ᵏ28 Isaiah 10:22,23
ˡ29 Isaiah 1:9

have obtained it, a righteousness that is by faith; 31 but Israel, who pursued a law of righteousness, has not attained it. 32 Why not? Because they pursued it not by faith but as if it were by works. They stumbled over the "stumbling-stone". 33 As it is written:

"See, I lay in Zion a stone that causes people to stumble
and a rock that makes them fall,
and the one who trusts in him will never be put to shame."*m*

10 Brothers and sisters, my heart's desire and prayer to God for the Israelites is that they may be saved. 2 For I can testify about them that they are zealous for God, but their zeal is not based on knowledge. 3 Since they did not know the righteousness that comes from God and sought to establish their own, they did not submit to God's righteousness. 4 Christ is the end of the law so that there may be righteousness for everyone who believes.

5 Moses describes in this way the righteousness that is by the law: "The one who does these things will live by them."*a* 6 But the righteousness that is by faith says: "Do not say in your heart, 'Who will ascend into heaven?'*b* " (that is, to bring Christ down) 7 "or 'Who will descend into the deep?'*c* " (that is, to bring Christ up from the dead). 8 But what does it say? "The word is near you; it is in your mouth and in your heart,"*d* that is, the word of faith we are proclaiming: 9 That if you confess with your mouth, "Jesus is Lord," and believe in your heart that God raised him from the dead, you will be saved. 10 For it is with your heart that you believe and are justified, and it is with your mouth that you confess and are saved. 11 As the Scripture says, "Anyone who trusts in him will never be put to shame."*e* 12 For there is no difference between Jew and Gentile—the same Lord is Lord of all and richly blesses all who call on him, 13 for, "Everyone who calls on the name of the Lord will be saved."*f* 14 How, then, can they call on the one

they have not believed in? And how can they believe in the one of whom they have not heard? And how can they hear without someone preaching to them? 15 And how can they preach unless they are sent? As it is written, "How beautiful are the feet of those who bring good news!"*g* 16 But not all the Israelites accepted the good news. For Isaiah says, "Lord, who has believed our message?"*h* 17 Consequently, faith comes from hearing the message, and the message is heard through the word of Christ. 18 But I ask: Did they not hear? Of course they did:

"Their voice has gone out into all the earth,
their words to the ends of the world."*i*

19 Again I ask: Did Israel not understand? First, Moses says,

"I will make you envious by those who are not a nation;
I will make you angry by a nation that has no understanding."*j*

20 And Isaiah boldly says,

"I was found by those who did not seek me;
I revealed myself to those who did not ask for me."*k*

21 But concerning Israel he says,

"All day long I have held out my hands to a disobedient and obstinate people."*l*

The Remnant of Israel

11 I ask then: Did God reject his people? By no means! I am an Israelite myself, a descendant of Abraham, from the tribe of Benjamin. 2 God did not reject his people, whom he foreknew. Don't you know what the Scripture says in the passage about Elijah—how he

*m*33 Isaiah 8:14; 28:16   *a*5 Lev. 18:5   *b*6 Deut. 30:12   *c*7 Deut. 30:13   *d*8 Deut. 30:14
*e*11 Isaiah 28:16   *f*13 Joel 2:32   *g*15 Isaiah 52:7   *h*16 Isaiah 53:1   *i*18 Psalm 19:4
*j*19 Deut. 32:21   *k*20 Isaiah 65:1   *l*21 Isaiah 65:2

appealed to God against Israel: [3]"Lord, they have killed your prophets and torn down your altars; I am the only one left, and they are trying to kill me"[a]? [4]And what was God's answer to him? "I have reserved for myself seven thousand who have not bowed the knee to Baal."[b] [5]So too, at the present time there is a remnant chosen by grace. [6]And if by grace, then it is no longer by works; if it were, grace would no longer be grace.[c]

[7]What then? What Israel sought so earnestly it did not obtain, but the elect did. The others were hardened, [8]as it is written:

"God gave them a spirit of stupor,
    eyes so that they could not see
    and ears so that they could not
        hear,
to this very day."[d]

[9]And David says:

"May their table become a snare and
        a trap,
    a stumbling-block and a retribution
        for them.
[10]May their eyes be darkened so they
        cannot see,
    and their backs be bent for ever."[e]

Ingrafted Branches

[11]Again I ask: Did they stumble so as to fall beyond recovery? Not at all! Rather, because of their transgression, salvation has come to the Gentiles to make Israel envious. [12]But if their transgression means riches for the world, and their loss means riches for the Gentiles, how much greater riches will their fulness bring!

[13]I am talking to you Gentiles. Inasmuch as I am the apostle to the Gentiles, I make much of my ministry [14]in the hope that I may somehow arouse my own people to envy and save some of them. [15]For if their rejection is the reconciliation of the world, what will their acceptance be but life from the dead? [16]If the part of

the dough offered as firstfruits is holy, then the whole batch is holy; if the root is holy, so are the branches.

[17]If some of the branches have been broken off, and you, though a wild olive shoot, have been grafted in among the others and now share in the nourishing sap from the olive root, [18]do not boast over those branches. If you do, consider this: You do not support the root, but the root supports you. [19]You will say then, "Branches were broken off so that I could be grafted in." [20]Granted. But they were broken off because of unbelief, and you stand by faith. Do not be arrogant, but be afraid. [21]For if God did not spare the natural branches, he will not spare you either.

[22]Consider therefore the kindness and sternness of God: sternness to those who fell, but kindness to you, provided that you continue in his kindness. Otherwise, you also will be cut off. [23]And if they do not persist in unbelief, they will be grafted in, for God is able to graft them in again. [24]After all, if you were cut out of an olive tree that is wild by nature, and contrary to nature were grafted into a cultivated olive tree, how much more readily will these, the natural branches, be grafted into their own olive tree!

All Israel Will Be Saved

[25]I do not want you to be ignorant of this mystery, brothers and sisters, so that you may not be conceited: Israel has experienced a hardening in part until the full number of the Gentiles has come in. [26]And so all Israel will be saved, as it is written:

"The deliverer will come from Zion;
    he will turn godlessness away from
        Jacob.
[27]And this is[f] my covenant with them
    when I take away their sins."[g]

[28]As far as the gospel is concerned, they are enemies on your account; but as far as

---

[a]3 1 Kings 19:10,14   [b]4 1 Kings 19:18
[c]6 Some manuscripts *by grace. But if by works, then it is no longer grace; if it were, work would no longer be work.*
[d]8 Deut. 29:4; Isaiah 29:10   [e]10 Psalm 69:22,23   [f]27 Or *will be*   [g]27 Isaiah 59:20,21; 27:9; Jer. 31:33,34

election is concerned, they are loved on account of the patriarchs, ²⁹for God's gifts and his call are irrevocable. ³⁰Just as you who were at one time disobedient to God have now received mercy as a result of their disobedience, ³¹so they too have now become disobedient in order that they too may now[h] receive mercy as a result of God's mercy to you. ³²For God has bound everyone over to disobedience so that he may have mercy on them all.

Doxology

³³Oh, the depth of the riches of the
    wisdom and[i] knowledge of
    God!
How unsearchable his judgments,
    and his paths beyond tracing out!
³⁴"Who has known the mind of the
    Lord?
    Or who has been his counsellor?"[j]
³⁵"Who has ever given to God,
    that God should repay the gift?"[k]
³⁶For from him and through him and to
    him are all things.
    To him be the glory for ever!
    Amen.

Living Sacrifices

12 Therefore, I urge you, brothers and sisters, in view of God's mercy, to offer your bodies as living sacrifices, holy and pleasing to God—this is your spiritual[a] act of worship. ²Do not conform any longer to the pattern of this world, but be transformed by the renewing of your mind. Then you will be able to test and approve what God's will is—his good, pleasing and perfect will.

³For by the grace given me I say to every one of you: Do not think of yourself more highly than you ought, but rather think of yourself with sober judgment, in accordance with the measure of faith God has given you. ⁴Just as each of us has one body with many members, and these members do not all have the same

function, ⁵so in Christ we who are many form one body, and each member belongs to all the others. ⁶We have different gifts, according to the grace given us. If your gift is prophesying, then use it in proportion to your[b] faith. ⁷If it is serving, then serve; if it is teaching, then teach; ⁸if it is encouraging, then encourage; if it is contributing to the needs of others, then give generously; if it is leadership, then govern diligently; if it is showing mercy, then do it cheerfully.

Love

⁹Love must be sincere. Hate what is evil; cling to what is good. ¹⁰Be devoted to one another with mutual affection. Honour one another above yourselves. ¹¹Never be lacking in zeal, but keep your spiritual fervour, serving the Lord. ¹²Be joyful in hope, patient in affliction, faithful in prayer. ¹³Share with God's people who are in need. Practise hospitality.

¹⁴Bless those who persecute you; bless and do not curse. ¹⁵Rejoice with those who rejoice; mourn with those who mourn. ¹⁶Live in harmony with one another. Do not be proud, but be willing to associate with people of low position.[c] Do not be conceited.

¹⁷Do not repay anyone evil for evil. Be careful to do what is right in the eyes of everybody. ¹⁸If it is possible, as far as it depends on you, live at peace with everyone. ¹⁹Do not take revenge, my friends, but leave room for God's wrath, for it is written: "It is mine to avenge; I will repay,"[d] says the Lord. ²⁰On the contrary:

"If your enemies are hungry, feed
    them;
if they are thirsty, give them
    something to drink.
In doing this, you will heap burning
    coals on their heads."[e]

²¹Do not be overcome by evil, but overcome evil with good.

---

[h]31 Some manuscripts do not have *now*.   *i*33 Or *riches and the wisdom and the*   [j]34 Isaiah 40:13
[k]35 Job 41:1   [a]1 Or *reasonable*   [b]6 Or *in agreement with the*   [c]16 Or *willing to do menial work*
[d]19 Deut. 32:35   [e]20 Prov. 25:21,22

Submission to the Authorities

13 Let everyone be subject to the governing authorities, for there is no authority except that which God has established. The authorities that exist have been established by God. [2] Consequently, whoever who rebels against the authority is rebelling against what God has instituted, and those who do so will bring judgment on themselves. [3] For rulers hold no terror for those who do right, but for those who do wrong. Do you want to be free from fear of the one in authority? Then do what is right and you will be commended. [4] For the one in authority is God's servant to do you good. But if you do wrong, be afraid, for rulers do not bear the sword for nothing. They are God's servants, agents of wrath to bring punishment on the wrongdoer. [5] Therefore, it is necessary to submit to the authorities, not only because of possible punishment but also because of conscience.

[6] This is also why you pay taxes, for the authorities are God's servants, who give their full time to governing. [7] Give to everyone what you owe: If you owe taxes, pay taxes; if revenue, then revenue; if respect, then respect; if honour, then honour.

Love, for the Day Is Near

[8] Let no debt remain outstanding, except the continuing debt to love one another, for whoever loves others has fulfilled the law. [9] The commandments, "Do not commit adultery," "Do not murder," "Do not steal," "Do not covet,"[a] and whatever other commandment there may be, are summed up in this one rule: "Love your neighbour as yourself."[b] [10] Love does no harm to its neighbour. Therefore love is the fulfilment of the law.

[11] And do this, understanding the present time. The hour has come for you to wake up from your slumber, because our salvation is nearer now than when we first believed. [12] The night is nearly over; the day is almost here. So let us put aside the deeds of darkness and put on the armour of light. [13] Let us behave decently, as in the daytime, not in orgies and drunkenness, not in sexual immorality and debauchery, not in dissension and jealousy. [14] Rather, clothe yourselves with the Lord Jesus Christ, and do not think about how to gratify the desires of the sinful nature.[c]

The Weak and the Strong

14 Accept those whose faith is weak, without passing judgment on disputable matters. [2] One person's faith allows the eating of everything, but another person, whose faith is weak, eats only vegetables. [3] The one who eats everything must not look down on one who does not, and the one who does not eat everything must not condemn the one who does, for God has accepted that person. [4] Who are you to judge someone else's servants? To their own master they stand or fall. And they will stand, for the Lord is able to make them stand.

[5] Some consider one day more sacred than another; others consider every day alike. Everybody should be fully convinced in their own minds. [6] Those who regard one day as special, do so to the Lord. Those who eat meat, eat to the Lord, for they give thanks to God; and those who abstain, do so to the Lord and give thanks to God. [7] For we do not live to ourselves alone and we do not die to ourselves alone. [8] If we live, we live to the Lord; and if we die, we die to the Lord. So, whether we live or die, we belong to the Lord.

[9] For this very reason, Christ died and returned to life so that he might be the Lord of both the dead and the living. [10] You, then, why do you judge your brother or sister? Or why do you look down on your brother or sister? For we will all stand before God's judgment seat. [11] It is written:

" 'As surely as I live,' says the Lord,
'Every knee will bow before me;
　　every tongue will confess to
　　　God.' "[a]

---

[a]9 Exodus 20:13–15,17; Deut. 5:17–19,21　　[b]9 Lev. 19:18　　[c]14 Or *the flesh*　　[a]11 Isaiah 45:23

¹²So then, we will all give an account of ourselves to God.

¹³Therefore let us stop passing judgment on one another. Instead, make up your mind not to put any stumbling-block or obstacle in another believer's way. ¹⁴As one who is in the Lord Jesus, I am fully convinced that no food[b] is unclean in itself. But if anyone regards something as unclean, then for that person it is unclean. ¹⁵If your brother or sister is distressed because of what you eat, you are no longer acting in love. Do not by your eating destroy your brother or sister for whom Christ died. ¹⁶Do not allow what you consider good to be spoken of as evil. ¹⁷For the kingdom of God is not a matter of eating and drinking, but of righteousness, peace and joy in the Holy Spirit, ¹⁸because anyone who serves Christ in this way is pleasing to God and receives human approval.

¹⁹Let us therefore make every effort to do what leads to peace and to mutual edification. ²⁰Do not destroy the work of God for the sake of food. All food is clean, but it is wrong for a person to eat anything that causes someone else to stumble. ²¹It is better not to eat meat or drink wine or to do anything else that will cause your brother or sister to fall.

²²So whatever you believe about these things keep between yourself and God. Blessed are those who do not condemn themselves by what they approve. ²³But those who have doubts are condemned if they eat, because their eating is not from faith; and everything that does not come from faith is sin.

15 We who are strong ought to bear with the failings of the weak and not to please ourselves. ²We should all please our neighbours for their good, to build them up. ³For even Christ did not please himself but, as it is written: "The insults of those who insult you have fallen on me."[a] ⁴For everything that was written in the past was written to teach us, so that through endurance and the encouragement of the Scriptures we might have hope.

⁵May the God who gives endurance and encouragement give you a spirit of unity among yourselves as you follow Christ Jesus, ⁶so that with one heart and mouth you may glorify the God and Father of our Lord Jesus Christ.

⁷Accept one another, then, just as Christ accepted you, in order to bring praise to God. ⁸For I tell you that Christ has become a servant of the Jews[b] on behalf of God's truth, to confirm the promises made to the patriarchs ⁹so that the Gentiles may glorify God for his mercy, as it is written:

"Therefore I will praise you among
    the Gentiles;
I will sing hymns to your name."[c]

¹⁰Again, it says,

"Rejoice, O Gentiles, with his
    people."[d]

¹¹And again,

"Praise the Lord, all you Gentiles,
    and sing praises to him, all you
    peoples."[e]

¹²And again, Isaiah says,

"The Root of Jesse will spring up,
    one who will arise to rule over the
    nations;
the Gentiles will hope in him."[f]

¹³May the God of hope fill you with all joy and peace as you trust in him, so that you may overflow with hope by the power of the Holy Spirit.

Paul the Minister to the Gentiles

¹⁴I myself am convinced, my brothers and sisters, that you yourselves are full of goodness, complete in knowledge and competent to instruct one another. ¹⁵I have written to you quite boldly on some points, as if to remind you of them again, because of the grace God gave me ¹⁶to be a minister of Christ Jesus to the Gentiles

---

[b]14 Or *that nothing*   [a]3 Psalm 69:9   [b]8 Greek *circumcision*   [c]9 2 Samuel 22:50; Psalm 18:49
[d]10 Deut. 32:43   [e]11 Psalm 117:1   [f]12 Isaiah 11:10

with the priestly duty of proclaiming the gospel of God, so that the Gentiles might become an offering acceptable to God, sanctified by the Holy Spirit.

[17] Therefore I glory in Christ Jesus in my service to God. [18] I will not venture to speak of anything except what Christ has accomplished through me in leading the Gentiles to obey God by what I have said and done—[19] by the power of signs and miracles, through the power of the Spirit. So from Jerusalem all the way round to Illyricum, I have fully proclaimed the gospel of Christ. [20] It has always been my ambition to preach the gospel where Christ was not known, so that I would not be building on someone else's foundation. [21] Rather, as it is written:

> "Those who were not told about him
>   will see,
>   and those who have not heard will
>   understand."[g]

[22] This is why I have often been hindered from coming to you.

Paul's Plan to Visit Rome

[23] But now that there is no more place for me to work in these regions, and since I have been longing for many years to see you, [24] I plan to do so when I go to Spain. I hope to visit you while passing through and to have you assist me on my journey there, after I have enjoyed your company for a while. [25] Now, however, I am on my way to Jerusalem in the service of the saints there. [26] For Macedonia and Achaia were pleased to make a contribution for the poor among the saints in Jerusalem. [27] They were pleased to do it, and indeed they owe it to them. For if the Gentiles have shared in the Jews' spiritual blessings, they owe it to the Jews to share with them their material blessings. [28] So after I have completed this task and have made sure that they have received this fruit, I will go to Spain and visit you on the way. [29] I know that when I come to you, I will come in the full measure of the blessing of Christ.

[30] I urge you, brothers and sisters, by our Lord Jesus Christ and by the love of the Spirit, to join me in my struggle by praying to God for me. [31] Pray that I may be rescued from the unbelievers in Judea and that my service in Jerusalem may be acceptable to the saints there, [32] so that by God's will I may come to you with joy and together with you be refreshed. [33] The God of peace be with you all. Amen.

Personal Greetings

16 I commend to you our sister Phoebe, a servant[a] of the church in Cenchrea. [2] I ask you to receive her in the Lord in a way worthy of the saints and to give her any help she may need from you, for she has been a great help to many people, including me.

[3] Greet Priscilla[b] and Aquila, my co-workers in Christ Jesus. [4] They risked their lives for me. Not only I but all the churches of the Gentiles are grateful to them.

[5] Greet also the church that meets at their house.

Greet my dear friend Epenetus, who was the first convert to Christ in the province of Asia.

[6] Greet Mary, who worked very hard for you.

[7] Greet Andronicus and Junia,[c] my relatives who have been in prison with me. They are outstanding among the apostles, and they were in Christ before I was.

[8] Greet Ampliatus, whom I love in the Lord.

[9] Greet Urbanus, our co-worker in Christ, and my dear friend Stachys.

[10] Greet Apelles, tested and approved in Christ.

Greet those who belong to the household of Aristobulus.

[11] Greet Herodion, my relative.

Greet those in the household of Narcissus who are in the Lord.

[12] Greet Tryphena and Tryphosa, those women who work hard in the Lord.

---

[g]21 Isaiah 52:15　　[a]1 Or *deaconess*　　[b]3 Greek *Prisca*, a variant of *Priscilla*　　[c]7 Or *Junias*; some manuscripts Julia

Greet my dear friend Persis, another woman who has worked very hard in the Lord.

[13] Greet Rufus, chosen in the Lord, and his mother, who has been a mother to me, too.

[14] Greet Asyncritus, Phlegon, Hermes, Patrobas, Hermas and the other believers with them.

[15] Greet Philologus, Julia, Nereus and his sister, and Olympas and all the saints with them.

[16] Greet one another with a holy kiss. All the churches of Christ send greetings.

[17] I urge you, brothers and sisters, to watch out for those who cause divisions and put obstacles in your way that are contrary to the teaching you have learned. Keep away from them. [18] For such people are not serving our Lord Christ, but their own appetites. By smooth talk and flattery they deceive the minds of naïve people. [19] Everyone has heard about your obedience, so I am full of joy over you; but I want you to be wise about what is good, and innocent about what is evil.

[20] The God of peace will soon crush Satan under your feet.

The grace of our Lord Jesus be with you.

[21] Timothy, my fellow-worker, sends his greetings to you, as do Lucius, Jason and Sosipater, my relatives.

[22] I, Tertius, who wrote down this letter, greet you in the Lord.

[23] Gaius, whose hospitality I and the whole church here enjoy, sends you his greetings.

Erastus, who is the city's director of public works, and our brother Quartus send you their greetings.[d]

[25] Now to him who is able to establish you by my gospel and the proclamation of Jesus Christ, according to the revelation of the mystery hidden for long ages past, [26] but now revealed and made known through the prophetic writings by the command of the eternal God, so that all nations might believe and obey him—[27] to the only wise God be glory for ever through Jesus Christ! Amen.

---

[d]23 Some manuscripts *their greetings.* [24]*May the grace of our Lord Jesus Christ be with all of you. Amen.*

1 Corinthians

1 Paul, called to be an apostle of Christ Jesus by the will of God, and our brother Sosthenes,

2 To the church of God in Corinth, to those sanctified in Christ Jesus and called to be holy, together with all those everywhere who call on the name of our Lord Jesus Christ—their Lord and ours:

3 Grace and peace to you from God our Father and the Lord Jesus Christ.

Thanksgiving

4 I always thank God for you because of his grace given you in Christ Jesus. 5 For in him you have been enriched in every way—in all your speaking and in all your knowledge—6 because our testimony about Christ was confirmed in you. 7 Therefore you do not lack any spiritual gift as you eagerly wait for our Lord Jesus Christ to be revealed. 8 He will keep you strong to the end, so that you will be blameless on the day of our Lord Jesus Christ. 9 God, who has called you into fellowship with his Son Jesus Christ our Lord, is faithful.

Divisions in the Church

10 I appeal to you, brothers and sisters, in the name of our Lord Jesus Christ, that all of you agree with one another so that there may be no divisions among you and that you may be perfectly united in mind and thought. 11 My dear friends, some from Chloe's household have informed me that there are quarrels among you 12 What I mean is this: One of you says, "I follow Paul"; another, "I follow Apollos"; another, "I follow Cephas";[a] still another, "I follow Christ."

13 Is Christ divided? Was Paul crucified for you? Were you baptised into[b] the name of Paul? 14 I am thankful that I did not baptise any of you except Crispus and Gaius, 15 so no-one can say that you were baptised into my name. (16 Yes, I also baptised the household of Stephanas; beyond that, I don't remember if I baptised anyone else.) 17 For Christ did not send me to baptise, but to preach the gospel—not with words of human wisdom, lest the cross of Christ be emptied of its power.

Christ the Wisdom and Power of God

18 For the message of the cross is foolishness to those who are perishing, but to us who are being saved it is the power of God. 19 For it is written:

"I will destroy the wisdom of the wise;
 the intelligence of the intelligent I
 will frustrate."[c]

20 Where are the wise? Where are the scholars? Where are the philosophers of this age? Has not God made foolish the wisdom of the world? 21 For since in the wisdom of God the world through its wisdom did not know him, God was pleased through the foolishness of what was preached to save those who believe. 22 Jews demand miraculous signs and

a12 That is, Peter   b13 Or in; also in verse 15   c19 Isaiah 29:14

Greeks look for wisdom, [23]but we preach Christ crucified: a stumbling-block to Jews and foolishness to Gentiles, [24]but to those whom God has called, both Jews and Greeks, Christ the power of God and the wisdom of God. [25]For the foolishness of God is wiser than human wisdom, and the weakness of God is stronger than human strength.

[26]Brothers and sisters, think of what you were when you were called. Not many of you were wise by human standards; not many were influential; not many were of noble birth. [27]But God chose the foolish things of the world to shame the wise; God chose the weak things of the world to shame the strong. [28]He chose the lowly things of this world and the despised things—and the things that are not—to nullify the things that are, [29]so that no-one may boast before him. [30]It is because of him that you are in Christ Jesus, who has become for us wisdom from God—that is, our righteousness, holiness and redemption. [31]Therefore, as it is written: "Let those who boast boast in the Lord."[d]

2 When I came to you, brothers and sisters, I did not come with eloquence or superior wisdom as I proclaimed to you the testimony about God.[a] [2]For I resolved to know nothing while I was with you except Jesus Christ and him crucified. [3]I came to you in weakness and fear, and with much trembling. [4]My message and my preaching were not with wise and persuasive words, but with a demonstration of the Spirit's power, [5]so that your faith might not rest on human wisdom, but on God's power.

Wisdom From the Spirit

[6]We do, however, speak a message of wisdom among the mature, but not the wisdom of this age or of the rulers of this age, who are coming to nothing. [7]No, we speak of God's secret wisdom, a wisdom that has been hidden and that God destined for our glory before time began. [8]None of the rulers of this age understood it, for if they had, they would not have crucified the Lord of glory. [9]However, as it is written:

"No eye has seen,
    no ear has heard,
no mind has conceived
    what God has prepared for those
        who love him"[b]—

[10]but God has revealed it to us by his Spirit.

The Spirit searches all things, even the deep things of God. [11]For who knows the thoughts of another human being except that person's own spirit within? In the same way no-one knows the thoughts of God except the Spirit of God. [12]We have not received the spirit of the world but the Spirit who is from God, that we may understand what God has freely given us. [13]This is what we speak, not in words taught us by human wisdom but in words taught by the Spirit, expressing spiritual truths in spiritual words.[c] [14]The person without the Spirit does not accept the things that come from the Spirit of God but considers them foolishness, and cannot understand them because they are spiritually discerned. [15]The person with the Spirit makes judgments about all things, but such a person is not subject to merely human judgements:

[16]"For who has known the mind of the Lord
    so as to instruct him?"[d]

But we have the mind of Christ.

On Divisions in the Church

3 Brothers and sisters, I could not address you as spiritual but as worldly—mere infants in Christ. [2]I gave you milk, not solid food, for you were not yet ready for it. Indeed, you are still not ready. [3]You are still worldly. For since there is jealousy and quarrelling among you, are you not worldly? Are you not acting like mere human beings? [4]For when one says, "I follow Paul," and another, "I follow Apollos," are you not mere human beings?

*d*31 Jer. 9:24   *a*1 Some manuscripts *as I proclaimed to you God's mystery*   *b*9 Isaiah 64:4
*c*13 Or *Spirit, interpreting spiritual truths to those who are spiritual*   *d*16 Isaiah 40:13

⁵ What, after all, is Apollos? And what is Paul? Only servants, through whom you came to believe—as the Lord has assigned to each his task. ⁶ I planted the seed, Apollos watered it, but God made it grow. ⁷ So neither the one who plants nor the one who waters is anything, but only God, who makes things grow. ⁸ The one who plants and the one who waters have one purpose, and they will each be rewarded according to their own labour. ⁹ For we are God's co-workers; you are God's field, God's building.

¹⁰ By the grace God has given me, I laid a foundation as an expert builder, and someone else is building on it. But each one should build with care. ¹¹ For no-one can lay any foundation other than the one already laid, which is Jesus Christ. ¹² If anyone builds on this foundation using gold, silver, costly stones, wood, hay or straw, ¹³ that person's work will be shown for what it is, because the Day will bring it to light. It will be revealed with fire, and the fire will test the quality of everyone's work. ¹⁴ If the building survives, the builder will receive a reward. ¹⁵ If it is burned up, the builder will suffer loss; the builder, however, will be saved, but only as one escaping through the flames.

¹⁶ Don't you know that you yourselves are God's temple and that God's Spirit lives in you? ¹⁷ If anyone destroys God's temple, God will destroy that person; for God's temple is sacred, and you are that temple.

¹⁸ Do not deceive yourselves. If any of you think you are wise by the standards of this age, you should become "fools" so that you may become wise. ¹⁹ For the wisdom of this world is foolishness in God's sight. As it is written: "He catches the wise in their craftiness";[a] ²⁰ and again, "The Lord knows that the thoughts of the wise are futile."[b] ²¹ So then, no more boasting about human leaders! All things are yours, ²² whether Paul or Apollos or Cephas[c] or the world or life or death or the present or the future—all are yours, ²³ and you are of Christ, and Christ is of God.

Apostles of Christ

4 So then, you ought to regard us as servants of Christ and as those entrusted with the secret things of God. ² Now it is required that those who have been given a trust must prove faithful. ³ I care very little if I am judged by you or by any human court; indeed, I do not even judge myself. ⁴ My conscience is clear, but that does not make me innocent. It is the Lord who judges me. ⁵ Therefore judge nothing before the appointed time; wait till the Lord comes. He will bring to light what is hidden in darkness and will expose the motives of people's hearts. At that time each will receive praise from God.

⁶ Now, brothers and sisters, I have applied these things to myself and Apollos for your benefit, so that you may learn from us the meaning of the saying, "Do not go beyond what is written." Then you will not take pride in one over against another. ⁷ For who makes you different from anyone else? What do you have that you did not receive? And if you did receive it, why do you boast as though you did not?

⁸ Already you have all you want! Already you have become rich! You have begun to reign—and that without us! How I wish that you really had begun to reign so that we might come to rule with you! ⁹ For it seems to me that God has put us apostles on display at the end of the procession, like those condemned to die in the arena. We have been made a spectacle to the whole universe, to angels as well as to human beings. ¹⁰ We are fools for Christ, but you are so wise in Christ! We are weak, but you are strong! You are honoured, we are dishonoured! ¹¹ To this very hour we go hungry and thirsty, we are in rags, we are brutally treated, we are homeless. ¹² We work hard with our own hands. When we are cursed, we bless; when we are persecuted, we endure it; ¹³ when we are slandered, we answer kindly. Up to this moment we have become the scum of the earth, the refuse of the world.

¹⁴ I am not writing this to shame you, but to warn you, as my dear children.

---

[a]19 Job 5:13   [b]20 Psalm 94:11   [c]22 That is, Peter

[15] Even though you have ten thousand guardians in Christ, you do not have many fathers, for in Christ Jesus I became your father through the gospel. [16] Therefore I urge you to imitate me. [17] For this reason I am sending to you Timothy, my son whom I love, who is faithful in the Lord. He will remind you of my way of life in Christ Jesus, which agrees with what I teach everywhere in every church.

[18] Some of you have become arrogant, as if I were not coming to you. [19] But I will come to you very soon, if the Lord is willing, and then I will find out not only how these arrogant people are talking, but what power they have. [20] For the kingdom of God is not a matter of talk but of power. [21] What do you prefer? Shall I come to you with a whip, or in love and with a gentle spirit?

Expel the Immoral Brother!

5 It is actually reported that there is sexual immorality among you, and of a kind that does not occur even among pagans: A man has his father's wife. [2] And you are proud! Shouldn't you rather have been filled with grief and have put out of your fellowship the man who did this? [3] Even though I am not physically present, I am with you in spirit. And I have already passed judgment on the one who did this, just as if I were present. [4] When you are assembled in the name of our Lord Jesus and I am with you in spirit, and the power of our Lord Jesus is present, [5] hand this man over to Satan, so that the sinful nature[a] may be destroyed and his spirit saved on the day of the Lord.

[6] Your boasting is not good. Don't you know that a little yeast works through the whole batch of dough? [7] Get rid of the old yeast that you may be a new batch without yeast—as you really are. For Christ, our Passover lamb, has been sacrificed. [8] Therefore let us keep the Festival, not with the old yeast, the yeast of malice and wickedness, but with bread without yeast, the bread of sincerity and truth.

[9] I have written to you in my letter not to associate with sexually immoral people— [10] not at all meaning the people of this world who are immoral, or the greedy and swindlers, or idolaters. In that case you would have to leave this world. [11] But now I am writing to you that you must not associate with any who call themselves believers but are sexually immoral or greedy, idolaters or slanderers, drunkards or swindlers. With such persons do not even eat.

[12] What business is it of mine to judge those outside the church? Are you not to judge those inside? [13] God will judge those outside. "Expel the wicked person from among you."[b]

Lawsuits Among Believers

6 If any of you has a dispute with another, dare you take it before the ungodly for judgment instead of before the saints? [2] Do you not know that the saints will judge the world? And if you are to judge the world, are you not competent to judge trivial cases? [3] Do you not know that we will judge angels? How much more the things of this life! [4] Therefore, if you have disputes about such matters, appoint as judges those of little account in the church![a] [5] I say this to shame you. Is it possible that there is nobody among you wise enough to judge a dispute between believers? [6] But instead, one believer goes to law against another believer—and this in front of unbelievers!

[7] The very fact that you have lawsuits among you means you have been completely defeated already. Why not rather be wronged? Why not rather be cheated? [8] Instead, you yourselves cheat and do wrong, and you do this to your brothers and sisters.

[9] Do you not know that the wicked will not inherit the kingdom of God? Do not be deceived: Neither the sexually immoral nor idolaters nor adulterers nor male prostitutes nor homosexual offenders [10] nor thieves nor the greedy nor drunkards nor slanderers nor swindlers will

[a]5 Or *that his body*; or *that the flesh*   [b]13 Deut. 17:7; 19:19; 21:21; 22:21,24; 24:7
[a]4 Or *matters, do you ask a ruling from those whose way of life is scorned in the church?*

inherit the kingdom of God. ¹¹And that is what some of you were. But you were washed, you were sanctified, you were justified in the name of the Lord Jesus Christ and by the Spirit of our God.

Sexual Immorality

¹²"Everything is permissible for me"— but not everything is beneficial. "Everything is permissible for me"—but I will not be mastered by anything. ¹³"Food for the stomach and the stomach for food"— but God will destroy them both. The body is not meant for sexual immorality, but for the Lord, and the Lord for the body. ¹⁴By his power God raised the Lord from the dead, and he will raise us also. ¹⁵Do you not know that your bodies are members of Christ himself? Shall I then take the members of Christ and unite them with a prostitute? Never! ¹⁶Do you not know that he who unites himself with a prostitute is one with her in body? For it is said, "The two will become one flesh."[c] ¹⁷But whoever is united with the Lord is one with him in spirit.

¹⁸Flee from sexual immorality. All other sins people commit are outside their bodies, but those who sin sexually sin against their own bodies. ¹⁹Do you not know that your bodies are temples of the Holy Spirit, who is in you, whom you have received from God? You are not your own; ²⁰you were bought at a price. Therefore honour God with your bodies.

Marriage

7 Now for the matters you wrote about: It is good for a man not to marry.[a] ²But since there is so much immorality, each man should have his own wife, and each woman her own husband. ³The husband should fulfil his marital duty to his wife, and likewise the wife to her husband. ⁴The wife's body does not belong to her alone but also to her husband. In the same way, the husband's body does not belong to him alone but also to his wife. ⁵Do not deprive each other except by mutual consent and for a time, so that

you may devote yourselves to prayer. Then come together again so that Satan will not tempt you because of your lack of self-control. ⁶I say this as a concession, not as a command. ⁷I wish that all of you were as I am. But each of you has your own gift from God; one has this gift, another has that.

⁸Now to the unmarried and the widows I say: It is good for them to stay unmarried, as I am. ⁹But if they cannot control themselves, they should marry, for it is better to marry than to burn with passion.

¹⁰To the married I give this command (not I, but the Lord): A wife must not separate from her husband. ¹¹But if she does, she must remain unmarried or else be reconciled to her husband. And a husband must not divorce his wife.

¹²To the rest I say this (I, not the Lord): If any brother has a wife who is not a believer and she is willing to live with him, he must not divorce her. ¹³And if a woman has a husband who is not a believer and he is willing to live with her, she must not divorce him. ¹⁴For the unbelieving husband has been sanctified through his wife, and the unbelieving wife has been sanctified through her believing husband. Otherwise your children would be unclean, but as it is, they are holy.

¹⁵But if the unbeliever leaves, let it be so. A believing man or woman is not bound in such circumstances; God has called us to live in peace. ¹⁶How do you know, wife, whether you will save your husband? Or, how do you know, husband, whether you will save your wife?

¹⁷Nevertheless, each of you should retain the place in life that the Lord has assigned you and to which God has called you. This is the rule I lay down in all the churches. ¹⁸Was a man already circumcised when he was called? He should not become uncircumcised. Was a man uncircumcised when he was called? He should not be circumcised. ¹⁹Circumcision is nothing and uncircumcision is nothing. Keeping God's commands is what counts. ²⁰Each of you should remain in the situation which you were in when God called

---

[c]16 Gen. 2:24   [a]1 Or "It is good for a man not to have sexual relations with a woman."

you. [21] Were you a slave when you were called? Don't let it trouble you—although if you can gain your freedom, do so. [22] For those who were slaves when called by the Lord are the Lord's freed people; similarly, those who were free when called are Christ's slaves. [23] You were bought at a price; do not become slaves of people. [24] Brothers and sisters, all of you, as responsible to God, should remain in the situation in which God called you.

[25] Now about virgins: I have no command from the Lord, but I give a judgment as one who by the Lord's mercy is trustworthy. [26] Because of the present crisis, I think that it is good for you to remain as you are. [27] Are you married? Do not seek a divorce. Are you unmarried? Do not look for a wife. [28] But if you do marry, you have not sinned; and if a virgin marries, she has not sinned. But those who marry will face many troubles in this life, and I want to spare you this.

[29] What I mean, brothers and sisters, is that the time is short. From now on those who have a husband or wife should live as if they did not; [30] those who mourn, as if they did not; those who are happy, as if they were not; those who buy something, as if it were not theirs to keep; [31] those who use the things of the world, as if not engrossed in them. For this world in its present form is passing away.

[32] I would like you to be free from concern. An unmarried man is concerned about the Lord's affairs—how he can please the Lord. [33] But a married man is concerned about the affairs of this world—how he can please his wife— [34] and his interests are divided. An unmarried woman or virgin is concerned about the Lord's affairs: Her aim is to be devoted to the Lord in both body and spirit. But a married woman is concerned about the affairs of this world—how she can please her husband. [35] I am saying this for your own good, not to restrict you, but that you may live in a right way in undivided devotion to the Lord.

[36] If anyone thinks he is acting improperly towards the virgin he is engaged to, and if she is getting on in years and he feels he ought to marry, he should do as he wants. He is not sinning. They should get married. [37] But the man who has settled the matter in his own mind, who is under no compulsion but has control over his own will, and who has made up his mind not to marry the virgin—this man also does the right thing. [38] So then, he who marries the virgin does right, but he who does not marry her does even better.[b]

[39] A woman is bound to her husband as long as he lives. But if her husband dies, she is free to marry anyone she wishes, but he must belong to the Lord. [40] In my judgment, she is happier if she stays as she is—and I think that I too have the Spirit of God.

Food Sacrificed to Idols

8 Now about food sacrificed to idols: We know that we all possess knowledge.[a] Knowledge puffs up, but love builds up. [2] Those who think they know something do not yet know as they ought to know. [3] But whoever loves God is known by God.

[4] So then, about eating food sacrificed to idols: We know that an idol is nothing at all in the world and that there is no God but one. [5] For even if there are so-called gods, whether in heaven or on earth (as indeed there are many "gods" and many "lords"), [6] yet for us there is but one God, the Father, from whom all things came and for whom we live; and there is but one Lord, Jesus Christ, through whom all things came and through whom we live.

[7] But not everyone knows this. Some people are still so accustomed to idols that when they eat such food they think of it as having been sacrificed to an idol, and since their conscience is weak, it is defiled. [8] But food does not bring us near to God;

---

[b]36–38 Or [36]*If anyone thinks he is not treating his daughter properly, and if she is getting on in years, and he feels she ought to marry, he should do as he wants. He is not sinning. He should let her get married.* [37]*But the man who has settled the matter in his own mind, who is under no compulsion but has control over his own will, and who has made up his mind to keep the virgin unmarried—this man also does the right thing.* [38]*So then, he who gives his virgin in marriage does right, but he who does not give her in marriage does even better.*   [a]1 Or *"We all possess knowledge," as you say*

we are no worse if we do not eat, and no better if we do.

⁹Be careful, however, that the exercise of your freedom does not become a stumbling-block to the weak. ¹⁰For if anyone with a weak conscience sees you who have this knowledge eating in an idol's temple, won't such a person be emboldened to eat what has been sacrificed to idols? ¹¹So this weak brother or sister, for whom Christ died, is destroyed by your knowledge. ¹²When you sin against other believers in this way and wound their weak conscience, you sin against Christ. ¹³Therefore, if what I eat causes my brother or sister to fall into sin, I will never eat meat again, so that I will not cause them to fall.

The Rights of an Apostle

9 Am I not free? Am I not an apostle? Have I not seen Jesus our Lord? Are you not the result of my work in the Lord? ²Even though I may not be an apostle to others, surely I am to you! For you are the seal of my apostleship in the Lord.

³This is my defence to those who sit in judgment on me. ⁴Don't we have the right to food and drink? ⁵Don't we have the right to take a believing wife along with us, as do the other apostles and the Lord's brothers and Cephas?ᵃ ⁶Or is it only I and Barnabas who must work for a living?

⁷Who serves as a soldier at his own expense? Who plants a vineyard and does not eat of its grapes? Who tends a flock and does not drink of the milk? ⁸Do I say this merely from a human point of view? Doesn't the Law say the same thing? ⁹For it is written in the Law of Moses: "Do not muzzle an ox while it is treading out the grain."ᵇ Is it about oxen that God is concerned? ¹⁰Surely he says this for us, doesn't he? Yes, this was written for us, because when farmers plough and thresh, they ought to do so in the hope of sharing in the harvest. ¹¹If we have sown spiritual seed among you, is it too much if we reap a material harvest from you? ¹²If others have this right of support from you, shouldn't we have it all the more?

But we did not use this right. On the contrary, we put up with anything rather than hinder the gospel of Christ. ¹³Don't you know that those who work in the temple get their food from the temple, and those who serve at the altar share in what is offered on the altar? ¹⁴In the same way, the Lord has commanded that those who preach the gospel should receive their living from the gospel.

¹⁵But I have not used any of these rights. And I am not writing this in the hope that you will do such things for me. I would rather die than have anyone deprive me of this boast. ¹⁶Yet when I preach the gospel, I cannot boast, for I am compelled to preach. Woe to me if I do not preach the gospel! ¹⁷If I preach voluntarily, I have a reward; if not voluntarily, I am simply discharging the trust committed to me. ¹⁸What then is my reward? Just this: that in preaching the gospel I may offer it free of charge, and so not make use of my rights in preaching it.

¹⁹Though I am free and belong to no-one, I make myself a slave to everyone, to win as many as possible. ²⁰To the Jews I became like a Jew, to win the Jews. To those under the law I became like one under the law (though I myself am not under the law), so as to win those under the law. ²¹To those not having the law I became like one not having the law (though I am not free from God's law but am under Christ's law), so as to win those not having the law. ²²To the weak I became weak, to win the weak. I have become all things to all people so that by all possible means I might save some. ²³I do all this for the sake of the gospel, that I may share in its blessings.

²⁴Do you not know that in a race all the runners run, but only one gets the prize? Run in such a way as to get the prize. ²⁵Everyone who competes in the games goes into strict training. They do it to get a crown that will not last; but we do it to get a crown that will last for ever. ²⁶Therefore I do not run like someone running aimlessly; I do not fight like someone beating the air. ²⁷No, I beat my body and

ᵃ5 That is, Peter   ᵇ9 Deut. 25:4

make it my slave so that after I have preached to others, I myself will not be disqualified for the prize.

Warnings From Israel's History

10 For I do not want you to be ignorant of the fact, brothers and sisters, that our ancestors were all under the cloud and that they all passed through the sea. [2]They were all baptised into Moses in the cloud and in the sea. [3]They all ate the same spiritual food [4]and drank the same spiritual drink; for they drank from the spiritual rock that accompanied them, and that rock was Christ. [5]Nevertheless, God was not pleased with most of them; their bodies were scattered over the desert.

[6]Now these things occurred as examples[a] to keep us from setting our hearts on evil things as they did. [7]Do not be idolaters, as some of them were; as it is written: "The people sat down to eat and drink and got up to indulge in pagan revelry."[b] [8]We should not commit sexual immorality, as some of them did—and in one day twenty-three thousand of them died. [9]We should not test the Lord, as some of them did—and were killed by snakes. [10]And do not grumble, as some of them did—and were killed by the destroying angel.

[11]These things happened to them as examples and were written down as warnings for us, on whom the fulfilment of the ages has come. [12]So, if you think you are standing firm, be careful that you don't fall! [13]No temptation has seized you except what is common to all people. And God is faithful; he will not let you be tempted beyond what you can bear. But when you are tempted, he will also provide a way out so that you can stand up under it.

Idol Feasts and the Lord's Supper

[14]Therefore, my dear friends, flee from idolatry. [15]I speak to sensible people; judge for yourselves what I say. [16]Is not the cup of thanksgiving for which we give thanks a participation in the blood of Christ? And is not the bread that we break a participation in the body of Christ?

[17]Because there is one loaf, we, who are many, are one body, for we all partake of the one loaf.

[18]Consider the people of Israel: Do not those who eat the sacrifices participate in the altar? [19]Do I mean then that a sacrifice offered to an idol is anything, or that an idol is anything? [20]No, but the sacrifices of pagans are offered to demons, not to God, and I do not want you to be participants with demons. [21]You cannot drink the cup of the Lord and the cup of demons too; you cannot have a part in both the Lord's table and the table of demons. [22]Are we trying to arouse the Lord's jealousy? Are we stronger than he?

The Believer's Freedom

[23]"Everything is permissible"—but not everything is beneficial. "Everything is permissible"—but not everything is constructive. [24]None of us should seek our own good, but the good of others.

[25]Eat anything sold in the meat market without raising questions of conscience, [26]for, "The earth is the Lord's, and everything in it."[c]

[27]If some unbeliever invites you to a meal and you want to go, eat whatever is put before you without raising questions of conscience. [28]But if anyone says to you, "This has been offered in sacrifice," then do not eat it, both for the sake of the one who told you and for conscience' sake[d]— [29]the other person's conscience, I mean, not yours. For why should my freedom be judged by another's conscience? [30]If I take part in the meal with thankfulness, why am I denounced because of something I thank God for?

[31]So whether you eat or drink or whatever you do, do it all for the glory of God. [32]Do not cause anyone to stumble, whether Jews, Greeks or the church of God—[33]even as I try to please everybody in every way. For I am not seeking my own good but the good of many, so

11 that they may be saved. [1]Follow my example, as I follow the example of Christ.

---

[a]6 Or *types*; also in verse 11   [b]7 Exodus 32:6   [c]26 Psalm 24:1
[d]28 Some manuscripts *conscience' sake, for "the earth is the Lord's and everything in it"*

Propriety in Worship

2 I praise you for remembering me in everything and for holding to the teachings,*a* just as I passed them on to you.

3 Now I want you to realise that the head of every man is Christ, and the head of the woman is man, and the head of Christ is God. 4 Every man who prays or prophesies with his head covered dishonours his head. 5 And every woman who prays or prophesies with her head uncovered dishonours her head—it is just as though her head were shaved. 6 If a woman does not cover her head, she should have her hair cut off; and if it is a disgrace for a woman to have her hair cut or shaved off, she should cover her head. 7 A man ought not to cover his head,*b* since he is the image and glory of God; but the woman is the glory of man. 8 For man did not come from woman, but woman from man; 9 neither was man created for woman, but woman for man. 10 For this reason, and because of the angels, the woman ought to have a sign of authority on her head.

11 In the Lord, however, woman is not independent of man, nor is man independent of woman. 12 For as woman came from man, so also man is born of woman. But everything comes from God. 13 Judge for yourselves: Is it proper for a woman to pray to God with her head uncovered? 14 Does not the very nature of things teach you that if a man has long hair, it is a disgrace to him, 15 but that if a woman has long hair, it is her glory? For long hair is given to her as a covering. 16 If anyone wants to be contentious about this, we have no other practice—nor do the churches of God.

The Lord's Supper

17 In the following directives I have no praise for you, for your meetings do more harm than good. 18 In the first place, I hear that when you come together as a church, there are divisions among you, and to some extent I believe it. 19 No doubt there have to be differences among you to show which of you have God's approval. 20 When you come together, it is not the Lord's Supper you eat, 21 for as you eat, each of you goes ahead without waiting for anybody else. One remains hungry, another gets drunk. 22 Don't you have homes to eat and drink in? Or do you despise the church of God and humiliate those who have nothing? What shall I say to you? Shall I praise you for this? Certainly not!

23 For I received from the Lord what I also passed on to you: The Lord Jesus, on the night he was betrayed, took bread, 24 and when he had given thanks, he broke it and said, "This is my body, which is for you; do this in remembrance of me." 25 In the same way, after supper he took the cup, saying, "This cup is the new covenant in my blood; do this, whenever you drink it, in remembrance of me." 26 For whenever you eat this bread and drink this cup, you proclaim the Lord's death until he comes.

27 Therefore, whoever eats the bread or drinks the cup of the Lord in an unworthy manner will be guilty of sinning against the body and blood of the Lord. 28 We ought to examine ourselves before we eat of the bread and drink of the cup. 29 For those who eat and drink without recognising the body of the Lord eat and drink judgment on themselves. 30 That is why many among you are weak and sick, and a number of you have fallen asleep. 31 But if we judged ourselves, we would not come under judgment. 32 When we are judged by the Lord, we are being disciplined so that we will not be condemned with the world.

33 So then, my brothers and sisters, when you come together to eat, wait for each other. 34 Those who are hungry should eat at home, so that when you meet together it may not result in judgment.

And when I come I will give further directions.

---

*a*2 Or *traditions*
*b*4 –7 Or *4Every man who prays or prophesies with long hair dishonours his head. 5And every woman who prays or prophesies with no covering ⌊of hair⌋ on her head dishonours her head—she is just like one of the "shorn women".* *6If a woman has no covering, let her be for now with short hair, but since it is a disgrace for a woman to have her hair shorn or shaved, she should grow it again. 7A man ought not to have long hair*

Spiritual Gifts

12 Now about spiritual gifts, brothers and sisters, I do not want you to be ignorant. ²You know that when you were pagans, somehow or other you were influenced and led astray to mute idols. ³Therefore I tell you that no-one who is speaking by the Spirit of God says, "Jesus be cursed," and no-one can say, "Jesus is Lord," except by the Holy Spirit.

⁴There are different kinds of gifts, but the same Spirit. ⁵There are different kinds of service, but the same Lord. ⁶There are different kinds of working, but the same God works all of them in everyone.

⁷Now to each one the manifestation of the Spirit is given for the common good. ⁸To one there is given through the Spirit the message of wisdom, to another the message of knowledge by means of the same Spirit, ⁹to another faith by the same Spirit, to another gifts of healing by that one Spirit, ¹⁰to another miraculous powers, to another prophecy, to another distinguishing between spirits, to another speaking in different kinds of tongues,ᵃ and to still another the interpretation of tongues.ᵃ ¹¹All these are the work of one and the same Spirit, and he gives them to each one, just as he determines.

One Body, Many Parts

¹²The body is a unit, though it is made up of many parts; and though all its parts are many, they form one body. So it is with Christ. ¹³For we were all baptised byᵇ one Spirit into one body—whether Jews or Greeks, slave or free—and we were all given the one Spirit to drink.

¹⁴Now the body is not made up of one part but of many. ¹⁵If the foot should say, "Because I am not a hand, I do not belong to the body," it would not for that reason cease to be part of the body. ¹⁶And if the ear should say, "Because I am not an eye, I do not belong to the body," it would not for that reason cease to be part of the body. ¹⁷If the whole body were an eye, where would the sense of hearing be? If the whole body were an ear, where would the sense of smell be? ¹⁸But in fact God has arranged the parts in the body, every one of them, just as he wanted them to be. ¹⁹If they were all one part, where would the body be? ²⁰As it is, there are many parts, but one body.

²¹The eye cannot say to the hand, "I don't need you!" And the head cannot say to the feet, "I don't need you!" ²²On the contrary, those parts of the body that seem to be weaker are indispensable, ²³and the parts that we think are less honourable we treat with special honour. And the parts that are unpresentable are treated with special modesty, ²⁴while our presentable parts need no special treatment. But God has combined the members of the body and has given greater honour to the parts that lacked it, ²⁵so that there should be no division in the body, but that its parts should have equal concern for each other. ²⁶If one part suffers, every part suffers with it; if one part is honoured, every part rejoices with it.

²⁷Now you are the body of Christ, and each one of you is a part of it. ²⁸And in the church God has appointed first of all apostles, second prophets, third teachers, then workers of miracles, also those having gifts of healing, those able to help others, those with gifts of administration, and those speaking in different kinds of tongues. ²⁹Are all apostles? Are all prophets? Are all teachers? Do all work miracles? ³⁰Do all have gifts of healing? Do all speak in tongues?ᶜ Do all interpret? ³¹But eagerly desireᵈ the greater gifts.

Love

And now I will show you the most excellent way.

13 If I speak in human or angelic tongues, but have not love, I am only a resounding gong or a clanging cymbal. ²If I have the gift of prophecy and can fathom all mysteries and all knowledge, and if I have a faith that can move mountains, but have not love, I am nothing. ³If I give all I possess to the poor

---

ᵃ10 Or *languages*; also in verse 28   ᵇ13 Or *with*; or *in*   ᶜ30 Or *other languages*
ᵈ31 Or *But you are eagerly desiring*   ᵃ1 Or *languages*

and surrender my body to the flames,[b] but have not love, I gain nothing.

[4] Love is patient, love is kind. It does not envy, it does not boast, it is not proud. [5] It is not rude, it is not self-seeking, it is not easily angered, it keeps no record of wrongs. [6] Love does not delight in evil but rejoices with the truth. [7] It always protects, always trusts, always hopes, always perseveres.

[8] Love never fails. But where there are prophecies, they will cease; where there are tongues, they will be stilled; where there is knowledge, it will pass away. [9] For we know in part and we prophesy in part, [10] but when perfection comes, the imperfect disappears. [11] When I was a child, I talked like a child, I thought like a child, I reasoned like a child. When I became an adult, I put childish ways behind me. [12] Now we see but a poor reflection as in a mirror; then we shall see face to face. Now I know in part; then I shall know fully, even as I am fully known.

[13] And now these three remain: faith, hope and love. But the greatest of these is love.

Gifts of Prophecy and Tongues

14 Follow the way of love and eagerly desire spiritual gifts, especially the gift of prophecy. [2] For those who speak in a tongue[a] do not speak to people but to God. Indeed, no-one understands them; they utter mysteries with their spirits.[b] [3] But those who prophesy speak to people for their strengthening, encouragement and comfort. [4] Those who speak in a tongue edify themselves, but those who prophesy edify the church. [5] I would like every one of you to speak in tongues,[c] but I would rather have you prophesy. Those who prophesy are greater than those who speak in tongues,[c] unless they interpret, so that the church may be edified.

[6] Now, brothers and sisters, if I come to you and speak in tongues, what good will I be to you, unless I bring you some revelation or knowledge or prophecy or word of instruction? [7] Even in the case of lifeless things that make sounds, such as the flute or harp, how will anyone know what tune is being played unless there is a distinction in the notes? [8] Again, if the trumpet does not sound a clear call, who will get ready for battle? [9] So it is with you. Unless you speak intelligible words with your tongue, how will anyone know what you are saying? You will just be speaking into the air. [10] Undoubtedly there are all sorts of languages in the world, yet none of them is without meaning. [11] If then I do not grasp the meaning of what someone is saying, I am a foreigner to the speaker, and the speaker is a foreigner to me. [12] So it is with you. Since you are eager to have spiritual gifts, try to excel in gifts that build up the church.

[13] For this reason those who speak in a tongue should pray that they may interpret what they say. [14] For if I pray in a tongue, my spirit prays, but my mind is unfruitful. [15] So what shall I do? I will pray with my spirit, but I will also pray with my mind; I will sing with my spirit, but I will also sing with my mind. [16] If you are praising God with your spirit, how can the others who find themselves among those who do not understand[d] say "Amen" to your thanksgiving, since they do not know what you are saying? [17] You are giving thanks well enough, but the others are not edified.

[18] I thank God that I speak in tongues more than all of you. [19] But in the church I would rather speak five intelligible words to instruct others than ten thousand words in a tongue.

[20] Brothers and sisters, stop thinking like children. In regard to evil be infants, but in your thinking be adults. [21] In the Law it is written:

"Through people of strange tongues
    and through the lips of foreigners
I will speak to this people,
    but even then they will not listen to
    me,"[e]
says the Lord.

b3 Some early manuscripts body that I may boast   a2 Or another language; also in verses 4, 13, 14, 19, 26 and 27   b2 Or by the Spirit   c5 Or other languages; also in verses 6, 18, 22, 23 and 39   d16 Or among the enquirers   e21 Isaiah 28:11,12

22 Tongues, then, are a sign, not for believers but for unbelievers; prophecy, however, is for believers, not for unbelievers. 23 So if the whole church comes together and everyone speaks in tongues, and some who do not understand*f* or some unbelievers come in, will they not say that you are out of your mind? 24 But if an unbeliever or someone who does not understand*g* comes in while everybody is prophesying, such people will be convinced by all that they are sinners and will be judged by all, 25 and the secrets of their hearts will be laid bare. So they will fall down and worship God, exclaiming, "God is really among you!"

Orderly Worship

26 What then shall we say, brothers and sisters? When you come together, everyone has a hymn, or a word of instruction, a revelation, a tongue or an interpretation. All of these must be done for the strengthening of the church. 27 If anyone speaks in a tongue, two—or at the most three—should speak, one at a time, and someone must interpret. 28 If there is no interpreter, the speakers should keep quiet in the church and speak to themselves and God.

29 Two or three prophets should speak, and the others should weigh carefully what is said. 30 And if a revelation comes to someone who is sitting down, the first speaker should stop. 31 For you can all prophesy in turn so that everyone may be instructed and encouraged. 32 The spirits of prophets are subject to the control of prophets. 33 For God is not a God of disorder but of peace.

As in all the congregations of the saints, 34 women should remain silent in the churches. They are not allowed to speak, but must be in submission, as the Law says. 35 If they want to enquire about something, they should ask their own husbands at home; for it is disgraceful for a woman to speak in the church.

36 Did the word of God originate with you? Or are you the only people it has reached? 37 If any think they are prophets or are spiritually gifted, let them acknowledge that what I am writing to you is the Lord's command. 38 Those who ignore this will themselves be ignored.*h*

39 Therefore, my brothers and sisters, be eager to prophesy, and do not forbid speaking in tongues. 40 But everything should be done in a fitting and orderly way.

The Resurrection of Christ

15 Now, brothers and sisters, I want to remind you of the gospel I preached to you, which you received and on which you have taken your stand. 2 By this gospel you are saved, if you hold firmly to the word I preached to you. Otherwise, you have believed in vain.

3 For what I received I passed on to you as of first importance:*a* that Christ died for our sins according to the Scriptures, 4 that he was buried, that he was raised on the third day according to the Scriptures, 5 and that he appeared to Peter,*b* and then to the Twelve. 6 After that, he appeared to more than five hundred of the brothers and sisters at the same time, most of whom are still living, though some have fallen asleep. 7 Then he appeared to James, then to all the apostles, 8 and last of all he appeared to me also, as to one abnormally born.

9 For I am the least of the apostles and do not even deserve to be called an apostle, because I persecuted the church of God. 10 But by the grace of God I am what I am, and his grace to me was not without effect. No, I worked harder than all of them—yet not I, but the grace of God that was with me. 11 Whether, then, it was I or they, this is what we preach, and this is what you believed.

The Resurrection of the Dead

12 But if it is preached that Christ has been raised from the dead, how can some of you say that there is no resurrection of the dead? 13 If there is no resurrection of the dead, then not even Christ has been

---

*f*23 Or *some enquirers*   *g*24 Or *or some enquirer*
*h*38 Some manuscripts *If he is ignorant of this, let him be ignorant*   *a*3 Or *you at the first*   *b*5 Greek *Cephas*

raised. [14] And if Christ has not been raised, our preaching is useless and so is your faith. [15] More than that, we are then found to be false witnesses about God, for we have testified about God that he raised Christ from the dead. But he did not raise him if in fact the dead are not raised. [16] For if the dead are not raised, then Christ has not been raised either. [17] And if Christ has not been raised, your faith is futile; you are still in your sins. [18] Then those also who have fallen asleep in Christ are lost. [19] If only for this life we have hope in Christ, we are to be pitied more than all people.

[20] But Christ has indeed been raised from the dead, the firstfruits of those who have fallen asleep. [21] For since death came through a human being, the resurrection of the dead comes also through a human being. [22] For as in Adam all die, so in Christ all will be made alive. [23] But in this order: Christ, the firstfruits; then, when he comes, those who belong to him. [24] Then the end will come, when he hands over the kingdom to God the Father after he has destroyed all dominion, authority and power. [25] For he must reign until he has put all his enemies under his feet. [26] The last enemy to be destroyed is death. [27] For he "has put everything under his feet". [c] Now when it says that "everything" has been put under him, it is clear that this does not include God himself, who put everything under Christ. [28] When he has done this, then the Son himself will be made subject to him who put everything under him, so that God may be all in all.

[29] Now if there is no resurrection, what will those do who are baptised for the dead? If the dead are not raised at all, why are people baptised for them? [30] And as for us, why do we endanger ourselves every hour? [31] I die every day—I mean that, brothers and sisters—just as surely as I glory over you in Christ Jesus our Lord. [32] If I fought wild beasts in Ephesus for merely human reasons, what have I gained? If the dead are not raised,

"Let us eat and drink,
    for tomorrow we die." [d]

[33] Do not be misled: "Bad company corrupts good character." [34] Come back to your senses as you ought, and stop sinning; for there are some who are ignorant of God—I say this to your shame.

The Resurrection Body

[35] But someone may ask, "How are the dead raised? With what kind of body will they come?" [36] How foolish! What you sow does not come to life unless it dies. [37] When you sow, you do not plant the body that will be, but just a seed, perhaps of wheat or of something else. [38] But God gives it a body as he has determined, and to each kind of seed he gives its own body. [39] All flesh is not the same: Human beings have one kind of flesh, animals have another, birds another and fish another. [40] There are also heavenly bodies and there are earthly bodies; but the splendour of the heavenly bodies is one kind, and the splendour of the earthly bodies is another. [41] The sun has one kind of splendour, the moon another and the stars another; and star differs from star in splendour.

[42] So will it be with the resurrection of the dead. The body that is sown is perishable, it is raised imperishable; [43] it is sown in dishonour, it is raised in glory; it is sown in weakness, it is raised in power; [44] it is sown a natural body, it is raised a spiritual body.

If there is a natural body, there is also a spiritual body. [45] So it is written: "The first Adam became a living being"; [e] the last Adam, a life-giving spirit. [46] The spiritual did not come first, but the natural, and after that the spiritual. [47] The first man was of the dust of the earth, the second man from heaven. [48] As was the earthly, so are those who are of the earth; and as is the one from heaven, so also are those who are of heaven. [49] And just as we have borne the likeness of the earthly, so shall we [f] bear the likeness of the heavenly.

[50] I declare to you, brothers and sisters, that flesh and blood cannot inherit the kingdom of God, nor does the perishable

---

[c] 27 Psalm 8:6   [d] 32 Isaiah 22:13   [e] 45 Gen. 2:7   [f] 49 Some early manuscripts *so let us*

inherit the imperishable. [51]Listen, I tell you a mystery: We will not all sleep, but we will all be changed—[52]in a flash, in the twinkling of an eye, at the last trumpet. For the trumpet will sound, the dead will be raised imperishable, and we will be changed. [53]For the perishable must clothe itself with the imperishable, and the mortal with immortality. [54]When the perishable has been clothed with the imperishable, and the mortal with immortality, then the saying that is written will come true: "Death has been swallowed up in victory."[g]

[55]"Where, O death, is your victory?
   Where, O death, is your sting?"[h]

[56]The sting of death is sin, and the power of sin is the law. [57]But thanks be to God! He gives us the victory through our Lord Jesus Christ.

[58]Therefore, my dear brothers and sisters, stand firm. Let nothing move you. Always give yourselves fully to the work of the Lord, because you know that your labour in the Lord is not in vain.

The Collection for God's People

16 Now about the collection for God's people: Do what I told the Galatian churches to do. [2]On the first day of every week, each one of you should set aside a sum of money in keeping with your income, saving it up, so that when I come no collections will have to be made. [3]Then, when I arrive, I will give letters of introduction to those you approve and send them with your gift to Jerusalem. [4]If it seems advisable for me to go also, they will accompany me.

Personal Requests

[5]After I go through Macedonia, I will come to you—for I will be going through Macedonia. [6]Perhaps I will stay with you awhile, or even spend the winter, so that you can help me on my journey, wherever I go. [7]I do not want to see you now and make only a passing visit; I hope to spend some time with you, if the Lord permits. [8]But I will stay on at Ephesus until Pentecost, [9]because a great door for effective work has opened to me, and there are many who oppose me.

[10]If Timothy comes, see to it that he has nothing to fear while he is with you, for he is carrying on the work of the Lord, just as I am. [11]No-one, then, should refuse to accept him. Send him on his way in peace so that he may return to me. I am expecting him along with the brothers.

[12]Now about our brother Apollos: I strongly urged him to go to you with the brothers. He was quite unwilling to go now, but he will go when he has the opportunity.

[13]Be on your guard; stand firm in the faith; be courageous; be strong. [14]Do everything in love.

[15]You know that the household of Stephanas were the first converts in Achaia, and they have devoted themselves to the service of the saints. I urge you, brothers and sisters, [16]to submit to such as these and to everyone who joins in the work, and labours at it. [17]I was glad when Stephanas, Fortunatus and Achaicus arrived, because they have supplied what was lacking from you. [18]For they refreshed my spirit and yours also. Such men deserve recognition.

Final Greetings

[19]The churches in the province of Asia send you greetings. Aquila and Priscilla[a] greet you warmly in the Lord, and so does the church that meets at their house. [20]All the brothers and sisters here send you greetings. Greet one another with a holy kiss.

[21]I, Paul, write this greeting in my own hand.

[22]If anyone does not love the Lord, let that person be cursed! Come, O Lord![b]

[23]The grace of the Lord Jesus be with you.

[24]My love to all of you in Christ Jesus. Amen.[c]

---

[g]54 Isaiah 25:8   [h]55 Hosea 13:14   [a]19 Greek *Prisca*, a variant of *Priscilla*
[b]22 In Aramaic the expression *Come, O Lord* is *Marana tha*.   [c]24 Some manuscripts do not have *Amen*.

2 Corinthians

1 Paul, an apostle of Christ Jesus by the will of God, and Timothy our brother,

To the church of God in Corinth, together with all the saints throughout Achaia:

² Grace and peace to you from God our Father and the Lord Jesus Christ.

The God of All Comfort

³ Praise be to the God and Father of our Lord Jesus Christ, the Father of compassion and the God of all comfort, ⁴ who comforts us in all our troubles, so that we can comfort those in any trouble with the comfort we ourselves have received from God. ⁵ For just as the sufferings of Christ flow over into our lives, so also through Christ our comfort overflows. ⁶ If we are distressed, it is for your comfort and salvation; if we are comforted, it is for your comfort, which produces in you patient endurance of the same sufferings we suffer. ⁷ And our hope for you is firm, because we know that just as you share in our sufferings, so also you share in our comfort.

⁸ We do not want you to be uninformed, brothers and sisters, about the hardships we suffered in the province of Asia. We were under great pressure, far beyond our ability to endure, so that we despaired even of life. ⁹ Indeed, in our hearts we felt the sentence of death. But this happened that we might not rely on ourselves but on God, who raises the dead. ¹⁰ He has delivered us from such a deadly peril, and he will deliver us. On him we have set our hope that he will continue to deliver us, ¹¹ as you help us by your prayers. Then many will give thanks on our*a* behalf for the gracious favour granted us in answer to the prayers of many.

Paul's Change of Plans

¹² Now this is our boast: Our conscience testifies that we have conducted ourselves in the world, and especially in our relations with you, in the holiness and sincerity that are from God. We have done so not according to worldly wisdom but according to God's grace. ¹³ For we do not write to you anything you cannot read or understand. And I hope that, ¹⁴ as you have understood us in part, you will come to understand fully that you can boast of us just as we will boast of you in the day of the Lord Jesus.

¹⁵ Because I was confident of this, I planned to visit you first so that you might benefit twice. ¹⁶ I planned to visit you on my way to Macedonia and to come back to you from Macedonia, and then to have you send me on my way to Judea. ¹⁷ When I planned this, did I do it lightly? Or do I make my plans in a worldly manner so that in the same breath I say, "Yes, yes" and "No, no"?

¹⁸ But as surely as God is faithful, our message to you is not "Yes" and "No".

---

*a*11 Many manuscripts *your*

[19]For the Son of God, Jesus Christ, who was preached among you by me and Silas[b] and Timothy, was not "Yes" and "No", but in him it has always been "Yes." [20]For no matter how many promises God has made, they are "Yes" in Christ. And so through him the "Amen" is spoken by us to the glory of God. [21]Now it is God who makes both us and you stand firm in Christ. He anointed us, [22]set his seal of ownership on us, and put his Spirit in our hearts as a deposit, guaranteeing what is to come.

[23]I call God as my witness that it was in order to spare you that I did not return to Corinth. [24]Not that we lord it over your faith, but we work with you for your joy, because it is by faith you stand firm. [2:1]So I made up my mind that I would not make another painful visit to you. [2]For if I grieve you, who is left to make me glad but you whom I have grieved? [3]I wrote as I did so that when I came I should not be distressed by those who ought to make me rejoice. I had confidence in all of you, that you would all share my joy. [4]For I wrote to you out of great distress and anguish of heart and with many tears, not to grieve you but to let you know the depth of my love for you.

Forgiveness for the Sinner

[5]If anyone has caused grief, he has not so much grieved me as he has grieved all of you, to some extent—not to put it too severely. [6]The punishment inflicted on him by the majority is sufficient. [7]Now instead, you ought to forgive and comfort him, so that he will not be overwhelmed by excessive sorrow. [8]I urge you, therefore, to reaffirm your love for him. [9]The reason I wrote to you was to see if you would stand the test and be obedient in everything. [10]Anyone you forgive I also forgive. And what I have forgiven—if there was anything to forgive—I have forgiven in the sight of Christ for your sake, [11]in order that Satan might not outwit us. For we are not unaware of his schemes.

Ministers of the New Covenant

[12]Now when I went to Troas to preach the gospel of Christ and found that the Lord had opened a door for me, [13]I still had no peace of mind, because I did not find my brother Titus there. So I said good-bye to them and went on to Macedonia.

[14]But thanks be to God, who always leads us in triumphal procession in Christ and through us spreads everywhere the fragrance of the knowledge of him. [15]For we are to God the aroma of Christ among those who are being saved and those who are perishing. [16]To the one we are the smell of death; to the other, the fragrance of life. And who is equal to such a task? [17]Unlike so many, we do not peddle the word of God for profit. On the contrary, in Christ we speak before God with sincerity, as those sent from God.

[3:1]Are we beginning to commend ourselves again? Or do we need, like some people, letters of recommendation to you or from you? [2]You yourselves are our letter, written on our hearts, known and read by everybody. [3]You show that you are a letter from Christ, the result of our ministry, written not with ink but with the Spirit of the living God, not on tablets of stone but on tablets of human hearts.

[4]Such confidence as this is ours through Christ before God. [5]Not that we are competent in ourselves to claim anything for ourselves, but our competence comes from God. [6]He has made us competent as ministers of a new covenant—not of the letter but of the Spirit; for the letter kills, but the Spirit gives life.

The Glory of the New Covenant

[7]Now if the ministry that brought death, which was engraved in letters on stone, came with glory, so that the Israelites could not look steadily at the face of Moses because of its glory, fading though it was, [8]will not the ministry of the Spirit be even more glorious? [9]If the ministry that brings condemnation is glorious, how much more glorious is the ministry that

brings righteousness! [10] For what was glorious has no glory now in comparison with the surpassing glory. [11] And if what was fading away came with glory, how much greater is the glory of that which lasts!

[12] Therefore, since we have such a hope, we are very bold. [13] We are not like Moses, who would put a veil over his face to keep the Israelites from gazing at it while the radiance was fading away. [14] But their minds were made dull, for to this day the same veil remains when the old covenant is read. It has not been removed, because only in Christ is it taken away. [15] Even to this day when Moses is read, a veil covers their hearts. [16] But whenever anyone turns to the Lord, the veil is taken away. [17] Now the Lord is the Spirit, and where the Spirit of the Lord is, there is freedom. [18] And we, who with unveiled faces all reflect[a] the Lord's glory, are being transformed into his likeness with ever-increasing glory, which comes from the Lord, who is the Spirit.

Treasures in Jars of Clay

4 Therefore, since through God's mercy we have this ministry, we do not lose heart. [2] Rather, we have renounced secret and shameful ways; we do not use deception, nor do we distort the word of God. On the contrary, by setting forth the truth plainly we commend ourselves to everyone's conscience in the sight of God. [3] And even if our gospel is veiled, it is veiled to those who are perishing. [4] The god of this age has blinded the minds of unbelievers, so that they cannot see the light of the gospel of the glory of Christ, who is the image of God. [5] For we do not preach ourselves, but Jesus Christ as Lord, and ourselves as your servants for Jesus' sake. [6] For God, who said, "Let light shine out of darkness,"[a] made his light shine in our hearts to give us the light of the knowledge of the glory of God in the face of Christ.

[7] But we have this treasure in jars of clay to show that this all-surpassing power is from God and not from us. [8] We are hard

pressed on every side, but not crushed; perplexed, but not in despair; [9] persecuted, but not abandoned; struck down, but not destroyed. [10] We always carry around in our body the death of Jesus, so that the life of Jesus may also be revealed in our body. [11] For we who are alive are always being given over to death for Jesus' sake, so that his life may be revealed in our mortal body. [12] So then, death is at work in us, but life is at work in you.

[13] It is written: "I believed; therefore I have spoken."[b] With that same spirit of faith we also believe and therefore speak, [14] because we know that the one who raised the Lord Jesus from the dead will also raise us with Jesus and present us with you in his presence. [15] All this is for your benefit, so that the grace that is reaching more and more people may cause thanksgiving to overflow to the glory of God.

[16] Therefore we do not lose heart. Though outwardly we are wasting away, yet inwardly we are being renewed day by day. [17] For our light and momentary troubles are achieving for us an eternal glory that far outweighs them all. [18] So we fix our eyes not on what is seen, but on what is unseen. For what is seen is temporary, but what is unseen is eternal.

Our Heavenly Dwelling

5 Now we know that if the earthly tent we live in is destroyed, we have a building from God, an eternal house in heaven, not built by human hands. [2] Meanwhile we groan, longing to be clothed with our heavenly dwelling, [3] because when we are clothed, we will not be found naked. [4] For while we are in this tent, we groan and are burdened, because we do not wish to be unclothed but to be clothed with our heavenly dwelling, so that what is mortal may be swallowed up by life. [5] Now it is God who has made us for this very purpose and has given us the Spirit as a deposit, guaranteeing what is to come.

[6] Therefore we are always confident and

---

know that as long as we are at home in the body we are away from the Lord. [7] We live by faith, not by sight. [8] We are confident, I say, and would prefer to be away from the body and at home with the Lord. [9] So we make it our goal to please him, whether we are at home in the body or away from it. [10] For we must all appear before the judgment seat of Christ, that everyone may receive what is due them for the things done while in the body, whether good or bad.

The Ministry of Reconciliation

[11] Since, then, we know what it is to fear the Lord, we try to persuade people. What we are is plain to God, and I hope it is also plain to your conscience. [12] We are not trying to commend ourselves to you again, but are giving you an opportunity to take pride in us, so that you can answer those who take pride in what is seen rather than in what is in the heart. [13] If we are out of our mind, it is for the sake of God; if we are in our right mind, it is for you. [14] For Christ's love compels us, because we are convinced that one died for all, and therefore all died. [15] And he died for all, that those who live should no longer live for themselves but for him who died for them and was raised again.

[16] So from now on we regard no-one from a worldly point of view. Though we once regarded Christ in this way, we do so no longer. [17] Therefore, if anyone is in Christ, there is a new creation: the old has gone, the new has come! [18] All this is from God, who reconciled us to himself through Christ and gave us the ministry of reconciliation: [19] that God was reconciling the world to himself in Christ, not counting people's sins against them. And he has committed to us the message of reconciliation. [20] We are therefore Christ's ambassadors, as though God were making his appeal through us. We implore you on Christ's behalf: Be reconciled to God. [21] God made him who had no sin to be sin[a] for us, so that in him we might become the righteousness of God.

6 As God's co-workers we urge you not to receive God's grace in vain. [2] For he says,

> "In the time of my favour I heard you,
> and in the day of salvation I helped
> you."[a]

I tell you, now is the time of God's favour, now is the day of salvation.

Paul's Hardships

[3] We put no stumbling-block in anyone's path, so that our ministry will not be discredited. [4] Rather, as servants of God we commend ourselves in every way: in great endurance; in troubles, hardships and distresses; [5] in beatings, imprisonments and riots; in hard work, sleepless nights and hunger; [6] in purity, understanding, patience and kindness; in the Holy Spirit and in sincere love; [7] in truthful speech and in the power of God; with weapons of righteousness in the right hand and in the left; [8] through glory and dishonour, bad report and good report; genuine, yet regarded as impostors; [9] known, yet regarded as unknown; dying, and yet we live on; beaten, and yet not killed; [10] sorrowful, yet always rejoicing; poor, yet making many rich; having nothing, and yet possessing everything.

[11] We have spoken freely to you, Corinthians, and opened wide our hearts to you. [12] We are not withholding our affection from you, but you are withholding yours from us. [13] As a fair exchange—I speak as to my children—open wide your hearts also.

Do Not Be Yoked With Unbelievers

[14] Do not be yoked together with unbelievers. For what do righteousness and wickedness have in common? Or what fellowship can light have with darkness? [15] What harmony is there between Christ and Belial?[b] What does a believer have in common with an unbeliever? [16] What agreement is there between the temple of

---

[a]21 Or *be a sin offering*   [a]2 Isaiah 49:8   [b]15 Greek *Beliar*, a variant of *Belial*

God and idols? For we are the temple of the living God. As God has said: "I will live with them and walk among them, and I will be their God, and they will be my people."[c]

17 "Therefore come out from them
   and be separate,
                   says the Lord.
   Touch no unclean thing,
   and I will receive you."[d]
18 "I will be a Father to you,
   and you will be my sons and
   daughters,
              says the Lord Almighty."[e]

7 Since we have these promises, dear friends, let us purify ourselves from everything that contaminates body and spirit, perfecting holiness out of reverence for God.

Paul's Joy

2 Make room for us in your hearts. We have wronged no-one, we have corrupted no-one, we have exploited no-one. 3 I do not say this to condemn you; I have said before that you have such a place in our hearts that we would live or die with you. 4 I have great confidence in you; I take great pride in you. I am greatly encouraged; in all our troubles my joy knows no bounds.

5 For when we came into Macedonia, this body of ours had no rest, but we were harassed at every turn—conflicts on the outside, fears within. 6 But God, who comforts the downcast, comforted us by the coming of Titus, 7 and not only by his coming but also by the comfort you had given him. He told us about your longing for me, your deep sorrow, your ardent concern for me, so that my joy was greater than ever.

8 Even if I caused you sorrow by my letter, I do not regret it. Though I did regret it—I see that my letter hurt you, but only for a little while—9 yet now I am happy, not because you were made sorry, but because your sorrow led you to repentance. For you became sorrowful as

God intended and so were not harmed in any way by us. 10 Godly sorrow brings repentance that leads to salvation and leaves no regret, but worldly sorrow brings death. 11 See what this godly sorrow has produced in you: what earnestness, what eagerness to clear yourselves, what indignation, what alarm, what longing, what concern, what readiness to see justice done. At every point you have proved yourselves to be innocent in this matter. 12 So even though I wrote to you, it was not on account of the one who did the wrong or of the injured party, but rather that before God you could see for yourselves how devoted to us you are. 13 By all this we are encouraged.

In addition to our own encouragement, we were especially delighted to see how happy Titus was, because his spirit has been refreshed by all of you. 14 I had boasted to him about you, and you have not embarrassed me. But just as everything we said to you was true, so our boasting about you to Titus has proved to be true as well. 15 And his affection for you is all the greater when he remembers that you were all obedient, receiving him with fear and trembling. 16 I am glad I can have complete confidence in you.

Generosity Encouraged

8 And now, brothers and sisters, we want you to know about the grace that God has given the Macedonian churches. 2 Out of the most severe trial, their overflowing joy and their extreme poverty welled up in rich generosity. 3 For I testify that they gave as much as they were able, and even beyond their ability. Entirely on their own, 4 they urgently pleaded with us for the privilege of sharing in this service to the saints. 5 And they did not do as we expected, but they gave themselves first to the Lord and then to us in keeping with God's will. 6 So we urged Titus, since he had earlier made a beginning, to bring also to completion this act of grace on your part. 7 But just as you excel in everything—in faith, in speech, in knowledge, in complete earnestness and in your love

[c]16 Lev. 26:12; Jer. 32:38; Ezek. 37:27   [d]17 Isaiah 52:11; Ezek. 20:34,41   [e]18 2 Samuel 7:14; 7:8

for us[a]—see that you also excel in this grace of giving.

[8] I am not commanding you, but I want to test the sincerity of your love by comparing it with the earnestness of others. [9] For you know the grace of our Lord Jesus Christ, that though he was rich, yet for your sakes he became poor, so that you through his poverty might become rich.

[10] And here is my advice about what is best for you in this matter: Last year you were the first not only to give but also to have the desire to do so. [11] Now finish the work, so that your eager willingness to do it may be matched by your completion of it, according to your means. [12] For if the willingness is there, the gift is acceptable according to what one has, not according to what one does not have.

[13] Our desire is not that others might be relieved while you are hard pressed, but that there might be equality. [14] At the present time your plenty will supply what they need, so that in turn their plenty will supply what you need. Then there will be equality, [15] as it is written: "The person who gathered much did not have too much, and the one who gathered little did not have too little."[b]

Titus Sent to Corinth

[16] I thank God, who put into the heart of Titus the same concern I have for you. [17] For Titus not only welcomed our appeal, but he is coming to you with much enthusiasm and on his own initiative. [18] And we are sending along with him the brother who is praised by all the churches for his service to the gospel. [19] What is more, he was chosen by the churches to accompany us as we carry the offering, which we administer in order to honour the Lord himself and to show our eagerness to help. [20] We want to avoid any criticism of the way we administer this liberal gift. [21] For we are taking pains to do what is right, not only in the eyes of the Lord but also in the eyes of others. [22] In addition, we are sending with them

our brother who has often proved to us in many ways that he is zealous, and now even more so because of his great confidence in you. [23] As for Titus, he is my partner and co-worker among you; as for our brothers, they are representatives of the churches and an honour to Christ. [24] Therefore show these men the proof of your love and the reason for our pride in you, so that the churches can see it.

[9] There is no need for me to write to you about this service to the saints. [2] For I know your eagerness to help, and I have been boasting about it to the Macedonians, telling them that since last year you in Achaia were ready to give; and your enthusiasm has stirred most of them to action. [3] But I am sending the brothers in order that our boasting about you in this matter should not prove hollow, but that you may be ready, as I said you would be. [4] For if any Macedonians come with me and find you unprepared, we—not to say anything about you—would be ashamed of having been so confident. [5] So I thought it necessary to urge the brothers to visit you in advance and finish the arrangements for the generous gift you had promised. Then it will be ready as a generous gift, not as one grudgingly given.

Sowing Generously

[6] Remember this: Whoever sows sparingly will also reap sparingly, and whoever sows generously will also reap generously. [7] Each of you should give what you have decided in your heart to give, not reluctantly or under compulsion, for God loves a cheerful giver. [8] And God is able to make all grace abound to you, so that in all things at all times, having all that you need, you will abound in every good work. [9] As it is written:

"They have scattered abroad their
    gifts to the poor;
  their righteousness endures for
    ever."[a]

---

[a]7 Some manuscripts *in our love for you*   [b]15 Exodus 16:18   [a]9 Psalm 112:9

¹⁰Now he who supplies seed to the sower and bread for food will also supply and increase your store of seed and will enlarge the harvest of your righteousness. ¹¹You will be made rich in every way so that you can be generous on every occasion, and through us your generosity will result in thanksgiving to God.

¹²This service that you perform is not only supplying the needs of God's people but is also overflowing in many expressions of thanks to God. ¹³Because of the service by which you have proved yourselves, people will praise God for the obedience that accompanies your confession of the gospel of Christ, and for your generosity in sharing with them and with everyone else. ¹⁴And in their prayers for you their hearts will go out to you, because of the surpassing grace God has given you. ¹⁵Thanks be to God for his indescribable gift!

Paul's Defence of His Ministry

10 By the meekness and gentleness of Christ, I appeal to you—I, Paul, who am "timid" when face to face with you, but "bold" when away! ²I beg you that when I come I may not have to be as bold as I expect to be towards some people who think that we live by the standards of this world. ³For though we live in the world, we do not wage war as the world does. ⁴The weapons we fight with are not the weapons of the world. On the contrary, they have divine power to demolish strongholds. ⁵We demolish arguments and every pretension that sets itself up against the knowledge of God, and we take captive every thought to make it obedient to Christ. ⁶And we will be ready to punish every act of disobedience, once your obedience is complete.

⁷You are looking only on the surface of things.ᵃ If any are confident that they belong to Christ, they should consider again that we belong to Christ just as much as they do. ⁸For even if I boast somewhat freely about the authority the Lord gave us for building you up rather than pulling you down, I will not be ashamed of it. ⁹I do not want to seem to be trying to frighten you with my letters. ¹⁰For some say, "His letters are weighty and forceful, but in person he is unimpressive and his speaking amounts to nothing." ¹¹Such people should realise that what we are in our letters when we are absent, we will be in our actions when we are present.

¹²We do not dare to classify or compare ourselves with some who commend themselves. When they measure themselves by themselves and compare themselves with themselves, they are not wise. ¹³We, however, will not boast beyond proper limits, but will confine our boasting to the field God has assigned to us, a field that reaches even to you. ¹⁴We are not going too far in our boasting, as would be the case if we had not come to you, for we did get as far as you with the gospel of Christ. ¹⁵Neither do we go beyond our limits by boasting of work done by others.ᵇ Our hope is that, as your faith continues to grow, our area of activity among you will greatly expand, ¹⁶so that we can preach the gospel in the regions beyond you. For we do not want to boast about work already done in someone else's territory. ¹⁷But, "Let those who boast boast in the Lord."ᶜ ¹⁸For it is not those who commend themselves who are approved, but those whom the Lord commends.

Paul and the False Apostles

11 I hope you will put up with a little of my foolishness; but you are already doing that. ²I am jealous for you with a godly jealousy. I promised you to one husband, to Christ, so that I might present you as a pure virgin to him. ³But I am afraid that just as Eve was deceived by the serpent's cunning, your minds may somehow be led astray from your sincere

---

ᵃ7 Or *Look at the obvious facts*
ᵇ13–15 Or *¹³We, however, will not boast about things that cannot be measured, but we will boast according to the standard of measurement that the God of measure has assigned us—a measurement that relates even to you. ¹⁴ . . . ¹⁵Neither do we boast about things that cannot be measured in regard to the work done by others.*   ᶜ17 Jer. 9:24

and pure devotion to Christ. [4]For if someone comes to you and preaches a Jesus other than the Jesus we preached, or if you receive a different spirit from the one you received, or a different gospel from the one you accepted, you put up with it easily enough. [5]But I do not think I am in the least inferior to those "super-apostles". [6]I may not be a trained speaker, but I do have knowledge. We have made this perfectly clear to you in every way.

[7]Was it a sin for me to lower myself in order to elevate you by preaching the gospel of God to you free of charge? [8]I robbed other churches by receiving support from them so as to serve you. [9]And when I was with you and needed something, I was not a burden to anyone, for the believers who came from Macedonia supplied what I needed. I have kept myself from being a burden to you in any way, and will continue to do so. [10]As surely as the truth of Christ is in me, nobody in the regions of Achaia will stop this boasting of mine. [11]Why? Because I do not love you? God knows I do! [12]And I will keep on doing what I am doing in order to cut the ground from under those who want an opportunity to be considered equal with us in the things they boast about.

[13]For such persons are false apostles, deceitful workers, masquerading as apostles of Christ. [14]And no wonder, for Satan himself masquerades as an angel of light. [15]It is not surprising, then, if his servants masquerade as servants of righteousness. Their end will be what their actions deserve.

Paul Boasts About His Sufferings

[16]I repeat: Let no-one take me for a fool. But if you do, then receive me just as you would a fool, so that I may do a little boasting. [17]In this self-confident boasting I am not talking as the Lord would, but as a fool. [18]Since many are boasting in the way the world does, I too will boast. [19]You gladly put up with fools since you are so wise! [20]In fact, you even put up with any who enslave you or exploit

you or take advantage of you or push themselves forward or slap you in the face. [21]To my shame I admit that we were too weak for that!

What anyone else dares to boast about—I am speaking as a fool—I also dare to boast about. [22]Are they Hebrews? So am I. Are they Israelites? So am I. Are they Abraham's descendants? So am I. [23]Are they servants of Christ? (I am out of my mind to talk like this.) I am more. I have worked much harder, been in prison more frequently, been flogged more severely, and been exposed to death again and again. [24]Five times I received from the Jews the forty lashes minus one. [25]Three times I was beaten with rods, once I was stoned, three times I was shipwrecked, I spent a night and a day in the open sea, [26]I have been constantly on the move. I have been in danger from rivers, in danger from bandits, in danger from my own people, in danger from Gentiles; in danger in the city, in danger in the country, in danger at sea; and in danger from false believers. [27]I have laboured and toiled and have often gone without sleep; I have known hunger and thirst and have often gone without food; I have been cold and naked. [28]Besides everything else, I face daily the pressure of my concern for all the churches. [29]Who is weak, and I do not feel weak? Who is led into sin, and I do not inwardly burn?

[30]If I must boast, I will boast of the things that show my weakness. [31]The God and Father of the Lord Jesus, who is to be praised for ever, knows that I am not lying. [32]In Damascus the governor under King Aretas had the city of the Damascenes guarded in order to arrest me. [33]But I was lowered in a basket from a window in the wall and slipped through his hands.

Paul's Vision and His Thorn

12 I must go on boasting. Although there is nothing to be gained, I will go on to visions and revelations from the Lord. [2]I know a man in Christ who fourteen years ago was caught up to the third heaven. Whether it was in the body or out of the body I do not know—God knows. [3] And I know that this person—whether in the body or apart from the body I do not know, but God knows—[4] was caught up to paradise and heard inexpressible things, things that human beings are not permitted to tell. [5] I will boast about someone like that, but I will not boast about myself, except about my weaknesses. [6] Even if I should choose to boast, I would not be a fool, because I would be speaking the truth. But I refrain, so no-one will think more of me than is warranted by what I do or say.

[7] To keep me from becoming conceited because of these surpassingly great revelations, there was given me a thorn in my flesh, a messenger of Satan, to torment me. [8] Three times I pleaded with the Lord to take it away from me. [9] But he said to me, "My grace is sufficient for you, for my power is made perfect in weakness." Therefore I will boast all the more gladly about my weaknesses, so that Christ's power may rest on me. [10] That is why, for Christ's sake, I delight in weaknesses, in insults, in hardships, in persecutions, in difficulties. For when I am weak, then I am strong.

Paul's Concern for the Corinthians

[11] I have made a fool of myself, but you drove me to it. I ought to have been commended by you, for I am not in the least inferior to the "super-apostles", even though I am nothing. [12] The things that mark an apostle—signs, wonders and miracles—were done among you with great perseverance. [13] How were you inferior to the other churches, except that I was never a burden to you? Forgive me this wrong!

[14] Now I am ready to visit you for the third time, and I will not be a burden to you, because what I want is not your possessions but you. After all, children should not have to save up for their parents, but parents for their children. [15] So I will very gladly spend for you everything I have and expend myself as well. If I love you more, will you love me less? [16] Be that as it may, I have not been a burden to you. Yet, crafty fellow that I am, I caught you by trickery! [17] Did I exploit you through any of those whom I sent you? [18] I urged Titus to go to you and I sent our brother with him. Titus did not exploit you, did he? Did we not act in the same spirit and follow the same course?

[19] Have you been thinking all along that we have been defending ourselves to you? We have been speaking in the sight of God as those in Christ; and everything we do, dear friends, is for your strengthening. [20] For I am afraid that when I come I may not find you as I want you to be, and you may not find me as you want me to be. I fear that there may be quarrelling, jealousy, outbursts of anger, factions, slander, gossip, arrogance and disorder. [21] I am afraid that when I come again my God will humble me before you, and I will be grieved over many who have sinned earlier and have not repented of the impurity, sexual sin and debauchery in which they have indulged.

Final Warnings

13 This will be my third visit to you. "Every matter must be established by the testimony of two or three witnesses."[a] [2] I already gave you a warning when I was with you the second time. I now repeat it while absent: On my return I will not spare those who sinned earlier or any of the others, [3] since you are demanding proof that Christ is speaking through me. He is not weak in dealing with you, but is powerful among you. [4] For to be sure, he was crucified in weakness, yet he lives by God's power. Likewise, we are weak in him, yet by God's power we will live with him to serve you.

[5] Examine yourselves to see whether you are in the faith; test yourselves. Do you not realise that Christ Jesus is in you—unless, of course, you fail the test? [6] And I trust that you will discover that we have not failed the test. [7] Now we pray to God that you will not do anything wrong.

[a]1 Deut. 19:15

Not that people will see that we have stood the test but that you will do what is right even though we may seem to have failed. 8 For we cannot do anything against the truth, but only for the truth. 9 We are glad whenever we are weak but you are strong; and our prayer is for your perfection. 10 This is why I write these things when I am absent, that when I come I may not have to be harsh in my use of authority—the authority the Lord gave me for building you up, not for tearing you down.

Final Greetings

11 Finally, brothers and sisters, goodbye. Aim for perfection, listen to my appeal, be of one mind, live in peace. And the God of love and peace will be with you.

12 Greet one another with a holy kiss. 13 All the saints send their greetings.

14 May the grace of the Lord Jesus Christ, and the love of God, and the fellowship of the Holy Spirit be with you all.

Galatians

1 Paul, an apostle—sent not with a human commission nor by a human authority, but by Jesus Christ and God the Father, who raised him from the dead— ²and all the brothers and sisters with me,

To the churches in Galatia:

³ Grace and peace to you from God our Father and the Lord Jesus Christ, ⁴who gave himself for our sins to rescue us from the present evil age, according to the will of our God and Father, ⁵ to whom be glory for ever and ever. Amen.

No Other Gospel

⁶ I am astonished that you are so quickly deserting the one who called you by the grace of Christ and are turning to a different gospel—⁷which is really no gospel at all. Evidently some people are throwing you into confusion and are trying to pervert the gospel of Christ. ⁸But even if we or an angel from heaven should preach a gospel other than the one we preached to you, let that person be eternally condemned! ⁹As we have already said, so now I say again: If anybody is preaching to you a gospel other than what you accepted, let that person be eternally condemned!

¹⁰ Am I now trying to win human approval, or God's approval? Or am I trying to please people? If I were still trying to please people, I would not be a servant of Christ.

Paul Called by God

¹¹ I want you to know, brothers and sisters, that the gospel I preached is not of human origin. ¹²I did not receive it from any human source, nor was I taught it; rather, I received it by revelation from Jesus Christ.

¹³ For you have heard of my previous way of life in Judaism, how intensely I persecuted the church of God and tried to destroy it. ¹⁴I was advancing in Judaism beyond many Jews of my own age and was extremely zealous for the traditions of my ancestors. ¹⁵But when God, who set me apart from birth*a* and called me by his grace, was pleased ¹⁶to reveal his Son in me so that I might preach him among the Gentiles, I did not consult any human being, ¹⁷nor did I go up to Jerusalem to see those who were apostles before I was, but I went immediately into Arabia and later returned to Damascus.

¹⁸ Then after three years, I went up to Jerusalem to get acquainted with Peter*b* and stayed with him fifteen days. ¹⁹I saw none of the other apostles—only James, the Lord's brother. ²⁰I assure you before God that what I am writing to you is no lie. ²¹Later I went to Syria and Cilicia. ²²I was personally unknown to the churches of Judea that are in Christ. ²³They only heard the report: "The man who formerly persecuted us is now preaching the faith he once tried to destroy." ²⁴And they praised God because of me.

Paul Accepted by the Apostles

2 Fourteen years later I went up again to Jerusalem, this time with Barnabas. I took Titus along also. ²I went in response to a revelation and set before them

---

*a*15 Or *from my mother's womb*   *b*18 Greek *Cephas*

the gospel that I preach among the Gentiles. But I did this privately to those who seemed to be leaders, for fear that I was running or had run my race in vain. ³Yet not even Titus, who was with me, was compelled to be circumcised, even though he was a Greek. ⁴⌐This matter arose⌐ because some false believers had infiltrated our ranks to spy on the freedom we have in Christ Jesus and to make us slaves. ⁵We did not give in to them for a moment, so that the truth of the gospel might remain with you.

⁶As for those who seemed to be important—whatever they were makes no difference to me; God does not judge by external appearance—they added nothing to my message. ⁷On the contrary, they saw that I had been entrusted with the task of preaching the gospel to the Gentiles,ᵃ just as Peter had been to the Jews.ᵇ ⁸For God, who was at work in the ministry of Peter as an apostle to the Jews, was also at work in my ministry as an apostle to the Gentiles. ⁹James, Peterᶜ and John, those reputed to be pillars, gave me and Barnabas the right hand of fellowship when they recognised the grace given to me. They agreed that we should go to the Gentiles, and they to the Jews. ¹⁰All they asked was that we should continue to remember the poor, the very thing I was eager to do.

Paul Opposes Peter

¹¹When Peter came to Antioch, I opposed him to his face, because he was clearly in the wrong. ¹²Before certain people came from James, he used to eat with the Gentiles. But when they arrived, he began to draw back and separate himself from the Gentiles because he was afraid of those who belonged to the circumcision group. ¹³The other Jews joined him in his hypocrisy, so that by their hypocrisy even Barnabas was led astray.

¹⁴When I saw that they were not acting in line with the truth of the gospel, I said to Peter in front of them all, "You are a Jew, yet you live like a Gentile and not

like a Jew. How is it, then, that you force Gentiles to follow Jewish customs?

¹⁵"We who are Jews by birth and not 'Gentile sinners' ¹⁶know that a person is not justified by observing the law, but by faith in Jesus Christ. So we, too, have put our faith in Christ Jesus that we may be justified by faith in Christ and not by observing the law, because by observing the law no-one will be justified.

¹⁷"If, while we seek to be justified in Christ, it becomes evident that we ourselves are sinners, does that mean that Christ promotes sin? Absolutely not! ¹⁸If I rebuild what I destroyed, I prove that I am a law-breaker. ¹⁹For through the law I died to the law so that I might live for God. ²⁰I have been crucified with Christ and I no longer live, but Christ lives in me. The life I live in the body, I live by faith in the Son of God, who loved me and gave himself for me. ²¹I do not set aside the grace of God, for if righteousness could be gained through the law, Christ died for nothing!"ᵈ

Faith or Observance of the Law

3 You foolish Galatians! Who has bewitched you? Before your very eyes Jesus Christ was clearly portrayed as crucified. ²I would like to learn just one thing from you: Did you receive the Spirit by observing the law, or by believing what you heard? ³Are you so foolish? After beginning with the Spirit, are you now trying to attain your goal by human effort? ⁴Have you suffered so much for nothing— if it really was for nothing? ⁵Does God give you his Spirit and work miracles among you because you observe the law, or because you believe what you heard?

⁶Consider Abraham: "He believed God, and it was credited to him as righteousness."ᵃ ⁷Understand, then, that those who believe are children of Abraham. ⁸The Scripture foresaw that God would justify the Gentiles by faith, and announced the gospel in advance to Abraham: "All nations will be blessed

---

ᵃ7 Greek *uncircumcised*   ᵇ7 Greek *circumcised* ; also in verses 8 and 9
ᶜ9 Greek *Cephas*; also in verses 11 and 14   ᵈ21 Some interpreters end the quotation after verse 14.   ᵃ6 Gen. 15:6

through you."*b* 9 So those who have faith are blessed along with Abraham, the man of faith.

10 All who rely on observing the law are under a curse, for it is written: "Cursed is everyone who does not continue to do everything written in the Book of the Law."*c* 11 Clearly no-one is justified before God by the law, because, "The righteous will live by faith."*d* 12 The law is not based on faith; on the contrary, "The one who does these things will live by them."*e* 13 Christ redeemed us from the curse of the law by becoming a curse for us, for it is written: "Cursed is everyone who is hung on a tree."*f* 14 He redeemed us in order that the blessing given to Abraham might come to the Gentiles through Christ Jesus, so that by faith we might receive the promise of the Spirit.

The Law and the Promise

15 Brothers and sisters, let me take an example from everyday life. Just as no-one can set aside or add to a human covenant that has been duly established, so it is in this case. 16 The promises were spoken to Abraham and to his seed. The Scripture does not say "and to seeds", meaning many people, but "and to your seed",*g* meaning one person, who is Christ. 17 What I mean is this: The law, introduced 430 years later, does not set aside the covenant previously established by God and thus do away with the promise. 18 For if the inheritance depends on the law, then it no longer depends on a promise; but God in his grace gave it to Abraham through a promise.

19 What, then, was the purpose of the law? It was added because of transgressions until the Seed to whom the promise referred had come. The law was put into effect through angels by a mediator. 20 A mediator, however, does not represent just one party; but God is one.

21 Is the law, therefore, opposed to the promises of God? Absolutely not! For if a law had been given that could impart life, then righteousness would certainly

have come by the law. 22 But the Scripture declares that the whole world is a prisoner of sin, so that what was promised, being given through faith in Jesus Christ, might be given to those who believe.

23 Before this faith came, we were held prisoners by the law, locked up until faith should be revealed. 24 So the law was put in charge to lead us to Christ*h* that we might be justified by faith. 25 Now that faith has come, we are no longer under the supervision of the law.

Children of God

26 You are all children of God through faith in Christ Jesus, 27 for all of you who were baptised into Christ have clothed yourselves with Christ. 28 There is neither Jew nor Greek, slave nor free, male nor female, for you are all one in Christ Jesus. 29 If you belong to Christ, then you are Abraham's seed, and heirs according to the promise.

4 What I am saying is that as long as heirs are minors, they are no different from slaves, although they own the whole estate. 2 They are subject to guardians and trustees until the time set by their fathers. 3 So also, when we were minors, we were in slavery under the basic principles of the world. 4 But when the time had fully come, God sent his Son, born of a woman, born under law, 5 to redeem those under law, that we might receive adoption as God's children. 6 Because you are sons, God sent the Spirit of his Son into our hearts, the Spirit who calls out, "*Abba*,*a* Father." 7 So you are no longer slaves, but God's children; and since you are his children, God has made you also heirs.

Paul's Concern for the Galatians

8 Formerly, when you did not know God, you were slaves to those who by nature are not gods. 9 But now that you know God—or rather are known by God—how is it that you are turning back to those weak and miserable principles? Do you wish to be enslaved by them all

---

*b*8 Gen. 12:3; 18:18; 22:18   *c*10 Deut. 27:26   *d*11 Hab. 2:4   *e*12 Lev. 18:5   *f*13 Deut. 21:23
*g*16 Gen. 12:7; 13:15; 24:7   *h*24 Or *charge until Christ came*   *a*6 Aramaic for *Father*

over again? [10] You are observing special days and months and seasons and years! [11] I fear for you, that somehow I have wasted my efforts on you.

[12] I plead with you, brothers and sisters, become like me, for I became like you. You have done me no wrong. [13] As you know, it was because of an illness that I first preached the gospel to you. [14] Even though my illness was a trial to you, you did not treat me with contempt or scorn. Instead, you welcomed me as if I were an angel of God, as if I were Christ Jesus himself. [15] What has happened to all your joy? I can testify that, if you could have done so, you would have torn out your eyes and given them to me. [16] Have I now become your enemy by telling you the truth?

[17] Those people are zealous to win you over, but for no good. What they want is to alienate you ⌐from us⌐, so that you may be zealous for them. [18] It is fine to be zealous, provided the purpose is good, and to be so always and not just when I am with you. [19] My dear children, for whom I am again in the pains of childbirth until Christ is formed in you, [20] how I wish I could be with you now and change my tone, because I am perplexed about you!

Hagar and Sarah

[21] Tell me, you who want to be under the law, are you not aware of what the law says? [22] For it is written that Abraham had two sons, one by the slave woman and the other by the free woman. [23] His son by the slave woman was born in the ordinary way; but his son by the free woman was born as the result of a promise.

[24] These things may be taken figuratively, for the women represent two covenants. One covenant is from Mount Sinai and bears children who are to be slaves: This is Hagar. [25] Now Hagar stands for Mount Sinai in Arabia and corresponds to the present city of Jerusalem, because she is in slavery with her children. [26] But the Jerusalem that is above is free, and she is our mother. [27] For it is written:

"Be glad, O barren woman,
   who bears no children;
break forth and cry aloud,
   you who have no labour pains;
because more are the children of the
   desolate woman
than of her who has a husband."[b]

[28] Now you, brothers and sisters, like Isaac, are children of promise. [29] At that time the son born in the ordinary way persecuted the son born by the power of the Spirit. It is the same now. [30] But what does the Scripture say? "Get rid of the slave woman and her son, for the slave woman's son will never share in the inheritance with the free woman's son."[c] [31] Therefore, brothers and sisters, we are not children of the slave woman, but of the free woman.

Freedom in Christ

[5] It is for freedom that Christ has set us free. Stand firm, then, and do not let yourselves be burdened again by a yoke of slavery.

[2] Mark my words! I, Paul, tell you that if you let yourselves be circumcised, Christ will be of no value to you at all. [3] Again I declare to every man who lets himself be circumcised that he is required to obey the whole law. [4] You who are trying to be justified by law have been alienated from Christ; you have fallen away from grace. [5] But by faith we eagerly await through the Spirit the righteousness for which we hope. [6] For in Christ Jesus neither circumcision nor uncircumcision has any value. The only thing that counts is faith expressing itself through love.

[7] You were running a good race. Who cut in on you and kept you from obeying the truth? [8] That kind of persuasion does not come from the one who calls you. [9] "A little yeast works through the whole batch of dough." [10] I am confident in the Lord that you will take no other view. The one who is throwing you into confusion will pay the penalty, whoever that may be. [11] Brothers and sisters, if I am still

b27 Isaiah 54:1   c30 Gen. 21:10

preaching circumcision, why am I still being persecuted? In that case the offence of the cross has been abolished. [12] As for those agitators, I wish they would go the whole way and emasculate themselves!

[13] You, my brothers and sisters, were called to be free. But do not use your freedom to indulge the sinful nature;[a] rather, serve one another in love. [14] The entire law is summed up in a single command: "Love your neighbour as yourself."[b] [15] If you keep on biting and devouring each other, watch out or you will be destroyed by each other.

Life by the Spirit

[16] So I say, live by the Spirit, and you will not gratify the desires of the sinful nature. [17] For the sinful nature desires what is contrary to the Spirit, and the Spirit what is contrary to the sinful nature. They are in conflict with each other, so that you do not do what you want. [18] But if you are led by the Spirit, you are not under law.

[19] The acts of the sinful nature are obvious: sexual immorality, impurity and debauchery; [20] idolatry and witchcraft; hatred, discord, jealousy, fits of rage, selfish ambition, dissensions, factions [21] and envy; drunkenness, orgies, and the like. I warn you, as I did before, that those who live like this will not inherit the kingdom of God.

[22] But the fruit of the Spirit is love, joy, peace, patience, kindness, goodness, faithfulness, [23] gentleness and self-control. Against such things there is no law. [24] Those who belong to Christ Jesus have crucified the sinful nature with its passions and desires. [25] Since we live by the Spirit, let us keep in step with the Spirit. [26] Let us not become conceited, provoking and envying each other.

Doing Good to All

6 Brothers and sisters, if someone is caught in a sin, you who are spiritual should restore that person gently. But watch yourself, or you also may be tempted. [2] Carry each other's burdens, and in this way you will fulfil the law of Christ. [3] If any of you think you are something when you are nothing, you deceive yourselves. [4] Each of you should test your own actions. Then you can take pride in yourself, without comparing yourself to somebody else, [5] for each of you should carry your own load.

[6] Those who receive instruction in the word must share all good things with their instructor.

[7] Do not be deceived: God cannot be mocked. People reap what they sow. [8] Those who sow to please their sinful nature, from that nature[a] will reap destruction; those who sow to please the Spirit, from the Spirit will reap eternal life. [9] Let us not become weary in doing good, for at the proper time we will reap a harvest if we do not give up. [10] Therefore, as we have opportunity, let us do good to all people, especially to those who belong to the family of believers.

Not Circumcision but a New Creation

[11] See what large letters I use as I write to you with my own hand!

[12] Those who want to make a good impression outwardly are trying to compel you to be circumcised. The only reason they do this is to avoid being persecuted for the cross of Christ. [13] Not even those who are circumcised obey the law, yet they want you to be circumcised that they may boast about your flesh. [14] May I never boast except in the cross of our Lord Jesus Christ, through which[b] the world has been crucified to me, and I to the world. [15] Neither circumcision nor uncircumcision means anything; what counts is a new creation. [16] Peace and mercy to all who follow this rule, even to the Israel of God.

[17] Finally, let no-one cause me trouble, for I bear on my body the marks of Jesus.

[18] The grace of our Lord Jesus Christ be with your spirit, brothers and sisters. Amen.

---

[a]13 Or *the flesh*; also in verses 16, 17, 19 and 24   [b]14 Lev. 19:18   [a]8 Or *his flesh, from the flesh*
[b]14 Or *whom*

Ephesians

1 Paul, an apostle of Christ Jesus by the will of God,

To the saints in Ephesus,[a] the faithful[b] in Christ Jesus:

[2] Grace and peace to you from God our Father and the Lord Jesus Christ.

Spiritual Blessings in Christ

[3] Praise be to the God and Father of our Lord Jesus Christ, who has blessed us in the heavenly realms with every spiritual blessing in Christ. [4] For he chose us in him before the creation of the world to be holy and blameless in his sight. In love [5] he[c] predestined us to be adopted as his children through Jesus Christ, in accordance with his pleasure and will—[6] to the praise of his glorious grace, which he has freely given us in the One he loves. [7] In him we have redemption through his blood, the forgiveness of sins, in accordance with the riches of God's grace [8] that he lavished on us with all wisdom and understanding. [9] And he[d] made known to us the mystery of his will according to his good pleasure, which he purposed in Christ, [10] to be put into effect when the times will have reached their fulfilment—to bring all things in heaven and on earth together under one head, even Christ.

[11] In him we were also chosen,[e] having been predestined according to the plan of him who works out everything in conformity with the purpose of his will, [12] in order that we, who were the first to hope in Christ, might be for the praise of his glory. [13] And you also were included in Christ when you heard the word of truth, the gospel of your salvation. Having believed, you were marked in him with a seal, the promised Holy Spirit, [14] who is a deposit guaranteeing our inheritance until the redemption of those who are God's possession—to the praise of his glory.

Thanksgiving and Prayer

[15] For this reason, ever since I heard about your faith in the Lord Jesus and your love for all the saints, [16] I have not stopped giving thanks for you, remembering you in my prayers. [17] I keep asking that the God of our Lord Jesus Christ, the glorious Father, may give you the Spirit[f] of wisdom and revelation, so that you may know him better. [18] I pray also that the eyes of your heart may be enlightened in order that you may know the hope to which he has called you, the riches of his glorious inheritance in the saints, [19] and his incomparably great power for us who believe. That power is like the working of his mighty strength, [20] which he exerted in Christ when he raised him from the dead and seated him at his right hand in the heavenly realms, [21] far above all rule and authority, power and dominion, and every title that can be given, not only in the present age but also in the one to come. [22] And God placed all things under his feet and appointed him to be head over

---

[a]1 Some early manuscripts do not have *in Ephesus*.   [b]1 Or *believers who are*   [c]4,5 Or *sight in love. [5]He*
[d]8, 9 Or *us. With all wisdom and understanding, [9]he*   [e]11 Or *were made heirs*   [f]17 Or *a spirit*

everything for the church, ²³which is his body, the fulness of him who fills everything in every way.

Made Alive in Christ

2 As for you, you were dead in your transgressions and sins, ²in which you used to live when you followed the ways of this world and of the ruler of the kingdom of the air, the spirit who is now at work in those who are disobedient. ³All of us also lived among them at one time, gratifying the cravings of our sinful nature*a* and following its desires and thoughts. Like the rest, we were by nature objects of wrath. ⁴But because of his great love for us, God, who is rich in mercy, ⁵made us alive with Christ even when we were dead in transgressions—it is by grace you have been saved. ⁶And God raised us up with Christ and seated us with him in the heavenly realms in Christ Jesus, ⁷in order that in the coming ages he might show the incomparable riches of his grace, expressed in his kindness to us in Christ Jesus. ⁸For it is by grace you have been saved, through faith—and this not from yourselves, it is the gift of God—⁹not by works, so that no-one can boast. ¹⁰For we are God's handiwork, created in Christ Jesus to do good works, which God prepared in advance for us to do.

One in Christ

¹¹Therefore, remember that formerly you who are Gentiles by birth and called "uncircumcised" by those who call themselves "the circumcision" (that done in the body by human hands)—¹²remember that at that time you were separate from Christ, excluded from citizenship in Israel and foreigners to the covenants of the promise, without hope and without God in the world. ¹³But now in Christ Jesus you who once were far away have been brought near through the blood of Christ. ¹⁴For he himself is our peace, who has made the two one and has destroyed the barrier, the dividing wall of hostility, ¹⁵by abolishing in his flesh the law with its commandments and regulations. His purpose was to create in himself one new humanity out of the two, thus making peace, ¹⁶and in this one body to reconcile both of them to God through the cross, by which he put to death their hostility. ¹⁷He came and preached peace to you who were far away and peace to those who were near. ¹⁸For through him we both have access to the Father by one Spirit.

¹⁹Consequently, you are no longer foreigners and aliens, but fellow-citizens with God's people and members of God's household, ²⁰built on the foundation of the apostles and prophets, with Christ Jesus himself as the chief cornerstone. ²¹In him the whole building is joined together and rises to become a holy temple in the Lord. ²²And in him you too are being built together to become a dwelling in which God lives by his Spirit.

Paul the Preacher to the Gentiles

3 For this reason I, Paul, the prisoner of Christ Jesus for the sake of you Gentiles—

²Surely you have heard about the administration of God's grace that was given to me for you, ³that is, the mystery made known to me by revelation, as I have already written briefly. ⁴In reading this, then, you will be able to understand my insight into the mystery of Christ, ⁵which was not made known to people in other generations as it has now been revealed by the Spirit to God's holy apostles and prophets. ⁶This mystery is that through the gospel the Gentiles are heirs together with Israel, members together of one body, and sharers together in the promise in Christ Jesus.

⁷I became a servant of this gospel by the gift of God's grace given me through the working of his power. ⁸Although I am less than the least of all God's people, this grace was given me: to preach to the Gentiles the unsearchable riches of Christ, ⁹and to make plain to everyone the administration of this mystery, which for

*a*3 Or *our flesh*

ages past was kept hidden in God, who created all things. [10] His intent was that now, through the church, the manifold wisdom of God should be made known to the rulers and authorities in the heavenly realms, [11] according to his eternal purpose which he accomplished in Christ Jesus our Lord. [12] In him and through faith in him we may approach God with freedom and confidence. [13] I ask you, therefore, not to be discouraged because of my sufferings for you, which are your glory.

A Prayer for the Ephesians

[14] For this reason I kneel before the Father, [15] from whom his whole family[a] in heaven and on earth derives its name. [16] I pray that out of his glorious riches he may strengthen you with power through his Spirit in your inner being, [17] so that Christ may dwell in your hearts through faith. And I pray that you, being rooted and established in love, [18] may have power, together with all the saints, to grasp how wide and long and high and deep is the love of Christ, [19] and to know this love that surpasses knowledge—that you may be filled to the measure of all the fulness of God.

[20] Now to him who is able to do immeasurably more than all we ask or imagine, according to his power that is at work within us, [21] to him be glory in the church and in Christ Jesus throughout all generations, for ever and ever! Amen.

Unity in the Body of Christ

4 As a prisoner for the Lord, then, I urge you to live a life worthy of the calling you have received. [2] Be completely humble and gentle; be patient, bearing with one another in love. [3] Make every effort to keep the unity of the Spirit through the bond of peace. [4] There is one body and one Spirit—just as you were called to one hope when you were called—[5] one Lord, one faith, one baptism; [6] one God and Father of all, who is over all and through all and in all.

[7] But to each one of us grace has been given as Christ apportioned it. [8] This is why it[a] says:

"When he ascended on high,
　he led captives in his train
　and gave gifts to people."[b]

[9] (What does "he ascended" mean except that he also descended to the lower, earthly regions?[c] [10] He who descended is the very one who ascended higher than all the heavens, in order to fill the whole universe.) [11] It was he who gave some to be apostles, some to be prophets, some to be evangelists, and some to be pastors and teachers, [12] to prepare God's people for works of service, so that the body of Christ may be built up [13] until we all reach unity in the faith and in the knowledge of the Son of God and become mature, attaining to the whole measure of the fulness of Christ.

[14] Then we will no longer be infants, tossed back and forth by the waves, and blown here and there by every wind of teaching and by the cunning and craftiness of people in their deceitful scheming. [15] Instead, speaking the truth in love, we will in all things grow up into him who is the Head, that is, Christ. [16] From him the whole body, joined and held together by every supporting ligament, grows and builds itself up in love, as each part does its work.

Living as Children of Light

[17] So I tell you this, and insist on it in the Lord, that you must no longer live as the Gentiles do, in the futility of their thinking. [18] They are darkened in their understanding and separated from the life of God because of the ignorance that is in them due to the hardening of their hearts. [19] Having lost all sensitivity, they have given themselves over to sensuality so as to indulge in every kind of impurity, with a continual lust for more.

[20] You, however, did not come to know Christ that way. [21] Surely you heard of him

[a]15 Or whom all fatherhood　　[a]8 Or God　　[b]8 Psalm 68:18　　[c]9 Or the depths of the earth

and were taught in him in accordance with the truth that is in Jesus. ²²You were taught, with regard to your former way of life, to put off your old self, which is being corrupted by its deceitful desires; ²³to be made new in the attitude of your minds; ²⁴and to put on the new self, created to be like God in true righteousness and holiness.

²⁵Therefore each of you must put off falsehood and speak truthfully to your neighbour, for we are all members of one body. ²⁶"In your anger do not sin"ᵈ: Do not let the sun go down while you are still angry, ²⁷and do not give the devil a foothold. ²⁸Those who have been stealing must steal no longer, but must work, doing something useful with their own hands, that they may have something to share with those in need.

²⁹Do not let any unwholesome talk come out of your mouths, but only what is helpful for building others up according to their needs, that it may benefit those who listen. ³⁰And do not grieve the Holy Spirit of God, with whom you were sealed for the day of redemption. ³¹Get rid of all bitterness, rage and anger, brawling and slander, along with every form of malice. ³²Be kind and compassionate to one another, forgiving each other, just as in Christ God forgave you.

5 Be imitators of God, therefore, as dearly loved children ²and live a life of love, just as Christ loved us and gave himself up for us as a fragrant offering and sacrifice to God.

³But among you there must not be even a hint of sexual immorality, or of any kind of impurity, or of greed, because these are improper for God's holy people. ⁴Nor should there be obscenity, foolish talk or coarse joking, which are out of place, but rather thanksgiving. ⁵For of this you can be sure: No immoral, impure or greedy person—such a person is an idolater— has any inheritance in the kingdom of Christ and of God.ᵃ ⁶Let no-one deceive you with empty words, for because of such things God's wrath comes on those who are disobedient. ⁷Therefore do not be partners with them.

⁸For you were once darkness, but now you are light in the Lord. Live as children of light ⁹(for the fruit of the light consists in all goodness, righteousness and truth) ¹⁰and find out what pleases the Lord. ¹¹Have nothing to do with the fruitless deeds of darkness, but rather expose them. ¹²For it is shameful even to mention what the disobedient do in secret. ¹³But everything exposed by the light becomes visible, ¹⁴for it is light that makes everything visible. This is why it is said:

"Wake up, O sleeper,
rise from the dead,
and Christ will shine on you."

¹⁵Be very careful, then, how you live— not as unwise but as wise, ¹⁶making the most of every opportunity, because the days are evil. ¹⁷Therefore do not be foolish, but understand what the Lord's will is. ¹⁸Do not get drunk on wine, which leads to debauchery. Instead, be filled with the Spirit. ¹⁹Speak to one another with psalms, hymns and spiritual songs. Sing and make music in your heart to the Lord, ²⁰always giving thanks to God the Father for everything, in the name of our Lord Jesus Christ.

²¹Submit to one another out of reverence for Christ.

Wives and Husbands

²²Wives, submit to your husbands as to the Lord. ²³For the husband is the head of the wife as Christ is the head of the church, his body, of which he is the Saviour. ²⁴Now as the church submits to Christ, so also wives should submit to their husbands in everything.

²⁵Husbands, love your wives, just as Christ loved the church and gave himself up for her ²⁶to make her holy, cleansingᵇ her by the washing with water through the word, ²⁷and to present her to himself as a radiant church, without stain or wrinkle or any other blemish, but holy and blameless. ²⁸In this same way, husbands ought to love their wives as their own bodies. He who loves his wife loves himself. ²⁹After

ᵈ26 Psalm 4:4   ᵃ5 Or *kingdom of the Christ and God*   ᵇ26 Or *having cleansed* all, people have never hated their own bodies, but feed and care for them, just as Christ does the church—30 for we are members of his body. 31 "For this reason a man will leave his father and mother and be united to his wife, and the two will become one flesh."*c* 32 This is a profound mystery—but I am talking about Christ and the church. 33 However, each one of you also must love his wife as he loves himself, and the wife must respect her husband.

Children and Parents

6 Children, obey your parents in the Lord, for this is right. 2 "Honour your father and mother"—which is the first commandment with a promise—3 "that it may go well with you and that you may enjoy long life on the earth."*a*

4 Fathers,*b* do not exasperate your children; instead, bring them up in the training and instruction of the Lord.

Slaves and Masters

5 Slaves, obey your earthly masters with respect and fear, and with sincerity of heart, just as you would obey Christ. 6 Obey them not only to win their favour when their eye is on you, but like slaves of Christ, doing the will of God from your heart. 7 Serve wholeheartedly, as if you were serving the Lord, not people, 8 because you know that the Lord will reward each one of you for whatever good you do, whether you are slave or free.

9 And masters, treat your slaves in the same way. Do not threaten them, since you know that he who is both their Master and yours is in heaven, and there is no favouritism with him.

The Armour of God

10 Finally, be strong in the Lord and in his mighty power. 11 Put on the full armour of God so that you can take your stand against the devil's schemes. 12 For our struggle is not against flesh and blood, but against the rulers, against the authorities, against the powers of this dark world and against the spiritual forces of evil in the heavenly realms. 13 Therefore put on the full armour of God, so that when the day of evil comes, you may be able to stand your ground, and after you have done everything, to stand. 14 Stand firm then, with the belt of truth buckled round your waist, with the breastplate of righteousness in place, 15 and with your feet fitted with the readiness that comes from the gospel of peace. 16 In addition to all this, take up the shield of faith, with which you can extinguish all the flaming arrows of the evil one. 17 Take the helmet of salvation and the sword of the Spirit, which is the word of God. 18 And pray in the Spirit on all occasions with all kinds of prayers and requests. With this in mind, be alert and always keep on praying for all the saints.

19 Pray also for me, that whenever I open my mouth, words may be given me so that I will fearlessly make known the mystery of the gospel, 20 for which I am an ambassador in chains. Pray that I may declare it fearlessly, as I should.

Final Greetings

21 Tychicus, the dear brother and faithful servant in the Lord, will tell you everything, so that you also may know how I am and what I am doing. 22 I am sending him to you for this very purpose, that you may know how we are, and that he may encourage you.

23 Peace to the brothers and sisters, and love with faith from God the Father and the Lord Jesus Christ. 24 Grace to all who love our Lord Jesus Christ with an undying love.

---

*c*31 Gen. 2:24   *a*3 Deut. 5:16   *b*4 Or *parents*

Philippians

1 Paul and Timothy, servants of Christ Jesus,

To all the saints in Christ Jesus at Philippi, together with the overseers*ᵃ* and deacons:

² Grace and peace to you from God our Father and the Lord Jesus Christ.

Thanksgiving and Prayer

³ I thank my God every time I remember you. ⁴ In all my prayers for all of you, I always pray with joy ⁵ because of your partnership in the gospel from the first day until now, ⁶ being confident of this, that he who began a good work in you will carry it on to completion until the day of Christ Jesus.

⁷ It is right for me to feel this way about all of you, since I have you in my heart; for whether I am in chains or defending and confirming the gospel, all of you share in God's grace with me. ⁸ God can testify how I long for all of you with the affection of Christ Jesus.

⁹ And this is my prayer: that your love may abound more and more in knowledge and depth of insight, ¹⁰ so that you may be able to discern what is best and may be pure and blameless until the day of Christ, ¹¹ filled with the fruit of righteousness that comes through Jesus Christ—to the glory and praise of God.

Paul's Chains Advance the Gospel

¹² Now I want you to know, brothers and sisters, that what has happened to me has really served to advance the gospel. ¹³ As a result, it has become clear throughout the whole palace guard*ᵇ* and to everyone else that I am in chains for Christ. ¹⁴ Because of my chains, most of the brothers and sisters in the Lord have been encouraged to speak the word of God more courageously and fearlessly.

¹⁵ It is true that some preach Christ out of envy and rivalry, but others out of goodwill. ¹⁶ The latter do so in love, knowing that I am put here for the defence of the gospel. ¹⁷ The former preach Christ out of selfish ambition, not sincerely, supposing that they can stir up trouble for me while I am in chains.*ᶜ* ¹⁸ But what does it matter? The important thing is that in every way, whether from false motives or true, Christ is preached. And because of this I rejoice.

Yes, and I will continue to rejoice, ¹⁹ for I know that through your prayers and the help given by the Spirit of Jesus Christ, what has happened to me will turn out for my deliverance.*ᵈ* ²⁰ I eagerly expect and hope that I will in no way be ashamed, but will have sufficient courage so that now as always Christ will be exalted in my body, whether by life or by death. ²¹ For to me, to live is Christ and to die is gain. ²² If I am to go on living in the body, this will mean fruitful labour for me. Yet what

---

*ᵃ*1 Traditionally *bishops*   *ᵇ*13 Or *whole palace*
*ᶜ*16,17 Some late manuscripts have verses 16 and 17 in reverse order.   *ᵈ*19 Or *salvation*

shall I choose? I do not know! ²³ I am torn between the two: I desire to depart and be with Christ, which is better by far; ²⁴ but it is more necessary for you that I remain in the body. ²⁵ Convinced of this, I know that I will remain, and I will continue with all of you for your progress and joy in the faith, ²⁶ so that through my being with you again your joy in Christ Jesus will overflow on account of me.

²⁷ Whatever happens, conduct yourselves in a manner worthy of the gospel of Christ. Then, whether I come and see you or only hear about you in my absence, I will know that you stand firm in one spirit, striving together with one accord for the faith of the gospel ²⁸ without being frightened in any way by those who oppose you. This is a sign to them that they will be destroyed, but that you will be saved—and that by God. ²⁹ For it has been granted to you on behalf of Christ not only to believe on him, but also to suffer for him, ³⁰ since you are going through the same struggle you saw I had, and now hear that I still have.

Imitating Christ's Humility

2 If you have any encouragement from being united with Christ, if any comfort from his love, if any fellowship with the Spirit, if any tenderness and compassion, ² then make my joy complete by being like-minded, having the same love, being one in spirit and purpose. ³ Do nothing out of selfish ambition or vain conceit, but in humility consider others better than yourselves. ⁴ Each of you should look not only to your own interests, but also to the interests of others.

⁵ Your attitude should be the same as that of Christ Jesus:

⁶ Who, being in very nature^a God,
did not consider equality with God
something to be grasped,
⁷ but made himself nothing,
taking the very nature^b of a servant,
being made in human likeness.
⁸ And being found in appearance as a
human being,

he humbled himself
and became obedient to death—
even death on a cross!
⁹ Therefore God exalted him to the
highest place
and gave him the name that is
above every name,
¹⁰ that at the name of Jesus every knee
should bow,
in heaven and on earth and under
the earth,
¹¹ and every tongue confess that Jesus
Christ is Lord,
to the glory of God the Father.

Shining as Stars

¹² Therefore, my dear friends, as you have always obeyed—not only in my presence, but now much more in my absence—continue to work out your salvation with fear and trembling, ¹³ for it is God who works in you to will and to act according to his good purpose.

¹⁴ Do everything without complaining or arguing, ¹⁵ so that you may become blameless and pure, children of God without fault in a crooked and depraved generation, in which you shine like stars in the universe ¹⁶ as you hold out^c the word of life—in order that I may boast on the day of Christ that I did not run or labour for nothing. ¹⁷ But even if I am being poured out like a drink offering on the sacrifice and service coming from your faith, I am glad and rejoice with all of you. ¹⁸ So you too should be glad and rejoice with me.

Timothy and Epaphroditus

¹⁹ I hope in the Lord Jesus to send Timothy to you soon, that I also may be cheered when I receive news about you. ²⁰ I have no-one else like him, who takes a genuine interest in your welfare. ²¹ For all are looking out for their own interests, not those of Jesus Christ. ²² But you know that Timothy has proved himself, because as a son with his father he has served with me in the work of the gospel. ²³ I hope, therefore, to send him as soon as I see how

^a6 Or *in the form of*   ^b7 Or *the form*   ^c16 Or *hold on to*

things go with me. 24 And I am confident in the Lord that I myself will come soon.

25 But I think it is necessary to send back to you Epaphroditus, my brother, fellow-worker and fellow-soldier, who is also your messenger, whom you sent to take care of my needs. 26 For he longs for all of you and is distressed because you heard he was ill. 27 Indeed he was ill, and almost died. But God had mercy on him, and not on him only but also on me, to spare me sorrow upon sorrow. 28 Therefore I am all the more eager to send him, so that when you see him again you may be glad and I may have less anxiety. 29 Welcome him in the Lord with great joy, and honour people like him, 30 because he almost died for the work of Christ, risking his life to make up for the help you could not give me.

No Confidence in the Flesh

3 Finally, my brothers and sisters, rejoice in the Lord! It is no trouble for me to write the same things to you again, and it is a safeguard for you.

2 Watch out for those dogs, those evildoers, those mutilators of the flesh. 3 For it is we who are the circumcision, we who worship by the Spirit of God, who glory in Christ Jesus, and who put no confidence in the flesh—4 though I myself have reasons for such confidence.

If others think they have reasons to put confidence in the flesh, I have more: 5 circumcised on the eighth day, of the people of Israel, of the tribe of Benjamin, a Hebrew of Hebrews; in regard to the law, a Pharisee; 6 as for zeal, persecuting the church; as for legalistic righteousness, faultless.

7 But whatever was to my profit I now consider loss for the sake of Christ. 8 What is more, I consider everything a loss compared to the surpassing greatness of knowing Christ Jesus my Lord, for whose sake I have lost all things. I consider them rubbish, that I may gain Christ 9 and be found in him, not having a righteousness of my own that comes from the law, but that which is through faith in Christ—the righteousness that comes from God and

is by faith. 10 I want to know Christ and the power of his resurrection and the fellowship of sharing in his sufferings, becoming like him in his death, 11 and so, somehow, to attain to the resurrection from the dead.

Pressing on Towards the Goal

12 Not that I have already obtained all this, or have already been made perfect, but I press on to take hold of that for which Christ Jesus took hold of me. 13 Brothers and sisters, I do not consider myself yet to have taken hold of it. But one thing I do: Forgetting what is behind and straining towards what is ahead, 14 I press on towards the goal to win the prize for which God has called me heavenwards in Christ Jesus.

15 All of us who are mature should take such a view of things. And if on some point you think differently, that too God will make clear to you. 16 Only let us live up to what we have already attained.

17 Join with others in following my example, brothers and sisters, and take note of those who live according to the pattern we gave you. 18 For, as I have often told you before and now say again even with tears, many live as enemies of the cross of Christ. 19 Their destiny is destruction, their god is their stomach, and their glory is in their shame. Their mind is on earthly things. 20 But our citizenship is in heaven. And we eagerly await a Saviour from there, the Lord Jesus Christ, 21 who, by the power that enables him to bring everything under his control, will transform our lowly bodies so that they will be like his glorious body.

4 Therefore, my brothers and sisters, you whom I love and long for, my joy and crown, that is how you should stand firm in the Lord, dear friends!

Exhortations

2 I plead with Euodia and I plead with Syntyche to agree with each other in the Lord. 3 Yes, and I ask you, true companion,[a] help these women who have

---

[a] 3 Or loyal Syzygus

contended at my side in the cause of the gospel, along with Clement and the rest of my co-workers, whose names are in the book of life.

⁴Rejoice in the Lord always. I will say it again: Rejoice! ⁵Let your gentleness be evident to all. The Lord is near. ⁶Do not be anxious about anything, but in everything, by prayer and petition, with thanksgiving, present your requests to God. ⁷And the peace of God, which transcends all understanding, will guard your hearts and your minds in Christ Jesus.

⁸Finally, brothers and sisters, whatever is true, whatever is noble, whatever is right, whatever is pure, whatever is lovely, whatever is admirable—if anything is excellent or praiseworthy—think about such things. ⁹Whatever you have learned or received or heard from me, or seen in me—put it into practice. And the God of peace will be with you.

Thanks for Their Gifts

¹⁰I rejoice greatly in the Lord that at last you have renewed your concern for me. Indeed, you have been concerned, but you had no opportunity to show it. ¹¹I am not saying this because I am in need, for I have learned to be content whatever the circumstances. ¹²I know what it is to be in need, and I know what it is to have plenty. I have learned the secret of being content in any and every situation, whether well fed or hungry, whether living in plenty or in want. ¹³I can do everything through him who gives me strength.

¹⁴Yet it was good of you to share in my troubles. ¹⁵Moreover, as you Philippians know, in the early days of your acquaintance with the gospel, when I set out from Macedonia, not one church shared with me in the matter of giving and receiving, except you only; ¹⁶for even when I was in Thessalonica, you sent me aid again and again when I was in need. ¹⁷Not that I am looking for a gift, but I am looking for what may be credited to your account. ¹⁸I have received full payment and even more; I am amply supplied, now that I have received from Epaphroditus the gifts you sent. They are a fragrant offering, an acceptable sacrifice, pleasing to God. ¹⁹And my God will meet all your needs according to his glorious riches in Christ Jesus.

²⁰To our God and Father be glory for ever and ever. Amen.

Final Greetings

²¹Greet all the saints in Christ Jesus. The brothers and sisters who are with me send greetings. ²²All the saints send you greetings, especially those who belong to Caesar's household.

²³The grace of the Lord Jesus Christ be with your spirit. Amen.*b*

---

*b*23 Some manuscripts do not have *Amen.*

Colossians

1 Paul, an apostle of Christ Jesus by the will of God, and Timothy our brother,

[2] To the holy and faithful*a* brothers and sisters in Christ at Colosse:

Grace and peace to you from God our Father.*b*

Thanksgiving and Prayer

[3] We always thank God, the Father of our Lord Jesus Christ, when we pray for you, [4] because we have heard of your faith in Christ Jesus and of the love you have for all the saints—[5] the faith and love that spring from the hope that is stored up for you in heaven and that you have already heard about in the word of truth, the gospel [6] that has come to you. All over the world this gospel is bearing fruit and growing, just as it has been doing among you since the day you heard it and understood God's grace in all its truth. [7] You learned it from Epaphras, our dear fellow-servant, who is a faithful minister of Christ on our*c* behalf, [8] and who also told us of your love in the Spirit.

[9] For this reason, since the day we heard about you, we have not stopped praying for you and asking God to fill you with the knowledge of his will through all spiritual wisdom and understanding. [10] And we pray this in order that you may live a life worthy of the Lord and may please him in every way: bearing fruit in every good work, growing in the knowledge of God,

[11] being strengthened with all power according to his glorious might so that you may have great endurance and patience, and joyfully [12] giving thanks to the Father, who has qualified you*d* to share in the inheritance of the saints in the kingdom of light. [13] For he has rescued us from the dominion of darkness and brought us into the kingdom of the Son he loves, [14] in whom we have redemption,*e* the forgiveness of sins.

The Supremacy of Christ

[15] He is the image of the invisible God, the firstborn over all creation. [16] For by him all things were created: things in heaven and on earth, visible and invisible, whether thrones or powers or rulers or authorities; all things were created by him and for him. [17] He is before all things, and in him all things hold together. [18] And he is the head of the body, the church; he is the beginning and the firstborn from among the dead, so that in everything he might have the supremacy. [19] For God was pleased to have all his fulness dwell in him, [20] and through him to reconcile to himself all things, whether things on earth or things in heaven, by making peace through his blood, shed on the cross.

[21] Once you were alienated from God and were enemies in your minds because of*f* your evil behaviour. [22] But now he has reconciled you by Christ's physical body through death to present you holy in his sight, without blemish and free from

---

*a*2 Or *believing*   *b*2 Some manuscripts *Father and the Lord Jesus Christ*   *c*7 Some manuscripts *your*
*d*12 Some manuscripts *us*   *e*14 A few late manuscripts *redemption through his blood*   *f*21 Or *minds, as shown by*

accusation—[23] if you continue in your faith, established and firm, not moved from the hope held out in the gospel. This is the gospel that you heard and that has been proclaimed to every creature under heaven, and of which I, Paul, have become a servant.

Paul's Labour for the Church

[24] Now I rejoice in what was suffered for you, and I fill up in my flesh what is still lacking in regard to Christ's afflictions, for the sake of his body, which is the church. [25] I have become its servant by the commission God gave me to present to you the word of God in its fulness—[26] the mystery that has been kept hidden for ages and generations, but is now disclosed to the saints. [27] To them God has chosen to make known among the Gentiles the glorious riches of this mystery, which is Christ in you, the hope of glory.

[28] We proclaim him, admonishing and teaching everyone with all wisdom, so that we may present everyone perfect in Christ. [29] To this end I labour, struggling with all his energy, which so powerfully works in me.

2 I want you to know how much I am struggling for you and for those at Laodicea, and for all who have not met me personally. [2] My purpose is that they may be encouraged in heart and united in love, so that they may have the full riches of complete understanding, in order that they may know the mystery of God, namely, Christ, [3] in whom are hidden all the treasures of wisdom and knowledge. [4] I tell you this so that no-one may deceive you by fine-sounding arguments. [5] For though I am absent from you in body, I am present with you in spirit and delight to see how orderly you are and how firm your faith in Christ is.

Freedom From Human Regulations Through Life With Christ

[6] So then, just as you received Christ Jesus as Lord, continue to live in him,

[7] rooted and built up in him, strengthened in the faith as you were taught, and overflowing with thankfulness.

[8] See to it that no-one takes you captive through hollow and deceptive philosophy, which depends on human tradition and the basic principles of this world rather than on Christ.

[9] For in Christ all the fulness of the Deity lives in bodily form, [10] and you have been given fulness in Christ, who is the Head over every power and authority. [11] In him you were also circumcised, in the putting off of the sinful nature,[a] not with a circumcision done by human hands but with the circumcision done by Christ, [12] having been buried with him in baptism and raised with him through your faith in the power of God, who raised him from the dead.

[13] When you were dead in your sins and in the uncircumcision of your sinful nature,[b] God made you[c] alive with Christ. He forgave us all our sins, [14] having cancelled the written code, with its regulations, that was against us and that stood opposed to us; he took it away, nailing it to the cross. [15] And having disarmed the powers and authorities, he made a public spectacle of them, triumphing over them by the cross.[d]

[16] Therefore do not let anyone judge you by what you eat or drink, or with regard to a religious festival, a New Moon celebration or a Sabbath day. [17] These are a shadow of the things that were to come; the reality, however, is found in Christ. [18] Do not let anyone who delights in false humility and the worship of angels disqualify you for the prize. Such people go into great detail about what they have seen, and their unspiritual minds puff them up with idle notions. [19] They have lost connection with the Head, from whom the whole body, supported and held together by its ligaments and sinews, grows as God causes it to grow.

[20] Since you died with Christ to the basic principles of this world, why, as though you still belonged to it, do you submit to its rules: [21] "Do not handle! Do not taste!

---

[a] 11 Or *the flesh*　　[b] 13 Or *your flesh*　　[c] 13 Some manuscripts *us*　　[d] 15 Or *them in him*

Do not touch!'"? [22] These are all destined to perish with use, because they are based on human commands and teachings. [23] Such regulations indeed have an appearance of wisdom, with their self-imposed worship, their false humility and their harsh treatment of the body, but they lack any value in restraining sensual indulgence.

Rules for Holy Living

3 Since, then, you have been raised with Christ, set your hearts on things above, where Christ is seated at the right hand of God. [2] Set your minds on things above, not on earthly things. [3] For you died, and your life is now hidden with Christ in God. [4] When Christ, who is your[a] life, appears, then you also will appear with him in glory.

[5] Put to death, therefore, whatever belongs to your earthly nature: sexual immorality, impurity, lust, evil desires and greed, which is idolatry. [6] Because of these, the wrath of God is coming.[b] [7] You used to walk in these ways, in the life you once lived. [8] But now you must rid yourselves of all such things as these: anger, rage, malice, slander and filthy language from your lips. [9] Do not lie to each other, since you have taken off your old self with its practices [10] and have put on the new self, which is being renewed in knowledge in the image of its Creator. [11] Here there is no Greek or Jew, circumcised or uncircumcised, barbarian, Scythian, slave or free, but Christ is all, and is in all.

[12] Therefore, as God's chosen people, holy and dearly loved, clothe yourselves with compassion, kindness, humility, gentleness and patience. [13] Bear with each other and forgive whatever grievances you may have against one another. Forgive as the Lord forgave you. [14] And over all these virtues put on love, which binds them all together in perfect unity.

[15] Let the peace of Christ rule in your hearts, since as members of one body you were called to peace. And be thankful.

[16] Let the word of Christ dwell in you richly as you teach and admonish one another with all wisdom, and as you sing psalms, hymns and spiritual songs with gratitude in your hearts to God. [17] And whatever you do, whether in word or deed, do it all in the name of the Lord Jesus, giving thanks to God the Father through him.

Rules for Christian Households

[18] Wives, submit to your husbands, as is fitting in the Lord.

[19] Husbands, love your wives and do not be harsh with them.

[20] Children, obey your parents in everything, for this pleases the Lord.

[21] Fathers,[c] do not embitter your children, or they will become discouraged.

[22] Slaves, obey your earthly masters in everything; and do it, not only when their eye is on you and to win their favour, but with sincerity of heart and reverence for the Lord. [23] Whatever you do, work at it with all your heart, as working for the Lord, not for human masters, [24] since you know that you will receive an inheritance from the Lord as a reward. It is the Lord Christ you are serving. [25] Those who do wrong will be repaid for their wrongs, and there is no favouritism.

4 Masters, provide your slaves with what is right and fair, because you know that you also have a Master in heaven.

Further Instructions

[2] Devote yourselves to prayer, being watchful and thankful. [3] And pray for us, too, that God may open a door for our message, so that we may proclaim the mystery of Christ, for which I am in chains. [4] Pray that I may proclaim it clearly, as I should. [5] Be wise in the way you act towards outsiders; make the most of every opportunity. [6] Let your conversation be always full of grace, seasoned with salt, so that you may know how to answer everyone.

---

[a] 4 Some manuscripts *our*   [b] 6 Some early manuscripts *coming on those who are disobedient*   [c] 7 Or *parents*

Final Greetings

[7] Tychicus will tell you all the news about me. He is a dear brother, a faithful minister and fellow-servant in the Lord. [8] I am sending him to you for the express purpose that you may know about our[a] circumstances and that he may encourage your hearts. [9] He is coming with Onesimus, our faithful and dear brother, who is one of you. They will tell you everything that is happening here.

[10] My fellow-prisoner Aristarchus sends you his greetings, as does Mark, the cousin of Barnabas. (You have received instructions about him; if he comes to you, welcome him.) [11] Jesus, who is called Justus, also sends greetings. These are the only Jews among my co-workers for the kingdom of God, and they have proved a comfort to me. [12] Epaphras, who is one of you and a servant of Christ Jesus, sends greetings. He is always wrestling in prayer for you, that you may stand firm in all the will of God, mature and fully assured. [13] I vouch for him that he is working hard for you and for those at Laodicea and Hierapolis. [14] Our dear friend Luke, the doctor, and Demas send greetings. [15] Give my greetings to the brothers and sisters at Laodicea, and to Nympha and the church in her house.

[16] After this letter has been read to you, see that it is also read in the church of the Laodiceans and that you in turn read the letter from Laodicea.

[17] Tell Archippus: "See to it that you complete the work you have received in the Lord."

[18] I, Paul, write this greeting in my own hand. Remember my chains. Grace be with you.

---

[a]8 Some manuscripts *that he may know about your*

1 Thessalonians

1

Paul, Silas[a] and Timothy,

To the church of the Thessalonians in God the Father and the Lord Jesus Christ:

Grace and peace to you.[b]

Thanksgiving for the Thessalonians' Faith

[2] We always thank God for all of you, mentioning you in our prayers. [3] We continually remember before our God and Father your work produced by faith, your labour prompted by love, and your endurance inspired by hope in our Lord Jesus Christ.

[4] For we know, brothers and sisters loved by God, that he has chosen you, [5] because our gospel came to you not simply with words, but also with power, with the Holy Spirit and with deep conviction. You know how we lived among you for your sake. [6] You became imitators of us and of the Lord; in spite of severe suffering, you welcomed the message with the joy given by the Holy Spirit. [7] And so you became a model to all the believers in Macedonia and Achaia. [8] The Lord's message rang out from you not only in Macedonia and Achaia—your faith in God has become known everywhere. Therefore we do not need to say anything about it, [9] for they themselves report what kind of reception you gave us. They tell how you turned to God from idols to serve the living and true God, [10] and to wait for his Son from heaven, whom he raised from the dead—Jesus, who rescues us from the coming wrath.

Paul's Ministry in Thessalonica

2

You know, brothers and sisters, that our visit to you was not a failure. [2] We had previously suffered and been insulted in Philippi, as you know, but with the help of our God we dared to tell you his gospel in spite of strong opposition. [3] For the appeal we make does not spring from error or impure motives, nor are we trying to trick you. [4] On the contrary, we speak as those approved by God to be entrusted with the gospel. We are not trying to please people but God, who tests our hearts. [5] You know we never used flattery, nor did we put on a mask to cover up greed—God is our witness. [6] We were not looking for human praise, not from you or anyone else.

As apostles of Christ we could have been a burden to you, [7] but we were gentle among you, like a mother caring for her little children. [8] We loved you so much that we were delighted to share with you not only the gospel of God but our lives as well, because you had become so dear to us. [9] Surely you remember, brothers and sisters, our toil and hardship; we worked night and day in order not to be a burden to anyone while we preached the gospel of God to you.

[10] You are witnesses, and so is God, of how holy, righteous and blameless we were among you who believed. [11] For you

---

[a]1 Greek *Silvanus*, a variant of *Silas*   [b]1 Some early manuscripts *you from God our Father and the Lord Jesus Christ*

know that we dealt with each of you as a father deals with his own children, 12 encouraging, comforting and urging you to live lives worthy of God, who calls you into his kingdom and glory.

13 And we also thank God continually because, when you received the word of God, which you heard from us, you accepted it not as a human word, but as it actually is, the word of God, which is at work in you who believe. 14 For you, brothers and sisters, became imitators of God's churches in Judea, which are in Christ Jesus: You suffered from your own people the same things those churches suffered from the Jews, 15 who killed the Lord Jesus and the prophets and also drove us out. They displease God and are hostile to everyone 16 in their effort to keep us from speaking to the Gentiles so that they may be saved. In this way they always heap up their sins to the limit. The wrath of God has come upon them at last.[a]

Paul's Longing to See the Thessalonians

17 But, brothers and sisters, when we were torn away from you for a short time (in person, not in thought), out of our intense longing we made every effort to see you. 18 For we wanted to come to you—certainly I, Paul, did, again and again—but Satan stopped us. 19 For what is our hope, our joy, or the crown in which we will glory in the presence of our Lord Jesus when he comes? Is it not you? 20 Indeed, you are our glory and joy.

3 So when we could stand it no longer, we thought it best to be left by ourselves in Athens. 2 We sent Timothy, who is our brother and God's fellow-worker[a] in spreading the gospel of Christ, to strengthen and encourage you in your faith, 3 so that no-one would be unsettled by these trials. You know quite well that we were destined for them. 4 In fact, when we were with you, we kept telling you that we would be persecuted. And it turned out that way, as you well know. 5 For this reason, when I could stand it no longer, I sent to find out about your faith.

I was afraid that in some way the tempter might have tempted you and our efforts might have been useless.

Timothy's Encouraging Report

6 But Timothy has just now come to us from you and has brought good news about your faith and love. He has told us that you always have pleasant memories of us and that you long to see us, just as we also long to see you. 7 Therefore, brothers and sisters, in all our distress and persecution we were encouraged about you because of your faith. 8 For now we really live, since you are standing firm in the Lord. 9 How can we thank God enough for you in return for all the joy we have in the presence of our God because of you? 10 Night and day we pray most earnestly that we may see you again and supply what is lacking in your faith.

11 Now may our God and Father himself and our Lord Jesus clear the way for us to come to you. 12 May the Lord make your love increase and overflow for each other and for everyone else, just as ours does for you. 13 May he strengthen your hearts so that you will be blameless and holy in the presence of our God and Father when our Lord Jesus comes with all his holy ones.

Living to Please God

4 Finally, brothers and sisters, we instructed you how to live in order to please God, as in fact you are living. Now we ask you and urge you in the Lord Jesus to do this more and more. 2 For you know what instructions we gave you by the authority of the Lord Jesus.

3 It is God's will that you should be sanctified: that you should avoid sexual immorality; 4 that each of you should learn to control your own body[a] in a way that is holy and honourable, 5 not in passionate lust like the heathen, who do not know God; 6 and that in this matter no-one should wrong or take advantage of a brother or sister. The Lord will punish

[a]16 Or them fully   [a]2 Some manuscripts brother and fellow-worker; other manuscripts brother and God's servant
[a]4 Or learn to live with his own wife; or learn to acquire a wife

those who commit all such sins, as we have already told you and warned you. ⁷For God did not call us to be impure, but to live a holy life. ⁸Therefore, he who rejects this instruction does not reject man but God, who gives you his Holy Spirit.

⁹Now about your mutual love we do not need to write to you, for you yourselves have been taught by God to love each other. ¹⁰And in fact, you do love all the brothers and sisters throughout Macedonia. Yet we urge you, dear friends, to do so more and more.

¹¹Make it your ambition to lead a quiet life, to mind your own business and to work with your hands, just as we told you, ¹²so that your daily life may win the respect of outsiders and so that you will not be dependent on anybody.

The Coming of the LORD

¹³Brothers and sisters, we do not want you to be ignorant about those who fall asleep, or to grieve like the rest, who have no hope. ¹⁴We believe that Jesus died and rose again and so we believe that God will bring with Jesus those who have fallen asleep in him. ¹⁵According to the Lord's own word, we tell you that we who are still alive, who are left till the coming of the Lord, will certainly not precede those who have fallen asleep. ¹⁶For the Lord himself will come down from heaven, with a loud command, with the voice of the archangel and with the trumpet call of God, and the dead in Christ will rise first. ¹⁷After that, we who are still alive and are left will be caught up together with them in the clouds to meet the Lord in the air. And so we will be with the Lord for ever. ¹⁸Therefore encourage each other with these words.

5 Now, brothers and sisters, about times and dates we do not need to write to you, ²for you know very well that the day of the Lord will come like a thief in the night. ³While people are saying, "Peace and safety", destruction will come on them suddenly, as labour pains on a pregnant woman, and they will not escape.

⁴But you, brothers and sisters, are not in darkness so that this day should surprise you like a thief. ⁵You are all children of the light and children of the day. We do not belong to the night or to the darkness. ⁶So then, let us not be like others, who are asleep, but let us be alert and self-controlled. ⁷For those who sleep, sleep at night, and those who get drunk, get drunk at night. ⁸But since we belong to the day, let us be self-controlled, putting on faith and love as a breastplate, and the hope of salvation as a helmet. ⁹For God did not appoint us to suffer wrath but to receive salvation through our Lord Jesus Christ. ¹⁰He died for us so that, whether we are awake or asleep, we may live together with him. ¹¹Therefore encourage one another and build each other up, just as in fact you are doing.

Final Instructions

¹²Now we ask you, brothers and sisters, to respect those who work hard among you, who are over you in the Lord and who admonish you. ¹³Hold them in the highest regard in love because of their work. Live in peace with each other. ¹⁴And we urge you, brothers and sisters, warn those who are idle, encourage the timid, help the weak, be patient with everyone. ¹⁵Make sure that nobody pays back wrong for wrong, but always try to be kind to each other and to everyone else.

¹⁶Be joyful always; ¹⁷pray continually; ¹⁸give thanks in all circumstances, for this is God's will for you in Christ Jesus.

¹⁹Do not put out the Spirit's fire; ²⁰do not treat prophecies with contempt. ²¹Test everything. Hold on to the good. ²²Avoid every kind of evil.

²³May God himself, the God of peace, sanctify you through and through. May your whole spirit, soul and body be kept blameless at the coming of our Lord Jesus Christ. ²⁴The one who calls you is faithful and he will do it.

²⁵Brothers and sisters, pray for us. ²⁶Greet all God's people with a holy kiss. ²⁷I charge you before the Lord to have this letter read to all the brothers and sisters.

²⁸The grace of our Lord Jesus Christ be with you.

2 Thessalonians

1 Paul, Silas[a] and Timothy,

To the church of the Thessalonians in God our Father and the Lord Jesus Christ:

²Grace and peace to you from God the Father and the Lord Jesus Christ.

Thanksgiving and Prayer

³We ought always to thank God for you, brothers and sisters, and rightly so, because your faith is growing more and more, and the love every one of you has for each other is increasing. ⁴Therefore, among God's churches we boast about your perseverance and faith in all the persecutions and trials you are enduring.

⁵All this is evidence that God's judgment is right, and as a result you will be counted worthy of the kingdom of God, for which you are suffering. ⁶God is just: He will pay back trouble to those who trouble you ⁷and give relief to you who are troubled, and to us as well. This will happen when the Lord Jesus is revealed from heaven in blazing fire with his powerful angels. ⁸He will punish those who do not know God and do not obey the gospel of our Lord Jesus. ⁹They will be punished with everlasting destruction and shut out from the presence of the Lord and from the majesty of his power ¹⁰on the day he comes to be glorified in his holy people and to be marvelled at among all those who have believed. This includes you, because you believed our testimony to you.

¹¹With this in mind, we constantly pray for you, that our God may count you worthy of his calling, and that by his power he may fulfil every good purpose of yours and every act prompted by your faith. ¹²We pray this so that the name of our Lord Jesus may be glorified in you, and you in him, according to the grace of our God and the Lord Jesus Christ.[b]

The Man of Lawlessness

2 Concerning the coming of our Lord Jesus Christ and our being gathered to him, we ask you, brothers and sisters, ²not to become easily unsettled or alarmed by some prophecy, report or letter supposed to have come from us, saying that the day of the Lord has already come. ³Don't let anyone deceive you in any way, for ⌐that day will not come⌐ until the rebellion occurs and the man of lawlessness[a] is revealed, the man doomed to destruction. ⁴He will oppose and will exalt himself over everything that is called God or is worshipped, so that he sets himself up in God's temple, proclaiming himself to be God.

⁵Don't you remember that when I was with you I used to tell you these things? ⁶And now you know what is holding him back, so that he may be revealed at the proper time. ⁷For the secret power of lawlessness is already at work; but the one who now holds it back will continue to do so till he is taken out of the way. ⁸And then the lawless one will be revealed, whom the Lord Jesus will overthrow with

---

[a]1 Greek *Silvanus*, a variant of *Silas*   [b]12 Or *God and Lord, Jesus Christ*   [a]3 Some manuscripts *sin*

the breath of his mouth and destroy by the splendour of his coming. [9] The coming of the lawless one will be in accordance with the work of Satan displayed in all kinds of counterfeit miracles, signs and wonders, [10] and in every sort of evil that deceives those who are perishing. They perish because they refused to love the truth and so be saved. [11] For this reason God sends them a powerful delusion so that they will believe the lie [12] and so that all will be condemned who have not believed the truth but have delighted in wickedness.

Stand Firm

[13] But we ought always to thank God for you, brothers and sisters loved by the Lord, because from the beginning God chose you[b] to be saved through the sanctifying work of the Spirit and through belief in the truth. [14] He called you to this through our gospel, that you might share in the glory of our Lord Jesus Christ. [15] So then, brothers and sisters, stand firm and hold to the teachings[c] we passed on to you, whether by word of mouth or by letter.

[16] May our Lord Jesus Christ himself and God our Father, who loved us and by his grace gave us eternal encouragement and good hope, [17] encourage your hearts and strengthen you in every good deed and word.

Request for Prayer

3 Finally, brothers and sisters, pray for us that the message of the Lord may spread rapidly and be honoured, just as it was with you. [2] And pray that we may be delivered from wicked and evil people, for not everyone has faith. [3] But the Lord is faithful, and he will strengthen and protect you from the evil one. [4] We have confidence in the Lord that you are doing and will continue to do the things we

command. [5] May the Lord direct your hearts into God's love and Christ's perseverance.

Warning Against Idleness

[6] In the name of the Lord Jesus Christ, we command you, brothers and sisters, to keep away from every believer who is idle and does not live according to the teaching[a] you received from us. [7] For you yourselves know how you ought to follow our example. We were not idle when we were with you, [8] nor did we eat anyone's food without paying for it. On the contrary, we worked night and day, labouring and toiling so that we would not be a burden to any of you. [9] We did this, not because we do not have the right to such help, but in order to make ourselves a model for you to follow. [10] For even when we were with you, we gave you this rule: "Anyone who will not work shall not eat."

[11] We hear that some among you are idle. They are not busy; they are busybodies. [12] Such people we command and urge in the Lord Jesus Christ to settle down and earn the bread they eat. [13] And as for you, brothers and sisters, never tire of doing what is right.

[14] Take special note of those who do not obey our instruction in this letter. Do not associate with them, in order that they may feel ashamed. [15] Yet do not regard them as enemies, but warn them as fellow believers.

Final Greetings

[16] Now may the Lord of peace himself give you peace at all times and in every way. The Lord be with all of you.

[17] I, Paul, write this greeting in my own hand, which is the distinguishing mark in all my letters. This is how I write.

[18] The grace of our Lord Jesus Christ be with you all.

---

[b]13 Some manuscripts *because God chose you as his firstfruits*   [c]15 Or *traditions*   [a]6 Or *tradition*

1 Timothy

1 Paul, an apostle of Christ Jesus by the command of God our Saviour and of Christ Jesus our hope,

[2] To Timothy my true son in the faith:

Grace, mercy and peace from God the Father and Christ Jesus our Lord.

Warning Against False Teachers of the Law

[3] As I urged you when I went into Macedonia, stay there in Ephesus so that you may command certain persons not to teach false doctrines any longer [4] nor to devote themselves to myths and endless genealogies. These promote controversies rather than God's work—which is by faith. [5] The goal of this command is love, which comes from a pure heart and a good conscience and a sincere faith. [6] Some have wandered away from these and turned to meaningless talk. [7] They want to be teachers of the law, but they do not know what they are talking about or what they so confidently affirm.

[8] We know that the law is good if one uses it properly. [9] We also know that law[a] is made not for the righteous but for lawbreakers and rebels, the ungodly and sinful, the unholy and irreligious; for those who kill their fathers or mothers, for murderers, [10] for adulterers and perverts, for slave traders and liars and perjurers— and for whatever else is contrary to the sound doctrine [11] that conforms to the glorious gospel of the blessed God, which he entrusted to me.

The Lord's Grace to Paul

[12] I thank Christ Jesus our Lord, who has given me strength, that he considered me faithful, appointing me to his service. [13] Even though I was once a blasphemer and a persecutor and a violent man, I was shown mercy because I acted in ignorance and unbelief. [14] The grace of our Lord was poured out on me abundantly, along with the faith and love that are in Christ Jesus.

[15] Here is a trustworthy saying that deserves full acceptance: Christ Jesus came into the world to save sinners—of whom I am the worst. [16] But for that very reason I was shown mercy so that in me, the worst of sinners, Christ Jesus might display his unlimited patience as an example for those who would believe on him and receive eternal life. [17] Now to the King eternal, immortal, invisible, the only God, be honour and glory for ever and ever. Amen.

[18] Timothy, my son, I give you this instruction in keeping with the prophecies once made about you, so that by following them you may fight the good fight, [19] holding on to faith and a good conscience. Some have rejected these and so have shipwrecked their faith. [20] Among them are Hymenaeus and Alexander, whom I have handed over to Satan to be taught not to blaspheme.

[a]9 Or that the law

Instructions on Worship

2 I urge, then, first of all, that requests, prayers, intercession and thanksgiving be made for everyone—²for kings and all those in authority, that we may live peaceful and quiet lives in all godliness and holiness. ³This is good, and pleases God our Saviour, ⁴who wants all people to be saved and to come to a knowledge of the truth. ⁵For there is one God and one mediator between God and human beings, Christ Jesus, himself human, ⁶who gave himself as a ransom for all— the testimony given in its proper time. ⁷And for this purpose I was appointed a herald and an apostle—I am telling the truth, I am not lying—and a teacher of the true faith to the Gentiles.

⁸I want men everywhere to lift up holy hands in prayer, without anger or disputing.

⁹I also want women to dress modestly, with decency and propriety, not with braided hair or gold or pearls or expensive clothes, ¹⁰but with good deeds, appropriate for women who profess to worship God.

¹¹A woman should learn in quietness and full submission. ¹²I do not permit a woman to teach or to have authority over a man; she must be silent. ¹³For Adam was formed first, then Eve. ¹⁴And Adam was not the one deceived; it was the woman who was deceived and became a sinner. ¹⁵But women*a* will be saved*b* through childbearing—if they continue in faith, love and holiness with propriety.

Overseers and Deacons

3 Here is a trustworthy saying: Whoever aspires to be an overseer*a* desires a noble task. ²Now the overseer must be above reproach, the husband of but one wife, temperate, self-controlled, respectable, hospitable, able to teach, ³not given to drunkenness, not violent but gentle, not quarrelsome, not a lover of money. ⁴He must manage his own family well and see that his children obey him with proper

respect. ⁵(If anyone does not know how to manage his own family, how can he take care of God's church?) ⁶He must not be a recent convert, or he may become conceited and fall under the same judgment as the devil. ⁷He must also have a good reputation with outsiders, so that he will not fall into disgrace and into the devil's trap.

⁸Deacons, likewise, are to be worthy of respect, sincere, not indulging in much wine, and not pursuing dishonest gain. ⁹They must keep hold of the deep truths of the faith with a clear conscience. ¹⁰They must first be tested; and then if there is nothing against them, let them serve as deacons.

¹¹In the same way, wives*b* are to be women worthy of respect, not malicious talkers but temperate and trustworthy in everything.

¹²A deacon must be the husband of but one wife and must manage his children and his household well. ¹³Those who have served well gain an excellent standing and great assurance in their faith in Christ Jesus.

¹⁴Although I hope to come to you soon, I am writing you these instructions so that, ¹⁵if I am delayed, you will know how people ought to conduct themselves in God's household, which is the church of the living God, the pillar and foundation of the truth. ¹⁶Beyond all question, the mystery of godliness is great:

He*c* appeared in a body,*d*
     was vindicated by the Spirit,
was seen by angels,
     was preached among the nations,
was believed on in the world,
     was taken up in glory.

Instructions to Timothy

4 The Spirit clearly says that in later times some will abandon the faith and follow deceiving spirits and things taught by demons. ²Such teachings come through hypocritical liars, whose consciences have been seared as with a hot iron. ³They

---

*a*15 Greek *she*   *b*15 Or *restored*   *a*1 Traditionally *bishop*; also in verse 2   *b*11 Or *deaconesses*
*c*16 Some manuscripts *God*   *d*16 Or *in the flesh*

forbid people to marry and order them to abstain from certain foods, which God created to be received with thanksgiving by those who believe and who know the truth. [4]For everything God created is good, and nothing is to be rejected if it is received with thanksgiving, [5]because it is consecrated by the word of God and prayer.

[6]If you point these things out to the brothers and sisters, you will be a good minister of Christ Jesus, brought up in the truths of the faith and of the good teaching that you have followed. [7]Have nothing to do with godless myths and old wives' tales; rather, train yourself to be godly. [8]For physical training is of some value, but godliness has value for all things, holding promise for both the present life and the life to come.

[9]This is a trustworthy saying that deserves full acceptance [10](and for this we labour and strive), that we have put our hope in the living God, who is the Saviour of all people, and especially of those who believe.

[11]Command and teach these things. [12]Don't let anyone look down on you because you are young, but set an example for the believers in speech, in life, in love, in faith and in purity. [13]Until I come, devote yourself to the public reading of Scripture, to preaching and to teaching. [14]Do not neglect your gift, which was given you through a prophetic message when the body of elders laid their hands on you.

[15]Be diligent in these matters; give yourself wholly to them, so that everyone may see your progress. [16]Watch your life and doctrine closely. Persevere in them, because if you do, you will save both yourself and your hearers.

Advice About Widows, Elders and Slaves

5 Do not rebuke an older man harshly, but exhort him as if he were your father. Treat younger men as brothers, [2]older women as mothers, and younger women as sisters, with absolute purity.

[3]Give proper recognition to those widows who are really in need. [4]But if a widow has children or grandchildren, these should learn first of all to put their religion into practice by caring for their own family and so repaying their parents and grandparents, for this is pleasing to God. [5]The widow who is really in need and left all alone puts her hope in God and continues night and day to pray and to ask God for help. [6]But the widow who lives for pleasure is dead even while she lives. [7]Give the people these instructions, too, so that no-one may be open to blame. [8]Anyone who does not provide for relatives, and especially for immediate family members, has denied the faith and is worse than an unbeliever.

[9]No widow may be put on the list of widows unless she is over sixty, has been faithful to her husband,[a] [10]and is well known for her good deeds, such as bringing up children, showing hospitality, washing the feet of the saints, helping those in trouble and devoting herself to all kinds of good deeds.

[11]As for younger widows, do not put them on such a list. For when their sensual desires overcome their dedication to Christ, they want to marry. [12]Thus they bring judgment on themselves, because they have broken their first pledge. [13]Besides, they get into the habit of being idle and going about from house to house. And not only do they become idlers, but also gossips and busybodies, saying things they ought not to. [14]So I counsel younger widows to marry, to have children, to manage their homes and to give the enemy no opportunity for slander. [15]Some have in fact already turned away to follow Satan.

[16]If any woman who is a believer has widows in her family, she should help them and not let the church be burdened with them, so that the church can help those widows who are really in need.

[17]The elders who direct the affairs of the church well are worthy of double honour, especially those whose work is preaching and teaching. [18]For the Scripture says, "Do not muzzle the ox while it is treading out the grain,"[b] and "Workers

[a]9 Or has had but one husband   [b]18 Deut. 25:4

deserve their wages."[c] [19] Do not entertain an accusation against an elder unless it is brought by two or three witnesses. [20] Those who sin are to be rebuked publicly, so that the others may take warning.

[21] I charge you, in the sight of God and Christ Jesus and the elect angels, to keep these instructions without partiality, and to do nothing out of favouritism.

[22] Do not be hasty in the laying on of hands, and do not share in the sins of others. Keep yourself pure.

[23] Stop drinking only water, and use a little wine because of your stomach and your frequent illnesses.

[24] The sins of some are obvious, reaching the place of judgment ahead of them; the sins of others trail behind them. [25] In the same way, good deeds are obvious, and even those that are not cannot be hidden.

[6] All who are under the yoke of slavery should consider their masters worthy of full respect, so that God's name and our teaching may not be slandered. [2] Those who have believing masters are not to show less respect for them because they are believers. Instead, they are to serve them even better, because those who benefit from their service are believers, and dear to them. These are the things you are to teach and urge on them.

Love of Money

[3] Anyone who teaches false doctrines and does not agree to the sound instruction of our Lord Jesus Christ and to godly teaching, [4] is conceited and understands nothing. Such people have an unhealthy interest in controversies and quarrels about words that result in envy, strife, malicious talk, evil suspicions [5] and constant friction between people of corrupt mind, who have been robbed of the truth and who think that godliness is a means to financial gain.

[6] But godliness with contentment is great gain. [7] For we brought nothing into the world, and we can take nothing out of it. [8] But if we have food and clothing, we will be content with that. [9] Those who

want to get rich fall into temptation and a trap and into many foolish and harmful desires that plunge people into ruin and destruction. [10] For the love of money is a root of all kinds of evil. Some people, eager for money, have wandered from the faith and pierced themselves with many griefs.

Paul's Charge to Timothy

[11] But you, man of God, flee from all this, and pursue righteousness, godliness, faith, love, endurance and gentleness. [12] Fight the good fight of the faith. Take hold of the eternal life to which you were called when you made your good confession in the presence of many witnesses. [13] In the sight of God, who gives life to everything, and of Christ Jesus, who while testifying before Pontius Pilate made the good confession, I charge you [14] to keep this command without spot or blame until the appearing of our Lord Jesus Christ, [15] which God will bring about in his own time—God, the blessed and only Ruler, the King of kings and Lord of lords, [16] who alone is immortal and who lives in unapproachable light, whom no-one has seen or can see. To him be honour and might for ever. Amen.

[17] Command those who are rich in this present world not to be arrogant nor to put their hope in wealth, which is so uncertain, but to put their hope in God, who richly provides us with everything for our enjoyment. [18] Command them to do good, to be rich in good deeds, and to be generous and willing to share. [19] In this way they will lay up treasure for themselves as a firm foundation for the coming age, so that they may take hold of the life that is truly life.

[20] Timothy, guard what has been entrusted to your care. Turn away from godless chatter and the opposing ideas of what is falsely called knowledge, [21] which some have professed and in so doing have wandered from the faith.

Grace be with you.

[c]18 Luke 10:7

2 Timothy

1 Paul, an apostle of Christ Jesus by the will of God, according to the promise of life that is in Christ Jesus,

²To Timothy, my dear son:

Grace, mercy and peace from God the Father and Christ Jesus our Lord.

Encouragement to Be Faithful

³I thank God, whom I serve, as my ancestors did, with a clear conscience, as night and day I constantly remember you in my prayers. ⁴Recalling your tears, I long to see you, so that I may be filled with joy. ⁵I have been reminded of your sincere faith, which first lived in your grandmother Lois and in your mother Eunice and, I am persuaded, now lives in you also. ⁶For this reason I remind you to fan into flame the gift of God, which is in you through the laying on of my hands. ⁷For God did not give us a spirit of timidity, but a spirit of power, of love and of self-discipline.

⁸So do not be ashamed to testify about our Lord, or ashamed of me his prisoner. But join with me in suffering for the gospel, by the power of God, ⁹who has saved us and called us to a holy life—not because of anything we have done but because of his own purpose and grace. This grace was given us in Christ Jesus before the beginning of time, ¹⁰but it has now been revealed through the appearing of our Saviour, Christ Jesus, who has destroyed death and has brought life and

immortality to light through the gospel. ¹¹And of this gospel I was appointed a herald and an apostle and a teacher. ¹²That is why I am suffering as I am. Yet I am not ashamed, because I know whom I have believed, and am convinced that he is able to guard what I have entrusted to him for that day.

¹³What you heard from me, keep as the pattern of sound teaching, with faith and love in Christ Jesus. ¹⁴Guard the good deposit that was entrusted to you—guard it with the help of the Holy Spirit who lives in us.

¹⁵You know that everyone in the province of Asia has deserted me, including Phygelus and Hermogenes.

¹⁶May the Lord show mercy to the household of Onesiphorus, because he often refreshed me and was not ashamed of my chains. ¹⁷On the contrary, when he was in Rome, he searched hard for me until he found me. ¹⁸May the Lord grant that he will find mercy from the Lord on that day! You know very well in how many ways he helped me in Ephesus.

2 You then, my son, be strong in the grace that is in Christ Jesus. ²And the things you have heard me say in the presence of many witnesses entrust to reliable people*a* who will also be qualified to teach others. ³Endure hardship with us like a good soldier of Christ Jesus. ⁴No-one serving as a soldier gets involved in civilian affairs, but rather tries to please the commanding officer. ⁵Similarly, anyone who competes as an athlete does not receive the victor's crown except by

*a*2 Or *men*

competing according to the rules. 6The hardworking farmer should be the first to receive a share of the crops. 7Reflect on what I am saying, for the Lord will give you insight into all this.

8Remember Jesus Christ, raised from the dead, descended from David. This is my gospel, 9for which I am suffering even to the point of being chained like a criminal. But God's word is not chained. 10Therefore I endure everything for the sake of the elect, that they too may obtain the salvation that is in Christ Jesus, with eternal glory.

11Here is a trustworthy saying:

If we died with him,
we will also live with him;
12if we endure,
we will also reign with him.
If we disown him,
he will also disown us;
13if we are faithless,
he will remain faithful,
for he cannot disown himself.

A Worker Approved by God

14Keep reminding them of these things. Warn them before God against quarrelling about words; it is of no value, and only ruins those who listen. 15Do your best to present yourself to God as one approved, a worker who does not need to be ashamed and who correctly handles the word of truth. 16Avoid godless chatter, because those who indulge in it will become more and more ungodly. 17Their teaching will spread like gangrene. Among them are Hymenaeus and Philetus, 18who have wandered away-from the truth. They say that the resurrection has already taken place, and they destroy the faith of some. 19Nevertheless, God's solid foundation stands firm, sealed with this inscription: "The Lord knows those who are his,"b and, "Everyone who confesses the name of the Lord must turn away from wickedness."

20In a large house there are articles not only of gold and silver, but also of wood

and clay; some are for noble purposes and some for ignoble. 21Any who cleanse themselves from the latter will be instruments for noble purposes, made holy, useful to the Master and prepared to do any good work.

22Flee the evil desires of youth, and pursue righteousness, faith, love and peace, along with those who call on the Lord out of a pure heart. 23Don't have anything to do with foolish and stupid arguments, because you know they produce quarrels. 24And the Lord's servants must not quarrel; instead, they must be kind to everyone, able to teach, not resentful. 25Opponents must be gently instructed, in the hope that God will grant them repentance leading them to a knowledge of the truth, 26and that they will come to their senses and escape from the trap of the devil, who has taken them captive to do his will.

Godlessness in the Last Days

3 But mark this: There will be terrible times in the last days. 2People will be lovers of themselves, lovers of money, boastful, proud, abusive, disobedient to their parents, ungrateful, unholy, 3without love, unforgiving, slanderous, without self-control, brutal, not lovers of the good, 4treacherous, rash, conceited, lovers of pleasure rather than lovers of God—5having a form of godliness but denying its power. Have nothing to do with them.

6They are the kind who worm their way into homes and gain control over weak-willed women, who are loaded down with sins and are swayed by all kinds of evil desires, 7always learning but never able to acknowledge the truth. 8Just as Jannes and Jambres opposed Moses, so also these people oppose the truth—people of depraved minds, who, as far as the faith is concerned, are rejected. 9But they will not get very far because, as in the case of those men, their folly will be clear to everyone.

b19 Num. 16:5 (see Septuagint)

Paul's Charge to Timothy

[10] You, however, know all about my teaching, my way of life, my purpose, faith, patience, love, endurance, [11] persecutions, sufferings—what kinds of things happened to me in Antioch, Iconium and Lystra, the persecutions I endured. Yet the Lord rescued me from all of them. [12] In fact, everyone who wants to live a godly life in Christ Jesus will be persecuted, [13] while evildoers and impostors will go from bad to worse, deceiving and being deceived. [14] But as for you, continue in what you have learned and have become convinced of, because you know those from whom you learned it, [15] and how from infancy you have known the holy Scriptures, which are able to make you wise for salvation through faith in Christ Jesus. [16] All Scripture is God-breathed and is useful for teaching, rebuking, correcting and training in righteousness, [17] so that God's servant may be thoroughly equipped for every good work.

4 In the presence of God and of Christ Jesus, who will judge the living and the dead, and in view of his appearing and his kingdom, I give you this charge: [2] Preach the Word; be prepared in season and out of season; correct, rebuke and encourage—with great patience and careful instruction. [3] For the time will come when people will not put up with sound doctrine. Instead, to suit their own desires, they will gather around them a great number of teachers to say what their itching ears want to hear. [4] They will turn their ears away from the truth and turn aside to myths. [5] But you, keep your head in all situations, endure hardship, do the work of an evangelist, discharge all the duties of your ministry.

[6] For I am already being poured out like a drink offering, and the time has come for my departure. [7] I have fought the good fight, I have finished the race, I have kept the faith. [8] Now there is in store for me the crown of righteousness, which the Lord, the righteous Judge, will award to me on that day—and not only to me, but also to all who have longed for his appearing.

Personal Remarks

[9] Do your best to come to me quickly, [10] for Demas, because he loved this world, has deserted me and has gone to Thessalonica. Crescens has gone to Galatia, and Titus to Dalmatia. [11] Only Luke is with me. Get Mark and bring him with you, because he is helpful to me in my ministry. [12] I sent Tychicus to Ephesus. [13] When you come, bring the cloak that I left with Carpus at Troas, and my scrolls, especially the parchments.

[14] Alexander the metalworker did me a great deal of harm. The Lord will repay him for what he has done. [15] You too should be on your guard against him, because he strongly opposed our message.

[16] At my first defence, no-one came to my support, but everyone deserted me. May it not be held against them. [17] But the Lord stood at my side and gave me strength, so that through me the message might be fully proclaimed and all the Gentiles might hear it. And I was delivered from the lion's mouth. [18] The Lord will rescue me from every evil attack and will bring me safely to his heavenly kingdom. To him be glory for ever and ever. Amen.

Final Greetings

[19] Greet Priscilla[a] and Aquila and the household of Onesiphorus. [20] Erastus stayed in Corinth, and I left Trophimus sick in Miletus. [21] Do your best to get here before winter. Eubulus greets you, and so do Pudens, Linus, Claudia and all the brothers and sisters.

[22] The Lord be with your spirit. Grace be with you.

---

[a] 19 Greek *Prisca*, a variant of *Priscilla*

Titus

1 Paul, a servant of God and an apostle of Jesus Christ for the faith of God's elect and the knowledge of the truth that leads to godliness—²a faith and knowledge resting on the hope of eternal life, which God, who does not lie, promised before the beginning of time, ³and at his appointed season he brought his word to light through the preaching entrusted to me by the command of God our Saviour,

⁴To Titus, my true son in our common faith:

Grace and peace from God the Father and Christ Jesus our Saviour.

Titus' Task on Crete

⁵The reason I left you in Crete was that you might straighten out what was left unfinished and appoint*a* elders in every town, as I directed you. ⁶An elder must be blameless, the husband of but one wife, a man whose children believe and are not open to the charge of being wild and disobedient. ⁷Since an overseer*b* is entrusted with God's work, he must be blameless—not overbearing, not quick-tempered, not given to drunkenness, not violent, not pursuing dishonest gain. ⁸Rather he must be hospitable, one who loves what is good, who is self-controlled, upright, holy and disciplined. ⁹He must hold firmly to the trustworthy message as it has been taught, so that he can encourage others by sound doctrine and refute those who oppose it.

¹⁰For there are many rebellious people, mere talkers and deceivers, especially those of the circumcision group. ¹¹They must be silenced, because they are ruining whole households by teaching things they ought not to teach—and that for the sake of dishonest gain. ¹²Even one of their own prophets has said, "Cretans are always liars, evil brutes, lazy gluttons." ¹³This testimony is true. Therefore, rebuke them sharply, so that they will be sound in the faith ¹⁴and will pay no attention to Jewish myths or to the commands of those who reject the truth. ¹⁵To the pure, all things are pure, but to those who are corrupted and do not believe, nothing is pure. In fact, both their minds and consciences are corrupted. ¹⁶They claim to know God, but by their actions they deny him. They are detestable, disobedient and unfit for doing anything good.

What Must Be Taught to Various Groups

2 You must teach what is in accord with sound doctrine. ²Teach the older men to be temperate, worthy of respect, self-controlled, and sound in faith, in love and in endurance.

³Likewise, teach the older women to be reverent in the way they live, not to be slanderers or addicted to much wine, but to teach what is good. ⁴Then they can train the younger women to love their husbands and children, ⁵to be self-controlled and pure, to be busy at home, to be kind, and to be subject to their husbands, so

---

*a*5 Or *ordain*   *b*7 Traditionally *bishop*

that no-one will malign the word of God.

⁶Similarly, encourage the young men to be self-controlled. ⁷In everything set them an example by doing what is good. In your teaching show integrity, seriousness ⁸and soundness of speech that cannot be condemned, so that those who oppose you may be ashamed because they have nothing bad to say about us.

⁹Teach slaves to be subject to their masters in everything, to try to please them, not to talk back to them, ¹⁰and not to steal from them, but to show that they can be fully trusted, so that in every way they will make the teaching about God our Saviour attractive.

¹¹For the grace of God that brings salvation has appeared to all people. ¹²It teaches us to say "No" to ungodliness and worldly passions, and to live self-controlled, upright and godly lives in this present age, ¹³while we wait for the blessed hope—the glorious appearing of our great God and Saviour, Jesus Christ, ¹⁴who gave himself for us to redeem us from all wickedness and to purify for himself a people that are his very own, eager to do what is good.

¹⁵These, then, are the things you should teach. Encourage and rebuke with all authority. Do not let anyone despise you.

Doing What is Good

3 Remind the people to be subject to rulers and authorities, to be obedient, to be ready to do whatever is good, ²to slander no-one, to be peaceable and considerate, and to show true humility towards everyone.

³At one time we too were foolish, disobedient, deceived and enslaved by all kinds of passions and pleasures. We lived in malice and envy, being hated and hating one another. ⁴But when the kindness and love of God our Saviour appeared, ⁵he saved us, not because of righteous things we had done, but because of his mercy. He saved us through the washing of rebirth and renewal by the Holy Spirit, ⁶whom he poured out on us generously through Jesus Christ our Saviour, ⁷so that, having been justified by his grace, we might become heirs having the hope of eternal life. ⁸This is a trustworthy saying. And I want you to stress these things, so that those who have trusted in God may be careful to devote themselves to doing what is good. These things are excellent and profitable for everyone.

⁹But avoid foolish controversies and genealogies and arguments and quarrels about the law, because these are unprofitable and useless. ¹⁰Warn divisive people once, and then warn them a second time. After that, have nothing to do with them. ¹¹You may be sure that such people are warped and sinful; they are self-condemned.

Final Remarks

¹²As soon as I send Artemas or Tychicus to you, do your best to come to me at Nicopolis, because I have decided to winter there. ¹³Do everything you can to help Zenas the lawyer and Apollos on their way and see that they have everything they need. ¹⁴Our people must learn to devote themselves to doing what is good, in order that they may provide for daily necessities and not live unproductive lives.

¹⁵Everyone with me sends you greetings. Greet those who love us in the faith.

Grace be with you all.

Philemon

¹ Paul, a prisoner of Christ Jesus, and Timothy our brother,

To Philemon our dear friend and fellow-worker, ² to Apphia our sister, to Archippus our fellow-soldier and to the church that meets in your home:

³ Grace to you and peace from God our Father and the Lord Jesus Christ.

Thanksgiving and Prayer

⁴ I always thank my God as I remember you in my prayers, ⁵ because I hear about your faith in the Lord Jesus and your love for all the saints. ⁶ I pray that you may be active in sharing your faith, so that you will have a full understanding of every good thing we have in Christ. ⁷ Your love has given me great joy and encouragement, because you, brother, have refreshed the hearts of the saints.

Paul's Plea for Onesimus

⁸ Therefore, although in Christ I could be bold and order you to do what you ought to do, ⁹ yet I appeal to you on the basis of love. I then, as Paul—an old man and now also a prisoner of Christ Jesus— ¹⁰ I appeal to you for my son Onesimus,ᵃ who became my son while I was in chains. ¹¹ Formerly he was useless to you, but now he has become useful both to you and to me.

¹² I am sending him—who is my very heart—back to you. ¹³ I would have liked to keep him with me so that he could take your place in helping me while I am in chains for the gospel. ¹⁴ But I did not want to do anything without your consent, so that any favour you do will be spontaneous and not forced. ¹⁵ Perhaps the reason he was separated from you for a little while was that you might have him back for good—¹⁶ no longer as a slave, but better than a slave, as a dear fellow believer. He is very dear to me but even dearer to you, both as a person and as a fellow believer in the Lord.

¹⁷ So if you consider me a partner, welcome him as you would welcome me. ¹⁸ If he has done you any wrong or owes you anything, charge it to me. ¹⁹ I, Paul, am writing this with my own hand. I will pay it back—not to mention that you owe me your very self. ²⁰ I do wish, brother, that I may have some benefit from you in the Lord; refresh my heart in Christ. ²¹ Confident of your obedience, I write to you, knowing that you will do even more than I ask.

²² And one thing more: Prepare a guest room for me, because I hope to be restored to you in answer to your prayers.

²³ Epaphras, my fellow-prisoner in Christ Jesus, sends you greetings. ²⁴ And so do Mark, Aristarchus, Demas and Luke, my fellow-workers.

²⁵ The grace of the Lord Jesus Christ be with your spirit.

ᵃ10 *Onesimus* means *useful*.

Hebrews

The Son Superior to Angels

1 In the past God spoke to our ancestors through the prophets at many times and in various ways, [2] but in these last days he has spoken to us by his Son, whom he appointed heir of all things, and through whom he made the universe. [3] The Son is the radiance of God's glory and the exact representation of his being, sustaining all things by his powerful word. After he had provided purification for sins, he sat down at the right hand of the Majesty in heaven. [4] So he became as much superior to the angels as the name he has inherited is superior to theirs.

[5] For to which of the angels did God ever say,

"You are my Son;
    today I have become your
        Father"[a,b]?

Or again,

"I will be his Father,
    and he will be my Son"[c]?

[6] And again, when God brings his firstborn into the world, he says,

"Let all God's angels worship him."[d]

[7] In speaking of the angels he says,

"He makes his angels winds,
    his servants flames of fire."[e]

[8] But about the Son he says,

"Your throne, O God, will last for
        ever and ever,
    and righteousness will be the
        sceptre of your kingdom.
[9] You have loved righteousness and
        hated wickedness;
    therefore God, your God, has set
        you above your companions
    by anointing you with the oil of joy."[f]

[10] He also says,

"In the beginning, O Lord, you laid
        the foundations of the earth,
    and the heavens are the work of
        your hands.
[11] They will perish, but you remain;
    they will all wear out like a garment.
[12] You will roll them up like a robe;
    like a garment they will be changed.
But you remain the same,
    and your years will never end."[g]

[13] To which of the angels did God ever say,

"Sit at my right hand
until I make your enemies
    a footstool for your feet"[h]?

[14] Are not all angels ministering spirits sent to serve those who will inherit salvation?

Warning to Pay Attention

2 We must pay more careful attention, therefore, to what we have heard, so that we do not drift away. [2] For if the message spoken by angels was binding, and every violation and disobedience received its just punishment, [3] how shall we escape

[a]5 Or *have begotten you*   [b]5 Psalm 2:7   [c]5 2 Samuel 7:14; 1 Chron. 17:13
[d]6 Deut. 32:43 (see Dead Sea Scrolls and Septuagint)   [e]7 Psalm 104:4   [f]9 Psalm 45:6,7
[g]12 Psalm 102:25–27   [h]13 Psalm 110:1

if we ignore such a great salvation? This salvation, which was first announced by the Lord, was confirmed to us by those who heard him. ⁴God also testified to it by signs, wonders and various miracles, and gifts of the Holy Spirit distributed according to his will.

Jesus Made Like His Brothers and Sisters

⁵It is not to angels that he has subjected the world to come, about which we are speaking. ⁶But there is a place where someone has testified:

> "What is a human being that you are mindful of him,
>   the son of man that you care for him?
> ⁷You made him a little*ᵃ* lower than the angels;
>   you crowned him with glory and honour
> ⁸   and put everything under his feet."*ᵇ*

In putting everything under him, God left nothing that is not subject to him. Yet at present we do not see everything subject to him. ⁹But we see Jesus, who was made a little lower than the angels, now crowned with glory and honour because he suffered death, so that by the grace of God he might taste death for everyone.

¹⁰In bringing many sons and daughters to glory, it was fitting that God, for whom and through whom everything exists, should make the author of their salvation perfect through suffering. ¹¹Both the one who makes people holy and those who are made holy are of the same family. So Jesus is not ashamed to call them brothers and sisters. ¹²He says,

> "I will declare your name to my brothers and sisters;
>   in the presence of the congregation I will sing your praises."*ᶜ*

¹³And again,

> "I will put my trust in him."*ᵈ*

And again he says,

> "Here am I, and the children God has given me."*ᵉ*

¹⁴Since the children have flesh and blood, he too shared in their humanity so that by his death he might destroy him who holds the power of death—that is, the devil—¹⁵and free those who all their lives were held in slavery by their fear of death. ¹⁶For surely it is not angels he helps, but Abraham's descendants. ¹⁷For this reason he had to be made like his brothers and sisters in every way, in order that he might become a merciful and faithful high priest in service to God, and that he might make atonement for*ᶠ* the sins of the people. ¹⁸Because he himself suffered when he was tempted, he is able to help those who are being tempted.

Jesus Greater Than Moses

3 Therefore, holy brothers and sisters, who share in the heavenly calling, fix your thoughts on Jesus, the apostle and high priest whom we confess. ²He was faithful to the one who appointed him, just as Moses was faithful in all God's house. ³Jesus has been found worthy of greater honour than Moses, just as the builder of a house has greater honour than the house itself. ⁴For every house is built by someone, but God is the builder of everything. ⁵Moses was faithful as a servant in all God's house, testifying to what would be said in the future. ⁶But Christ is faithful as a son over God's house. And we are his house, if we hold on to our courage and the hope of which we boast.

Warning Against Unbelief

⁷So, as the Holy Spirit says:

> "Today, if you hear his voice,
> ⁸   do not harden your hearts
>   as you did in the rebellion,

---

*ᵃ*7 Or *him for a little while*; also in verse 9
*ᵇ*8 Or *What are mere mortals that you are mindful of them, human beings that you care for them? / You made them a little lower than the angels; you crowned them with glory and honour and put everything under their feet.* Psalm 8:4 – 6
*ᶜ*12 Psalm 22:22   *ᵈ*13 Isaiah 8:17   *ᵉ*13 Isaiah 8:18   *ᶠ*17 Or *and that he might turn aside God's wrath, taking away*

during the time of testing in the
desert,
[9] where your ancestors tested and tried
me
and for forty years saw what I did.
[10] That is why I was angry with that
generation,
and I said, 'Their hearts are always
going astray,
and they have not known my ways.'
[11] So I declared on oath in my anger,
'They shall never enter my rest.' " [a]

[12] See to it, brothers and sisters, that
none of you has a sinful, unbelieving heart
that turns away from the living God. [13] But
encourage one another daily, as long as it
is called Today, so that none of you may
be hardened by sin's deceitfulness. [14] We
have come to share in Christ if we hold
firmly till the end the confidence we had
at first. [15] As has just been said:

"Today, if you hear his voice,
do not harden your hearts
as you did in the rebellion." [b]

[16] Who were they who heard and rebelled? Were they not all those Moses led
out of Egypt? [17] And with whom was he
angry for forty years? Was it not with
those who sinned, whose bodies fell in the
desert? [18] And to whom did God swear
that they would never enter his rest if not
to those who disobeyed? [c] [19] So we see that
they were not able to enter, because of
their unbelief.

A Sabbath-rest for the People of God

4 Therefore, since the promise of entering his rest still stands, let us be
careful that none of you be found to have
fallen short of it. [2] For we also have had
the gospel preached to us, just as they did;
but the message they heard was of no
value to them, because those who heard
did not combine it with faith. [a] [3] Now we
who have believed enter that rest, just as
God has said,

"So I declared on oath in my anger,
'They shall never enter my rest.' " [b]

And yet his work has been finished since
the creation of the world. [4] For somewhere he has spoken about the seventh
day in these words: "And on the seventh
day God rested from all his work." [c] [5] And
again in the passage above he says, "They
shall never enter my rest."

[6] It still remains that some will enter that
rest, and those who formerly had the
gospel preached to them did not go in,
because of their disobedience. [7] Therefore
God again set a certain day, calling it
Today, when a long time later he spoke
through David, as was said before:

"Today, if you hear his voice,
do not harden your hearts." [d]

[8] For if Joshua had given them rest, God
would not have spoken later about another day. [9] There remains, then, a Sab-
bath-rest for the people of God; [10] for
those who enter God's rest also rest from
their own work, just as God did from his.
[11] Let us, therefore, make every effort to
enter that rest, so that no-one will fall by
following their example of disobedience.

[12] For the word of God is living and
active. Sharper than any double-edged
sword, it penetrates even to dividing soul
and spirit, joints and marrow; it judges
the thoughts and attitudes of the heart.
[13] Nothing in all creation is hidden from
God's sight. Everything is uncovered and
laid bare before the eyes of him to whom
we must give account.

Jesus the Great High Priest

[14] Therefore, since we have a great high
priest who has gone through the heavens, [e]
Jesus the Son of God, let us hold firmly to
the faith we profess. [15] For we do not have
a high priest who is unable to sympathise
with our weaknesses, but we have one who
has been tempted in every way, just as we
are—yet was without sin. [16] Let us then
approach the throne of grace with confidence, so that we may receive mercy and
find grace to help us in our time of need.

[a]11 Psalm 95:7–11   [b]15 Psalm 95:7,8   [c]18 Or *disbelieved*
[a]2 Many manuscripts *because they did not share in the faith of those who obeyed*   [b]3 Psalm 95:11; also in verse 5
[c]4 Gen. 2:2   [d]7 Psalm 95:7,8   [e]14 Or *gone into heaven*

5 Every high priest is selected from among human beings and is appointed to represent them in matters related to God, to offer gifts and sacrifices for sins. [2] He is able to deal gently with those who are ignorant and are going astray, since he himself is subject to weakness. [3] This is why he has to offer sacrifices for his own sins, as well as for the sins of the people.

[4] No-one takes this honour upon himself; he must be called by God, just as Aaron was. [5] So Christ also did not take upon himself the glory of becoming a high priest. But God said to him,

"You are my Son;
    today I have become your
      Father."[a, b]

[6] And he says in another place,

"You are a priest for ever,
    in the order of Melchizedek."[c]

[7] During the days of Jesus' life on earth, he offered up prayers and petitions with loud cries and tears to the one who could save him from death, and he was heard because of his reverent submission. [8] Although he was a son, he learned obedience from what he suffered [9] and, once made perfect, he became the source of eternal salvation for all who obey him [10] and was designated by God to be high priest in the order of Melchizedek.

Warning Against Falling Away

[11] We have much to say about this, but it is hard to explain because you are slow to learn. [12] In fact, though by this time you ought to be teachers, you need someone to teach you the elementary truths of God's word all over again. You need milk, not solid food! [13] Anyone who lives on milk, being still an infant, is not acquainted with the teaching about righteousness. [14] But solid food is for the mature, who by constant use have trained themselves to distinguish good from evil.

6 Therefore let us leave the elementary teachings about Christ and go on to maturity, not laying again the foundation of repentance from acts that lead to death,[a] and of faith in God, [2] instruction about baptisms, the laying on of hands, the resurrection of the dead, and eternal judgment. [3] And God permitting, we will do so.

[4] It is impossible for those who have once been enlightened, who have tasted the heavenly gift, who have shared in the Holy Spirit, [5] who have tasted the goodness of the word of God and the powers of the coming age, [6] if they fall away, to be brought back to repentance, because[b] to their loss they are crucifying the Son of God all over again and subjecting him to public disgrace.

[7] Land that drinks in the rain often falling on it and that produces a crop useful to those for whom it is farmed receives the blessing of God. [8] But land that produces thorns and thistles is worthless and is in danger of being cursed. In the end it will be burned.

[9] Even though we speak like this, dear friends, we are confident of better things in your case—things that accompany salvation. [10] God is not unjust; he will not forget your work and the love you have shown him as you have helped his people and continue to help them. [11] We want each of you to show this same diligence to the very end, in order to make your hope sure. [12] We do not want you to become lazy, but to imitate those who through faith and patience inherit what has been promised.

The Certainty of God's Promise

[13] When God made his promise to Abraham, since there was no-one greater for him to swear by, he swore by himself, [14] saying, "I will surely bless you and give you many descendants."[c] [15] And so after waiting patiently, Abraham received what was promised.

[16] People swear by someone greater than themselves, and the oath confirms what is said and puts an end to all argument.

[a]5 Or have begotten you   [b]5 Psalm 2:7   [c]6 Psalm 110:4   [a]1 Or from useless rituals
[b]6 Or repentance while   [c]14 Gen. 22:17

17 Because God wanted to make the unchanging nature of his purpose very clear to the heirs of what was promised, he confirmed it with an oath. 18 God did this so that, by two unchangeable things in which it is impossible for God to lie, we who have fled to take hold of the hope offered to us may be greatly encouraged. 19 We have this hope as an anchor for the soul, firm and secure. It enters the inner sanctuary behind the curtain, 20 where Jesus, who went before us, has entered on our behalf. He has become a high priest for ever, in the order of Melchizedek.

Melchizedek the Priest

7 This Melchizedek was king of Salem and priest of God Most High. He met Abraham returning from the defeat of the kings and blessed him, 2 and Abraham gave him a tenth of everything. First, his name means "king of righteousness"; then also, "king of Salem" means "king of peace". 3 Without father or mother, without genealogy, without beginning of days or end of life, like the Son of God he remains a priest for ever.

4 Just think how great he was: Even the patriarch Abraham gave him a tenth of the plunder! 5 Now the law requires the descendants of Levi who become priests to collect a tenth from the people—that is, from the members of their own nation—even though they are descended from Abraham. 6 This man, however, did not trace his descent from Levi, yet he collected a tenth from Abraham and blessed him who had the promises. 7 And without doubt the lesser person is blessed by the greater. 8 In the one case, the tenth is collected by those who die; but in the other case, by him who is declared to be living. 9 One might even say that Levi, who collects the tenth, paid the tenth through Abraham, 10 because when Melchizedek met Abraham, Levi was still in the body of his ancestor.

Jesus Like Melchizedek

11 If perfection could have been attained through the Levitical priesthood

(for on the basis of it the law was given to the people), why was there still need for another priest to come—one in the order of Melchizedek, not in the order of Aaron? 12 For when there is a change of the priesthood, there must also be a change of the law. 13 He of whom these things are said belonged to a different tribe, and no-one from that tribe has ever served at the altar. 14 For it is clear that our Lord descended from Judah, and in regard to that tribe Moses said nothing about priests. 15 And what we have said is even more clear if another priest like Melchizedek appears, 16 one who has become a priest not on the basis of a regulation as to his ancestry but on the basis of the power of an indestructible life. 17 For it is declared:

> "You are a priest for ever,
>   in the order of Melchizedek."[a]

18 The former regulation is set aside because it was weak and useless 19 (for the law made nothing perfect), and a better hope is introduced, by which we draw near to God.

20 And it was not without an oath! Others became priests without any oath, 21 but he became a priest with an oath when God said to him:

> "The Lord has sworn
>   and will not change his mind:
> 'You are a priest for ever.' "[b]

22 Because of this oath, Jesus has become the guarantee of a better covenant.

23 Now there have been many of those priests, since death prevented them from continuing in office; 24 but because Jesus lives for ever, he has a permanent priesthood. 25 Therefore he is able to save completely[c] those who come to God through him, because he always lives to intercede for them.

26 Such a high priest meets our need—one who is holy, blameless, pure, set apart from sinners, exalted above the heavens. 27 Unlike the other high priests, he does not need to offer sacrifices day after day,

---

*a*17 Psalm 110:4   *b*21 Psalm 110:4   *c*25 Or *for ever* first for his own sins, and then for the sins of the people. He sacrificed for their sins once for all when he offered himself. 28 For the law appoints as high priests men who are weak; but the oath, which came after the law, appointed the Son, who has been made perfect for ever.

The High Priest of a New Covenant

8 The point of what we are saying is this: We do have such a high priest, who sat down at the right hand of the throne of the Majesty in heaven, 2 and who serves in the sanctuary, the true tabernacle set up by the Lord, not by any human being.

3 Every high priest is appointed to offer both gifts and sacrifices, and so it was necessary for this one also to have something to offer. 4 If he were on earth, he would not be a priest, for there are already priests who offer the gifts prescribed by the law. 5 They serve at a sanctuary that is a copy and shadow of what is in heaven. This is why Moses was warned when he was about to build the tabernacle: "See to it that you make everything according to the pattern shown you on the mountain."[a] 6 But the ministry Jesus has received is as superior to theirs as the covenant of which he is mediator is superior to the old one, and it is founded on better promises.

7 For if there had been nothing wrong with that first covenant, no place would have been sought for another. 8 But God found fault with the people and said:[b]

"The time is coming, declares the Lord,
when I will make a new covenant
with the house of Israel
and with the house of Judah.
9 It will not be like the covenant
I made with their ancestors
when I took them by the hand
to lead them out of Egypt,
because they did not remain faithful
to my covenant,
and I turned away from them,
declares the Lord.

10 This is the covenant I will make with
the house of Israel
after that time, declares the Lord.
I will put my laws in their minds
and write them on their hearts.
I will be their God,
and they will be my people.
11 No longer will they teach their
neighbours,
or say to one another, 'Know the
Lord,'
because they will all know me,
from the least of them to the
greatest.
12 For I will forgive their wickedness
and will remember their sins no
more."[c]

13 By calling this covenant "new", he has made the first one obsolete; and what is obsolete and ageing will soon disappear.

Worship in the Earthly Tabernacle

9 Now the first covenant had regulations for worship and also an earthly sanctuary. 2 A tabernacle was set up. In its first room were the lampstand, the table and the consecrated bread; this was called the Holy Place. 3 Behind the second curtain was a room called the Most Holy Place, 4 which had the golden altar of incense and the gold-covered ark of the covenant. This ark contained the gold jar of manna, Aaron's staff that had budded, and the stone tablets of the covenant. 5 Above the ark were the cherubim of the Glory, overshadowing the atonement cover.[a] But we cannot discuss these things in detail now.

6 When everything had been arranged like this, the priests entered regularly into the outer room to carry on their ministry. 7 But only the high priest entered the inner room, and that only once a year, and never without blood, which he offered for himself and for the sins the people had committed in ignorance. 8 The Holy Spirit was showing by this that the way into the Most Holy Place had not yet been disclosed as long as the first tabernacle was still standing. 9 This is an illustration for

[a]5 Exodus 25:40   [b]8 Some manuscripts may be translated *fault and said to the people.*   [c]12 Jer. 31:31–34
[a]5 Traditionally *the mercy seat*

the present time, indicating that the gifts and sacrifices being offered were not able to clear the conscience of the worshipper. [10] They are only a matter of food and drink and various ceremonial washings—external regulations applying until the time of the new order.

The Blood of Christ

[11] When Christ came as high priest of the good things that are already here,[b] he went through the greater and more perfect tabernacle that is not made with human hands, that is to say, not a part of this creation. [12] He did not enter by means of the blood of goats and calves; but he entered the Most Holy Place once for all by his own blood, having obtained eternal redemption. [13] The blood of goats and bulls and the ashes of a heifer sprinkled on those who are ceremonially unclean sanctify them so that they are outwardly clean. [14] How much more, then, will the blood of Christ, who through the eternal Spirit offered himself unblemished to God, cleanse our consciences from acts that lead to death,[c] so that we may serve the living God!

[15] For this reason Christ is the mediator of a new covenant, that those who are called may receive the promised eternal inheritance—now that he has died as a ransom to set them free from the sins committed under the first covenant.

[16] In the case of a will,[d] it is necessary to prove the death of the one who made it, [17] because a will is in force only when somebody has died; it never takes effect while the one who made it is living. [18] This is why even the first covenant was not put into effect without blood. [19] When Moses had proclaimed every commandment of the law to all the people, he took the blood of calves, together with water, scarlet wool and branches of hyssop, and sprinkled the scroll and all the people. [20] He said, "This is the blood of the covenant, which God has commanded you to keep."[e] [21] In the same way, he sprinkled with the blood both the tabernacle and everything used in its ceremonies. [22] In fact, the law requires that nearly everything be cleansed with blood, and without the shedding of blood there is no forgiveness.

[23] It was necessary, then, for the copies of the heavenly things to be purified with these sacrifices, but the heavenly things themselves with better sacrifices than these. [24] For Christ did not enter a sanctuary made with human hands that was only a copy of the true one; he entered heaven itself, now to appear for us in God's presence. [25] Nor did he enter heaven to offer himself again and again, the way the high priest enters the Most Holy Place every year with blood that is not his own. [26] Then Christ would have had to suffer many times since the creation of the world. But now he has appeared once for all at the end of the ages to do away with sin by the sacrifice of himself. [27] Just as people are destined to die once, and after that to face judgment, [28] so Christ was sacrificed once to take away the sins of many people; and he will appear a second time, not to bear sin, but to bring salvation to those who are waiting for him.

Christ's Sacrifice Once for All

10 The law is only a shadow of the good things that are coming—not the realities themselves. For this reason it can never, by the same sacrifices repeated endlessly year after year, make perfect those who draw near to worship. [2] If it could, would they not have stopped being offered? For the worshippers would have been cleansed once for all, and would no longer have felt guilty for their sins. [3] But those sacrifices are an annual reminder of sins, [4] because it is impossible for the blood of bulls and goats to take away sins. [5] Therefore, when Christ came into the world, he said:

"Sacrifice and offering you did not
    desire,
    but a body you prepared for me;

---

[b]11 Some early manuscripts *are to come*   [c]14 Or *from useless rituals*
[d]16 Same Greek word as *covenant* ; also in verse 17   [e]20 Exodus 24:8

6 with burnt offerings and sin offerings you were not pleased.

7 Then I said, 'Here I am—it is written about me in the scroll—
I have come to do your will,
O God.' "*a*

8 First he said, "Sacrifices and offerings, burnt offerings and sin offerings you did not desire, nor were you pleased with them" (although the law required them to be made). 9 Then he said, "Here I am, I have come to do your will." He sets aside the first to establish the second. 10 And by that will, we have been made holy through the sacrifice of the body of Jesus Christ once for all.

11 Day after day every priest stands and performs his religious duties; again and again he offers the same sacrifices, which can never take away sins. 12 But when this priest had offered for all time one sacrifice for sins, he sat down at the right hand of God. 13 Since that time he waits for his enemies to be made his footstool, 14 because by one sacrifice he has made perfect for ever those who are being made holy.

15 The Holy Spirit also testifies to us about this. First he says:

16 "This is the covenant I will make with them
after that time, says the Lord.
I will put my laws in their hearts,
and I will write them on their
minds." *b*

17 Then he adds:

"Their sins and lawless acts
I will remember no more." *c*

18 And where these have been forgiven, there is no longer any sacrifice for sin.

A Call to Persevere

19 Therefore, brothers and sisters, since we have confidence to enter the Most Holy Place by the blood of Jesus, 20 by a new and living way opened for us through the curtain, that is, his body, 21 and since we have a great priest over the house of God, 22 let us draw near to God with a sincere heart in full assurance of faith, having our hearts sprinkled to cleanse us from a guilty conscience and having our bodies washed with pure water. 23 Let us hold unswervingly to the hope we profess, for he who promised is faithful. 24 And let us consider how we may spur one another on towards love and good deeds. 25 Let us not give up meeting together, as some are in the habit of doing, but let us encourage one another—and all the more as you see the Day approaching.

26 If we deliberately keep on sinning after we have received the knowledge of the truth, no sacrifice for sins is left, 27 but only a fearful expectation of judgment and of raging fire that will consume the enemies of God. 28 Anyone who rejected the law of Moses died without mercy on the testimony of two or three witnesses. 29 How much more severely do you think those deserve to be punished who have trampled the Son of God under foot, who have treated as an unholy thing the blood of the covenant that sanctified them, and who have insulted the Spirit of grace? 30 For we know him who said, "It is mine to avenge; I will repay," *d* and again, "The Lord will judge his people." *e* 31 It is a dreadful thing to fall into the hands of the living God.

32 Remember those earlier days after you had received the light, when you stood your ground in a great contest in the face of suffering. 33 Sometimes you were publicly exposed to insult and persecution; at other times you stood side by side with those who were so treated. 34 You sympathised with those in prison and joyfully accepted the confiscation of your property, because you knew that you yourselves had better and lasting possessions.

35 So do not throw away your confidence; it will be richly rewarded. 36 You need to persevere so that when you have

---

a 7 Psalm 40:6 –8 (see Septuagint) *b* 16 Jer. 31:33 *c* 17 Jer. 31:34 *d* 30 Deut. 32:35
e 30 Deut. 32:36; Psalm 135:14

done the will of God, you will receive what he has promised. [37] For in just a very little while,

"He who is coming will come and will not delay.
[38] But my righteous one[f] will live by faith.
And I take no pleasure
in the one who shrinks back."[g]

[39] But we are not of those who shrink back and are destroyed, but of those who believe and are saved.

By Faith

11 Now faith is being sure of what we hope for and certain of what we do not see. [2] This is what the ancients were commended for.

[3] By faith we understand that the universe was formed at God's command, so that what is seen was not made out of what was visible.

[4] By faith Abel offered God a better sacrifice than Cain did. By faith he was commended as righteous, when God spoke well of his offerings. And by faith he still speaks, even though he is dead.

[5] By faith Enoch was taken from this life, so that he did not experience death; he could not be found, because God had taken him away. For before he was taken, he was commended as one who pleased God. [6] And without faith it is impossible to please God, because anyone who comes to him must believe that he exists and that he rewards those who earnestly seek him.

[7] By faith Noah, when warned about things not yet seen, in holy fear built an ark to save his family. By his faith he condemned the world and became heir of the righteousness that comes by faith.

[8] By faith Abraham, when called to go to a place he would later receive as his inheritance, obeyed and went, even though he did not know where he was going. [9] By faith he made his home in the promised land like a stranger in a foreign country; he lived in tents, as did Isaac and Jacob, who were heirs with him of the same promise. [10] For he was looking forward to the city with foundations, whose architect and builder is God.

[11] By faith Abraham, even though he was past age—and Sarah herself was barren—was enabled to become a father because he[a] considered him faithful who had made the promise. [12] And so from this one man, and he as good as dead, came descendants as numerous as the stars in the sky and as countless as the sand on the seashore.

[13] All these people were still living by faith when they died. They did not receive the things promised; they only saw them and welcomed them from a distance. And they admitted that they were aliens and strangers on earth. [14] People who say such things show that they are looking for a country of their own. [15] If they had been thinking of the country they had left, they would have had opportunity to return. [16] Instead, they were longing for a better country—a heavenly one. Therefore God is not ashamed to be called their God, for he has prepared a city for them.

[17] By faith Abraham, when God tested him, offered Isaac as a sacrifice. He who had received the promises was about to sacrifice his one and only son, [18] even though God had said to him, "It is through Isaac that your offspring[b] will be reckoned."[c] [19] Abraham reasoned that God could raise the dead, and figuratively speaking, he did receive Isaac back from death.

[20] By faith Isaac blessed Jacob and Esau in regard to their future.

[21] By faith Jacob, when he was dying, blessed each of Joseph's sons, and worshipped as he leaned on the top of his staff.

[22] By faith Joseph, when his end was near, spoke about the exodus of the Israelites from Egypt and gave instructions about his bones.

[23] By faith Moses' parents hid him for

[f]38 One early manuscript *But the righteous*   [g]38 Hab. 2:3,4
[a]11 Or *By faith even Sarah, who was past age, was enabled to bear children because she*
[b]18 Greek *seed*   [c]18 Gen. 21:12

three months after he was born, because they saw he was no ordinary child, and they were not afraid of the king's edict.

24 By faith Moses, when he had grown up, refused to be known as the son of Pharaoh's daughter. 25 He chose to be ill-treated along with the people of God rather than to enjoy the pleasures of sin for a short time. 26 He regarded disgrace for the sake of Christ as of greater value than the treasures of Egypt, because he was looking ahead to his reward. 27 By faith he left Egypt, not fearing the king's anger; he persevered because he saw him who is invisible. 28 By faith he kept the Passover and the sprinkling of blood, so that the destroyer of the firstborn would not touch the firstborn of Israel.

29 By faith the people passed through the Red Sea*d* as on dry land; but when the Egyptians tried to do so, they were drowned.

30 By faith the walls of Jericho fell, after the people had marched around them for seven days.

31 By faith the prostitute Rahab, because she welcomed the spies, was not killed with those who were disobedient.*e*

32 And what more shall I say? I do not have time to tell about Gideon, Barak, Samson, Jephthah, David, Samuel and the prophets, 33 who through faith conquered kingdoms, administered justice, and gained what was promised; who shut the mouths of lions, 34 quenched the fury of the flames, and escaped the edge of the sword; whose weakness was turned to strength; and who became powerful in battle and routed foreign armies. 35 Women received back their dead, raised to life again. Others were tortured and refused to be released, so that they might gain a better resurrection. 36 Some faced jeers and flogging, while still others were chained and put in prison. 37 They were stoned;*f* they were sawn in two; they were put to death by the sword. They went about in sheepskins and goatskins, destitute, persecuted and ill-treated—38 the world was not worthy of them. They wandered in deserts and mountains, and in caves and holes in the ground.

39 These were all commended for their faith, yet none of them received what had been promised. 40 God had planned something better for us so that only together with us would they be made perfect.

God Disciplines His Children

12 Therefore, since we are surrounded by such a great cloud of witnesses, let us throw off everything that hinders and the sin that so easily entangles, and let us run with perseverance the race marked out for us. 2 Let us fix our eyes on Jesus, the author and perfecter of our faith, who for the joy set before him endured the cross, scorning its shame, and sat down at the right hand of the throne of God. 3 Consider him who endured such opposition from sinners, so that you will not grow weary and lose heart.

4 In your struggle against sin, you have not yet resisted to the point of shedding your blood. 5 And you have forgotten that word of encouragement that addresses you as children:

"My child, do not make light of the
    Lord's discipline,
  and do not lose heart when he
    rebukes you,
6 because the Lord disciplines those he
    loves,
  and he punishes everyone he
    accepts as a child."*a*

7 Endure hardship as discipline; God is treating you as children. For what children are not disciplined by their parents? 8 If you are not disciplined (and everyone undergoes discipline), then you are illegitimate and not true children. 9 Moreover, we have all had human parents who disciplined us and we respected them for it. How much more should we submit to the Father of our spirits and live! 10 Our parents disciplined us for a little while as they thought best; but God disciplines us

---

*d*29 That is, Sea of Reeds   *e*31 Or *unbelieving*   *f*37 Some early manuscripts *stoned; they were put to the test;*
*a*6 Prov. 3:11,12

for our good, that we may share in his holiness. ¹¹No discipline seems pleasant at the time, but painful. Later on, however, it produces a harvest of righteousness and peace for those who have been trained by it.

¹²Therefore, strengthen your feeble arms and weak knees! ¹³"Make level paths for your feet,"*b* so that the lame may not be disabled, but rather healed.

Warning Against Refusing God

¹⁴Make every effort to live in peace with everyone and to be holy; without holiness no-one will see the Lord. ¹⁵See to it that no-one misses the grace of God and that no bitter root grows up to cause trouble and defile many. ¹⁶See that no-one is sexually immoral, or is godless like Esau, who for a single meal sold his inheritance rights as the oldest son. ¹⁷Afterwards, as you know, when he wanted to inherit this blessing, he was rejected. He could bring about no change of mind, though he sought the blessing with tears.

¹⁸You have not come to a mountain that can be touched and that is burning with fire; to darkness, gloom and storm; ¹⁹to a trumpet blast or to such a voice speaking words that those who heard it begged that no further word be spoken to them, ²⁰because they could not bear what was commanded: "If even an animal touches the mountain, it must be stoned."*c* ²¹The sight was so terrifying that Moses said, "I am trembling with fear."*d*

²²But you have come to Mount Zion, to the heavenly Jerusalem, the city of the living God. You have come to thousands upon thousands of angels in joyful assembly, ²³to the church of the firstborn, whose names are written in heaven. You have come to God, the judge of all people, to the spirits of the righteous made perfect, ²⁴to Jesus the mediator of a new covenant, and to the sprinkled blood that speaks a better word than the blood of Abel.

²⁵See to it that you do not refuse him who speaks. If they did not escape when they refused him who warned them on earth, how much less will we, if we turn away from him who warns us from heaven? ²⁶At that time his voice shook the earth, but now he has promised, "Once more I will shake not only the earth but also the heavens."*e* ²⁷The words "once more" indicate the removing of what can be shaken—that is, created things—so that what cannot be shaken may remain.

²⁸Therefore, since we are receiving a kingdom that cannot be shaken, let us be thankful, and so worship God acceptably with reverence and awe, ²⁹for our "God is a consuming fire."*f*

Concluding Exhortations

13 Keep on loving each other as brothers and sisters. ²Do not forget to entertain strangers, for by so doing some people have entertained angels without knowing it. ³Remember those in prison as if you were together with them in prison, and those who are ill-treated as if you yourselves were suffering.

⁴Marriage should be honoured by all, and the marriage bed kept pure, for God will judge the adulterer and all the sexually immoral. ⁵Keep your lives free from the love of money and be content with what you have, because God has said,

"Never will I leave you;
   never will I forsake you."*a*

⁶So we say with confidence,

"The Lord is my helper; I will not be
   afraid.
What can human beings do to
   me?"*b*

⁷Remember your leaders, who spoke the word of God to you. Consider the outcome of their way of life and imitate their faith. ⁸Jesus Christ is the same yesterday and today and for ever. ⁹Do not be carried away by all kinds of

---

*b*13 Prov. 4:26   *c*20 Exodus 19:12,13   *d*21 Deut. 9:19   *e*26 Haggai 2:6   *f*29 Deut. 4:24
*a*5 Deut. 31:6   *b*6 Psalm 118:6,7

strange teachings. It is good for our hearts to be strengthened by grace, not by ceremonial foods, which are of no value to those who eat them. [10] We have an altar from which those who minister at the tabernacle have no right to eat.

[11] The high priest carries the blood of animals into the Most Holy Place as a sin offering, but the bodies are burned outside the camp. [12] And so Jesus also suffered outside the city gate to make the people holy through his own blood. [13] Let us, then, go to him outside the camp, bearing the disgrace he bore. [14] For here we do not have an enduring city, but we are looking for the city that is to come.

[15] Through Jesus, therefore, let us continually offer to God a sacrifice of praise—the fruit of lips that confess his name. [16] And do not forget to do good and to share with others, for with such sacrifices God is pleased.

[17] Obey your leaders and submit to their authority. They keep watch over you as those who must give an account. Obey them so that their work will be a joy, not a burden, for that would be of no advantage to you.

[18] Pray for us. We are sure that we have a clear conscience and desire to live honourably in every way. [19] I particularly urge you to pray so that I may be restored to you soon.

[20] May the God of peace, who through the blood of the eternal covenant brought back from the dead our Lord Jesus, that great Shepherd of the sheep, [21] equip you with everything good for doing his will, and may he work in us what is pleasing to him, through Jesus Christ, to whom be glory for ever and ever. Amen.

[22] Brothers and sisters, I urge you to bear with my word of exhortation, for I have written you only a short letter.

[23] I want you to know that our brother Timothy has been released. If he arrives soon, I will come with him to see you.

[24] Greet all your leaders and all God's people. Those from Italy send you their greetings.

[25] Grace be with you all.

James

1 James, a servant of God and of the Lord Jesus Christ,

To the twelve tribes scattered among the nations:

Greetings.

Trials and Temptations

2 Consider it pure joy, my brothers and sisters, whenever you face trials of many kinds, 3 because you know that the testing of your faith develops perseverance. 4 Perseverance must finish its work so that you may be mature and complete, not lacking anything. 5 If any of you lacks wisdom, you should ask God, who gives generously to all without finding fault, and it will be given to you. 6 But when you ask, you must believe and not doubt, because the one who doubts is like a wave of the sea, blown and tossed by the wind. 7 Those who doubt should not think they will receive anything from the Lord; 8 They are double-minded and unstable in all they do.

9 Believers in humble circumstances ought to take pride in their high position. 10 But those who are rich should take pride in their low position, because they will pass away like a wild flower. 11 For the sun rises with scorching heat and withers the plant; its blossom falls and its beauty is destroyed. In the same way, the rich will fade away even while they go about their business.

12 Blessed are those who persevere under trial, because when they have stood the test, they will receive the crown of life that God has promised to those who love him.

13 When tempted, no-one should say, "God is tempting me." For God cannot be tempted by evil, nor does he tempt anyone; 14 but each of you is tempted when, by your own evil desire, you are dragged away and enticed. 15 Then, after desire has conceived, it gives birth to sin; and sin, when it is full-grown, gives birth to death.

16 Don't be deceived, my dear brothers and sisters. 17 Every good and perfect gift is from above, coming down from the Father of the heavenly lights, who does not change like shifting shadows. 18 He chose to give us birth through the word of truth, that we might be a kind of first-fruits of all he created.

Listening and Doing

19 My dear brothers and sisters, take note of this: Everyone should be quick to listen, slow to speak and slow to become angry, 20 for human anger does not bring about the righteous life that God desires. 21 Therefore, get rid of all moral filth and the evil that is so prevalent, and humbly accept the word planted in you, which can save you.

22 Do not merely listen to the word, and so deceive yourselves. Do what it says. 23 Those who listen to the word but do not do what it says are like people who look at their faces in a mirror 24 and, after looking at themselves, go away and immediately forget what they look like. 25 But those who look intently into the perfect law that

gives freedom, and continue to do this, not forgetting what they have heard, but doing it—they will be blessed in what they do.

26 Those who consider themselves religious and yet do not keep a tight rein on their tongues deceive themselves, and their religion is worthless. 27 Religion that God our Father accepts as pure and faultless is this: to look after orphans and widows in their distress and to keep oneself from being polluted by the world.

Favouritism Forbidden

2 My brothers and sisters, as believers in our glorious Lord Jesus Christ, don't show favouritism. 2 Suppose someone comes into your meeting wearing a gold ring and fine clothes, and a poor person in shabby clothes also comes in. 3 If you show special attention to the one wearing fine clothes and say, "Here's a good seat for you," but say to the one who is poor, "You stand there" or "Sit on the floor by my feet," 4 have you not discriminated among yourselves and become judges with evil thoughts?

5 Listen, my dear brothers and sisters: Has not God chosen those who are poor in the eyes of the world to be rich in faith and to inherit the kingdom he promised those who love him? 6 But you have insulted the poor. Is it not the rich who are exploiting you? Are they not the ones who are dragging you into court? 7 Are they not the ones who are slandering the noble name of him to whom you belong?

8 If you really keep the royal law found in Scripture, "Love your neighbour as yourself,"*a* you are doing right. 9 But if you show favouritism, you sin and are convicted by the law as law-breakers. 10 For whoever keeps the whole law and yet stumbles at just one point is guilty of breaking all of it. 11 For he who said, "Do not commit adultery,"*b* also said, "Do not murder."*c* If you do not commit adultery but do commit murder, you have become a law-breaker.

12 Speak and act as those who are going to be judged by the law that gives freedom, 13 because judgment without mercy will be shown to anyone who has not been merciful. Mercy triumphs over judgment!

Faith and Deeds

14 What good is it, my brothers and sisters, if people claim to have faith but have no deeds? Can such faith save them? 15 Suppose a brother or sister is without clothes and daily food. 16 If one of you says to them, "Go, I wish you well; keep warm and well fed," but does nothing about their physical needs, what good is it? 17 In the same way, faith by itself, if it is not accompanied by action, is dead.

18 But someone will say, "You have faith; I have deeds."

Show me your faith without deeds, and I will show you my faith by what I do. 19 You believe that there is one God. Good! Even the demons believe that—and shudder. 20 You foolish person, do you want evidence that faith without deeds is useless?*d* 21 Was not our father Abraham considered righteous for what he did when he offered his son Isaac on the altar? 22 You see that his faith and his actions were working together, and his faith was made complete by what he did. 23 And the scripture was fulfilled that says, "Abraham believed God, and it was credited to him as righteousness,"*e* and he was called God's friend. 24 You see that people are justified by what they do and not by faith alone.

25 In the same way, was not even Rahab the prostitute considered righteous for what she did when she gave lodging to the spies and sent them off in a different direction? 26 As the body without the spirit is dead, so faith without deeds is dead.

Taming the Tongue

3 Not many of you should presume to be teachers, my brothers and sisters, because you know that we who teach will be judged more strictly. 2 We all stumble in many ways. Those who are never at

---

*a*8 Lev. 19:18   *b*11 Exodus 20:14; Deut. 5:18   *c*11 Exodus 20:13; Deut. 5:17
*d*20 Some early manuscripts *dead*   *e*23 Gen. 15:6

fault in what they say are perfect, able to keep their whole body in check.

3 When we put bits into the mouths of horses to make them obey us, we can turn the whole animal. 4 Or take ships as an example. Although they are so large and are driven by strong winds, they are steered by a very small rudder wherever the pilot wants to go. 5 Likewise the tongue is a small part of the body, but it makes great boasts. Consider what a great forest is set on fire by a small spark. 6 The tongue also is a fire, a world of evil among the parts of the body. It corrupts the whole person, sets the whole course of one's life on fire, and is itself set on fire by hell.

7 All kinds of animals, birds, reptiles and creatures of the sea are being tamed and have been tamed by people, 8 but no one can tame the tongue. It is a restless evil, full of deadly poison.

9 With the tongue we praise our Lord and Father, and with it we curse people, who have been made in God's likeness. 10 Out of the same mouth come praise and cursing. My brothers and sisters, this should not be. 11 Can both fresh water and salt[a] water flow from the same spring? 12 My brothers and sisters, can a fig-tree bear olives, or a grapevine bear figs? Neither can a salt spring produce fresh water.

Two Kinds of Wisdom

13 Who are wise and understanding among you? Let them show it by their good life, by deeds done in the humility that comes from wisdom. 14 But if you harbour bitter envy and selfish ambition in your hearts, do not boast about it or deny the truth. 15 Such "wisdom" does not come down from heaven but is earthly, unspiritual, of the devil. 16 For where you have envy and selfish ambition, there you find disorder and every evil practice.

17 But the wisdom that comes from heaven is first of all pure; then peace-loving, considerate, submissive, full of mercy and good fruit, impartial and sincere. 18 Peacemakers who sow in peace raise a harvest of righteousness.

Submit Yourselves to God

4 What causes fights and quarrels among you? Don't they come from your desires that battle within you? 2 You want something but don't get it. You kill and covet, but you cannot have what you want. You quarrel and fight. You do not have, because you do not ask God. 3 When you ask, you do not receive, because you ask with wrong motives, that you may spend what you get on your pleasures.

4 You adulterous people, don't you know that friendship with the world is hatred towards God? Anyone who chooses to be a friend of the world becomes an enemy of God. 5 Or do you think Scripture says without reason that the spirit he caused to live in us envies intensely?[a] 6 But he gives us more grace. That is why Scripture says:

"God opposes the proud
   but gives grace to the humble."[b]

7 Submit yourselves, then, to God. Resist the devil, and he will flee from you. 8 Come near to God and he will come near to you. Wash your hands, you sinners, and purify your hearts, you double-minded. 9 Grieve, mourn and wail. Change your laughter to mourning and your joy to gloom. 10 Humble yourselves before the Lord, and he will lift you up.

11 Brothers and sisters, do not slander one another. Anyone who speaks against a brother or sister or judges them speaks against the law and judges it. When you judge the law, you are not keeping it, but sitting in judgment on it. 12 There is only one Lawgiver and Judge, the one who is able to save and destroy. But you—who are you to judge your neighbour?

Boasting About Tomorrow

13 Now listen, you who say, "Today or tomorrow we will go to this or that city, spend a year there, carry on business and make money." 14 Why, you do not even know what will happen tomorrow. What

---

[a]11 Greek bitter (see also verse 14)
[a]5 Or that God jealously longs for the spirit that he made to live in us; or that the Spirit he caused to live in us longs jealously   [b]6 Prov. 3:34

is your life? You are a mist that appears for a little while and then vanishes. 15 Instead, you ought to say, "If it is the Lord's will, we will live and do this or that." 16 As it is, you boast and brag. All such boasting is evil. 17 So, then, if you know the good you ought to do and don't do it, you sin.

Warning to Rich Oppressors

5 Now listen, you rich people, weep and wail because of the misery that is coming upon you. 2 Your wealth has rotted, and moths have eaten your clothes. 3 Your gold and silver are corroded. Their corrosion will testify against you and eat your flesh like fire. You have hoarded wealth in the last days. 4 Look! The wages you failed to pay the workers who mowed your fields are crying out against you. The cries of the harvesters have reached the ears of the Lord Almighty. 5 You have lived on earth in luxury and self-indulgence. You have fattened yourselves in the day of slaughter.[a] 6 You have condemned and murdered innocent people, who were not opposing you.

Patience in Suffering

7 Be patient, then, brothers and sisters, until the Lord's coming. See how the farmer waits for the land to yield its valuable crop, patiently waiting for the autumn and spring rains. 8 You too, be patient and stand firm, because the Lord's coming is near. 9 Don't grumble against each other, brothers and sisters, or you will be judged. The Judge is standing at the door!

10 Brothers and sisters, as an example of patience in the face of suffering, take the prophets who spoke in the name of the Lord. 11 As you know, we consider blessed those who have persevered. You have heard of Job's perseverance and have seen what the Lord finally brought about. The Lord is full of compassion and mercy.

12 Above all, my brothers and sisters, do not swear—not by heaven or by earth or by anything else. Let your "Yes" be yes, and your "No", no, or you will be condemned.

The Prayer of Faith

13 Is any one of you in trouble? You should pray. Is anyone happy? Sing songs of praise. 14 Is any one of you sick? Call the elders of the church to pray over you and anoint you with oil in the name of the Lord. 15 And the prayer offered in faith will make you well; the Lord will raise you up. If you have sinned, you will be forgiven. 16 Therefore confess your sins to each other and pray for each other so that you may be healed. The prayer of a righteous person is powerful and effective.

17 Elijah was human just as we are. He prayed earnestly that it would not rain, and it did not rain on the land for three and a half years. 18 Again he prayed, and the heavens gave rain, and the earth produced its crops.

19 My brothers and sisters, if one of you should wander from the truth and someone should bring that person back, 20 remember this: Those who turn sinners from the error of their ways will save them from death and cover over a multitude of sins.

[a]5 Or yourselves as in a day of feasting

1 Peter

1 Peter, an apostle of Jesus Christ,

To God's elect, strangers in the world, scattered throughout Pontus, Galatia, Cappadocia, Asia and Bithynia, ²who have been chosen according to the foreknowledge of God the Father, through the sanctifying work of the Spirit, for obedience to Jesus Christ and sprinkling by his blood:

Grace and peace be yours in abundance.

Praise to God for a Living Hope

³Praise be to the God and Father of our Lord Jesus Christ! In his great mercy he has given us new birth into a living hope through the resurrection of Jesus Christ from the dead, ⁴and into an inheritance that can never perish, spoil or fade—kept in heaven for you, ⁵who through faith are shielded by God's power until the coming of the salvation that is ready to be revealed in the last time. ⁶In this you greatly rejoice, though now for a little while you may have had to suffer grief in all kinds of trials. ⁷These have come so that your faith—of greater worth than gold, which perishes even though refined by fire—may be proved genuine and may result in praise, glory and honour when Jesus Christ is revealed. ⁸Though you have not seen him, you love him; and even though you do not see him now, you believe in him and are filled with an inexpressible and glorious joy, ⁹for you are receiving the goal of your faith, the salvation of your souls.

¹⁰Concerning this salvation, the prophets, who spoke of the grace that was to come to you, searched intently and with the greatest care, ¹¹trying to find out the time and circumstances to which the Spirit of Christ in them was pointing when he predicted the sufferings of Christ and the glories that would follow. ¹²It was revealed to them that they were not serving themselves but you, when they spoke of the things that have now been told you by those who have preached the gospel to you by the Holy Spirit sent from heaven. Even angels long to look into these things.

Be Holy

¹³Therefore, prepare your minds for action; be self-controlled; set your hope fully on the grace to be given you when Jesus Christ is revealed. ¹⁴As obedient children, do not conform to the evil desires you had when you lived in ignorance. ¹⁵But just as he who called you is holy, so be holy in all you do; ¹⁶for it is written: "Be holy, because I am holy."*a*

¹⁷Since you call on a Father who judges each person's work impartially, live your lives as strangers here in reverent fear. ¹⁸For you know that it was not with perishable things such as silver or gold that you were redeemed from the empty way of life handed down to you from your ancestors, ¹⁹but with the precious blood of

*a*16 Lev. 11:44,45; 19:2; 20:7

Christ, a lamb without blemish or defect. [20] He was chosen before the creation of the world, but was revealed in these last times for your sake. [21] Through him you believe in God, who raised him from the dead and glorified him, and so your faith and hope are in God.

[22] Now that you have purified yourselves by obeying the truth so that you have sincere mutual affection, love one another deeply, from the heart.[b] [23] For you have been born again, not of perishable seed, but of imperishable, through the living and enduring word of God. [24] For,

> "All human beings are like grass,
>   and all their glory is like the flowers of the field;
> the grass withers and the flowers fall,
> [25]   but the word of the Lord stands for ever."[c]

And this is the word that was preached to you.

2 Therefore, rid yourselves of all malice and all deceit, hypocrisy, envy, and slander of every kind. [2] Like newborn babies, crave pure spiritual milk, so that by it you may grow up in your salvation, [3] now that you have tasted that the Lord is good.

The Living Stone and a Chosen People

[4] As you come to him, the living Stone —rejected by human beings but chosen by God and precious to him—[5] you also, like living stones, are being built into a spiritual house to be a holy priesthood, offering spiritual sacrifices acceptable to God through Jesus Christ. [6] For in Scripture it says:

> "See, I lay a stone in Zion,
>   a chosen and precious cornerstone,
> and the one who trusts in him
>   will never be put to shame."[a]

[7] Now to you who believe, this stone is precious. But to those who do not believe,

> "The stone the builders rejected
>   has become the capstone,"[b, c]

[8] and,

> "A stone that causes people to stumble
>   and a rock that makes them fall."[d]

They stumble because they disobey the message—which is also what they were destined for.

[9] But you are a chosen people, a royal priesthood, a holy nation, a people belonging to God, that you may declare the praises of him who called you out of darkness into his wonderful light. [10] Once you were not a people, but now you are the people of God; once you had not received mercy, but now you have received mercy.

[11] Dear friends, I urge you, as aliens and strangers in the world, to abstain from sinful desires, which war against your soul. [12] Live such good lives among the pagans that, though they accuse you of doing wrong, they may see your good deeds and glorify God on the day he visits us.

Submission to Rulers and Masters

[13] Submit yourselves for the Lord's sake to every human authority: whether to the king, as the supreme authority, [14] or to governors, who are sent by him to punish those who do wrong and to commend those who do right. [15] For it is God's will that by doing good you should silence the ignorant talk of foolish people. [16] Live as free persons, but do not use your freedom as a cover-up for evil; live as servants of God. [17] Show proper respect to everyone: Love the brothers and sisters, fear God, honour the king.

[18] Slaves, submit yourselves to your masters with all respect, not only to those who are good and considerate, but also to those who are harsh. [19] For it is commendable if you bear up under the pain of unjust suffering because you are conscious of God. [20] But how is it to your credit if you receive a beating for doing wrong and

---

[b]22 Some early manuscripts *from a pure heart*   [c]25 Isaiah 40:6–8   [a]6 Isaiah 28:16   [b]7 Or *cornerstone*
[c]7 Psalm 118:22   [d]8 Isaiah 8:14

endure it? But if you suffer for doing good and you endure it, this is commendable before God. ²¹ To this you were called, because Christ suffered for you, leaving you an example, that you should follow in his steps.

²² "He committed no sin,
and no deceit was found in his
mouth."^e

²³ When they hurled their insults at him, he did not retaliate; when he suffered, he made no threats. Instead, he entrusted himself to him who judges justly. ²⁴ He himself bore our sins in his body on the tree, so that we might die to sins and live for righteousness; by his wounds you have been healed. ²⁵ For you were like sheep going astray, but now you have returned to the Shepherd and Overseer of your souls.

Wives and Husbands

3 Wives, in the same way be submissive to your husbands so that, if any of them do not believe the word, they may be won over without words by the behaviour of their wives, ² when they see the purity and reverence of your lives. ³ Your beauty should not come from outward adornment, such as braided hair and the wearing of gold jewellery and fine clothes. ⁴ Instead, it should be that of your inner self, the unfading beauty of a gentle and quiet spirit, which is of great worth in God's sight. ⁵ For this is the way the holy women of the past who put their hope in God used to make themselves beautiful. They were submissive to their own husbands, ⁶ like Sarah, who obeyed Abraham and called him her master. You are her daughters if you do what is right and do not give way to fear.

⁷ Husbands, in the same way be considerate as you live with your wives, and treat them with respect as the weaker partner and as heirs with you of the gracious gift of life, so that nothing will hinder your prayers.

Suffering for Doing Good

⁸ Finally, all of you, live in harmony with one another; be sympathetic, love one another, be compassionate and humble. ⁹ Do not repay evil with evil or insult with insult, but with blessing, because to this you were called so that you may inherit a blessing. ¹⁰ For,

"Whoever among you would love life
and see good days
must keep your tongue from evil
and your lips from deceitful speech.
¹¹ Turn from evil and do good;
seek peace and pursue it.
¹² For the eyes of the Lord are on the
righteous
and his ears are attentive to their
prayer,
but the face of the Lord is against
those who do evil."^a

¹³ Who is going to harm you if you are eager to do good? ¹⁴ But even if you should suffer for what is right, you are blessed. "Do not fear what they fear;^b do not be frightened."^c ¹⁵ But in your hearts set apart Christ as Lord. Always be prepared to give an answer to everyone who asks you to give the reason for the hope that you have. But do this with gentleness and respect, ¹⁶ keeping a clear conscience, so that those who speak maliciously against your good behaviour in Christ may be ashamed of their slander. ¹⁷ It is better, if it is God's will, to suffer for doing good than for doing evil. ¹⁸ For Christ died for sins once for all, the righteous for the unrighteous, to bring you to God. He was put to death in the body but made alive by the Spirit, ¹⁹ through whom^d also he went and preached to the spirits in prison ²⁰ who disobeyed long ago when God waited patiently in the days of Noah while the ark was being built. In it only a few people, eight in all, were saved through water, ²¹ and this water symbolises baptism that now saves you also—not the removal of dirt from the body but the pledge^e of a good conscience towards God. It saves you by the resurrection of

^e22 Isaiah 53:9   ^a12 Psalm 34:12–16   ^b14 Or *not fear their threats*   ^c14 Isaiah 8:12
^d18,19 Or *alive in the spirit,* ¹⁹*through which*   ^e21 Or *response*

Jesus Christ, [22]who has gone into heaven and is at God's right hand—with angels, authorities and powers in submission to him.

Living for God

4 Therefore, since Christ suffered in his body, arm yourselves also with the same attitude, because all who have suffered in their bodies are done with sin. [2]As a result, they do not live the rest of their earthly lives for evil human desires, but rather for the will of God. [3]For you have spent enough time in the past doing what pagans choose to do—living in debauchery, lust, drunkenness, orgies, carousing and detestable idolatry. [4]They think it strange that you do not plunge with them into the same flood of dissipation, and they heap abuse on you. [5]But they will have to give account to him who is ready to judge the living and the dead. [6]For this is the reason the gospel was preached even to those who are now dead, so that they might be judged according to human standards in regard to the body, but live according to God in regard to the spirit.

[7]The end of all things is near. Therefore be clear minded and self-controlled so that you can pray. [8]Above all, love each other deeply, because love covers over a multitude of sins. [9]Offer hospitality to one another without grumbling. [10]Each of you should use whatever gift you have received to serve others, faithfully administering God's grace in its various forms. [11]If you speak, you should do it as those who speak the very words of God. If you serve, you should do it with the strength God provides, so that in all things God may be praised through Jesus Christ. To him be the glory and the power for ever and ever. Amen.

Suffering for Being a Christian

[12]Dear friends, do not be surprised at the painful trial you are suffering, as though something strange were happening to you. [13]But rejoice that you

participate in the sufferings of Christ, so that you may be overjoyed when his glory is revealed. [14]If you are insulted because of the name of Christ, you are blessed, for the Spirit of glory and of God rests on you. [15]If you suffer, it should not be as a murderer or thief or any other kind of criminal, or even as a meddler. [16]However, if you suffer as a Christian, do not be ashamed, but praise God that you bear that name. [17]For it is time for judgment to begin with the family of God; and if it begins with us, what will the outcome be for those who do not obey the gospel of God? [18]And,

"If it is hard for the righteous to be
    saved,
  what will become of the ungodly
    and the sinner?"[a]

[19]So then, those who suffer according to God's will should commit themselves to their faithful Creator and continue to do good.

To Elders and Young Men

5 To the elders among you, I appeal as an elder myself, a witness of Christ's sufferings and one who also will share in the glory to be revealed: [2]Be shepherds of God's flock that is under your care, serving as overseers—not because you must, but because you are willing, as God wants you to be; not greedy for money, but eager to serve; [3]not lording it over those entrusted to you, but being examples to the flock. [4]And when the Chief Shepherd appears, you will receive the crown of glory that will never fade away.

[5]In the same way, you who are younger, be submissive to those who are older. All of you, clothe yourselves with humility towards one another, because,

"God opposes the proud
  but gives grace to the humble."[a]

[6]Humble yourselves, therefore, under God's mighty hand, that he may lift you up in due time. [7]Cast all your anxiety on him because he cares for you.

[a]18 Prov. 11:31   [a]5 Prov. 3:34

[8] Be self-controlled and alert. Your enemy the devil prowls around like a roaring lion looking for someone to devour. [9] Resist him, standing firm in the faith, because you know that your brothers and sisters throughout the world are undergoing the same kind of sufferings.

[10] And the God of all grace, who called you to his eternal glory in Christ, after you have suffered a little while, will himself restore you and make you strong, firm and steadfast. [11] To him be the power for ever and ever. Amen.

Final Greetings

[12] With the help of Silas,[b] whom I regard as a faithful brother, I have written to you briefly, encouraging you and testifying that this is the true grace of God. Stand fast in it.

[13] She who is in Babylon, chosen together with you, sends you her greetings, and so does my son Mark. [14] Greet one another with a kiss of love.

Peace to all of you who are in Christ.

---

[b] 12 Greek *Silvanus*, a variant of *Silas*

2 Peter

1 Simon Peter, a servant and apostle of Jesus Christ,

To those who through the righteousness of our God and Saviour Jesus Christ have received a faith as precious as ours:

[2] Grace and peace be yours in abundance through the knowledge of God and of Jesus our Lord.

Making One's Calling and Election Sure

[3] His divine power has given us everything we need for life and godliness through our knowledge of him who called us by his own glory and goodness. [4] Through these he has given us his very great and precious promises, so that through them you may participate in the divine nature and escape the corruption in the world caused by evil desires.

[5] For this very reason, make every effort to add to your faith goodness; and to goodness, knowledge; [6] and to knowledge, self-control; and to self-control, perseverance; and to perseverance, godliness; [7] and to godliness, mutual affection; and to mutual affection, love. [8] For if you possess these qualities in increasing measure, they will keep you from being ineffective and unproductive in your knowledge of our Lord Jesus Christ. [9] But if any of you do not have them, you are short-sighted and blind, and you have forgotten that you have been cleansed from your past sins.

[10] Therefore, my brothers and sisters,

be all the more eager to make your calling and election sure. For if you do these things, you will never fall, [11] and you will receive a rich welcome into the eternal kingdom of our Lord and Saviour Jesus Christ.

Prophecy of Scripture

[12] So I will always remind you of these things, even though you know them and are firmly established in the truth you now have. [13] I think it is right to refresh your memory as long as I live in the tent of this body, [14] because I know that I will soon put it aside, as our Lord Jesus Christ has made clear to me. [15] And I will make every effort to see that after my departure you will always be able to remember these things.

[16] We did not follow cleverly invented stories when we told you about the power and coming of our Lord Jesus Christ, but we were eye-witnesses of his majesty. [17] For he received honour and glory from God the Father when the voice came to him from the Majestic Glory, saying, "This is my Son, whom I love; with him I am well pleased."[a] [18] We ourselves heard this voice that came from heaven when we were with him on the sacred mountain.

[19] And we have the word of the prophets made more certain, and you will do well to pay attention to it, as to a light shining in a dark place, until the day dawns and the morning star rises in your hearts. [20] Above all, you must understand that no prophecy of Scripture came about by the prophet's own interpretation.

[a] 17 Matt. 17:5; Mark 9:7; Luke 9:35

21 For prophecy never had its origin in the human will, but prophets, though human, spoke from God as they were carried along by the Holy Spirit.

False Teachers and Their Destruction

2 But there were also false prophets among the people, just as there will be false teachers among you. They will secretly introduce destructive heresies, even denying the sovereign Lord who bought them—bringing swift destruction on themselves. 2 Many will follow their shameful ways and will bring the way of truth into disrepute. 3 In their greed these teachers will exploit you with stories they have made up. Their condemnation has long been hanging over them, and their destruction has not been sleeping.

4 For if God did not spare angels when they sinned, but sent them to hell,*a* putting them into gloomy dungeons*b* to be held for judgment; 5 if he did not spare the ancient world when he brought the flood on its ungodly people, but protected Noah, a preacher of righteousness, and seven others; 6 if he condemned the cities of Sodom and Gomorrah by burning them to ashes, and made them an example of what is going to happen to the ungodly; 7 and if he rescued Lot, a righteous man, who was distressed by the filthy lives of the lawless 8 (for that righteous man, living among them day after day, was tormented in his righteous soul by the lawless deeds he saw and heard)—9 if this is so, then the Lord knows how to rescue the godly from trials and to hold the unrighteous for the day of judgment, while continuing their punishment.*c* 10 This is especially true of those who follow the corrupt desire of the sinful nature*d* and despise authority.

Bold and arrogant, they are not afraid to slander celestial beings; 11 yet even angels, although they are stronger and more powerful, do not bring slanderous accusations against such beings in the presence of the Lord. 12 But these people blaspheme in matters they do not understand.

They are like brute beasts, creatures of instinct, born only to be caught and destroyed, and like beasts they too will perish. 13 They will be paid back with harm for the harm they have done. Their idea of pleasure is to carouse in broad daylight. They are blots and blemishes, revelling in their pleasures while they feast with you.*e* 14 With eyes full of adultery, they never stop sinning; they seduce the unstable; they are experts in greed—an accursed brood! 15 They have left the straight way and wandered off to follow the way of Balaam son of Beor, who loved the wages of wickedness. 16 But he was rebuked for his wrongdoing by a donkey—a beast without speech—who spoke with a human voice and restrained the prophet's madness.

17 These people are springs without water and mists driven by a storm. Blackest darkness is reserved for them. 18 For they mouth empty, boastful words and, by appealing to the lustful desires of sinful human nature, they entice people who are just escaping from those who live in error. 19 They promise freedom, while they themselves are slaves of depravity—for people are slaves to whatever has mastered them. 20 If they have escaped the corruption of the world by knowing our Lord and Saviour Jesus Christ and are again entangled in it and overcome, they are worse off at the end than they were at the beginning. 21 It would have been better for them not to have known the way of righteousness, than to have known it and then to turn their backs on the sacred command that was passed on to them. 22 Of them the proverbs are true: "A dog returns to its vomit,"*f* and, "A sow that is washed goes back to her wallowing in the mud."

The Day of the LORD

3 Dear friends, this is now my second letter to you. I have written both of them as reminders to stimulate you to wholesome thinking. 2 I want you to recall the words spoken in the past by the holy

---

*a*4 Greek *Tartarus*   *b*4 Some manuscripts *into chains of darkness*
*c*9 Or *unrighteous for punishment until the day of judgment*   *d*10 Or *the flesh*
*e*13 Some manuscripts *in their love feasts*   *f*22 Prov. 26:11

prophets and the command given by our Lord and Saviour through your apostles.

3 First of all, you must understand that in the last days scoffers will come, scoffing and following their own evil desires. 4 They will say, "Where is this 'coming' he promised? Ever since our ancestors died, everything goes on as it has since the beginning of creation." 5 But they deliberately forget that long ago by God's word the heavens existed and the earth was formed out of water and by water. 6 By these waters also the world of that time was deluged and destroyed. 7 By the same word the present heavens and earth are reserved for fire, being kept for the day of judgment and destruction of the ungodly.

8 But do not forget this one thing, dear friends: With the Lord a day is like a thousand years, and a thousand years are like a day. 9 The Lord is not slow in keeping his promise, as some understand slowness. He is patient with you, not wanting anyone to perish, but everyone to come to repentance.

10 But the day of the Lord will come like a thief. The heavens will disappear with a roar; the elements will be destroyed by fire, and the earth and everything in it will be laid bare.*a*

11 Since everything will be destroyed in this way, what kind of people ought you to be? You ought to live holy and godly lives 12 as you look forward to the day of God and speed its coming.*b* That day will bring about the destruction of the heavens by fire, and the elements will melt in the heat. 13 But in keeping with his promise we are looking forward to a new heaven and a new earth, the home of righteousness.

14 So then, dear friends, since you are looking forward to this, make every effort to be found spotless, blameless and at peace with him. 15 Bear in mind that our Lord's patience means salvation, just as our dear brother Paul also wrote to you with the wisdom that God gave him. 16 He writes the same way in all his letters, speaking in them of these matters. His letters contain some things that are hard to understand, which ignorant and unstable people distort, as they do the other Scriptures, to their own destruction.

17 Therefore, dear friends, since you already know this, be on your guard so that you may not be carried away by the error of the lawless and fall from your secure position. 18 But grow in the grace and knowledge of our Lord and Saviour Jesus Christ. To him be glory both now and for ever! Amen.

---

*a*10 Some manuscripts *be burned up*   *b*12 Or *as you wait eagerly for the day of God to come*

1 John

The Word of Life

1 That which was from the beginning, which we have heard, which we have seen with our eyes, which we have looked at and our hands have touched—this we proclaim concerning the Word of life. ²The life appeared; we have seen it and testify to it, and we proclaim to you the eternal life, which was with the Father and has appeared to us. ³We proclaim to you what we have seen and heard, so that you also may have fellowship with us. And our fellowship is with the Father and with his Son, Jesus Christ. ⁴We write this to make our*a* joy complete.

Walking in the Light

⁵This is the message we have heard from him and declare to you: God is light; in him there is no darkness at all. ⁶If we claim to have fellowship with him yet walk in the darkness, we lie and do not live by the truth. ⁷But if we walk in the light, as he is in the light, we have fellowship with one another, and the blood of Jesus, his Son, purifies us from all*b* sin.

⁸If we claim to be without sin, we deceive ourselves and the truth is not in us. ⁹If we confess our sins, he is faithful and just and will forgive us our sins and purify us from all unrighteousness. ¹⁰If we claim we have not sinned, we make him out to be a liar and his word has no place in our lives.

2 My dear children, I write this to you so that you will not sin. But if anybody does sin, we have one who speaks to the Father in our defence—Jesus Christ, the Righteous One. ²He is the atoning sacrifice for our sins, and not only for ours but also for*a* the sins of the whole world.

³We know that we have come to know him if we obey his commands. ⁴Those who say, "I know him," but do not do what he commands are liars, and the truth is not in them. ⁵But if anyone obeys his word, God's love*b* is truly made complete in that person. This is how we know we are in him: ⁶Whoever claims to live in him must walk as Jesus did.

⁷Dear friends, I am not writing you a new command but an old one, which you have had since the beginning. This old command is the message you have heard. ⁸Yet I am writing you a new command; its truth is seen in him and you, because the darkness is passing and the true light is already shining.

⁹Those who claim to be in the light but hate a brother or sister are still in the darkness. ¹⁰Those who love their brothers and sisters live in the light, and there is nothing in them*c* to make them stumble. ¹¹But those who hate a brother or sister are in the darkness and walk around in the darkness; they do not know where they are going, because the darkness has blinded them.

¹²I write to you, dear children,
because your sins have been
forgiven on account of his name.

---

*a*4 Some manuscripts *your*   *b*7 Or *every*
*a*2 Or *He is the one who turns aside God's wrath, taking away our sins, and not only ours but also*
*b*5 Or *word, love for God*   *c*10 Or *it*

13 I write to you, fathers,
    because you have known him who
      is from the beginning.
I write to you, young people,
    because you have overcome the
      evil one.
I write to you, dear children,
    because you have known the Father.
14 I write to you, fathers,
    because you have known him who
      is from the beginning.
I write to you, young people,
    because you are strong,
    and the word of God lives in you,
    and you have overcome the evil one.

Do Not Love the World

15 Do not love the world or anything in the world. If you love the world, the love of the Father is not in you. 16 For everything in the world—the cravings of sinful people, the lust of their eyes and the boasting of what they have and do—comes not from the Father but from the world. 17 The world and its desires pass away, but whoever does the will of God lives for ever.

Warning Against Antichrists

18 Dear children, this is the last hour; and as you have heard that the antichrist is coming, even now many antichrists have come. This is how we know it is the last hour. 19 They went out from us, but they did not really belong to us. For if they had belonged to us, they would have remained with us; but their going showed that none of them belonged to us.

20 But you have an anointing from the Holy One, and all of you know the truth.*d* 21 I do not write to you because you do not know the truth, but because you do know it and because no lie comes from the truth. 22 Who is the liar? It is whoever denies that Jesus is the Christ. Such a person is the antichrist—denying the Father and the Son. 23 No-one who denies the Son has the Father; whoever acknowledges the Son has the Father also.

24 See that what you have heard from the beginning remains in you. If it does, you also will remain in the Son and in the Father. 25 And this is what he promised us—even eternal life.

26 I am writing these things to you about those who are trying to lead you astray. 27 As for you, the anointing you received from him remains in you, and you do not need anyone to teach you. But as his anointing teaches you about all things and as that anointing is real, not counterfeit— just as it has taught you, remain in him.

Children of God

28 And now, dear children, continue in him, so that when he appears we may be confident and unashamed before him at his coming.

29 If you know that he is righteous, you know that everyone who does what is right has been born of him.

3 How great is the love the Father has lavished on us, that we should be called children of God! And that is what we are! The reason the world does not know us is that it did not know him. 2 Dear friends, now we are children of God, and what we will be has not yet been made known. But we know that when he appears,*a* we shall be like him, for we shall see him as he is. 3 All who have this hope in them purify themselves, just as he is pure.

4 Everyone who sins breaks the law; in fact, sin is lawlessness. 5 But you know that he appeared so that he might take away our sins. And in him is no sin. 6 No-one who lives in him keeps on sinning. No-one who continues to sin has either seen him or known him.

7 Dear children, do not let anyone lead you astray. The one who does what is right is righteous, just as he is righteous. 8 The one who does what is sinful is of the devil, because the devil has been sinning from the beginning. The reason the Son of God appeared was to destroy the devil's work. 9 Those who are born of God will not continue to sin, because God's seed remains

---

*d*20 Some manuscripts *and you know all things*   *a*2 Or *when it is made known* in them; they cannot go on sinning, because they have been born of God. [10] This is how we know who the children of God are and who the children of the devil are: Those who do not do what is right are not God's children; nor are those who do not love their brothers and sisters.

Love One Another

[11] This is the message you heard from the beginning: We should love one another. [12] Do not be like Cain, who belonged to the evil one and murdered his brother. And why did he murder him? Because his own actions were evil and his brother's were righteous. [13] Do not be surprised, my brothers and sisters, if the world hates you. [14] We know that we have passed from death to life, because we love each other. Anyone who does not love remains in death. [15] Anyone who hates a brother or sister is a murderer, and you know that no murderers have eternal life in them.

[16] This is how we know what love is: Jesus Christ laid down his life for us. And we ought to lay down our lives for one another. [17] If anyone of you has material possessions and sees a brother or sister in need but has no pity on them, how can the love of God be in you? [18] Dear children, let us not love with words or tongue but with actions and in truth. [19] This then is how we know that we belong to the truth, and how we set our hearts at rest in his presence [20] whenever our hearts condemn us. For God is greater than our hearts, and he knows everything.

[21] Dear friends, if our hearts do not condemn us, we have confidence before God [22] and receive from him anything we ask, because we obey his commands and do what pleases him. [23] And this is his command: to believe in the name of his Son, Jesus Christ, and to love one another as he commanded us. [24] Those who obey his commands live in him, and he in them. And this is how we know that he lives in us: We know it by the Spirit he gave us.

Test the Spirits

4 Dear friends, do not believe every spirit, but test the spirits to see whether they are from God, because many false prophets have gone out into the world. [2] This is how you can recognise the Spirit of God: Every spirit that acknowledges that Jesus Christ has come in the flesh is from God, [3] but every spirit that does not acknowledge Jesus is not from God. This is the spirit of the antichrist, which you have heard is coming and even now is already in the world.

[4] You, dear children, are from God and have overcome them, because the one who is in you is greater than the one who is in the world. [5] They are from the world and therefore speak from the viewpoint of the world, and the world listens to them. [6] We are from God, and whoever knows God listens to us; but whoever is not from God does not listen to us. This is how we recognise the Spirit[a] of truth and the spirit of falsehood.

God's Love and Ours

[7] Dear friends, let us love one another, for love comes from God. Everyone who loves has been born of God and knows God. [8] Whoever does not love does not know God, because God is love. [9] This is how God showed his love among us: He sent his one and only Son[b] into the world that we might live through him. [10] This is love: not that we loved God, but that he loved us and sent his Son as an atoning sacrifice for[c] our sins. [11] Dear friends, since God so loved us, we also ought to love one another. [12] No-one has ever seen God; but if we love one another, God lives in us and his love is made complete in us.

[13] We know that we live in him and he in us, because he has given us of his Spirit. [14] And we have seen and testify that the Father has sent his Son to be the Saviour of the world. [15] If any acknowledge that Jesus is the Son of God, God lives in them

---

[a]6 Or *spirit*   [b]9 Or *his only begotten Son*   [c]10 Or *as the one who would turn aside his wrath, taking away*

and they in God. [16] And so we know and rely on the love God has for us.

God is love. Those who live in love live in God, and God in them. [17] In this way, love is made complete among us so that we will have confidence on the day of judgment, because in this world we are like him. [18] There is no fear in love. But perfect love drives out fear, because fear has to do with punishment. The one who fears is not made perfect in love.

[19] We love because he first loved us. [20] If we say we love God yet hate a brother or sister, we are liars. For any of us who do not love a brother or sister, whom we have seen, cannot love God, whom we have not seen. [21] And he has given us this command: Those who love God must also love one another.

Faith in the Son of God

5 Everyone who believes that Jesus is the Christ is born of God, and everyone who loves the father loves his child as well. [2] This is how we know that we love the children of God: by loving God and carrying out his commands. [3] This is love for God: to obey his commands. And his commands are not burdensome, [4] for everyone born of God overcomes the world. This is the victory that has overcome the world, even our faith. [5] Who is it that overcomes the world? Only the one who believes that Jesus is the Son of God.

[6] This is the one who came by water and blood—Jesus Christ. He did not come by water only, but by water and blood. And it is the Spirit who testifies, because the Spirit is the truth. [7] For there are three that testify: [8] the[a] Spirit, the water and the blood; and the three are in agreement. [9] We accept human testimony, but God's testimony is greater because it is the testimony of God, which he has given about his Son. [10] Those who believe in the Son of God have this testimony in their hearts. Those who do not believe God have made him out to be a liar, because they have not believed the testimony God has given about his Son. [11] And this is the testimony: God has given us eternal life, and this life is in his Son. [12] Those who have the Son have life; those who do not have the Son of God do not have life.

Concluding remarks

[13] I write these things to you who believe in the name of the Son of God so that you may know that you have eternal life. [14] This is the confidence we have in approaching God: that if we ask anything according to his will, he hears us. [15] And if we know that he hears us—whatever we ask—we know that we have what we asked of him.

[16] If you see your brother or sister commit a sin that does not lead to death, you should pray and God will give them life. I refer to those whose sin does not lead to death. There is a sin that leads to death. I am not saying that you should pray about that. [17] All wrongdoing is sin, and there is sin that does not lead to death.

[18] We know that those who are born of God do not continue to sin; the one who was born of God keeps them safe, and the evil one cannot harm them. [19] We know that we are children of God, and that the whole world is under the control of the evil one. [20] We know also that the Son of God has come and has given us understanding, so that we may know him who is true. And we are in him who is true—even in his Son Jesus Christ. He is the true God and eternal life.

[21] Dear children, keep yourselves from idols.

---

[a] 7,8 Late manuscripts of the Vulgate *testify in heaven: the Father, the Word and the Holy Spirit, and these three are one.* [8] *And there are three that testify on earth: the* (not found in any Greek manuscript before the sixteenth century)

2 John

¹The elder,

To the chosen lady and her children, whom I love in the truth—and not I only, but also all who know the truth—²because of the truth, which lives in us and will be with us for ever:

³Grace, mercy and peace from God the Father and from Jesus Christ, the Father's Son, will be with us in truth and love.

⁴It has given me great joy to find some of your children walking in the truth, just as the Father commanded us. ⁵And now, dear lady, I am not writing you a new command but one we have had from the beginning. I ask that we love one another. ⁶And this is love: that we walk in obedience to his commands. As you have heard from the beginning, his command is that you walk in love.

⁷Many deceivers, who do not acknowledge Jesus Christ as coming in the flesh, have gone out into the world. Any such person is the deceiver and the antichrist. ⁸Watch out that you do not lose what you have worked for, but that you may be rewarded fully. ⁹Anyone who runs ahead and does not continue in the teaching of Christ does not have God; whoever continues in the teaching has both the Father and the Son. ¹⁰If anyone comes to you and does not bring this teaching, do not take them into your house or welcome them. ¹¹Anyone who welcomes them shares in their wicked work.

¹²I have much to write to you, but I do not want to use paper and ink. Instead, I hope to visit you and talk with you face to face, so that our joy may be complete.

¹³The children of your chosen sister send their greetings.

3 John

¹The elder,

To my dear friend Gaius, whom I love in the truth.

²Dear friend, I pray that you may enjoy good health and that all may go well with you, even as your soul is getting along well. ³It gave me great joy to have some believers come and tell about your faithfulness to the truth and how you continue to walk in the truth. ⁴I have no greater joy than to hear that my children are walking in the truth.

⁵Dear friend, you are faithful in what you are doing for the believers, even though they are strangers to you. ⁶They have told the church about your love. You will do well to send them on their way in a manner worthy of God. ⁷It was for the sake of the Name that they went out, receiving no help from the pagans. ⁸We ought therefore to show hospitality to such people so that we may work together for the truth.

⁹I wrote to the church, but Diotrephes, who loves to be first, will have nothing to do with us. ¹⁰So if I come, I will call attention to what he is doing, gossiping maliciously about us. Not satisfied with that, he refuses to welcome other believers. He also stops those who want to do so and puts them out of the church.

¹¹Dear friend, do not imitate what is evil but what is good. Anyone who does what is good is from God. Anyone who does what is evil has not seen God. ¹²Demetrius is well spoken of by everyone—and even by the truth itself. We also speak well of him, and you know that our testimony is true.

¹³I have much to write to you, but I do not want to do so with pen and ink. ¹⁴I hope to see you soon, and we will talk face to face.

Peace to you. The friends here send their greetings. Greet the friends there by name.

Jude

¹Jude, a servant of Jesus Christ and a brother of James,

To those who have been called, who are loved by God the Father and kept by*ᵃ* Jesus Christ:

²Mercy, peace and love be yours in abundance.

The Sin and Doom of Godless Men

³Dear friends, although I was very eager to write to you about the salvation we share, I felt I had to write and urge you to contend for the faith that was once for all entrusted to the saints. ⁴For certain persons whose condemnation was written about*ᵇ* long ago have secretly slipped in among you. They are godless people, who change the grace of our God into a licence for immorality and deny Jesus Christ our only Sovereign and Lord.

⁵Though you already know all this, I want to remind you that the Lord*ᶜ* delivered his people out of Egypt, but later destroyed those who did not believe. ⁶And the angels who did not keep their positions of authority but abandoned their own home—these he has kept in darkness, bound with everlasting chains for judgment on the great Day. ⁷In a similar way, Sodom and Gomorrah and the surrounding towns gave themselves up to sexual immorality and perversion. They serve as an example of those who suffer the punishment of eternal fire.

⁸In the very same way, these dreamers pollute their own bodies, reject authority and slander celestial beings. ⁹But even the archangel Michael, when he was disputing with the devil about the body of Moses, did not dare to bring a slanderous accusation against him, but said, "The Lord rebuke you!" ¹⁰Yet these people speak abusively against whatever they do not understand; and what things they do understand by instinct, like unreasoning animals—these are the very things that destroy them.

¹¹Woe to them! They have taken the way of Cain; they have rushed for profit into Balaam's error; they have been destroyed in Korah's rebellion.

¹²These people are blemishes at your love feasts, eating with you without the slightest qualm—shepherds who feed only themselves. They are clouds without rain, blown along by the wind; autumn trees, without fruit and uprooted—twice dead. ¹³They are wild waves of the sea, foaming up their shame; wandering stars, for whom blackest darkness has been reserved for ever.

¹⁴Enoch, the seventh from Adam, prophesied about them: "See, the Lord is coming with thousands upon thousands of his holy ones ¹⁵to judge everyone, and to convict all the ungodly of all the ungodly acts they have done in the ungodly way, and of all the harsh words ungodly sinners have spoken against him." ¹⁶These people are grumblers and fault-finders; they follow their own evil desires; they boast

---

*ᵃ*1 Or *for; or in*   *ᵇ*4 Or *men who were marked out for condemnation*   *ᶜ*5 Some early manuscripts *Jesus* about themselves and flatter others for their own advantage.

A Call to Persevere

[17] But, dear friends, remember what the apostles of our Lord Jesus Christ foretold. [18] They said to you, "In the last times there will be scoffers who will follow their own ungodly desires." [19] These are the people who divide you, who follow mere natural instincts and do not have the Spirit.

[20] But you, dear friends, build yourselves up in your most holy faith and pray in the Holy Spirit. [21] Keep yourselves in God's love as you wait for the mercy of our Lord Jesus Christ to bring you to eternal life.

[22] Be merciful to those who doubt; [23] snatch others from the fire and save them; to others show mercy, mixed with fear—hating even the clothing stained by corrupted flesh.

Doxology

[24] To him who is able to keep you from falling and to present you before his glorious presence without fault and with great joy—[25] to the only God our Saviour be glory, majesty, power and authority, through Jesus Christ our Lord, before all ages, now and for evermore! Amen.

Revelation

Prologue

1 The revelation of Jesus Christ, which God gave him to show his servants what must soon take place. He made it known by sending his angel to his servant John, ² who testifies to everything he saw—that is, the word of God and the testimony of Jesus Christ. ³ Blessed is the one who reads the words of this prophecy, and blessed are those who hear it and take to heart what is written in it, because the time is near.

Greetings and Doxology

⁴ John,

To the seven churches in the province of Asia:

Grace and peace to you from him who is, and who was, and who is to come, and from the seven spirits*a* before his throne, ⁵ and from Jesus Christ, who is the faithful witness, the firstborn from the dead, and the ruler of the kings of the earth.

To him who loves us and has freed us from our sins by his blood, ⁶ and has made us to be a kingdom and priests to serve his God and Father—to him be glory and power for ever and ever! Amen.

⁷ Look, he is coming with the clouds,
    and every eye will see him,
even those who pierced him;
    and all the peoples of the earth
    will mourn because of him.
           So shall it be! Amen.

⁸ "I am the Alpha and the Omega," says the Lord God, "who is, and who was, and who is to come, the Almighty."

One Like a Son of Man

⁹ I, John, your brother and companion in the suffering and kingdom and patient endurance that are ours in Jesus, was on the island of Patmos because of the word of God and the testimony of Jesus. ¹⁰ On the Lord's Day I was in the Spirit, and I heard behind me a loud voice like a trumpet, ¹¹ which said: "Write on a scroll what you see and send it to the seven churches: to Ephesus, Smyrna, Pergamum, Thyatira, Sardis, Philadelphia and Laodicea."

¹² I turned round to see the voice that was speaking to me. And when I turned I saw seven golden lampstands, ¹³ and among the lampstands was someone "like a son of man",*b* dressed in a robe reaching down to his feet and with a golden sash round his chest. ¹⁴ His head and hair were white like wool, as white as snow, and his eyes were like blazing fire. ¹⁵ His feet were like bronze glowing in a furnace, and his voice was like the sound of rushing waters. ¹⁶ In his right hand he held seven stars, and out of his mouth came a sharp double-edged sword. His face was like the sun shining in all its brilliance.

¹⁷ When I saw him, I fell at his feet as though dead. Then he placed his right hand on me and said: "Do not be afraid. I am the First and the Last. ¹⁸ I am the Living One; I was dead, and behold I am

*a*4 Or *the sevenfold Spirit*   *b*13 Daniel 7:13

alive for ever and ever! And I hold the keys of death and Hades.

19 "Write, therefore, what you have seen, what is now and what will take place later. 20 The mystery of the seven stars that you saw in my right hand and of the seven golden lampstands is this: The seven stars are the angels[c] of the seven churches, and the seven lampstands are the seven churches.

To the Church in Ephesus

2 "To the angel[a] of the church in Ephesus write:

These are the words of him who holds the seven stars in his right hand and walks among the seven golden lampstands: 2 I know your deeds, your hard work and your perseverance. I know that you cannot tolerate wicked people, that you have tested those who claim to be apostles but are not, and have found them false. 3 You have persevered and have endured hardships for my name, and have not grown weary.

4 Yet I hold this against you: You have forsaken your first love. 5 Remember the height from which you have fallen! Repent and do the things you did at first. If you do not repent, I will come to you and remove your lampstand from its place. 6 But you have this in your favour: You hate the practices of the Nicolaitans, which I also hate.

7 Those who have ears, let them hear what the Spirit says to the churches. To those who overcome, I will give the right to eat from the tree of life, which is in the paradise of God.

To the Church in Smyrna

8 "To the angel of the church in Smyrna write:

These are the words of him who is the First and the Last, who died and came to life again. 9 I know your afflictions and your poverty—yet you are rich! I know the slander of those who say they are Jews and are not, but are a synagogue of Satan. 10 Do not be afraid of what you are about to suffer. I tell you, the devil will put some of you in prison to test you, and you will suffer persecution for ten days. Be faithful, even to the point of death, and I will give you the crown of life.

11 Those who have ears, let them hear what the Spirit says to the churches. Those who overcome will not be hurt at all by the second death.

To the Church in Pergamum

12 "To the angel of the church in Pergamum write:

These are the words of him who has the sharp, double-edged sword. 13 I know where you live—where Satan has his throne. Yet you remain true to my name. You did not renounce your faith in me, even in the days of Antipas, my faithful witness, who was put to death in your city— where Satan lives.

14 Nevertheless, I have a few things against you: You have people there who hold to the teaching of Balaam, who taught Balak to entice the Israelites to sin by eating food sacrificed to idols and by committing sexual immorality. 15 Likewise you also have those who hold to the teaching of the Nicolaitans. 16 Repent therefore! Otherwise, I will soon come to you and will fight against them with the sword of my mouth.

17 Those who have ears, let them hear what the Spirit says to the churches. To those who overcome, I will give some of the hidden manna. I will also give each of them a white stone with a new name written on it, known only to the one who receives it.

---

c20 Or *messengers*   a1 Or *messenger*; also in verses 8, 12 and 18

To the Church in Thyatira

18 "To the angel of the church in Thyatira write:

These are the words of the Son of God, whose eyes are like blazing fire and whose feet are like burnished bronze. 19 I know your deeds, your love and faith, your service and perseverance, and that you are now doing more than you did at first.

20 Nevertheless, I have this against you: You tolerate that woman Jezebel, who calls herself a prophetess. By her teaching she misleads my servants into sexual immorality and the eating of food sacrificed to idols. 21 I have given her time to repent of her immorality, but she is unwilling. 22 So I will cast her on a bed of suffering, and I will make those who commit adultery with her suffer intensely, unless they repent of her ways. 23 I will strike her children dead. Then all the churches will know that I am he who searches hearts and minds, and I will repay each of you according to your deeds. 24 Now I say to the rest of you in Thyatira, to you who do not hold to her teaching and have not learned Satan's so-called deep secrets (I will not impose any other burden on you): 25 Only hold on to what you have until I come.

26 To those who overcome and do my will to the end, I will give authority over the nations—

27'They will rule them with an iron
    sceptre;
  they will dash them to pieces like
    pottery'b—

just as I have received authority from my Father. 28 I will also give them the morning star. 29 Those who have ears, let them hear what the Spirit says to the churches.

To the Church in Sardis

3 "To the angela of the church in Sardis write:

These are the words of him who holds the seven spiritsb of God and the seven stars. I know your deeds; you have a reputation of being alive, but you are dead. 2 Wake up! Strengthen what remains and is about to die, for I have not found your deeds complete in the sight of my God. 3 Remember, therefore, what you have received and heard; obey it, and repent. But if you do not wake up, I will come like a thief, and you will not know at what time I will come to you.

4 Yet you have a few people in Sardis who have not soiled their clothes. They will walk with me, dressed in white, for they are worthy. 5 Those who overcome will, like them, be dressed in white. I will never blot out their names from the book of life, but will acknowledge their names before my Father and his angels. 6 Those who have ears, let them hear what the Spirit says to the churches.

To the Church in Philadelphia

7 "To the angel of the church in Philadelphia write:

These are the words of him who is holy and true, who holds the key of David. What he opens no-one can shut, and what he shuts no-one can open. 8 I know your deeds. See, I have placed before you an open door that no-one can shut. I know that you have little strength, yet you have kept my word and have not denied my name. 9 I will make those who are of the synagogue of Satan, who claim to be Jews though they are not, but are liars—I will make them come and fall down at your feet and acknowledge that I have loved you.

b27 Psalm 2:9   a1 Or messenger; also in verses 7 and 14   b1 Or the sevenfold Spirit

[10] Since you have kept my command to endure patiently, I will also keep you from the hour of trial that is going to come upon the whole world to test those who live on the earth.

[11] I am coming soon. Hold on to what you have, so that no-one will take your crown. [12] Those who overcome I will make pillars in the temple of my God. Never again will they leave it. I will write on them the name of my God and the name of the city of my God, the new Jerusalem, which is coming down out of heaven from my God; and I will also write on them my new name. [13] Those who have ears, let them hear what the Spirit says to the churches.

To the Church in Laodicea

[14] "To the angel of the church in Laodicea write:

These are the words of the Amen, the faithful and true witness, the ruler of God's creation. [15] I know your deeds, that you are neither cold nor hot. I wish you were either one or the other! [16] So, because you are lukewarm—neither hot nor cold—I am about to spit you out of my mouth. [17] You say, 'I am rich; I have acquired wealth and do not need a thing.' But you do not realise that you are wretched, pitiful, poor, blind and naked. [18] I counsel you to buy from me gold refined in the fire, so that you can become rich; and white clothes to wear, so that you can cover your shameful nakedness; and salve to put on your eyes, so that you can see.

[19] Those whom I love I rebuke and discipline. So be earnest, and repent. [20] Here I am! I stand at the door and knock. If anyone hears my voice and opens the door, I will come in and eat with them, and they with me.

[21] To those who overcome, I will give the right to sit with me on my throne, just as I overcame and sat down with my Father on his throne. [22] Those who have ears, let them hear what the Spirit says to the churches."

The Throne in Heaven

4 After this I looked, and there before me was a door standing open in heaven. And the voice I had first heard speaking to me like a trumpet said, "Come up here, and I will show you what must take place after this." [2] At once I was in the Spirit, and there before me was a throne in heaven with someone sitting on it. [3] And the one who sat there had the appearance of jasper and carnelian. A rainbow, resembling an emerald, encircled the throne. [4] Surrounding the throne were twenty-four other thrones, and seated on them were twenty-four elders. They were dressed in white and had crowns of gold on their heads. [5] From the throne came flashes of lightning, rumblings and peals of thunder. Before the throne, seven lamps were blazing. These are the seven spirits[a] of God. [6] Also before the throne there was what looked like a sea of glass, clear as crystal.

In the centre, around the throne, were four living creatures, and they were covered with eyes, in front and behind. [7] The first living creature was like a lion, the second was like an ox, the third had a face like a human being, the fourth was like a flying eagle. [8] Each of the four living creatures had six wings and was covered with eyes all around, even under his wings. Day and night they never stop saying:

"Holy, holy, holy
is the Lord God Almighty,
who was, and is, and is to come."

[9] Whenever the living creatures give glory, honour and thanks to him who sits on the throne and who lives for ever and ever, [10] the twenty-four elders fall down before him who sits on the throne, and worship him who lives for ever and ever. They lay their crowns before the throne and say:

---

[a]5 Or *the sevenfold Spirit*

11 "You are worthy, our Lord and God,
     to receive glory and honour and
          power,
  for you created all things,
     and by your will they were created
     and have their being."

The Scroll and the Lamb

5 Then I saw in the right hand of him
  who sat on the throne a scroll with
writing on both sides and sealed with seven
seals. 2 And I saw a mighty angel proclaiming in a loud voice, "Who is worthy to
break the seals and open the scroll?" 3 But
no-one in heaven or on earth or under the
earth could open the scroll or even look
inside it. 4 I wept and wept because
no-one was found who was worthy to open
the scroll or look inside. 5 Then one of the
elders said to me, "Do not weep! See,
the Lion of the tribe of Judah, the Root of
David, has triumphed. He is able to open
the scroll and its seven seals."

6 Then I saw a Lamb, looking as if it had
been slain, standing in the centre of the
throne, encircled by the four living creatures and the elders. He had seven horns
and seven eyes, which are the seven spirits[a] of God sent out into all the earth. 7 He
came and took the scroll from the right
hand of him who sat on the throne. 8 And
when he had taken it, the four living
creatures and the twenty-four elders fell
down before the Lamb. Each one had a
harp and they were holding golden bowls
full of incense, which are the prayers of the
saints. 9 And they sang a new song:

  "You are worthy to take the scroll
     and to open its seals,
  because you were slain,
     and with your blood you purchased
     for God
     members of every tribe and
     language and people and nation.
10 You have made them to be a kingdom
     and priests to serve our God,
  and they will reign on the earth."

11 Then I looked and heard the voice of
many angels, numbering thousands upon

thousands, and ten thousand times ten
thousand. They encircled the throne and
the living creatures and the elders. 12 In a
loud voice they sang:

  "Worthy is the Lamb, who was slain,
     to receive power and wealth and
          wisdom and strength
  and honour and glory and praise!"

13 Then I heard every creature in heaven
and on earth and under the earth and on
the sea, and all that is in them, singing:

  "To him who sits on the throne and
     to the Lamb
  be praise and honour and glory and
          power,
          for ever and ever!"

14 The four living creatures said, "Amen",
and the elders fell down and worshipped.

The Seals

6 I watched as the Lamb opened the first
  of the seven seals. Then I heard one
of the four living creatures say in a voice
like thunder, "Come!" 2 I looked, and
there before me was a white horse! Its
rider held a bow, and he was given a
crown, and he rode out as a conqueror
bent on conquest.

3 When the Lamb opened the second
seal, I heard the second living creature
say, "Come!" 4 Then another horse came
out, a fiery red one. Its rider was given
power to take peace from the earth and
to make people slay each other. To him
was given a large sword.

5 When the Lamb opened the third seal,
I heard the third living creature say,
"Come!" I looked, and there before me
was a black horse! Its rider was holding a
pair of scales in his hand. 6 Then I heard
what sounded like a voice among the four
living creatures, saying, "A quart[a] of
wheat for a day's wages,[b] and three quarts
of barley for a day's wages,[b] and do not
damage the oil and the wine!"

7 When the Lamb opened the fourth
seal, I heard the voice of the fourth living

---

[a]6 Or *the sevenfold Spirit*   [a]6 Greek *a choinix* (probably about a litre)   [b]6 Greek *a denarius*

creature say, "Come!" 8I looked, and there before me was a pale horse! Its rider was named Death, and Hades was following close behind him. They were given power over a fourth of the earth to kill by sword, famine and plague, and by the wild beasts of the earth.

9When he opened the fifth seal, I saw under the altar the souls of those who had been slain because of the word of God and the testimony they had maintained. 10They called out in a loud voice, "How long, Sovereign Lord, holy and true, until you judge the inhabitants of the earth and avenge our blood?" 11Then each of them was given a white robe, and they were told to wait a little longer, until the number of their fellow-servants and brothers and sisters who were to be killed as they had been was completed.

12I watched as he opened the sixth seal. There was a great earthquake. The sun turned black like sackcloth made of goat hair, the whole moon turned blood red, 13and the stars in the sky fell to earth, as late figs drop from a fig-tree when shaken by a strong wind. 14The sky receded like a scroll, rolling up, and every mountain and island was removed from its place.

15Then the kings of the earth, the princes, the generals, the rich, the mighty, and everyone, slave and free, hid in caves and among the rocks of the mountains. 16They called to the mountains and the rocks, "Fall on us and hide us from the face of him who sits on the throne and from the wrath of the Lamb! 17For the great day of their wrath has come, and who can stand?"

144,000 Sealed

7 After this I saw four angels standing at the four corners of the earth, holding back the four winds of the earth to prevent any wind from blowing on the land or on the sea or on any tree. 2Then I saw another angel coming up from the east, having the seal of the living God. He called out in a loud voice to the four angels who had been given power to harm the land and the sea: 3"Do not harm the land or the sea or the trees until we put a seal

on the foreheads of the servants of our God." 4Then I heard the number of those who were sealed: 144,000 from all the tribes of Israel.

5From the tribe of Judah 12,000 were
    sealed,
  from the tribe of Reuben 12,000,
  from the tribe of Gad 12,000,
  6from the tribe of Asher 12,000,
  from the tribe of Naphtali 12,000,
  from the tribe of Manasseh 12,000,
  7from the tribe of Simeon 12,000,
  from the tribe of Levi 12,000,
  from the tribe of Issachar 12,000,
  8from the tribe of Zebulun 12,000,
  from the tribe of Joseph 12,000,
  from the tribe of Benjamin 12,000.

The Great Multitude in White Robes

9After this I looked and there before me was a great multitude that no-one could count, from every nation, tribe, people and language, standing before the throne and in front of the Lamb. They were wearing white robes and were holding palm branches in their hands. 10And they cried out in a loud voice:

"Salvation belongs to our God,
  who sits on the throne,
  and to the Lamb."

11All the angels were standing round the throne and around the elders and the four living creatures. They fell down on their faces before the throne and worshipped God, 12saying:

"Amen!
Praise and glory
and wisdom and thanks and honour
and power and strength
be to our God for ever and ever.
Amen!"

13Then one of the elders asked me, "These in white robes—who are they, and where did they come from?"

14I answered, "Sir, you know."

And he said, "These are they who have come out of the great tribulation; they have washed their robes and made them white in the blood of the Lamb. [15] Therefore,

"they are before the throne of God
and serve him day and night in his temple;
and he who sits on the throne will spread his tent over them.
[16] Never again will they hunger;
never again will they thirst.
The sun will not beat upon them,
nor any scorching heat.
[17] For the Lamb at the centre of the throne will be their shepherd;
he will lead them to springs of living water.
And God will wipe away every tear from their eyes."

The Seventh Seal and the Golden Censer

8 When he opened the seventh seal, there was silence in heaven for about half an hour.

[2] And I saw the seven angels who stand before God, and to them were given seven trumpets.

[3] Another angel, who had a golden censer, came and stood at the altar. He was given much incense to offer, with the prayers of all the saints, on the golden altar before the throne. [4] The smoke of the incense, together with the prayers of the saints, went up before God from the angel's hand. [5] Then the angel took the censer, filled it with fire from the altar, and hurled it on the earth; and there came peals of thunder, rumblings, flashes of lightning and an earthquake.

The Trumpets

[6] Then the seven angels who had the seven trumpets prepared to sound them.

[7] The first angel sounded his trumpet, and there came hail and fire mixed with blood, and it was hurled down upon the earth. A third of the earth was burned up, a third of the trees were burned up, and all the green grass was burned up.

[8] The second angel sounded his trumpet, and something like a huge mountain, all ablaze, was thrown into the sea. A third of the sea turned into blood, [9] a third of the living creatures in the sea died, and a third of the ships were destroyed.

[10] The third angel sounded his trumpet, and a great star, blazing like a torch, fell from the sky on a third of the rivers and on the springs of water—[11] the name of the star is Wormwood.[a] A third of the waters turned bitter, and many people died from the waters that had become bitter.

[12] The fourth angel sounded his trumpet, and a third of the sun was struck, a third of the moon, and a third of the stars, so that a third of them turned dark. A third of the day was without light, and also a third of the night.

[13] As I watched, I heard an eagle that was flying in mid-air call out in a loud voice: "Woe! Woe! Woe to the inhabitants of the earth, because of the trumpet blasts about to be sounded by the other three angels!"

9 The fifth angel sounded his trumpet, and I saw a star that had fallen from the sky to the earth. The star was given the key to the shaft of the Abyss. [2] When he opened the Abyss, smoke rose from it like the smoke from a gigantic furnace. The sun and sky were darkened by the smoke from the Abyss. [3] And out of the smoke locusts came down upon the earth and were given power like that of scorpions of the earth. [4] They were told not to harm the grass of the earth or any plant or tree, but only those people who did not have the seal of God on their foreheads. [5] They were not given power to kill them, but only to torture them for five months. And the agony they suffered was like that of the sting of a scorpion when it strikes someone. [6] During those days people will seek death, but will not find it; they will long to die, but death will elude them.

[7] The locusts looked like horses prepared for battle. On their heads they wore something like crowns of gold, and their faces resembled human faces. [8] Their hair was like women's hair, and their teeth

[a] 11 That is, Bitterness

were like lions' teeth. 9They had breast-plates like breastplates of iron, and the sound of their wings was like the thundering of many horses and chariots rushing into battle. 10They had tails and stings like scorpions, and in their tails they had power to torment people for five months. 11They had as king over them the angel of the Abyss, whose name in Hebrew is Abaddon, and in Greek, Apollyon.[a]

12The first woe is past; two other woes are yet to come.

13The sixth angel sounded his trumpet, and I heard a voice coming from the horns[b] of the golden altar that is before God. 14It said to the sixth angel who had the trumpet, "Release the four angels who are bound at the great river Euphrates." 15And the four angels who had been kept ready for this very hour and day and month and year were released to kill a third of the world's people. 16The number of the mounted troops was two hundred million. I heard their number.

17The horses and riders I saw in my vision looked like this: Their breastplates were fiery red, dark blue, and yellow as sulphur. The heads of the horses resembled the heads of lions, and out of their mouths came fire, smoke and sulphur. 18A third of the people were killed by the three plagues of fire, smoke and sulphur that came out of their mouths. 19The power of the horses was in their mouths and in their tails; for their tails were like snakes, having heads with which they inflict injury.

20The rest of the people that were not killed by these plagues still did not repent of the work of their hands; they did not stop worshipping demons, and idols of gold, silver, bronze, stone and wood—idols that cannot see or hear or walk. 21Nor did they repent of their murders, their magic arts, their sexual immorality or their thefts.

The Angel and the Little Scroll

10 Then I saw another mighty angel coming down from heaven. He was robed in a cloud, with a rainbow above his head; his face was like the sun, and his legs were like fiery pillars. 2He was holding a little scroll, which lay open in his hand. He planted his right foot on the sea and his left foot on the land, 3and he gave a loud shout like the roar of a lion. When he shouted, the voices of the seven thunders spoke. 4And when the seven thunders spoke, I was about to write; but I heard a voice from heaven say, "Seal up what the seven thunders have said and do not write it down."

5Then the angel I had seen standing on the sea and on the land raised his right hand to heaven. 6And he swore by him who lives for ever and ever, who created the heavens and all that is in them, the earth and all that is in it, and the sea and all that is in it, and said, "There will be no more delay! 7But in the days when the seventh angel is about to sound his trumpet, the mystery of God will be accomplished, just as he announced to his servants the prophets."

8Then the voice that I had heard from heaven spoke to me once more: "Go, take the scroll that lies open in the hand of the angel who is standing on the sea and on the land."

9So I went to the angel and asked him to give me the little scroll. He said to me, "Take it and eat it. It will turn your stomach sour, but in your mouth it will be as sweet as honey." 10I took the little scroll from the angel's hand and ate it. It tasted as sweet as honey in my mouth, but when I had eaten it, my stomach turned sour. 11Then I was told, "You must prophesy again about many peoples, nations, languages and kings."

The Two Witnesses

11 I was given a reed like a measuring rod and was told, "Go and measure the temple of God and the altar, and count the worshippers there. 2But exclude the outer court; do not measure it, because it has been given to the Gentiles. They will trample on the holy city for 42 months. 3And I will give power to my two

---

[a]11 *Abaddon* and *Apollyon* mean *Destroyer*.   [b]13 That is, projections

witnesses, and they will prophesy for 1,260 days, clothed in sackcloth." ⁴These are the two olive trees and the two lampstands that stand before the Lord of the earth. ⁵If anyone tries to harm them, fire comes from their mouths and devours their enemies. This is how anyone who wants to harm them must die. ⁶They have power to shut up the sky so that it will not rain during the time they are prophesying; and they have power to turn the waters into blood and to strike the earth with every kind of plague as often as they want.

⁷Now when they have finished their testimony, the beast that comes up from the Abyss will attack them, and overpower and kill them. ⁸Their bodies will lie in the street of the great city, which is figuratively called Sodom and Egypt, where also their Lord was crucified. ⁹For three and a half days people from every race, tribe, language and nation will gaze on their bodies and refuse them burial. ¹⁰The inhabitants of the earth will gloat over them and will celebrate by sending each other gifts, because these two prophets had tormented those who live on earth.

¹¹But after the three and a half days a breath of life from God entered them, and they stood on their feet, and terror struck those who saw them. ¹²Then they heard a loud voice from heaven saying to them, "Come up here." And they went up to heaven in a cloud, while their enemies looked on.

¹³At that very hour there was a severe earthquake and a tenth of the city collapsed. Seven thousand people were killed in the earthquake, and the survivors were terrified and gave glory to the God of heaven.

¹⁴The second woe has passed; the third woe is coming soon.

The Seventh Trumpet

¹⁵The seventh angel sounded his trumpet, and there were loud voices in heaven, which said:

"The kingdom of the world has
    become the kingdom of our Lord
    and of his Christ,
    and he will reign for ever and ever."

¹⁶And the twenty-four elders, who were seated on their thrones before God, fell on their faces and worshipped God, ¹⁷saying:

"We give thanks to you, Lord God
    Almighty,
    the One who is and who was,
because you have taken your great
    power
    and have begun to reign.
¹⁸The nations were angry;
    and your wrath has come.
The time has come for judging the
    dead,
    and for rewarding your servants the
    prophets
and your saints and those who
    reverence your name,
    both small and great—
and for destroying those who destroy
    the earth."

¹⁹Then God's temple in heaven was opened, and within his temple was seen the ark of his covenant. And there came flashes of lightning, rumblings, peals of thunder, an earthquake and a great hailstorm.

The Woman and the Dragon

12 A great and wondrous sign appeared in heaven: a woman clothed with the sun, with the moon under her feet and a crown of twelve stars on her head. ²She was pregnant and cried out in pain as she was about to give birth. ³Then another sign appeared in heaven: an enormous red dragon with seven heads and ten horns and seven crowns on his heads. ⁴His tail swept a third of the stars out of the sky and flung them to the earth. The dragon stood in front of the woman who was about to give birth, so that he might devour her child the moment it was born. ⁵She gave birth to a son, a male child, who will rule all the nations with an iron sceptre. And her child was snatched up to God and to his throne. ⁶The woman fled into the desert to a place prepared for her by God, where she might be taken care of for 1,260 days.

[7] And there was war in heaven. Michael and his angels fought against the dragon, and the dragon and his angels fought back. [8] But he was not strong enough, and they lost their place in heaven. [9] The great dragon was hurled down—that ancient serpent called the devil, or Satan, who leads the whole world astray. He was hurled to the earth, and his angels with him.

[10] Then I heard a loud voice in heaven say:

"Now have come the salvation and
　　the power and the kingdom of our
　　　God,
　and the authority of his Christ.
For the accuser of our brothers and
　　sisters,
　who accuses them before our God
　　day and night,
　has been hurled down.
[11] They overcame him
　by the blood of the Lamb
　and by the word of their testimony;
they did not love their lives so much
　　as to shrink from death.
[12] Therefore rejoice, you heavens
　and you who dwell in them!
But woe to the earth and the sea,
　because the devil has gone down to
　　you!
He is filled with fury,
　because he knows that his time is
　　short."

[13] When the dragon saw that he had been hurled to the earth, he pursued the woman who had given birth to the male child. [14] The woman was given the two wings of a great eagle, so that she might fly to the place prepared for her in the desert, where she would be taken care of for a time, times and half a time, out of the serpent's reach. [15] Then from his mouth the serpent spewed water like a river, to overtake the woman and sweep her away with the torrent. [16] But the earth helped the woman by opening its mouth and swallowing the river that the dragon had spewed out of his mouth. [17] Then the dragon was enraged at the woman and went off to make war against the rest of her offspring—those who obey God's commandments and hold to the testimony of Jesus. [1] And the dragon[a] stood on the shore of the sea.

13

The Beast out of the Sea

And I saw a beast coming out of the sea. He had ten horns and seven heads, with ten crowns on his horns, and on each head a blasphemous name. [2] The beast I saw resembled a leopard, but had feet like those of a bear and a mouth like that of a lion. The dragon gave the beast his power and his throne and great authority. [3] One of the heads of the beast seemed to have had a fatal wound, but the fatal wound had been healed. The whole world was astonished and followed the beast. [4] People worshipped the dragon because he had given authority to the beast, and they also worshipped the beast and asked, "Who is like the beast? Who can make war against him?"

[5] The beast was given a mouth to utter proud words and blasphemies and to exercise his authority for forty-two months. [6] He opened his mouth to blaspheme God, and to slander his name and his dwelling-place and those who live in heaven. [7] He was given power to make war against the saints and to conquer them. And he was given authority over every tribe, people, language and nation. [8] All inhabitants of the earth will worship the beast—all whose names have not been written in the book of life belonging to the Lamb that was slain from the creation of the world.[b] [9] Those who have ears, let them hear.

[10] If any are to go into captivity,
　　into captivity they will go.
If any are to be killed[c] with the sword,
　　with the sword they will be killed.

This calls for patient endurance and faithfulness on the part of the saints.

---

[a]1　Some late manuscripts *And I*
[b]8　Or *written from the creation of the world in the book of life belonging to the Lamb that was slain*
[c]10　Some manuscripts *anyone kills*

The Beast out of the Earth

11 Then I saw another beast, coming out of the earth. He had two horns like a lamb, but he spoke like a dragon. 12 He exercised all the authority of the first beast on his behalf, and made the earth and its inhabitants worship the first beast, whose fatal wound had been healed. 13 And he performed great and miraculous signs, even causing fire to come down from heaven to earth in full view of all people. 14 Because of the signs he was given power to do on behalf of the first beast, he deceived the inhabitants of the earth. He ordered them to set up an image in honour of the beast who was wounded by the sword and yet lived. 15 He was given power to give breath to the image of the first beast, so that it could speak and cause all who refused to worship the image to be killed. 16 He also forced everyone, small and great, rich and poor, free and slave, to receive a mark on their right hands or on their foreheads, 17 so that they could not buy or sell unless they had the mark, which is the name of the beast or the number of his name.

18 This calls for wisdom. Let those who have insight calculate the number of the beast, for it is humanity's number. The number is 666.

The Lamb and the 144,000

14 Then I looked, and there before me was the Lamb, standing on Mount Zion, and with him 144,000 who had his name and his Father's name written on their foreheads. 2 And I heard a sound from heaven like the roar of rushing waters and like a loud peal of thunder. The sound I heard was like that of harpists playing their harps. 3 And they sang a new song before the throne and before the four living creatures and the elders. No-one could learn the song except the 144,000 who had been redeemed from the earth. 4 These are those who did not defile themselves with women, for they kept themselves pure. They follow the Lamb wherever he goes. They were purchased from among the human race and offered as firstfruits to God and the Lamb. 5 No lie was found in their mouths; they are blameless.

The Three Angels

6 Then I saw another angel flying in mid-air, and he had the eternal gospel to proclaim to those who live on the earth— to every nation, tribe, language and people. 7 He said in a loud voice, "Fear God and give him glory, because the hour of his judgment has come. Worship him who made the heavens, the earth, the sea and the springs of water."

8 A second angel followed and said, "Fallen! Fallen is Babylon the Great, which made all the nations drink the maddening wine of her adulteries."

9 A third angel followed them and said in a loud voice: "If any worship the beast and his image and receive his mark on the forehead or on the hand, 10 they, too, will drink of the wine of God's fury, which has been poured full strength into the cup of his wrath. They will be tormented with burning sulphur in the presence of the holy angels and of the Lamb. 11 And the smoke of their torment rises for ever and ever. There is no rest day or night for those who worship the beast and his image, or for anyone who receives the mark of his name." 12 This calls for patient endurance on the part of the saints who obey God's commandments and remain faithful to Jesus.

13 Then I heard a voice from heaven say, "Write: Blessed are the dead who die in the Lord from now on."

"Yes," says the Spirit, "they will rest from their labour, for their deeds will follow them."

The Harvest of the Earth

14 I looked, and there before me was a white cloud, and seated on the cloud was one "like a son of man"*a* with a crown of gold on his head and a sharp sickle in his hand. 15 Then another angel came out of the temple and called in a loud voice to

---

a 14 Daniel 7:13

him who was sitting on the cloud, "Take your sickle and reap, because the time to reap has come, for the harvest of the earth is ripe." [16]So he who was seated on the cloud swung his sickle over the earth, and the earth was harvested.

[17]Another angel came out of the temple in heaven, and he too had a sharp sickle. [18]Still another angel, who had charge of the fire, came from the altar and called in a loud voice to him who had the sharp sickle, "Take your sharp sickle and gather the clusters of grapes from the earth's vine, because its grapes are ripe." [19]The angel swung his sickle on the earth, gathered its grapes and threw them into the great winepress of God's wrath. [20]They were trampled in the winepress outside the city, and blood flowed out of the press, rising as high as the horses' bridles for a distance of 1,600 stadia.[b]

Seven Angels With Seven Plagues

15 I saw in heaven another great and marvellous sign: seven angels with the seven last plagues—last, because with them God's wrath is completed. [2]And I saw what looked like a sea of glass mixed with fire and, standing beside the sea, those who had been victorious over the beast and his image and over the number of his name. They held harps given them by God [3]and sang the song of Moses the servant of God and the song of the Lamb:

"Great and marvellous are your deeds,
　Lord God Almighty.
Just and true are your ways,
　King of the ages.
[4]Who will not fear you, O Lord,
　and bring glory to your name?
For you alone are holy.
All nations will come
　and worship before you,
for your righteous acts have been
　revealed."

[5]After this I looked and in heaven the temple, that is, the tabernacle of the Testimony, was opened. [6]Out of the temple

came the seven angels with the seven plagues. They were dressed in clean, shining linen and wore golden sashes round their chests. [7]Then one of the four living creatures gave to the seven angels seven golden bowls filled with the wrath of God, who lives for ever and ever. [8]And the temple was filled with smoke from the glory of God and from his power, and no-one could enter the temple until the seven plagues of the seven angels were completed.

The Seven Bowls of God's Wrath

16 Then I heard a loud voice from the temple saying to the seven angels, "Go, pour out the seven bowls of God's wrath on the earth."

[2]The first angel went and poured out his bowl on the land, and ugly and painful sores broke out on the people who had the mark of the beast and worshipped his image.

[3]The second angel poured out his bowl on the sea, and it turned into blood like that of a dead person, and every living thing in the sea died.

[4]The third angel poured out his bowl on the rivers and springs of water, and they became blood. [5]Then I heard the angel in charge of the waters say:

"You are just in these judgments,
　you who are and who were, the
　　Holy One,
　because you have so judged;
[6]for they have shed the blood of your
　saints and prophets,
　and you have given them blood to
　drink as they deserve."

[7]And I heard the altar respond:

"Yes, Lord God Almighty,
　true and just are your judgments."

[8]The fourth angel poured out his bowl on the sun, and the sun was given power to scorch people with fire. [9]They were seared by the intense heat and they cursed the name of God, who had control over

[b]20 That is, about 180 miles (about 300 kilometres)

these plagues, but they refused to repent and glorify him.

[10] The fifth angel poured out his bowl on the throne of the beast, and his kingdom was plunged into darkness. People gnawed their tongues in agony [11] and cursed the God of heaven because of their pains and their sores, but they refused to repent of what they had done.

[12] The sixth angel poured out his bowl on the great river Euphrates, and its water was dried up to prepare the way for the kings from the East. [13] Then I saw three evil[a] spirits that looked like frogs; they came out of the mouth of the dragon, out of the mouth of the beast and out of the mouth of the false prophet. [14] They are spirits of demons performing miraculous signs, and they go out to the kings of the whole world, to gather them for the battle on the great day of God Almighty.

[15] "Behold, I come like a thief! Blessed are those who stay awake and keep their clothes with them, so that they may not go naked and be shamefully exposed."

[16] Then they gathered the kings together to the place that in Hebrew is called Armageddon.

[17] The seventh angel poured out his bowl into the air, and out of the temple came a loud voice from the throne, saying, "It is done!" [18] Then there came flashes of lightning, rumblings, peals of thunder and a severe earthquake. No earthquake like it has ever occurred since the human race has been on earth, so tremendous was the quake. [19] The great city split into three parts, and the cities of the nations collapsed. God remembered Babylon the Great and gave her the cup filled with the wine of the fury of his wrath. [20] Every island fled away and the mountains could not be found. [21] From the sky huge hailstones of about a hundred pounds each fell upon people. And they cursed God on account of the plague of hail, because the plague was so terrible.

The Woman on the Beast

17 One of the seven angels who had the seven bowls came and said to me, "Come, I will show you the punishment of the great prostitute, who sits on many waters. [2] With her the kings of the earth committed adultery and the inhabitants of the earth were intoxicated with the wine of her adulteries."

[3] Then the angel carried me away in the Spirit into a desert. There I saw a woman sitting on a scarlet beast that was covered with blasphemous names and had seven heads and ten horns. [4] The woman was dressed in purple and scarlet, and was glittering with gold, precious stones and pearls. She held a golden cup in her hand, filled with abominable things and the filth of her adulteries. [5] This title was written on her forehead:

MYSTERY
BABYLON THE GREAT
THE MOTHER OF PROSTITUTES
AND OF THE ABOMINATIONS OF THE EARTH.

[6] I saw that the woman was drunk with the blood of the saints, the blood of those who bore testimony to Jesus.

When I saw her, I was greatly astonished. [7] Then the angel said to me: "Why are you astonished? I will explain to you the mystery of the woman and of the beast she rides, which has the seven heads and ten horns. [8] The beast, which you saw, once was, now is not, and will come up out of the Abyss and go to his destruction. The inhabitants of the earth whose names have not been written in the book of life from the creation of the world will be astonished when they see the beast, because he once was, now is not, and yet will come.

[9] "This calls for a mind with wisdom. The seven heads are seven hills on which the woman sits. [10] They are also seven kings. Five have fallen, one is, the other has not yet come; but when he does come, he must remain for a little while. [11] The beast who once was, and now is not, is an eighth king. He belongs to the seven and is going to his destruction.

[12] "The ten horns you saw are ten kings who have not yet received a kingdom, but who for one hour will receive authority as kings along with the beast. [13] They have one purpose and will give their power and

[a] 13 Greek unclean

authority to the beast. ¹⁴They will make war against the Lamb, but the Lamb will overcome them because he is Lord of lords and King of kings—and with him will be his called, chosen and faithful followers."

¹⁵Then the angel said to me, "The waters you saw, where the prostitute sits, are peoples, multitudes, nations and languages. ¹⁶The beast and the ten horns you saw will hate the prostitute. They will bring her to ruin and leave her naked; they will eat her flesh and burn her with fire. ¹⁷For God has put it into their hearts to accomplish his purpose by agreeing to give the beast their power to rule, until God's words are fulfilled. ¹⁸The woman you saw is the great city that rules over the kings of the earth."

The Fall of Babylon

18 After this I saw another angel coming down from heaven. He had great authority, and the earth was illuminated by his splendour. ²With a mighty voice he shouted:

"Fallen! Fallen is Babylon the Great!
　She has become a home for demons
and a haunt for every evil*a* spirit,
　a haunt for every unclean and
　　detestable bird.
³For all the nations have drunk
　the maddening wine of her
　　adulteries.
The kings of the earth committed
　adultery with her,
　and the merchants of the earth
　　grew rich from her excessive
　　luxuries."

⁴Then I heard another voice from heaven say:

"Come out of her, my people,
　so that you will not share in her
　　sins,
　so that you will not receive any of
　　her plagues;
⁵for her sins are piled up to heaven,

　　and God has remembered her
　　　crimes.
⁶Give back to her as she has given;
　pay her back double for what she
　　has done.
　Mix her a double portion from her
　　own cup.
⁷Give her as much torture and grief
　as the glory and luxury she gave
　　herself.
In her heart she boasts,
　'I sit as queen; I am not a widow,
　and I will never mourn.'
⁸Therefore in one day her plagues will
　　overtake her:
　death, mourning and famine.
She will be consumed by fire,
　for mighty is the Lord God who
　　judges her.

⁹"When the kings of the earth who committed adultery with her and shared her luxury see the smoke of her burning, they will weep and mourn over her. ¹⁰Terrified at her torment, they will stand far off and cry:

"'Woe! Woe, O great city,
　O Babylon, city of power!
In one hour your doom has come!'

¹¹"The merchants of the earth will weep and mourn over her because no-one buys their cargoes any more—¹²cargoes of gold, silver, precious stones and pearls; fine linen, purple, silk and scarlet cloth; every sort of citron wood, and articles of every kind made of ivory, costly wood, bronze, iron and marble; ¹³cargoes of cinnamon and spice, of incense, myrrh and frankincense, of wine and olive oil, of fine flour and wheat; cattle and sheep; horses and carriages; and slaves—human beings!

¹⁴"They will say, 'The fruit you longed for is gone from you. All your riches and splendour have vanished, never to be recovered.' ¹⁵The merchants who sold these things and gained their wealth from her will stand far off, terrified at her torment. They will weep and mourn ¹⁶and cry out:

*a*2 Greek unclean

" 'Woe! Woe, O great city,
    dressed in fine linen, purple and
        scarlet,
    and glittering with gold, precious
        stones and pearls!
¹⁷ In one hour such great wealth has
    been brought to ruin!'

"Every sea captain, and all who travel
by ship, the sailors, and all who earn their
living from the sea, will stand far off.
¹⁸ When they see the smoke of her
burning, they will exclaim, 'Was there
ever a city like this great city?' ¹⁹ They will
throw dust on their heads, and with
weeping and mourning cry out:

" 'Woe! Woe, O great city,
    where all who had ships on the sea
    became rich through her wealth!
In one hour she has been brought to
        ruin!
²⁰ Rejoice over her, O heaven!
    Rejoice, saints and apostles and
        prophets!
God has judged her for the way she
    treated you.' "

²¹ Then a mighty angel picked up a
boulder the size of a large millstone and
threw it into the sea, and said:

"With such violence
    the great city of Babylon will be
        thrown down,
    never to be found again.
²² The music of harpists and musicians,
        flute players and trumpeters,
    will never be heard in you again.
No worker of any trade
    will ever be found in you again.
The sound of a millstone
    will never be heard in you again.
²³ The light of a lamp
    will never shine in you again.
The voice of bridegroom and bride
    will never be heard in you again.
Your merchants were the world's
        important people.
    By your magic spell all the nations
        were led astray.
²⁴ In her was found the blood of
    prophets and of the saints,

and of all who have been killed on
    the earth."

Hallelujah!

19 After this I heard what sounded
like the roar of a great multitude in
heaven shouting:

"Hallelujah!
Salvation and glory and power belong
    to our God,
²   for true and just are his judgments.
He has condemned the great
        prostitute
    who corrupted the earth by her
        adulteries.
He has avenged on her the blood of
    his servants."

³ And again they shouted:

"Hallelujah!
The smoke from her goes up for ever
    and ever."

⁴ The twenty-four elders and the four
living creatures fell down and worshipped
God, who was seated on the throne. And
they cried:

"Amen, Hallelujah!"

⁵ Then a voice came from the throne,
saying:

"Praise our God,
    all you his servants,
you who fear him,
    both small and great!"

⁶ Then I heard what sounded like a great
multitude, like the roar of rushing waters
and like loud peals of thunder, shouting:

"Hallelujah!
    For our Lord God Almighty reigns.
⁷ Let us rejoice and be glad
    and give him glory!
For the wedding of the Lamb has
        come,
    and his bride has made herself
        ready.

8 Fine linen, bright and clean,
  was given her to wear."

(Fine linen stands for the righteous acts of the saints.)

9 Then the angel said to me, "Write: 'Blessed are those who are invited to the wedding supper of the Lamb!' " And he added, "These are the true words of God."

10 At this I fell at his feet to worship him. But he said to me, "Do not do it! I am a fellow-servant with you and with your brothers and sisters who hold to the testimony of Jesus. Worship God! For the testimony of Jesus is the spirit of prophecy."

The Rider on the White Horse

11 I saw heaven standing open and there before me was a white horse, whose rider is called Faithful and True. With justice he judges and makes war. 12 His eyes are like blazing fire, and on his head are many crowns. He has a name written on him that no-one knows but he himself. 13 He is dressed in a robe dipped in blood, and his name is the Word of God. 14 The armies of heaven were following him, riding on white horses and dressed in fine linen, white and clean. 15 Out of his mouth comes a sharp sword with which to strike down the nations. "He will rule them with an iron sceptre." [a] He treads the winepress of the fury of the wrath of God Almighty. 16 On his robe and on his thigh he has this name written:

KING OF KINGS AND LORD OF LORDS.

17 And I saw an angel standing in the sun, who cried in a loud voice to all the birds flying in mid-air, "Come, gather together for the great supper of God, 18 so that you may eat the flesh of kings, generals, and the mighty, of horses and their riders, and the flesh of all people, free and slave, small and great."

19 Then I saw the beast and the kings of the earth and their armies gathered together to make war against the rider on

[a] 15 Psalm 2:9

the horse and his army. 20 But the beast was captured, and with him the false prophet who had performed the miraculous signs on his behalf. With these signs he had deluded those who had received the mark of the beast and worshipped his image. The two of them were thrown alive into the fiery lake of burning sulphur. 21 The rest of them were killed with the sword that came out of the mouth of the rider on the horse, and all the birds gorged themselves on their flesh.

The Thousand Years

20 And I saw an angel coming down out of heaven, having the key to the Abyss and holding in his hand a great chain. 2 He seized the dragon, that ancient serpent, who is the devil, or Satan, and bound him for a thousand years. 3 He threw him into the Abyss, and locked and sealed it over him, to keep him from deceiving the nations any more until the thousand years were ended. After that, he must be set free for a short time.

4 I saw thrones on which were seated those who had been given authority to judge. And I saw the souls of those who had been beheaded because of their testimony for Jesus and because of the word of God. They had not worshipped the beast or his image and had not received his mark on their foreheads or their hands. They came to life and reigned with Christ for a thousand years. 5 (The rest of the dead did not come to life until the thousand years were ended.) This is the first resurrection. 6 Blessed and holy are those who have part in the first resurrection. The second death has no power over them, but they will be priests of God and of Christ and will reign with him for a thousand years.

Satan's Doom

7 When the thousand years are over, Satan will be released from his prison 8 and will go out to deceive the nations in the four corners of the earth—Gog and Magog—to gather them for battle. In

number they are like the sand on the seashore. ⁹They marched across the breadth of the earth and surrounded the camp of God's people, the city he loves. But fire came down from heaven and devoured them. ¹⁰And the devil, who deceived them, was thrown into the lake of burning sulphur, where the beast and the false prophet had been thrown. They will be tormented day and night for ever and ever.

The Dead Are Judged

¹¹Then I saw a great white throne and him who was seated on it. Earth and sky fled from his presence, and there was no place for them. ¹²And I saw the dead, great and small, standing before the throne, and books were opened. Another book was opened, which is the book of life. The dead were judged according to what they had done as recorded in the books. ¹³The sea gave up the dead that were in it, and death and Hades gave up the dead that were in them, and everyone was judged according to what they had done. ¹⁴Then death and Hades were thrown into the lake of fire. The lake of fire is the second death. ¹⁵All whose names were not found written in the book of life were thrown into the lake of fire.

The New Jerusalem

21 Then I saw a new heaven and a new earth, for the first heaven and the first earth had passed away, and there was no longer any sea. ²I saw the Holy City, the new Jerusalem, coming down out of heaven from God, prepared as a bride beautifully dressed for her husband. ³And I heard a loud voice from the throne saying, "Now the dwelling of God is with human beings, and he will live with them. They will be his people, and God himself will be with them and be their God. ⁴He will wipe every tear from their eyes. There will be no more death or mourning

or crying or pain, for the old order of things has passed away."

⁵He who was seated on the throne said, "I am making everything new!" Then he said, "Write this down, for these words are trustworthy and true."

⁶He said to me: "It is done. I am the Alpha and the Omega, the Beginning and the End. To those who are thirsty I will give to drink without cost from the spring of the water of life. ⁷Those who overcome will inherit all this, and I will be their God and they will be my children. ⁸But the cowardly, the unbelieving, the vile, the murderers, the sexually immoral, those who practise magic arts, the idolaters and all liars—their place will be in the fiery lake of burning sulphur. This is the second death."

⁹One of the seven angels who had the seven bowls full of the seven last plagues came and said to me, "Come, I will show you the bride, the wife of the Lamb." ¹⁰And he carried me away in the Spirit to a mountain great and high, and showed me the Holy City, Jerusalem, coming down out of heaven from God. ¹¹It shone with the glory of God, and its brilliance was like that of a very precious jewel, like a jasper, clear as crystal. ¹²It had a great, high wall with twelve gates, and with twelve angels at the gates. On the gates were written the names of the twelve tribes of Israel. ¹³There were three gates on the east, three on the north, three on the south and three on the west. ¹⁴The wall of the city had twelve foundations, and on them were the names of the twelve apostles of the Lamb.

¹⁵The angel who talked with me had a measuring rod of gold to measure the city, its gates and its walls. ¹⁶The city was laid out like a square, as long as it was wide. He measured the city with the rod and found it to be 12,000 stadia*ᵃ* in length, and as wide and high as it is long. ¹⁷He measured its wall and it was 144 cubits*ᵇ* thick,*ᶜ* by human measurement, which the angel was using. ¹⁸The wall was made of jasper, and the city of pure gold, as pure as glass.

---

*ᵃ*16 That is, about 1,400 miles (about 2,200 kilometres)   *ᵇ*17 That is, about 200 feet (about 65 metres)
*ᶜ*17 Or *high*

[19] The foundations of the city walls were decorated with every kind of precious stone. The first foundation was jasper, the second sapphire, the third chalcedony, the fourth emerald, [20] the fifth sardonyx, the sixth carnelian, the seventh chrysolite, the eighth beryl, the ninth topaz, the tenth chrysoprase, the eleventh jacinth, and the twelfth amethyst.[d] [21] The twelve gates were twelve pearls, each gate made of a single pearl. The great street of the city was of pure gold, like transparent glass.

[22] I did not see a temple in the city, because the Lord God Almighty and the Lamb are its temple. [23] The city does not need the sun or the moon to shine on it, for the glory of God gives it light, and the Lamb is its lamp. [24] The nations will walk by its light, and the kings of the earth will bring their splendour into it. [25] On no day will its gates ever be shut, for there will be no night there. [26] The glory and honour of the nations will be brought into it. [27] Nothing impure will ever enter it, nor will anyone who does what is shameful or deceitful, but only those whose names are written in the Lamb's book of life.

The River of Life

22 Then the angel showed me the river of the water of life, as clear as crystal, flowing from the throne of God and of the Lamb [2] down the middle of the great street of the city. On each side of the river stood the tree of life, bearing twelve crops of fruit, yielding its fruit every month. And the leaves of the tree are for the healing of the nations. [3] No longer will there be any curse. The throne of God and of the Lamb will be in the city, and his servants will serve him. [4] They will see his face, and his name will be on their foreheads. [5] There will be no more night. They will not need the light of a lamp or the light of the sun, for the Lord God will give them light. And they will reign for ever and ever.

[6] The angel said to me, "These words are trustworthy and true. The Lord, the God of the spirits of the prophets, sent his angel to show his servants the things that must soon take place."

Jesus Is Coming

[7] "Behold, I am coming soon! Blessed are those who keep the words of the prophecy in this book."

[8] I, John, am the one who heard and saw these things. And when I had heard and seen them, I fell down to worship at the feet of the angel who had been showing them to me. [9] But he said to me, "Do not do it! I am a fellow-servant with you and with your fellow prophets and of all who keep the words of this book. Worship God!"

[10] Then he told me, "Do not seal up the words of the prophecy of this book, because the time is near. [11] Let those who do wrong continue to do wrong; let those who are vile continue to be vile; let those who do right continue to do right; and let those who are holy continue to be holy."

[12] "Behold, I am coming soon! My reward is with me, and I will give to everyone according to what they have done. [13] I am the Alpha and the Omega, the First and the Last, the Beginning and the End.

[14] "Blessed are those who wash their robes, that they may have the right to the tree of life and may go through the gates into the city. [15] Outside are the dogs, those who practise magic arts, the sexually immoral, the murderers, the idolaters and everyone who loves and practises falsehood.

[16] "I, Jesus, have sent my angel to give you[a] this testimony for the churches. I am the Root and the Offspring of David, and the bright Morning Star."

[17] The Spirit and the bride say, "Come!" And let those who hear say, "Come!" Let those who are thirsty come; and let all who wish take the free gift of the water of life.

---

[d]20 The precise identification of some of these precious stones is uncertain.   [a]16 The Greek is plural.

[18] I warn everyone who hears the words of the prophecy of this book: If any one of you adds anything to them, God will add to you the plagues described in this book. [19] And if any one of you takes words away from this book of prophecy, God will take away from you your share in the tree of life and in the holy city, which are described in this book.

[20] He who testifies to these things says, "Yes, I am coming soon."

Amen. Come, Lord Jesus.

[21] The grace of the Lord Jesus be with God's people. Amen.

THE
BOOKS OF PSALMS
AND PROVERBS

Psalms

BOOK I

Psalms 1–41

Psalm 1

¹Blessed are those
  who do not walk in the counsel of
    the wicked
 or stand in the way of sinners
  or sit in the seat of mockers.
²But their delight is in the law of the
    Lord,
  and on his law they meditate day
    and night.
³They are like trees planted by streams
    of water,
  which yield their fruit in season
 and whose leaves do not wither.
  Whatever they do prospers.

⁴Not so the wicked!
  They are like chaff
  that the wind blows away.
⁵Therefore the wicked will not stand
    in the judgment,
  nor sinners in the assembly of the
    righteous.

⁶For the Lord watches over the way
    of the righteous,
  but the way of the wicked will
    perish.

Psalm 2

¹Why do the nations conspire*a*
  and the peoples plot in vain?

²The kings of the earth take their stand
  and the rulers gather together
    against the Lord
  and against his Anointed One.*b*
³"Let us break their chains," they say,
  "and throw off their fetters."

⁴The One enthroned in heaven laughs;
  the Lord scoffs at them.
⁵Then he rebukes them in his anger
  and terrifies them in his wrath,
    saying,
⁶"I have installed my King*c*
  on Zion, my holy hill."

⁷I will proclaim the decree of the Lord:

  He said to me, "You are my Son;*d*
    today I have become your Father.*e*
⁸Ask of me,
  and I will make the nations your
    inheritance,
  the ends of the earth your
    possession.
⁹You will rule them with an iron
    sceptre;*f*
  you will dash them to pieces like
    pottery."

¹⁰Therefore, you kings, be wise;
  be warned, you rulers of the earth.
¹¹Serve the Lord with fear
  and rejoice with trembling.
¹²Kiss the Son, lest he be angry
  and you be destroyed in your way,
 for his wrath can flare up in a moment.
  Blessed are all who take refuge in
    him.

---

*a*1 Hebrew; Septuagint *rage*   *b*2 Or *anointed one*   *c*6 Or *king*   *d*7 Or *son*; also in verse 12
*e*7 Or *have begotten you*   *f*9 Or *will break them with a rod of iron*

Psalm 3

A psalm of David. When he fled from his son Absalom.

[1] O LORD, how many are my foes!
How many rise up against me!
[2] Many are saying of me,
"God will not deliver him." *Selah*[a]

[3] But you are a shield around me,
O LORD;
you bestow glory on me and lift[b] up
my head.
[4] To the LORD I cry aloud,
and he answers me from his holy hill.
Selah

[5] I lie down and sleep;
I wake again, because the LORD
sustains me.
[6] I will not fear the tens of thousands
drawn up against me on every side.

[7] Arise, O LORD!
Deliver me, O my God!
Strike all my enemies on the jaw;
break the teeth of the wicked.

[8] From the LORD comes deliverance.
May your blessing be on your
people. *Selah*

Psalm 4

*For the director of music. With stringed instruments.
A psalm of David.*

[1] Answer me when I call to you,
O my righteous God.
Give me relief from my distress;
be merciful to me and hear my
prayer.

[2] How long, O men, will you turn my
glory into shame?[a]
How long will you love delusions
and seek false gods?[b] *Selah*
[3] Know that the LORD has set apart the
godly for himself;
the LORD will hear when I call to
him.

[4] In your anger do not sin;
when you are on your beds,
search your hearts and be silent.
Selah

[5] Offer right sacrifices
and trust in the LORD.

[6] Many are asking, "Who can show us
any good?"
Let the light of your face shine upon
us, O LORD.
[7] You have filled my heart with greater
joy
than when their grain and new wine
abound.
[8] I will lie down and sleep in peace,
for you alone, O LORD,
make me dwell in safety.

Psalm 5

*For the director of music. For flutes. A psalm
of David.*

[1] Give ear to my words, O LORD,
consider my sighing.
[2] Listen to my cry for help,
my King and my God,
for to you I pray.
[3] In the morning, O LORD, you hear my
voice;
in the morning I lay my requests
before you
and wait in expectation.

[4] You are not a God who takes pleasure
in evil;
with you the wicked cannot dwell.
[5] The arrogant cannot stand in your
presence;
you hate all who do wrong.
[6] You destroy those who tell lies;
those who are bloodthirsty and
deceitful
the LORD abhors.

[7] But I, by your great mercy,
will come into your house;
in reverence will I bow down
towards your holy temple.
[8] Lead me, O LORD, in your
righteousness

---

[a]2 A word of uncertain meaning, occurring frequently in the Psalms; possibly a musical term
[b]3 Or *LORD, / my Glorious One, who lifts*   [a]2 Or *you dishonour my Glorious One*   [b]2 Or *seek lies*

because of my enemies—
make straight your way before me.

⁹Not a word from their mouth can be
    trusted;
  their heart is filled with destruction.
  Their throat is an open grave;
    with their tongue they speak deceit.
¹⁰Declare them guilty, O God!
    Let their intrigues be their
      downfall.
  Banish them for their many sins,
    for they have rebelled against you.

¹¹But let all who take refuge in you be
    glad;
  let them ever sing for joy.
  Spread your protection over them,
    that those who love your name may
      rejoice in you.
¹²For surely, O LORD, you bless the
    righteous;
  you surround them with your
    favour as with a shield.

Psalm 6

For the director of music. With stringed instruments.
According to sheminith.ᵃ
A psalm of David.

¹O LORD, do not rebuke me in your
    anger
  or discipline me in your wrath.
²Be merciful to me, LORD, for I am
    faint;
  O LORD, heal me, for my bones are
    in agony.
³My soul is in anguish.
  How long, O LORD, how long?

⁴Turn, O LORD, and deliver me;
  save me because of your unfailing
    love.
⁵The dead do not remember you.
  Who praises you from the grave?ᵇ

⁶I am worn out from groaning;
  all night long I flood my bed with
    weeping
  and drench my couch with tears.

⁷My eyes grow weak with sorrow;
  they fail because of all my foes.

⁸Away from me, all you who do evil,
  for the LORD has heard my
    weeping.
⁹The LORD has heard my cry for
    mercy;
  the LORD accepts my prayer.
¹⁰All my enemies will be ashamed and
    dismayed;
  they will turn back in sudden
    disgrace.

Psalm 7

A shiggaionᵃ *of David, which he sang to the* LORD
concerning Cush, a Benjamite.

¹O LORD my God, I take refuge in you;
  save and deliver me from all who
    pursue me,
²or they will tear me like a lion
  and rip me to pieces with no-one to
    rescue me.

³O LORD my God, if I have done this
  and there is guilt on my hands—
⁴if I have done evil to those who are at
    peace with me
  or without cause have robbed my
    foes—
⁵then let my enemies pursue and
    overtake me;
  let them trample my life to the
    ground
  and make me sleep in the dust.
                                    Selah

⁶Arise, O LORD, in your anger;
  rise up against the rage of my
    enemies.
  Awake, my God; decree justice.
⁷Let the assembled peoples gather
    round you.
  Rule over them from on high;
⁸   let the LORD judge the peoples.
  Judge me, O LORD, according to my
    righteousness,
  according to my integrity, O Most
    High.

ᵃTitle: Probably a musical term   ᵇ5 Hebrew *Sheol*   ᵃTitle: Probably a literary or musical term

⁹O righteous God,
 who searches minds and hearts,
bring to an end the violence of the
 wicked
 and make the righteous secure.

¹⁰My shield*b* is God Most High,
 who saves the upright in heart.
¹¹God is a righteous judge,
 a God who expresses his wrath
 every day.
¹²If he does not relent,
 he*c* will sharpen his sword;
 he will bend and string his bow.
¹³He has prepared his deadly weapons;
 he makes ready his flaming arrows.

¹⁴Those who are pregnant with evil
 and conceive trouble give birth to
 disillusionment.
¹⁵Those who dig a hole and scoop it out
 fall into the pit they have made.
¹⁶The trouble they cause recoils on them;
 their violence comes down on their
 own heads.

¹⁷I will give thanks to the LORD because
 of his righteousness
 and will sing praise to the name of
 the LORD Most High.

Psalm 8

For the director of music. According to gittith.*a*
A psalm of David.

¹O LORD, our Lord,
 how majestic is your name in all the
 earth!

You have set your glory
 above the heavens.
²From the lips of children and infants
 you have ordained praise*b*
because of your enemies,
 to silence the foe and the avenger.

³When I consider your heavens,
 the work of your fingers,
the moon and the stars,
 which you have set in place,

⁴what are mere mortals that you are
 mindful of them,
 human beings that you care for
 them?*c*
⁵You made them*d* a little lower than
 the heavenly beings*e*
 and crowned them*f* with glory and
 honour.

⁶You made them rulers*g* over the
 works of your hands;
 you put everything under their*h*
 feet:
⁷all flocks and herds,
 and the beasts of the field,
⁸the birds of the air,
 and the fish of the sea,
 all that swim the paths of the seas.

⁹O LORD, our Lord,
 how majestic is your name in all the
 earth!

Psalm 9*a*

For the director of music. To ˌthe tune of ˌ *"The Death
of the Son". A psalm of David.*

¹I will praise you, O LORD, with all my
 heart;
 I will tell of all your wonders.
²I will be glad and rejoice in you;
 I will sing praise to your name,
 O Most High.

³My enemies turn back;
 they stumble and perish before you.
⁴For you have upheld my right and my
 cause;
 you have sat on your throne,
 judging righteously.
⁵You have rebuked the nations and
 destroyed the wicked;
 you have blotted out their name for
 ever and ever.
⁶Endless ruin has overtaken the
 enemy,
 you have uprooted their cities;
 even the memory of them has
 perished.

*b*10 Or *sovereign*   *c*12 Or *If anyone does not repent, / God*   *a*Title: Probably a musical term   *b*2 Or *strength*
*c*4 Or *what is a human being that you are mindful of him, / the son of man that you care for him?*   *d*5 Or *him*
*e*5 Or *than God*   *f*5 Or *him*   *g*6 Or *made him ruler*   *h*6 Or *his*
*a*Psalms 9 and 10 may have been originally a single acrostic poem, the stanzas of which begin with the successive letters
of the Hebrew alphabet. In the Septuagint they constitute one psalm.

⁷The Lᴏʀᴅ reigns for ever;
　he has established his throne for
　　judgment.
⁸He will judge the world in
　righteousness;
　he will govern the peoples with
　　justice.
⁹The Lᴏʀᴅ is a refuge for the oppressed,
　a stronghold in times of trouble.
¹⁰Those who know your name will trust
　in you,
　for you, Lᴏʀᴅ, have never forsaken
　those who seek you.

¹¹Sing praises to the Lᴏʀᴅ, enthroned
　in Zion;
　proclaim among the nations what
　he has done.
¹²For he who avenges blood remembers;
　he does not ignore the cry of the
　afflicted.

¹³O Lᴏʀᴅ, see how my enemies
　persecute me!
　Have mercy and lift me up from the
　gates of death,
¹⁴that I may declare your praises
　in the gates of the Daughter of Zion
　and there rejoice in your salvation.
¹⁵The nations have fallen into the pit
　they have dug;
　their feet are caught in the net they
　have hidden.
¹⁶The Lᴏʀᴅ is known by his justice;
　the wicked are ensnared by the
　work of their hands.
　　　　　　　　*Higgaion.*ᵇ *Selah*

¹⁷The wicked return to the grave,ᶜ
　all the nations that forget God.
¹⁸But the needy will not always be
　forgotten,
　nor the hope of the afflicted ever
　perish.

¹⁹Arise, O Lᴏʀᴅ, let not mortals
　triumph;
　let the nations be judged in your
　presence.
²⁰Strike them with terror, O Lᴏʀᴅ;

let the nations know they are only
　mortals.　　　　　　　　　*Selah*

Psalm 10ᵃ

¹Why, O Lᴏʀᴅ, do you stand far off?
　Why do you hide yourself in times
　of trouble?

²In their arrogance the wicked hunt
　down the weak,
　who are caught in the schemes they
　devise.
³They boast of the cravings of their
　hearts;
　they bless the greedy and revile the
　Lᴏʀᴅ.
⁴In their pride the wicked do not seek
　him;
　in all their thoughts there is no
　room for God.
⁵Their ways are always prosperous;
　they are haughty and your laws are
　far from them;
　they sneer at all their enemies.
⁶They say to themselves, "Nothing will
　shake us;
　We'll always be happy and never
　have trouble."
⁷Their mouths are full of curses and lies
　and threats;
　trouble and evil are under their
　tongues.
⁸They lie in wait near the villages;
　from ambush they murder the
　innocent,
　watching in secret for their victims.
⁹They lie in wait like a lion in cover;
　they lie in wait to catch the helpless;
　they catch the helpless and drag
　them off in their nets.
¹⁰Their victims are crushed, they
　collapse;
　they fall under superior strength.
¹¹The wicked say to themselves, "God
　has forgotten;
　he covers his face and never sees."

¹²Arise, Lᴏʀᴅ! Lift up your hand,
　O God.
　Do not forget the helpless.

ᵇ16 Or *Meditation*; possibly a musical notation　　ᶜ17 Hebrew *Sheol*
ᵃPsalms 9 and 10 may have been originally a single acrostic poem, the stanzas of which begin with the successive letters
of the Hebrew alphabet. In the Septuagint they constitute one psalm.

13 Why do the wicked revile God?
   Why do they say to themselves,
   "He won't call us to account"?
14 But you, O God, do see trouble and
   grief;
   you consider it to take it in hand.
The victims commit themselves to
   you;
   you are the helper of the fatherless.
15 Break the arms of the wicked and
   evildoers;
   call them to account for their
   wickedness
   that would not be found out.

16 The LORD is King for ever and ever;
   the nations will perish from his
   land.
17 You hear, O LORD, the desire of the
   afflicted;
   you encourage them, and you listen
   to their cry,
18 defending the fatherless and the
   oppressed,
   in order that those who are of the
   earth may terrify no more.

Psalm 11

For the director of music. Of David.

1 In the LORD I take refuge.
   How then can you say to me:
   "Flee like a bird to your mountain.
2 For look, the wicked bend their bows;
   they set their arrows against the
   strings
to shoot from the shadows
   at the upright in heart.
3 When the foundations are being
   destroyed,
   what can the righteous do?"*a*

4 The LORD is in his holy temple;
   the LORD is on his heavenly throne.
He observes all human beings;
   his eyes examine them.
5 The LORD examines the righteous,
   but the wicked*b* and those who love
   violence
   his soul hates.
6 On the wicked he will rain

fiery coals and burning sulphur;
   a scorching wind will be their lot.

7 For the LORD is righteous,
   he loves justice;
   the upright will see his face.

Psalm 12

For the director of music. According to sheminith.*a*
A psalm of David.

1 Help, LORD, for the godly are no more;
   the faithful have vanished from the
   human race.
2 People all lie to their neighbours;
   their flattering lips speak with
   deception.

3 May the LORD cut off all flattering lips
   and every boastful tongue
4 that says, "We will triumph with our
   tongues;
   we own our lips*b*—who is our
   master?"

5 "Because of the oppression of the weak
   and the groaning of the needy,
I will now arise," says the LORD.
   "I will protect them from those
   who malign them."
6 And the words of the LORD are flawless,
   like silver refined in a furnace of clay,
   purified seven times.

7 O LORD, you will keep us safe
   and protect us from such people for
   ever.
8 The wicked freely strut about
   when what is vile is honoured
   among the human race.

Psalm 13

For the director of music. A psalm of David.

1 How long, O LORD? Will you forget
   me for ever?
   How long will you hide your face
   from me?
2 How long must I wrestle with my
   thoughts

---

*a*3 Or *what is the Righteous One doing*   *b*5 Or *The LORD, the Righteous One, examines the wicked, /*
*a*Title: Probably a musical term   *b*4 Or */ our lips are our ploughshares*

and every day have sorrow in my
heart?
How long will my enemy triumph
over me?

3 Look on me and answer, O Lord my
God.
Give light to my eyes, or I will sleep
in death;
4 my enemy will say, "I have overcome
him,"
and my foes will rejoice when I
fall.

5 But I trust in your unfailing love;
my heart rejoices in your salvation.
6 I will sing to the Lord,
for he has been good to me.

Psalm 14

For the director of music. Of David.

1 Fools*a* say in their hearts,
"There is no God."
They are corrupt, their deeds are vile;
there is no-one who does good.

2 The Lord looks down from heaven
on the human race
to see if there are any who
understand,
any who seek God.
3 All have turned aside,
they have together become
corrupt;
there is no-one who does good,
not even one.

4 Will evildoers never learn—
those who devour my people as if
eating bread
and who do not call on the Lord?
5 There they are, overwhelmed with
dread,
for God is present in the company
of the righteous.
6 You evildoers frustrate the plans of
the poor,
but the Lord is their refuge.

7 Oh, that salvation for Israel would
come out of Zion!
When the Lord restores the
fortunes of his people,
let Jacob rejoice and Israel be glad!

Psalm 15

A psalm of David.

1 Lord, who may dwell in your
sanctuary?
Who may live on your holy hill?

2 Those whose walk is blameless
and who do what is righteous,
who speak the truth from their
hearts
3   and have no slander on their
tongues,
who do their neighbours no wrong
and cast no slur on others,
4 who despise those who are vile
but honour those who fear the
Lord,
who keep their oaths
even when it hurts,
5 who lend their money without usury
and do not accept bribes against the
innocent.

Those who do these things
will never be shaken.

Psalm 16

*A miktam*a* of David.*

1 Keep me safe, O God,
for in you I take refuge.

2 I said to the Lord, "You are my Lord;
apart from you I have no good
thing."
3 As for the saints who are in the land,
they are the glorious ones in whom
is all my delight.*b*
4 The sorrows of those will increase
who run after other gods.

---

*a*1 The Hebrew words rendered *fool* in Psalms denote one who is morally deficient.
*a*Title: Probably a literary or musical term
*b*3 Or *As for the pagan priests who are in the land / and the nobles in whom all delight, I said:*

I will not pour out their libations of
blood
or take up their names on my lips.

⁵LORD, you have assigned me my
portion and my cup;
you have made my lot secure.
⁶The boundary lines have fallen for me
in pleasant places;
surely I have a delightful
inheritance.

⁷I will praise the LORD, who counsels
me;
even at night my heart instructs me.
⁸I have set the LORD always before me.
Because he is at my right hand,
I shall not be shaken.

⁹Therefore my heart is glad and my
tongue rejoices;
my body also will rest secure,
¹⁰because you will not abandon me to
the grave,^{c}
nor will you let your Holy One^d see
decay.
¹¹You have made known^e to me the
path of life;
you will fill me with joy in your
presence,
with eternal pleasures at your right
hand.

Psalm 17

A prayer of David.

¹Hear, O LORD, my righteous plea;
listen to my cry.
Give ear to my prayer—
it does not rise from deceitful lips.
²May my vindication come from you;
may your eyes see what is right.

³Though you probe my heart and
examine me at night,
though you test me, you will find
nothing;
I have resolved that my mouth will
not sin.

⁴As for what others do—
by the word of your lips
I have kept myself
from the ways of the violent.
⁵My steps have held to your paths;
my feet have not slipped.

⁶I call on you, O God, for you will
answer me;
give ear to me and hear my
prayer.
⁷Show the wonder of your great love,
you who save by your right hand
those who take refuge in you from
their foes.
⁸Keep me as the apple of your eye;
hide me in the shadow of your
wings
⁹from the wicked who assail me,
from my mortal enemies who
surround me.

¹⁰They close up their callous hearts,
and their mouths speak with
arrogance.
¹¹They have tracked me down, they
now surround me,
with eyes alert, to throw me to the
ground.
¹²They are like a lion hungry for prey,
like a great lion crouching in cover.

¹³Rise up, O LORD, confront them,
bring them down;
rescue me from the wicked by your
sword.
¹⁴O LORD, by your hand save me from
such people,
from those of this world whose
reward is in this life.

You still the hunger of those you
cherish;
their little ones have plenty,
and they store up wealth for their
children.
¹⁵And I—in righteousness I shall see
your face;
when I awake, I shall be satisfied
with seeing your likeness.

^{c}10 Hebrew *Sheol* ^{d}10 Or *your faithful one* ^{e}11 Or *You will make known*

Psalm 18

For the director of music. Of David the servant of the
LORD. He sang to the LORD the words of this song
when the LORD delivered him from the hand of all his
enemies and from the hand of Saul. He said:

¹ I love you, O LORD, my strength.

² The LORD is my rock, my fortress and
my deliverer;
my God is my rock, in whom I take
refuge.
He is my shield and the horn*ᵃ* of my
salvation, my stronghold.
³ I call to the LORD, who is worthy of
praise,
and I am saved from my enemies.

⁴ The cords of death entangled me;
the torrents of destruction
overwhelmed me.
⁵ The cords of the grave*ᵇ* coiled around
me;
the snares of death confronted me.
⁶ In my distress I called to the LORD;
I cried to my God for help.
From his temple he heard my voice;
my cry came before him, into his
ears.

⁷ The earth trembled and quaked,
and the foundations of the
mountains shook;
they trembled because he was
angry.
⁸ Smoke rose from his nostrils;
consuming fire came from his
mouth,
burning coals blazed out of it.
⁹ He parted the heavens and came
down;
dark clouds were under his feet.
¹⁰ He mounted the cherubim and flew;
he soared on the wings of the wind.
¹¹ He made darkness his covering, his
canopy around him —
the dark rain clouds of the sky.
¹² Out of the brightness of his presence
clouds advanced,
with hailstones and bolts of
lightning.

¹³ The LORD thundered from heaven;
the voice of the Most High
resounded.*ᶜ*
¹⁴ He shot his arrows and scattered ˻the
enemies˼,
great bolts of lightning and routed
them.
¹⁵ The valleys of the sea were exposed
and the foundations of the earth
laid bare
at your rebuke, O LORD,
at the blast of breath from your
nostrils.

¹⁶ He reached down from on high and
took hold of me;
he drew me out of deep waters.
¹⁷ He rescued me from my powerful
enemy,
from my foes, who were too strong
for me.
¹⁸ They confronted me in the day of my
disaster,
but the LORD was my support.
¹⁹ He brought me out into a spacious
place;
he rescued me because he delighted
in me.

²⁰ The LORD has dealt with me according
to my righteousness;
according to the cleanness of my
hands he has rewarded me.
²¹ For I have kept the ways of the LORD;
I have not done evil by turning from
my God.
²² All his laws are before me;
I have not turned away from his
decrees.
²³ I have been blameless before him
and have kept myself from sin.
²⁴ The LORD has rewarded me according
to my righteousness,
according to the cleanness of my
hands in his sight.

²⁵ To the faithful you show yourself
faithful,
to the blameless you show yourself
blameless,

*ᵃ*2 *Horn* here symbolises strength.   *ᵇ*5 Hebrew *Sheol*
*ᶜ*13 Some Hebrew manuscripts and Septuagint (see also 2 Samuel 22:14); most Hebrew manuscripts *resounded, /*
amid hailstones and bolts of lightning

26 to the pure you show yourself pure,
  but to the crooked you show
    yourself shrewd.
27 You save the humble
  but bring low those whose eyes are
    haughty.
28 You, O Lord, keep my lamp burning;
  my God turns my darkness into light.
29 With your help I can advance against
    a troop;[d]
  with my God I can scale a wall.

30 As for God, his way is perfect;
  the word of the Lord is flawless.
  He is a shield
  for all who take refuge in him.
31 For who is God besides the Lord?
  And who is the Rock except our
    God?
32 It is God who arms me with strength
  and makes my way perfect.
33 He makes my feet like the feet of a
    deer;
  he enables me to stand on the
    heights.
34 He trains my hands for battle;
  my arms can bend a bow of bronze.
35 You give me your shield of victory,
  and your right hand sustains me;
  you stoop down to make me great.
36 You broaden the path beneath me,
  so that my ankles do not turn over.

37 I pursued my enemies and overtook
    them;
  I did not turn back till they were
    destroyed.
38 I crushed them so that they could not
    rise;
  they fell beneath my feet.
39 You armed me with strength for battle;
  you made my adversaries bow at
    my feet.
40 You made my enemies turn their
    backs in flight,
  and I destroyed my foes.
41 They cried for help, but there was
    no-one to save them—
  to the Lord, but he did not answer.
42 I beat them as fine as dust borne on
    the wind;

I poured them out like mud in the
    streets.

43 You have delivered me from the
    attacks of the people;
  you have made me the head of
    nations;
  people I did not know are subject
    to me.
44 As soon as they hear me, they obey me;
  foreigners cringe before me.
45 They all lose heart;
  they come trembling from their
    strongholds.

46 The Lord lives! Praise be to my Rock!
  Exalted be God my Saviour!
47 He is the God who avenges me,
  who subdues nations under me,
48   who saves me from my enemies.
  You exalted me above my foes;
  from violent people you rescued
    me.
49 Therefore I will praise you among the
    nations, O Lord;
  I will sing praises to your name.
50 He gives his king great victories;
  he shows unfailing kindness to his
    anointed,
  to David and his descendants for
    ever.

Psalm 19

For the director of music. A psalm of David.

1 The heavens declare the glory of God;
  the skies proclaim the work of his
    hands.
2 Day after day they pour forth speech;
  night after night they display
    knowledge.
3 There is no speech or language
  where their voice is not heard.[a]
4 Their voice[b] goes out into all the
    earth,
  their words to the ends of the world.

In the heavens he has pitched a tent
    for the sun,
5   which is like a bridegroom coming
    forth from his pavilion,

---

d29 Or *can run through a barricade*   a3 Or *They have no speech, there are no words; / no sound is heard from them*
b4 Septuagint, Jerome and Syriac; Hebrew *line*

like a champion rejoicing to run his
    course.
6 It rises at one end of the heavens
    and makes its circuit to the other;
    nothing is hidden from its heat.

7 The law of the LORD is perfect,
    reviving the soul.
The statutes of the LORD are
    trustworthy,
    making wise the simple.
8 The precepts of the LORD are right,
    giving joy to the heart.
The commands of the LORD are
    radiant,
    giving light to the eyes.
9 The fear of the LORD is pure,
    enduring for ever.
The ordinances of the LORD are sure
    and altogether righteous.
10 They are more precious than gold,
    than much pure gold;
they are sweeter than honey,
    than honey from the comb.
11 By them is your servant warned;
    in keeping them there is great
    reward.

12 Who can discern their errors?
    Forgive my hidden faults.
13 Keep your servant also from wilful sins;
    may they not rule over me.
Then will I be blameless,
    innocent of great transgression.

14 May the words of my mouth and the
    meditation of my heart
    be pleasing in your sight,
    O LORD, my Rock and my
    Redeemer.

Psalm 20

For the director of music. A psalm of David.

1 May the LORD answer you when you
    are in distress;
    may the name of the God of Jacob
    protect you.
2 May he send you help from the
    sanctuary
    and grant you support from Zion.

3 May he remember all your sacrifices
    and accept your burnt offerings.
                                        Selah
4 May he give you the desire of your
    heart
    and make all your plans succeed.
5 We will shout for joy when you are
    victorious
    and will lift up our banners in the
    name of our God.
May the LORD grant all your requests.

6 Now I know that the LORD saves his
    anointed;
    he answers him from his holy heaven
    with the saving power of his right
    hand.
7 Some trust in chariots and some in
    horses,
    but we trust in the name of the LORD
    our God.
8 They are brought to their knees and
    fall,
    but we rise up and stand firm.

9 O LORD, save the king!
    Answer*a* us when we call!

Psalm 21

For the director of music. A psalm of David.

1 O LORD, the king rejoices in your
    strength.
How great is his joy in the victories
    you give!
2 You have granted him the desire of
    his heart
    and have not withheld the request
    of his lips.   *Selah*
3 You welcomed him with rich blessings
    and placed a crown of pure gold on
    his head.
4 He asked you for life, and you gave it
    to him—
    length of days, for ever and ever.
5 Through the victories you gave, his
    glory is great;
    you have bestowed on him
    splendour and majesty.
6 Surely you have granted him eternal
    blessings

---

*a*9 Or *save! / O King, answer*

and made him glad with the joy of
  your presence.
7 For the king trusts in the LORD;
  through the unfailing love of the
    Most High
  he will not be shaken.

8 Your hand will lay hold on all your
  enemies;
  your right hand will seize your foes.
9 At the time of your appearing
  you will make them like a fiery
    furnace.
In his wrath the LORD will swallow
  them up,
  and his fire will consume them.
10 You will destroy their descendants
  from the earth,
  their posterity from the human
    race.
11 Though they plot evil against you
  and devise wicked schemes, they
    cannot succeed;
12 for you will make them turn their backs
  when you aim at them with drawn
    bow.

13 Be exalted, O LORD, in your strength;
  we will sing and praise your might.

Psalm 22

*For the director of music. To ⌊the tune of⌋ "The Doe
of the Morning". A psalm of David.*

1 My God, my God, why have you
  forsaken me?
Why are you so far from saving me,
  so far from the words of my
    groaning?
2 O my God, I cry out by day, but you
  do not answer,
  by night, and am not silent.

3 Yet you are enthroned as the Holy
  One;
  you are the praise of Israel.*a*
4 In you our ancestors put their trust;
  they trusted and you delivered them.
5 They cried to you and were saved;
  in you they trusted and were not
    disappointed.

6 But I am a worm and not a human
  being,
  scorned by everyone and despised
    by the people.
7 All who see me mock me;
  they hurl insults, shaking their heads:
8 "He trusts in the LORD;
  let the LORD rescue him.
Let him deliver him,
  since he delights in him."

9 Yet you brought me out of the womb;
  you made me trust in you
  even at my mother's breast.
10 From birth I was cast upon you;
  from my mother's womb you have
    been my God.
11 Do not be far from me,
  for trouble is near
  and there is no-one to help.

12 Many bulls surround me;
  strong bulls of Bashan encircle me.
13 Roaring lions tearing their prey
  open their mouths wide against me.
14 I am poured out like water,
  and all my bones are out of joint.
My heart has turned to wax;
  it has melted away within me.
15 My strength is dried up like a
    potsherd,
  and my tongue sticks to the roof of
    my mouth;
  you lay me*b* in the dust of death.
16 Dogs have surrounded me;
  a band of evil people has encircled
    me,
  they have pierced*c* my hands and
    my feet.
17 I can count all my bones;
  people stare and gloat over me.
18 They divide my garments among them
  and cast lots for my clothing.

19 But you, O LORD, be not far off;
  O my Strength, come quickly to
    help me.
20 Deliver my life from the sword,
  my precious life from the power of
    the dogs.

*a*3 Or *Yet you are holy, / enthroned on the praises of Israel*   *b*15 Or / *I am laid*
*c*16 Some Hebrew manuscripts, Septuagint and Syriac; most Hebrew manuscripts / *like the lion,*

²¹ Rescue me from the mouth of the lions;
  save*d* me from the horns of the wild
    oxen.

²² I will declare your name to my people;
  in the congregation I will praise you.
²³ You who fear the LORD, praise him!
  All you descendants of Jacob,
    honour him!
  Revere him, all you descendants of
    Israel!
²⁴ For he has not despised or disdained
  the suffering of the afflicted one;
  he has not hidden his face from him
  but has listened to his cry for help.

²⁵ From you comes the theme of my
    praise in the great assembly;
  before those who fear you*e* will I
    fulfil my vows.
²⁶ The poor will eat and be satisfied;
    they who seek the LORD will praise
      him—
    may your hearts live for ever!
²⁷ All the ends of the earth
    will remember and turn to the
      LORD,
  and all the families of the nations
    will bow down before him,
²⁸ for dominion belongs to the LORD
    and he rules over the nations.

²⁹ All the rich of the earth will feast and
    worship;
    all who go down to the dust will
      kneel before him—
    those who cannot keep themselves
      alive.
³⁰ Posterity will serve him;
    future generations will be told
      about the Lord.
³¹ They will proclaim his righteousness
    to a people yet unborn—
    for he has done it.

Psalm 23

A psalm of David.

¹ The LORD is my shepherd, I shall not
    be in want.
²   He makes me lie down in green
        pastures,

he leads me beside quiet waters,
³   he restores my soul.
  He guides me in paths of
      righteousness
    for his name's sake.
⁴ Even though I walk
    through the valley of the shadow of
      death,*a*
  I will fear no evil,
    for you are with me;
  your rod and your staff,
    they comfort me.

⁵ You prepare a table before me
    in the presence of my enemies.
  You anoint my head with oil;
    my cup overflows.
⁶ Surely goodness and love will follow
      me
    all the days of my life,
  and I will dwell in the house of the LORD
    for ever.

Psalm 24

Of David. A psalm.

¹ The earth is the LORD's, and
    everything in it,
    the world, and all who live in it;
² for he founded it upon the seas
    and established it upon the waters.

³ Who may ascend the hill of the
      LORD?
  Who may stand in his holy place?
⁴ Those who have clean hands and pure
      hearts,
    who do not lift up their souls to an
      idol
    or swear by what is false.*a*
⁵ They will receive blessing from the
      LORD
    and vindication from God their
      Saviour.
⁶ Such is the generation of those who
      seek him,
    who seek your face, O God of
      Jacob.*b*   *Selah*

⁷ Lift up your heads, O you gates;
    be lifted up, you ancient doors,
    that the King of glory may come in.

---

*d*21 Or *I you have heard*   *e*25 Hebrew *him*   *a*4 Or *through the darkest valley*   *a*4 Or *swear falsely*
*b*6 Two Hebrew manuscripts and Syriac (see also Septuagint); most Hebrew manuscripts *face, Jacob*

8 Who is this King of glory?
The LORD strong and mighty,
the LORD mighty in battle.
9 Lift up your heads, O you gates;
lift them up, you ancient doors,
that the King of glory may come in.
10 Who is he, this King of glory?
The LORD Almighty—
he is the King of glory.   *Selah*

Psalm 25 [a]

Of David.

1 To you, O LORD, I lift up my soul;
2   in you I trust, O my God.
Do not let me be put to shame,
nor let my enemies triumph over me.
3 No-one whose hope is in you
will ever be put to shame,
but they will be put to shame
who are treacherous without excuse.

4 Show me your ways, O LORD,
teach me your paths;
5 guide me in your truth and teach me,
for you are God my Saviour,
and my hope is in you all day long.
6 Remember, O LORD, your great
mercy and love,
for they are from of old.
7 Remember not the sins of my youth
and my rebellious ways;
according to your love remember me,
for you are good, O LORD.

8 Good and upright is the LORD;
therefore he instructs sinners in his
ways.
9 He guides the humble in what is right
and teaches them his way.
10 All the ways of the LORD are loving
and faithful
for those who keep the demands of
his covenant.
11 For the sake of your name, O LORD,
forgive my iniquity, though it is
great.
12 Who, then, are those who fear the
LORD?
He will instruct them in the way
chosen for them.

13 They will spend their days in
prosperity,
and their descendants will inherit
the land.
14 The LORD confides in those who fear
him;
he makes his covenant known to
them.
15 My eyes are ever on the LORD,
for only he will release my feet from
the snare.

16 Turn to me and be gracious to me,
for I am lonely and afflicted.
17 The troubles of my heart have
multiplied;
free me from my anguish.
18 Look upon my affliction and my
distress
and take away all my sins.
19 See how my enemies have
increased
and how fiercely they hate me!
20 Guard my life and rescue me;
let me not be put to shame,
for I take refuge in you.
21 May integrity and uprightness protect
me,
because my hope is in you.

22 Redeem Israel, O God,
from all their troubles!

Psalm 26

Of David.

1 Vindicate me, O LORD,
for I have led a blameless life;
I have trusted in the LORD
without wavering.
2 Test me, O LORD, and try me,
examine my heart and my mind;
3 for your love is ever before me,
and I walk continually in your
truth.
4 I do not sit with the deceitful,
nor do I consort with hypocrites;
5 I abhor the assembly of evildoers
and refuse to sit with the wicked.
6 I wash my hands in innocence,
and go about your altar, O LORD,
7 proclaiming aloud your praise

[a] This psalm is an acrostic poem, the verses of which begin with the successive letters of the Hebrew alphabet.

and telling of all your wonderful
   deeds.
8 I love the house where you live,
   O LORD,
   the place where your glory dwells.

9 Do not take away my soul along with
   sinners,
   my life with those who are
   bloodthirsty,
10 in whose hands are wicked schemes,
   whose right hands are full of
   bribes.
11 But I lead a blameless life;
   redeem me and be merciful to me.

12 My feet stand on level ground;
   in the great assembly I will praise
   the LORD.

Psalm 27

Of David.

1 The LORD is my light and my
   salvation—
   whom shall I fear?
The LORD is the stronghold of my
   life—
   of whom shall I be afraid?
2 When the wicked advance against me
   to devour my flesh,*a*
when my enemies and my foes attack
   me,
   they will stumble and fall.
3 Though an army besiege me,
   my heart will not fear;
though war break out against me,
   even then will I be confident.

4 One thing I ask of the LORD,
   this is what I seek:
that I may dwell in the house of the
   LORD
   all the days of my life,
to gaze upon the beauty of the LORD
   and to seek him in his temple.
5 For in the day of trouble
   he will keep me safe in his dwelling;
he will hide me in the shelter of his
   tabernacle
   and set me high upon a rock.
6 Then my head will be exalted

above the enemies who surround
   me;
at his tabernacle will I sacrifice with
   shouts of joy;
   I will sing and make music to the
   LORD.

7 Hear my voice when I call, O LORD;
   be merciful to me and answer me.
8 My heart says of you, "Seek his*b*
   face!"
   Your face, LORD, I will seek.
9 Do not hide your face from me,
   do not turn your servant away in
   anger;
   you have been my helper.
Do not reject me or forsake me,
   O God my Saviour.
10 Though my father and mother forsake
   me,
   the LORD will receive me.
11 Teach me your way, O LORD;
   lead me in a straight path
   because of my oppressors.
12 Do not hand me over to the desire of
   my foes,
   for false witnesses rise up against
   me,
   breathing out violence.

13 I am still confident of this:
   I will see the goodness of the LORD
   in the land of the living.
14 Wait for the LORD;
   be strong and take heart
   and wait for the LORD.

Psalm 28

Of David.

1 To you I call, O LORD my Rock;
   do not turn a deaf ear to me.
For if you remain silent,
   I shall be like those who have gone
   down to the pit.
2 Hear my cry for mercy
   as I call to you for help,
as I lift up my hands
   towards your Most Holy Place.

3 Do not drag me away with the wicked,
   with those who do evil,

---

*a*2 Or *to slander me*   *b*8 Or *To you, O my heart, he has said, "Seek my*

who speak cordially with their
neighbours
but harbour malice in their hearts.
4 Repay them for their deeds
and for their evil work;
repay them for what their hands have
done
and bring back upon them what
they deserve.
5 Since they show no regard for the
works of the LORD
and what his hands have done,
he will tear them down
and never build them up again.

6 Praise be to the LORD,
for he has heard my cry for mercy.
7 The LORD is my strength and my shield;
my heart trusts in him, and I am
helped.
My heart leaps for joy
and I will give thanks to him in song.

8 The LORD is the strength of his people,
a fortress of salvation for his
anointed one.
9 Save your people and bless your
inheritance;
be their shepherd and carry them
for ever.

Psalm 29

A psalm of David.

1 Ascribe to the LORD, O mighty ones,
ascribe to the LORD glory and
strength.
2 Ascribe to the LORD the glory due to
his name;
worship the LORD in the splendour
of his*a* holiness.

3 The voice of the LORD is over the
waters;
the God of glory thunders,
the LORD thunders over the mighty
waters.
4 The voice of the LORD is powerful;
the voice of the LORD is majestic.
5 The voice of the LORD breaks the
cedars;

the LORD breaks in pieces the
cedars of Lebanon.
6 He makes Lebanon skip like a calf,
Sirion*b* like a young wild ox.
7 The voice of the LORD strikes
with flashes of lightning.
8 The voice of the LORD shakes the
desert;
the LORD shakes the Desert of
Kadesh.
9 The voice of the LORD twists the oaks*c*
and strips the forests bare.
And in his temple all cry, "Glory!"

10 The LORD sits*d* enthroned over the
flood;
the LORD is enthroned as King for
ever.
11 The LORD gives strength to his
people;
the LORD blesses his people with
peace.

Psalm 30

*A psalm. A song. For the dedication of the temple.*a
Of David.

1 I will exalt you, O LORD,
for you lifted me out of the
depths
and did not let my enemies gloat
over me.
2 O LORD my God, I called to you for
help
and you healed me.
3 O LORD, you brought me up from the
grave;*b*
you spared me from going down
into the pit.

4 Sing to the LORD, you saints of his;
praise his holy name.
5 For his anger lasts only a moment,
but his favour lasts a lifetime;
weeping may remain for a night,
but rejoicing comes in the
morning.

6 When I felt secure, I said,
"I shall never be shaken."
7 O LORD, when you favoured me,

---

*a*2 Or LORD *with the splendour of*　　*b*6 That is, Mount Hermon　　*c*9 Or LORD *makes the deer give birth*
*d*10 Or *sat*　　*a*Title: Or *palace*　　*b*3 Hebrew *Sheol*

you made my mountain[c] stand firm;
but when you hid your face,
  I was dismayed.

8 To you, O Lord, I called;
  to the Lord I cried for mercy:
9 "What gain is there in my
    destruction,[d]
  in my going down into the pit?
Will the dust praise you?
  Will it proclaim your faithfulness?
10 Hear, O Lord, and be merciful to me;
  O Lord, be my help."

11 You turned my wailing into dancing;
  you removed my sackcloth and
    clothed me with joy,
12 that my heart may sing to you and not
  be silent.
  O Lord my God, I will give you
    thanks for ever.

Psalm 31

For the director of music. A psalm of David.

1 In you, O Lord, I have taken refuge;
  let me never be put to shame;
  deliver me in your righteousness.
2 Turn your ear to me,
  come quickly to my rescue;
  be my rock of refuge,
  a strong fortress to save me.
3 Since you are my rock and my
    fortress,
  for the sake of your name lead and
    guide me.
4 Free me from the trap that is set for
  me,
  for you are my refuge.
5 Into your hands I commit my spirit;
  redeem me, O Lord, the God of
    truth.

6 I hate those who cling to worthless
    idols;
  I trust in the Lord.
7 I will be glad and rejoice in your love,
  for you saw my affliction
  and knew the anguish of my soul.
8 You have not handed me over to the
  enemy

but have set my feet in a spacious
  place.

9 Be merciful to me, O Lord, for I am
  in distress;
  my eyes grow weak with sorrow,
  my soul and my body with grief.
10 My life is consumed by anguish
  and my years by groaning;
  my strength fails because of my
    affliction,[a]
  and my bones grow weak.
11 Because of all my enemies,
  I am the utter contempt of my
    neighbours;
  I am a dread to my friends—
  those who see me on the street flee
    from me.
12 I am forgotten by them as though I
  were dead;
  I have become like broken
    pottery.
13 For I hear the slander of many;
  there is terror on every side;
  they conspire against me
  and plot to take my life.

14 But I trust in you, O Lord;
  I say, "You are my God."
15 My times are in your hands;
  deliver me from my enemies
  and from those who pursue me.
16 Let your face shine on your servant;
  save me in your unfailing love.
17 Let me not be put to shame, O Lord,
  for I have cried out to you;
  but let the wicked be put to shame
  and lie silent in the grave.[b]
18 Let their lying lips be silenced,
  for with pride and contempt
  they speak arrogantly against the
    righteous.

19 How great is your goodness,
  which you have stored up for those
    who fear you,
  which you bestow in the sight of all
    on those who take refuge in you.
20 In the shelter of your presence you
  hide them
  from human intrigues;

---

[c]7 Or *hill country*   [d]9 Or *there if I am silenced*   [a]10 Or *guilt*   [b]17 Hebrew *Sheol*

in your dwelling you keep them safe
 from accusing tongues.

21 Praise be to the LORD,
   for he showed his wonderful love to
     me
   when I was in a besieged city.
22 In my alarm I said,
   "I am cut off from your sight!"
 Yet you heard my cry for mercy
   when I called to you for help.

23 Love the LORD, all his saints!
   The LORD preserves the faithful,
   but the proud he pays back in full.
24 Be strong and take heart,
   all you who hope in the LORD.

Psalm 32

Of David. A maskil.[a]

1 Blessed are those
   whose transgressions are forgiven,
   whose sins are covered.
2 Blessed are those
   whose sin the LORD does not count
     against them
   and in whose spirit is no deceit.

3 When I kept silent,
   my bones wasted away
   through my groaning all day long.
4 For day and night
   your hand was heavy upon me;
 my strength was sapped
   as in the heat of summer.   *Selah*
5 Then I acknowledged my sin to
     you
   and did not cover up my iniquity.
 I said, "I will confess
   my transgressions to the LORD"—
 and you forgave
   the guilt of my sin.   *Selah*

6 Therefore let everyone who is godly
     pray to you
   while you may be found;
 surely the rising of the mighty waters
   will not reach them.
7 You are my hiding-place;

you will protect me from trouble
 and surround me with songs of
   deliverance.   *Selah*

8 I will instruct you and teach you in the
     way you should go;
   I will counsel you and watch over
     you.
9 Do not be like the horse or the mule,
   which have no understanding
 but must be controlled by bit and
     bridle
   or they will not come to you.
10 Many are the woes of the wicked,
   but the LORD's unfailing love
   surrounds those who trust in him.

11 Rejoice in the LORD and be glad, you
     righteous;
   sing, all you who are upright in
     heart!

Psalm 33

1 Sing joyfully to the LORD, you
     righteous;
   it is fitting for the upright to praise
     him.
2 Praise the LORD with the harp;
   make music to him on the
     ten-stringed lyre.
3 Sing to him a new song;
   play skilfully, and shout for joy.

4 For the word of the LORD is right and
     true;
   he is faithful in all he does.
5 The LORD loves righteousness and
     justice;
   the earth is full of his unfailing love.

6 By the word of the LORD were the
     heavens made,
   their starry host by the breath of his
     mouth.
7 He gathers the waters of the sea into
     jars;[a]
   he puts the deep into storehouses.
8 Let all the earth fear the LORD;
   let all the people of the world revere
     him.

---

[a] Title: Probably a literary or musical term   [a]7 Or *sea as into a heap*

9 For he spoke, and it came to be;
  he commanded, and it stood firm.
10 The LORD foils the plans of the
   nations;
   he thwarts the purposes of the
   peoples.
11 But the plans of the LORD stand firm
   for ever,
   the purposes of his heart through all
   generations.

12 Blessed is the nation whose God is the
   LORD,
   the people he chose for his
   inheritance.
13 From heaven the LORD looks down
   and sees all humanity;
14 from his dwelling-place he watches
   all who live on earth—
15 he who forms the hearts of all,
   who considers everything they do.
16 No king is saved by the size of his
   army;
   no warrior escapes by his great
   strength.
17 A horse is a vain hope for deliverance;
   despite all its great strength it
   cannot save.
18 But the eyes of the LORD are on those
   who fear him,
   on those whose hope is in his
   unfailing love,
19 to deliver them from death
   and keep them alive in famine.

20 We wait in hope for the LORD;
   he is our help and our shield.
21 In him our hearts rejoice,
   for we trust in his holy name.
22 May your unfailing love rest upon us,
   O LORD,
   even as we put our hope in you.

Psalm 34[a]

*Of David. When he pretended to be insane before
Abimelech, who drove him away, and he left.*

1 I will extol the LORD at all times;
  his praise will always be on my lips.
2 My soul will boast in the LORD;
  let the afflicted hear and rejoice.

3 Glorify the LORD with me:
  let us exalt his name together.

4 I sought the LORD, and he answered me;
  he delivered me from all my fears.
5 Those who look to him are radiant;
  their faces are never covered with
  shame.
6 This poor man called, and the LORD
  heard him;
  he saved him out of all his troubles.
7 The angel of the LORD encamps
  around those who fear him,
  and he delivers them.

8 Taste and see that the LORD is good;
  blessed are those who take refuge
  in him.
9 Fear the LORD, you his saints,
  for those who fear him lack nothing.
10 The lions may grow weak and hungry,
   but those who seek the LORD lack
   no good thing.

11 Come, my children, listen to me;
   I will teach you the fear of the LORD.
12 Whoever among you loves life
   and desires to see many good days,
13 keep your tongue from evil
   and your lips from speaking lies.
14 Turn from evil and do good;
   seek peace and pursue it.

15 The eyes of the LORD are on the
   righteous
   and his ears are attentive to their
   cry;
16 the face of the LORD is against those
   who do evil,
   to cut off the memory of them from
   the earth.

17 The righteous cry out, and the LORD
   hears them;
   he delivers them from all their
   troubles.
18 The LORD is close to the broken-
   hearted
   and saves those who are crushed in
   spirit.

---

[a] This psalm is an acrostic poem, the verses of which begin with the successive letters of the Hebrew alphabet.

¹⁹ The righteous may have many troubles,
  but the LORD delivers them from them all;
²⁰ he protects all their bones,
  not one of them will be broken.

²¹ Evil will slay the wicked;
  the foes of the righteous will be condemned.
²² The LORD redeems his servants;
  no-one will be condemned who takes refuge in him.

Psalm 35

Of David.

¹ Contend, O LORD, with those who contend with me;
  fight against those who fight against me.
² Take up shield and buckler;
  arise and come to my aid.
³ Brandish spear and javelin[a]
  against those who pursue me.
 Say to my soul,
  "I am your salvation."

⁴ May those who seek my life
  be disgraced and put to shame;
 may those who plot my ruin
  be turned back in dismay.
⁵ May they be like chaff before the wind,
  with the angel of the LORD driving them away;
⁶ may their path be dark and slippery,
  with the angel of the LORD pursuing them.
⁷ Since they hid their net for me without cause
  and without cause dug a pit for me,
⁸ may ruin overtake them by surprise—
  may the net they hid entangle them,
  may they fall into the pit, to their ruin.
⁹ Then my soul will rejoice in the LORD
  and delight in his salvation.
¹⁰ My whole being will exclaim,
  "Who is like you, O LORD?
 You rescue the poor from those too strong for them,

the poor and needy from those who rob them."

¹¹ Ruthless witnesses come forward;
  they question me on things I know nothing about.
¹² They repay me evil for good
  and leave my soul forlorn.
¹³ Yet when they were ill, I put on sackcloth
  and humbled myself with fasting.
 When my prayers returned to me unanswered,
¹⁴ I went about mourning
  as though for my friend or brother.
 I bowed my head in grief
  as though weeping for my mother.
¹⁵ But when I stumbled, they gathered in glee;
  attackers gathered against me when I was unaware.
 They slandered me without ceasing.
¹⁶ Like the ungodly they maliciously mocked;[b]
  they gnashed their teeth at me.
¹⁷ O Lord, how long will you look on?
  Rescue my life from their ravages,
  my precious life from these lions.
¹⁸ I will give you thanks in the great assembly;
  among throngs of people I will praise you.

¹⁹ Let not those gloat over me
  who are my enemies without cause;
 let not those who hate me without reason
  maliciously wink the eye.
²⁰ They do not speak peaceably,
  but devise false accusations
 against those who live quietly in the land.
²¹ They gape at me and say, "Aha! Aha!
  With our own eyes we have seen it."

²² O LORD, you have seen this; be not silent.
  Do not be far from me, O Lord.
²³ Awake, and rise to my defence!
  Contend for me, my God and Lord.

---

*a*3 Or *and block the way*   *b*16 Septuagint; Hebrew may mean *ungodly circle of mockers.*

24 Vindicate me in your righteousness,
   O Lord my God;
do not let them gloat over me.
25 Do not let them think, "Aha, just
   what we wanted!"
   or say, "We have swallowed him
   up."

26 May all who gloat over my distress
   be put to shame and confusion;
   may all who exalt themselves over me
   be clothed with shame and disgrace.
27 May those who delight in my
   vindication
   shout for joy and gladness;
   may they always say, "The Lord be
   exalted,
   who delights in the well-being of his
   servant."
28 My tongue will speak of your
   righteousness
   and of your praises all day long.

Psalm 36

*For the director of music. Of David the
servant of the Lord.*

1 An oracle is within my heart
   concerning the sinfulness of the
   wicked:*a*
There is no fear of God
   before their eyes.
2 For in their own eyes they flatter
   themselves
   too much to detect or hate their sin.
3 The words of their mouths are wicked
   and deceitful;
   they have ceased to be wise and to
   do good.
4 Even on their beds they plot evil;
   they commit themselves to a sinful
   course
   and do not reject what is wrong.

5 Your love, O Lord, reaches to the
   heavens,
   your faithfulness to the skies.
6 Your righteousness is like the mighty
   mountains,
   your justice like the great deep.

O Lord, you preserve both people
   and animals.
7   How priceless is your unfailing
   love!
Both highborn and low
   find*b* refuge in the shadow of your
   wings.
8 They feast in the abundance of your
   house;
   you give them drink from your river
   of delights.
9 For with you is the fountain of life;
   in your light we see light.

10 Continue your love to those who
   know you,
   your righteousness to the upright in
   heart.
11 May the foot of the proud not come
   against me,
   nor the hand of the wicked drive me
   away.
12 See how the evildoers lie fallen—
   thrown down, not able to rise!

Psalm 37*a*

Of David.

1 Do not fret because of those who are
   evil
   or be envious of those who do wrong;
2 for like the grass they will soon wither,
   like green plants they will soon die
   away.

3 Trust in the Lord and do good;
   dwell in the land and enjoy safe
   pasture.
4 Delight yourself in the Lord
   and he will give you the desires of
   your heart.

5 Commit your way to the Lord;
   trust in him and he will do this:
6 He will make your righteousness shine
   like the dawn,
   the justice of your cause like the
   noonday sun.

7 Be still before the Lord and wait
   patiently for him;

*a*1 Or *heart: / Sin proceeds from the wicked.*
*b*7 Or *love, O God! / Human beings find*; or *love! / Both heavenly and earthly beings / find*
*a*This psalm is an acrostic poem, the stanzas of which begin with the successive letters of the Hebrew alphabet.

do not fret when people succeed in
   their ways,
when they carry out their wicked
   schemes.

8 Refrain from anger and turn from
   wrath;
   do not fret—it leads only to evil.
9 For those who are evil will be cut off,
   but those who hope in the LORD will
     inherit the land.

10 A little while, and the wicked will be
   no more;
   though you look for them, they will
     not be found.
11 But the meek will inherit the land
   and enjoy great peace.

12 The wicked plot against the righteous
   and gnash their teeth at them;
13 but the Lord laughs at the wicked,
   for he knows their day is coming.

14 The wicked draw the sword
   and bend the bow
to bring down the poor and needy,
   to slay those whose ways are
     upright.
15 But their swords will pierce their own
   hearts,
   and their bows will be broken.

16 Better the little that the righteous
   have
   than the wealth of many wicked;
17 for the power of the wicked will be
   broken,
   but the LORD upholds the righteous.

18 The days of the blameless are known
   to the LORD,
   and their inheritance will endure
     for ever.
19 In times of disaster they will not
   wither;
   in days of famine they will enjoy
     plenty.

20 But the wicked will perish:
   The LORD's enemies will be like the
     beauty of the fields,
   they will vanish—vanish like smoke.

21 The wicked borrow and do not repay,
   but the righteous give generously;
22 those the LORD blesses will inherit the
   land,
   but those he curses will be cut off.

23 The LORD makes firm the steps
   of those who delight in him;
24 though they stumble, they will not fall,
   for the LORD upholds them with his
     hand.

25 I was young and now I am old,
   yet I have never seen the righteous
     forsaken
   or their children begging bread.
26 They are always generous and lend
   freely;
   their children will be blessed.

27 Turn from evil and do good;
   then you will dwell in the land for
     ever.
28 For the LORD loves the just
   and will not forsake his faithful
     ones.

They will be protected for ever,
   but the offspring of the wicked will
     be cut off;
29 the righteous will inherit the land
   and dwell in it for ever.

30 The mouths of the righteous utter
   wisdom,
   and their tongues speak what is
     just.
31 The law of their God is in their hearts;
   their feet do not slip.

32 The wicked lie in wait for the
   righteous,
   seeking their very lives;
33 but the LORD will not leave them in
   their power
   or let them be condemned when
     brought to trial.

34 Wait for the LORD
   and keep his way.
He will exalt you to inherit the land;
   when the wicked are cut off, you
     will see it.

35 I have seen the wicked and ruthless
   flourishing like a green tree in its
   native soil,
36 but they soon passed away and were
   no more;
      though I looked for them, they
      could not be found.

37 Consider the blameless, observe the
   upright;
      there is a future*b* for those who seek
      peace.
38 But all sinners will be destroyed;
      the future*c* of the wicked will be cut
      off.

39 The salvation of the righteous comes
   from the LORD;
      he is their stronghold in time of
      trouble.
40 The LORD helps them and delivers
   them;
      he delivers them from the wicked
      and saves them,
      because they take refuge in him.

Psalm 38

A psalm of David. A petition.

1 O LORD, do not rebuke me in your
   anger
   or discipline me in your wrath.
2 For your arrows have pierced me,
      and your hand has come down upon
      me.
3 Because of your wrath there is no
      health in my body;
      my bones have no soundness
      because of my sin.
4 My guilt has overwhelmed me
   like a burden too heavy to bear.

5 My wounds fester and are loathsome
   because of my sinful folly.
6 I am bowed down and brought very
   low;
      all day long I go about mourning.
7 My back is filled with searing pain;
      there is no health in my body.
8 I am feeble and utterly crushed;
      I groan in anguish of heart.

9 All my longings lie open before you,
   O Lord:
      my sighing is not hidden from you.
10 My heart pounds, my strength fails
    me;
      even the light has gone from my
      eyes.
11 My friends and companions avoid me
      because of my wounds;
      my neighbours stay far away.
12 Those who seek my life set their traps,
      those who would harm me talk of
      my ruin;
      all day long they plot deception.

13 I am like the deaf, who cannot hear,
      like the mute, who cannot
      speak;
14 I have become like one who does not
      hear,
      whose mouth can offer no reply.
15 I wait for you, O LORD;
      you will answer, O Lord my God.
16 For I said, "Do not let them gloat
      or exalt themselves over me when
      my foot slips."

17 For I am about to fall,
      and my pain is ever with me.
18 I confess my iniquity;
      I am troubled by my sin.
19 Many are those who are my vigorous
      enemies;
      those who hate me without reason
      are numerous.
20 Those who repay my good with evil
      slander me when I pursue what is
      good.

21 O LORD, do not forsake me;
      be not far from me, O my God.
22 Come quickly to help me,
      O Lord my Saviour.

Psalm 39

*For the director of music. For Jeduthun. A psalm
of David.*

1 I said, "I will watch my ways
      and keep my tongue from sin;
      I will put a muzzle on my mouth

---

*b*37 Or *there will be posterity*   *c*38 Or *posterity*

as long as the wicked are in my
    presence."
2 But when I was silent and still,
    not even saying anything good,
    my anguish increased.
3 My heart grew hot within me,
    and as I meditated, the fire burned;
    then I spoke with my tongue:

4 "Show me, O LORD, my life's end
    and the number of my days;
    let me know how fleeting is my life.
5 You have made my days a mere
    handbreadth;
    the span of my years is as nothing
      before you.
    Everyone's life is but a breath. *Selah*
6 Human beings are mere phantoms
    as they go to and fro:
    They bustle about, but only in
      vain;
    they heap up wealth, not knowing
      who will get it.

7 "But now, Lord, what do I look for?
    My hope is in you.
8 Save me from all my transgressions;
    do not make me the scorn of fools.
9 I was silent; I would not open my
    mouth,
    for you are the one who has done
      this.
10 Remove your scourge from me;
    I am overcome by the blow of your
      hand.
11 You rebuke and discipline people for
    their sins;
    you consume their wealth like a
      moth—
    every mortal is but a breath.   *Selah*

12 "Hear my prayer, O LORD,
    listen to my cry for help;
    be not deaf to my weeping.
    For I dwell with you as an alien,
    a stranger, as all my ancestors
      were.
13 Look away from me, that I may
    rejoice again
    before I depart and am no more."

Psalm 40

For the director of music. Of David. A psalm.

1 I waited patiently for the LORD;
    he turned to me and heard my cry.
2 He lifted me out of the slimy pit,
    out of the mud and mire;
    he set my feet on a rock
    and gave me a firm place to stand.
3 He put a new song in my mouth,
    a hymn of praise to our God.
    Many will see and fear
    and put their trust in the LORD.

4 Blessed are those
    who make the LORD their trust,
    who do not look to the proud,
    to those who turn aside to false
      gods.*a*
5 Many, O LORD my God,
    are the wonders you have done.
    The things you planned for us
    no-one can recount to you;
    were I to speak and tell of them,
    they would be too many to declare.

6 Sacrifice and offering you did not
    desire,
    but my ears you have pierced;*b, c*
    burnt offerings and sin offerings
    you did not require.
7 Then I said, "Here I am, I have come—
    it is written about me in the scroll.*d*
8 I desire to do your will, O my God;
    your law is within my heart."

9 I proclaim righteousness in the great
    assembly;
    I do not seal my lips,
    as you know, O LORD.
10 I do not hide your righteousness in my
    heart;
    I speak of your faithfulness and
      salvation.
    I do not conceal your love and your
      truth
    from the great assembly.

11 Do not withhold your mercy from me,
    O LORD;

---

*a*4 Or *to falsehood*
*b*6 Hebrew; Septuagint *but a body you have prepared for me* (see also Symmachus and Theodotion)   *c*6 Or *opened*
*d*7 Or *come / with the scroll written for me*

may your love and your truth
    always protect me.
[12] For troubles without number
    surround me;
    my sins have overtaken me, and I
      cannot see.
They are more than the hairs of my
    head,
    and my heart fails within me.

[13] Be pleased, O LORD, to save me;
    O LORD, come quickly to help me.
[14] May all who seek to take my life
    be put to shame and confusion;
    may all who desire my ruin
    be turned back in disgrace.
[15] May those who say to me, "Aha!
    Aha!"
    be appalled at their own shame.
[16] But may all who seek you
    rejoice and be glad in you;
    may those who love your salvation
    always say,
    "The LORD be exalted!"

[17] Yet I am poor and needy;
    may the Lord think of me.
You are my help and my deliverer;
    O my God, do not delay.

Psalm 41

For the director of music. A psalm of David.

[1] Blessed are those who have regard for
    the weak;
    the LORD delivers them in times of
    trouble.
[2] The LORD will protect them and
    preserve their lives;
    he will bless them in the land
    and not surrender them to the
    desire of their foes.
[3] The LORD will sustain them on their
    sick-bed
    and restore them from their bed of
    illness.

[4] I said, "O LORD, have mercy on me;
    heal me, for I have sinned against
    you."
[5] My enemies say of me in malice,

"When will he die and his name
    perish?"
[6] Whenever they come to see me,
    they speak falsely, while their
    hearts gather slander;
    then they go out and spread it
    abroad.

[7] All my enemies whisper together
    against me;
    they imagine the worst for me,
    saying,
[8] "A vile disease has beset him;
    he will never get up from the place
    where he lies."
[9] Even my close friend, whom I
    trusted,
    he who shared my bread,
    has lifted up his heel against me.

[10] But you, O LORD, have mercy on me;
    raise me up, that I may repay them.
[11] I know that you are pleased with me,
    for my enemy does not triumph
    over me.
[12] In my integrity you uphold me
    and set me in your presence for
    ever.

[13] Praise be to the LORD, the God of
    Israel,
    from everlasting to everlasting.
    Amen and Amen.

BOOK II

Psalms 42–72

Psalm 42 [a]

*For the director of music. A maskil[b] of the
Sons of Korah.*

[1] As the deer pants for streams of
    water,
    so my soul pants for you, O God.
[2] My soul thirsts for God, for the living
    God.
    When can I go and meet with God?
[3] My tears have been my food
    day and night,

---

[a] In many Hebrew manuscripts Psalms 42 and 43 constitute one psalm.
[b] Title: Probably a literary or musical term

while people say to me all day long,
    "Where is your God?"
[4] These things I remember
    as I pour out my soul:
how I used to go with the multitude,
    leading the procession to the house
        of God,
with shouts of joy and thanksgiving
    among the festive throng.

[5] Why are you downcast, O my soul?
    Why so disturbed within me?
Put your hope in God,
    for I will yet praise him,
    my Saviour and [6] my God.

My[c] soul is downcast within me;
    therefore I will remember you
from the land of the Jordan,
    the heights of Hermon—from
        Mount Mizar.
[7] Deep calls to deep
    in the roar of your waterfalls;
all your waves and breakers
    have swept over me.

[8] By day the LORD directs his love,
    at night his song is with me—
    a prayer to the God of my life.

[9] I say to God my Rock,
    "Why have you forgotten me?
Why must I go about mourning,
    oppressed by the enemy?"
[10] My bones suffer mortal agony
    as my foes taunt me,
saying to me all day long,
    "Where is your God?"

[11] Why are you downcast, O my soul?
    Why so disturbed within me?
Put your hope in God,
    for I will yet praise him,
    my Saviour and my God.

Psalm 43[a]

[1] Vindicate me, O God,
    and plead my cause against an
        ungodly nation;

rescue me from those who are
    deceitful and wicked.
[2] You are God my stronghold.
    Why have you rejected me?
Why must I go about mourning,
    oppressed by the enemy?
[3] Send forth your light and your truth,
    let them guide me;
let them bring me to your holy
    mountain,
    to the place where you dwell.
[4] Then will I go to the altar of God,
    to God, my joy and my delight.
I will praise you with the harp,
    O God, my God.

[5] Why are you downcast, O my soul?
    Why so disturbed within me?
Put your hope in God,
    for I will yet praise him,
    my Saviour and my God.

Psalm 44

*For the director of music. Of the Sons of Korah.
A maskil.[a]*

[1] We have heard with our ears, O God;
    our ancestors have told us
what you did in their days,
    in days long ago.
[2] With your hand you drove out the
        nations
    and planted our ancestors;
you crushed the peoples
    and made our ancestors flourish.
[3] It was not by their sword that they won
        the land,
    nor did their arm bring them
        victory;
it was your right hand, your arm,
    and the light of your face, for you
        loved them.

[4] You are my King and my God,
    who decrees[b] victories for Jacob.
[5] Through you we push back our
        enemies;
    through your name we trample our
        foes.

---

[c]5,6 A few Hebrew manuscripts, Septuagint and Syriac; most Hebrew manuscripts *praise him for his saving help.* /
[6]*O my God, my*   [a]In many Hebrew manuscripts Psalms 42 and 43 constitute one psalm.
[a]Title: Probably a literary or musical term   [b]4 Septuagint, Aquila and Syriac; Hebrew *King, O God; / command*

⁶I do not trust in my bow,
my sword does not bring me
victory;
⁷but you give us victory over our
enemies,
you put our adversaries to shame.
⁸In God we make our boast all day long,
and we will praise your name for
ever.   *Selah*

⁹But now you have rejected and
humbled us;
you no longer go out with our armies.
¹⁰You made us retreat before the enemy,
and our adversaries have
plundered us.
¹¹You gave us up to be devoured like
sheep
and have scattered us among the
nations.
¹²You sold your people for a pittance,
gaining nothing from their sale.

¹³You have made us a reproach to our
neighbours,
the scorn and derision of those
around us.
¹⁴You have made us a byword among
the nations;
the peoples shake their heads at us.
¹⁵My disgrace is before me all day long,
and my face is covered with shame
¹⁶at the taunts of those who reproach
and revile me,
because of the enemy, who is bent
on revenge.

¹⁷All this happened to us,
though we had not forgotten you
or been false to your covenant.
¹⁸Our hearts had not turned back;
our feet had not strayed from your
path.
¹⁹But you crushed us and made us a
haunt for jackals
and covered us over with deep
darkness.

²⁰If we had forgotten the name of our
God
or spread out our hands to a foreign
god,

²¹would not God have discovered it,
since he knows the secrets of the
heart?
²²Yet for your sake we face death all day
long;
we are considered as sheep to be
slaughtered.

²³Awake, O Lord! Why do you sleep?
Rouse yourself! Do not reject us
for ever.
²⁴Why do you hide your face
and forget our misery and
oppression?

²⁵We are brought down to the dust;
our bodies cling to the ground.
²⁶Rise up and help us;
redeem us because of your unfailing
love.

Psalm 45

*For the director of music. To ⌐the tune of⌐ "Lilies".
Of the Sons of Korah. A maskil.ᵃ A wedding song.*

¹My heart is stirred by a noble theme
as I recite my verses for the king;
my tongue is the pen of a skilful
writer.

²You are the most excellent of men
and your lips have been anointed
with grace,
since God has blessed you for ever.
³Gird your sword upon your side,
O mighty one;
clothe yourself with splendour and
majesty.
⁴In your majesty ride forth
victoriously
on behalf of truth, humility and
righteousness;
let your right hand display awesome
deeds.
⁵Let your sharp arrows pierce the
hearts of the king's enemies;
let the nations fall beneath your
feet.
⁶Your throne, O God, will last for ever
and ever;
a sceptre of justice will be the
sceptre of your kingdom.

ᵃTitle: Probably a literary or musical term

7 You love righteousness and hate
   wickedness;
   therefore God, your God, has set
   you above your companions
   by anointing you with the oil of joy.
8 All your robes are fragrant with myrrh
   and aloes and cassia;
   from palaces adorned with ivory
   the music of the strings makes you
   glad.
9 Daughters of kings are among your
   honoured women;
   at your right hand is the royal bride
   in gold of Ophir.

10 Listen, O daughter, consider and give
   ear:
   Forget your people and your
   father's house.
11 The king is enthralled by your beauty;
   honour him, for he is your lord.
12 The Daughter of Tyre will come with
   a gift,[b]
   people of wealth will seek your
   favour.
13 All glorious is the princess within ⌞her
   chamber⌟;
   her gown is interwoven with gold.
14 In embroidered garments she is led to
   the king;
   her virgin companions follow her
   and are brought to you.
15 They are led in with joy and gladness;
   they enter the palace of the king.

16 Your sons will take the place of your
   fathers;
   you will make them princes
   throughout the land.
17 I will perpetuate your memory
   through all generations;
   therefore the nations will praise you
   for ever and ever.

Psalm 46

*For the director of music. Of the Sons of Korah.
According to* alamoth.[a] *A song.*

1 God is our refuge and strength,
   an ever-present help in trouble.

2 Therefore we will not fear, though the
   earth give way
   and the mountains fall into the
   heart of the sea,
3 though its waters roar and foam
   and the mountains quake with their
   surging.   *Selah*

4 There is a river whose streams make
   glad the city of God,
   the holy place where the Most High
   dwells.
5 God is within her, she will not fall;
   God will help her at break of day.
6 Nations are in uproar, kingdoms fall;
   he lifts his voice, the earth melts.

7 The LORD Almighty is with us;
   the God of Jacob is our fortress.
                              Selah

8 Come and see the works of the LORD,
   the desolations he has brought on
   the earth.
9 He makes wars cease to the ends of
   the earth;
   he breaks the bow and shatters the
   spear,
   he burns the shields[b] with fire.
10 "Be still, and know that I am God;
   I will be exalted among the nations,
   I will be exalted in the earth."

11 The LORD Almighty is with us;
   the God of Jacob is our fortress.
                              Selah

Psalm 47

*For the director of music. Of the Sons of Korah.
A psalm.*

1 Clap your hands, all you nations;
   shout to God with cries of joy.
2 How awesome is the LORD Most
   High,
   the great King over all the earth!
3 He subdued nations under us,
   peoples under our feet.
4 He chose our inheritance for us,
   the pride of Jacob, whom he loved.
                              Selah

5 God has ascended amid shouts of joy,
    the Lord amid the sounding of
    trumpets.
6 Sing praises to God, sing praises;
    sing praises to our King, sing
    praises.

7 For God is the King of all the earth;
    sing to him a psalm[a] of praise.
8 God reigns over the nations;
    God is seated on his holy throne.
9 The nobles of the nations assemble
    as the people of the God of
    Abraham,
  for the kings[b] of the earth belong to
    God;
    he is greatly exalted.

Psalm 48

A song. A psalm of the Sons of Korah.

1 Great is the Lord, and most worthy
    of praise,
    in the city of our God, his holy
    mountain.
2 It is beautiful in its loftiness,
    the joy of the whole earth.
  Like the utmost heights of Zaphon[a] is
    Mount Zion,
    the[b] city of the Great King.
3 God is in her citadels;
    he has shown himself to be her
    fortress.

4 When the kings joined forces,
    when they advanced together,
5 they saw ⌊her⌋ and were astounded;
    they fled in terror.
6 Trembling seized them there,
    pain like that of a woman in labour.
7 You destroyed them like ships of
    Tarshish
    shattered by an east wind.

8 As we have heard,
    so have we seen
  in the city of the Lord Almighty,
    in the city of our God:
    God makes her secure for ever.
                                        Selah

9 Within your temple, O God,
    we meditate on your unfailing
    love.
10 Like your name, O God,
    your praise reaches to the ends of
    the earth;
    your right hand is filled with
    righteousness.
11 Mount Zion rejoices,
    the villages of Judah are glad
    because of your judgments.

12 Walk about Zion, go round her,
    count her towers,
13 consider well her ramparts,
    view her citadels,
    that you may tell of them to the next
    generation.
14 For this God is our God for ever and
    ever;
    he will be our guide even to the
    end.

Psalm 49

*For the director of music. Of the Sons of Korah.
A psalm.*

1 Hear this, all you peoples;
    listen, all who live in this world,
2 both low and high,
    rich and poor alike:
3 My mouth will speak words of
    wisdom;
    the utterance from my heart will
    give understanding.
4 I will turn my ear to a proverb;
    with the harp I will expound my
    riddle:

5 Why should I fear when evil days
    come,
    when wicked deceivers surround
    me—
6 those who trust in their wealth
    and boast of their great riches?
7 No-one can redeem the life of another
    or give to God a sufficient
    ransom—
8 the ransom for a life is costly,
    no payment is ever enough—

---

[a]7 Or *a maskil* (probably a literary or musical term)   [b]9 Or *shields*
[a]2 *Zaphon* can refer to a sacred mountain or the direction north.
[b]2 Or *earth, / Mount Zion, on the northern side / of the*

⁹that someone should live on for ever
    and not see decay.

¹⁰For all can see that the wise die;
    the foolish and the senseless alike
        perish
    and leave their wealth to others.
¹¹Their tombs will remain their houses*a*
        for ever,
    their dwellings for endless
        generations,
    though they had*b* named lands after
        themselves.

¹²But human beings, despite their
        riches, do not endure;
    they are*c* like the beasts that perish.

¹³This is the fate of those who trust in
        themselves,
    and of their followers, who approve
        their sayings.   *Selah*
¹⁴Like sheep they are destined for the
        grave,*d*
    and death will feed on them.
    The upright will rule over them in the
        morning;
    their forms will decay in the grave,*d*
        far from their princely mansions.
¹⁵But God will redeem my life*e* from the
        grave;
    he will surely take me to himself.
                                        Selah

¹⁶Do not be overawed when others
        grow rich,
    when the splendour of their houses
        increases;
¹⁷for they will take nothing with them
        when they die,
    their splendour will not descend
        with them.
¹⁸Though while they lived they counted
        themselves blessed—
    and people praise you when you
        prosper—
¹⁹they will join those who have gone
        before,
    who will never see the light ⌊of life⌋.

²⁰Human beings who have riches
        without understanding
    are like the beasts that perish.

Psalm 50

A psalm of Asaph.

¹The Mighty One, God, the Lᴏʀᴅ,
    speaks and summons the earth
    from the rising of the sun to the
        place where it sets.
²From Zion, perfect in beauty,
    God shines forth.
³Our God comes and will not be silent;
    a fire devours before him,
    and around him a tempest rages.
⁴He summons the heavens above,
    and the earth, that he may judge his
        people:
⁵"Gather to me my consecrated ones,
    who made a covenant with me by
        sacrifice."
⁶And the heavens proclaim his
        righteousness,
    for God himself is judge.   *Selah*

⁷"Hear, O my people, and I will
        speak,
    O Israel, and I will testify against
        you:
    I am God, your God.
⁸I do not rebuke you for your sacrifices
    or your burnt offerings, which are
        ever before me.
⁹I have no need of a bull from your
        stall
    or of goats from your pens,
¹⁰for every animal of the forest is mine,
    and the cattle on a thousand hills.
¹¹I know every bird in the mountains,
    and the creatures of the field are
        mine.
¹²If I were hungry I would not tell you,
    for the world is mine, and all that is
        in it.
¹³Do I eat the flesh of bulls
    or drink the blood of goats?
¹⁴Sacrifice thank-offerings to God,
    fulfil your vows to the Most High,

*a*11 Septuagint and Syriac; Hebrew *In their thoughts their houses will remain*   *b*11 Or / *for they have*
*c*12 Hebrew; Septuagint and Syriac read verse 12 the same as verse 20.   *d*14 Hebrew *Sheol*; also in verse 15
*e*15 Or *soul*

15 and call upon me in the day of trouble;
 I will deliver you, and you will
  honour me."

16 But to the wicked, God says:

"What right have you to recite my
 laws
 or take my covenant on your lips?
17 You hate my instruction
 and cast my words behind you.
18 When you see thieves, you join with
  them;
 you throw in your lot with
  adulterers.
19 You use your mouth for evil
 and harness your tongue to deceit.
20 You speak continually against your
  brother
 and slander your own mother's son.
21 These things you have done and I kept
  silent;
 you thought I was altogether*a* like
  you.
But I will rebuke you
 and accuse you to your face.

22 "Consider this, you who forget God,
 or I will tear you to pieces, with
  none to rescue:
23 Those who sacrifice thank-offerings
  honour me,
 and they prepare the way
 so that I may show them*b* the
  salvation of God."

Psalm 51

*For the director of music. A psalm of David. When
the prophet Nathan came to him after David had
committed adultery with Bathsheba.*

1 Have mercy on me, O God,
 according to your unfailing love;
according to your great compassion
 blot out my transgressions.
2 Wash away all my iniquity
 and cleanse me from my sin.

3 For I know my transgressions,
 and my sin is always before me.

4 Against you, you only, have I
  sinned
 and done what is evil in your
  sight,
so that you are proved right when you
  speak
 and justified when you judge.
5 Surely I was sinful at birth,
 sinful from the time my mother
  conceived me.
6 Surely you desire truth in the inner
  parts;*a*
 you teach*b* me wisdom in the inmost
  place.

7 Cleanse me with hyssop, and I shall
  be clean;
 wash me, and I shall be whiter than
  snow.
8 Let me hear joy and gladness;
 let the bones you have crushed
  rejoice.
9 Hide your face from my sins
 and blot out all my iniquity.

10 Create in me a pure heart, O God,
 and renew a steadfast spirit within
  me.
11 Do not cast me from your
  presence
 or take your Holy Spirit from me.
12 Restore to me the joy of your
  salvation
 and grant me a willing spirit, to
  sustain me.

13 Then I will teach transgressors your
  ways,
 and sinners will turn back to
  you.
14 Save me from bloodguilt, O God,
 the God who saves me,
 and my tongue will sing of your
  righteousness.
15 O Lord, open my lips,
 and my mouth will declare your
  praise.
16 You do not delight in sacrifice, or I
  would bring it;

---

*a*21 Or *thought the 'I AM' was* *b*23 Or *and to those who consider their ways / I will show*
*a*6 The meaning of the Hebrew for this phrase is uncertain. *b*6 Or *you desired . . .; / you taught*

you do not take pleasure in burnt
offerings.
[17] The sacrifices of God are[c] a broken
spirit;
a broken and contrite heart,
O God, you will not despise.

[18] In your good pleasure make Zion
prosper;
build up the walls of Jerusalem.
[19] Then there will be righteous
sacrifices,
whole burnt offerings to delight
you;
then bulls will be offered on your
altar.

Psalm 52

For the director of music. A maskil[a] of David.
When Doeg the Edomite had gone to Saul and told
him: "David has gone to the house of Ahimelech."

[1] Why do you boast of evil, you mighty
one?
Why do you boast all day long,
you who are a disgrace in the eyes
of God?
[2] Your tongue plots destruction;
it is like a sharpened razor,
you who practise deceit.
[3] You love evil rather than good,
falsehood rather than speaking the
truth. *Selah*
[4] You love every harmful word,
O you deceitful tongue!

[5] Surely God will bring you down to
everlasting ruin:
He will snatch you up and tear you
from your tent;
he will uproot you from the land of
the living. *Selah*
[6] The righteous will see and fear;
they will laugh at you, saying,
[7] "Here now is the one
who did not make God his
stronghold
but trusted in his great wealth
and grew strong by destroying
others!"

[8] But I am like an olive tree
flourishing in the house of God;
I trust in God's unfailing love
for ever and ever.
[9] I will praise you for ever for what you
have done;
in your name I will hope, for your
name is good.
I will praise you in the presence of
your saints.

Psalm 53

For the director of music. According to mahalath.[a]
A maskil[b] of David.

[1] Fools say in their hearts,
"There is no God."
They are corrupt, and their ways are
vile;
there is no-one who does good.

[2] God looks down from heaven
on the human race
to see if there are any who
understand,
any who seek God.
[3] Everyone has turned away,
they have together become
corrupt;
there is no-one who does good,
not even one.

[4] Will the evildoers never learn—
those who devour my people as if
eating bread
and who do not call on God?
[5] There they were, overwhelmed with
dread,
where there was nothing to dread.
God scattered the bones of those who
attacked you;
you put them to shame, for God
despised them.

[6] Oh, that salvation for Israel would
come out of Zion!
When God restores the fortunes of
his people,
let Jacob rejoice and Israel be
glad!

---

[c]17 Or *My sacrifice, O God, is*   [a]Title: Probably a literary or musical term   [a]Title: Probably a musical term
[a]Title: Probably a literary or musical term

Psalm 54

For the director of music. With stringed instruments.
A maskil[a] of David. When the Ziphites had gone to
Saul and said, "Is not David hiding among us?"

¹ Save me, O God, by your name;
    vindicate me by your might.
² Hear my prayer, O God;
    listen to the words of my mouth.

³ Strangers are attacking me;
    ruthless people seek my life—
    people without regard for God.
                                    Selah

⁴ Surely God is my help;
    the Lord is the one who sustains me.

⁵ Let evil recoil on those who slander
    me;
    in your faithfulness destroy them.

⁶ I will sacrifice a freewill offering to
    you;
    I will praise your name, O Lord,
    for it is good.
⁷ For he has delivered me from all my
    troubles,
    and my eyes have looked in triumph
    on my foes.

Psalm 55

For the director of music. With stringed instruments.
A maskil[a] of David.

¹ Listen to my prayer, O God,
    do not ignore my plea;
²   hear me and answer me.
  My thoughts trouble me and I am
    distraught
³   at the voice of the enemy,
    at the stares of the wicked;
  for they bring down suffering upon me
    and revile me in their anger.

⁴ My heart is in anguish within me;
    the terrors of death assail me.
⁵ Fear and trembling have beset me;
    horror has overwhelmed me.
⁶ I said, "Oh, that I had the wings of a
    dove!
    I would fly away and be at rest—

⁷ I would flee far away
    and stay in the desert;   *Selah*
⁸ I would hurry to my place of shelter,
    far from the tempest and storm."

⁹ Confuse the wicked, O Lord,
    confound their speech,
    for I see violence and strife in the
    city.
¹⁰ Day and night they prowl about on its
    walls;
    malice and abuse are within it.
¹¹ Destructive forces are at work in the
    city;
    threats and lies never leave its
    streets.

¹² If an enemy were insulting me,
    I could endure it;
  if a foe were rising against me,
    I could hide.
¹³ But it is you, one like myself,
    my companion, my close friend,
¹⁴ with whom I once enjoyed sweet
    fellowship
  as we walked with the throng at the
    house of God.

¹⁵ Let death take my enemies by
    surprise;
    let them go down alive to the
    grave,[b]
    for evil finds lodging among them.

¹⁶ But I call to God,
    and the Lord saves me.
¹⁷ Evening, morning and noon
    I cry out in distress,
    and he hears my voice.
¹⁸ He ransoms me unharmed
    from the battle waged against me,
    even though many oppose me.
¹⁹ God, who is enthroned for ever,
    will hear them and afflict them—
                                    Selah
  people who never change their
    ways
    and have no fear of God.

²⁰ My companion attacks his friends;
    he violates his covenant.

---

*a*Title: Probably a literary or musical term   *a*Title: Probably a literary or musical term   *b*15 Hebrew *Sheol*

21 His speech is smooth as butter,
  yet war is in his heart;
his words are more soothing than oil,
  yet they are drawn swords.

22 Cast your cares on the LORD
  and he will sustain you;
he will never let the righteous fall.
23 But you, O God, will bring down the
    wicked
  into the pit of corruption;
the bloodthirsty and deceitful
  will not live out half their days.

But as for me, I trust in you.

Psalm 56

*For the director of music. To ⌊the tune of⌋ "A Dove
on Distant Oaks". Of David. A miktam.ᵃ When the
Philistines had seized him in Gath.*

1 Be merciful to me, O God, for
    enemies hotly pursue me;
  all day long they press their attack.
2 My slanderers pursue me all day long;
    many are attacking me in their
    pride.

3 When I am afraid,
  I will trust in you.
4 In God, whose word I praise,
  in God I trust; I will not be afraid.
  What can mortals do to me?

5 All day long they twist my words;
  they are always plotting to harm me.
6 They conspire, they lurk,
  they watch my steps,
  eager to take my life.

7 On no account let them escape;
  in your anger, O God, bring down
    the nations.
8 Record my lament;
  list my tears on your scrollᵇ—
  are they not in your record?

9 Then my enemies will turn back
  when I call for help.
By this I will know that God is for
  me.

10 In God, whose word I praise,
  in the LORD, whose word I praise—
11 in God I trust; I will not be afraid.
  What can human beings do to me?

12 I am under vows to you, O God;
  I will present my thank-offerings to
    you.
13 For you have delivered meᶜ from death
  and my feet from stumbling,
that I may walk before God
  in the light of life.ᵈ

Psalm 57

*For the director of music. ⌊To the tune of⌋ "Do Not
Destroy". Of David. A miktam.ᵃ When he had fled
from Saul into the cave.*

1 Have mercy on me, O God, have
    mercy on me,
  for in you my soul takes refuge.
I will take refuge in the shadow of
    your wings
until the disaster has passed.

2 I cry out to God Most High,
  to God, who fulfils ⌊his purpose⌋ for
    me.
3 He sends from heaven and saves me,
  rebuking those who hotly pursue me;
                                    Selah
God sends his love and his
    faithfulness.

4 I am in the midst of lions;
  I lie among ravenous beasts—
people whose teeth are spears and
    arrows,
  whose tongues are sharp swords.

5 Be exalted, O God, above the heavens;
  let your glory be over all the earth.

6 They spread a net for my feet—
  I was bowed down in distress.
They dug a pit in my path—
  but they have fallen into it
    themselves.   *Selah*

7 My heart is steadfast, O God,
  my heart is steadfast;

ᵃTitle: Probably a literary or musical term   ᵇ8 Or / *put my tears in your wineskin*   ᶜ13 Or *my soul*
ᵈ13 Or *the land of the living*   ᵃTitle: Probably a literary or musical term

I will sing and make music.
⁸Awake, my soul!
　Awake, harp and lyre!
　I will awaken the dawn.

⁹I will praise you, O Lord, among the
　nations;
　I will sing of you among the peoples.
¹⁰For great is your love, reaching to the
　heavens;
　your faithfulness reaches to the
　skies.

¹¹Be exalted, O God, above the
　heavens;
　let your glory be over all the earth.

Psalm 58

*For the director of music. ⌐To the tune of⌐ "Do Not
Destroy". Of David. A miktam.ᵃ*

¹Do you rulers indeed speak justly?
　Do you judge people uprightly?
²No, in your heart you devise injustice,
　and your hands mete out violence
　on the earth.
³Even from birth the wicked go astray;
　from the womb they are wayward
　and speak lies.
⁴Their venom is like the venom of a
　snake,
　like that of a cobra that has stopped
　its ears,
⁵that will not heed the tune of the
　charmer,
　however skilful the enchanter may
　be.

⁶Break the teeth in their mouths,
　O God;
　tear out, O Lord, the fangs of the
　lions!
⁷Let them vanish like water that flows
　away;
　when they draw the bow, let their
　arrows be blunted.
⁸Like a slug melting away as it moves
　along,
　like a stillborn child, may they not
　see the sun.

⁹Before your pots can feel ⌐the heat of⌐
　the thorns—
　whether they be green or dry—the
　wicked will be swept away.ᵇ
¹⁰The righteous will be glad when they
　are avenged,
　when they bathe their feet in the
　blood of the wicked.
¹¹Then people will say,
　"Surely the righteous still are
　rewarded;
　surely there is a God who judges the
　earth."

Psalm 59

*For the director of music. ⌐To the tune of⌐ "Do Not
Destroy". Of David. A miktam.ᵃ When Saul had sent
men to watch David's house in order to kill him.*

¹Deliver me from my enemies, O God;
　protect me from those who rise up
　against me.
²Deliver me from evildoers
　and save me from the bloodthirsty.

³See how they lie in wait for me!
　Powerful people conspire against
　me
　for no offence or sin of mine,
　O Lord.
⁴I have done no wrong, yet they are
　ready to attack me.
　Arise to help me; look on my plight!
⁵O Lord God Almighty, the God of
　Israel,
　rouse yourself to punish all the
　nations;
　show no mercy to wicked traitors.
　　　　　　　　　　　　Selah

⁶They return at evening,
　snarling like dogs,
　and prowl about the city.
⁷See what they spew from their
　mouths—
　they spew out swords from their
　lips,
　and they say, "Who can hear us?"
⁸But you, O Lord, laugh at them;
　you scoff at all those nations.

9 O my Strength, I watch for you;
  you, O God, are my fortress, 10 my
    loving God.

God will go before me
  and will let me gloat over those who
    slander me.
11 But do not kill them, O Lord our
    shield,*b*
  or my people will forget.
In your might make them wander
    about,
  and bring them down.
12 For the sins of their mouths,
  for the words of their lips,
    let them be caught in their pride.
For the curses and lies they utter,
13   consume them in wrath,
  consume them till they are no more.
Then it will be known to the ends of
    the earth
  that God rules over Jacob.   *Selah*

14 They return at evening,
  snarling like dogs,
    and prowl about the city.
15 They wander about for food
  and howl if not satisfied.
16 But I will sing of your strength,
  in the morning I will sing of your
    love;
  for you are my fortress,
    my refuge in times of trouble.

17 O my Strength, I sing praise to you;
  you, O God, are my fortress, my
    loving God.

Psalm 60

*For the director of music. To the tune of, "The Lily
of the Covenant". A miktam*a *of David. For teaching.
When he fought Aram Naharaim*b *and Aram Zobah,*c
*and when Joab returned and struck down twelve
thousand Edomites in the Valley of Salt.*

1 You have rejected us, O God, and
    burst forth upon us;
  you have been angry—now restore
    us!
2 You have shaken the land and torn it
    open;
  mend its fractures, for it is quaking.

3 You have shown your people
    desperate times;
  you have given us wine that makes
    us stagger.

4 But for those who fear you, you have
    raised a banner
  to be unfurled against the bow.
                              Selah

5 Save us and help us with your right
    hand,
  that those you love may be
    delivered.
6 God has spoken from his sanctuary:
  "In triumph I will parcel out
    Shechem
  and measure off the Valley of
    Succoth.
7 Gilead is mine, and Manasseh is mine;
  Ephraim is my helmet,
    Judah my sceptre.
8 Moab is my washbasin,
  upon Edom I toss my sandal;
    over Philistia I shout in triumph."

9 Who will bring me to the fortified
    city?
  Who will lead me to Edom?
10 Is it not you, O God, you who have
    rejected us
  and no longer go out with our
    armies?
11 Give us aid against the enemy,
  for human help is worthless.
12 With God we shall gain the victory,
  and he will trample down our
    enemies.

Psalm 61

*For the director of music. With stringed instruments.
Of David.*

1 Hear my cry, O God;
  listen to my prayer.

2 From the ends of the earth I call to
    you,
  I call as my heart grows faint;
    lead me to the rock that is higher
    than I.

*b*11 Or *sovereign*   *a*Title: Probably a literary or musical term
*b*Title: That is, Arameans of North-west Mesopotamia   *c*Title: That is, Arameans of central Syria

3 For you have been my refuge,
  a strong tower against the foe.

4 I long to dwell in your tent for ever
  and take refuge in the shelter of your
    wings.   *Selah*
5 For you have heard my vows, O God;
  you have given me the heritage of
    those who fear your name.

6 Increase the days of the king's life,
  his years for many generations.
7 May he be enthroned in God's
    presence for ever;
  appoint your love and faithfulness
    to protect him.

8 Then will I ever sing praise to your
    name
  and fulfil my vows day after
    day.

Psalm 62

*For the director of music. For Jeduthun. A psalm
of David.*

1 My soul finds rest in God alone;
  my salvation comes from him.
2 He alone is my rock and my
    salvation;
  he is my fortress, I shall never be
    shaken.

3 How long will you assault me?
  Would all of you throw me down—
  this leaning wall, this tottering
    fence?
4 They fully intend to topple me
  from my lofty place;
  they take delight in lies.
  With their mouths they bless,
  but in their hearts they curse. *Selah*

5 Find rest, O my soul, in God alone;
  my hope comes from him.
6 He alone is my rock and my salvation;
  he is my fortress, I shall not be
    shaken.
7 My salvation and my honour depend
    on God;[a]
  he is my mighty rock, my refuge.
8 Trust in him at all times, O people;

[a]7 Or / *God Most High is my salvation and my honour*

pour out your hearts to him,
  for God is our refuge.   *Selah*

9 The lowborn are but a breath,
  the highborn are but a lie;
  if weighed on a balance, they are
    nothing;
  together they are only a breath.
10 Do not trust in extortion
  or take pride in stolen goods;
  though your riches increase,
  do not set your heart on them.

11 One thing God has spoken,
  two things have I heard:
  that you, O God, are strong,
12 and that you, O Lord, are loving.
  Surely you will reward everyone
    according to what they have
    done.

Psalm 63

*A psalm of David. When he was in the Desert
of Judah.*

1 O God, you are my God,
  earnestly I seek you;
  my soul thirsts for you,
  my body longs for you,
  in a dry and weary land
  where there is no water.

2 I have seen you in the sanctuary
  and beheld your power and your
    glory.
3 Because your love is better than life,
  my lips will glorify you.
4 I will praise you as long as I live,
  and in your name I will lift up my
    hands.
5 My soul will be satisfied as with the
    richest of foods;
  with singing lips my mouth will
    praise you.

6 On my bed I remember you;
  I think of you through the watches
    of the night.
7 Because you are my help,
  I sing in the shadow of your wings.
8 My soul clings to you;
  your right hand upholds me.

9 They who seek my life will be
   destroyed;
   they will go down to the depths of
     the earth.
10 They will be given over to the sword
   and become food for jackals.

11 But the king will rejoice in God;
   all who swear by God's name will
     praise him,
   while the mouths of liars will be
     silenced.

Psalm 64

For the director of music. A psalm of David.

1 Hear me, O God, as I voice my
   complaint;
   protect my life from the threat of
     the enemy.
2 Hide me from the conspiracy of the
   wicked,
   from that noisy crowd of evildoers.

3 They sharpen their tongues like
   swords
   and aim their words like deadly
     arrows.
4 They shoot from ambush at the
   innocent;
   they shoot suddenly, without
     fear.

5 They encourage each other in evil
   plans,
   they talk about hiding their snares;
   they say, "Who will see them?"*a*
6 They plot injustice and say,
   "We have devised a perfect plan!"
   Surely the human mind and heart
     are cunning.

7 But God will shoot them with
   arrows;
   suddenly they will be struck down.
8 He will turn their own tongues against
   them
   and bring them to ruin;
   all who see them will shake their
     heads in scorn.

9 All people will fear;
   they will proclaim the works of
     God
   and ponder what he has done.
10 Let the righteous rejoice in the
   LORD
   and take refuge in him;
   let all the upright in heart praise
     him!

Psalm 65

For the director of music. A psalm of David. A song.

1 Praise awaits*a* you, O God, in Zion;
   to you our vows will be fulfilled.
2 O you who hear prayer,
   to you all people will come.
3 When we were overwhelmed by sins,
   you forgave*b* our transgressions.
4 Blessed are those you choose
   and bring near to live in your
     courts!
We are filled with the good things of
   your house,
   of your holy temple.

5 You answer us with awesome deeds of
   righteousness,
   O God our Saviour,
the hope of all the ends of the earth
   and of the farthest seas,
6 who formed the mountains by your
   power,
   having armed yourself with
     strength,
7 who stilled the roaring of the seas,
   the roaring of their waves,
   and the turmoil of the nations.
8 Those living far away fear your
   wonders;
   where morning dawns and evening
     fades
   you call forth songs of joy.

9 You care for the land and water it;
   you enrich it abundantly.
The streams of God are filled with
   water
   to provide the people with corn,
   for so you have ordained it.*c*

*a*5 Or *us*   *a*1 Or *befits*; the meaning of the Hebrew for this word is uncertain.   *b*3 Or *made atonement for*
*c*9 Or *for that is how you prepare the land*

10 You drench its furrows
  and level its ridges;
 you soften it with showers
  and bless its crops.
11 You crown the year with your bounty,
  and your carts overflow with
    abundance.
12 The grasslands of the desert overflow;
  the hills are clothed with gladness.
13 The meadows are covered with flocks
  and the valleys are mantled with
    corn;
  they shout for joy and sing.

Psalm 66

For the director of music. A song. A psalm.

1 Shout with joy to God, all the earth!
2   Sing the glory of his name;
  make his praise glorious!
3 Say to God, "How awesome are your
    deeds!
  So great is your power
  that your enemies cringe before you.
4 All the earth bows down to you;
  they sing praise to you,
  they sing praise to your name."
                                    Selah

5 Come and see what God has done,
  how awesome his works for human
    beings!
6 He turned the sea into dry land,
  they passed through the waters on
    foot—
  come, let us rejoice in him.
7 He rules for ever by his power,
  his eyes watch the nations—
  let not the rebellious rise up against
    him.   *Selah*

8 Praise our God, O peoples,
  let the sound of his praise be heard;
9 he has preserved our lives
  and kept our feet from slipping.
10 For you, O God, tested us;
  you refined us like silver.
11 You brought us into prison
  and laid burdens on our backs.
12 You let people ride over our heads;
  we went through fire and water,
  but you brought us to a place of
    abundance.

13 I will come to your temple with burnt
    offerings
  and fulfil my vows to you—
14 vows my lips promised and my mouth
    spoke
  when I was in trouble.
15 I will sacrifice fat animals to you
  and an offering of rams;
  I will offer bulls and goats.   *Selah*

16 Come and listen, all you who fear
    God;
  let me tell you what he has done for
    me.
17 I cried out to him with my mouth;
  his praise was on my tongue.
18 If I had cherished sin in my heart,
  the Lord would not have
    listened;
19 but God has surely listened
  and heard my voice in prayer.
20 Praise be to God,
  who has not rejected my prayer
  or withheld his love from me!

Psalm 67

For the director of music. With stringed instruments.
A psalm. A song.

1 May God be gracious to us and bless
    us
  and make his face shine upon us,
                                    Selah
2 that your ways may be known on
    earth,
  your salvation among all nations.

3 May the peoples praise you,
    O God;
  may all the peoples praise you.
4 May the nations be glad and sing for
    joy,
  for you rule the peoples justly
  and guide the nations of the earth.
                                    Selah
5 May the peoples praise you, O God;
  may all the peoples praise you.

6 Then the land will yield its harvest,
  and God, our God, will bless us.
7 God will bless us,
  and all the ends of the earth will fear
    him.

Psalm 68

For the director of music. Of David. A psalm. A song.

¹ May God arise, may his enemies be
   scattered;
   may his foes flee before him.
² As smoke is blown away by the wind,
   may you blow them away;
as wax melts before the fire,
   may the wicked perish before
   God.
³ But may the righteous be glad
   and rejoice before God;
   may they be happy and joyful.

⁴ Sing to God, sing praise to his name,
   extol him who rides on the clouds*ᵃ*—
his name is the LORD—
   and rejoice before him.
⁵ A father to the fatherless, a defender
   of widows,
   is God in his holy dwelling.
⁶ God sets the lonely in families,*ᵇ*
   he leads forth the prisoners with
   singing;
but the rebellious live in a
   sun-scorched land.

⁷ When you went out before your
   people, O God,
   when you marched through the
   wasteland,   *Selah*
⁸ the earth shook,
   the heavens poured down rain,
before God, the One of Sinai,
   before God, the God of Israel.
⁹ You gave abundant showers, O God;
   you refreshed your weary
   inheritance.
¹⁰ Your people settled in it,
   and from your bounty, O God, you
   provided for the poor.

¹¹ The Lord announced the word,
   and great was the company of those
   who proclaimed it:
¹² "Kings and armies flee in haste;
   in the camps men divide the
   plunder.
¹³ Even while you sleep among the
   campfires,*ᶜ*

the wings of ˻my˼ dove are sheathed
   with silver,
   its feathers with shining gold."
¹⁴ When the Almighty*ᵈ* scattered the
   kings in the land,
   it was like snow fallen on Zalmon.

¹⁵ The mountains of Bashan are majestic
   mountains;
   rugged are the mountains of
   Bashan.
¹⁶ Why gaze in envy, O rugged
   mountains,
   at the mountain where God chooses
   to reign,
   where the LORD himself will dwell
   for ever?
¹⁷ The chariots of God are tens of
   thousands
   and thousands of thousands;
   the Lord ˻has come˼ from Sinai into
   his sanctuary.
¹⁸ When you ascended on high,
   you led captives in your train;
   you received gifts from people,
even from*ᵉ* the rebellious—
   that you,*ᶠ* O LORD God, might
   dwell there.

¹⁹ Praise be to the Lord, to God our
   Saviour,
   who daily bears our burdens.   *Selah*
²⁰ Our God is a God who saves;
   from the Sovereign LORD comes
   escape from death.

²¹ Surely God will crush the heads of his
   enemies,
   the hairy crowns of those who go on
   in their sins.
²² The Lord says, "I will bring them from
   Bashan;
   I will bring them from the depths of
   the sea,
²³ that you may plunge your feet in the
   blood of your foes,
   while the tongues of your dogs have
   their share."

²⁴ Your procession has come into view,
   O God,

---

*ᵃ*4 Or / *prepare the way for him who rides through the deserts*   *ᵇ*6 Or *the desolate in a homeland*
*ᶜ*13 Or *saddlebags*   *ᵈ*14 Hebrew *Shaddai*   *ᵉ*18 Or *gifts for people, / even*   *ᶠ*18 Or *they*

the procession of my God and King
  into the sanctuary.
25 In front are the singers, after them the
  musicians;
  with them are the young women
  playing tambourines.
26 Praise God in the great congregation;
  praise the LORD in the assembly of
  Israel.
27 There is the little tribe of Benjamin,
  leading them,
  there the great throng of Judah's
  princes,
  and there the princes of Zebulun
  and of Naphtali.

28 Summon your power, O God;*g*
  show us your strength, O God, as
  you have done before.
29 Because of your temple at Jerusalem
  kings will bring you gifts.
30 Rebuke the beast among the reeds,
  the herd of bulls among the calves
  of the nations.
  Humbled, may it bring bars of silver.
  Scatter the nations who delight in war.
31 Envoys will come from Egypt;
  Cush*h* will submit herself to God.

32 Sing to God, O kingdoms of the earth,
  sing praise to the Lord,   *Selah*
33 to him who rides the ancient skies
  above,
  who thunders with mighty voice.
34 Proclaim the power of God,
  whose majesty is over Israel,
  whose power is in the skies.
35 You are awesome, O God, in your
  sanctuary;
  the God of Israel gives power and
  strength to his people.

  Praise be to God!

Psalm 69

For the director of music. To ⌊the tune of⌋ "Lilies".
Of David.

1 Save me, O God,
  for the waters have come up to my
  neck.

2 I sink in the miry depths,
  where there is no foothold.
  I have come into the deep waters;
  the floods engulf me.
3 I am worn out calling for help;
  my throat is parched.
  My eyes fail,
  looking for my God.
4 Those who hate me without reason
  outnumber the hairs of my head;
  many are my enemies without cause,
  those who seek to destroy me.
  I am forced to restore
  what I did not steal.

5 You know my folly, O God;
  my guilt is not hidden from you.

6 May those who hope in you
  not be disgraced because of me,
  O Lord, the LORD Almighty;
  may those who seek you
  not be put to shame because of me,
  O God of Israel.
7 For I endure scorn for your sake,
  and shame covers my face.
8 I am a stranger to my own family,
  an alien to my mother's children;
9 for zeal for your house consumes me,
  and the insults of those who insult
  you fall on me.
10 When I weep and fast,
  I must endure scorn;
11 when I put on sackcloth,
  people make sport of me.
12 Those who sit at the gate mock me,
  and I am the song of the drunkards.

13 But I pray to you, O LORD,
  in the time of your favour;
  in your great love, O God,
  answer me with your sure salvation.
14 Rescue me from the mire,
  do not let me sink;
  deliver me from those who hate me,
  from the deep waters.
15 Do not let the floodwaters engulf me
  or the depths swallow me up
  or the pit close its mouth over me.

---

*g*28 Many Hebrew manuscripts, Septuagint and Syriac; most Hebrew manuscripts *Your God has summoned power*
for you   *h*31 That is, the upper Nile region

16 Answer me, O Lord, out of the
       goodness of your love;
   in your great mercy turn to me.
17 Do not hide your face from your
       servant;
   answer me quickly, for I am in
       trouble.
18 Come near and rescue me;
   redeem me because of my foes.

19 You know how I am scorned,
       disgraced and shamed;
   all my enemies are before you.
20 Scorn has broken my heart
       and has left me helpless;
   I looked for sympathy, but there was
       none,
   for comforters, but I found none.
21 They put gall in my food
   and gave me vinegar for my thirst.

22 May the table set before them become
       a snare;
   may it become retribution and[a] a
       trap.
23 May their eyes be darkened so that
       they cannot see,
   and their backs be bent for ever.
24 Pour out your wrath on them;
   let your fierce anger overtake them.
25 May their place be deserted;
   let there be no-one to dwell in their
       tents.
26 For they persecute those you wound
   and talk about the pain of those you
       hurt.
27 Charge them with crime upon crime;
   do not let them share in your
       salvation.
28 May they be blotted out of the book
       of life
   and not be listed with the righteous.

29 I am in pain and distress;
   may your salvation, O God, protect
       me.

30 I will praise God's name in song
   and glorify him with thanksgiving.
31 This will please the Lord more than
       an ox,

more than a bull with its horns and
       hoofs.
32 The poor will see and be glad—
   you who seek God, may your hearts
       live!
33 The Lord hears the needy
   and does not despise his captive
       people.

34 Let heaven and earth praise him,
   the seas and all that move in them,
35 for God will save Zion
   and rebuild the cities of Judah.
   Then people will settle there and
       possess it;
36   the children of his servants will
       inherit it,
   and those who love his name will
       dwell there.

Psalm 70

For the director of music. Of David. A petition.

1 Hasten, O God, to save me;
   O Lord, come quickly to help me.
2 May those who seek my life
   be put to shame and confusion;
   may all who desire my ruin
   be turned back in disgrace.
3 May those who say to me, "Aha!
       Aha!"
   turn back because of their shame.
4 But may all who seek you
   rejoice and be glad in you;
   may those who love your salvation
       always say,
   "Let God be exalted!"

5 Yet I am poor and needy;
   come quickly to me, O God.
   You are my help and my deliverer;
   O Lord, do not delay.

Psalm 71

1 In you, O Lord, I have taken refuge;
   let me never be put to shame.
2 Rescue me and deliver me in your
       righteousness;
   turn your ear to me and save me.
3 Be my rock of refuge,
   to which I can always go;

[a]22 Or *snare / and their fellowship become*

give the command to save me,
  for you are my rock and my fortress.
[4] Deliver me, O my God, from the hand
    of the wicked,
  from the grasp of those who are evil
    and cruel.

[5] For you have been my hope,
    O Sovereign LORD,
  my confidence since my youth.
[6] From my birth I have relied on you;
  you brought me forth from my
    mother's womb.
  I will ever praise you.
[7] I have become like a portent to many,
  but you are my strong refuge.
[8] My mouth is filled with your praise,
  declaring your splendour all day
    long.

[9] Do not cast me away when I am old;
  do not forsake me when my
    strength is gone.
[10] For my enemies speak against me;
  those who wait to kill me conspire
    together.
[11] They say, "God has forsaken him;
  pursue him and seize him,
  for no-one will rescue him."
[12] Be not far from me, O God;
  come quickly, O my God, to help
    me.
[13] May my accusers perish in shame;
  may those who want to harm me
  be covered with scorn and disgrace.

[14] But as for me, I shall always have hope;
  I will praise you more and more.
[15] My mouth will tell of your
    righteousness,
  of your salvation all day long,
  though I know not its measure.
[16] I will come and proclaim your mighty
    acts, O Sovereign LORD;
  I will proclaim your righteousness,
    yours alone.
[17] Since my youth, O God, you have
    taught me,
  and to this day I declare your
    marvellous deeds.
[18] Even when I am old and grey,

  do not forsake me, O God,
  till I declare your power to the next
    generation,
  your might to all who are to come.

[19] Your righteousness reaches to the
    skies, O God,
  you who have done great things.
  Who, O God, is like you?
[20] Though you have made me see
    troubles, many and bitter,
  you will restore my life again;
  from the depths of the earth
  you will again bring me up.
[21] You will increase my honour
  and comfort me once again.

[22] I will praise you with the harp
  for your faithfulness, O my God;
  I will sing praise to you with the lyre,
    O Holy One of Israel.
[23] My lips will shout for joy
  when I sing praise to you—
  I, whom you have redeemed.
[24] My tongue will tell of your righteous acts
    all day long,
  for those who wanted to harm me
  have been put to shame and
    confusion.

Psalm 72

Of Solomon.

[1] Endow the king with your justice,
    O God,
  the royal son with your
    righteousness.
[2] He will[a] judge your people in
    righteousness,
  your afflicted ones with justice.
[3] The mountains will bring prosperity to
    the people,
  the hills the fruit of righteousness.
[4] He will defend the afflicted among the
    people
  and save the children of the needy;
  he will crush the oppressor.

[5] He will endure[b] as long as the sun,
  as long as the moon, through all
    generations.

---

[a]2 Or *May he*; similarly in verses 3–11 and 17   [b]5 Septuagint; Hebrew *You will be feared*

6 He will be like rain falling on a mown field,
    like showers watering the earth.
7 In his days the righteous will flourish;
    prosperity will abound till the moon is no more.

8 He will rule from sea to sea
    and from the River[c] to the ends of the earth.[d]
9 The desert tribes will bow before him
    and his enemies will lick the dust.
10 The kings of Tarshish and of distant shores
    will bring tribute to him;
the kings of Sheba and Seba
    will present him gifts.
11 All kings will bow down to him
    and all nations will serve him.

12 For he will deliver the needy who cry out,
    the afflicted who have no-one to help.
13 He will take pity on the weak and the needy
    and save the needy from death.
14 He will rescue them from oppression and violence,
    for precious is their blood in his sight.

15 Long may he live!
    May gold from Sheba be given to him.
May people ever pray for him
    and bless him all day long.
16 Let corn abound throughout the land;
    on the tops of the hills may it sway.
Let its fruit flourish like Lebanon;
    let it thrive like the grass of the field.
17 May his name endure for ever;
    may it continue as long as the sun.

All nations will be blessed through him,
    and they will call him blessed.

18 Praise be to the LORD God, the God of Israel,
    who alone does marvellous deeds.
19 Praise be to his glorious name for ever;
    may the whole earth be filled with his glory.
          Amen and Amen.

20 This concludes the prayers of David son of Jesse.

BOOK III

Psalms 73–89

Psalm 73

A psalm of Asaph.

1 Surely God is good to Israel,
    to those who are pure in heart.

2 But as for me, my feet had almost slipped;
    I had nearly lost my foothold.
3 For I envied the arrogant
    when I saw the prosperity of the wicked.

4 They have no struggles;
    their bodies are healthy and strong.[a]
5 They are free from common human burdens;
    they are not plagued by human ills.
6 Therefore pride is their necklace;
    they clothe themselves with violence.
7 From their callous hearts comes iniquity;[b]
    the evil conceits of their minds know no limits.
8 They scoff, and speak with malice;
    in their arrogance they threaten oppression.
9 Their mouths lay claim to heaven,
    and their tongues take possession of the earth.
10 Therefore their people turn to them
    and drink up waters in abundance.[c]
11 They say, "How can God know?
    Does the Most High have knowledge?"

12 This is what the wicked are like—
    always carefree, they increase in wealth.

---

[c]8 That is, the Euphrates   [d]8 Or *the end of the land*
[a]4 With a different word division of the Hebrew; Masoretic Text *struggles at their death; / their bodies are healthy*
[b]7 Syriac (see also Septuagint); Hebrew *Their eyes bulge with fat*
[c]10 The meaning of the Hebrew for this verse is uncertain.

¹³Surely in vain have I kept my heart
    pure;
    in vain have I washed my hands in
    innocence.
¹⁴All day long I have been plagued;
    I have been punished every morning.

¹⁵If I had said, "I will speak thus,"
    I would have betrayed your
    children.
¹⁶When I tried to understand all this,
    it was oppressive to me
¹⁷till I entered the sanctuary of God;
    then I understood their final destiny.

¹⁸Surely you place them on slippery
    ground;
    you cast them down to ruin.
¹⁹How suddenly are they destroyed,
    completely swept away by terrors!
²⁰As a dream when one awakes,
    so when you arise, O Lord,
    you will despise them as fantasies.

²¹When my heart was grieved
    and my spirit embittered,
²²I was senseless and ignorant;
    I was a brute beast before you.

²³Yet I am always with you;
    you hold me by my right hand.
²⁴You guide me with your counsel,
    and afterwards you will take me
    into glory.
²⁵Whom have I in heaven but you?
    And earth has nothing I desire
    besides you.
²⁶My flesh and my heart may fail,
    but God is the strength of my heart
    and my portion for ever.

²⁷Those who are far from you will perish;
    you destroy all who are unfaithful
    to you.
²⁸But as for me, it is good to be near God.
    I have made the Sovereign LORD my
    refuge;
    I will tell of all your deeds.

Psalm 74

A maskil[a] of Asaph.

¹Why have you rejected us for ever,
    O God?

[a]Title: Probably a literary or musical term

Why does your anger smoulder
    against the sheep of your pasture?
²Remember the people you purchased
    of old,
    the tribe of your inheritance, whom
    you redeemed—
    Mount Zion, where you dwelt.
³Turn your steps towards these
    everlasting ruins,
    all this destruction the enemy has
    brought on the sanctuary.

⁴Your foes roared in the place where
    you met with us;
    they set up their standards as signs.
⁵They behaved like people wielding axes
    to cut through a thicket of trees.
⁶They smashed all the carved panelling
    with their axes and hatchets.
⁷They burned your sanctuary to the
    ground;
    they defiled the dwelling-place of
    your Name.
⁸They said in their hearts, "We will
    crush them completely!"
    They burned every place where God
    was worshipped in the land.
⁹We are given no miraculous signs;
    no prophets are left,
    and none of us knows how long this
    will be.

¹⁰How long will the enemy mock you,
    O God?
    Will the foe revile your name for
    ever?
¹¹Why do you hold back your hand,
    your right hand?
    Take it from the folds of your
    garment and destroy them!

¹²But you, O God, are my king from of
    old;
    you bring salvation upon the earth.
¹³It was you who split open the sea by
    your power;
    you broke the heads of the monster
    in the waters.
¹⁴It was you who crushed the heads of
    Leviathan
    and gave it as food to the creatures
    of the desert.

¹⁵It was you who opened up springs and
        streams;
    you dried up the ever-flowing rivers.
¹⁶The day is yours, and yours also the
        night;
    you established the sun and moon.
¹⁷It was you who set all the boundaries
        of the earth;
    you made both summer and winter.

¹⁸Remember how the enemy has
        mocked you, O LORD,
    how foolish people have reviled
        your name.
¹⁹Do not hand over the life of your dove
        to wild beasts;
    do not forget the lives of your
        afflicted people for ever.
²⁰Have regard for your covenant,
    because haunts of violence fill the
        dark places of the land.
²¹Do not let the oppressed retreat in
        disgrace;
    may the poor and needy praise your
        name.

²²Rise up, O God, and defend your
        cause;
    remember how fools mock you all
        day long.
²³Do not ignore the clamour of your
        adversaries,
    the uproar of your enemies, which
        rises continually.

Psalm 75

*For the director of music. To the tune of "Do Not
Destroy". A psalm of Asaph. A song.*

¹We give thanks to you, O God,
    we give thanks, for your Name is
        near;
    people tell of your wonderful
        deeds.

²You say, "I choose the appointed
        time;
    it is I who judge uprightly.
³When the earth and all its people
        quake,
    it is I who hold its pillars firm. *Selah*
⁴To the arrogant I say, 'Boast no
        more,'

and to the wicked, 'Do not lift up
        your horns.
⁵Do not lift your horns against heaven;
    do not speak with outstretched
        neck.' "

⁶No-one from the east or the west
    or from the desert can exalt a
        human being.
⁷But it is God who judges:
    He brings one down, he exalts
        another.
⁸In the hand of the LORD is a cup
    full of foaming wine mixed with
        spices;
he pours it out, and all the wicked of
        the earth
    drink it down to its very dregs.

⁹As for me, I will declare this for ever;
    I will sing praise to the God of Jacob.
¹⁰I will cut off the horns of all the wicked,
    but the horns of the righteous shall
        be lifted up.

Psalm 76

*For the director of music. With stringed instruments.
A psalm of Asaph. A song.*

¹In Judah God is known;
    his name is great in Israel.
²His tent is in Salem,
    his dwelling-place in Zion.
³There he broke the flashing arrows,
    the shields and the swords, the
        weapons of war.   *Selah*

⁴You are resplendent with light,
    more majestic than mountains rich
        with game.
⁵The valiant lie plundered,
    they sleep their last sleep;
not one of the warriors
    can lift his hands.
⁶At your rebuke, O God of Jacob,
    both horse and chariot lie still.
⁷You alone are to be feared.
    Who can stand before you when
        you are angry?
⁸From heaven you pronounced
        judgment,
    and the land feared and was
        quiet—

⁹when you, O God, rose up to judge,
    to save all the afflicted of the land.
                                        Selah
¹⁰Surely your wrath against human
    beings brings you praise,
    and the survivors of your wrath are
        restrained.ᵃ

¹¹Make vows to the Lᴏʀᴅ your God and
    fulfil them;
    let all the neighbouring lands
    bring gifts to the One to be feared.
¹²He breaks the spirit of rulers;
    he is feared by the kings of the earth.

Psalm 77

For the director of music. For Jeduthun. Of Asaph.
A psalm.

¹I cried out to God for help;
    I cried out to God to hear me.
²When I was in distress, I sought the
        Lord;
    at night I stretched out untiring hands
    and my soul refused to be
        comforted.

³I remembered you, O God, and I
        groaned;
    I mused, and my spirit grew faint.
                                        Selah
⁴You kept my eyes from closing;
    I was too troubled to speak.
⁵I thought about the former days,
    the years of long ago;
⁶I remembered my songs in the night.
    My heart mused and my spirit
        enquired:

⁷"Will the Lord reject for ever?
    Will he never show his favour again?
⁸Has his unfailing love vanished for
        ever?
    Has his promise failed for all time?
⁹Has God forgotten to be merciful?
    Has he in anger withheld his
        compassion?"   *Selah*

¹⁰Then I thought, "To this I will appeal:
    the years of the right hand of the
        Most High."

¹¹I will remember the deeds of the
        Lᴏʀᴅ;
    yes, I will remember your miracles
        of long ago.
¹²I will meditate on all your works
    and consider all your mighty deeds.

¹³Your ways, O God, are holy.
    What god is so great as our God?
¹⁴You are the God who performs
        miracles;
    you display your power among the
        peoples.
¹⁵With your mighty arm you redeemed
        your people,
    the descendants of Jacob and Joseph.
                                        Selah

¹⁶The waters saw you, O God,
    the waters saw you and writhed;
    the very depths were convulsed.
¹⁷The clouds poured down water,
    the skies resounded with thunder;
    your arrows flashed back and forth.
¹⁸Your thunder was heard in the
        whirlwind,
    your lightning lit up the world;
    the earth trembled and quaked.
¹⁹Your path led through the sea,
    your way through the mighty waters,
    though your footprints were not seen.

²⁰You led your people like a flock
    by the hand of Moses and Aaron.

Psalm 78

A maskilᵃ of Asaph.

¹O my people, hear my teaching;
    listen to the words of my mouth.
²I will open my mouth in parables,
    I will utter hidden things, things
        from of old—
³what we have heard and known,
    what our ancestors have told us.
⁴We will not hide them from their
        children;
    we will tell the next generation
    the praiseworthy deeds of the Lᴏʀᴅ,
    his power, and the wonders he has
        done.

ᵃ10 Or *Surely human wrath brings you praise, / and with the remainder of wrath you arm yourself*
ᵃTitle: Probably a literary or musical term

⁵He decreed statutes for Jacob
 and established the law in Israel,
which he commanded our ancestors
 to teach their children,
⁶so that the next generation would
  know them,
 even the children yet to be born,
 and they in turn would tell their
  children.
⁷Then they would put their trust in God
 and would not forget his deeds
 but would keep his commands.
⁸They would not be like their
  ancestors—
 a stubborn and rebellious generation,
 whose hearts were not loyal to God,
 whose spirits were not faithful to him.

⁹The men of Ephraim, though armed
  with bows,
 turned back on the day of battle;
¹⁰they did not keep God's covenant
 and refused to live by his law.
¹¹They forgot what he had done,
 the wonders he had shown them.
¹²He did miracles in the sight of their
  ancestors
 in the land of Egypt, in the region
  of Zoan.
¹³He divided the sea and led them
  through;
 he made the water stand firm like a
  wall.
¹⁴He guided them with the cloud by day
 and with light from the fire all night.
¹⁵He split the rocks in the desert
 and gave them water as abundant
  as the seas;
¹⁶he brought streams out of a rocky crag
 and made water flow down like rivers.

¹⁷But they continued to sin against him,
 rebelling in the desert against the
  Most High.
¹⁸They wilfully put God to the test
 by demanding the food they craved.
¹⁹They spoke against God, saying,
 "Can God spread a table in the
  desert?
²⁰When he struck the rock, water
  gushed out,
 and streams flowed abundantly.
 But can he also give us food?
 Can he supply meat for his people?"

²¹When the LORD heard them, he was
  very angry;
 his fire broke out against Jacob,
 and his wrath rose against Israel,
²²for they did not believe in God
 or trust in his deliverance.
²³Yet he gave a command to the skies
  above
 and opened the doors of the
  heavens;
²⁴he rained down manna for the people
  to eat,
 he gave them the grain of heaven.
²⁵Human beings ate the bread of angels;
 he sent them all the food they could
  eat.
²⁶He let loose the east wind from the
  heavens
 and led forth the south wind by his
  power.
²⁷He rained meat down on them like
  dust,
 flying birds like sand on the seashore.
²⁸He made them come down inside their
  camp,
 all around their tents.
²⁹They ate till they had more than
  enough,
 for he had given them what they
  craved.
³⁰But before they turned from the food
  they craved,
 even while it was still in their mouths,
³¹God's anger rose against them;
 he put to death the sturdiest among
  them,
 cutting down the young men of Israel.

³²In spite of all this, they kept on sinning;
 in spite of his wonders, they did not
  believe.
³³So he ended their days in futility
 and their years in terror.
³⁴Whenever God slew them, they would
  seek him;
 they eagerly turned to him again.
³⁵They remembered that God was their
  Rock,
 that God Most High was their
  Redeemer.
³⁶But then they would flatter him with
  their mouths,
 lying to him with their tongues;

37 their hearts were not loyal to him,
    they were not faithful to his
    covenant.
38 Yet he was merciful;
    he forgave their iniquities
    and did not destroy them.
    Time after time he restrained his anger
    and did not stir up his full wrath.
39 He remembered that they were but
    flesh,
    a passing breeze that does not
    return.

40 How often they rebelled against him
    in the desert
    and grieved him in the wasteland!
41 Again and again they put God to the
    test;
    they vexed the Holy One of Israel.
42 They did not remember his power—
    the day he redeemed them from the
    oppressor,
43 the day he displayed his miraculous
    signs in Egypt,
    his wonders in the region of Zoan.
44 He turned their rivers to blood;
    they could not drink from their
    streams.
45 He sent swarms of flies that devoured
    them,
    and frogs that devastated them.
46 He gave their crops to the grasshopper,
    their produce to the locust.
47 He destroyed their vines with hail
    and their sycamore-figs with
    sleet.
48 He gave over their cattle to the hail,
    their livestock to bolts of lightning.
49 He unleashed against them his hot
    anger,
    his wrath, indignation and hostility—
    a band of destroying angels.
50 He prepared a path for his anger;
    he did not spare them from death
    but gave them over to the plague.
51 He struck down all the firstborn of
    Egypt,
    the firstfruits of manhood in the
    tents of Ham.
52 But he brought his people out like a
    flock;
    he led them like sheep through the
    desert.

53 He guided them safely, so they were
    unafraid;
    but the sea engulfed their enemies.
54 Thus he brought them to the border
    of his holy land,
    to the hill country his right hand had
    taken.
55 He drove out nations before them
    and allotted their lands to them as
    an inheritance;
    he settled the tribes of Israel in their
    homes.

56 But they put God to the test
    and rebelled against the Most High;
    they did not keep his statutes.
57 Like their ancestors they were disloyal
    and faithless,
    as unreliable as a faulty bow.
58 They angered him with their high
    places;
    they aroused his jealousy with their
    idols.
59 When God heard them, he was very
    angry;
    he rejected Israel completely.
60 He abandoned the tabernacle of
    Shiloh,
    the tent he had set up among people.
61 He sent ⌊the ark of⌋ his might into
    captivity,
    his splendour into the hands of the
    enemy.
62 He gave his people over to the sword;
    he was very angry with his
    inheritance.
63 Fire consumed their young men,
    and their young women had no
    wedding songs;
64 their priests were put to the sword,
    and their widows could not weep.

65 Then the Lord awoke as from sleep,
    as someone wakes from the stupor
    of wine.
66 He beat back his enemies;
    he put them to everlasting shame.
67 Then he rejected the tents of Joseph,
    he did not choose the tribe of
    Ephraim;
68 but he chose the tribe of Judah,
    Mount Zion, which he loved.
69 He built his sanctuary like the heights,

like the earth that he established for
    ever.
70 He chose David his servant
    and took him from the sheep pens;
71 from tending the sheep he brought
        him
    to be the shepherd of his people
        Jacob,
    of Israel his inheritance.
72 And David shepherded them with
        integrity of heart;
    with skilful hands he led them.

Psalm 79

A psalm of Asaph.

1 O God, the nations have invaded your
        inheritance;
    they have defiled your holy temple,
    they have reduced Jerusalem to
        rubble.
2 They have given the dead bodies of
        your servants
    as food to the birds of the air,
    the flesh of your saints to the beasts
        of the earth.
3 They have poured out blood like
        water
    all around Jerusalem,
    and there is no-one to bury the dead.
4 We are objects of reproach to our
        neighbours,
    of scorn and derision to those
        around us.

5 How long, O LORD? Will you be angry
        for ever?
    How long will your jealousy burn
        like fire?
6 Pour out your wrath on the nations
        that do not acknowledge you,
    on the kingdoms
        that do not call on your name;
7 for they have devoured Jacob
    and destroyed his homeland.
8 Do not hold against us the sins of past
        generations;
    may your mercy come quickly to
        meet us,
    for we are in desperate need.

9 Help us, O God our Saviour,
    for the glory of your name;

deliver us and forgive our sins
    for your name's sake.
10 Why should the nations say,
    "Where is their God?"
Before our eyes, make known among
        the nations
    that you avenge the outpoured
        blood of your servants.
11 May the groans of the prisoners come
        before you;
    by the strength of your arm
    preserve those condemned to die.

12 Pay back into the laps of our
        neighbours seven times
    the reproach they have hurled at
        you, O Lord.
13 Then we your people, the sheep of
        your pasture,
    will praise you for ever;
    from generation to generation
    we will recount your praise.

Psalm 80

*For the director of music. To ⌐the tune of⌐ "The Lilies
    of the Covenant". Of Asaph. A psalm.*

1 Hear us, O Shepherd of Israel,
    you who lead Joseph like a
        flock;
    you who sit enthroned between the
        cherubim, shine forth
2   before Ephraim, Benjamin and
        Manasseh.
    Awaken your might;
    come and save us.

3 Restore us, O God;
    make your face shine upon us,
    that we may be saved.

4 O LORD God Almighty,
    how long will your anger
        smoulder
    against the prayers of your
        people?
5 You have fed them with the bread of
        tears;
    you have made them drink tears by
        the bowlful.
6 You have made us a source of
        contention to our neighbours,
    and our enemies mock us.

⁷Restore us, O God Almighty;
  make your face shine upon us,
  that we may be saved.

⁸You brought a vine out of Egypt;
  you drove out the nations and
    planted it.
⁹You cleared the ground for it,
  and it took root and filled the land.
¹⁰The mountains were covered with its
    shade,
  the mighty cedars with its
    branches.
¹¹It sent out its boughs to the Sea,ᵃ
  its shoots as far as the River.ᵇ

¹²Why have you broken down its walls
  so that all who pass by pick its
    grapes?
¹³Boars from the forest ravage it
  and the creatures of the field feed
    on it.
¹⁴Return to us, O God Almighty!
  Look down from heaven and see!
  Watch over this vine,
¹⁵ the root your right hand has
    planted,
  the sonᶜ you have raised up for
    yourself.

¹⁶Your vine is cut down, it is burned
  with fire;
  at your rebuke your people perish.
¹⁷Let your hand rest on the man at your
  right hand,
  the son of man you have raised up
    for yourself.
¹⁸Then we will not turn away from you;
  revive us, and we will call on your
    name.

¹⁹Restore us, O Lᴏʀᴅ God Almighty;
  make your face shine upon us,
  that we may be saved.

Psalm 81

For the director of music. According to gittith.ᵃ
Of Asaph.

¹Sing for joy to God our strength;
  shout aloud to the God of Jacob!

²Begin the music, strike the
    tambourine,
  play the melodious harp and lyre.

³Sound the ram's horn at the New
    Moon,
  and when the moon is full, on the
    day of our Feast;
⁴this is a decree for Israel,
  an ordinance of the God of Jacob.
⁵He established it as a statute for
    Joseph
  when he went out against Egypt,
  where we heard a language we did
    not understand.ᵇ

⁶He says, "I removed the burden from
  their shoulders;
  their hands were set free from the
    basket.
⁷In your distress you called and I
  rescued you,
  I answered you out of a
    thundercloud;
  I tested you at the waters of Meribah.
                    Selah

⁸"Hear, O my people, and I will warn
  you—
  if you would but listen to me,
    O Israel!
⁹You shall have no foreign god among
  you;
  you shall not bow down to an alien
    god.
¹⁰I am the Lᴏʀᴅ your God,
  who brought you up out of Egypt.
  Open wide your mouth and I will
    fill it.

¹¹"But my people would not listen to
  me;
  Israel would not submit to me.
¹²So I gave them over to their stubborn
    hearts
  to follow their own devices.

¹³"If my people would but listen to me,
  if Israel would follow my ways,
¹⁴how quickly would I subdue their
    enemies

ᵃ11 Probably the Mediterranean   ᵇ11 That is, the Euphrates   ᶜ15 Or *branch*
ᵃTitle: Probably a musical term   ᵇ5 Or / *and we heard a voice we had not known*

and turn my hand against their
foes!

15 Those who hate the LORD would
cringe before him,
and their punishment would last for
ever.

16 But you would be fed with the finest
of wheat;
with honey from the rock I would
satisfy you."

Psalm 82

A psalm of Asaph.

1 God presides in the great assembly;
he gives judgment among the
"gods":

2 "How long will you[a] defend the
unjust
and show partiality to the wicked?
Selah

3 Defend the cause of the weak and
fatherless;
maintain the rights of the poor and
oppressed.

4 Rescue the weak and needy;
deliver them from the hand of the
wicked.

5 "They know nothing, they understand
nothing.
They walk about in darkness;
all the foundations of the earth are
shaken.

6 "I said, 'You are "gods";
you are all sons of the Most High.'

7 But you will die like mere mortals;
you will fall like every other ruler."

8 Rise up, O God, judge the earth,
for all the nations are your
inheritance.

Psalm 83

A song. A psalm of Asaph.

1 O God, do not keep silent;
be not quiet, O God, be not still.

2 See how your enemies are astir,

how your foes rear their heads.

3 With cunning they conspire against
your people;
they plot against those you cherish.

4 "Come," they say, "let us destroy
them as a nation,
that the name of Israel be
remembered no more."

5 With one mind they plot together;
they form an alliance against you—

6 the tents of Edom and the
Ishmaelites,
of Moab and the Hagrites,

7 Gebal,[a] Ammon and Amalek,
Philistia, with the people of Tyre.

8 Even Assyria has joined them
to lend strength to the descendants
of Lot.   *Selah*

9 Do to them as you did to Midian,
as you did to Sisera and Jabin at the
river Kishon,

10 who perished at Endor
and became like refuse on the
ground.

11 Make their nobles like Oreb and
Zeeb,
all their princes like Zebah and
Zalmunna,

12 who said, "Let us take possession
of the pasture-lands of God."

13 Make them like tumble-weed, O my
God,
like chaff before the wind.

14 As fire consumes the forest
or a flame sets the mountains
ablaze,

15 so pursue them with your tempest
and terrify them with your storm.

16 Cover their faces with shame
so that people will seek your name,
O LORD.

17 May they ever be ashamed and
dismayed;
may they perish in disgrace.

18 Let them know that you, whose name
is the LORD—
that you alone are the Most High
over all the earth.

---

*a*2 The Hebrew is plural.   *a*7 That is, Byblos

Psalm 84

For the director of music. According to gittith.[a] *Of the Sons of Korah. A psalm.*

[1] How lovely is your dwelling-place,
O LORD Almighty!
[2] My soul yearns, even faints,
for the courts of the LORD;
my heart and my flesh cry out
for the living God.

[3] Even the sparrow has found a home,
and the swallow a nest for herself,
where she may have her young—
a place near your altar,
O LORD Almighty, my King and my
God.
[4] Blessed are those who dwell in your
house;
they are ever praising you.   *Selah*

[5] Blessed are those whose strength is in
you,
who have set their hearts on
pilgrimage.
[6] As they pass through the Valley of
Baca,
they make it a place of springs;
the autumn rains also cover it with
pools.[b]
[7] They go from strength to strength,
till each appears before God in
Zion.

[8] Hear my prayer, O LORD God
Almighty;
listen to me, O God of Jacob.
                         Selah
[9] Look upon our shield,[c] O God;
look with favour on your anointed
one.

[10] Better is one day in your courts
than a thousand elsewhere;
I would rather be a doorkeeper in the
house of my God
than dwell in the tents of the
wicked.
[11] For the LORD God is a sun and shield;
the LORD bestows favour and
honour;
no good thing does he withhold

from those whose walk is
blameless.

[12] O LORD Almighty,
blessed are those who trust in you.

Psalm 85

*For the director of music. Of the Sons of Korah.
A psalm.*

[1] You showed favour to your land,
O LORD;
you restored the fortunes of Jacob.
[2] You forgave the iniquity of your
people
and covered all their sins.   *Selah*
[3] You set aside all your wrath
and turned from your fierce anger.

[4] Restore us again, O God our Saviour,
and put away your displeasure
towards us.
[5] Will you be angry with us for ever?
Will you prolong your anger
through all generations?
[6] Will you not revive us again,
that your people may rejoice in
you?
[7] Show us your unfailing love, O LORD,
and grant us your salvation.

[8] I will listen to what God the LORD will
say;
he promises peace to his people, his
saints—
but let them not return to folly.
[9] Surely his salvation is near those who
fear him,
that his glory may dwell in our land.

[10] Love and faithfulness meet together;
righteousness and peace kiss each
other.
[11] Faithfulness springs forth from the
earth,
and righteousness looks down from
heaven.
[12] The LORD will indeed give what is
good,
and our land will yield its harvest.
[13] Righteousness goes before him
and prepares the way for his steps.

[a]Title: Probably a musical term   [b]6 Or *blessings*   [c]9 Or *sovereign*

Psalm 86

A prayer of David.

1 Hear, O LORD, and answer me,
for I am poor and needy.
2 Guard my life, for I am devoted to
you.
You are my God; save your servant
who trusts in you.
3 Have mercy on me, O Lord,
for I call to you all day long.
4 Bring joy to your servant,
for to you, O Lord,
I lift up my soul.

5 You are forgiving and good,
O Lord,
abounding in love to all who call to
you.
6 Hear my prayer, O LORD;
listen to my cry for mercy.
7 In the day of my trouble I will call to
you,
for you will answer me.

8 Among the gods there is none like
you, O Lord;
no deeds can compare with
yours.
9 All the nations you have made
will come and worship before you,
O Lord;
they will bring glory to your
name.
10 For you are great and do marvellous
deeds;
you alone are God.

11 Teach me your way, O LORD,
and I will walk in your truth;
give me an undivided heart,
that I may fear your name.
12 I will praise you, O Lord my God,
with all my heart;
I will glorify your name for
ever.
13 For great is your love towards me;
you have delivered me from the
depths of the grave.[a]

14 The arrogant are attacking me,
O God;
a band of ruthless people seeks my
life—
people without regard for you.
15 But you, O Lord, are a compassionate
and gracious God,
slow to anger, abounding in love
and faithfulness.
16 Turn to me and have mercy on me;
grant your strength to your
servant
and save the son of your woman
servant.[b]
17 Give me a sign of your goodness,
that my enemies may see it and be
put to shame,
for you, O LORD, have helped me
and comforted me.

Psalm 87

Of the Sons of Korah. A psalm. A song.

1 He has set his foundation on the holy
mountain;
2 the LORD loves the gates of
Zion
more than all the dwellings of
Jacob.
3 Glorious things are said of you,
O city of God: *Selah*
4 "I will record Rahab[a] and Babylon
among those who acknowledge
me—
Philistia too, and Tyre, along with
Cush[b]—
and will say, 'This[c] one was born in
Zion.' "

5 Indeed, of Zion it will be said,
"This one and that one were born
in her,
and the Most High himself will
establish her."
6 The LORD will write in the register of
the peoples:
"This one was born in Zion." *Selah*
7 As they make music they will sing,
"All my fountains are in you."

[a]13 Hebrew *Sheol*   [b]16 Or *save your faithful one*
[a]4 A poetic name for Egypt   [b]4 That is, the upper Nile region
[c]4 Or *"O Rahab and Babylon, / Philistia, Tyre and Cush, / I will record concerning those who acknowledge me: / 'This*

Psalm 88

*A song. A psalm of the Sons of Korah. For the
director of music. According to mahalath
leannoth.[a] A maskil[b] of Heman the Ezrahite.*

[1] O LORD, the God who saves me,
    day and night I cry out before you.
[2] May my prayer come before you;
    turn your ear to my cry.

[3] For my soul is full of trouble
    and my life draws near the grave.[c]
[4] I am counted among those who go
        down to the pit;
    I am like one without strength.
[5] I am set apart with the dead,
    like the slain who lie in the grave,
    whom you remember no more,
    who are cut off from your care.

[6] You have put me in the lowest pit,
    in the darkest depths.
[7] Your wrath lies heavily upon me;
    you have overwhelmed me with all
        your waves.   *Selah*
[8] You have taken from me my closest
        friends
    and have made me repulsive to
        them.
    I am confined and cannot escape;
[9]   my eyes are dim with grief.

    I call to you, O LORD, every day;
    I spread out my hands to you.
[10] Do you show your wonders to the
        dead?
    Do those who are dead rise up and
        praise you?   *Selah*
[11] Is your love declared in the grave,
    your faithfulness in Destruction?[d]
[12] Are your wonders known in the place
        of darkness,
    or your righteous deeds in the land
        of oblivion?

[13] But I cry to you for help, O LORD;
    in the morning my prayer comes
        before you.
[14] Why, O LORD, do you reject me
    and hide your face from me?

[15] From my youth I have been afflicted
    and close to death;

I have suffered your terrors and am
    in despair.
[16] Your wrath has swept over me;
    your terrors have destroyed me.
[17] All day long they surround me like a
        flood;
    they have completely engulfed me.
[18] You have taken my companions and
        loved ones from me;
    the darkness is my closest friend.

Psalm 89

A maskil[a] of Ethan the Ezrahite.

[1] I will sing of the LORD's great love for
        ever;
    with my mouth I will make your
        faithfulness known through all
        generations.
[2] I will declare that your love stands
        firm for ever,
    that you established your
        faithfulness in heaven itself.

[3] You said, "I have made a covenant
        with my chosen one,
    I have sworn to David my servant,
[4] 'I will establish your line for ever
    and make your throne firm through
        all generations.' "   *Selah*

[5] The heavens praise your wonders,
        O LORD,
    your faithfulness too, in the
        assembly of the holy ones.
[6] For who in the skies above can
        compare with the LORD?
    Who is like the LORD among the
        heavenly beings?
[7] In the council of the holy ones God is
        greatly feared;
    he is more awesome than all who
        surround him.
[8] O LORD God Almighty, who is like
        you?
    You are mighty, O LORD, and your
        faithfulness surrounds you.

[9] You rule over the surging sea;
    when its waves mount up, you still
        them.

---

[a] Title: Possibly a tune, "The Suffering of Affliction"   [b] Title: Probably a literary or musical term
[c] 3 Hebrew *Sheol*   [d] 11 Hebrew *Abaddon*   [a] Title: Probably a literary or musical term

¹⁰ You crushed Rahab like one of the
slain;
    with your strong arm you scattered
your enemies.
¹¹ The heavens are yours, and yours also
the earth;
    you founded the world and all that
is in it.
¹² You created the north and the south;
    Tabor and Hermon sing for joy at
your name.
¹³ Your arm is endued with power;
    your hand is strong, your right hand
exalted.

¹⁴ Righteousness and justice are the
foundation of your throne;
    love and faithfulness go before you.
¹⁵ Blessed are those who have learned to
acclaim you,
    who walk in the light of your
presence, O LORD.
¹⁶ They rejoice in your name all day long;
    they exult in your righteousness.
¹⁷ For you are their glory and strength,
    and by your favour you exalt our
horn.*b*
¹⁸ Indeed, our shield*c* belongs to the
LORD,
    our king to the Holy One of Israel.

¹⁹ Once you spoke in a vision,
    to your faithful people you said:
"I have bestowed strength on a
warrior;
    I have exalted a young man from
among the people.
²⁰ I have found David my servant;
    with my sacred oil I have anointed
him.
²¹ My hand will sustain him;
    surely my arm will strengthen him.
²² No enemy will subject him to tribute;
    no wicked person will oppress him.
²³ I will crush his foes before him
    and strike down his adversaries.
²⁴ My faithful love will be with him,
    and through my name his horn*d* will
be exalted.
²⁵ I will set his hand over the sea,
    his right hand over the rivers.

²⁶ He will call out to me, 'You are my
Father,
    my God, the Rock my Saviour.'
²⁷ I will also appoint him my firstborn,
    the most exalted of the kings of the
earth.
²⁸ I will maintain my love to him for ever,
    and my covenant with him will
never fail.
²⁹ I will establish his line for ever,
    his throne as long as the heavens
endure.

³⁰ "If his sons forsake my law
    and do not follow my statutes,
³¹ if they violate my decrees
    and fail to keep my commands,
³² I will punish their sin with the rod,
    their iniquity with flogging;
³³ but I will not take my love from him,
    nor will I ever betray my
faithfulness.
³⁴ I will not violate my covenant
    or alter what my lips have uttered.
³⁵ Once for all, I have sworn by my
holiness—
    and I will not lie to David—
³⁶ that his line will continue for ever
    and his throne endure before me
like the sun;
³⁷ it will be established for ever like the
moon,
    the faithful witness in the sky."   *Selah*

³⁸ But you have rejected, you have
spurned,
    you have been very angry with your
anointed one.
³⁹ You have renounced the covenant
with your servant
    and have defiled his crown in the
dust.
⁴⁰ You have broken through all his walls
    and reduced his strongholds to
ruins.
⁴¹ All who pass by have plundered him;
    he has become the scorn of his
neighbours.
⁴² You have exalted the right hand of his
foes;
    you have made all his enemies rejoice.

---

*b*17 *Horn* here symbolises strong one.   *c*18 Or *sovereign*   *d*24 *Horn* here symbolises strength.

43 You have turned back the edge of his
    sword
  and have not supported him in battle.
44 You have put an end to his splendour
    and cast his throne to the ground.
45 You have cut short the days of his
    youth;
  you have covered him with a mantle
    of shame.   *Selah*

46 How long, O LORD? Will you hide
    yourself for ever?
  How long will your wrath burn like
    fire?
47 Remember how fleeting is my life.
  For what futility you have created
    all humanity!
48 Who can live and not see death,
  or who can escape from the power
    of the grave?*e*   *Selah*

49 O Lord, where is your former great
    love,
  which in your faithfulness you
    swore to David?
50 Remember, Lord, how your servant
    has*f* been mocked,
  how I bear in my heart the taunts of
    all the nations,
51 the taunts with which your enemies
    have mocked, O LORD,
  with which they have mocked every
    step of your anointed one.

52 Praise be to the LORD for ever!
  Amen and Amen.

BOOK IV

Psalms 90–106

Psalm 90

A prayer of Moses the man of God.

1 Lord, you have been our
    dwelling-place
  throughout all generations.
2 Before the mountains were born
  or you brought forth the earth and
    the world,

from everlasting to everlasting you
    are God.

3 You turn people back to dust,
  saying, "Return to dust, you
    mortals."
4 For a thousand years in your sight
  are like a day that has just gone by,
  or like a watch in the night.
5 You sweep people away in the sleep
    of death;
  they are like the new grass of the
    morning—
6 though in the morning it springs up
    new,
  by evening it is dry and withered.

7 We are consumed by your anger
  and terrified by your indignation.
8 You have set our iniquities before
    you,
  our secret sins in the light of your
    presence.
9 All our days pass away under your
    wrath;
  we finish our years with a moan.
10 The length of our days is seventy
    years—
  or eighty, if we have the strength;
  yet their span*a* is but trouble and
    sorrow,
  for they quickly pass, and we fly
    away.

11 Who knows the power of your anger?
  For your wrath is as great as the fear
    that is due to you.
12 Teach us to number our days aright,
  that we may gain a heart of wisdom.

13 Relent, O LORD! How long will it be?
  Have compassion on your servants.
14 Satisfy us in the morning with your
    unfailing love,
  that we may sing for joy and be glad
    all our days.
15 Make us glad for as many days as you
    have afflicted us,
  for as many years as we have seen
    trouble.
16 May your deeds be shown to your
    servants,

---

e 48 Hebrew *Sheol*   *f* 50 Or *your servants have*   *a* 10 Or *yet the best of them*

your splendour to their
children.

17 May the favour[b] of the Lord our God
rest upon us;
establish the work of our hands for
us—
yes, establish the work of our
hands.

Psalm 91

1 Whoever dwells in the shelter of the
Most High
will rest in the shadow of the
Almighty.[a]
2 I will say[b] of the LORD, "He is my
refuge and my fortress,
my God, in whom I trust."

3 Surely he will save you from the
fowler's snare
and from the deadly pestilence.
4 He will cover you with his feathers,
and under his wings you will find
refuge;
his faithfulness will be your shield
and rampart.
5 You will not fear the terror of night,
nor the arrow that flies by day,
6 nor the pestilence that stalks in the
darkness,
nor the plague that destroys at
midday.
7 A thousand may fall at your side,
ten thousand at your right hand,
but it will not come near you.
8 You will only observe with your
eyes
and see the punishment of the
wicked.

9 If you make the Most High your
dwelling—
even the LORD, who is my refuge—
10 then no harm will befall you,
no disaster will come near your
tent.
11 For he will command his angels
concerning you
to guard you in all your ways;
12 they will lift you up in their hands,

so that you will not strike your foot
against a stone.
13 You will tread upon the lion and the
cobra;
you will trample the great lion and
the serpent.

14 "Because you love me," says the
LORD, "I will rescue you;
I will protect you, for you
acknowledge my name.
15 You will call upon me, and I will
answer you;
I will be with you in trouble,
I will deliver you and honour you.
16 With long life will I satisfy you
and show you my salvation."

Psalm 92

A psalm. A song. For the Sabbath day.

1 It is good to praise the LORD
and make music to your name,
O Most High,
2 to proclaim your love in the morning
and your faithfulness at night,
3 to the music of the ten-stringed lyre
and the melody of the harp.

4 For you make me glad by your deeds,
O LORD;
I sing for joy at the work of your
hands.
5 How great are your works, O LORD,
how profound your thoughts!
6 Senseless people do not know,
fools do not understand,
7 that though the wicked spring up like
grass
and all evildoers flourish,
they will be for ever destroyed.

8 But you, O LORD, are exalted for
ever.

9 For surely your enemies, O LORD,
surely your enemies will perish;
all evildoers will be scattered.
10 You have exalted my horn[a] like that
of a wild ox;
fine oils have been poured upon
me.

---

b17 Or *beauty*   a1 Hebrew *Shaddai*   b2 Or *That one says*   a10 *Horn* here symbolises strength.

¹¹My eyes have seen the defeat of my
    adversaries;
    my ears have heard the rout of my
      wicked foes.

¹²The righteous will flourish like a palm
    tree,
    they will grow like a cedar of
      Lebanon;
¹³planted in the house of the LORD,
    they will flourish in the courts of our
      God.
¹⁴They will still bear fruit in old age,
    they will stay fresh and green,
¹⁵proclaiming, "The LORD is upright;
    he is my Rock, and there is no
      wickedness in him."

Psalm 93

¹The LORD reigns, he is robed in
    majesty;
    the LORD is robed in majesty
    and is armed with strength.
The world is firmly established;
    it cannot be moved.
²Your throne was established long
    ago;
    you are from all eternity.

³The seas have lifted up, O LORD,
    the seas have lifted up their voice;
    the seas have lifted up their
      pounding waves.
⁴Mightier than the thunder of the great
    waters,
    mightier than the breakers of the
      sea—
    the LORD on high is mighty.

⁵Your statutes stand firm;
    holiness adorns your house
    for endless days, O LORD.

Psalm 94

¹O LORD, the God who avenges,
    O God who avenges, shine forth.
²Rise up, O Judge of the earth;
    pay back to the proud what they
      deserve.
³How long will the wicked, O LORD,
    how long will the wicked be
      jubilant?

⁴They pour out arrogant words;
    all the evildoers are full of boasting.
⁵They crush your people, O LORD;
    they oppress your inheritance.
⁶They slay the widow and the alien;
    they murder the fatherless.
⁷They say, "The LORD does not see;
    the God of Jacob pays no heed."

⁸Take heed, you senseless ones among
    the people;
    you fools, when will you become
      wise?
⁹Does he who implanted the ear not
    hear?
    Does he who formed the eye not see?
¹⁰Does he who disciplines nations not
    punish?
    Does he who teaches human beings
      lack knowledge?
¹¹The LORD knows all human thoughts;
    he knows that they are futile.

¹²Blessed are those you discipline,
    O LORD,
    those you teach from your law;
¹³you grant them relief from days of
    trouble,
    till a pit is dug for the wicked.
¹⁴For the LORD will not reject his people;
    he will never forsake his inheritance.
¹⁵Judgment will again be founded on
    righteousness,
    and all the upright in heart will
      follow it.

¹⁶Who will rise up for me against the
    wicked?
    Who will take a stand for me against
      evildoers?
¹⁷Unless the LORD had given me help,
    I would soon have dwelt in the
      silence of death.
¹⁸When I said, "My foot is slipping,"
    your love, O LORD, supported me.
¹⁹When anxiety was great within me,
    your consolation brought joy to my
      soul.

²⁰Can a corrupt throne be allied with
    you—
    one that brings on misery by its
      decrees?

21 They band together against the
       righteous
   and condemn the innocent to
       death.
22 But the LORD has become my fortress,
   and my God the rock in whom I take
       refuge.
23 He will repay them for their sins
   and destroy them for their
       wickedness;
   the LORD our God will destroy them.

Psalm 95

1 Come, let us sing for joy to the LORD;
   let us shout aloud to the Rock of
       our salvation.
2 Let us come before him with
       thanksgiving
   and extol him with music and song.

3 For the LORD is the great God,
   the great King above all gods.
4 In his hand are the depths of the earth,
   and the mountain peaks belong to
       him.
5 The sea is his, for he made it,
   and his hands formed the dry land.

6 Come, let us bow down in worship,
   let us kneel before the LORD our
       Maker;
7 for he is our God
   and we are the people of his pasture,
   the flock under his care.

   Today, if you hear his voice,
8   do not harden your hearts as you
           did at Meribah,[a]
       as you did that day at Massah[b] in
           the desert,
9 where your ancestors tested and tried
       me,
   though they had seen what I did.
10 For forty years I was angry with that
       generation;
   I said, "They are a people whose
       hearts go astray,
   and they have not known my
       ways."
11 So I declared on oath in my anger,
   "They shall never enter my rest."

Psalm 96

1 Sing to the LORD a new song;
   sing to the LORD, all the earth.
2 Sing to the LORD, praise his name;
   proclaim his salvation day after day.
3 Declare his glory among the nations,
   his marvellous deeds among all
       peoples.

4 For great is the LORD and most worthy
       of praise;
   he is to be feared above all gods.
5 For all the gods of the nations are
       idols,
   but the LORD made the heavens.
6 Splendour and majesty are before him;
   strength and glory are in his
       sanctuary.

7 Ascribe to the LORD, O families of
       nations,
   ascribe to the LORD glory and
       strength.
8 Ascribe to the LORD the glory due to
       his name;
   bring an offering and come into his
       courts.
9 Worship the LORD in the splendour of
       his[a] holiness;
   tremble before him, all the earth.

10 Say among the nations, "The LORD
       reigns."
   The world is firmly established, it
       cannot be moved;
   he will judge the peoples with
       equity.
11 Let the heavens rejoice, let the earth
       be glad;
   let the sea resound, and all that is
       in it;
12   let the fields be jubilant, and
       everything in them.
   Then all the trees of the forest will sing
       for joy;
13   they will sing before the LORD, for
       he comes,
   he comes to judge the earth.
   He will judge the world in
       righteousness
   and the peoples in his truth.

[a]8 *Meribah* means *quarrelling*.   [b]8 *Massah* means *testing*.   [a]9 Or LORD *with the splendour of*

Psalm 97

¹The LORD reigns, let the earth be glad;
let the distant shores rejoice.

²Clouds and thick darkness surround
him;
righteousness and justice are the
foundation of his throne.
³Fire goes before him
and consumes his foes on every
side.
⁴His lightning lights up the world;
the earth sees and trembles.
⁵The mountains melt like wax before
the LORD,
before the Lord of all the earth.
⁶The heavens proclaim his
righteousness,
and all the peoples see his glory.

⁷All who worship images are put to
shame,
those who boast in idols—
worship him, all you gods!

⁸Zion hears and rejoices
and the villages of Judah are glad
because of your judgments,
O LORD.
⁹For you, O LORD, are the Most High
over all the earth;
you are exalted far above all gods.

¹⁰Let those who love the LORD hate
evil,
for he guards the lives of his faithful
ones
and delivers them from the hand of
the wicked.
¹¹Light is shed upon the righteous
and joy on the upright in heart.
¹²Rejoice in the LORD, you who are
righteous,
and praise his holy name.

Psalm 98

A psalm.

¹Sing to the LORD a new song,
for he has done marvellous things;
his right hand and his holy arm
have worked salvation for him.

²The LORD has made his salvation known
and revealed his righteousness to
the nations.
³He has remembered his love
and his faithfulness to the house of
Israel;
all the ends of the earth have seen
the salvation of our God.

⁴Shout for joy to the LORD, all the earth,
burst into jubilant song with music;
⁵make music to the LORD with the harp,
with the harp and the sound of
singing,
⁶with trumpets and the blast of the
ram's horn—
shout for joy before the LORD, the
King.

⁷Let the sea resound, and everything
in it,
the world, and all who live in it.
⁸Let the rivers clap their hands,
let the mountains sing together for
joy;
⁹let them sing before the LORD,
for he comes to judge the earth.
He will judge the world in
righteousness
and the peoples with equity.

Psalm 99

¹The LORD reigns,
let the nations tremble;
he sits enthroned between the
cherubim,
let the earth shake.
²Great is the LORD in Zion;
he is exalted over all the nations.
³Let them praise your great and
awesome name—
he is holy.

⁴The King is mighty, he loves justice—
you have established equity;
in Jacob you have done
what is just and right.
⁵Exalt the LORD our God
and worship at his footstool;
he is holy.

⁶Moses and Aaron were among his
priests,

Samuel was among those who
   called on his name;
they called on the LORD
   and he answered them.
⁷He spoke to them from the pillar of
   cloud;
   they kept his statutes and the
   decrees he gave them.

⁸O LORD our God,
   you answered them;
you were to Israelᵃ a forgiving God,
   though you punished their
   misdeeds.ᵇ
⁹Exalt the LORD our God
   and worship at his holy mountain,
   for the LORD our God is holy.

Psalm 100

A psalm. For giving thanks.

¹Shout for joy to the LORD, all the
   earth.
²   Worship the LORD with gladness;
   come before him with joyful
   songs.
³Know that the LORD is God.
   It is he who made us, and we are
   his;ᵃ
   we are his people, the sheep of his
   pasture.

⁴Enter his gates with thanksgiving
   and his courts with praise;
   give thanks to him and praise his
   name.
⁵For the LORD is good and his love
   endures for ever;
   his faithfulness continues through
   all generations.

Psalm 101

Of David. A psalm.

¹I will sing of your love and justice;
   to you, O LORD, I will sing praise.
²I will be careful to lead a blameless
   life—
   when will you come to me?

I will walk in my house
   with blameless heart.

³I will set before my eyes
   no vile thing.

The deeds of the faithless I hate;
   they shall not cling to me.
⁴The perverse of heart shall be far from
   me;
   I will have nothing to do with evil.

⁵Whoever slanders a neighbour in
   secret
   I will put to silence;
whoever has haughty eyes and a proud
   heart
   I will not endure.

⁶My eyes will be on the faithful in the
   land,
   that they may dwell with me;
those whose walk is blameless
   will minister to me.

⁷No-one who practises deceit
   will dwell in my house;
no-one who speaks falsely
   will stand in my presence.

⁸Every morning I will put to silence
   all the wicked in the land;
I will cut off every evildoer
   from the city of the LORD.

Psalm 102

*A prayer of an afflicted person who is faint and pours
out a lament before the LORD.*

¹Hear my prayer, O LORD;
   let my cry for help come to you.
²Do not hide your face from me
   when I am in distress.
   Turn your ear to me;
   when I call, answer me quickly.

³For my days vanish like smoke;
   my bones burn like glowing
   embers.
⁴My heart is blighted and withered like
   grass;
   I forget to eat my food.
⁵Because of my loud groaning
   I am reduced to skin and
   bones.

ᵃ8 Hebrew *them*   ᵇ8 Or / *an avenger of the wrongs done to them*   ᵃ3 Or *and not we ourselves*

⁶ I am like a desert owl,
   like an owl among the ruins.
⁷ I lie awake; I have become
   like a bird alone on a roof.
⁸ All day long my enemies taunt me;
   those who rail against me use my
    name as a curse.
⁹ For I eat ashes as my food
   and mingle my drink with tears
¹⁰ because of your great wrath,
   for you have taken me up and
    thrown me aside.
¹¹ My days are like the evening shadow;
   I wither away like grass.

¹² But you, O Lord, sit enthroned for
    ever;
   your renown endures through all
    generations.
¹³ You will arise and have compassion
    on Zion,
   for it is time to show favour to her;
   the appointed time has come.
¹⁴ For her stones are dear to your
    servants;
   her very dust moves them to pity.
¹⁵ The nations will fear the name of the
    Lord,
   all the kings of the earth will revere
    your glory.
¹⁶ For the Lord will rebuild Zion
   and appear in his glory.
¹⁷ He will respond to the prayer of the
    destitute;
   he will not despise their plea.

¹⁸ Let this be written for a future
    generation,
   that a people not yet created may
    praise the Lord:
¹⁹ "The Lord looked down from his
    sanctuary on high,
   from heaven he viewed the earth,
²⁰ to hear the groans of the prisoners
   and release those condemned to
    death."
²¹ So the name of the Lord will be
    declared in Zion
   and his praise in Jerusalem
²² when the peoples and the kingdoms
   assemble to worship the Lord.

²³ In the course of my life[a] he broke my
    strength;
   he cut short my days.
²⁴ So I said:
   "Do not take me away, O my God,
    in the midst of my days;
   your years go on through all
    generations.
²⁵ In the beginning you laid the
    foundations of the earth,
   and the heavens are the work of
    your hands.
²⁶ They will perish, but you remain;
   they will all wear out like a
    garment.
   Like clothing you will change them
   and they will be discarded.
²⁷ But you remain the same,
   and your years will never end.
²⁸ The children of your servants will live
    in your presence;
   their descendants will be
    established before you."

Psalm 103

Of David.

¹ Praise the Lord, O my soul;
   all my inmost being, praise his holy
    name.
² Praise the Lord, O my soul,
   and forget not all his benefits—
³ who forgives all your sins
   and heals all your diseases,
⁴ who redeems your life from the pit
   and crowns you with love and
    compassion,
⁵ who satisfies your desires with good
    things
   so that your youth is renewed like
    the eagle's.

⁶ The Lord works righteousness
   and justice for all the oppressed.

⁷ He made known his ways to Moses,
   his deeds to the people of Israel:
⁸ The Lord is compassionate and
    gracious,
   slow to anger, abounding in love.

[a]23 Or *By his power*

⁹He will not always accuse,
  nor will he harbour his anger for
    ever;
¹⁰he does not treat us as our sins deserve
  or repay us according to our
    iniquities.
¹¹For as high as the heavens are above
    the earth,
  so great is his love for those who
    fear him;
¹²as far as the east is from the west,
  so far has he removed our
    transgressions from us.
¹³As parents have compassion on their
    children,
  so the LORD has compassion on
    those who fear him;
¹⁴for he knows how we are formed,
  he remembers that we are dust.
¹⁵As for mortals, their days are like
    grass,
  they flourish like a flower of the
    field;
¹⁶the wind blows over it and it is gone,
  and its place remembers it no more.
¹⁷But from everlasting to everlasting
  the LORD's love is with those who
    fear him,
  and his righteousness with their
    children's children—
¹⁸with those who keep his covenant
  and remember to obey his precepts.

¹⁹The LORD has established his throne
    in heaven,
  and his kingdom rules over all.

²⁰Praise the LORD, you his angels,
  you mighty ones who do his bidding,
  who obey his word.
²¹Praise the LORD, all his heavenly hosts,
  you his servants who do his will.
²²Praise the LORD, all his works
  everywhere in his dominion.

  Praise the LORD, O my soul.

Psalm 104

¹Praise the LORD, O my soul.

  O LORD my God, you are very great;
  you are clothed with splendour and
    majesty.

²He wraps himself in light as with a
    garment;
  he stretches out the heavens like a
    tent
³ and lays the beams of his upper
    chambers on their waters.
  He makes the clouds his chariot
  and rides on the wings of the wind.
⁴He makes winds his messengers,ᵃ
  flames of fire his servants.

⁵He set the earth on its foundations;
  it can never be moved.
⁶You covered it with the deep as with
    a garment;
  the waters stood above the
    mountains.
⁷But at your rebuke the waters fled,
  at the sound of your thunder they
    took to flight;
⁸they flowed over the mountains,
  they went down into the valleys,
  to the place you assigned for them.
⁹You set a boundary they cannot
    cross;
  never again will they cover the earth.

¹⁰He makes springs pour water into the
    ravines;
  it flows between the mountains.
¹¹They give water to all the beasts of the
    field;
  the wild donkeys quench their
    thirst.
¹²The birds of the air nest by the waters;
  they sing among the branches.
¹³He waters the mountains from his
    upper chambers;
  the earth is satisfied by the fruit of
    his work.
¹⁴He makes grass grow for the cattle,
  and plants for people to cultivate—
  bringing forth food from the earth:
¹⁵wine that gladdens human hearts,
  oil to make their faces shine,
  and bread that sustains their hearts.
¹⁶The trees of the LORD are well watered,
  the cedars of Lebanon that he
    planted.
¹⁷There the birds make their nests;
  the stork has its home in the pine
    trees.

ᵃ4 Or angels

18 The high mountains belong to the wild
      goats;
   the crags are a refuge for the conies.b

19 The moon marks off the seasons,
      and the sun knows when to go down.
20 You bring darkness, it becomes night,
      and all the beasts of the forest
      prowl.
21 The lions roar for their prey
      and seek their food from God.
22 The sun rises, and they steal away;
      they return and lie down in their
      dens.
23 Then people go out to their work,
      to their labour until evening.

24 How many are your works, O LORD!
      In wisdom you made them all;
      the earth is full of your creatures.
25 There is the sea, vast and spacious,
      teeming with creatures beyond
      number—
      living things both large and small.
26 There the ships go to and fro,
      and the leviathan, which you
      formed to frolic there.

27 These all look to you
      to give them their food at the
      proper time.
28 When you give it to them,
      they gather it up;
   when you open your hand,
      they are satisfied with good things.
29 When you hide your face,
      they are terrified;
   when you take away their breath,
      they die and return to the dust.
30 When you send your Spirit,
      they are created,
      and you renew the face of the earth.

31 May the glory of the LORD endure for
      ever;
   may the LORD rejoice in his works—
32 he who looks at the earth, and it
      trembles,
   who touches the mountains, and
      they smoke.

33 I will sing to the LORD all my life;
   I will sing praise to my God as long
      as I live.
34 May my meditation be pleasing to him,
      as I rejoice in the LORD.
35 But may sinners vanish from the earth
      and the wicked be no more.

Praise the LORD, O my soul.

Praise the LORD. c

Psalm 105

1 Give thanks to the LORD, call on his
      name;
   make known among the nations
      what he has done.
2 Sing to him, sing praise to him;
      tell of all his wonderful acts.
3 Glory in his holy name;
      let the hearts of those who seek the
      LORD rejoice.
4 Look to the LORD and his strength;
      seek his face always.

5 Remember the wonders he has done,
      his miracles, and the judgments he
      pronounced,
6 O descendants of Abraham his servant,
   O children of Jacob, his chosen
      ones.
7 He is the LORD our God;
      his judgments are in all the earth.

8 He remembers his covenant for ever,
      the word he commanded, for a
      thousand generations,
9 the covenant he made with Abraham,
      the oath he swore to Isaac.
10 He confirmed it to Jacob as a decree,
      to Israel as an everlasting covenant:
11 "To you I will give the land of Canaan
      as the portion you will inherit."

12 When they were but few in number,
      few indeed, and strangers in it,
13 they wandered from nation to nation,
      from one kingdom to another.
14 He allowed no-one to oppress them;
      for their sake he rebuked kings:

b 18 That is, the hyrax or rock badger
c 35 Hebrew Hallelu Yah; in the Septuagint this line stands at the beginning of Psalm 105.

15 "Do not touch my anointed ones;
    do my prophets no harm."

16 He called down famine on the land
    and destroyed all their supplies of
      food;
17 and he sent a man before them—
    Joseph, sold as a slave.
18 They bruised his feet with shackles,
    his neck was put in irons,
19 till what he foretold came to pass,
    till the word of the LORD proved
      him true.
20 The king sent and released him,
    the ruler of peoples set him free.
21 He made him master of his household,
    ruler over all he possessed,
22 to instruct his princes as he pleased
    and teach his elders wisdom.

23 Then Israel entered Egypt;
    Jacob lived as an alien in the land
      of Ham.
24 The LORD made his people very
      fruitful;
    he made them too numerous for
      their foes,
25 whose hearts he turned to hate his
      people,
    to conspire against his servants.
26 He sent Moses his servant,
    and Aaron, whom he had chosen.
27 They performed his miraculous signs
      among them,
    his wonders in the land of Ham.
28 He sent darkness and made the land
      dark—
    for had they not rebelled against his
      words?
29 He turned their waters into blood,
    causing their fish to die.
30 Their land teemed with frogs,
    which went up into the bedrooms of
      their rulers.
31 He spoke, and there came swarms of
      flies,
    and gnats throughout their country.
32 He turned their rain into hail,
    with lightning throughout their
      land;
33 he struck down their vines and fig-trees

and shattered the trees of their
      country.
34 He spoke, and the locusts came,
    grasshoppers without number;
35 they ate up every green thing in their
      land,
    ate up the produce of their soil.
36 Then he struck down all the firstborn
      in their land,
    the firstfruits of all their manhood.

37 He brought out Israel, laden with
      silver and gold,
    and from among their tribes no-one
      faltered.
38 Egypt was glad when they left,
    because dread of Israel had fallen
      on them.
39 He spread out a cloud as a covering,
    and a fire to give light at night.
40 They asked, and he brought them
      quail
    and satisfied them with the bread of
      heaven.
41 He opened the rock, and water
      gushed out;
    like a river it flowed in the desert.

42 For he remembered his holy promise
    given to his servant Abraham.
43 He brought out his people with
      rejoicing,
    his chosen ones with shouts of joy;
44 he gave them the lands of the nations,
    and they fell heir to what others had
      toiled for—
45 that they might keep his precepts
    and observe his laws.

Praise the LORD.[a]

Psalm 106

1 Praise the LORD.[a]

Give thanks to the LORD, for he is
      good;
    his love endures for ever.
2 Who can proclaim the mighty acts of
      the LORD
    or fully declare his praise?
3 Blessed are those who maintain justice,

[a]45 Hebrew *Hallelu Yah*   [a]1 Hebrew *Hallelu Yah*; also in verse 48

who constantly do what is right.

⁴Remember me, O Lᴏʀᴅ, when you
show favour to your people,
come to my aid when you save them,
⁵that I may enjoy the prosperity of your
chosen ones,
that I may share in the joy of your
nation
and join your inheritance in giving
praise.

⁶We have sinned, even as our ancestors
did;
we have done wrong and acted
wickedly.
⁷When our ancestors were in Egypt,
they gave no thought to your
miracles;
they did not remember your many
kindnesses,
and they rebelled by the sea, the
Red Sea.ᵇ
⁸Yet he saved them for his name's sake,
to make his mighty power known.
⁹He rebuked the Red Sea, and it dried
up;
he led them through the depths as
through a desert.
¹⁰He saved them from the hand of the
foe;
from the hand of the enemy he
redeemed them.
¹¹The waters covered their adversaries;
not one of them survived.
¹²Then they believed his promises
and sang his praise.

¹³But they soon forgot what he had done
and did not wait for his counsel.
¹⁴In the desert they gave in to their
craving;
in the wasteland they put God to
the test.
¹⁵So he gave them what they asked for,
but sent a wasting disease upon them.

¹⁶In the camp they grew envious of Moses
and of Aaron, who was consecrated
to the Lᴏʀᴅ.
¹⁷The earth opened up and swallowed
Dathan;

it buried the company of Abiram.
¹⁸Fire blazed among their followers;
a flame consumed the wicked.

¹⁹At Horeb they made a calf
and worshipped an idol cast from
metal.
²⁰They exchanged their Glory
for an image of a bull, which eats
grass.
²¹They forgot the God who saved them,
who had done great things in Egypt,
²²miracles in the land of Ham
and awesome deeds by the Red Sea.
²³So he said he would destroy them—
had not Moses, his chosen one,
stood in the breach before him
to keep his wrath from destroying
them.

²⁴Then they despised the pleasant land;
they did not believe his promise.
²⁵They grumbled in their tents
and did not obey the Lᴏʀᴅ.
²⁶So he swore to them with uplifted hand
that he would make them fall in the
desert,
²⁷make their descendants fall among the
nations
and scatter them throughout the
lands.

²⁸They yoked themselves to the Baal of
Peor
and ate sacrifices offered to lifeless
gods;
²⁹they provoked the Lᴏʀᴅ to anger by
their wicked deeds,
and a plague broke out among them.
³⁰But Phinehas stood up and intervened,
and the plague was checked.
³¹This was credited to him as
righteousness
for endless generations to come.

³²By the waters of Meribah they
angered the Lᴏʀᴅ,
and trouble came to Moses because
of them;
³³for they rebelled against the Spirit of
God,

ᵇ7 Hebrew *Yam Suph*; that is, Sea of Reeds; also in verses 9 and 22

and rash words came from Moses'
  lips.[c]

34 They did not destroy the peoples
  as the LORD had commanded them,
35 but they mingled with the nations
  and adopted their customs.
36 They worshipped their idols,
  which became a snare to them.
37 They sacrificed their sons
  and their daughters to demons.
38 They shed innocent blood,
  the blood of their sons and daughters,
  whom they sacrificed to the idols of
      Canaan,
  and the land was desecrated by their
      blood.
39 They defiled themselves by what they
      did;
  by their deeds they prostituted
      themselves.

40 Therefore the LORD was angry with his
      people
  and abhorred his inheritance.
41 He handed them over to the nations,
  and their foes ruled over them.
42 Their enemies oppressed them
  and subjected them to their power.
43 Many times he delivered them,
  but they were bent on rebellion
  and they wasted away in their sin.

44 But he took note of their distress
  when he heard their cry;
45 for their sake he remembered his
      covenant
  and out of his great love he relented.
46 He caused them to be pitied
  by all who held them captive.

47 Save us, O LORD our God,
  and gather us from the nations,
  that we may give thanks to your holy
      name
  and glory in your praise.

48 Praise be to the LORD, the God of Israel,
  from everlasting to everlasting.
  Let all the people say, "Amen!"

Praise the LORD.

BOOK V

Psalms 107–150

Psalm 107

1 Give thanks to the LORD, for he is good;
  his love endures for ever.
2 Let the redeemed of the LORD say
      this—
  those he redeemed from the hand
      of the foe,
3 those he gathered from the lands,
  from east and west, from north and
      south.[a]

4 Some wandered in desert wastelands,
  finding no way to a city where they
      could settle.
5 They were hungry and thirsty,
  and their lives ebbed away.
6 Then they cried out to the LORD in
      their trouble,
  and he delivered them from their
      distress.
7 He led them by a straight way
  to a city where they could settle.
8 Let them give thanks to the LORD for
      his unfailing love
  and his wonderful deeds for human
      beings,
9 for he satisfies the thirsty
  and fills the hungry with good
      things.

10 Some sat in darkness and the deepest
      gloom,
  prisoners suffering in iron chains,
11 for they had rebelled against the
      words of God
  and despised the counsel of the
      Most High.
12 So he subjected them to bitter labour;
  they stumbled, and there was
      no-one to help.
13 Then they cried to the LORD in their
      trouble,
  and he saved them from their
      distress.
14 He brought them out of darkness and
      the deepest gloom

---

[c]33 Or *against his spirit, / and rash words came from his lips*   [a]3 Hebrew *north and the sea*

and broke away their chains.
¹⁵ Let them give thanks to the Lord for
his unfailing love
and his wonderful deeds for human
beings,
¹⁶ for he breaks down gates of bronze
and cuts through bars of iron.

¹⁷ Some became fools through their
rebellious ways
and suffered affliction because of
their iniquities.
¹⁸ They loathed all food
and drew near the gates of death.
¹⁹ Then they cried to the Lord in their
trouble,
and he saved them from their
distress.
²⁰ He sent forth his word and healed them;
he rescued them from the grave.
²¹ Let them give thanks to the Lord for
his unfailing love
and his wonderful deeds for human
beings.
²² Let them sacrifice thank-offerings
and tell of his works with songs of joy.

²³ Others went out on the sea in ships;
they were merchants on the mighty
waters.
²⁴ They saw the works of the Lord,
his wonderful deeds in the deep.
²⁵ For he spoke and stirred up a tempest
that lifted high the waves.
²⁶ They mounted up to the heavens and
went down to the depths;
in their peril their courage melted
away.
²⁷ They reeled and staggered like
drunkards;
they were at their wits' end.
²⁸ Then they cried out to the Lord in
their trouble,
and he brought them out of their
distress.
²⁹ He stilled the storm to a whisper;
the waves of the sea were hushed.
³⁰ They were glad when it grew calm,
and he guided them to their desired
haven.
³¹ Let them give thanks to the Lord for
his unfailing love
and his wonderful deeds for human
beings.

³² Let them exalt him in the assembly of
the people
and praise him in the council of the
elders.

³³ He turned rivers into a desert,
flowing springs into thirsty ground,
³⁴ and fruitful land into a salt waste,
because of the wickedness of those
who lived there.
³⁵ He turned the desert into pools of water
and the parched ground into flowing
springs;
³⁶ there he brought the hungry to live,
and they founded a city where they
could settle.
³⁷ They sowed fields and planted
vineyards
that yielded a fruitful harvest;
³⁸ he blessed them, and their numbers
greatly increased,
and he did not let their herds
diminish.

³⁹ Then their numbers decreased, and
they were humbled
by oppression, calamity and sorrow;
⁴⁰ he who pours contempt on nobles
made them wander in a trackless
waste.
⁴¹ But he lifted the needy out of their
affliction
and increased their families like
flocks.
⁴² The upright see and rejoice,
but all the wicked shut their mouths.

⁴³ Let those who are wise heed these
things
and consider the great love of the
Lord.

Psalm 108

A song. A psalm of David.

¹ My heart is steadfast, O God;
I will sing and make music with all
my soul.
² Awake, harp and lyre!
I will awaken the dawn.
³ I will praise you, O Lord, among the
nations;
I will sing of you among the peoples.

⁴For great is your love, higher than the
   heavens;
   your faithfulness reaches to the skies.
⁵Be exalted, O God, above the heavens,
   and let your glory be over all the
    earth.

⁶Save us and help us with your right
   hand,
   that those you love may be delivered.
⁷God has spoken from his sanctuary:
   "In triumph I will parcel out Shechem
   and measure off the Valley of
    Succoth.
⁸Gilead is mine, Manasseh is mine;
   Ephraim is my helmet,
   Judah my sceptre.
⁹Moab is my washbasin,
   upon Edom I toss my sandal;
   over Philistia I shout in triumph."

¹⁰Who will bring me to the fortified
   city?
   Who will lead me to Edom?
¹¹Is it not you, O God, you who have
   rejected us
   and no longer go out with our
    armies?
¹²Give us aid against the enemy,
   for human help is worthless.
¹³With God we shall gain the victory,
   and he will trample down our
    enemies.

Psalm 109

For the director of music. Of David. A psalm.

¹O God, whom I praise,
   do not remain silent,
²for people who are wicked and
   deceitful
   have opened their mouths against
    me;
   they have spoken against me with
    lying tongues.
³With words of hatred they surround
   me;
   they attack me without cause.
⁴In return for my friendship they
   accuse me,
   but I turn to prayer.

⁵They repay me evil for good,
   and hatred for my friendship.

⁶Appoint*ᵃ* someone evil*ᵇ* to oppose
   him;
   let an accuser*ᶜ* stand at his right hand.
⁷When he is tried, let him be found
   guilty,
   and may his prayers condemn him.
⁸May his days be few;
   may another take his place of
    leadership.
⁹May his children be fatherless
   and his wife a widow.
¹⁰May his children be wandering beggars;
   may they be driven*ᵈ* from their
    ruined homes.
¹¹May a creditor seize all he has;
   may strangers plunder the fruits of
    his labour.
¹²May no-one extend kindness to him
   or take pity on his fatherless children.
¹³May his descendants be cut off,
   their names blotted out from the
    next generation.
¹⁴May the iniquity of his fathers be
   remembered before the LORD;
   may the sin of his mother never be
    blotted out.
¹⁵May their sins always remain before
   the LORD,
   that he may cut off the memory of
    them from the earth.

¹⁶For he never thought of doing a
   kindness,
   but hounded to death the poor
   and the needy and the
    broken-hearted.
¹⁷He loved to pronounce a curse—
   may it*ᵉ* come on him;
   he found no pleasure in blessing—
   may it be*ᶠ* far from him.
¹⁸He wore cursing as his garment;
   it entered into his body like water,
   into his bones like oil.
¹⁹May it be like a cloak wrapped about
   him,
   like a belt tied for ever round him.
²⁰May this be the LORD's payment to my
   accusers,
   to those who speak evil of me.

---

*ᵃ*6 Or ⸢*They say:*⸣ "*Appoint* (with quotation marks at the end of verse 19)   *ᵇ*6 Or *the Evil One*   *ᶜ*6 Or *let Satan*
*ᵈ*10 Septuagint; Hebrew *sought*   *ᵉ*17 Or *curse, / and it has*   *ᶠ*17 Or *blessing, / and it is*

²¹ But you, O Sovereign LORD,
　　deal well with me for your name's
　　　sake;
　　out of the goodness of your love,
　　　deliver me.
²² For I am poor and needy,
　　and my heart is wounded within
　　　me.
²³ I fade away like an evening shadow;
　　I am shaken off like a locust.
²⁴ My knees give way from fasting;
　　my body is thin and gaunt.
²⁵ I am an object of scorn to my
　　　accusers;
　　when they see me, they shake their
　　　heads.

²⁶ Help me, O LORD my God;
　　save me in accordance with your
　　　love.
²⁷ Let them know that it is your hand,
　　that you, O LORD, have done it.
²⁸ They may curse, but you will bless;
　　when they attack they will be put to
　　　shame,
　　but your servant will rejoice.
²⁹ My accusers will be clothed with
　　　disgrace
　　and wrapped in shame as in a cloak.

³⁰ With my mouth I will greatly extol the
　　　LORD;
　　in the great throng I will praise him.
³¹ For he stands at the right hand of the
　　　needy,
　　to save their lives from those who
　　　condemn them.

Psalm 110

Of David. A psalm.

¹ The LORD says to my Lord:
　　"Sit at my right hand
　　until I make your enemies
　　　a footstool for your feet."

² The LORD will extend your mighty
　　sceptre from Zion;

you will rule in the midst of your
　　enemies.
³ Your troops will be willing
　　on your day of battle.
　Arrayed in holy majesty,
　　from the womb of the dawn
　　you will receive the dew of your
　　　youth.^a

⁴ The LORD has sworn
　　and will not change his mind:
　"You are a priest for ever,
　　in the order of Melchizedek."

⁵ The Lord is at your right hand;
　　he will crush kings on the day of his
　　　wrath.
⁶ He will judge nations, heaping up the
　　　dead
　　and crushing the rulers of the whole
　　　earth.
⁷ He will drink from a brook beside the
　　　way;^b
　　therefore he will lift up his head.

Psalm 111^a

¹ Praise the LORD.^b

　I will extol the LORD with all my heart
　　in the council of the upright and in
　　　the assembly.

² Great are the works of the LORD;
　　they are pondered by all who
　　　delight in them.
³ Glorious and majestic are his deeds,
　　and his righteousness endures for
　　　ever.
⁴ He has caused his wonders to be
　　　remembered;
　　the LORD is gracious and
　　　compassionate.
⁵ He provides food for those who fear
　　　him;
　　he remembers his covenant for
　　　ever.
⁶ He has shown his people the power of
　　　his works,

^a3 Or / *your young men will come to you like the dew*
^b7 Or / *The One who grants succession will set him in authority*
^aThis psalm is an acrostic poem, the lines of which begin with the successive letters of the Hebrew alphabet.
^b1 Hebrew *Hallelu Yah*

giving them the lands of other
nations.
7 The works of his hands are faithful
and just;
all his precepts are trustworthy.
8 They are steadfast for ever and ever,
done in faithfulness and uprightness.
9 He provided redemption for his people;
he ordained his covenant for ever—
holy and awesome is his name.

10 The fear of the LORD is the beginning
of wisdom;
all who follow his precepts have
good understanding.
To him belongs eternal praise.

Psalm 112[a]

1 Praise the LORD.[b]

Blessed are those who fear the LORD,
who find great delight in his
commands.

2 Their children will be mighty in the
land;
the generation of the upright will be
blessed.
3 Wealth and riches are in their houses,
and their righteousness endures for
ever.
4 Even in darkness light dawns for the
upright,
for those who are gracious and
compassionate and righteous.[c]
5 Good will come to those who are
generous and lend freely,
who conduct their affairs with justice.
6 Surely they will never be shaken;
the righteous will be remembered
for ever.
7 They will have no fear of bad news;
their hearts are steadfast, trusting
in the LORD.
8 Their hearts are secure, they will have
no fear;
in the end they will look in triumph
on their foes.
9 They have scattered abroad their gifts
to the poor,

their righteousness endures for
ever;
their horn[d] will be lifted high in
honour.

10 The wicked will see and be vexed,
they will gnash their teeth and
waste away;
the longings of the wicked will come
to nothing.

Psalm 113

1 Praise the LORD.[a]

Praise, O servants of the LORD,
praise the name of the LORD.
2 Let the name of the LORD be praised,
both now and for evermore.
3 From the rising of the sun to the place
where it sets,
the name of the LORD is to be
praised.

4 The LORD is exalted over all the
nations,
his glory above the heavens.
5 Who is like the LORD our God,
the One who sits enthroned on
high,
6 who stoops down to look
on the heavens and the earth?

7 He raises the poor from the dust
and lifts the needy from the ash
heap;
8 he seats them with princes,
with the princes of their people.
9 He settles the barren woman in her
home
as a happy mother of children.

Praise the LORD.

Psalm 114

1 When Israel came out of Egypt,
the house of Jacob from a people of
foreign tongue,
2 Judah became God's sanctuary,
Israel his dominion.

---

[a]This psalm is an acrostic poem, the lines of which begin with the successive letters of the Hebrew alphabet.
[b]1 Hebrew *Hallelu Yah*   [c]4 Or / *for ¡the* LORD ¡*is gracious and compassionate and righteous*
[d]9 *Horn* here symbolises dignity.   [a]1 Hebrew *Hallelu Yah*; also in verse 9

3 The sea looked and fled,
the Jordan turned back;
4 the mountains skipped like rams,
the hills like lambs.

5 Why was it, O sea, that you fled,
O Jordan, that you turned back,
6 you mountains, that you skipped like
rams,
you hills, like lambs?

7 Tremble, O earth, at the presence of
the Lord,
at the presence of the God of Jacob,
8 who turned the rock into a pool,
the hard rock into springs of water.

Psalm 115

1 Not to us, O Lord, not to us
but to your name be the glory,
because of your love and
faithfulness.

2 Why do the nations say,
"Where is their God?"
3 Our God is in heaven;
he does whatever pleases him.
4 But their idols are silver and gold,
made by human hands.
5 They have mouths, but cannot speak,
eyes, but they cannot see;
6 they have ears, but cannot hear,
noses, but they cannot smell;
7 they have hands, but cannot feel,
feet, but they cannot walk;
nor can they utter a sound with their
throats.
8 Those who make them will be like
them,
and so will all who trust in them.

9 O house of Israel, trust in the Lord—
he is their help and shield.
10 O house of Aaron, trust in the Lord—
he is their help and shield.
11 You who fear him, trust in the
Lord—
he is their help and shield.

12 The Lord remembers us and will bless
us:

He will bless the house of Israel,
he will bless the house of Aaron,
13 he will bless those who fear the Lord—
small and great alike.

14 May the Lord make you increase,
both you and your children.
15 May you be blessed by the Lord,
the Maker of heaven and earth.

16 The highest heavens belong to the
Lord,
but the earth he has given to the
human race.
17 It is not the dead who praise the Lord,
those who go down to silence;
18 it is we who extol the Lord,
both now and for evermore.

Praise the Lord.^a

Psalm 116

1 I love the Lord, for he heard my voice;
he heard my cry for mercy.
2 Because he turned his ear to me,
I will call on him as long as I live.

3 The cords of death entangled me,
the anguish of the grave^a came
upon me;
I was overcome by trouble and
sorrow.
4 Then I called on the name of the Lord:
"O Lord, save me!"

5 The Lord is gracious and righteous;
our God is full of compassion.
6 The Lord protects the
simple-hearted;
when I was in great need, he saved
me.

7 Be at rest once more, O my soul,
for the Lord has been good to you.

8 For you, O Lord, have delivered my
soul from death,
my eyes from tears,
my feet from stumbling,
9 that I may walk before the Lord
in the land of the living.

¹⁰ I believed; therefore[b] I said,
   "I am greatly afflicted."
¹¹ And in my dismay I said,
   "All people are liars."

¹² How can I repay the LORD
   for all his goodness to me?
¹³ I will lift up the cup of salvation
   and call on the name of the LORD.
¹⁴ I will fulfil my vows to the LORD
   in the presence of all his people.

¹⁵ Precious in the sight of the LORD
   is the death of his saints.
¹⁶ O LORD, truly I am your servant;
   I am your servant, the son of your
      woman servant;[c]
   you have freed me from my chains.

¹⁷ I will sacrifice a thank-offering to you
   and call on the name of the LORD.
¹⁸ I will fulfil my vows to the LORD
   in the presence of all his people,
¹⁹ in the courts of the house of the
      LORD—
   in your midst, O Jerusalem.

Praise the LORD.[d]

Psalm 117

¹ Praise the LORD, all you nations;
   extol him, all you peoples.
² For great is his love towards us,
   and the faithfulness of the LORD
      endures for ever.

Praise the LORD.[d]

Psalm 118

¹ Give thanks to the LORD, for he is
      good;
   his love endures for ever.

² Let Israel say:
   "His love endures for ever."
³ Let the house of Aaron say:
   "His love endures for ever."
⁴ Let those who fear the LORD say:
   "His love endures for ever."

⁵ In my anguish I cried to the LORD,
   and he answered by setting me free.
⁶ The LORD is with me; I will not be
      afraid.
   What can human beings do to me?
⁷ The LORD is with me; he is my helper.
   I will look in triumph on my enemies.

⁸ It is better to take refuge in the LORD
   than to trust in human beings.
⁹ It is better to take refuge in the LORD
   than to trust in princes.

¹⁰ All the nations surrounded me,
   but in the name of the LORD I cut
      them off.
¹¹ They surrounded me on every side,
   but in the name of the LORD I cut
      them off.
¹² They swarmed around me like bees,
   but they died out as quickly as
      burning thorns;
   in the name of the LORD I cut them
      off.

¹³ I was pushed back and about to fall,
   but the LORD helped me.
¹⁴ The LORD is my strength and my song;
   he has become my salvation.

¹⁵ Shouts of joy and victory
   resound in the tents of the righteous:
   "The LORD's right hand has done
      mighty things!
¹⁶   The LORD's right hand is lifted high;
   the LORD's right hand has done
      mighty things!"

¹⁷ I will not die but live,
   and will proclaim what the LORD
      has done.
¹⁸ The LORD has chastened me severely,
   but he has not given me over to death.

¹⁹ Open for me the gates of righteousness;
   I will enter and give thanks to the
      LORD.
²⁰ This is the gate of the LORD
   through which the righteous may
      enter.

---

*b*10 Or *believed even when*   *c*16 Or *servant, your faithful one*   *d*19,2 Hebrew *Hallelu Yah*

21 I will give you thanks, for you
    answered me;
  you have become my salvation.

22 The stone the builders rejected
    has become the capstone;
23 the LORD has done this,
    and it is marvellous in our eyes.
24 This is the day the LORD has made;
    let us rejoice and be glad in it.

25 O LORD, save us;
  O LORD, grant us success.
26 Blessed is he who comes in the name
    of the LORD.
  From the house of the LORD we
    bless you.*a*
27 The LORD is God,
    and he has made his light shine
      upon us.
  With boughs in hand, join in the festal
    procession
  up*b* to the horns of the altar.

28 You are my God, and I will give thanks;
  you are my God, and I will exalt you.

29 Give thanks to the LORD, for he is
    good;
  his love endures for ever.

Psalm 119*a*

א Aleph

1 Blessed are those whose ways are
    blameless,
  who walk according to the law of
    the LORD.
2 Blessed are those who keep his
    statutes
  and seek him with all their heart.
3 They do nothing wrong;
  they walk in his ways.
4 You have laid down precepts
  that are to be fully obeyed.
5 Oh, that my ways were steadfast
  in obeying your decrees!
6 Then I would not be put to shame
  when I consider all your
    commands.
7 I will praise you with an upright heart

as I learn your righteous laws.
8 I will obey your decrees;
  do not utterly forsake me.

ב Beth

9 How can the young keep their way
    pure?
  By living according to your word.
10 I seek you with all my heart;
  do not let me stray from your
    commands.
11 I have hidden your word in my heart
    that I might not sin against you.
12 Praise be to you, O LORD;
  teach me your decrees.
13 With my lips I recount
    all the laws that come from your
      mouth.
14 I rejoice in following your statutes
    as one rejoices in great riches.
15 I meditate on your precepts
    and consider your ways.
16 I delight in your decrees;
  I will not neglect your word.

ג Gimel

17 Do good to your servant, and I will
    live;
  I will obey your word.
18 Open my eyes that I may see
    wonderful things in your law.
19 I am a stranger on earth;
  do not hide your commands from
    me.
20 My soul is consumed with longing
    for your laws at all times.
21 You rebuke the arrogant, who are
    cursed
  and who stray from your
    commands.
22 Remove from me scorn and contempt,
    for I keep your statutes.
23 Though rulers sit together and slander
    me,
  your servant will meditate on your
    decrees.
24 Your statutes are my delight;
  they are my counsellors.

*a*26 The Hebrew is plural.   *b*27 Or *Bind the festal sacrifice with ropes / and take it*
*a*This psalm is an acrostic poem; the verses of each stanza begin with the same letter of the Hebrew alphabet.

ד Daleth

25 I am laid low in the dust;
preserve my life according to your
word.
26 I recounted my ways and you
answered me;
teach me your decrees.
27 Let me understand the teaching of
your precepts;
then I will meditate on your wonders.
28 My soul is weary with sorrow;
strengthen me according to your
word.
29 Keep me from deceitful ways;
be gracious to me through your law.
30 I have chosen the way of truth;
I have set my heart on your laws.
31 I hold fast to your statutes, O LORD;
do not let me be put to shame.
32 I run in the path of your commands,
for you have set my heart free.

ה He

33 Teach me, O LORD, to follow your
decrees;
then I will keep them to the end.
34 Give me understanding, and I will
keep your law
and obey it with all my heart.
35 Direct me in the path of your
commands,
for there I find delight.
36 Turn my heart towards your statutes
and not towards selfish gain.
37 Turn my eyes away from worthless
things;
preserve my life according to your
word.*b*
38 Fulfil your promise to your servant,
so that you may be feared.
39 Take away the disgrace I dread,
for your laws are good.
40 How I long for your precepts!
Preserve my life in your
righteousness.

ו Waw

41 May your unfailing love come to me,
O LORD,

your salvation according to your
promise;
42 then I will answer the one who taunts
me,
for I trust in your word.
43 Do not snatch the word of truth from
my mouth,
for I have put my hope in your laws.
44 I will always obey your law,
for ever and ever.
45 I will walk about in freedom,
for I have sought out your precepts.
46 I will speak of your statutes before
kings
and will not be put to shame,
47 for I delight in your commands
because I love them.
48 I lift up my hands to*c* your commands,
which I love,
and I meditate on your decrees.

ז Zayin

49 Remember your word to your servant,
for you have given me hope.
50 My comfort in my suffering is this:
Your promise preserves my life.
51 The arrogant mock me without
restraint,
but I do not turn from your law.
52 I remember your ancient laws, O LORD,
and I find comfort in them.
53 Indignation grips me because of the
wicked,
who have forsaken your law.
54 Your decrees are the theme of my song
wherever I lodge.
55 In the night I remember your name,
O LORD,
and I will keep your law.
56 This has been my practice:
I obey your precepts.

ח Heth

57 You are my portion, O LORD;
I have promised to obey your words.
58 I have sought your face with all my heart;
be gracious to me according to your
promise.

*b*37 Two manuscripts of the Masoretic Text and Dead Sea Scrolls; most manuscripts of the Masoretic Text *life in your
way*   *c*48 Or *for*

⁵⁹ I have considered my ways
    and have turned my steps to your
      statutes.
⁶⁰ I will hasten and not delay
    to obey your commands.
⁶¹ Though the wicked bind me with ropes,
    I will not forget your law.
⁶² At midnight I rise to give you thanks
    for your righteous laws.
⁶³ I am a friend to all who fear you,
    to all who follow your precepts.
⁶⁴ The earth is filled with your love,
    O LORD;
    teach me your decrees.

ט Teth

⁶⁵ Do good to your servant
    according to your word, O LORD.
⁶⁶ Teach me knowledge and good
      judgment,
    for I believe in your commands.
⁶⁷ Before I was afflicted I went astray,
    but now I obey your word.
⁶⁸ You are good, and what you do is good;
    teach me your decrees.
⁶⁹ Though the arrogant have smeared
      me with lies,
    I keep your precepts with all my
      heart.
⁷⁰ Their hearts are callous and unfeeling,
    but I delight in your law.
⁷¹ It was good for me to be afflicted
    so that I might learn your decrees.
⁷² The law from your mouth is more
      precious to me
    than thousands of pieces of silver
      and gold.

י Yodh

⁷³ Your hands made me and formed me;
    give me understanding to learn
      your commands.
⁷⁴ May those who fear you rejoice when
      they see me,
    for I have put my hope in your word.
⁷⁵ I know, O LORD, that your laws are
      righteous,
    and in faithfulness you have
      afflicted me.
⁷⁶ May your unfailing love be my comfort,

according to your promise to your
    servant.
⁷⁷ Let your compassion come to me that
    I may live,
    for your law is my delight.
⁷⁸ May the arrogant be put to shame for
    wronging me without cause;
    but I will meditate on your precepts.
⁷⁹ May those who fear you turn to me,
    those who understand your
      statutes.
⁸⁰ May my heart be blameless towards
    your decrees,
    that I may not be put to shame.

כ Kaph

⁸¹ My soul faints with longing for your
      salvation,
    but I have put my hope in your word.
⁸² My eyes fail, looking for your promise;
    I say, "When will you comfort me?"
⁸³ Though I am like a wineskin in the
      smoke,
    I do not forget your decrees.
⁸⁴ How long must your servant wait?
    When will you punish my
      persecutors?
⁸⁵ The arrogant dig pitfalls for me,
    contrary to your law.
⁸⁶ All your commands are trustworthy;
    help me, for people persecute me
      without cause.
⁸⁷ They almost wiped me from the earth,
    but I have not forsaken your
      precepts.
⁸⁸ Preserve my life according to your love,
    and I will obey the statutes of your
      mouth.

ל Lamedh

⁸⁹ Your word, O LORD, is eternal;
    it stands firm in the heavens.
⁹⁰ Your faithfulness continues through
    all generations;
    you established the earth, and it
      endures.
⁹¹ Your laws endure to this day,
    for all things serve you.
⁹² If your law had not been my delight,
    I would have perished in my
      affliction.

93 I will never forget your precepts,
   for by them you have preserved my
      life.
94 Save me, for I am yours;
   I have sought out your precepts.
95 The wicked are waiting to destroy me,
   but I will ponder your statutes.
96 To all perfection I see a limit;
   but your commands are boundless.

מ Mem

97 Oh, how I love your law!
   I meditate on it all day long.
98 Your commands make me wiser than
      my enemies,
   for they are ever with me.
99 I have more insight than all my
      teachers,
   for I meditate on your statutes.
100 I have more understanding than the
      elders,
   for I obey your precepts.
101 I have kept my feet from every evil
      path
   so that I might obey your word.
102 I have not departed from your laws,
   for you yourself have taught me.
103 How sweet are your words to my taste,
   sweeter than honey to my mouth!
104 I gain understanding from your
      precepts;
   therefore I hate every wrong path.

נ Nun

105 Your word is a lamp to my feet
   and a light for my path.
106 I have taken an oath and confirmed it,
   that I will follow your righteous
      laws.
107 I have suffered much;
   preserve my life, O LORD,
      according to your word.
108 Accept, O LORD, the willing praise
      of my mouth,
   and teach me your laws.
109 Though I constantly take my life in
      my hands,
   I will not forget your law.
110 The wicked have set a snare for me,
   but I have not strayed from your
      precepts.

111 Your statutes are my heritage for ever;
   they are the joy of my heart.
112 My heart is set on keeping your
      decrees
   to the very end.

ס Samekh

113 I hate double-minded people,
   but I love your law.
114 You are my refuge and my shield;
   I have put my hope in your word.
115 Away from me, you evildoers,
   that I may keep the commands of
      my God!
116 Sustain me according to your
      promise, and I shall live;
   do not let my hopes be dashed.
117 Uphold me, and I shall be delivered;
   I shall always have regard for your
      decrees.
118 You reject all who stray from your
      decrees,
   for their deceitfulness is in vain.
119 All the wicked of the earth you
      discard like dross;
   therefore I love your statutes.
120 My flesh trembles in fear of you;
   I stand in awe of your laws.

ע Ayin

121 I have done what is righteous and just;
   do not leave me to my oppressors.
122 Ensure your servant's well-being;
   let not the arrogant oppress me.
123 My eyes fail, looking for your
      salvation,
   looking for your righteous promise.
124 Deal with your servant according to
      your love
   and teach me your decrees.
125 I am your servant; give me
      discernment
   that I may understand your statutes.
126 It is time for you to act, O LORD;
   your law is being broken.
127 Because I love your commands
   more than gold, more than pure
      gold,
128 and because I consider all your
      precepts right,
   I hate every wrong path.

פ Pe

129 Your statutes are wonderful;
    therefore I obey them.
130 The unfolding of your words gives
    light;
    it gives understanding to the
    simple.
131 I open my mouth and pant,
    longing for your commands.
132 Turn to me and have mercy on me,
    as you always do to those who love
    your name.
133 Direct my footsteps according to
    your word;
    let no sin rule over me.
134 Redeem me from human
    oppression,
    that I may obey your precepts.
135 Make your face shine upon your
    servant
    and teach me your decrees.
136 Streams of tears flow from my eyes,
    for your law is not obeyed.

צ Tsadhe

137 Righteous are you, O LORD,
    and your laws are right.
138 The statutes you have laid down are
    righteous;
    they are fully trustworthy.
139 My zeal wears me out,
    for my enemies ignore your words.
140 Your promises have been
    thoroughly tested,
    and your servant loves them.
141 Though I am lowly and despised,
    I do not forget your precepts.
142 Your righteousness is everlasting
    and your law is true.
143 Trouble and distress have come
    upon me,
    but your commands are my delight.
144 Your statutes are for ever right;
    give me understanding that I may
    live.

ק Qoph

145 I call with all my heart; answer me,
    O LORD,
    and I will obey your decrees.
146 I call out to you; save me

and I will keep your statutes.
147 I rise before dawn and cry for help;
    I have put my hope in your word.
148 My eyes stay open through the
    watches of the night,
    that I may meditate on your
    promises.
149 Hear my voice in accordance with
    your love;
    preserve my life, O LORD,
    according to your laws.
150 Those who devise wicked schemes
    are near,
    but they are far from your law.
151 Yet you are near, O LORD,
    and all your commands are true.
152 Long ago I learned from your statutes
    that you established them to last
    for ever.

ר Resh

153 Look upon my suffering and deliver
    me,
    for I have not forgotten your law.
154 Defend my cause and redeem me;
    preserve my life according to your
    promise.
155 Salvation is far from the wicked,
    for they do not seek out your
    decrees.
156 Your compassion is great, O LORD;
    preserve my life according to your
    laws.
157 Many are the foes who persecute me,
    but I have not turned from your
    statutes.
158 I look on the faithless with loathing,
    for they do not obey your word.
159 See how I love your precepts;
    preserve my life, O LORD,
    according to your love.
160 All your words are true;
    all your righteous laws are eternal.

ש Sin and Shin

161 Rulers persecute me without cause,
    but my heart trembles at your word.
162 I rejoice in your promise
    like one who finds great spoil.
163 I hate and abhor falsehood
    but I love your law.

164 Seven times a day I praise you
for your righteous laws.
165 Great peace have they who love your
law,
and nothing can make them stumble.
166 I wait for your salvation, O LORD,
and I follow your commands.
167 I obey your statutes,
for I love them greatly.
168 I obey your precepts and your
statutes,
for all my ways are known to you.

ת Taw

169 May my cry come before you, O LORD;
give me understanding according to
your word.
170 May my supplication come before
you;
deliver me according to your
promise.
171 May my lips overflow with praise,
for you teach me your decrees.
172 May my tongue sing of your word,
for all your commands are
righteous.
173 May your hand be ready to help me,
for I have chosen your precepts.
174 I long for your salvation, O LORD,
and your law is my delight.
175 Let me live that I may praise you,
and may your laws sustain me.
176 I have strayed like a lost sheep.
Seek your servant,
for I have not forgotten your
commands.

Psalm 120

A song of ascents.

1 I call on the LORD in my distress,
and he answers me.
2 Save me, O LORD, from lying lips
and from deceitful tongues.

3 What will he do to you,
and what more besides, O deceitful
tongue?
4 He will punish you with a warrior's
sharp arrows,
with burning coals of the broom tree.

5 Woe to me that I dwell in Meshech,
that I live among the tents of Kedar!
6 Too long have I lived
among those who hate peace.
7 I am for peace;
but when I speak, they are for war.

Psalm 121

A song of ascents.

1 I lift up my eyes to the hills—
where does my help come from?
2 My help comes from the LORD,
the Maker of heaven and earth.

3 He will not let your foot slip—
he who watches over you will not
slumber;
4 indeed, he who watches over Israel
will neither slumber nor sleep.

5 The LORD watches over you—
the LORD is your shade at your right
hand;
6 the sun will not harm you by day,
nor the moon by night.

7 The LORD will keep you from all
harm—
he will watch over your life;
8 the LORD will watch over your coming
and going
both now and for evermore.

Psalm 122

A song of ascents. Of David.

1 I rejoiced with those who said to me,
"Let us go to the house of the LORD."
2 Our feet are standing
in your gates, O Jerusalem.

3 Jerusalem is built like a city
that is closely compacted together.
4 That is where the tribes go up,
the tribes of the LORD,
to praise the name of the LORD
according to the statute given to
Israel.
5 There the thrones for judgment
stand,
the thrones of the house of David.

6 Pray for the peace of Jerusalem:
  "May those who love you be secure.
7 May there be peace within your walls
  and security within your citadels."
8 For the sake of my relatives and
    friends,
  I will say, "Peace be within you."
9 For the sake of the house of the LORD
    our God,
  I will seek your prosperity.

Psalm 123

A song of ascents.

1 I lift up my eyes to you,
  to you whose throne is in heaven.
2 As the eyes of slaves look to the hand
    of their master,
  as the eyes of a servant woman look
    to the hand of her mistress,
  so our eyes look to the LORD our
    God,
  till he shows us his mercy.

3 Have mercy on us, O LORD, have
    mercy on us,
  for we have endured much
    contempt.
4 We have endured much ridicule from
    the proud,
  much contempt from the arrogant.

Psalm 124

A song of ascents. Of David.

1 If the LORD had not been on our side—
  let Israel say—
2 if the LORD had not been on our side
  when people attacked us,
3 when their anger flared against us,
  they would have swallowed us
    alive;
4 the flood would have engulfed us,
  the torrent would have swept over
    us,
5 the raging waters
  would have swept us away.

6 Praise be to the LORD,
  who has not let us be torn by their
    teeth.

7 We have escaped like a bird
  out of the fowler's snare;
  the snare has been broken,
  and we have escaped.
8 Our help is in the name of the LORD,
  the Maker of heaven and earth.

Psalm 125

A song of ascents.

1 Those who trust in the LORD are like
    Mount Zion,
  which cannot be shaken but
    endures for ever.
2 As the mountains surround Jerusalem,
  so the LORD surrounds his people
  both now and for evermore.

3 The sceptre of the wicked will not
    remain
  over the land allotted to the
    righteous,
  for then the righteous might use
    their hands to do evil.

4 Do good, O LORD, to those who are
    good,
  to those who are upright in heart.
5 But those who turn to crooked ways
  the LORD will banish with the
    evildoers.

Peace be upon Israel.

Psalm 126

A song of ascents.

1 When the LORD brought back the
    captives to*a* Zion,
  we were like those who dreamed.*b*
2 Our mouths were filled with laughter,
  our tongues with songs of joy.
  Then it was said among the nations,
    "The LORD has done great things for
    them."
3 The LORD has done great things for
    us,
  and we are filled with joy.

4 Restore our fortunes,*c* O LORD,
  like streams in the Negev.

*a*1 Or *LORD restored the fortunes of*   *b*1 Or *those restored to health*   *c*4 Or *Bring back our captives*

⁵Those who sow in tears
  will reap with songs of joy.
⁶Those who go out weeping,
  carrying seed to sow,
will return with songs of joy,
  carrying sheaves with them.

Psalm 127

A song of ascents. Of Solomon.

¹Unless the LORD builds the house,
  its builders labour in vain.
Unless the LORD watches over the
  city,
  the guards stand watch in vain.
²In vain you rise early
  and stay up late,
toiling for food to eat—
  for he grants sleep to*ᵃ* those he
  loves.

³Children are a heritage from the
  LORD,
  offspring a reward from him.
⁴Like arrows in the hands of a warrior
  are children born in one's youth.
⁵Blessed are those
  whose quivers are full of them.
They will not be put to shame
  when they contend with their
    enemies in the gate.

Psalm 128

A song of ascents.

¹Blessed are all who fear the LORD,
  who walk in his ways.
²You will eat the fruit of your labour;
  blessings and prosperity will be
    yours.
³Your wife will be like a fruitful vine
  within your house;
your children will be like olive shoots
  round your table.
⁴Thus are those blessed
  who fear the LORD.

⁵May the LORD bless you from Zion
  all the days of your life;
may you see the prosperity of
  Jerusalem,

⁶and may you live to see your
  children's children.

Peace be upon Israel.

Psalm 129

A song of ascents.

¹They have greatly oppressed me from
  my youth—
  let Israel say—
²they have greatly oppressed me from
  my youth,
  but they have not gained the victory
    over me.
³Those who plough have ploughed my
  back
  and made their furrows long.
⁴But the LORD is righteous;
  he has cut me free from the cords
    of the wicked.

⁵May all who hate Zion
  be turned back in shame.
⁶May they be like grass on the roof,
  which withers before it can grow;
⁷with it reapers cannot fill their hands,
  nor those who gather fill their arms.
⁸May those who pass by not say,
  "The blessing of the LORD be upon
    you;
  we bless you in the name of the
    LORD."

Psalm 130

A song of ascents.

¹Out of the depths I cry to you,
  O LORD;
² O Lord, hear my voice.
Let your ears be attentive
  to my cry for mercy.

³If you, O LORD, kept a record of sins,
  O Lord, who could stand?
⁴But with you there is forgiveness;
  therefore you are feared.

⁵I wait for the LORD, my soul waits,
  and in his word I put my hope.
⁶My soul waits for the Lord
  more than those on watch wait for
    the morning,

*ᵃ*2 Or *eat — / for while they sleep he provides for*

more than those on watch wait for
   the morning.

⁷O Israel, put your hope in the LORD,
   for with the LORD is unfailing love
   and with him is full redemption.
⁸He himself will redeem Israel
   from all their sins.

Psalm 131

A song of ascents. Of David.

¹My heart is not proud, O LORD,
   my eyes are not haughty;
I do not concern myself with great
   matters
   or things too wonderful for me.
²But I have stilled and quietened my
   soul;
   like a weaned child with its mother,
   like a weaned child is my soul within
   me.

³O Israel, put your hope in the LORD
   both now and for evermore.

Psalm 132

A song of ascents.

¹O LORD, remember David
   and all the hardships he endured.

²He swore an oath to the LORD
   and made a vow to the Mighty One
   of Jacob:
³"I will not enter my house
   or go to my bed—
⁴I will allow no sleep to my eyes,
   no slumber to my eyelids,
⁵till I find a place for the LORD,
   a dwelling for the Mighty One of
   Jacob."

⁶We heard it in Ephrathah,
   we came upon it in the fields of
   Jaar:[a, b]
⁷"Let us go to his dwelling-place;
   let us worship at his footstool—
⁸arise, O LORD, and come to your
   resting place,

you and the ark of your might.
⁹May your priests be clothed with
   righteousness;
   may your saints sing for joy."

¹⁰For the sake of David your servant,
   do not reject your anointed one.

¹¹The LORD swore an oath to David,
   a sure oath that he will not revoke:
   "One of your own descendants
   I will place on your throne—
¹²if your sons keep my covenant
   and the statutes I teach them,
   then their sons shall sit
   on your throne for ever and
   ever."

¹³For the LORD has chosen Zion,
   he has desired it for his dwelling:
¹⁴"This is my resting place for ever and
   ever;
   here I will sit enthroned, for I have
   desired it—
¹⁵I will bless her with abundant
   provisions;
   her poor will I satisfy with food.
¹⁶I will clothe her priests with salvation,
   and her saints shall ever sing for
   joy.

¹⁷"Here I will make a horn[c] grow for
   David
   and set up a lamp for my anointed
   one.
¹⁸I will clothe his enemies with shame,
   but the crown on his head shall be
   resplendent."

Psalm 133

A song of ascents. Of David.

¹How good and pleasant it is
   when God's people live together in
   unity!
²It is like precious oil poured on the
   head,
   running down on the beard,
   running down on Aaron's beard,
   down upon the collar of his robes.

---

[a]6 That is, Kiriath Jearim
[b]6 Or *heard of it in Ephrathah,* / *we found it in the fields of Jaar.* (and no quotation marks around verses 7–9)
[c]17 *Horn* here symbolises strong one, that is, king.

3 It is as if the dew of Hermon
were falling on Mount Zion.
For there the LORD bestows his
blessing,
even life for evermore.

Psalm 134

A song of ascents.

1 Praise the LORD, all you servants of
the LORD
who minister by night in the house
of the LORD.
2 Lift up your hands in the sanctuary
and praise the LORD.

3 May the LORD, the Maker of heaven
and earth,
bless you from Zion.

Psalm 135

1 Praise the LORD.[a]

Praise the name of the LORD;
praise him, you servants of the
LORD,
2 you who minister in the house of the
LORD,
in the courts of the house of our
God.

3 Praise the LORD, for the LORD is
good;
sing praise to his name, for that is
pleasant.
4 For the LORD has chosen Jacob to be
his own,
Israel to be his treasured
possession.

5 I know that the LORD is great,
that our Lord is greater than all
gods.
6 The LORD does whatever pleases him,
in the heavens and on the earth,
in the seas and all their depths.
7 He makes clouds rise from the ends of
the earth;
he sends lightning with the rain
and brings out the wind from his
storehouses.

8 He struck down the firstborn of
Egypt,
the firstborn of people and animals.
9 He sent his signs and wonders into
your midst, O Egypt,
against Pharaoh and all his
servants.
10 He struck down many nations
and killed mighty kings—
11 Sihon king of the Amorites,
Og king of Bashan
and all the kings of Canaan—
12 and he gave their land as an
inheritance,
an inheritance to his people Israel.

13 Your name, O LORD, endures for ever,
your renown, O LORD, through all
generations.
14 For the LORD will vindicate his people
and have compassion on his
servants.

15 The idols of the nations are silver and
gold,
made by human hands.
16 They have mouths, but cannot speak,
eyes, but they cannot see;
17 they have ears, but cannot hear,
nor is there breath in their mouths.
18 Those who make them will be like
them,
and so will all who trust in them.

19 O house of Israel, praise the LORD;
O house of Aaron, praise the LORD;
20 O house of Levi, praise the LORD;
you who fear him, praise the LORD.
21 Praise be to the LORD from Zion,
to him who dwells in Jerusalem.

Praise the LORD.

Psalm 136

1 Give thanks to the LORD, for he is
good.
His love endures for ever.
2 Give thanks to the God of gods.
His love endures for ever.
3 Give thanks to the Lord of lords:
His love endures for ever.

[a] 1 Hebrew *Hallelu Yah*; also in verses 3 and 21

4 to him who alone does great
  wonders,
> *His love endures for ever.*

5 who by his understanding made the
  heavens,
> *His love endures for ever.*

6 who spread out the earth upon the
  waters,
> *His love endures for ever.*

7 who made the great lights—
> *His love endures for ever.*

8 the sun to govern the day,
> *His love endures for ever.*

9 the moon and stars to govern the
  night;
> *His love endures for ever.*

10 to him who struck down the firstborn
   of Egypt
> *His love endures for ever.*

11 and brought Israel out from among
   them
> *His love endures for ever.*

12 with a mighty hand and outstretched
   arm;
> *His love endures for ever.*

13 to him who divided the Red Sea*a*
   asunder
> *His love endures for ever.*

14 and brought Israel through the midst
   of it,
> *His love endures for ever.*

15 but swept Pharaoh and his army into
   the Red Sea;
> *His love endures for ever.*

16 to him who led his people through the
   desert,
> *His love endures for ever.*

17 who struck down great kings,
> *His love endures for ever.*

18 and killed mighty kings—
> *His love endures for ever.*

19 Sihon king of the Amorites
> *His love endures for ever.*

20 and Og king of Bashan—
> *His love endures for ever.*

21 and gave their land as an
   inheritance,
> *His love endures for ever.*

22 an inheritance to his servant Israel;
> *His love endures for ever.*

23 to the One who remembered us in our
   low estate
> *His love endures for ever.*

24 and freed us from our enemies,
> *His love endures for ever.*

25 and who gives food to every creature.
> *His love endures for ever.*

26 Give thanks to the God of heaven.
> *His love endures for ever.*

Psalm 137

1 By the rivers of Babylon we sat and
  wept
  when we remembered Zion.
2 There on the poplars
  we hung our harps,
3 for there our captors asked us for
  songs,
  our tormentors demanded songs of
  joy;
  they said, "Sing us one of the songs
  of Zion!"

4 How can we sing the songs of the
  LORD
  while in a foreign land?
5 If I forget you, O Jerusalem,
  may my right hand forget ⌊its skill⌋.
6 May my tongue cling to the roof of my
  mouth
  if I do not remember you,
  if I do not consider Jerusalem
  my highest joy.

7 Remember, O LORD, what the
  Edomites did
  on the day Jerusalem fell.
  "Tear it down," they cried,
  "tear it down to its foundations!"

8 O Daughter of Babylon, doomed to
  destruction,
  happy are those who repay you
  for what you have done to us—
9 those who seize your infants
  and dash them against the rocks.

---

a 13 Hebrew *Yam Suph*; that is, Sea of Reeds; also in verse 15

Psalm 138

Of David.

1 I will praise you, O Lord, with all my
heart;
    before the "gods" I will sing your
    praise.
2 I will bow down towards your holy
temple
    and will praise your name
    for your love and your faithfulness,
    for you have exalted above all things
    your name and your word.
3 When I called, you answered me;
    you made me bold and
    stout-hearted.

4 May all the kings of the earth praise
you, O Lord,
    when they hear the words of your
    mouth.
5 May they sing of the ways of the
Lord,
    for the glory of the Lord is great.

6 Though the Lord is on high, he looks
upon the lowly,
    but the proud he knows from afar.
7 Though I walk in the midst of trouble,
you preserve my life;
    you stretch out your hand against the
    anger of my foes,
    with your right hand you save me.
8 The Lord will fulfil ⌐his purpose⌐ for
me;
    your love, O Lord, endures for
    ever—
    do not abandon the works of your
    hands.

Psalm 139

For the director of music. Of David. A psalm.

1 O Lord, you have searched me
    and you know me.
2 You know when I sit and when I rise;
    you perceive my thoughts from
    afar.
3 You discern my going out and my
lying down;
    you are familiar with all my ways.

4 Before a word is on my tongue
    you know it completely, O Lord.

5 You hem me in—behind and before;
    you have laid your hand upon me.
6 Such knowledge is too wonderful for
me,
    too lofty for me to attain.

7 Where can I go from your Spirit?
    Where can I flee from your
    presence?
8 If I go up to the heavens, you are there;
    if I make my bed in the depths,[a] you
    are there.
9 If I rise on the wings of the dawn,
    if I settle on the far side of the sea,
10 even there your hand will guide me,
    your right hand will hold me fast.

11 If I say, "Surely the darkness will hide
me
    and the light become night around
    me,"
12 even the darkness will not be dark to
you;
    the night will shine like the day,
    for darkness is as light to you.

13 For you created my inmost being;
    you knit me together in my
    mother's womb.
14 I praise you because I am fearfully and
wonderfully made;
    your works are wonderful,
    I know that full well.
15 My frame was not hidden from you
    when I was made in the secret place.
    When I was woven together in the
    depths of the earth,
16   your eyes saw my unformed body.
    All the days ordained for me
    were written in your book
    before one of them came to be.

17 How precious to[b] me are your
    thoughts, O God!
    How vast is the sum of them!
18 Were I to count them,
    they would outnumber the grains of
    sand.

---

[a]8 Hebrew *Sheol*   [b]17 Or *concerning*

When I awake,
   I am still with you.

19 If only you would slay the wicked,
   O God!
   Away from me, you who are
     bloodthirsty!
20 They speak of you with evil intent;
   your adversaries misuse your
     name.
21 Do I not hate those who hate you,
   O LORD,
   and abhor those who rise up against
     you?
22 I have nothing but hatred for them;
   I count them my enemies.

23 Search me, O God, and know my
   heart;
   test me and know my anxious
     thoughts.
24 See if there is any offensive way in me,
   and lead me in the way everlasting.

Psalm 140

For the director of music. A psalm of David.

1 Rescue me, O LORD, from evildoers;
   protect me from the violent,
2 who devise evil plans in their hearts
   and stir up war every day.
3 They make their tongues as sharp as a
   serpent's;
   the poison of vipers is on their lips.
            Selah

4 Keep me, O LORD, from the hands of
   the wicked;
   protect me from the violent
   who plan to trip my feet.
5 The proud have hidden a snare for me;
   they have spread out the cords of
     their net
   and have set traps for me along my
     path.   *Selah*

6 O LORD, I say to you, "You are my
   God."
   Hear, O LORD, my cry for mercy.
7 O Sovereign LORD, my strong deliverer,
   who shields my head in the day of
     battle—

a5 Or Let the Righteous One

8 do not grant the wicked their desires,
   O LORD;
   do not let their plans succeed,
   or they will become proud.   *Selah*

9 Let the heads of those who surround
   me
   be covered with the trouble their
     lips have caused.
10 Let burning coals fall upon them;
   may they be thrown into the fire,
   into miry pits, never to rise.
11 Let slanderers not be established in
   the land;
   may disaster hunt down the violent.

12 I know that the LORD secures justice
   for the poor
   and upholds the cause of the needy.
13 Surely the righteous will praise your
   name
   and the upright will live before you.

Psalm 141

A psalm of David.

1 O LORD, I call to you; come quickly to
   me.
   Hear my voice when I call to you.
2 May my prayer be set before you like
   incense;
   may the lifting up of my hands be
     like the evening sacrifice.

3 Set a guard over my mouth, O LORD;
   keep watch over the door of my lips.
4 Let not my heart be drawn to what is
   evil,
   to take part in wicked deeds
  with those who are evildoers;
   let me not eat of their delicacies.

5 Let a righteous person*a* strike me—
   that is a kindness;
   let them rebuke me—that is oil on
     my head.
   My head will not refuse it.

Yet my prayer is ever against the
   deeds of evildoers;
6   their rulers will be thrown down
     from the cliffs,

and the wicked will learn that my
words were well spoken.
⁷ ⌊They will say,⌋ "As one ploughs and
breaks up the earth,
so our bones have been scattered at
the mouth of the grave."*b*

⁸ But my eyes are fixed on you,
O Sovereign LORD;
in you I take refuge—do not give
me over to death.
⁹ Keep me from the snares they have
laid for me,
from the traps set by evildoers.
¹⁰ Let the wicked fall into their own
nets,
while I pass by in safety.

Psalm 142

*A maskil*ᵃ *of David. When he was in the cave.
A prayer.*

¹ I cry aloud to the LORD;
I lift up my voice to the LORD for
mercy.
² I pour out my complaint before
him;
before him I tell my trouble.

³ When my spirit grows faint within
me,
it is you who know my way.
In the path where I walk
people have hidden a snare for me.
⁴ Look to my right and see;
no-one is concerned for me.
I have no refuge;
no-one cares for my life.

⁵ I cry to you, O LORD;
I say, "You are my refuge,
my portion in the land of the living."
⁶ Listen to my cry,
for I am in desperate need;
rescue me from those who pursue me,
for they are too strong for me.
⁷ Set me free from my prison,
that I may praise your name.

Then the righteous will gather about
me
because of your goodness to me.

Psalm 143

A psalm of David.

¹ O LORD, hear my prayer,
listen to my cry for mercy;
in your faithfulness and righteousness
come to my relief.
² Do not bring your servant into
judgment,
for no-one living is righteous before
you.

³ The enemy pursues me,
he crushes me to the ground;
he makes me dwell in darkness
like those long dead.
⁴ So my spirit grows faint within me;
my heart within me is dismayed.

⁵ I remember the days of long ago;
I meditate on all your works
and consider what your hands have
done.
⁶ I spread out my hands to you;
my soul thirsts for you like a parched
land.   *Selah*

⁷ Answer me quickly, O LORD;
my spirit fails.
Do not hide your face from me
or I will be like those who go down
to the pit.
⁸ Let the morning bring me word of
your unfailing love,
for I have put my trust in you.
Show me the way I should go,
for to you I lift up my soul.
⁹ Rescue me from my enemies, O LORD,
for I hide myself in you.
¹⁰ Teach me to do your will,
for you are my God;
may your good Spirit
lead me on level ground.

¹¹ For your name's sake, O LORD,
preserve my life;
in your righteousness, bring me out
of trouble.
¹² In your unfailing love, silence my
enemies;
destroy all my foes,
for I am your servant.

*b*7 Hebrew *Sheol*   ᵃTitle: Probably a literary or musical term

Psalm 144

Of David.

¹ Praise be to the LORD my Rock,
  who trains my hands for war,
  my fingers for battle.
² He is my loving God and my fortress,
  my stronghold and my deliverer,
 my shield, in whom I take refuge,
  who subdues peoples*ᵃ* under me.

³ O LORD, what are human beings that
    you care for them,
  mere mortals that you think of
    them?
⁴ They are like a breath;
  their days are like a fleeting
    shadow.

⁵ Part your heavens, O LORD, and come
    down;
  touch the mountains, so that they
    smoke.
⁶ Send forth lightning and scatter ⌐the
    enemies⌐;
  shoot your arrows and rout
    them.
⁷ Reach down your hand from on high;
  deliver me and rescue me
 from the mighty waters,
  from the hands of foreigners
⁸ whose mouths are full of lies,
  whose right hands are deceitful.

⁹ I will sing a new song to you, O God;
  on the ten-stringed lyre I will make
    music to you,
¹⁰ to the One who gives victory to kings,
  who delivers his servant David from
    the deadly sword.

¹¹ Deliver me and rescue me
  from the hands of foreigners
 whose mouths are full of lies,
  whose right hands are deceitful.

¹² Then our sons in their youth
  will be like well-nurtured plants,

and our daughters will be like pillars
  carved to adorn a palace.
¹³ Our barns will be filled
  with every kind of provision.
Our sheep will increase by thousands,
  by tens of thousands in our fields;
14   our oxen will draw heavy loads.*ᵇ*
There will be no breaching of walls,
  no going into captivity,
  no cry of distress in our streets.

¹⁵ Blessed are the people of whom this
    is true;
  blessed are the people whose God
    is the LORD.

Psalm 145*ᵃ*

A psalm of praise. Of David.

¹ I will exalt you, my God the King;
  I will praise your name for ever and
    ever.
² Every day I will praise you
  and extol your name for ever and
    ever.

³ Great is the LORD and most worthy of
    praise;
  his greatness no-one can fathom.
⁴ One generation will commend your
    works to another;
  they will tell of your mighty acts.
⁵ They will speak of the glorious
    splendour of your majesty,
  and I will meditate on your
    wonderful works.*ᵇ*
⁶ They will tell of the power of your
    awesome works,
  and I will proclaim your great
    deeds.
⁷ They will celebrate your abundant
    goodness
  and joyfully sing of your
    righteousness.

⁸ The LORD is gracious and
    compassionate,
  slow to anger and rich in love.

---

*ᵃ*2 Many manuscripts of the Masoretic Text, Dead Sea Scrolls, Aquila, Jerome and Syriac; most manuscripts of the
Masoretic Text *subdues my people*   *ᵇ*14 Or *our chieftains will be firmly established*
*ᵃ*This psalm is an acrostic poem, the verses of which (including verse 13b) begin with the successive letters of the
Hebrew alphabet.
*ᵇ*5 Dead Sea Scrolls and Syriac (see also Septuagint); Masoretic Text *On the glorious splendour of your majesty / and
on your wonderful works I will meditate*

⁹ The LORD is good to all;
    he has compassion on all he has
      made.
¹⁰ All you have made will praise you,
    O LORD;
    your saints will extol you.
¹¹ They will tell of the glory of your
      kingdom
    and speak of your might,
¹² so that all people may know of your
      mighty acts
    and the glorious splendour of your
      kingdom.
¹³ Your kingdom is an everlasting
      kingdom,
    and your dominion endures
      through all generations.

    The LORD is faithful to all his
      promises
    and loving towards all he has
      made.ᶜ
¹⁴ The LORD upholds all those who fall
    and lifts up all who are bowed
      down.
¹⁵ The eyes of all look to you,
    and you give them their food at the
      proper time.
¹⁶ You open your hand
    and satisfy the desires of every
      living thing.

¹⁷ The LORD is righteous in all his ways
    and loving towards all he has made.
¹⁸ The LORD is near to all who call on
      him,
    to all who call on him in truth.
¹⁹ He fulfils the desires of those who fear
      him;
    he hears their cry and saves
      them.
²⁰ The LORD watches over all who love
      him,
    but all the wicked he will destroy.

²¹ My mouth will speak in praise of the
    LORD.
    Let every creature praise his holy
      name
    for ever and ever.

Psalm 146

¹ Praise the LORD.ᵃ

Praise the LORD, O my soul.
²   I will praise the LORD all my life;
    I will sing praise to my God as long
      as I live.

³ Do not put your trust in princes,
    in human beings, who cannot save.
⁴ When their spirit departs, they return
      to the ground,
    on that very day their plans come to
      nothing.

⁵ Blessed are those whose help is the
      God of Jacob,
    whose hope is in the LORD their God,
⁶ the Maker of heaven and earth,
    the sea, and everything in them—
    the LORD, who remains faithful for
      ever.
⁷ He upholds the cause of the
      oppressed
    and gives food to the hungry.
    The LORD sets prisoners free,
⁸   the LORD gives sight to the blind,
    the LORD lifts up those who are bowed
      down,
    the LORD loves the righteous.
⁹ The LORD watches over the alien
    and sustains the fatherless and the
      widow,
    but he frustrates the ways of the
      wicked.

¹⁰ The LORD reigns for ever,
    your God, O Zion, for all
      generations.

Praise the LORD.

Psalm 147

¹ Praise the LORD.ᵃ

How good it is to sing praises to our
    God,
    how pleasant and fitting to praise
      him!

ᶜ13 One manuscript of the Masoretic Text, Dead Sea Scrolls and Syriac (see also Septuagint); most manuscripts of the Masoretic Text do not have the last two lines of verse 13.   ᵃ1 Hebrew *Hallelu Yah*; also in verse 10
ᵃ1 Hebrew *Hallelu Yah*; also in verse 20

2 The LORD builds up Jerusalem;
  he gathers the exiles of Israel.
3 He heals the broken-hearted
  and binds up their wounds.

4 He determines the number of the
    stars
  and calls them each by name.
5 Great is our Lord and mighty in
    power;
  his understanding has no limit.
6 The LORD sustains the humble
  but casts the wicked to the ground.

7 Sing to the LORD with thanksgiving;
  make music to our God on the
    harp.
8 He covers the sky with clouds;
  he supplies the earth with rain
  and makes grass grow on the hills.
9 He provides food for the cattle
  and for the young ravens when they
    call.

10 His pleasure is not in the strength of
    the horse,
  nor his delight in the power of
    human legs;
11 the LORD delights in those who fear
    him,
  who put their hope in his unfailing
    love.

12 Extol the LORD, O Jerusalem;
  praise your God, O Zion,
13 for he strengthens the bars of your
    gates
  and blesses your people within you.
14 He grants peace to your borders
  and satisfies you with the finest of
    wheat.

15 He sends his command to the earth;
  his word runs swiftly.
16 He spreads the snow like wool
  and scatters the frost like ashes.
17 He hurls down hail like pebbles.
  Who can withstand his icy blast?
18 He sends his word and melts them;
  he stirs up his breezes, and the
    waters flow.

19 He has revealed his word to Jacob,
  his laws and decrees to Israel.
20 He has done this for no other nation;
  they do not know his laws.

Praise the LORD.

Psalm 148

1 Praise the LORD.*a*

Praise the LORD from the heavens,
  praise him in the heights above.
2 Praise him, all his angels,
  praise him, all his heavenly hosts.
3 Praise him, sun and moon,
  praise him, all you shining stars.
4 Praise him, you highest heavens
  and you waters above the skies.
5 Let them praise the name of the LORD,
  for he commanded and they were
    created.
6 He set them in place for ever and ever;
  he gave a decree that will never pass
    away.

7 Praise the LORD from the earth,
  you great sea creatures and all
    ocean depths,
8 lightning and hail, snow and clouds,
  stormy winds that do his bidding,
9 you mountains and all hills,
  fruit trees and all cedars,
10 wild animals and all cattle,
  small creatures and flying birds,
11 kings of the earth and all nations,
  you princes and all rulers on earth,
12 young men and women,
  old men and children.

13 Let them praise the name of the LORD,
  for his name alone is exalted;
  his splendour is above the earth and
    the heavens.
14 He has raised up for his people a
    horn,*b*
  the praise of all his saints,
  of Israel, the people close to his
    heart.

Praise the LORD.

*a*1 Hebrew *Hallelu Yah*; also in verse 14   *b*14 *Horn* here symbolises strong one, that is, king.

Psalm 149

[1] Praise the LORD.[a]

Sing to the LORD a new song,
  his praise in the assembly of the
    saints.

[2] Let Israel rejoice in their Maker;
  let the people of Zion be glad in
    their King.
[3] Let them praise his name with dancing
  and make music to him with
    tambourine and harp.
[4] For the LORD takes delight in his
    people;
  he crowns the humble with
    salvation.
[5] Let the saints rejoice in this honour
  and sing for joy on their beds.

[6] May the praise of God be in their
    mouths
  and a double-edged sword in their
    hands,
[7] to inflict vengeance on the nations
  and punishment on the peoples,
[8] to bind their kings with fetters,
  their nobles with shackles of iron,

[9] to carry out the sentence written
    against them.
This is the glory of all his saints.

Praise the LORD.

Psalm 150

[1] Praise the LORD.[a]

Praise God in his sanctuary;
  praise him in his mighty heavens.
[2] Praise him for his acts of power;
  praise him for his surpassing
    greatness.
[3] Praise him with the sounding of the
    trumpet,
  praise him with the harp and lyre,
[4] praise him with tambourine and
    dancing,
  praise him with the strings and
    flute,
[5] praise him with the clash of cymbals,
  praise him with resounding
    cymbals.

[6] Let everything that has breath praise
    the LORD.

Praise the LORD.

---

[a]1 Hebrew *Hallelu Yah*; also in verse 9 [a]1 Hebrew *Hallelu Yah*; also in verse 6

Proverbs

Prologue: Purpose and Theme

1 The proverbs of Solomon son of
David, king of Israel:

2 for attaining wisdom and discipline;
for understanding words of insight;
3 for acquiring a disciplined and
prudent life,
doing what is right and just and fair;
4 for giving prudence to the simple,
knowledge and discretion to the
young—
5 let the wise listen and add to their
learning,
and let the discerning get
guidance—
6 for understanding proverbs and
parables,
the sayings and riddles of the wise.

7 The fear of the LORD is the beginning
of knowledge,
but fools[a] despise wisdom and
discipline.

Exhortations to Embrace Wisdom

Warning Against Enticement

8 Listen, my son, to your father's
instruction
and do not forsake your mother's
teaching.
9 They will be a garland to grace your
head
and a chain to adorn your neck.

10 My son, if sinners entice you,
do not give in to them.
11 If they say, "Come along with us;
let's lie in wait for someone's blood,
let's waylay some harmless soul;
12 let's swallow them alive, like the
grave,[b]
and whole, like those who go down
to the pit;
13 we will get all sorts of valuable things
and fill our houses with plunder;
14 throw in your lot with us,
and we will share a common
purse"—
15 my son, do not go along with them,
do not set foot on their paths;
16 for their feet rush into sin,
they are swift to shed blood.
17 How useless to spread a net
in full view of all the birds!
18 These sinners lie in wait for their own
blood;
they waylay only themselves!
19 Such is the end of all who go after
ill-gotten gain;
it takes away the lives of those who
get it.

Warning Against Rejecting Wisdom

20 Wisdom calls aloud in the street,
she raises her voice in the public
squares;
21 at the head of the noisy streets[c] she
cries out,
in the gateways of the city she
makes her speech:

[a]7 The Hebrew words rendered *fool* in Proverbs, and often elsewhere in the Old Testament, denote one who is
morally deficient.   [b]12 Hebrew *Sheol*   [c]21 Hebrew; Septuagint / *on the tops of the walls*

22 "How long will you simple ones[d] love
    your simple ways?
  How long will mockers delight in
    mockery
  and fools hate knowledge?
23 If you had responded to my rebuke,
    I would have poured out my heart
      to you
  and made my thoughts known to you.
24 But since you rejected me when I called
    and no-one gave heed when I
      stretched out my hand,
25 since you ignored all my advice
    and would not accept my rebuke,
26 I in turn will laugh at your disaster;
    I will mock when calamity
      overtakes you—
27 when calamity overtakes you like a
    storm,
  when disaster sweeps over you like
    a whirlwind,
  when distress and trouble
    overwhelm you.

28 "Then they will call to me but I will
    not answer;
  they will look for me but will not
    find me.
29 Since they hated knowledge
    and did not choose to fear the LORD,
30 since they would not accept my advice
    and spurned my rebuke,
31 they will eat the fruit of their ways
    and be filled with the fruit of their
      schemes.
32 For the waywardness of the simple
    will kill them,
  and the complacency of fools will
    destroy them;
33 but whoever listens to me will live in
    safety
  and be at ease, without fear of harm."

Moral Benefits of Wisdom

2 My son, if you accept my words
  and store up my commands within
    you,
2 turning your ear to wisdom
  and applying your heart to
    understanding,

3 and if you call out for insight
    and cry aloud for understanding,
4 and if you look for it as for silver
    and search for it as for hidden
      treasure,
5 then you will understand the fear of
    the LORD
  and find the knowledge of God.
6 For the LORD gives wisdom,
    and from his mouth come
      knowledge and understanding.
7 He holds victory in store for the
    upright,
  he is a shield to those whose walk is
    blameless,
8 for he guards the course of the just
    and protects the way of his faithful
      ones.

9 Then you will understand what is right
    and just
  and fair—every good path.
10 For wisdom will enter your heart,
    and knowledge will be pleasant to
      your soul.
11 Discretion will protect you,
    and understanding will guard you.

12 Wisdom will save you from the ways
    of wicked men,
  from men whose words are perverse,
13 who leave the straight paths
    to walk in dark ways,
14 who delight in doing wrong
    and rejoice in the perverseness of
      evil,
15 whose paths are crooked
    and who are devious in their ways.

16 It will save you also from the
    adulteress,
  from the wayward wife with her
    seductive words,
17 who has left the partner of her youth
    and ignored the covenant she made
      before God.[a]
18 For her house leads down to death
    and her paths to the spirits of the
      dead.
19 None who go to her return
    or attain the paths of life.

---

d22 The Hebrew word rendered *simple* in Proverbs generally denotes one without moral direction and inclined to evil.   a17 Or *covenant of her God*

²⁰ Thus you will walk in the ways of the
just
and keep to the paths of the
righteous.
²¹ For the upright will live in the land,
and the blameless will remain in it;
²² but the wicked will be cut off from the
land,
and the unfaithful will be torn
from it.

Further Benefits of Wisdom

3 My son, do not forget my teaching,
but keep my commands in your
heart,
² for they will prolong your life many
years
and bring you prosperity.

³ Let love and faithfulness never leave
you;
bind them around your neck,
write them on the tablet of your
heart.
⁴ Then you will win favour and a good
name
in the sight of God and other people.

⁵ Trust in the LORD with all your heart
and lean not on your own
understanding;
⁶ in all your ways acknowledge him,
and he will make your paths straight.ᵃ

⁷ Do not be wise in your own eyes;
fear the LORD and shun evil.
⁸ This will bring health to your body
and nourishment to your bones.

⁹ Honour the LORD with your wealth,
with the firstfruits of all your crops;
¹⁰ then your barns will be filled to
overflowing,
and your vats will brim over with
new wine.

¹¹ My son, do not despise the LORD's
discipline
and do not resent his rebuke,
¹² because the LORD disciplines those he
loves,

as parents the children they delight
in.ᵇ

¹³ Blessed are those who find wisdom,
those who gain understanding,
¹⁴ for she is more profitable than silver
and yields better returns than gold.
¹⁵ She is more precious than rubies;
nothing you desire can compare
with her.
¹⁶ Long life is in her right hand;
in her left hand are riches and
honour.
¹⁷ Her ways are pleasant ways,
and all her paths are peace.
¹⁸ She is a tree of life to those who
embrace her;
those who lay hold of her will be
blessed.

¹⁹ By wisdom the LORD laid the earth's
foundations,
by understanding he set the
heavens in place;
²⁰ by his knowledge the deeps were
divided,
and the clouds let drop the dew.

²¹ My son, preserve sound judgment and
discernment,
do not let them out of your sight;
²² they will be life for you,
an ornament to grace your neck.
²³ Then you will go on your way in
safety,
and your foot will not stumble;
²⁴ when you lie down, you will not be
afraid;
when you lie down, your sleep will
be sweet.
²⁵ Have no fear of sudden disaster
or of the ruin that overtakes the
wicked,
²⁶ for the LORD will be your confidence
and will keep your foot from being
snared.

²⁷ Do not withhold good from those who
deserve it,
when it is in your power to act.
²⁸ Do not say to your neighbour,

ᵃ6 Or *will direct your paths.*   ᵇ12 Hebrew; Septuagint / *and he punishes everyone he accepts as a child*

"Come back later; I'll give it
  tomorrow"—
when you now have it with you.

29 Do not plot harm against your
    neighbour,
who lives trustfully near you.
30 Do not accuse someone for no
    reason—
when that person has done you no
    harm.

31 Do not envy the violent
or choose any of their ways,
32 for the LORD detests the perverse
but takes the upright into his
    confidence.

33 The LORD's curse is on the house of
    the wicked,
but he blesses the home of the
    righteous.
34 He mocks proud mockers
but gives grace to the humble.
35 The wise inherit honour,
but fools he holds up to shame.

Wisdom is Supreme

4 Listen, my sons, to a father's
  instruction;
pay attention and gain
    understanding.
2 I give you sound learning,
so do not forsake my teaching.
3 When I was a boy in my father's
    house,
still tender, and an only child of my
    mother,
4 he taught me and said,
    "Lay hold of my words with all your
    heart;
keep my commands and you will
    live.
5 Get wisdom, get understanding;
do not forget my words or swerve
    from them.
6 Do not forsake wisdom, and she will
    protect you;
love her, and she will watch over
    you.

7 Wisdom is supreme; therefore get
    wisdom.
Though it cost all you have,[a] get
    understanding.
8 Esteem her, and she will exalt you;
embrace her, and she will honour
    you.
9 She will set a garland of grace on your
    head
and present you with a crown of
    splendour."

10 Listen, my son, accept what I say,
and the years of your life will be
    many.
11 I guide you in the way of wisdom
and lead you along straight paths.
12 When you walk, your steps will not be
    hampered;
when you run, you will not
    stumble.
13 Hold on to instruction, do not let it
    go;
guard it well, for it is your life.
14 Do not set foot on the path of the
    wicked
or walk in the way of evildoers.
15 Avoid it, do not travel on it;
turn from it and go on your way.
16 For they cannot sleep till they do evil;
they are robbed of slumber till they
    make someone fall.
17 They eat the bread of wickedness
and drink the wine of violence.

18 The path of the righteous is like the
    first gleam of dawn,
shining ever brighter till the full
    light of day.
19 But the way of the wicked is like deep
    darkness;
they do not know what makes them
    stumble.

20 My son, pay attention to what I say;
listen closely to my words.
21 Do not let them out of your sight,
keep them within your heart;
22 for they are life to those who find
    them
and health to one's whole body.

_a_7 Or _Whatever else you get_

23 Above all else, guard your heart,
    for it is the wellspring of life.
24 Put away perversity from your mouth;
    keep corrupt talk far from your lips.
25 Let your eyes look straight ahead,
    fix your gaze directly before you.
26 Make level[b] paths for your feet
    and take only ways that are firm.
27 Do not swerve to the right or the left;
    keep your foot from evil.

Warning Against Adultery

5 My son, pay attention to my
    wisdom,
    listen well to my words of insight,
2 that you may maintain discretion
    and your lips may preserve
      knowledge.
3 For the lips of an adulteress drip honey,
    and her speech is smoother than oil;
4 but in the end she is bitter as gall,
    sharp as a double-edged sword.
5 Her feet go down to death;
    her steps lead straight to the grave.[a]
6 She gives no thought to the way of life;
    her paths are crooked, but she
      knows it not.

7 Now then, my sons, listen to me;
    do not turn aside from what I say.
8 Keep to a path far from her,
    do not go near the door of her
      house,
9 lest you give your best strength to
      others
    and your years to one who is cruel,
10 lest strangers feast on your wealth
    and your toil enrich the house of
      another.
11 At the end of your life you will groan,
    when your flesh and body are spent.
12 You will say, "How I hated discipline!
    How my heart spurned correction!
13 I would not obey my teachers
    or listen to my instructors.
14 I have come to the brink of utter ruin
    in the midst of the whole assembly."

15 Drink water from your own cistern,
    running water from your own well.
16 Should your springs overflow in the
      streets,
    your streams of water in the public
      squares?
17 Let them be yours alone,
    never to be shared with strangers.
18 May your fountain be blessed,
    and may you rejoice in the wife of
      your youth.
19 A loving doe, a graceful deer—
    may her breasts satisfy you always,
    may you ever be captivated by her
      love.
20 Why be captivated, my son, by an
      adulteress?
    Why embrace the bosom of another
      man's wife?

21 For your ways are in full view of the
      LORD,
    and he examines all your paths.
22 The evil deeds of the wicked ensnare
      them;
    the cords of their sins hold them
      fast.
23 They will die for lack of discipline,
    led astray by their own great folly.

Warnings Against Folly

6 My son, if you have put up security
    for your neighbour,
    if you have struck hands in pledge
      for another,
2 if you have been trapped by what you
      said,
    ensnared by the words of your mouth,
3 then do this, my son, to free yourself,
    since you have fallen into your
      neighbour's hands:
  Go and humble yourself;
    press your plea with your neighbour!
4 Allow no sleep to your eyes,
    no slumber to your eyelids.
5 Free yourself, like a gazelle from the
      hand of the hunter,
    like a bird from the snare of the
      fowler.

6 Go to the ant, you sluggard;
    consider its ways and be wise!

---

[b]26 Or *Consider the*   [a]5 Hebrew *Sheol*

7 It has no commander,
  no overseer or ruler,
8 yet it stores its provisions in summer
  and gathers its food at harvest.

9 How long will you lie there, you
  sluggard?
  When will you get up from your
  sleep?
10 A little sleep, a little slumber,
  a little folding of the hands to rest—
11 and poverty will come on you like a
  bandit
  and scarcity like an armed man.*a*

12 Scoundrels and villains,
  who go about with corrupt mouths,
13 who wink with their eyes,
  signal with their feet
  and motion with their fingers,
14 who plot evil with deceit in their
  hearts—
  they always stir up dissension.
15 Therefore disaster will overtake them
  in an instant;
  they will suddenly be destroyed—
  without remedy.

16 There are six things the LORD hates,
  seven that are detestable to him:
17 haughty eyes,
  a lying tongue,
  hands that shed innocent blood,
18 a heart that devises wicked
  schemes,
  feet that are quick to rush into evil,
19 a false witness who pours out lies
  and a person who stirs up dissension
  among the people.

Warning Against Adultery

20 My son, keep your father's commands
  and do not forsake your mother's
  teaching.
21 Bind them upon your heart for ever;
  fasten them around your neck.
22 When you walk, they will guide you;
  when you sleep, they will watch
  over you;
  when you awake, they will speak to
  you.

23 For these commands are a lamp,
  this teaching is a light,
  and the corrections of discipline
  are the way to life,
24 keeping you from the immoral woman,
  from the smooth tongue of the
  wayward wife.
25 Do not lust in your heart after her
  beauty
  or let her captivate you with her
  eyes,
26 for the prostitute reduces you to a loaf
  of bread,
  and the adulteress preys upon your
  very life.
27 Can a man scoop fire into his lap
  without his clothes being burned?
28 Can a man walk on hot coals
  without his feet being scorched?
29 So is he who sleeps with another man's
  wife;
  no-one who touches her will go
  unpunished.

30 People do not despise a thief if he
  steals
  to satisfy his hunger when he is
  starving.
31 Yet if he is caught, he must pay
  sevenfold,
  though it costs him all the wealth of
  his house.
32 But a man who commits adultery lacks
  judgment;
  whoever does so destroys himself.
33 Blows and disgrace are his lot,
  and his shame will never be wiped
  away;
34 for jealousy arouses a husband's fury,
  and he will show no mercy when he
  takes revenge.
35 He will not accept any compensation;
  he will refuse the bribe, however
  great it is.

Warning against the adulteress

7 My son, keep my words
  and store up my commands within
  you.
2 Keep my commands and you will live;

---

a 11 Or *like a vagrant / and scarcity like a beggar*

guard my teachings as the apple of
  your eye.
³Bind them on your fingers;
  write them on the tablet of your
    heart.
⁴Say to wisdom, "You are my sister,"
  and call understanding your
    kinsman;
⁵they will keep you from the
    adulteress,
  from the wayward wife with her
    seductive words.

⁶At the window of my house
  I looked out through the lattice.
⁷I saw among the simple,
  I noticed among the young men,
  a youth who lacked judgment.
⁸He was going down the street near her
    corner,
  walking along in the direction of her
    house
⁹at twilight, as the day was fading,
  as the dark of night set in.

¹⁰Then out came a woman to meet him,
  dressed like a prostitute and with
    crafty intent.
¹¹(She is loud and defiant,
  her feet never stay at home;
¹²now in the street, now in the squares,
  at every corner she lurks.)
¹³She took hold of him and kissed him
  and with a brazen face she said:

¹⁴"I have fellowship offerings*ᵃ* at
    home;
  today I fulfilled my vows.
¹⁵So I came out to meet you;
  I looked for you and have found
    you!
¹⁶I have covered my bed
  with coloured linens from Egypt.
¹⁷I have perfumed my bed
  with myrrh, aloes and cinnamon.
¹⁸Come, let's drink deep of love till
    morning;
  let's enjoy ourselves with love!
¹⁹My husband is not at home;
  he has gone on a long journey.

²⁰He took his purse filled with money
  and will not be home till full
    moon."

²¹With persuasive words she led him
    astray;
  she seduced him with her smooth
    talk.
²²All at once he followed her
  like an ox going to the slaughter,
  like a deer*ᵇ* stepping into a noose*ᶜ*
²³   till an arrow pierces his liver,
  like a bird darting into a snare,
  little knowing it will cost him his
    life.

²⁴Now then, my sons, listen to me;
  pay attention to what I say.
²⁵Do not let your heart turn to her ways
  or stray into her paths.
²⁶Many are the victims she has brought
    down;
  her slain are a mighty throng.
²⁷Her house is a highway to the grave,*ᵈ*
  leading down to the chambers of
    death.

Wisdom's Call

8 Does not wisdom call out?
  Does not understanding raise her
    voice?
²On the heights along the way,
  where the paths meet, she takes her
    stand;
³beside the gates leading into the city,
  at the entrances, she cries aloud:
⁴"To you, O people, I call out;
  I raise my voice to all humanity.
⁵You who are simple, gain prudence;
  you who are foolish, gain
    understanding.
⁶Listen, for I have worthy things to say;
  I open my lips to speak what is right.
⁷My mouth speaks what is true,
  for my lips detest wickedness.
⁸All the words of my mouth are just;
  none of them is crooked or perverse.
⁹To the discerning all of them are
    right;

---

*ᵃ*14 Traditionally *peace offerings*   *ᵇ*22 Syriac (see also Septuagint); Hebrew *fool*
*ᶜ*22 The meaning of the Hebrew for this line is uncertain.   *ᵈ*27 Hebrew *Sheol*

they are faultless to those who have
knowledge.
¹⁰ Choose my instruction instead of
silver,
knowledge rather than choice gold,
¹¹ for wisdom is more precious than
rubies,
and nothing you desire can
compare with her.

¹² "I, wisdom, dwell together with
prudence;
I possess knowledge and
discretion.
¹³ To fear the LORD is to hate evil;
I hate pride and arrogance,
evil behaviour and perverse speech.
¹⁴ Counsel and sound judgment are
mine;
I have understanding and power.
¹⁵ By me kings reign
and rulers make laws that are just;
¹⁶ by me princes govern,
and all nobles who rule on earth.ᵃ
¹⁷ I love those who love me,
and those who seek me find me.
¹⁸ With me are riches and honour,
enduring wealth and prosperity.
¹⁹ My fruit is better than fine gold;
what I yield surpasses choice silver.
²⁰ I walk in the way of righteousness,
along the paths of justice,
²¹ bestowing wealth on those who love
me
and making their treasuries full.

²² "The LORD brought me forth as the
first of his works,ᵇ,ᶜ
before his deeds of old;
²³ I was appointedᵈ from eternity,
from the beginning, before the
world began.
²⁴ When there were no oceans, I was
given birth,
when there were no springs
abounding with water;
²⁵ before the mountains were settled in
place,
before the hills, I was given birth,

²⁶ before he made the earth or its fields
or any of the dust of the world.
²⁷ I was there when he set the heavens
in place,
when he marked out the horizon on
the face of the deep,
²⁸ when he established the clouds above
and fixed securely the fountains of
the deep,
²⁹ when he gave the sea its boundary
so that the waters would not
overstep his command,
and when he marked out the
foundations of the earth.
³⁰ Then I was the master worker at his
side.
I was filled with delight day after day,
rejoicing always in his presence,
³¹ rejoicing in his whole world
and delighting in the human race.

³² "Now then, my sons, listen to me;
blessed are those who keep my
ways.
³³ Listen to my instruction and be wise;
do not ignore it.
³⁴ Blessed are those who listen to me,
watching daily at my doors,
waiting at my doorway.
³⁵ For those who find me find life
and receive favour from the LORD.
³⁶ But those who fail to find me harm
themselves;
all who hate me love death."

Invitations of Wisdom and of Folly

9 Wisdom has built her house;
she has hewn out its seven pillars.
² She has prepared her meat and mixed
her wine;
she has also set her table.
³ She has sent out her servants, and she
calls
from the highest point of the city.
⁴ "Let all who are simple come in here!"
she says to those who lack judgment.
⁵ "Come, eat my food
and drink the wine I have mixed.

ᵃ16 Many Hebrew manuscripts and Septuagint; most Hebrew manuscripts *and nobles—all righteous rulers*
ᵇ22 Or *way;* or *dominion*
ᶜ22 Or *The LORD possessed me at the beginning of his work;* or *The LORD brought me forth at the beginning of his
work* ᵈ23 Or *fashioned*

⁶Leave your simple ways and you will
live;
  walk in the way of understanding.

⁷"Whoever corrects mockers invites
insult;
  whoever rebukes the wicked incurs
  abuse.
⁸Do not rebuke mockers or they will
hate you;
  rebuke the wise and they will love
  you.
⁹Instruct the wise and they will be wiser
still;
  teach the righteous and they will
  add to their learning.

¹⁰"The fear of the LORD is the beginning
of wisdom,
  and knowledge of the Holy One is
  understanding.
¹¹For through me your days will be many,
  and years will be added to your life.
¹²If you are wise, your wisdom will
reward you;
  if you are a mocker, you alone will
  suffer."

¹³The woman Folly is loud;
  she is undisciplined and without
  knowledge.
¹⁴She sits at the door of her house,
  on a seat at the highest point of the
  city,
¹⁵calling out to those who pass by,
  who go straight on their way.
¹⁶"Let all who are simple come in here!"
  she says to those who lack judgment.
¹⁷"Stolen water is sweet;
  food eaten in secret is delicious!"
¹⁸But little do they know that the dead
are there,
  that her guests are in the depths of
  the grave.ᵃ

Proverbs of Solomon

10 The proverbs of Solomon:

Wise children bring joy to their fathers,
  but the foolish bring grief to their
  mothers.

²Ill-gotten treasures are of no value,
  but righteousness delivers from
  death.

³The LORD does not let the righteous
go hungry
  but he thwarts the craving of the
  wicked.

⁴Lazy hands make for poverty,
  but diligent hands bring wealth.

⁵He who gathers crops in summer is a
wise son,
  but he who sleeps during harvest is
  a disgraceful son.

⁶Blessings crown the head of the
righteous,
  but violence overwhelms the mouth
  of the wicked.ᵃ

⁷The memory of the righteous will be
a blessing,
  but the name of the wicked will rot.

⁸The wise in heart accept commands,
  but a chattering fool comes to
  ruin.

⁹Whoever walks in integrity walks
securely,
  but whoever takes crooked paths
  will be found out.

¹⁰Whoever winks maliciously causes
grief,
  and a chattering fool comes to ruin.

¹¹The mouth of the righteous is a
fountain of life,
  but violence overwhelms the mouth
  of the wicked.

¹²Hatred stirs up dissension,
  but love covers over all wrongs.

¹³Wisdom is found on the lips of the
discerning,
  but a rod is for the back of one who
  lacks judgment.

ᵃ18 Hebrew *Sheol*   ᵃ6 Or *but the mouth of the wicked conceals violence*; also in verse 11

14 The wise store up knowledge,
but the mouth of a fool invites ruin.

15 The wealth of the rich is their fortified
city,
but poverty is the ruin of the poor.

16 The wages of the righteous bring them
life,
but the income of the wicked brings
them punishment.

17 The one who heeds discipline shows
the way to life,
but whoever ignores correction
leads others astray.

18 The one who conceals hatred has lying
lips,
and whoever spreads slander is a
fool.

19 When words are many, sin is not
absent,
but the wise hold their tongues.

20 The tongue of the righteous is choice
silver,
but the heart of the wicked is of
little value.

21 The lips of the righteous nourish
many,
but fools die for lack of judgment.

22 The blessing of the LORD brings wealth,
and he adds no trouble to it.

23 Fools find pleasure in evil conduct,
but those who have insight delight
in wisdom.

24 What the wicked dread will overtake
them;
what the righteous desire will be
granted.

25 When the storm has swept by, the
wicked are gone,
but the righteous stand firm for
ever.

26 As vinegar to the teeth and smoke to
the eyes,

so are sluggards to those who send
them.

27 The fear of the LORD adds length to
life,
but the years of the wicked are cut
short.

28 The prospect of the righteous is joy,
but the hopes of the wicked come
to nothing.

29 The way of the LORD is a refuge for
the righteous,
but it is the ruin of those who do
evil.

30 The righteous will never be
uprooted,
but the wicked will not remain in
the land.

31 The mouth of the righteous brings
forth wisdom,
but a perverse tongue will be cut out.

32 The lips of the righteous know what is
fitting,
but the mouth of the wicked only
what is perverse.

11 The LORD abhors dishonest
scales,
but accurate weights are his delight.

2 When pride comes, then comes
disgrace,
but with humility comes wisdom.

3 The integrity of the upright guides
them,
but the unfaithful are destroyed by
their duplicity.

4 Wealth is worthless in the day of
wrath,
but righteousness delivers from
death.

5 The righteousness of the blameless
makes a straight way for them,
but the wicked are brought down by
their own wickedness.

⁶The righteousness of the upright
    delivers them,
    but the unfaithful are trapped by
      evil desires.

⁷When the wicked die, their hope
    perishes;
    all they expected from their power
      comes to nothing.

⁸The righteous are rescued from
    trouble,
    and it comes on the wicked instead.

⁹With their mouths the godless destroy
    their neighbours,
    but through knowledge the
      righteous escape.

¹⁰When the righteous prosper, the city
    rejoices;
    when the wicked perish, there are
      shouts of joy.

¹¹Through the blessing of the upright a
    city is exalted,
    but by the mouth of the wicked it is
      destroyed.

¹²Those who lack judgment deride their
    neighbours,
    but those who have insight hold
      their tongues.

¹³Gossips betray a confidence,
    but the trustworthy keep a secret.

¹⁴For lack of guidance a nation falls,
    but many advisers make victory
      sure.

¹⁵The one who puts up security for
    another will surely suffer,
    but whoever refuses to strike hands
      in pledge is safe.

¹⁶A kind-hearted woman gains respect,
    but ruthless men gain only wealth.

¹⁷Those who are kind benefit
    themselves,
    but the cruel bring trouble on
      themselves.

¹⁸The wicked earn deceptive wages,
    but those who sow righteousness
      reap a sure reward.

¹⁹The truly righteous attain life,
    but those who pursue evil go to
      their death.

²⁰The LORD detests those whose hearts
    are perverse
    but he delights in those whose ways
      are blameless.

²¹Be sure of this: The wicked will not go
    unpunished,
    but those who are righteous will go
      free.

²²Like a gold ring in a pig's snout
    is a beautiful woman who shows no
      discretion.

²³The desire of the righteous ends only
    in good,
    but the hope of the wicked only in
      wrath.

²⁴One gives freely, yet gains even
    more;
    another withholds unduly, but
      comes to poverty.

²⁵A generous person will prosper;
    the one who refreshes others will be
      refreshed.

²⁶People curse those who hoard grain,
    but blessing crowns those who are
      willing to sell.

²⁷Whoever seeks good finds goodwill,
    but evil comes to the one who
      searches for it.

²⁸Those who trust in their riches will
    fall,
    but the righteous will thrive like a
      green leaf.

²⁹Those who bring trouble on their
    families will inherit only wind,
    and the fool will be servant to the
      wise.

30 The fruit of the righteous is a tree of
life,
  and those who win souls are wise.

31 If the righteous receive their due on
earth,
  how much more the ungodly and
  the sinner!

12 Whoever loves discipline loves
knowledge,
  but whoever hates correction is
  stupid.

2 Good people obtain favour from the
LORD,
  but the LORD condemns the crafty.

3 No-one can be established through
wickedness,
  but the righteous cannot be
  uprooted.

4 A wife of noble character is her
husband's crown,
  but a disgraceful wife is like decay
  in his bones.

5 The plans of the righteous are just,
  but the advice of the wicked is
  deceitful.

6 The words of the wicked lie in wait for
blood,
  but the speech of the upright
  rescues them.

7 The wicked are overthrown and are
no more,
  but the house of the righteous
  stands firm.

8 One is praised according to one's
wisdom,
  but people with warped minds are
  despised.

9 Better to be a nobody and yet have a
servant
  than pretend to be somebody and
  have no food.

10 The righteous care for the needs of
their animals,

but the kindest acts of the wicked
are cruel.

11 Those who work their land will have
abundant food,
  but those who chase fantasies lack
  judgment.

12 The wicked desire the plunder of
evildoers,
  but the root of the righteous
  flourishes.

13 Evildoers are trapped by their sinful
talk,
  but the righteous escape trouble.

14 From the fruit of their lips people are
filled with good things
  as surely as the work of their hands
  brings them reward.

15 The way of fools seems right to them,
  but the wise listen to advice.

16 Fools show their annoyance at once,
  but the prudent overlook an insult.

17 A truthful witness gives honest
testimony,
  but a false witness tells lies.

18 Reckless words pierce like a sword,
  but the tongue of the wise brings
  healing.

19 Truthful lips endure for ever,
  but a lying tongue lasts only a
  moment.

20 There is deceit in the hearts of those
who plot evil,
  but joy for those who promote
  peace.

21 No harm befalls the righteous,
  but the wicked have their fill of
  trouble.

22 The LORD detests lying lips,
  but he delights in those who are
  truthful.

23 The prudent keep their knowledge to
themselves,

but the heart of fools blurts out
folly.

24 Diligent hands will rule,
but laziness ends in slave labour.

25 Anxiety weighs down the heart,
but a kind word cheers it up.

26 The righteous are cautious in
friendship,[a]
but the way of the wicked leads
them astray.

27 The lazy do not roast[b] their game,
but the diligent prize their
possessions.

28 In the way of righteousness there is
life;
along that path is immortality.

13 A wise child heeds a parent's
instruction,
but a mocker does not listen to
rebuke.

2 From the fruit of their lips people
enjoy good things,
but the unfaithful have a craving for
violence.

3 Those who guard their lips guard their
lives,
but those who speak rashly will
come to ruin.

4 The sluggard craves and gets nothing,
but the desires of the diligent are
fully satisfied.

5 The righteous hate what is false,
but the wicked bring shame and
disgrace.

6 Righteousness guards the person of
integrity,
but wickedness overthrows the
sinner.

7 One pretends to be rich, yet has
nothing;

another pretends to be poor, yet
has great wealth.

8 The rich may ransom their lives,
but the poor hear no threats.

9 The light of the righteous shines
brightly,
but the lamp of the wicked is
snuffed out.

10 Pride only breeds quarrels,
but wisdom is found in those who
take advice.

11 Dishonest money dwindles away,
but whoever gathers money little by
little makes it grow.

12 Hope deferred makes the heart
sick,
but a longing fulfilled is a tree of
life.

13 Whoever scorns instruction will pay
for it,
but whoever respects a command is
rewarded.

14 The teaching of the wise is a fountain
of life,
turning people from the snares of
death.

15 Good understanding wins favour,
but the way of the unfaithful is
hard.[a]

16 All who are prudent act out of
knowledge,
but fools expose their folly.

17 A wicked messenger falls into
trouble,
but a trustworthy envoy brings
healing.

18 The one who ignores discipline comes
to poverty and shame,
but whoever heeds correction is
honoured.

---

[a]26 Or *The righteous are a guide to their neighbours*
[a]15 Or *unfaithful does not endure*
[b]27 The meaning of the Hebrew for this word is uncertain.

¹⁹ A longing fulfilled is sweet to the soul,
but fools detest turning from evil.

²⁰ Whoever walks with the wise grows wise,
but a companion of fools suffers harm.

²¹ Misfortune pursues the sinner,
but prosperity is the reward of the righteous.

²² Good people leave an inheritance for their children's children,
but a sinner's wealth is stored up for the righteous.

²³ The field of the poor may produce abundant food,
but injustice sweeps it away.

²⁴ Those who spare the rod hate their children,
but those who love them are careful to discipline them.

²⁵ The righteous eat to their hearts' content,
but the stomach of the wicked goes hungry.

14 The wise woman builds her house,
but with her own hands the foolish one tears hers down.

² The person whose walk is upright fears the LORD,
but the one whose ways are devious despises him.

³ The talk of fools brings a rod to their backs,
but the lips of the wise protect them.

⁴ Where there are no oxen, the manger is empty,
but from the strength of an ox comes an abundant harvest.

⁵ A truthful witness does not deceive,
but a false witness pours out lies.

⁶ The mocker seeks wisdom and finds none,
but knowledge comes easily to the discerning.

⁷ Stay away from the foolish,
for you will not find knowledge on their lips.

⁸ The wisdom of the prudent is to give thought to their ways,
but the folly of fools is deception.

⁹ Fools mock at making amends for sin,
but goodwill is found among the upright.

¹⁰ Each heart knows its own bitterness,
and no-one else can share its joy.

¹¹ The house of the wicked will be destroyed,
but the tent of the upright will flourish.

¹² There is a way that seems right to a person,
but in the end it leads to death.

¹³ Even in laughter the heart may ache,
and joy may end in grief.

¹⁴ The faithless will be fully repaid for their ways,
and the good rewarded for theirs.

¹⁵ The simple believe anything,
but the prudent give thought to their steps.

¹⁶ The wise fear the LORD and shun evil,
but a fool is hotheaded and reckless.

¹⁷ The quick-tempered do foolish things,
and the crafty are hated.

¹⁸ The simple inherit folly,
but the prudent are crowned with knowledge.

¹⁹ Evildoers will bow down in the presence of the good,

and the wicked at the gates of the righteous.

20 The poor are shunned even by their neighbours,
but the rich have many friends.

21 To despise the poor is to sin,
but blessed are those who are kind to the needy.

22 Do not those who plot evil go astray?
But those who plan what is good find*a* love and faithfulness.

23 All hard work brings a profit,
but mere talk leads only to poverty.

24 The wealth of the wise is their crown,
but the folly of fools yields folly.

25 A truthful witness saves lives,
but a false witness is deceitful.

26 Those who fear the LORD have a secure fortress,
and for their children it will be a refuge.

27 The fear of the LORD is a fountain of life,
turning people from the snares of death.

28 A large population is a king's glory,
but without subjects a prince is ruined.

29 Those who are patient have great understanding,
but the quick-tempered display folly.

30 A heart at peace gives life to the body,
but envy rots the bones.

31 Whoever oppresses the poor shows contempt for their Maker,
but whoever is kind to the needy honours God.

32 When calamity comes, the wicked are brought down,
but even in death the righteous have a refuge.

33 Wisdom reposes in the heart of the discerning
and even among fools she lets herself be known.*b*

34 Righteousness exalts a nation,
but sin is a disgrace to any people.

35 A king delights in a wise servant,
but a shameful servant incurs his wrath.

15 A gentle answer turns away wrath,
but a harsh word stirs up anger.

2 The tongue of the wise commends knowledge,
but the mouth of the fool gushes folly.

3 The eyes of the LORD are everywhere,
keeping watch on the wicked and the good.

4 The tongue that brings healing is a tree of life,
but a deceitful tongue crushes the spirit.

5 A fool spurns a parent's discipline,
but whoever heeds correction shows prudence.

6 The house of the righteous contains great treasure,
but the income of the wicked brings them trouble.

7 The lips of the wise spread knowledge;
not so the hearts of fools.

8 The LORD detests the sacrifice of the wicked,

*a*22 Or *show*   *b*33 Hebrew; Septuagint and Syriac / *but in the heart of fools she is not known*

but the prayer of the upright pleases
him.

9 The LORD detests the way of the
wicked
but he loves those who pursue
righteousness.

10 Stern discipline awaits those who
leave the path;
those who hate correction will die.

11 Death and Destruction[a] lie open
before the LORD—
how much more do human
hearts!

12 Mockers resent correction;
they will not consult the wise.

13 A happy heart makes the face
cheerful,
but heartache crushes the spirit.

14 The discerning heart seeks
knowledge,
but the mouth of a fool feeds on
folly.

15 All the days of the oppressed are
wretched,
but the cheerful heart has a
continual feast.

16 Better a little with the fear of the
LORD
than great wealth with turmoil.

17 Better a meal of vegetables where
there is love
than a fattened calf with hatred.

18 The hot-tempered stir up dissension,
but those who are patient calm a
quarrel.

19 The way of the sluggard is blocked
with thorns,
but the path of the upright is a
highway.

20 Wise children bring joy to their
fathers,
but the foolish despise their
mothers.

21 Folly delights those who lack
judgment,
but those who have insight keep a
straight course.

22 Plans fail for lack of counsel,
but with many advisers they
succeed.

23 A person finds joy in giving an apt
reply—
and how good is a timely word!

24 The path of life leads upward for the
wise
to keep them from going down to
the grave.[b]

25 The LORD tears down the house of the
proud
but he keeps the widow's
boundaries intact.

26 The LORD detests the thoughts of the
wicked,
but those of the pure are pleasing
to him.

27 The greedy bring trouble to their
families,
but those who hate bribes will
live.

28 The heart of the righteous weighs its
answers,
but the mouth of the wicked gushes
evil.

29 The LORD is far from the wicked
but he hears the prayer of the
righteous.

30 A cheerful look brings joy to the
heart,
and good news gives health to the
bones.

[a]11 Hebrew *Sheol* and *Abaddon*   [b]24 Hebrew *Sheol*

31 Whoever listens to a life-giving
rebuke
will be at home among the wise.

32 Those who ignore discipline despise
themselves,
but those who heed correction gain
understanding.

33 The fear of the LORD teaches
wisdom,^c
and humility comes before
honour.

16 To human beings belong the plans
of the heart,
but from the LORD comes the reply
of the tongue.

2 People think all their ways are
innocent,
but motives are weighed by the
LORD.

3 Commit to the LORD whatever you
do,
and your plans will succeed.

4 The LORD works out everything for his
own ends—
even the wicked for a day of
disaster.

5 The LORD detests all the proud of
heart.
Be sure of this: They will not go
unpunished.

6 Through love and faithfulness sin is
atoned for;
through the fear of the LORD evil is
avoided.

7 When people's ways are pleasing to
the LORD,
he makes even their enemies live at
peace with them.

8 Better a little with righteousness
than much gain with injustice.

9 In your heart you may plan your
course,
but the LORD determines your
steps.

10 The lips of a king speak as an oracle,
and his mouth should not betray
justice.

11 Honest scales and balances are from
the LORD;
all the weights in the bag are of his
making.

12 Kings detest wrongdoing,
for a throne is established through
righteousness.

13 Kings take pleasure in honest lips;
they value one who speaks the
truth.

14 A king's wrath is a messenger of
death,
but the wise will appease it.

15 When a king's face brightens, it means
life;
his favour is like a rain cloud in
spring.

16 How much better to get wisdom than
gold,
to choose understanding rather
than silver!

17 The highway of the upright avoids
evil;
those who guard their ways guard
their lives.

18 Pride goes before destruction,
a haughty spirit before a fall.

19 Better to be lowly in spirit and among
the oppressed
than to share plunder with the
proud.

20 Those who give heed to instruction
prosper,

^c33 Or *Wisdom teaches the fear of the* LORD

and blessed are those who trust in
the LORD.

21 The wise in heart are called
discerning,
and pleasant words promote
instruction.*a*

22 Understanding is a fountain of life to
those who have it,
but folly brings punishment to
fools.

23 The hearts of the wise guide their
mouths,
and their lips promote instruction.*b*

24 Pleasant words are a honeycomb,
sweet to the soul and healing to the
bones.

25 There is a way that at the time seems
right,
but in the end it leads to death.

26 The appetite of labourers works for
them;
their hunger drives them on.

27 Scoundrels plot evil,
and their speech is like a scorching
fire.

28 The perverse stir up dissension,
and gossips separate close friends.

29 The violent entice their neighbours
and lead them down a path that is
not good.

30 Those who wink with their eyes are
plotting perversity;
those who purse their lips are bent
on evil.

31 Grey hair is a crown of splendour;
it is attained by a righteous life.

32 Better a patient person than a
warrior,

those who control their temper than
those who take a city.

33 The lot is cast into the lap,
but its every decision is from the
LORD.

17 Better a dry crust with peace and
quiet
than a house full of feasting,*a* with
strife.

2 A wise servant will rule over a
disgraceful child,
and will share the inheritance as
one of the family.

3 The crucible for silver and the furnace
for gold,
but the LORD tests the heart.

4 A wicked person listens to evil lips;
a liar pays attention to a malicious
tongue.

5 Whoever mocks the poor shows
contempt for their Maker;
whoever gloats over disaster will
not go unpunished.

6 Children's children are a crown to the
aged,
and parents are the pride of their
children.

7 Arrogant*b* lips are unsuited to a fool—
how much worse lying lips to a ruler!

8 A bribe is a charm to those who give
it;
wherever they turn, they succeed.

9 Whoever covers over an offence
promotes love,
but whoever repeats the matter
separates close friends.

10 A rebuke impresses a discerning
person
more than a hundred lashes a fool.

---

*a*21 Or *words make one persuasive*   *b*23 Or *mouths / and make their lips persuasive*   *a*1 Hebrew *sacrifices*
*b*7 Or *Eloquent*

¹¹ Evildoers are bent only on rebellion;
    merciless officials will be sent
        against them.

¹² Better to meet a bear robbed of her
        cubs
    than a fool bent on folly.

¹³ Evil will never leave the house
    of one who pays back evil for good.

¹⁴ Starting a quarrel is like breaching a
        dam;
    so drop the matter before a dispute
        breaks out.

¹⁵ Acquitting the guilty and condemning
        the innocent—
    the Lᴏʀᴅ detests them both.

¹⁶ Of what use is money in the hands of
        fools,
    since they have no desire to get
        wisdom?

¹⁷ A friend loves at all times,
    and a relative is born for
        adversity.

¹⁸ One who lacks judgment strikes hands
        in pledge
    and puts up security for a
        neighbour.

¹⁹ The one who loves a quarrel loves sin;
    whoever builds a high gate invites
        destruction.

²⁰ One whose heart is perverse does not
        prosper;
    one whose tongue is deceitful falls
        into trouble.

²¹ To have a fool for a child brings grief;
    there is no joy for the parent of a
        fool.

²² A cheerful heart is good medicine,
    but a crushed spirit dries up the
        bones.

²³ The wicked accept bribes in secret
    to pervert the course of justice.

²⁴ A discerning person keeps wisdom in
        view,
    but a fool's eyes wander to the ends
        of the earth.

²⁵ Foolish children bring grief to their
        fathers
    and bitterness to those who bore
        them.

²⁶ It is not good to punish the innocent,
    or to flog officials for their integrity.

²⁷ Those who have knowledge use words
        with restraint,
    and those who have insight are
        even-tempered.

²⁸ Even fools are thought wise if they
        keep silent,
    and discerning if they hold their
        tongues.

18 An unfriendly person pursues
    selfish ends
    and defies all sound judgment.

² Fools find no pleasure in
        understanding
    but delight in airing their own
        opinions.

³ When wickedness comes, so does
        contempt,
    and with shame comes disgrace.

⁴ The words of the mouth are deep
        waters,
    but the fountain of wisdom is a
        bubbling brook.

⁵ It is not good to be partial to the
        wicked
    or to deprive the innocent of
        justice.

⁶ The lips of fools bring them strife,
    and their mouths invite a beating.

⁷ The mouths of fools are their
        undoing,
    and their lips are a snare to their
        souls.

8 The words of a gossip are like choice
morsels;
    they go down to the inmost parts.

9 One who is slack in work
    is closely related to one who
    destroys.

10 The name of the LORD is a strong
tower;
    the righteous run to it and are safe.

11 The wealth of the rich is their fortified
city;
    they imagine it an unscalable wall.

12 Before a downfall one's heart is
proud,
    but humility comes before honour.

13 To answer before listening—
    that is folly and shame.

14 One's spirit provides strength in times
of sickness,
    but a crushed spirit who can bear?

15 The heart of the discerning acquires
knowledge;
    the ears of the wise seek it out.

16 A gift opens the way
    and ushers the giver into the
    presence of the great.

17 The first to present a case seems right,
    till another comes forward and asks
    questions.

18 Casting the lot settles disputes
    and keeps strong opponents apart.

19 An offended relative is more
unyielding than a fortified city,
    and disputes are like the barred
    gates of a citadel.

20 From the fruit of the mouth one's
stomach is filled;
    with the harvest from the lips one is
    satisfied.

21 The tongue has the power of life and
death,
    and those who love it will eat its
    fruit.

22 He who finds a wife finds what is good
    and receives favour from the LORD.

23 The poor plead for mercy,
    but the rich answer harshly.

24 One who has many companions may
come to ruin,
    but there is a friend who sticks
    closer than a brother or sister.

19 Better the poor whose walk is
blameless
    than a fool whose lips are perverse.

2 It is not good to have zeal without
knowledge,
    nor to be hasty and miss the way.

3 One's own folly leads to ruin,
    yet the heart rages against the
    LORD.

4 Wealth brings many friends,
    but the friends of the poor desert
    them.

5 A false witness will not go
unpunished,
    and whoever pours out lies will not
    go free.

6 Many curry favour with a ruler,
    and everyone is the friend of one
    who gives gifts.

7 The poor are shunned by all their
relatives—
    how much more do their friends
    avoid them!
Though they pursue them with
pleading,
    they are nowhere to be found.[a]

8 Those who get wisdom love their own
souls;

---

[a] 7 The meaning of the Hebrew for this sentence is uncertain.

those who cherish understanding prosper.

9 A false witness will not go unpunished,
and whoever pours out lies will perish.

10 It is not fitting for a fool to live in luxury—
how much worse for a slave to rule over princes!

11 A person's wisdom yields patience;
it is to one's glory to overlook an offence.

12 A king's rage is like the roar of a lion,
but his favour is like dew on the grass.

13 A foolish child is a father's ruin,
and a quarrelsome wife is like a constant dripping.

14 Houses and wealth are inherited from parents,
but a prudent wife is from the LORD.

15 Laziness brings on deep sleep,
and the shiftless go hungry.

16 Those who obey instructions guard their lives,
but those who are contemptuous of their ways will die.

17 Those who are kind to the poor lend to the LORD,
and he will reward them for what they have done.

18 Discipline your children, for in that there is hope;
do not be a willing party to their death.

19 The hot-tempered must pay the penalty;
rescue them, and you will have to do it again.

20 Listen to advice and accept instruction,
and in the end you will be wise.

21 Many are the plans in a human heart,
but it is the LORD's purpose that prevails.

22 What a person desires is unfailing love;b
better to be poor than a liar.

23 The fear of the LORD leads to life:
Then one rests content, untouched by trouble.

24 Sluggards bury their hands in the dish
and will not even bring them back to their mouths!

25 Flog a mocker, and the simple will learn prudence;
rebuke the discerning, and they will gain knowledge.

26 Those who rob their father and drive out their mother
are children who bring shame and disgrace.

27 Stop listening to instruction, my son,
and you will stray from the words of knowledge.

28 A corrupt witness mocks at justice,
and the mouth of the wicked gulps down evil.

29 Penalties are prepared for mockers,
and beatings for the backs of fools.

20 Wine is a mocker and beer a brawler;
whoever is led astray by them is not wise.

2 A king's wrath is like the roar of a lion;
those who anger him forfeit their lives.

3 It is to one's honour to avoid strife,
but every fool is quick to quarrel.

b22 Or *Greed is a person's shame*

4 Sluggards do not plough in season;
so at harvest time they look but find
nothing.

5 The purposes of the human heart are
deep waters,
but those who have insight draw
them out.

6 Many claim to have unfailing love,
but a faithful person who can find?

7 The righteous lead blameless lives;
blessed are their children after
them.

8 When a king sits on his throne to
judge,
he winnows out all evil with his
eyes.

9 Who can say, "I have kept my heart
pure;
I am clean and without sin"?

10 Differing weights and differing
measures—
the LORD detests them both.

11 Even children are known by their
actions,
by whether their conduct is pure
and right.

12 Ears that hear and eyes that see—
the LORD has made them both.

13 Do not love sleep or you will grow
poor;
stay awake and you will have food
to spare.

14 "It's no good, it's no good!" says the
buyer;
then goes off and boasts about the
purchase.

15 Gold there is, and rubies in
abundance,
but lips that speak knowledge are a
rare jewel.

16 Take the garment of one who puts up
security for a stranger;
hold it in pledge if it is done for a
wayward woman.

17 Food gained by fraud tastes sweet,
but one ends up with a mouth full
of gravel.

18 Make plans by seeking advice;
if you wage war, obtain guidance.

19 A gossip betrays a confidence;
so avoid anyone who talks too
much.

20 If you curse your father or mother,
your lamp will be snuffed out in
pitch darkness.

21 An inheritance quickly gained at the
beginning
will not be blessed at the end.

22 Do not say, "I'll pay you back for this
wrong!"
Wait for the LORD, and he will
deliver you.

23 The LORD detests differing weights,
and dishonest scales do not please
him.

24 A person's steps are directed by the
LORD.
How then can any understand their
own way?

25 It is a trap to dedicate something
rashly
and only later to consider one's vows.

26 A wise king winnows out the wicked;
he drives the threshing wheel over
them.

27 The lamp of the LORD searches the
human spirit;[a]
it searches out the inmost being.

28 Love and faithfulness keep a king
safe;

---

[a] 27 Or *The human spirit is the LORD's lamp*

through love his throne is made
　secure.

29 The glory of young men is their
　strength,
　　grey hair the splendour of the old.

30 Blows and wounds cleanse away evil,
　and beatings purge the inmost
　　being.

21 The king's heart is in the hand of
　the LORD;
　he directs it like a watercourse
　　wherever he pleases.

2 All your ways seem right to you,
　but the LORD weighs the heart.

3 To do what is right and just
　is more acceptable to the LORD than
　　sacrifice.

4 Haughty eyes and a proud heart,
　the lamp of the wicked, are sin!

5 The plans of the diligent lead to profit
　as surely as haste leads to poverty.

6 A fortune made by a lying tongue
　is a fleeting vapour and a deadly
　　snare. [a]

7 The violence of the wicked will drag
　them away,
　　for they refuse to do what is right.

8 The way of the guilty is devious,
　but the conduct of the innocent is
　　upright.

9 Better to live on a corner of the roof
　than share a house with a
　　quarrelsome wife.

10 The wicked crave evil;
　their neighbours get no mercy from
　　them.

11 When a mocker is punished, the
　simple gain wisdom;

when the wise are instructed, they
　get knowledge.

12 The Righteous One [b] takes note of the
　house of the wicked
　and brings the wicked to ruin.

13 If you shut your ears to the cry of the
　poor,
　you too will cry out and not be
　　answered.

14 A gift given in secret soothes
　anger,
　and a bribe concealed in the cloak
　　pacifies great wrath.

15 When justice is done, it brings joy to
　the righteous
　but terror to evildoers.

16 Whoever strays from the path of
　understanding
　comes to rest in the company of the
　　dead.

17 Whoever loves pleasure will become
　poor;
　whoever loves wine and oil will
　　never be rich.

18 The wicked become a ransom for the
　righteous,
　and the unfaithful for the upright.

19 Better to live in a desert
　than with a quarrelsome and
　　ill-tempered wife.

20 In the house of the wise are stores of
　choice food and oil,
　but fools devour all they have.

21 Whoever pursues righteousness and
　love
　finds life, prosperity [c] and honour.

22 One who is wise can attack the city of
　the mighty
　and pull down the stronghold in
　　which they trust.

_a_ 6 Some Hebrew manuscripts, Septuagint and Vulgate; most Hebrew manuscripts _vapour for those who seek death_
_b_ 12 Or _The righteous person_　_c_ 21 Or _righteousness_

23 Those who guard their mouths and
their tongues
keep themselves from calamity.

24 The proud and arrogant—"Mocker"
is their name;
they behave with overweening
pride.

25 The craving of sluggards will be the
death of them,
because their hands refuse to
work.
26 All day long they crave for more,
but the righteous give without
sparing.

27 The sacrifice of the wicked is
detestable—
how much more so when brought
with evil intent!

28 Those who give false witness will
perish,
and whoever listens to them will be
destroyed for ever.*d*

29 The wicked put up a bold front,
but the upright give thought to their
ways.

30 There is no wisdom, no insight, no
plan
that can succeed against the LORD.

31 The horse is made ready for the day
of battle,
but victory rests with the LORD.

22 A good name is more desirable
than great riches;
to be esteemed is better than silver
or gold.

2 Rich and poor have this in common:
The LORD is the Maker of them all.

3 The prudent see danger and take
refuge,
but the simple keep going and
suffer for it.

4 Humility and the fear of the LORD
bring wealth and honour and life.

5 In the paths of the wicked lie thorns
and snares,
but those who guard their souls stay
far from them.

6 Train*a* children in the way they should
go,
and when they are old they will not
turn from it.

7 The rich rule over the poor,
and the borrower is servant to the
lender.

8 Whoever sows wickedness reaps
trouble,
and the rod wielded in fury will be
destroyed.

9 The generous will themselves be
blessed,
for they share their food with the
poor.

10 Drive out the mocker, and out goes
strife;
quarrels and insults are ended.

11 Whoever loves a pure heart and
whose speech is gracious
will have the king for a friend.

12 The eyes of the LORD keep watch over
knowledge,
but he frustrates the words of the
unfaithful.

13 The sluggard says, "There is a lion
outside!"
or, "I will be murdered in the streets!"

14 The mouth of an adulteress is a deep
pit;
whoever is under the LORD's wrath
will fall into it.

15 Folly is bound up in the heart of a
child,

---

*d*28 Or / but the words of the obedient will live on   *a*6 Or Start

but the rod of discipline will drive
it far away.

16 Those who oppress the poor to
increase their wealth
and those who give gifts to the
rich—both come to poverty.

Sayings of the wise

17 Pay attention and listen to the sayings
of the wise;
apply your heart to what I teach,
18 for it is pleasing when you keep them
in your heart
and have all of them ready on your
lips.
19 So that your trust may be in the LORD,
I teach you today, even you.
20 Have I not written thirty[b] sayings for
you,
sayings of counsel and knowledge,
21 teaching you true and reliable words,
so that you can give sound answers
to those who sent you?

22 Do not exploit the poor because they
are poor
and do not crush the needy in court,
23 for the LORD will take up their case
and will plunder those who plunder
them.

24 Do not make friends with the
hot-tempered,
do not associate with those who are
easily angered,
25 or you may learn their ways
and get yourself ensnared.

26 Do not be one who strikes hands in
pledge
or puts up security for debts;
27 if you lack the means to pay,
your very bed will be snatched from
under you.

28 Do not move an ancient boundary stone
set up by your ancestors.

29 Do you see those who are skilled in
their work?

They will serve before kings;
they will not serve before obscure
people.

23 When you sit to dine with a ruler,
note well what[a] is before you,
2 and put a knife to your throat
if you are given to gluttony.
3 Do not crave his delicacies,
for that food is deceptive.

4 Do not wear yourself out to get rich;
have the wisdom to show restraint.
5 Cast but a glance at riches, and they
are gone,
for they will surely sprout wings
and fly off to the sky like an eagle.

6 Do not eat the food of the stingy,
do not crave their delicacies;
7 for they are the kind of people
who are always thinking about the
cost.[b]
"Eat and drink," they say to you,
but their hearts are not with you.
8 You will vomit up the little you have
eaten
and will have wasted your
compliments.

9 Do not speak to fools,
for they will scorn the wisdom of
your words.

10 Do not move an ancient boundary
stone
or encroach on the fields of the
fatherless,
11 for their Defender is strong;
he will take up their case against you.

12 Apply your heart to instruction
and your ears to words of
knowledge.

13 Do not withhold discipline from
children;
if you punish them with the rod,
they will not die.
14 Punish them with the rod
and save their souls from death.[c]

b20 Or *not formerly written*; or *not written excellent*   a1 Or *who*
b7 Or *for as they think within themselves, / so they are*; or *for as they put on a feast, / so they are*
c14 Hebrew *Sheol*

15 My son, if your heart is wise,
 then my heart will be glad;
16 my inmost being will rejoice
 when your lips speak what is right.

17 Do not let your heart envy sinners,
 but always be zealous for the fear
 of the LORD.
18 There is surely a future hope for you,
 and your hope will not be cut off.

19 Listen, my son, and be wise,
 and keep your heart on the right
 path.
20 Do not join those who drink too much
 wine
 or gorge themselves on meat,
21 for drunkards and gluttons become
 poor,
 and drowsiness clothes them in
 rags.

22 Listen to your father, who gave you
 life,
 and do not despise your mother
 when she is old.
23 Buy the truth and do not sell it;
 get wisdom, discipline and
 understanding.
24 The father of a righteous child has
 great joy;
 whoever has a wise son delights in
 him.
25 May your father and mother be glad;
 may she who gave you birth rejoice!

26 My son, give me your heart
 and let your eyes keep to my ways,
27 for a prostitute is a deep pit
 and a wayward wife is a narrow
 well.
28 Like a bandit she lies in wait,
 and multiplies the unfaithful among
 men.

29 Who has woe? Who has sorrow?
 Who has strife? Who has
 complaints?
 Who has needless bruises? Who has
 bloodshot eyes?
30 Those who linger over wine,
 who go to sample bowls of mixed
 wine.

31 Do not gaze at wine when it is red,
 when it sparkles in the cup,
 when it goes down smoothly!
32 In the end it bites like a snake
 and poisons like a viper.
33 Your eyes will see strange sights
 and your mind imagine confusing
 things.
34 You will be like one sleeping on the
 high seas,
 lying on top of the rigging.
35 "They hit me," you will say, "but I'm
 not hurt!
 They beat me, but I don't feel it!
 When will I wake up
 so I can find another drink?"

24 Do not envy the wicked,
 do not desire their company;
2 for their hearts plot violence,
 and their lips talk about making
 trouble.

3 By wisdom a house is built,
 and through understanding it is
 established;
4 through knowledge its rooms are
 filled
 with rare and beautiful treasures.

5 A wise person has great power,
 and one who has knowledge
 increases strength;
6 for waging war you need
 guidance,
 and for victory many advisers.

7 Wisdom is too high for fools;
 in the assembly at the gate they
 have nothing to say.

8 Whoever plots evil
 will be known as a schemer.
9 The schemes of folly are sin,
 and people detest a mocker.

10 If you falter in times of trouble,
 how small is your strength!

11 Rescue those being led away to
 death;
 hold back those staggering towards
 slaughter.

12 If you say, "But we knew nothing
about this,"
does not he who weighs the heart
perceive it?
Does not he who guards your life
know it?
Will he not repay everyone
according to what they have
done?

13 Eat honey, my son, for it is good;
honey from the comb is sweet to
your taste.
14 Know also that wisdom is sweet to
your soul;
if you find it, there is a future hope
for you,
and your hope will not be cut off.

15 Do not lie in wait like an outlaw
against the houses of the
righteous,
do not raid their dwelling-places;
16 for though the righteous fall seven
times, they rise again,
but the wicked are brought down by
calamity.

17 Do not gloat when your enemies fall;
when they stumble, do not let your
heart rejoice,
18 or the Lord will see and disapprove
and turn his wrath away from them.

19 Do not fret because of evildoers
or be envious of the wicked,
20 for the evildoer has no future hope,
and the lamp of the wicked will be
snuffed out.

21 Fear the Lord and the king, my son,
and do not join with the rebellious,
22 for those two will send sudden
destruction upon them,
and who knows what calamities
they can bring?

Further Sayings of the Wise

23 These also are sayings of the wise:

To show partiality in judging is not
good:

24 Whoever says to the guilty, "You are
innocent,"
will be cursed by peoples and
denounced by nations.
25 But it will go well with those who
convict the guilty,
and rich blessing will come upon
them.

26 An honest answer
is like a kiss on the lips.

27 Finish your outdoor work
and get your fields ready;
after that, build your house.

28 Do not testify against your neighbours
without cause,
or use your lips to deceive.
29 Do not say, "I'll do to them as they
have done to me;
I'll pay them back for what they
did."

30 I went past the field of a sluggard,
past the vineyard of someone who
lacks judgment;
31 thorns had come up everywhere,
the ground was covered with
weeds,
and the stone wall was in ruins.
32 I applied my heart to what I
observed
and learned a lesson from what I
saw:
33 A little sleep, a little slumber,
a little folding of the hands to
rest—
34 and poverty will come on you like a
bandit
and scarcity like an armed man.[a]

More Proverbs of Solomon

25 These are more proverbs of
Solomon, copied by the men of
Hezekiah king of Judah:

2 It is the glory of God to conceal a
matter;
to search out a matter is the glory
of kings.

[a]34 Or *like a vagrant | and scarcity like a beggar*

³ As the heavens are high and the earth
   is deep,
   so the hearts of kings are
   unsearchable.

⁴ Remove the dross from the silver,
   and out comes material for*ᵃ* the
   silversmith;
⁵ remove the wicked from the king's
   presence,
   and his throne will be established
   through righteousness.

⁶ Do not exalt yourself in the king's
   presence,
   and do not claim a place among the
   great;
⁷ it is better for him to say to you,
   "Come up here,"
   than for him to humiliate you
   before nobles.

What you have seen with your eyes
⁸   do not bringᵇ hastily to court,
   for what will you do in the end
   if your neighbour puts you to
   shame?

⁹ If you argue your case with a
   neighbour,
   do not betray another's confidence,
¹⁰ or someone who hears it may shame
   you
   and you will never lose your bad
   reputation.

¹¹ A word aptly spoken
   is like apples of gold in settings of
   silver.

¹² Like an ear-ring of gold or an
   ornament of fine gold
   is a wise rebuke to a listening
   ear.

¹³ Like the coolness of snow at harvest
   time
   are trustworthy messengers to
   those who send them;
   they refresh the spirits of their
   masters.

¹⁴ Like clouds and wind without rain
   is one who boasts of gifts never
   given.

¹⁵ Through patience a ruler can be
   persuaded,
   and a gentle tongue can break a
   bone.

¹⁶ If you find honey, eat just enough—
   too much of it, and you will vomit.
¹⁷ Seldom set foot in your neighbour's
   house—
   too much of you, and you will be
   hated.

¹⁸ Like a club or a sword or a sharp
   arrow
   is one who gives false testimony
   against a neighbour.

¹⁹ Like a bad tooth or a lame foot
   is reliance on the unfaithful in times
   of trouble.

²⁰ Like one who takes away a garment
   on a cold day,
   or like vinegar poured on soda,
   is one who sings songs to a heavy
   heart.

²¹ If your enemies are hungry, give them
   food to eat;
   if they are thirsty, give them water
   to drink.
²² In doing this, you will heap burning
   coals on their heads,
   and the LORD will reward you.

²³ As a north wind brings rain,
   so a sly tongue brings angry looks.

²⁴ Better to live on a corner of the roof
   than share a house with a
   quarrelsome wife.

²⁵ Like cold water to a weary soul
   is good news from a distant land.

²⁶ Like a muddied spring or a polluted
   well

---

*ᵃ*4 Or *comes a vessel from*   *ᵇ*7, 8 Or *nobles / on whom you had set your eyes. / ⁸Do not go*

are the righteous who give way to
the wicked.

²⁷ It is not good to eat too much honey,
nor is it honourable to seek one's
own honour.

²⁸ Like a city whose walls are broken
down
is a person who lacks self-control.

26 Like snow in summer or
rain in harvest,
honour is not fitting for a fool.

² Like a fluttering sparrow or a darting
swallow,
an undeserved curse does not come
to rest.

³ A whip for the horse, a halter for the
donkey,
and a rod for the backs of fools!

⁴ Do not answer fools according to their
folly,
or you will be like them yourself.

⁵ Answer fools according to their
folly,
or they will be wise in their own
eyes.

⁶ Like cutting off one's feet or drinking
violence
is the sending of a message by the
hand of a fool.

⁷ Like a lame person's legs that hang
limp
is a proverb in the mouth of a fool.

⁸ Like tying a stone in a sling
is the giving of honour to a fool.

⁹ Like a thornbush in a drunkard's
hand
is a proverb in the mouth of a fool.

¹⁰ Like an archer who wounds at
random

is one who hires a fool or any
passer-by.

¹¹ As a dog returns to its vomit,
so fools repeat their folly.

¹² Do you see those who are wise in their
own eyes?
There is more hope for fools than
for them.

¹³ A sluggard says, "There is a lion in the
road,
a fierce lion roaming the streets!"

¹⁴ As a door turns on its hinges,
so a sluggard turns on the bed.

¹⁵ Sluggards bury their hands in the dish
and are too lazy to bring them back
to their mouths.

¹⁶ Sluggards are wiser in their own eyes
than seven people who answer
discreetly.

¹⁷ Like one who seizes a dog by the
ears
is a passer-by who meddles in
another's quarrel.

¹⁸ Like a maniac shooting
firebrands or deadly arrows
¹⁹ is one who deceives a neighbour
and says, "I was only joking!"

²⁰ Without wood a fire goes out;
without gossip a quarrel dies down.

²¹ As charcoal to embers and as wood to
fire,
so is a quarrelsome person for
kindling strife.

²² The words of a gossip are like choice
morsels;
they go down to the inmost parts.

²³ Like a coating of glaze*a* over
earthenware
are fervent lips with an evil heart.

---

*a*23 With a different word division of the Hebrew; Masoretic Text *of silver dross*

24 The malicious disguise themselves
    with their lips,
  but in their hearts they harbour
    deceit.
25 Though their speech is charming, do
    not believe them,
  for seven abominations fill their
    hearts.
26 Their malice may be concealed by
    deception,
  but their wickedness will be
    exposed in the assembly.

27 If you dig a pit, you will fall into it;
  if you roll a stone, it will roll back
    on you.

28 A lying tongue hates those it hurts,
  and a flattering mouth works ruin.

27 Do not boast about tomorrow,
    for you do not know what a day
    may bring forth.

2 Let another praise you, and not your
    own mouth;
  someone else, and not your own
    lips.

3 Stone is heavy and sand a burden,
  but provocation by a fool is heavier
    than both.

4 Anger is cruel and fury
    overwhelming,
  but who can stand before jealousy?

5 Better is open rebuke
  than hidden love.

6 Wounds from a friend can be trusted,
  but an enemy multiplies kisses.

7 The one who is full loathes honey,
  but to the hungry even what is bitter
    tastes sweet.

8 Like a bird that strays from its nest
  is a person who strays from home.

9 Perfume and incense bring joy to the
    heart,
and the pleasantness of one's
    friends springs from their
    earnest counsel.

10 Do not forsake your friend and the
    friend of your parent,
  and do not go to your relative's
    house when disaster strikes you—
  better a neighbour nearby than a
    relative far away.

11 Be wise, my child, and bring joy to my
    heart;
  then I can answer anyone who
    treats me with contempt.

12 The prudent see danger and take
    refuge,
  but the simple keep going and
    suffer for it.

13 Take the garment of one who puts up
    security for a stranger;
  hold it in pledge if it is done for a
    wayward woman.

14 If anyone loudly blesses a neighbour
    early in the morning,
  it will be taken as a curse.

15 A quarrelsome wife is like
  a constant dripping on a rainy day;
16 restraining her is like restraining the
    wind
  or grasping oil with the hand.

17 As iron sharpens iron,
  so one person sharpens another.

18 Those who tend a fig-tree will eat its
    fruit,
  and those who look after their
    masters will be honoured.

19 As water reflects your face,
  so your heart reflects you.

20 Death and Destruction[a] are never
    satisfied,
  and neither are human eyes.

21 The crucible for silver and the furnace
    for gold,

[a] 20 Hebrew *Sheol and Abaddon*

but people are tested by the praise
they receive.

22 Though you grind fools in a mortar,
grinding them like grain with a
pestle,
you will not remove their folly from
them.

23 Be sure you know the condition of
your flocks,
give careful attention to your
herds;
24 for riches do not endure for ever,
and a crown is not secure for all
generations.
25 When the hay is removed and new
growth appears
and the grass from the hills is
gathered in,
26 the lambs will provide you with
clothing,
and the goats with the price of a
field.
27 You will have plenty of goats' milk
to feed you and your family
and to nourish your servant
women.

28 The wicked flee though no-one
pursues,
but the righteous are as bold as a
lion.

2 When a country is rebellious, it has
many rulers,
but one with insight and knowledge
maintains order.

3 A ruler[a] who oppresses the poor
is like a driving rain that leaves no
crops.

4 Those who forsake the law praise the
wicked,
but those who keep the law resist
them.

5 Evildoers do not understand justice,
but those who seek the LORD
understand it fully.

6 Better the poor whose walk is
blameless
than the rich whose ways are
perverse.

7 Those who keep the law are
discerning children,
but companions of gluttons
disgrace their parents.

8 Whoever increases wealth by
exorbitant interest
amasses it for another, who will be
kind to the poor.

9 If any turn a deaf ear to the law,
even their prayers are detestable.

10 Those who lead the upright along an
evil path
will fall into their own trap,
but the blameless will receive a
good inheritance.

11 The rich may be wise in their own eyes,
but the poor who have discernment
see how deluded they are.

12 When the righteous triumph, there is
great elation;
but when the wicked rise to power,
people go into hiding.

13 Those who conceal their sins do not
prosper,
but those who confess and
renounce them find mercy.

14 Blessed are those who always fear the
LORD,
but those who harden their hearts
fall into trouble.

15 Like a roaring lion or a charging
bear
is a wicked ruler over a helpless
people.

16 A tyrannical ruler lacks judgment,
but whoever hates ill-gotten gain
will enjoy a long life.

[a]3 Or *A poor person*

17 Anyone tormented by the guilt of
    murder
    will be a fugitive till death;
    let no-one support that person.

18 Those whose walk is blameless are
    kept safe,
    but those whose ways are perverse
    will suddenly fall.

19 Those who work their land will have
    abundant food,
    but those who chase fantasies will
    have their fill of poverty.

20 A faithful person will be richly
    blessed,
    but one eager to get rich will not go
    unpunished.

21 To show partiality is not good—
    yet a person will do wrong for a
    piece of bread.

22 The stingy are eager to get rich
    and are unaware that poverty
    awaits them.

23 Whoever rebukes a person will in the
    end gain more favour
    than one who has a flattering
    tongue.

24 Whoever robs father or mother
    and says, "It's not wrong"
    is partner to one who destroys.

25 The greedy stir up dissension,
    but those who trust in the LORD will
    prosper.

26 Those who trust in themselves are
    fools,
    but those who walk in wisdom are
    kept safe.

27 Those who give to the poor will lack
    nothing,
    but those who close their eyes to
    them receive many curses.

28 When the wicked rise to power,
    people go into hiding;

but when the wicked perish, the
    righteous thrive.

29 Whoever remains stiff-necked
    after many rebukes
    will suddenly be destroyed—
    without remedy.

2 When the righteous thrive, the people
    rejoice;
    when the wicked rule, the people
    groan.

3 Those who love wisdom bring joy to
    their parents,
    but companions of prostitutes
    squander their wealth.

4 By justice a king gives a country
    stability,
    but one who is greedy for bribes
    tears it down.

5 Those who flatter their neighbours
    are spreading nets for their feet.

6 Evildoers are snared by their own sin,
    but the righteous can sing and be
    glad.

7 The righteous care about justice for
    the poor,
    but the wicked have no such
    concern.

8 Mockers stir up a city,
    but the wise turn away anger.

9 If a wise person goes to court with a
    fool,
    the fool rages and scoffs, and there
    is no peace.

10 The bloodthirsty hate people of
    integrity
    and seek to kill the upright.

11 Fools give full vent to their anger,
    but the wise keep themselves under
    control.

12 If a ruler listens to lies,
    all his officials become wicked.

13 The poor and the oppressor have this
    in common:
    The LORD gives sight to the eyes of
    both.

14 If a king judges the poor with
    fairness,
    his throne will always be secure.

15 The rod of correction imparts
    wisdom,
    but children left to themselves
    disgrace their mothers.

16 When the wicked thrive, so does sin,
    but the righteous will see their
    downfall.

17 Discipline your children, and they will
    give you peace;
    they will bring delight to your soul.

18 Where there is no revelation, the
    people cast off restraint;
    but blessed are those who keep the
    law.

19 Servants cannot be corrected by mere
    words;
    though they understand, they will
    not respond.

20 Do you see one who speaks in haste?
    There is more hope for a fool.

21 A servant pampered from youth
    will bring grief[a] in the end.

22 Angry people stir up dissension,
    and the hot-tempered commit
    many sins.

23 Pride brings people low,
    but the lowly in spirit gain
    honour.

24 The accomplices of thieves are their
    own enemies;
    they are put under oath and dare
    not testify.

25 To fear anyone will prove to be a
    snare,
    but whoever trusts in the LORD is
    kept safe.

26 Many seek an audience with a ruler,
    but it is from the LORD that one gets
    justice.

27 The righteous detest the dishonest;
    the wicked detest the upright.

Sayings of Agur

30 The sayings of Agur son of
    Jakeh—an oracle:[a]

This man declared to Ithiel,
    to Ithiel and to Ucal:[b]

2 "I am the most ignorant of human
    beings;
    I do not have their understanding.
3 I have not learned wisdom,
    nor have I knowledge of the Holy
    One.
4 Who has gone up to heaven and come
    down?
    Whose hands have gathered up the
    wind?
Who has wrapped up the waters in a
    cloak?
    Who has established all the ends of
    the earth?
What is that person's name, and what
    is the name of that person's son?
    Tell me if you know!

5 "Every word of God is flawless;
    he is a shield to those who take
    refuge in him.
6 Do not add to his words,
    or he will rebuke you and prove you
    a liar.

7 "Two things I ask of you, O LORD;
    do not refuse me before I die:
8 Keep falsehood and lies far from me;
    give me neither poverty nor riches,
    but give me only my daily bread.

---

*a*21 The meaning of the Hebrew for this word is uncertain.   *a*1 Or *Jakeh of Massa*
*b*1 Masoretic Text; with a different word division of the Hebrew *declared, "I am weary, O God; I I am weary, O God,
and faint.*

9 Otherwise, I may have too much and
     disown you
and say, 'Who is the LORD?'
Or I may become poor and steal,
     and so dishonour the name of my
     God.

10 "Do not slander servants to their
     masters,
     or they will curse you, and you will
     pay for it.

11 "There are those who curse their
     fathers
     and do not bless their mothers;
12 those who are pure in their own eyes
     and yet are not cleansed of their
     filth;
13 those whose eyes are ever so haughty,
     whose glances are so disdainful;
14 those whose teeth are swords
     and whose jaws are set with knives
to devour the poor from the earth,
     the needy from among the human
     race.

15 "The leech has two daughters.
     'Give! Give!' they cry.

"There are three things that are never
     satisfied,
     four that never say, 'Enough!':
16 the grave,^{c} the barren womb,
     land, which is never satisfied with
     water,
     and fire, which never says,
     'Enough!'

17 "The eye that mocks a father,
     that scorns obedience to a mother,
will be pecked out by the ravens of the
     valley,
     will be eaten by the vultures.

18 "There are three things that are too
     amazing for me,
     four that I do not understand:
19 the way of an eagle in the sky,
     the way of a snake on a rock,
     the way of a ship on the high seas,

and the way of a man with a young
     woman.

20 "This is the way of an adulteress:
     She eats and wipes her mouth
     and says, 'I've done nothing
     wrong.'

21 "Under three things the earth
     trembles,
     under four it cannot bear up:
22 a servant who becomes king,
     a fool who is full of food,
23 an unloved woman who is married,
     and a servant woman who displaces
     her mistress.

24 "Four things on earth are small,
     yet they are extremely wise:
25 Ants are creatures of little strength,
     yet they store up their food in the
     summer;
26 conies^d are creatures of little power,
     yet they make their home in the
     crags;
27 locusts have no king,
     yet they advance together in
     ranks;
28 a lizard can be caught with the hand,
     yet it is found in kings' palaces.

29 "There are three things that are
     stately in their stride,
     four that move with stately bearing:
30 a lion, mighty among beasts,
     who retreats before nothing;
31 a strutting cock, a he-goat,
     and a king with his army around
     him.^{e}

32 "If you have played the fool and
     exalted yourself,
     or if you have planned evil,
     clap your hand over your mouth!
33 For as churning the milk produces
     butter,
     and as twisting the nose produces
     blood,
     so stirring up anger produces
     strife."

---

^{c}16 Hebrew *Sheol* ^{d}26 That is, the hyrax or rock badger ^{e}31 Or *king secure against revolt.*

Sayings of King Lemuel

31 The sayings of King Lemuel—an oracle[a] his mother taught him:

2 "O my son, O son of my womb,
  O son of my vows,[b]
3 do not spend your strength on women,
  your vigour on those who ruin
    kings.

4 "It is not for kings, O Lemuel—
  not for kings to drink wine,
  not for rulers to crave beer,
5 lest they drink and forget what the law
    decrees,
  and deprive all the oppressed of
    their rights.
6 Give beer to those who are perishing,
  wine to those who are in anguish;
7 let them drink and forget their poverty
  and remember their misery no
    more.

8 "Speak up for those who cannot speak
    for themselves,
  for the rights of all who are
    destitute.
9 Speak up and judge fairly;
  defend the rights of the poor and
    needy."

Epilogue: the wife of noble character

10 [c]A wife of noble character who can
    find?
  She is worth far more than rubies.
11 Her husband has full confidence in
    her
  and lacks nothing of value.
12 She brings him good, not harm,
  all the days of her life.
13 She selects wool and flax
  and works with eager hands.
14 She is like the merchant ships,
  bringing her food from afar.
15 She gets up while it is still dark;
  she provides food for her family
  and portions for her serving
    women.

16 She considers a field and buys it;
  out of her earnings she plants a
    vineyard.
17 She sets about her work vigorously;
  her arms are strong for her tasks.
18 She sees that her trading is profitable,
  and her lamp does not go out at
    night.
19 In her hand she holds the distaff
  and grasps the spindle with her
    fingers.
20 She opens her arms to the poor
  and extends her hands to the needy.
21 When it snows, she has no fear for her
    household;
  for all of them are clothed in scarlet.
22 She makes coverings for her bed;
  she is clothed in fine linen and
    purple.
23 Her husband is respected at the city
    gate,
  where he takes his seat among the
    elders of the land.
24 She makes linen garments and sells
    them,
  and supplies the merchants with
    sashes.
25 She is clothed with strength and
    dignity;
  she can laugh at the days to come.
26 She speaks with wisdom,
  and faithful instruction is on her
    tongue.
27 She watches over the affairs of her
    household
  and does not eat the bread of
    idleness.
28 Her children arise and call her
    blessed;
  her husband also, and he praises her:
29 "Many women do noble things,
  but you surpass them all."
30 Charm is deceptive, and beauty is
    fleeting;
  but a woman who fears the LORD is
    to be praised.
31 Give her the reward she has earned,
  and let her works bring her praise
    at the city gate.

---

[a]1 Or *of Lemuel king of Massa, which*   [b]2 Or / *the answer to my prayers*
[c]10 Verses 10 –31 are an acrostic, each verse beginning with a successive letter of the Hebrew alphabet.